STRATEGIC HUMAN RESOURCING

Principles, Perspectives and Practices

Edited by

JOHN LEOPOLD

LYNETTE HARRIS

TONY WATSON

Department of Human Resource Management
Nottingham Business School
The Nottingham Trent University

FINANCIAL TIMES
PITMAN PUBLISHING

For Margaret, Dennis and Diane

FINANCIAL TIMES
MANAGEMENT
LONDON · SAN FRANCISCO
KUALA LUMPUR · JOHANNESBURG

*Financial Times Management delivers the knowledge,
skills and understanding that enable students,
managers and organisations to achieve their ambitions,
whatever their needs, wherever they are.*

London Office:
128 Long Acre, London WC2E 9AN
Tel: +44 (0)171 447 2000
Fax: +44 (0)171 240 5771
Website: www.ftmanagement.com

An imprint of Pearson Education Limited

First published in Great Britain in 1999

© Pearson Education Limited, 1999
© Chapter 15, Brian Towers 1999

ISBN 0 273 63164 0

British Library Cataloguing in Publication Data
A CIP catalogue record for this book can be obtained
from the British Library.

1 3 5 7 9 10 8 6 4 2

Typeset by M Rules
Printed and bound in Great Britain by
William Clowes Ltd, Beccles

*The Publishers' policy is to use paper manufactured
from sustainable forests.*

CONTENTS

Contributing authors   xi
List of figures   xiv
List of tables   xv
List of case studies   xvii
Acknowledgements   xix

FOREWORD: Achieving the human advantage   xxi
Paul Turner

Plan of the book   xxiv

INTRODUCTION   1
John Leopold, Lynette Harris and Tony Watson
    The aims and objectives of this book   1
    The intended readership   2
    Using this book   3
    The structure of the book   3
    Strategy, planning and flexibility at home and abroad   4
    Human resourcing policies in practice   7
    Training and development   8
    Law, ethics and equality   10
    Employment relations   12

Part I
STRATEGY, PLANNING AND FLEXIBILITY AT HOME AND ABROAD

1 HUMAN RESOURCING STRATEGIES: Choice, chance and circumstance   17
    Tony Watson
    Introduction   18
    Human resourcing strategies and employment management   19
    Organising, managing and strategy making   21
    Strategy as plan and strategy as pattern   23
    Human resource strategy making – mainstream thinking   25
    A processual approach to human resource strategy making: choice,
      chance and circumstances   27
    Conclusion   36
    Summary   37
    Discussion questions   38
    Further reading   38

2 HUMAN RESOURCE PLANNING: Strategies, systems and processes   39
Carole Tansley
Introduction   40
Manpower planning and/or human resource planning?   40
Systems and processual perspectives   43
Integration between strategy making and HR planning   47
HR planning in the context of action   51
Budgetary control and HR planning   53
The importance of computerised HR information systems
    in HR planning   55
Summary   61
Discussion questions   61
Further reading   62

3 MANAGING UNCERTAINTY OR MANAGING UNCERTAINLY?   63
Colin Bryson
Introduction   64
Conceptualising flexibility   65
Factors promoting a different approach in human resourcing   69
A working definition of flexible employment and
    managing uncertainty   71
Implications and outcomes of different approaches to
    managing uncertainty   81
Conclusion   84
Summary   86
Discussion questions   87
Further reading   88

4 INTERNATIONAL HUMAN RESOURCING   89
David Walsh
Introduction   90
From domestic to international human resourcing   90
Globalisation and organisational approaches to international
    human resourcing   99
Staffing for transnational companies   109
Host-country employment – contingent factors   114
Summary   124
Discussion questions   126
Further reading   126

Part II
HUMAN RESOURCING POLICIES IN PRACTICE

5 ASSESSMENT, SELECTION AND EVALUATION: Problems and pitfalls   129
Sue Newell and Chris Rice
Introduction   130

Two different perspectives on selection	130
Selection and learning	135
A critical exploration of 'normal' practice	151
Conclusion	163
Summary	163
Discussion questions	164
Further reading	165

6 PERFORMANCE MANAGEMENT AND PERFORMING MANAGEMENT — 166
Colin Fisher

Introduction	167
Clarifying and publishing objectives	170
Performance measurement	172
Target setting	177
360° appraisal	180
Personal development plans	181
Managing problem staff	182
Staff appraisal	183
Conclusion – does performance management work?	188
Summary	189
Discussion questions	189
Further reading	190

7 PERFORMANCE PAY AND PERFORMING FOR PAY — 191
Lynette Harris

Introduction – PRP in context	192
What do we mean by performance-related pay?	193
The growth in performance-related pay	193
PRP and the employee commitment agenda	195
Motivational principles and PRP	196
The felt-fair concept	199
The continuing use of PRP	200
Measuring and rating	201
PRP in practice	203
PRP and line management	205
Whose responsibility?	208
Developments in paying for performance	208
Conclusion	212
Summary	212
Discussion questions	213
Further reading	214

Part III
TRAINING AND DEVELOPMENT

8 EMPLOYEE TRAINING AND DEVELOPMENT   217
Jim Stewart, Eileen Manhire and Rachael Hall
   Introduction   218
   Training or development – a matter of perception?   218
   Employee development roles   222
   Employee training and development and organisational change   231
   Conclusion   236
   Summary   237
   Discussion questions   238
   Further reading   238

9 MANAGEMENT DEVELOPMENT   239
Jim Stewart
   Introduction   240
   Management development – an overview   240
   Management development – definitions and meanings   244
   Management development approaches and methods   248
   Management development and human resourcing strategy   255
   Conclusion   260
   Summary   261
   Discussion questions   261
   Further reading   262

Part IV
LAW, ETHICS AND EQUALITY

10 EMPLOYMENT LAW AND HUMAN RESOURCING:
   Challenges and constraints   265
Lynette Harris
   Introduction   266
   The development of employment law in the post-war period   269
   The impact of the EU   271
   The UK's new agenda   275
   The impact of employment law on the specialist function   278
   The call for a different approach   280
   Enter the line manager   282
   Different directions for the specialist function   285
   Conclusion   289
   Summary   289
   Discussion questions   290
   Further reading   290

11 ACHIEVING EQUALITY OF OPPORTUNITY? 291
Mary Crow
  Introduction 292
  Reasons for taking equality initiatives 292
  Equal opportunity policies and initiatives 296
  Perspectives on the promotion of equality 298
  Espoused EO policies and operational practices 301
  Managing diversity 304
  Conclusions 304
  Summary 308
  Discussion questions 308
  Further reading 309

12 MANAGING MESSY MORAL MATTERS: Ethics and HRM 310
Colin Fisher and Chris Rice
  Organisation, management, strategy and ethics 311
  Perceptions of ethical issues 315
  Moral reasoning 324
  Thinking through ethical issues 328
  Conclusions 331
  Summary 334
  Discussion questions 335
  Further reading 335

Part V
EMPLOYMENT RELATIONS

13 EMPLOYEE PARTICIPATION, INVOLVEMENT AND COMMUNICATION 339
John Leopold and Susan Kirk
  Industrial democracy, employee participation and employee
    involvement 340
  Representative participation 343
  Employee involvement 344
  The spectre of Europe 354
  Conclusion 356
  Summary 360
  Discussion questions 361
  Further reading 361

14 CONFLICT AND CO-OPERATION IN EMPLOYMENT RELATIONS 362
Tony Watson, John Leopold and Kirsty Newsome
  Introduction 363
  The interplay of conflict and co-operation 366
  Two levels of conflict and its variety of expressions 369
  Strategic human resourcing options in management–union relations 371
  New workplace regimes and the suppression of conflict 379

Evidence of continuing conflict in new workplace regimes   384
Partnership as a way forward?   386
Conclusion   388
Summary   388
Discussion questions   389
Further reading   390

**15 CONFLICT, CHANGE AND COMPROMISE: Comparative industrial
relations and the world automobile industry**   391
Brian Towers
Introduction   392
Comparative study: approaches, problems and value   394
The world automobile industry: a comparative case study   400
Summary   412
Discussion questions   414
Further reading   414

AFTERWORD: Successful human resourcing   417
Ward Griffiths

References   421
Subject index   451
Name index   461

CONTRIBUTING AUTHORS

All contributing authors are members of the Department of Human Resource Management, Nottingham Business School, at The Nottingham Trent University.

Colin Bryson is Senior Lecturer in Human Resource Management and is researching flexible employment, specifically the use of temporary employment in areas such as higher education in the UK. An active trade unionist, he is secretary of Nottingham Trent Local Association of the Association of University Teachers and has acted as a consultant for the AUT on flexible employment. He has previously researched in industrial relations, HRM in the NHS and the management of IT. He teaches employee resourcing and reward, the employment relationship and all aspects of flexible employment for undergraduate, postgraduate and postexperience students.

Mary Crow is Senior Lecturer in Human Resource Management and teaches human resource management, organisational sociology and employee relations to both undergraduate and postgraduate students. Prior to entering higher education at Coventry University in 1991, she worked as an administrator and researcher with Barclays Bank plc and as a Divisional Personnel and Training Officer with Thorn EMI. She has a particular research interest in equality management and managing diversity and has published work on gender issues in management in Poland.

Colin Fisher is Principal Lecturer in Human Resource Management, author of *Resource Allocation in the Public Sector: Value of priorities and markets in the management of the Public Services* (1998: Routledge), and is engaged on CIMA-funded research on the ethical problems of accountancy and personnel practitioners. Colin has extensive experience teaching management, research methods and ethics to postgraduate students.

Rachael Hall is Senior Lecturer in Human Resource Management. After working as a food technologist, a merchandising manager with Coats Viyella and a human resource and quality manager with an engineering consultancy, Rachael has taught employee resourcing and development to both undergraduate and postgraduate students at NBS. She is module leader of an innovative undergraduate module, Developing Learning for Business, and is researching lifelong learning and the role of higher education.

Lynette Harris is Director of HR Professional Practice, founder of the MA in HRM, and is a consultant to a number of organisations in the public and private sector. Following a career in personnel management with a number of leading organisations, Lynette joined NBS in 1988 and has extensive experience teaching human resource management in professional and postgraduate programmes. She has particular expertise in teaching on in-company programmes. She is an ACAS arbitrator and member of the IPD's Quality

Assurance Panel and Policy Adviser to the Derbyshire and Nottinghamshire Branch. Through the directorship of a Teaching Company Scheme at Wayzgoose plc and other work, she is researching performance management and the role of personnel specialists and employment law.

Susan Kirk teaches human resource management to undergraduate and postgraduate students. Prior to joining NBS she worked in export sales with Marconi and in the textile industry.

John Leopold is Professor of Human Resource Management and Head of Department of HRM. His research interests are union renewal in the UK and New Zealand; HRM in greenfield sites in the UK and New Zealand; and control over working time in the UK and The Netherlands. Previously employed at the Universities of Glasgow and Stirling, his teaching interests include British and comparative industrial relations, employee involvement and consultation and human resourcing strategy. He is a former member of the AUT National Executive and a member of the IPD's Quality Assurance Panel.

Eileen Manhire is Senior Lecturer in Human Resource Management, Director of the IPD Professional Accreditation of Competence Centre and Course Leader of the IPD Core Management programme. Between 1973 and 1984, Eileen worked for the Hotel and Catering Industry Training Board and then as a consultant training associate. Her specialist teaching is in the area of employee training and development.

Sue Newell joined NBS in July 1998 as Professor of Innovation and Organisational Analysis. Previously she lectured at the Universities of Warwick, Birmingham, Aston and Portsmouth. She co-holds ESRC research grants on the role of professional associations in the diffusion of technological innovation and the role of networks in the creation of expertise. She is editor of the *International Journal of Assessment and Selection* and has researched in this field as well as in innovation management.

Kirsty Newsome is Course Leader of the MSc in Employment Relations and teaches organisational sociology and employment relations on a range of undergraduate and postgraduate courses. She recently completed her PhD – a study of just-in-time systems of work organisation on buyer/supplier relationships and the labour process of suppliers. Her current research interest is in the area of labour process theory and new workplace regimes.

Chris Rice teaches employee resourcing to postgraduate and postexperience students, has experience of course leadership of IPD programmes and teaches on a wide range of degree and professional programmes in NBS. He has undertaken in-company training for organisations such as Bass, Marks & Spencer, GPT, Lloyds TSB and Siemens. He has assisted the establishment of postgraduate and postexperience management education programmes in Poland, the Czech Republic, Bulgaria and Zimbabwe. He is engaged in a CIMA-funded research project on the ethical problems of accountancy and personnel practitioners.

Jim Stewart is Reader in Human Resource Development, Reviews Editor of the *International Journal of Training and Development* and the *Journal of Applied Management Studies*, and Convenor of the Research Committee of the University Forum for HRD. He is author of *Employee Development Practice* (1999: FT Pitman). He is a National Assignment Moderator and a member of the Quality Assurance Panel of the IPD. He founded the MSc in Human Resource Development at NBS and teaches human resource development on this and other programmes, drawing on his prior experience as a management and employee development professional in both local government and the retail sectors.

Carole Tansley is Senior Lecturer in Human Resource Management and Course Leader of the MA in Strategic Human Resource Management. She teaches in the area of human resourcing strategies, planning, policy and practice to both undergraduate and post-graduate students. She is also an Academic Associate to the Head of Quality Systems at Rolls-Royce plc. Before joining NBS, Carole was an area manager for a search and selection consultancy, a senior human resourcing officer with Rolls-Royce and Associates Ltd and an executive officer in the civil service. Based on her ethnographic study of Cargill, she has completed her PhD on 'Identity, power and exchange in the development of human resource management systems'.

Brian Towers is Professor of Industrial Relations and editor of the *Industrial Relations Journal* and the *Annual European Industrial Relations Review*. Prior to joining NBS, Brian lectured from 1966–89 on the University of Nottingham's programmes for trade unions and industrial workers and was Chair in Industrial Relations at the University of Strathclyde. He has been a Visiting Professor at a number of US universities and his main research interest is a comparative study of statutory recognition procedures in the USA and the UK. He is author of *The Representation Gap: Change and reform in the British and American workplace* (1997: Oxford University Press). He has been on the ACAS panel of arbitrators since 1974 and has conducted well over 100 cases.

David Walsh is Principal Lecturer in Human Resource Management and Course Leader of the Postgraduate Diploma in Personnel Management. He teaches employee relations on this programme and international human resource management on the undergraduate BABS degree. He is a member of the IPD's Quality Assurance Panel and leads the department's involvement in teaching on the Lloyds TSB IPD programmes.

Tony Watson is Professor of Organisational and Managerial Behaviour and author of *In Search of Management* (1994: International Thompson), *Sociology, Work and Industry* (1995: Routledge and *The Emergent Manager* (1999: Sage), as well as various articles in journals such as *Organisational Studies* and *Journal of Management Studies*. He teaches organisational behaviour, human resourcing strategies and research methods to post-graduate students and plays a leading role in doctoral research in NBS. He makes a significant contribution to srategy making and human resourcing policies within the management of The Nottingham Trent University.

LIST OF FIGURES

1.1	Factors shaping an organisation's human resourcing strategy	31
2.1	Three levels of change in the HR function	48
2.2	A *systems* perspective of the HR planning process	51
2.3	A *processual* perspective of the HR planning process	52
5.1	The traditional, 'psychometric' view of the selection process: fitting a square peg to a square hole	132
5.2	Recruitment and selection as a process of exchange and negotiation	134
5.3	Kolb's learning cycle	135
5.4	Typology of selection methods	150
6.1	The purposes of staff appraisal	184
6.2	Design options for designers of appraisal schemes	185
7.1	Middle managers' perceptions of organisational initiatives on appraisal-related pay	206
8.1	Why and how organisations train	220
9.1	Dimensions of management development	245
9.2	Classification of management development methods	255
10.1	Levels of employment law and the HR specialist's role	278
12.1	Dependency theory	316
12.2	Managers' perceptions of ethical issues – a framework	317
12.3	Kohlberg's stages in the development of moral reasoning	324
12.4	Mapping Kohlberg's stages of moral reasoning on to the framework of ethical categorisation	327
13.1	Movements of employee involvement and participation schemes within an organisation over time	357
14.1	Why individuals join unions	372
14.2	Options for managing the employment relationship identified by Guest	378
15.1	Leading carmakers are investing in eastern Europe	402

LIST OF TABLES

1.1	Four usages of the term human resource management	20
1.2	Key terms to be used in this book	21
1.3	Two ways of looking at organisational strategies	23
1.4	Defining human resources and human resourcing strategy	28
1.5	The scope of the human resourcing strategy	29
1.6	Two key and alternative human resourcing principles	29
1.7	HRM-style or 'high-commitment' practices	30
1.8	Possible fits between human resourcing strategies and perceived contingencies	32
1.9	The option of a single or a dual human resourcing strategy	33
2.1	Defining human resources and the HR task	40
2.2	Hard or soft human resource planning?	41
2.3	Five phases of HR planning	51
3.1	Management options for flexibility	72
3.2	Examples of multiskilling/functional flexibility	73
3.3	Facilitating factors promoting use of zero-hours contracts versus overtime	80
3.4	Barriers to use of zero-hours contracts versus overtime	80
3.5	Zero-hours contracts and overtime: advantages and disadvantages	80
4.1	Human resourcing levers in the multinational firm	107
5.1	16PF traits	141
6.1	A systems approach to performance measurement	173
6.2	The desirability and practicability of performance indicators in hospitals	174
6.3	Customer care programme	179
7.1	Rating of individual performance	200
7.2	The extent of performance pay schemes, October 1997	201
7.3	The impact of IPRP on employee behaviour in the private and public sector	205
8.1	Roles within HRD work	225
9.1	Management development agendas	241
9.2	Approaches to management development	244
9.3	Typologies of management development	251
10.1	Key developments in legislation relating to employment from 1960 onwards	268
10.2	A framework for categorising labour law	269
10.3	EU legislation and equal opportunities	272
10.4	The Working Time Directive	273
11.1	Legislative developments in the UK concerned with equal opportunities	293
11.2	Women-only training	298
13.1	Employee involvement and participation compared	341

13.2	Employee participation and involvement continuum	341
13.3	Models of consultation	344
13.4	The differences between quality circles and TQM	347
13.5	Use of Inland Revenue-approved profit-sharing and share-ownership schemes	352
14.1	Two levels at which conflict exists in employment relations	369
14.2	Changing levels of union membership	371
14.3	The UK's strike record post WW2	374
15.1	The world's top 10: production and new registrations of passenger cars, 1995–7 (000s)	403
15.2	Mass production and lean production compared	404
15.3	Auto transplants in North America, 1990	405

LIST OF CASE STUDIES

1.1 Seeing the wood for the trees: human resourcing in O&V Joifel 33
2.1 Electronic Instruments Limited –'hard' and 'soft' human resource planning? 42
2.2 Cargill Inc. 46
2.3 Vertical and horizontal integration at Cargill Europe 47
2.4 A strategic human resource plan? 49
2.5 Cargill HR vision, mission and values statements 52
2.6 The Cargill HR budget-planning process 54
2.7 Cargill Strategic Human Resource Information Management Project (SHRIMP) 57
3.1 O&V Joifel – 10 years on 85
4.1 Going international? 98
4.2 Human resourcing in a major US multinational 117
4.3 Saving face in Malaysia 118
4.4 The Bee-K-Gee Corporation 122
5.1 Monks Brewery 163
6.1 The validity of financial measures in the private sector 174
6.2 Designing an appraisal scheme for a university 186
7.1 The Mutual Alliance Bank 204
7.2 The Eastward Housing Association 210
8.1 Bainbridge NHS Trust Hospital 235
9.1 Highfield College of FE 259
10.1 The Arctel Company Ltd – conflict in the maintenance section 287
11.1 Developing equal opportunities at Star Entertainment Ltd 306
12.1 Whistleblowing: the Graham Pink case 325
12.2 Reverse headhunting 332
13.1 Ragtime Textiles 359
14.1 Conflict and co-operation in the Dogger Bank loans department – Part I 367
14.1 Conflict and co-operation in the Dogger Bank loans department – Part II 368
14.2 Union recognition in Kleensweep 378
14.3 Co-operation and conflict in Data-Cables 382
15.1 Comparative industrial relations policy 412

ACKNOWLEDGEMENTS

The authors and publishers wish to thank the following for permission to reproduce copyright material:

Cargill plc for extracts from company documents; N. Anderson and C. Ostroff 'Selection as Socialization', Chapter 20 of N. Anderson and P. Herriot (1997) *International Handbook of Selection and Assessment*, John Wiley and Sons Ltd, for Table 5.1; MCB University Press and *Personnel Review*, Vol. 24, No.1, for Figures 6.1 and 6.2; IPD Publications for Tables 7.1 and 7.2 from IPD (1998) Performance Pay Survey, Executive Summary; MCB University Press and *Journal of European Industrial Training* for Figure 8.1 from R. Bennett and T. Leduchowicz (1983) What Makes for An Effective Trainer?; American Society for Training and Development and P. McLagan and R. McCullough for Table 8.1 from *Models of Excellence: the Conclusions and Recommendations of the ASTD Training and Development Competency Study*, Copyright 1983, the American Society for Training and Development; IPD Publications for Table 10.3 from *IPD European Update*, July 1998; Lynette Harris for Case Study 11.1; MCB University Press and A. Carroll for Ranking ethical principles from 'Principles of Business Ethics: their role in decision making and an initial consensus' in *Management Decision*, Vol. 28, No. 8, 1990; D. McGregor (1960) *The Human Side of the Enterprise*, McGraw-Hill for Figure 12.1; C. Fisher, A. Lovell and C. Rice for Figures 12.2 and 12.4; Sage Publications for Table 13.1 from J. Hyman and R. Mason *Managing Employee Involvement and Participation* (1995); M. Marchington and *People Management* for Table 13.3 from M. Marchington (1988) 'The Four Faces of Employee Consultation', *People Management*, May, p. 47; Industrial Relations Services and the *Human Resource Management Journal* for Table 13.4 from A. Wilkinson, M. Marchington, J. Goodman and P. Ackers, 'Total quality management and employee involvement' (1992).

Every effort has been made to trace all the copyright-holders, but if any have been inadvertently overlooked the publishers will be pleased to make the necessary arrangements at the first opportunity.

We are indebted to the quiet efficient skills of Debbie Wojtulewicz who prepared the final manuscript from the assorted disks and e-mail attachments of the contributing authors. Without her dedication the final deadline would have been missed.

Finally, we thank our editor Michelle Graham at Financial Times Management for her support and our Publisher Sadie McClelland, who came to this project late, but who helped steer it to a successful conclusion with her support, advice and encouragement.

FOREWORD

Achieving the human advantage

Paul Turner

HR Business Director, Lloyds TSB Group and
Visiting Professor of Human Resource Practice,
Nottingham Business School

The dynamic nature of the competitive environment, the emphasis on inclusivity in strategy setting and the need to ensure a convergence of interests in the way in which organisations are run are three particular challenges to the modern organisation. Ensuring that appropriate people strategies are in place to deal with these challenges is increasingly recognised as critical to success. This book is a significant contribution to the crafting of such strategies. In identifying key human resourcing themes, the book provides important insights into dialogues in which organisations, managers and others are likely to be involved as they tackle the subject. The circumstances facing public and private organisations as they enter the twenty-first century make its timing particularly appropriate.

Developing a strategy against which an organisation's resources can be allocated is a complex affair. First, the environment in which public- and private-sector organisations operate is extremely dynamic. This leads to a situation whereby, for many, change is the norm, change is complex, radical change is probable or likely. Furthermore, it is becoming increasingly difficult for organisations to sustain their performance using conventional sources of advantage. Even the theoretical constructs of business strategy don't seem to provide the answers that they once did. Analysing external forces, identifying opportunities, defining core competencies and matching them in the form of a business strategy now seems too pedestrian a process for strategy setting. So organisations face a double jeopardy whereby both their traditional sources of competitive advantage and the theoretical basis of that advantage are less certain than they once seemed; a situation compounded by a rapid pace of change.

Among the changes facing organisations from an employer's perspective are new or increased competition, technology advances, a greater focus on customer service requiring different types of knowledge, skill, attitude and behaviour, new types of production processes necessary to survive against global competition in the manufacturing sector, and the radical change that has taken place in the running of public services during the past 20 years. At the same time, there have been real changes from the employee's viewpoint. These include greater flexibility of employment, individual rather than collectivist approaches to reward, a decline in long-term employment and the adoption of new organisational patterns moving away from hierarchical structures. Even a cursory environmental scan, therefore, will show a highly complex situation facing organisations.

One way of meeting this challenge has been to decide on a particular strategic direction and allocate resources either to achieving that advantage or sustaining it if it has already been delivered. Ideally, there would be rationality on the part of the environment, markets and the decision-making process to enable the strategy to be delivered. Often, however, the environment is far from rational. Achieving long-term success or sustained business efficiency therefore continues to be an issue that taxes academics and practitioners alike.

Some of the key components of competitive advantage are less advantageous than they used to be. For example, one of the conventional sources of advantage, technology, is actually becoming a great leveller, giving unprecedented amounts of information as well as enabling businesses to access markets regardless of whether they have had a historical presence in those markets. Technology developments such as the Internet are likely to offer further potential in this regard. Another source of advantage has been the enhanced use of financial competence. Aiming to be a low-cost provider, focusing on shareholder value or using financial engineering as a way of leveraging the organisation's capital base or potential cash flow seemed to be areas that provided differential advantage. A third source of advantage used to be greater effectiveness in marketing. Case studies abound of the marketing prowess of some world-class brands and the problems that were likely to occur if others did not learn these lessons. And so a great deal of effort went into these areas at strategy time to try to decide from where sources of differentiation could come. It is the massive upskilling that has taken place in the areas of technology, finance and marketing that has, ironically, led to their being able to deliver less advantage in today's environment. As a focus of activity they are still on the critical path and their importance has not diminished. Increasingly, however, the management activity in these areas, which was once designed to achieve differentiation, is now necessary merely to stay in business. The differentiators have become core to business survival.

The challenge to organisations in both the public and private sectors is to find a formula that maximises the benefits from the appropriate uses of technology, finance and marketing and adds to them an extra dimension that will provide a successful future. It is not about replacing strategies in these areas, but ensuring that they converge with another ingredient and together deliver advantage. The question is: 'what is the ingredient?' The answer would seem to lie in the organisation's human resources and it is possible that this will become the key differentiator sought by organisations in their strategy. If this is indeed the case, then the process by which people are acquired, deployed and retained, the values that enable them to contribute to performance coupled with continued motivation at times of great change, and a business philosophy that ensures convergence of interests between diverse organisational stakeholders, of which the workplace is an important one, will all be critical to achieving this differentiation.

A significant contributor to how these processes, values and business philosophies are put in place will be the professionalism by which human resources are managed. There are two elements to this. First, there is the short- and long-term dialogue that ensures that human effort matches organisational objectives. This is largely, but not uniquely, the process of general management. The second element is the framework within which people skills, capabilities and behaviours are contained. It is this which defines the role of the human resources specialist, which articulates the nature of the dialogue about human resources and the boundaries within which this dialogue takes place. It is to these areas that this book is addressed. But why has such a book been produced?

Recent developments in human resource management and human resourcing strategy have already provided some of the ideas, tools and techniques on which the frameworks referred to above are built. Evolving over a period of 20 years, the human resourcing function has recognised some of the limitations of traditional personnel and training methods and has adapted them accordingly. Reacting to the growing demands (and criticisms) from a range of organisations, human resourcing has become more 'strategic', has become more business oriented, has become a partner in decision making. It has taken a much more robust approach to its role and to some extent this has been acknowledged. Academics and practitioners of HR have been on quite a journey to get to this position. This has been no means easy, because of the sheer diversity of views and options about what should constitute the role of HR, how much it should be a partner to business or a neutral adviser, how much traditional activity should be devolved to the line, and most important, what the strategic role of HR should be. None the less, progress has been made and a functional health check would show HR to be relatively fit, even though each question answered generates others. The result is that the debate about HR continues.

This book is a welcome contribution to the debate in three ways. First, it provides a new method of dealing with the organisation's longer-term human resource issues. By introducing the concept of 'human resourcing strategy', the various strands of the debate are pulled together into a coherent format. Further, the book uses a broad brush on the canvas of HR and a full range of perspectives are included in the overall picture. Second, it provides both a pedagogic and an academic approach and as such the book is a valuable source of references, ideas and practical examples of the ways in which effective human resourcing can be achieved. Third, it addresses the subject thematically rather than following a product or technical approach. In so doing, it is able to guide managerial thought from a cross-functional perspective. By dealing with human resourcing strategy in this way, the book represents a contribution to the shift in the HR paradigm that is taking place as we move into the twenty-first century. Its contributors have combined pragmatism within an innovative framework and the output is a very original view of a subject that is growing in importance.

PLAN OF THE BOOK

PART I – STRATEGY, PLANNING AND FLEXIBILITY AT HOME AND ABROAD			
Chapter 1 Human resourcing strategies: choice, chance and circumstance	Chapter 2 Human resource planning: strategies, systems and processes	Chapter 3 Managing uncertainty or managing uncertainly?	Chapter 4 International human resourcing

PART II – HUMAN RESOURCING POLICIES IN PRACTICE		
Chapter 5 Assessment, selection and evaluation: problems and pitfalls	Chapter 6 Performance management and performing management	Chapter 7 Performing pay and performing for pay

PART III – TRAINING AND DEVELOPMENT	
Chapter 8 Employee training and development	Chapter 9 Management development

PART IV – LAW, ETHICS AND EQUALITY		
Chapter 10 Employment law and human resourcing: challenges and constraints	Chapter 11 Achieving equality of opportunity?	Chapter 12 Managing messy moral matters: ethics and HRM

PART V – EMPLOYMENT RELATIONS		
Chapter 13 Employee participation, involvement and communication	Chapter 14 Conflict and co-operation in employment relations	Chapter 15 Conflict, change and compromise: comparative industrial relations and the world automobile industry

INTRODUCTION

*John Leopold, Lynette Harris
and Tony Watson*

The aims and objectives of this book

One of the most important requirements of all work organisations is that they have a continuous supply of human skills, capabilities and committed behaviours that will take them forward into the future. This applies to all employing organisations – from manufacturing concerns to service providers, from small firms to giant corporations, from private enterprises to public bodies. The providing and maintaining of these capabilities, commitments and behaviours is what we call *human resourcing*. And when we speak of *strategic* human resourcing, we are referring to a process of resource acquisition and development which is concerned with more than simply meeting day-to-day demands or short-term staffing pressures. Strategic human resourcing is about shaping the human dimension of the organisation as a whole and taking the enterprise forward towards a healthy long-term future.

It is with this broad perspective on strategic human resourcing that a group of like-minded colleagues within the Department of Human Resource Management at Nottingham Business School have collaborated to identify and write about a whole range of further perspectives, principles and practices that follow from it. This book is a distinctive contribution to the literature on human resource management for a number of reasons. First, it is structured around a basic perspective that frames all the contributions that follow it. A processual view of work organisations and of human resource strategy making is explained and vividly illustrated in Chapter 1 and the approach it advocates is developed in various ways, and with reference to a number of specific aspects of human resourcing, in subsequent contributions. Second, each chapter is based on an examination of the principles, policies and practices of human resource management: 'principles', to examine a number of concepts that lie behind what managers do or seek to do; 'policies', because these principles may be manifest in a number of different ways and from the processual approach we stress the question of choices that managers can make to deal with the employment relationship, even though these choices are bounded by contingencies and constraints; and finally 'practices', because there are indeed many practices arising from the implementation of policy options. These themes mean that in each chapter we try to examine a range of principles that may be used to guide managerial thought and action, we discuss the policies that might be adopted and examine the practices that a range of research evidence reveals in organisations. All this is done to enable the reader to make better informed judgements about what is appropriate or feasible or even desirable in their organisation.

Third, we try to achieve these objectives by writing at a time when the study of human resource management has matured following two decades of debate, often with little purpose or outcome, about the meaning of HRM. Writing at the end of the 1990s, we are better able to reflect on the emergent trends and to analyse critically the principles, policies and practices that are to be found in a range of organisations, both in the UK and around the world.

Each chapter is written around a common structure of learning and teaching features that will assist readers in addressing the issues raised in the chapters, relating these to their past experience and considering and projecting them into their future practice. These features include clear student learning objectives for each chapter, activities to engage students, clearly laid-out definitions of key terms, chapter summaries, a major case study, discussion points and a guide to further reading at the end of each chapter. The bibliography is at the end of the book rather than after each chapter. Many of the chapters are based on recent research by members of the writing team, but all are designed to be authoritative overviews of the current situation in their field. The material in them, especially the activities and case studies, has been piloted, and subsequently refined, in our teaching on advanced undergraduate and specialised human resource management master's and professional programmes, as well as with members of more general MBA-type courses. In short, the book is the product of a team experienced in teaching the students at whom it is aimed, and the chapters have been shaped by the authors' pedagogic experience and research work.

The intended readership

The book will be of value to practising personnel practitioners and line managers seeking to develop further their knowledge and understanding of current operational HR practice. It is aimed at the reflective practitioner and is designed to evaluate the processual approach to human resource strategy making and to consider the implications of principles, perspectives and practices on human resource management that may relate to their own practice. These words are deliberately plural, as we do not set out to offer a prescriptive set of tools applicable in all circumstances, but to create the opportunity for readers to reflect on the choices, chances and circumstances that affect their own situation.

The book will therefore be of relevance and interest to managers studying on generalist management programmes such as the DMS or MBA, to those on specialist HRM courses, such as students taking the IPD specialist electives en route to graduateship of the IPD, and to students following specialist master's programmes in human resource management. The book has also been written to support final-year-level undergraduates and people who have an interest in management but have not yet started on a managerial career. It is therefore envisaged that distinctive groups of students will benefit from reading significant sections of this book, but that the relevant chapters will depend on the specific course they follow, their personal interests and the guidance of tutors.

Using this book

The book is a postgraduate and advanced undergraduate textbook and each chapter contains a number of common features that will help readers to gain most benefit from it. In addition, there is an accompanying tutors' guide that offers advice and suggestions for using the exercises, case studies and discussion questions in the classroom situation. Each chapter begins with a set of objectives that readers should be able to achieve on completion of the chapter and its associated exercises. Throughout the chapters are activities that can be used in a number of ways depending on the learning context of the reader. At the end of each chapter is a major case study that attempts to draw on the key learning points in the chapter and offers the opportunity to examine and discuss a range of questions around each case. Activities and case studies can be used as either individual or group-work exercises by course members as directed independent learning activities, or as part of tutor-guided workshop discussions. To that end, the case studies are of varying length and the number of questions set for discussion can be varied by tutors to suit the needs of the student group and the time available. Guidance on this is to be found in the accompanying tutors' guide. The end-of-chapter case studies are ideal for use with a supporting lecture followed by workshop activity. Most chapters conclude with a set of questions that can be used to open up new areas for discussion or as reflective exercises on what has been learned. Finally, each chapter ends with suggestions for further reading.

In producing the exercises and case studies, we have attempted to draw on a range of organisational contexts, including manufacturing, public-sector, SMEs and non-profit-making bodies to reflect the range of settings where the employment relationship is managed. Throughout the book we have tried to analyse the respective role and responsibilities of specialist and line managers in the selected areas of practice that we examine. This is to reflect the intended readership, potential specialists and managers who have to manage the employment relationship as part of their overall managerial role, as well as the way the relationship is practised. Connected to this is a further common feature, in that managers have to make a whole series of informed judgements, and the book seeks to inform the choices, chances and circumstances that shape and influence these judgements. Each chapter also recognises that the personnel specialist may have to operate as a consultant, either external or internal, to persuade line managers to pursue various policies and practices.

The structure of the book

The book is structured into five parts, each containing a number of chapters. Part I introduces the overall concepts used in the book and examines the strategic aspects of human resource management. Issues related to human resource planning, the use of flexibility and the international dimension of these issues are explored in subsequent chapters. Part II discusses human resourcing policies in practice through a consideration of assessment, selection and evaluation, performance management and performance pay. In Part III, employee training and development and management development are examined in detail. Part IV focuses on the law, ethics and equality management, with a chapter on each of these important topics. Finally, in Part V there is a consideration of the employment relations dimensions of human resourcing through a discussion of employee participation and involvement, industrial conflict, and through a detailed examination of industrial relations in the global automobile industry.

Strategy, planning and flexibility at home and abroad

■ A processual view of human resource strategy-making

Chapter 1 introduces the reader to the processual view of management that underpins the rest of the book. The processual view is set out as an alternative to orthodox systems views of human resource strategy making. Human resource strategy making, it is argued, is better viewed not as a 'plan to be implemented', but as the pattern to be seen over time in the way organisational managements handle the human resources of effort, skill and capability that are needed for the organisation to continue in the long term. A second distinguishing feature of this view of management is that human resource strategy making is seen as a facet of the general managing of an employing organisation and not as an activity of human resource specialists or one practised only by 'top managers'. Rather, it is seen as being the concern of all managers, but it is recognised that within this the human resource specialist can make a particular contribution.

None the less, the concern with the fit between strategies and organisational contingencies that is central to the orthodox views of strategy is retained, but the interplay of choice chance and circumstance is stressed in shaping the emergent pattern of outcomes, both planned and unplanned. The search for fit may take place at two levels: vertical integration between the human resourcing strategy and the organisational context; and horizontal integration between different elements of the human resourcing principles and practices. Examples of approaches to both vertical and horizontal integration appear throughout the book.

As explained more fully in the chapter, we prefer to use the term *human resourcing strategy* rather than HRM strategy, as there cannot be a HRM strategy that stands outside of the overall organisational strategy. This approach also recognises that a range of human resourcing strategies are possible depending on choice, chance and circumstance, and that what has in some circles come to be known as 'HRM' is better regarded as but one possible approach and therefore called HRM-style practices. It is suggested that the fundamental choice that mangers face in practising human resource strategy making is between approaches based on direct-control/low-commitment principles and those based on indirect-control/high-commitment principles. Moreover, it is suggested that managers may seek to adopt either a single or a dual approach.

■ Human resource planning

Human resource strategy making is related to human resource planning in Chapter 2. An explanation and critique of the conceptualisation of 'hard ' and 'soft' human resource planning are offered and it is suggested that such a conceptualisation is not particularly helpful, as managers use both approaches simultaneously and alternately in addressing issues of human resource planning. Continuing the themes of Chapter 1, systems and processual approaches to understanding human resource planning are explored in order to gain a better understanding of the relationships involved. Particular attention is given to the vertical and horizontal integration aspects of the relationship between corporate strategies and human resourcing activities. Both of these issues are explored through an integrating case study of Cargill Europe, to illustrate the different understandings gained from trying to analyse the case study example from both a systems and processual perspective. The concept of strategic exchange is used to develop the processual view.

Specific aspects of human resource planning, such as ethics, vision and vision making and budgetary control, are examined and particular attention is given to the use of computerised human resource information systems, again from both the systems and processual perspectives through the Cargill example. Although throughout the chapter explanations and understandings from both the systems and processual perspectives are offered, it is suggested that a better understanding of the relationships involved in human resource planning comes from the processual perspective, as this involves the incorporation of continual experimentation, revision and rethinking in which processes of argument, debate and conflict between different managers and interest groups play a part.

■ Flexible employment

Both of the first two chapters mention the notion of the *flexible firm*. Chapter 3 takes up this position and focuses on it. Atkinson's model (1984) is outlined and then a number of critiques of this model that have been advanced over the last decade are summarised, before readers are invited to address some debates around the flexible firm. These include assessing the evidence for and against the model in terms of the empirical evidence; judging whether or not the model might be viable in particular circumstances; considering whether there are other explanations for the adoption of types of flexibility associated with the flexible firm; and reflecting on whether adopting the processual view lends support to the model.

Notwithstanding the debate about the flexible firm, the chapter then uses the Atkinson terminology of functional, numerical and temporal flexibility, as well as reward and locational flexibility, to present arguments around a series of options from which managers may choose to employ and utilise human resources. Detailed examples are given of five forms of flexibility and these are considered in terms of the extent of usage of the form; the facilitating factors that promote their use; the barriers against them; their advantages and disadvantages from both the employer's and employee's perspective; and a final summary overview of our state of knowledge on the particular form.

In concluding, it is suggested, in line with a central argument of this book, that a processual view of strategy formation can better explain the research evidence on the use of forms of flexible employment, rather than a view that seeks to find top-down senior management strategy on the issue. It is stressed that while managers have choices over the use of forms of flexibility, they only do so in the circumstances set by balancing the needs and imperatives of the employer and those of the employee.

■ International human resourcing

In Chapter 4, the central argument about choice, chance and circumstance is extended to the management of the employment relationship in firms operating internationally. The similarities and the differences between national and international human resourcing are discussed, but the differences are presented as differences of degree rather than of essence. International human resourcing is therefore presented in a way that builds on, rather than replaces, our understanding of its practice in a national UK context. It therefore uses the models presented in these initial chapters and relates these to the specifics of human resourcing that follow. It is argued that managers make human resourcing decisions based on their interpretation of societal and organisational factors; their choices are influenced by circumstances and their opportunities reined in by constraints.

Globalisation, the growing economic interdependence among countries as reflected in increasing cross-border flows of goods, services, capital and knowhow, is discussed as the critical context for organisational approaches to international human resourcing. First, the structural form of the international company is examined in terms of being either multinational, global, international or transnational, and it is demonstrated how each of these possible structural choices can act as a major constraint on the subsequent operation of international human resourcing.

The second set of strategic choices is around the dominant cultural viewpoint or approach adopted by headquarters management towards its foreign subsidiaries. These choices are discussed in terms of Heenan and Perlmutter's (1979) classification of polycentric, ethnocentric, geocentric and regiocentric. Again, the implications for international human resourcing are explored, with particular reference to developing a way of thinking or 'mindset' appropriate for a geocentric organisational culture.

The third set of strategic choices faced by managers in international companies is that of staffing policies, expressed in terms of the possible combinations of parent-country nationals, host-country nationals and third-country nationals. It is argued that the adoption of particular staffing policies is constrained and shaped by the decisions made over structural forms and dominant management orientation. Possible outcomes of these interactions are discussed in terms of the pre-departure, expatriation and repatriation phases of the relocation process.

The concluding section concentrates on the formulation of human resourcing policies and practices for host-country subsidiaries, based on a careful analysis of local conditions and circumstances. One approach is to amend parent-company practices in the light of contingent factors; and particular attention is drawn to the significance of the local culture as it relates to the management of work and the maintenance of favourable employee relations. Comparative studies of national cultures are then considered, primarily through the work of Hofstede. The author asserts that such a study may be useful for the human resourcing decision maker as a general guide, but that it should ideally be no more than a starting point for a comprehensive analysis of the circumstances affecting the foreign subsidiary.

Human resourcing policies in practice

■ Assessment, selection and evaluation

In this book we have stressed that an essential part of managing is about making choices, albeit in constrained circumstances. Assessment, selection and evaluation are fundamental aspects within any decision-making process and the ways in which these relate to decisions about whom to employ, promote, reassign, train and dismiss are explored in this chapter. Approaches to this are examined through two lenses: the 'normal' or systemic approach to selection, encapsulated by the metaphor of fitting the square peg (the 'right' individual) into the square hole (the job); and the exchange or process approach, based on negotiation between the employing organisation and the potential recruit. Both approaches are, however, based on the notion of 'fit' between the person and the job environment; this notion of 'fit' is one that recurs throughout this book. The exchange or process perspective is advocated because, rather than attempting to deny the subjectivity inherent in human judgements, it recognises it, so that selection is seen as a process of two-way negotiation.

Kolb's (1984) learning cycle model is then applied to the learning that takes place in the selection process. Experience is related to the concept of impression management; reflective observation is linked to attribution theory; generalisation is related to personal construct theory and the two approaches to selection are analysed; and, finally experimentation is discussed in terms of validity and criteria for selection. The insights from this analysis and discussion are then used to consider how selection is generally carried out within organisations and the problems associated with this.

The systemic perspective is the traditional and still dominant approach to selection based on defining the job and the ideal candidate to fill it. It is explained and criticised in terms of the insights offered by the process approach. Following job analysis is the stage of deciding how candidates are going to be measured or assessed against the determined requirements of the post and candidate. An extensive range of possible methods are introduced and examined, including application forms and biodata, psychometric measures, performance tests, group methods, references, interviews and assessment centres. It is suggested that adopting the process perspective does not necessarily alter the methods adopted, but does alter the way they are used.

■ Performance management

In Chapter 6, various approaches and techniques of performance management are described and criticised. Following Walters (1995), performance management is defined as the process of improving the quality and quantity of work done and bringing all activity in line with an organisation's objectives, but is presented and analysed in this chapter as a corpus of folk prescription and recipes. Difficulties in clarifying and publishing objectives and of measuring performance are examined. A number of other features of the practice of performance management are then discussed in some detail. These include target setting and monitoring, 360° appraisal, personal development planning, dealing with problem staff and staff appraisal. Each is discussed in terms of the claims made by their advocates, but also the observed difficulties and drawbacks from their operation in practice.

The chapter concludes that there is no solid evidence that performance management improves an organisation's performance, but that there is evidence that people can find it helpful in interpreting and evaluating their organisational roles. But analysing performance management as folk lore makes possible the suggestion that performance management lore provides people with the rhetorical raw material from which they can craft personally relevant interpretations of their organisational and personal roles.

■ Performance pay

Within the overall context of performance management, performance-related pay (PRP) has been an extensively used system for rewarding employees and for encouraging them to perform to standards set by senior managers. Chapter 7 focuses on individual PRP. It is demonstrated that such reward systems were a feature of employers' responses to the market pressures of the 1980s and were used in an attempt to convey organisational objectives and reward the behaviours that employers sought from their workforces. The contradictions between commitment and reward in the search for HRM-style policies are explored and related particularly to two motivational theories: expectancy theory (Vroom, 1964) and goal-setting theory (Locke *et al.*, 1981, Locke and Latham, 1984, 1990). The 'felt-fair' principle is also used to examine problems and difficulties with PRP in practice. Issues of subjectivity and inconsistency in measuring and rating PRP schemes are also discussed.

The theme of the relationship between line managers and personnel specialists is discussed in the context of the view that the manager is invariably identified as the weak link in the application of performance-management systems, and the tension between the stated objectives of schemes and the hidden agenda perceived by many managers is examined in a range of contexts. The chapter concludes that the search for a pay system that improves employee motivation, productivity and commitment remains elusive, but although PRP has failed to provide a panacea, it remains firmly on the agenda of many organisations. It is suggested that PRP makes the employment relationship more transactional and then this stands in contrast to the relational position desired by those searching for high commitment.

Training and development

The two chapters in Part III introduce the reader to particular debates about the specialist function of employee training and development and management development. In both chapters, it is argued that the development of individuals and ultimately organisations can only be achieved when training and development and its practitioners are able to contribute to human resource strategy making. Tensions between the terms training and development are explored and working definitions are given of these and other terms used in Chapter 8. A modified version of the Bennett and Leduchowicz (1983) model is utilised to consider the 'caretaker', 'educator', 'evangelist', and 'innovator' roles and to explore these tensions further.

From the observation that trainers have increasingly had change agent roles comes the establishment and exploration of this particular model of training and development. This leads back to the continuing theme of whether these activities are, or should be, performed by line managers or specialist practitioners. In this context, a case is made for 'partnership arrangements' (Jones, 1991). Whoever is responsible for training and development activities, it is argued that in order to make the best contribution to organisational effectiveness, the profile of the training and development function needs to be raised. The prospects for this being achieved are examined, and in particular issues around the evaluation of training and development activities are explored.

After examining various examples of employee development and managing the change process, the chapter concludes by linking the development approach to the indirect-control/high-commitment human resourcing strategy introduced in Chapter 1. In contrast, the training focus discussed earlier in this chapter can be related to the direct-control/low-commitment strategy, but it is suggested that in being able to differentiate between a training and a development strategy, managers in an organisation are able to exercise some degree of strategic choice. Indeed, by stressing the possibility of choice it is also possible to envisage a dual human resourcing strategy, with an emphasis on training for some employees but on development for others.

■ Management development

In some organisations the term development is reserved for managers. In Chapter 9, the concept and practice of management development are examined. It is suggested that management development is a term with no clear meaning and a number of approaches to the concept are explored. In part, it is argued, this is related to unclarity and ambiguity about the nature of management, especially if one moves away from a conventional view of management as a rational and technical activity to adopt a processual view, in which managing is seen as confusing and uncertain and therefore what should constitute development for managers in such a situation is equally uncertain. Similar uncertainties exist around the concept of development and Lee's (1997) four approaches to management development – maturation, shaping, voyage and emergent – are used to assist in understanding the issues.

A key issue in the debate is whether the focus is, or should be, on the individual or the organisation. This is examined by means of a framework that links the individual/organisation focus to the changed behaviour/career progression tension in the primary purpose of management development. It is argued that this framework allows the practice of management development to be categorised whether it is being approached from a conventional perspective or from a processual perspective.

The framework is then utilised to examine various approaches and methods in management development. Typologies provided by Mabey and Salaman (1995), Burgoyne (1988) and Mumford (1993, 1997) are discussed and related to prior debates. Linkages from these approaches and typologies are then drawn to the range of methods that may be adopted, and differences between changes in the job, changes in job content and changes within the job are explored. The framework introduced to categorise the focus and purpose of management development is linked to possible methods.

In the final section, issues around the horizontal integration of management development and human resourcing strategy are examined. The direct-control/low-commitment and indirect-control/high-commitment approaches to human resource strategy introduced in Chapter 1 are related to management development in terms of the competency approach and the development approach. But these are not seen as categorical either/ors, but as a continuum with tendencies in one direction or another being traceable between organisations and, linked to the concept of a dual human resourcing strategy, within them.

Law, ethics and equality

■ The challenges and constraints of employment law

Chapter 10 is not a detailed account of employment law, but an examination of the ways in which employment law, both UK and European, has had an impact on human resource strategy making; how the responsibilities of interpreting and applying employment law have varied and may continue to vary between line managers and human resource specialists; and how changes in employment law might affect the relative status and positions of line managers and HR specialists. The development of employment law in the post-war period is discussed briefly in both its UK and EU dimensions. The legislation presented is correct as of August 1998.

A model is offered that maps four decades of legal regulation/deregulation against the dominant role played by personnel/HR managers in each period and the focus of their activity. For example, in the 1990s we are witnessing increasing EU regulation and a consequent growth in individual rights. This, it is suggested, will leave personnel/HR managers at a crossroads between focusing on keeping the rule book or strategically integrating the new regulations. The analysis of the impact of the legislative environment on the role of the personnel specialist is related to longstanding debates about how such specialists demonstrate their value and contribution to other managers. This is traced through the four decades of the model.

Central to the search for a clear role of the status of personnel specialists is their relationship with line managers. The view of human resource management as a particular form of managing the employment relationship has identified the devolvement of personnel activities to line management as a key characteristic. Ways in which this relationship might be interpreted and developed in the context of employment law are examined. It is suggested, however, that while knowledge of the law may provide a potential source of organisational influence, it also has the potential to handcuff the HR function into a policing role that can make its contribution seem to be bureaucratic rather than strategic.

■ Achieving equality of opportunity

In Chapter 11, the issue of equality of opportunity is examined. It is presented as an issue that is integral to all areas of managing the employment relationship. Equality of opportunity is discussed throughout in terms of a range of factors that may be used as the basis for unfair discrimination in the labour market, such as race, disability, sex and class. This chapter is linked to the discussion of law and ethics and these are related to reasons that employers have promoted greater employment opportunity – to achieve penalty avoidance through compliance, or in the positive pursuit of organisational benefits (Dickens, 1994). Policy initiatives associated with these motives are explored, such as target setting and equality training. The approaches that may be adopted are examined in terms of the liberal – treating everybody the same – and radical – achieving equal outcomes – approaches. Adopting either of these approaches leads to a different set of policy prescriptions, while a third perspective suggests a transformative EO strategy (Cockburn, 1989).

Despite such initiatives, there has been only limited success in achieving equality in the workplace. The difficulties in translating espoused EO policies into practice are then explored through the tensions between line and personnel managers, the role played by managers of the dominant group in perpetuating their position, and disadvantaged groups resisting initiatives that are intended to assist them. An alternative perspective on equality based on management of diversity rather than equal opportunities is then examined. This shifts the focus from positive action to managing diversity, or maximising employee potential and being seen as relevant to all employees and involving all managers. However, Crompton's (1996) warning that the celebration of 'difference' may result in the intensification of material inequalities is added as a rider to the view that managing diversity is an approach that will necessarily overcome the difficulties identified in earlier approaches.

■ Managing messy moral matters

The issues and problems with which human resource managers have been grappling in the previous two chapters are underscored by the subject matter of Chapter 12 – ethics. While not arguing that HR managers are the sole repository of ethical standards in organisations, this chapter seeks to identify the types of ethical issues that all managers face at work, and to identify the main ethical principles that are appropriate for organisational contexts. In particular, a framework for categorising managers' perceptions of ethical issues is introduced. The eight categories in this framework are discussed in detail, as are the possibilities and meanings of movement between categories. The framework of ethical categorisation is related to models of moral reasoning, particularly that put forward by Kohlberg (1969, 1984). The tension between Kohlberg's model, with means proceeding to a pre-determined final purpose, and the circular model presented in this chapter is examined.

Finally, three ways of improving awareness of, and the quality of analysis of, ethical issues are considered. One approach is to follow the Kohlberg hierarchical model and seek to raise our levels of moral reasoning. The second is to consider the role of values and heuristics, or tools for thinking, as a way of comprehending moral and ethical decision making. Deservingness, individual need, utility, fairness, ecology and personal satisfaction and gain are presented as heuristics that assist in making decisions. Finally, the role of professional body ethical codes is considered. It is pointed out that ethical reasoning is not the same as ethical action, and the chapter concludes by arguing that ethical organisations will only emerge when they have members who are skilled at thinking morally for themselves and who are able to act on their thoughts.

Employment relations

■ Employee participation, involvement and communication

The final chapters of the book consider employment relations issues in the context of human resource strategy making. In Chapter 13, issues related to employee participation, involvement and communication are considered. The difference in meaning between industrial democracy, employee participation and employee involvement are clearly established, as is the point that managers, employees and trade unions often have different objectives from those of participation and involvement schemes. These differences are related to the Hyman & Mason (1995) differentiation of the two terms, and to a model of a participation continuum that permits an understanding of which participants are seeking what type of scheme and why. In particular, throughout the chapter the distinction is drawn between direct and indirect schemes and job-related and business-related levels of decision making. Movements in the popularity of different schemes are discussed in terms of the cycles and waves models.

In the context of these general distinctions, a number of particular schemes of participation and involvement are examined, including representative participation, downward communication, upward problem solving, task participation and financial involvement. The prospects for a change in approach in the way that British managers, trade unionists and employees regard employee participation and involvement are considered in the light of developments in policy and practice in the European Union.

Finally, the notion of horizontal fit between different forms of employee participation and involvement and the relationship of these to overall human resourcing strategy is considered. In particular, the potential mismatch from a fads and fashions approach is highlighted, as are the tensions in operating schemes derived from the employee participation approach alongside the employee involvement one. The Marchington *et al.* (1993) model of the dynamics of schemes over time is used to assist our understanding of the processes involved.

■ Conflict and co-operation in employment relations

The central argument of Chapter 14 is that there is a complex interrelationship between conflict and co-operation in the employment relationship and that this can best be understood by using a processual and pluralist approach rather than a systems and unitarist one. Conflict is neither the opposite of, nor the absence of, co-operation, but the two co-exist and, indeed, interact with each other. Conflict may be covert or overt, but the processual view leads us to suggest the continuous need for people to manage their differences. These can be between a variety of individuals and groups in the organisation, not simply between unions and management. Conflict may exist at the level of interests and at the level of behaviour and this understanding helps us distinguish between manifest conflict and latent conflict. These issues are explored through the device of a dialogue between two reflective practitioners of HRM and a case study of organisational conflict.

One arrangement that employers use to manage conflict is to institutionalise it through collective bargaining with trade unions. However, union recognition is only one of a number of possible strategic directions that employers can and do follow. Others considered here are union derecognition, in the context where employers may wish to end or marginalise previously established relationships with unions, substitution strategies, under which employers seek to create an employment relationship where employees do not seek to represent their views through unions or use them as a vehicle for improvement of terms and conditions of employment; or a 'black hole' strategy, where unions are rejected and avoided by whatever means possible. The context for these possible strategic directions is examined in the light of the decline in union membership since the 1979 peak, the weakening and decentralisation of collective bargaining, and the reduction of the overt manifestation of conflict through strikes. It is suggested that employers might wish to reconsider their strategies in the light of statutory support for union recognition and derecognition, but employers and trade unions are also likely to take account of the overall industrial relations context discussed above. Students are invited to explore these possible strategic directions through a case study.

One approach that has been adopted in the 1990s is to combine the 'HRM-style' focus on the individual efforts of employees with new production concepts such as lean production or total quality management. These are known as *new workplace regimes* and are analysed here in the context of their being understood as attempts to contain or deny overt forms of conflict. Ways in which these approaches, apparently based on indirect control, actually lead to increased control and intensification of the work process are analysed. Students are encouraged to examine these issues through a research-based case study and then to consider ways in which conflict may be suppressed, but also to reflect on how it may erupt in the longer term. Examples of ways in which conflict is manifest in new workplace regimes are then reviewed, reinforcing our central point that conflict and co-operation always co-exist. Similarly, the ambiguous use of 'partnership' to describe employer–employee and/or employer–trade union relations is discussed, and it is suggested that any attempt to mask conflict is unlikely to be successful.

Conflict, change and compromise

The concluding chapter presents a compelling case for the continued inclusion of the study of industrial relations in a book of this type. This is done through arguing that trade union membership and collective bargaining still cover six million workers in the UK and that the 'social partner' approach favoured in continental Europe signifies a continuing importance. This leads directly to the second main justification for this chapter, the value of comparative study. Study of comparative industrial relations has paradoxically been growing due to the increasing internationalisation of national economies and the study of how global industries such as the automobile industry operate. International competitiveness also gives rise to a second main concern in comparative study, the relative position of national economies and how this might be affected by the industrial relations institutions of one country compared with another. This in turn gives rise to a concern on the part of international bodies to establish internationally acceptable labour standards and thus further comparative study is required to inform these policy decisions.

The virtues and problems of comparative study are examined in this chapter, a discussion that has a wider resonance beyond the specifics of comparative industrial relations. In the context of choice and circumstance established in Chapter 1 as a key dimensions of human resource strategy making, the operation of multinationals needs to be considered on a comparative basis. Comparative industrial relations also focuses on different forms of employee organisation and the degree to which they are compatible within one system, or transferable to another. Comparative study is not without its problems, such as the different approaches of the academic disciplines, the limited value of creating macro models and the consequent need to have studies that combine micro changes within firms in a cross-national context.

A study of the automobile industry, which adopted such a strategy (Kochan *et al.* 1997) is the focus for the rest of the chapter. The automobile industry is chosen because of the value of the new comparative methods, because it is significant in substantive terms and because study of its attempts to reconcile conflicts of interest between capital and labour reflects a continuing wider phenomenon. The study examines issues around mass and lean production, their associated personnel policies and ways in which organised workers might resist these.

Part I

STRATEGY, PLANNING AND FLEXIBILITY AT HOME AND ABROAD

1

HUMAN RESOURCING STRATEGIES
Choice, chance and circumstance

Tony Watson

2

HUMAN RESOURCE PLANNING
Strategies, systems and processes

Carole Tansley

3

MANAGING UNCERTAINTY OR MANAGING UNCERTAINLY?

Colin Bryson

4

INTERNATIONAL HUMAN RESOURCING

David Walsh

HUMAN RESOURCING STRATEGIES

Choice, chance and circumstance

Tony Watson

OBJECTIVES

Having completed this chapter and its associated activities, readers should be able to:

- consider themselves familiar with a way of thinking about human resource strategy making that can best inform analysis and practice in the management of work. This can be done by reviewing recent conceptual thinking on both human resourcing issues and strategic management, as well as on research studies in these areas;

- use concepts and terms that avoid some of the confusions that often arise in such discussions,

- recognise that strategic matters, in the human resourcing area as much as in any other, are most usefully seen as a concern of all managers, rather than as the special responsibility of senior managers and expert advisers (while nevertheless recognising a key role for the human resources specialist);

- appreciate the value of viewing strategies as patterns in organisational activity rather than as plans that precede activity;

- understand the orthodox way of thinking about human resource strategy making and identify its shortcomings;

- use a 'processual' alternative to orthodox thinking that retains the 'orthodox' concern with *fit* between strategies and organisational contingencies, but that sees these as only one element in the emergence of strategies – a factor that has to be combined with others such as the broad political-economic and cultural context of the organisation, the choices, values and preferences of managers themselves and the conflicts, disputes and unforeseen events that arise in the human resourcing arena of contestation;

- recognise that an organisation's management may adopt a single human resourcing strategy or structure the organisation so that it can follow a dual human resourcing (or 'flexible firm') strategy;

- appreciate, through a case study, the way in which the variety of factors that influence a human resourcing strategy can come into play.

Introduction

Human resources are the efforts, skills or capabilities that people contribute to an employing organisation to enable it to continue in existence. The purpose of this chapter is to argue that the most helpful way to think about the strategic management of such resources is to focus first and foremost on the work organisation as a whole and how its managers tackle the problem of securing, maintaining and developing them. Within this, it is possible to examine the way in which strategic management processes involve both active managerial choice as well as the influence of various circumstances (or 'contingencies'). The key options in human resource strategy making are identified. The adoption of 'new-style human resource management practices' is just one of these. Attention is given to what factors may influence the adoption, or the rejection, of this broad approach. While it is stressed that the human resourcing strategy adopted in any particular organisation is a facet of the organisation's overall management, and that this strategy may be either a relatively conscious and explicit one or a relatively unplanned or 'emergent' one, it is nevertheless recognised that a key part is still played by human preferences, values, ideologies and by the cultural and political context of the organisation.

The main spirit of this chapter is a critical and analytical one. It is *critical-evaluative* in Legge's terms (1995: 2, 5). But it nevertheless contains a prescriptive or practice-related element. It is critical in that it takes a sceptical view of orthodoxies about both strategic processes in general and human resourcing trends in particular. And it is analytical in that it develops concepts and frameworks to help us understand strategy-making processes in the human resourcing sphere. The concern is not, however, with putting forward concepts and theoretical ideas that are *right* and that are intended to replace those that are *wrong*. The view taken here is that concepts, models and frameworks that a social scientist can bring to the understanding of work organisations and their management are not to be judged in terms of whether they are right or wrong, but in terms of *how helpful they are* to anybody who wishes either to understand or to act with regard to those activities (Watson, 1997: 6–7). Thus, the approach to strategic thinking and human resourcing issues advocated here is felt to be more helpful to someone wishing to come to terms with such matters than are others looked at in the chapter. The chapter's approach is put forward as a more useful one than others – in the sense of how well it informs practice. It is not an approach that is more 'true' or more correct than others.

This chapter is *analytical* because:

- it focuses on what tends to happen in the 'real world' of managerial practice, as opposed to setting out – as we see in many management texts – an armchair-based set of guidelines on how things might be done in an ideally harmonious, unambiguous and conflict-free world;

■ it is concerned with how certain factors, choices and circumstances appear to be associated with particular outcomes for organisations;

■ it is informed, directly and indirectly, by consideration of a large amount of academic research and theory.

The chapter is at the same time *prescriptive* because:

■ it is claimed that readers who adopt the style of thinking being put forward will be better placed to understand the principles underlying human resource strategy making processes than if they adopt the approaches to which the present one is being offered as an alternative;

■ someone using this style of thinking will be better placed to engage in practices in this sphere of human activity.

Having carefully explained the ways in which principles, perspectives and practices interrelate in our consideration of the strategic aspects of human resourcing, we can turn to the issue of the key concepts and terminology that are to be used.

Human resourcing strategies and employment management

In the spirit of what has been said so far, we now need to establish some useful terms and key concepts for the analysis of human resourcing strategies. It is seen as utterly beside the point to try to identity the *correct* definition of, say, 'personnel strategy' or 'human resource management'. The question is one of deciding which is the most useful way of conceptualising these matters. A concept, whether it is a broad one like 'strategy' or a more specific one like 'human resource', is a working definition of a phenomenon that is adopted to assist in a particular analysis of phenomena and human actions in the world.

The most obvious way for us to proceed would be simply to follow the normal practice and talk about 'human resource management' and to focus in the chapter on 'strategic human resource management' and the developing of 'human resource management strategies'. But to proceed in this way can be dangerous. Most of the dangers arise from problems with the notion of HRM itself. The main problem is that this term is widely used to mean quite different things at different times. It can create havoc in any analysis of social life if a key term's meaning is prone to shift from time to time. In economics, for example, it has to be made clear for any sensible analysis to occur whether the term 'money' is going to be used to refer to, say, only the notes and coins that are in circulation in an economy or to such items together with the credits that people have in their bank accounts. One cannot slip and slide between definitions in a piece of economic analysis. And just as 'money' can be defined in a variety of different ways in economics, so HRM, as a term, can be used in various ways (but without the explicit distinctions of M1, M2, M3, M4, etc. that economists use when speaking of money). There are four main uses of the term HRM, as shown in Table 1.1.

Table 1.1 Four usages of the term human resource management

'HRM' is variously used:

- ■ as a more fashionable name for personnel management

- ■ to refer to all managerial activity – beyond as well as within a personnel function – that involves relationships between the organisation and its employees

- ■ to describe an area of academic study, integrating the 'subjects' of personnel management, industrial relations and elements of organisational behaviour

- ■ as an umbrella term for 'new management' practices, involving higher commitment from employees and giving them greater task discretion, which have been given increased emphasis in the USA and UK in the latter decades of the twentieth century

Activity 1.1

Think about the various ways you hear or read about people using the term 'HRM'. How many of each of the types of usage shown in Table 1.1 can you identify?

The ambiguities that arise with the use of the term HRM are ones most of us can come to terms with in everyday life. Most readers of this book will recognise that the term 'HRM' in its title is referring to the second of these uses (yet some may suspect that it has more to do with the first). And they will easily recognise the third use when they see that the authors all work in a university department of HRM. But where things could get a little more difficult would be when the prospective reader of this or of any other book with HRM in its title wonders whether it is primarily about the 'new approaches' to employment practices or whether it gives equal attention to the more orthodox procedures and practices. In this chapter we cannot afford this kind of ambiguity. If we are interested in the choices and alternatives available to an employing organisation, we have to consider the extent to which a given organisation has adopted or might adopt the 'new' HRM type of practice and the extent to which it follows 'pre-HRM' styles (cf. Boxall, 1996). We can hardly label this choice process one of 'HRM strategy'. If we do, we hear the sort of nonsensical statement that one has indeed come across in the words, 'The HRM strategy of my company is one that does not follow HRM principles'. The speaker here was explaining that the organisation resourced itself with people and skills in a traditional 'hire and fire' manner and that little or no attention was given to new-style HRM practices.

To avoid this kind of problem, it is helpful to replace the term 'HRM strategy' with the concept *human resourcing strategy*. This is suggested for four reasons:

1 Dropping the 'HRM' expression from the general term for the overall human resourcing direction followed by the organisation enables us to retain it for the newer 'HRM-style practices' that we see in *some* human resourcing strategies.

2 The term *human resourcing strategy* better recognises that decisions might be made to bring 'human inputs' into the organisation – through subcontracting, for example – where the resources are not really 'managed' in a direct sense at all by the organisation.

3 *Human resourcing strategy* avoids the implication in the expression 'HRM strategy' that such a strategy is something that stands on its own. In the final analysis, there cannot be an HRM strategy, only a human resourcing element of an overall organisational strategy. We do not speak of a 'marketing management strategy' or an 'engineering management strategy'. Why should the functional area concerned with human resources have the word 'management' in it when others do not? 'Management' is most usefully seen as the management of the organisation as a whole, as we shall see later, and human resourcing, marketing, engineering, accounting and the rest are components of this and are not 'managements' in themselves.

4 The term human *resourcing* has much stronger implications of action and process than the term human *resource management*. For the same reason, it is more helpful to speak of 'human resource strategy making' in place of the more conventional 'strategic HRM'.

The concepts indicated in Table 1.2 are thus suggested as the most helpful for analytical purposes.

Table 1.2 Key terms to be used in this book

Preferred term	In place of
■ Human resourcing strategy	■ HRM strategy
■ Human resource strategy making	■ Strategic HRM
■ HRM-style practices	■ HRM (used as a label for new-style practices)

Organising, managing and strategy making

It might seem that we have spent an inordinate amount of time sorting out concepts, but this is not so. Unless our language is clarified and meanings established, there can be little meaningful communication. And the 'HRM' field has suffered badly from the sort of ambiguities and confusions we have striven to overcome. But in the process of sorting out the terms that can best help our analysis, certain quite important substantive points have already been raised. The most important one was the argument that the most useful way to think about 'management' is not as a series of 'professional' specialisms, like personnel, accounting and marketing, but as the general directing or 'steering' of an organisation. As I argued in my *In Search of Management* study (Watson, 1994a), we can best understand what management is if we identify the essential role of a manager not as one of being 'in charge' of a particular department or function, but as contributing, certainly in part through departmental responsibility or specialist expertise, to the overall performance of the organisation.

To think in this way has real implications for practice. It can be argued that managers will do a 'better job' if they think in this way. A purchasing manager, for example, will be better at their job if they understand the products and markets that their company is involved in – and might be even better if they felt that they were actually contributing to the shape of these products and markets through bringing their purchasing expertise into broader decision making. And the same applies to human resourcing specialists. Can we possibly imagine that a human resourcing manager responsible, say, for recruiting and training retail staff, but who knew little of the products being sold and the customers being served, would do as well as one who knew the shops, products and customers well? And would not such a manager be even more effective if they could influence policies on shop and customer development through their specialist knowledge of labour market conditions or the 'trainability' of different kinds of staff?

Management, then, is best seen as a process. It is a process where people, who often have special expertise in an aspect of business or work organisation, contribute to the overall performance of an organisation in both the short term and the long term. A manager is someone who is first and foremost a 'manager of the organisation' and is only second a manager of recruitment, training, employee relations or whatever. Their departments or functions only exist as subsystems of the bigger system or as subprocesses of a bigger process. They should not, therefore, manage their own 'patch' simply for the benefit of that patch, but should manage it so as to contribute to the directing of the broader activities of the corporation. This means that both the terms personnel manager and human resource manager are misnomers. Such managers are there neither to manage 'personnel' nor to manage 'human resources'. They are there to help manage the organisation, through helping to ensure that it is resourced with whatever human skills, competencies and efforts are needed to help it survive into the long term. Equally, it is unhelpful to speak of 'people management'. No one – whether in a human resourcing or line management role – is employed to 'manage people'. It is *work* that is managed, through utilising the skills and efforts of people, as opposed to people being managed as such.

A major implication of adopting this perspective on management in general and human resourcing in particular – and especially the stress on the importance of long-term organisational performance – is to give a role in strategy making to every manager. Managers are part of an organisation's 'management', which is, in turn, that part of an organisation's workforce concerned with shaping and directing the organisation in the face of all the opportunities and threats that arise both in the organisation's 'environment' and in its internal circumstances and constituencies. Every manager is thus a contributor, however humble, to an organisation's strategic processes. And to adopt this perspective is inevitably to question the orthodox or 'mainstream' perspective that sees strategy making in organisations as the responsibility of top managers and strategic experts and, essentially, as the development by such people of corporate plans. It is increasingly being recognised that we can more usefully understand strategies as the outcomes of ongoing organisational processes involving a range of contributors, rather than as pre-decided plans produced by specialist 'strategy makers'. When we want to understand how organisations are – or might be – shaped and directed over time (the point, surely, of all strategic analysis), it is more helpful to utilise a concept of strategies as *realised patterns* than to stick with the idea of strategies as managerial *plans*.

Strategy as plan and strategy as pattern

In a much-quoted definition of corporate strategy, Quinn suggests that it is simply 'the pattern or plan that integrates an organisation's major goals, policies and action sequences' (1991: 5). Although one might have some trouble with the notion of an organisation 'having goals', this is nevertheless a helpful formulation in that it focuses on 'strategy' as something that 'pulls together' or gives shape to all the various aspirations, intentions, actions and activities that constitute the organisation. And it is interesting that Quinn uses the phrase 'pattern *or* plan'. The study that follows Quinn's definition of strategy, presented early in his book, tends strongly to encourage us to see the value of looking for patterns as opposed to plans when trying to understand how organisations are shaped and reshaped and perform over time. This is not, however, to deny that plans and planning play a part in the unfolding of strategies. What Quinn and his fellow researcher, Mintzberg (1994), show from their studies is that strategy making involves a great deal more than simply developing and implementing plans. However, their research recognises that formal or deliberate planning may play a part in it. The strategy of an organisation is thus *not the plan that an organisation follows* but a *pattern that unfolds over time* in which formal planning can be found to occur to a greater or lesser extent.

The shift in perspective that is occurring here involves turning to a processual view of strategy making, in which both planned and unplanned activities of people at all levels contribute to the shaping and directing of the enterprise, and away from the mainstream view in which the planning activity of top managers and specialists is analytically privileged (Table 1.3).

Table 1.3 Two ways of looking at organisational strategies

Strategy as plan – *mainstream view*	Strategy as pattern – *processual view*
■ Strategies are *plans* made by top managers and their corporate strategy advisers ■ Strategy is a matter of *policy* and it precedes action ■ Strategy and *implementation* are separate	■ Strategies are more usefully seen as the *outcomes* of both planned and unplanned activities ■ Policies often *emerge* out of actions that have already been taken ■ Strategy and implementation tend to happen simultaneously

To adopt this perspective means to accept that to understand broad strategic human resourcing patterns we do not have to look for explicit and conscious plans on the part of the organisation's management. We can identify strategic directions that 'emerge' as readily as we can identify patterns that follow more or less from managerial plans. What the observer is interested in when looking for a strategic pattern is consistency. A strategy can be identified, says Mintzberg, where there is '*consistency* of behaviour, *whether or not* intended' (1987: 11). Consistency, in this sense, can be seen in human resource management practices without our using those conventional frameworks for integrating business and human resourcing strategies which, as Legge observes, 'assume a classical, rationalistic, top-down mode of strategy-making' that is 'normative rather than empirically grounded' (1995: 135). There is little evidence that very deliberate processes of carefully sequenced strategic analysis and implementation are followed in practice – including in the human resourcing sphere. As Whipp puts it, 'the application of over-rational, linear programmes of HRM as a means of securing competitive success is shown to be at odds with experience both in the UK and elsewhere' (1992: 33). More processual frameworks, Legge argues, like those adopted in research by Hendry and Pettigrew (1992) and Pettigrew and Whipp (1991), show that integrating human resourcing with broader strategies is a 'highly complex and iterative process, much dependent on the interplay and resources of different stakeholders' (1995: 135). There is rarely an 'easily isolated logic to strategic change' and, instead, the process is one which 'takes its motive force from an amalgam of economic, personal and political imperatives' (Whipp 1992: 33). All kinds of conflict and difference arise in the managerial political arena and lead to shifting priorities and varying practices.

Patterns are often imposed on unplanned outcomes by the legitimisations and rationalisations offered by managements after the event. In fact, one of the chief benefits of this type of analysis, according to Tyson, is that it shows that strategic issues are as much a function of the mindsets that produce them as an outcome of some form of objective reality (1995: 9). But this is not to imply that there is a single shared managerial 'mindset'. Although 'the selection of strategy is primarily by means of management judgement', it is likely, as Johnson emphasises, 'to be bound up in a process of bargaining within the organisation' (1987: 29). Strategies are less likely to be selected 'on the basis of some sort of objective yardstick, but because they are acceptable to those who influence the decision or have to implement it (Johnson, 1987: 29). Strategy making in practice, then, is a 'tentative and exploratory process, often existing in retrospective rationalisations, couched in the appropriate rhetoric' (Whittington, 1993: 135). The policies or strategies that senior managers sometimes tell us were behind certain corporate developments may well be little more than stories they have created to give legitimacy and an air of 'rationality' to the outcomes of a whole range of wrangles, surprises, muddles and unintended circumstances. At other times, however, they are straightforwardly explaining how certain plans and policies laid down years before have now come to fruition. More typically, perhaps, we find elements of both of these tendencies whenever we investigate how any particular organisation has come to be in the shape it is and is performing in the way we find it.

Research does indeed suggest that there are variations across organisations in the way strategic patterns take shape. However, it has been demonstrated that a relatively incremental, trial-and-error approach – albeit one within a strong managerial sense of direction – tends to lead to greater strategic success than approaches that follow a 'muddling through' type of incrementalism or rigid, pre-decided strategic plans. Research by Quinn (1980), for example, shows that organisations whose strategy-formation efforts are relatively successful in terms of conventional business criteria follow processes of *logical incrementalism*. This is 'a process of the gradual evolution of strategy driven by conscious managerial thought', as opposed to one involving operating with systematic, pre-shaped strategic plans. At the centre of the 'process realm' is a 'network of information' that extends the perspective of operating managers and helps reduce their uncertainty about the future, as well as stimulating long-term 'special studies' (Quinn, 1980: 38–9). Mintzberg's 'McGill studies', which tracked the strategies of several organisations, similarly and 'in general . . . found strategy making to be a complex, interactive, and evolutionary process, best described as one of adaptive learning' (Mintzberg, 1994: 110). Strategy again *emerges* from complex processes rather than grand plans and 'the apt metaphor for the process, in sharp contrast with the one of architecture in the design school and keeping a ship on course in the planning school, might well be crafting' (Mintzberg, 1994: 110).

The processual perspective on strategy making, whether it is applied to a corporate whole or to the human resourcing aspect of an organisation's activities, views strategies as 'the pattern in a stream of actions', as Mintzberg and Waters (1985) put it or, as I have expressed it previously, 'the pattern to be seen emerging over time as actions are taken to enable the organisation to continue into the future' (Watson, 1994a: 87). The mainstream literature on human resourcing strategies has tended to take the alternative approach, however, and conceptualise strategy as plan – with human resourcing being something that *follows from* and is shaped to *fit* pre-established corporate plans that have been devised to handle the 'business environment'. Stacey is especially critical of what he calls a 'strong tendency' to slip into talking about strategy making as 'a response that "the organisation" makes to an "environment"' (1996: 2). He sees the inevitable result of this as 'a lack of insight into the real complexities of strategic management because in reality organisations and their environments are not things, one adapting to the other, but groupings of people interacting one with another' (Stacey 1996: 2). Nevertheless, mainstream thinking has taken precisely this risk.

Human resource strategy making – mainstream thinking

The mainstream 'strategic HRM' literature has at its heart the notion of human resource strategy makers seeking to achieve a 'fit' between human resource strategy and the broader business strategy. The 'aim of strategic human resource management', in the influential words of Armstrong, is 'to contribute fully to the achievement of business objectives' (1992: 47). 'The key', Miller argues, 'is to make operational the concept of "fit" – the fit of human resource management – with the strategic thrust of the organisation' (1989: 51). This broad corporate 'strategic thrust' comes about as top management seeks to achieve a 'fit' between the organisation itself and the business environment in which it finds itself. Thus, if the organisation is felt to be facing challenges of inefficiency and inability to match competitors' costs, its business and human resourcing policies might be expected to focus on control of labour costs. If the risk comes from failing to match competitors' innovations, business and human resourcing policy will need to address these rather different issues, perhaps involving attention to employee 'empowerment' and other indirect-control or 'HRM-style' innovations. Beer and Spector (1985) offer this kind of analysis, arguing, for example, that the approach to how people are paid and the degree of employment security that would be appropriate if the 'competitive strategy' of a business was that of a 'low-cost producer' would be different from the one they would need to adopt if they were following a 'product innovation' type of competitive strategy.

The main strategic choices or routes to 'competitive advantage' discussed by Beer and Spector are those identified in the seminal writing of Porter (1980, 1985): innovation, quality enhancement and cost reduction. These are also utilised in Schuler and Jackson's (1987) model, which offers a typology of human resourcing practices said to fit with each of the three main corporate strategic alternatives; while Kochan and Barocci (1985) focus instead on the different types of human resourcing practice that they believe fit the different stages – growth, maturity and decline – of an organisation's product life cycle.

The aspirations of the 'strategic HRM' mainstream are seen in the classic formulation of Fombrun *et al.* and their identification of the 'critical management task' as the attempt to 'align the formal structure and the HR systems so that they drive the strategic objective of the organisation' (1984: 37). This statement reveals quite a lot about the image of the employing organisation that tends to be associated with mainstream thinking on human resourcing strategies. The image is one of an organisation unified around some shared objective or 'goal' and designed and driven just as if it were a big machine. Mechanical metaphors like those we see here – drive and thrust – are very popular in this kind of discourse. Top managers, it is implied, are both the designers of the big corporate machine and the drivers who take it down the road towards its undisputed destination. Human resourcing managers are there to 'fuel' this machine with a supply of human resources. And the human resource strategy is the set of plans for finding the right sort of human fuel, in the right quantity, available at the appropriate octane when it is needed.

None of this is, in some total sense, 'wrong'. It is perfectly reasonable to consider what circumstantial or *contingent* factors, for example, might be relevant to the success of one type of human resourcing strategy rather than another. A hire-and-fire and low-job-discretion type of human resourcing strategy, for example, could reasonably be expected to create considerable difficulties for the managers of an advanced technology business operating in a rapidly changing market context, and these would not arise in a business utilising simple technologies to provide goods for a stable and long-term market. A fully fledged processual perspective on human resource strategy making needs to incorporate a notion of a 'fit' between the human resourcing aspect of an organisational strategy and the broader organisational strategy. But we have to be careful about two things.

First, we have to be careful not to let the rather physical metaphor of 'fit' take us over and encourage us to think that we can carefully 'blueprint' our human resourcing strategies to support a larger blueprint devised by corporate planners. Strategies are outcomes of human interpretations, conflicts, confusions, guesses and rationalisations, rather than clear pictures unambiguously traced out on an engineer's drawing board.

Second, we have to be careful not to see human resourcing strategies as necessarily *deriving* from broader corporate strategies. Although the evidence seems to indicate clearly that human resourcing strategies are very much subservient, on the one hand to larger business pressures and on the other hand to day-to-day pressures and exigencies (Purcell, 1989, 1995; Marchington and Parker, 1990), we must recognise that this is an *empirical* matter (it is the observed pattern that currently pertains) and is not something that is *in principle* (or theoretically) inevitable. Indeed, Beaumont advocates a 'close, two-way relationship between business strategy' and 'HRM planning' (1993: 4) and Lengnick-Hall and Lengnick-Hall argue that organisations that 'systematically and reciprocally consider human resources and competitive strategy will perform better over the long term than firms that manage human resources primarily as a means to solve competitive strategy issues' (1988: 468).

A processual perspective should make us aware that, in principle at least, a human resourcing strategy favoured by a particular set of managers could influence the direction of corporate strategy making. Say, for example, that the managers of an organisation decided that, for ethical or even industry fashion reasons, they wanted to adopt 'progressive' empowerment policies for their employees. This might entail them in looking for markets for more complex products or services, ones which would better fit with a high-discretion and high-commitment workforce than the currently unchallenging tasks that employees undertake. This accords with Hendry and Pettigrew's notion that management could choose methodically to 'identify wherein its HR strengths lie and gear its HRM policies and business strategies towards utilising and developing these advantages' (1986: 7). My example of this not only promotes human resource considerations to a 'driver' position (flying in the face of the environmental determinism tendency of mainstream thinking), it also requires us to take into account such matters as choice, value and fashion. Let us see if we can develop a processual perspective that has a place for such matters while still recognising the relevance of some notion of contingency and 'fit'.

A processual approach to human resource strategy making: choice, chance and circumstances

At the heart of the processual view of human resource strategy making is the principle of looking for patterns that take shape over time. We do not refuse to see 'strategy' where there is a shape to events that has not been deliberately planned or explicitly stated. Although managements sometimes choose a deliberate direction and make explicit an employment philosophy, it is equally possible for a direction and an 'operating philosophy' to *emerge* over time – in the same way that an individual's 'career strategy' can be said to emerge when we look for a pattern in the way they have partly chosen and partly been 'pushed' by circumstance and accident into a certain career pattern (Watson and Harris, 1996). Procter *et al.* (1994) valuably apply this perspective to the debate about *flexibility* in British human resourcing practices and attack the naïveté of the critique of the flexible firm model (Atkinson, 1987), which argued that the lack of explicit human-resource-oriented managerial intentions behind such innovations means that they do not have strategic organisational significance. It is demonstrated that the 'flexible firm' model assists our understanding of human resourcing strategies because it highlights an emergent pattern – a strategic direction. Just because something is not carefully and deliberately planned and is consciously, holistically and deliberately engineered does not mean that it has not happened and does not constitute something worth identifying as 'strategic'. To limit our perspectives on strategic processes to ones where there are clear and explicit intentions is severely to limit our analyses and understanding of human resourcing practices.

The most useful way of conceptualising human resourcing strategy, therefore, is as the broad pattern to be observed in the various practices undertaken to ensure that human efforts, skills and commitments are obtained, developed and sometimes discarded to help bring about the long-term survival of the organisation (Table 1.4). As I have argued in detail elsewhere (Watson, 1986, 1994), the basic *logic* of all managerial work is one of working towards such long-term continuation through processes of exchange with parties internal and external to the organisation itself. And the logic of the human resourcing dimension of management is one of ensuring that appropriate exchanges (material and symbolic, economic and psychological) with employees and associated bodies, such as trade unions, training organisations or labour subcontractors, are achieved so as to provide human resources necessary for that long-term performance. A human resourcing strategy is the pattern that emerges over time in the way this is developed.

Table 1.4 Defining human resources and human resourcing strategy

Human resources	Human resourcing strategy
The efforts, skills or capabilities that people contribute to an employing organisation to enable it to continue in existence	The general direction followed by an organisation in how it secures, develops and, from time to time, dispenses with human resources to help it continue in the long term

To adopt this perspective is to weaken the normal distinction between strategy and tactics. In mainstream thinking, it is assumed that operational or 'tactical' actions follow from the strategy that has been adopted. This can indeed happen if the strategy-making process in any given organisational situation has involved working closely to a clear 'big plan'. On the other hand, a whole series of tactics can surely add up to a 'strategy' – in the organisational world as much as in the world of warfare, where the strategy concept comes from. If, as the research reviewed earlier suggests, the strategy process is typically a more incremental one, then we can see a pattern of relatively small-scale innovations adding up to movement in a strategic direction. It is therefore helpful to stress that the scope of a human resourcing strategy ranges from what would readily be recognised as 'big' or obviously strategic matters, like the choice of a particular organisational structure or the favouring of a specific cultural style, down to very particular and detailed matters such as how people are expected to dress at work (Table 1.5).

So far, we could envisage on the basis of all this that almost 'anything goes', and that every organisation would have its own unique pattern or strategic direction. Each organisation's human resourcing strategy would be a unique mixture of different practices and styles. But this would be to deny any kind of notion of 'fit' or integration, whether this be *vertical integration* between the human resourcing strategy and the organisational context or *horizontal integration* between different elements of human resourcing principles and practices. To help us with this, we can turn to a type of distinction that builds on a long-existing tendency in organisational analysis to contrast management practices tending to give high discretion to roles and practices minimising such discretion (Jaques, 1956; Hickson, 1966; Fox, 1974; Friedman, 1990).

The two alternative key principles that give us our analytical starting point for comparing human resourcing strategies (and, hence, informing the strategic choices that might be made) are those of *direct control/low commitment* and *indirect control/high commitment* (Table 1.6).

Table 1.5 The scope of the human resourcing strategy

Human resourcing strategy's scope ranges
From such matters as: ■ the overall organisational structure ■ the corporate culture ■ recruitment policies
To: ■ whether employees clock in or not ■ the smoking/non-smoking policy ■ dress codes

Table 1.6 Two key and alternative human resourcing principles

Direct control/low commitment	Indirect control/high commitment
■ Employees given little discretion, closely supervised and monitored	■ Employees 'empowered' – encouraged to use discretion
■ Limited 'psychological' commitment sought from employees	■ High 'psychological' commitment sought from employees

Recruitment, selection, employee development and deployment policies and practices all follow from this basic choice. This is not to say that the choice is a simple 'either/or' one. It might, for example, lead to practices that combine aspects of the two principles. The pattern of 'lean production' seen in some car-assembly plants would be an example of this (Womack, *et al.*, 1990; Chapter 15 in this book). Nevertheless, the right-hand side of Table 1.6 brings in what we referred to earlier as *HRM-style practices*. As we saw, the term 'human resource management' is often used to refer to human resourcing practices based on *indirect-control and high-commitment* principles. This is done in Storey's most recent definition of 'HRM' as 'a distinctive approach to employment management which seeks to achieve competitive advantage through the strategic development of a highly committed and capable workforce, using an integrated array of cultural, structural and personnel techniques' (1995: 5). Such practices are, however, perhaps more helpfully labelled by Wood and Albanese (1995) as 'high commitment management' practices, the basic characteristics of which are indicated in Table 1.7.

To follow a direct-control/high-commitment human resourcing strategy, then, would be to move in such a direction by taking on various of these practices. It would not have to be done in a highly conscious way or as an explicit philosophy. Indeed, all the evidence is that it is not done in this 'strategy-as-plan' way. As Storey and Sisson say, commenting on the research finding that the majority of the employing organisations

Table 1.7 HRM-style or 'high-commitment' practices

> **HRM-style practices involve:**
>
> - personnel or human resourcing issues becoming the concern of all managers (as opposed to being delegated to a personnel function)
>
> - human resourcing issues becoming central to all strategic-level deliberations in the organisation
>
> - the development of a strong culture encouraging employees to be highly committed to the organisation and its continuous improvement
>
> - the development of a culture of high trust, teamworking and willing cooperation, making close supervision, detailed procedures and strict hierarchies unnecessary
>
> - a stress on the personal development of employees, involving them in continually developing their skills to achieve both personal 'growth' and task flexibility

in their study said they had adopted a significant proportion of HRM-style practices, 'most cases failed to show much in the way of an integrated approach to employment management, and still less was there evidence of strategic integration with the corporate plan' (1993: 22). These authors further stress that the 'multifarious practices' that were being adopted 'arose for diverse reasons'.

Although the reasons for adopting one human resourcing practice rather than another, and for moving in one general direction rather than another, are diverse, we can logically identify the range of factors that are likely, in varying combinations, to play a part. The most important thing to recognise is that human resourcing patterns do not simply arise to 'fit' organisational circumstances. The 'contingencies' of organisational size (Pugh and Hickson, 1976), technology (Woodward, 1994; Perrow, 1986) or market context (Burns and Stalker, 1994) do not determine organisational shapes or managerial practices. As vague and confused as these patterns may be and as influenced as they inevitably are by chance, political wrangling and cultural assumptions, human resourcing patterns are outcomes of *strategic choices* by managers (Child, 1972, 1984). To varying degrees, managers will take into account contingencies such as size, technology and environment. These things do influence organisational patterns. But it is an influence that is always *mediated* by managerial interpretation and political manoeuvring (Watson, 1977). Contingencies are, in Weick's (1979) terms, always *enacted* by human actors. Figure 1.1 suggests how managerial choices, together with political-economic, cultural and organisational contingency factors, come together within an arena of contestation and unforeseen circumstances to shape the pattern that we understand as the realised human resourcing strategy of an organisation.

The human resourcing policies and practices of an organisation can only be fully understood if seen as part of a broader social, political and economic order, as the top section of Fig. 1.1 suggests. For example, an organisation located in a society whose government leans towards socialist principles and attempts directly to influence business and employing practices will operate differently from one existing in a much more market-dominated setting. In fact, the overall pattern of power and inequality in a society will influence both the opportunities and the constraints that managers consider

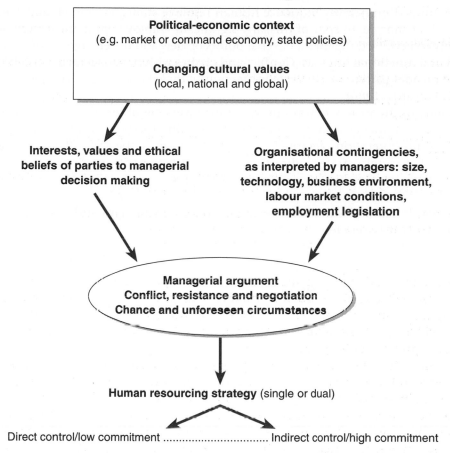

Fig. 1.1 Factors shaping an organisation's human resourcing strategy

when shaping human resources strategies. The 'structure of domination' (Alvesson and Willmott, 1996) of a particular political-economic order both significantly influences and is an outcome of the employment policies and practices of organisations and their managers. Similarly acting as both 'inputs' to and 'outputs' of human resourcing strategies are cultural trends operating at local, national or global levels. An example here would be the relationship between 'HRM-style' innovations and the emphasis given to enterprise and markets in the periods of Thatcherism or Reaganism in the UK and USA (Keenoy and Anthony, 1992; Legge, 1995).

It is in this broad context that managers make choices, taking into account to a greater or a lesser extent organisational contingencies like technology, size or business environment. But such 'choices' are themselves made in a corporate setting where some managers are more powerful than others (Watson, 1995: 263–8), where decision makers are influenced by personal values or fashionable ideas (Watson, 1994b, 1995b), where all sorts of ambiguities and chance factors come into play (March and Olsen, 1976) and where specific industry traditions play a part. Research has shown that the personal philosophies of the chief executives of business units, in combination with the history of the units, significantly influence human resource strategies (Purcell and Ahlstrand, 1994), for example. In spite of this, any significant employment management decision is likely to involve different managerial points of view and the emergence of various personal and functional interests. Conflict and clashes within managements also take place in the broader pattern of 'structured antagonism' that characterises all employment relations (Edwards, 1986).

In spite of the variety of ways in which managers might 'read' or 'enact' the societal and organisational circumstances in which they find themselves, and however fiercely different interpretations are fought over in boardrooms, there is still a basic logic suggesting that certain strategic directions might fit better with particular circumstances than others. Possible 'fits' are outlined in Table 1.8.

Table 1.8 Possible fits between human resourcing strategies and perceived contingencies

Fit with direct control . . . .**Fit with indirect control**
■ *Organisational contingencies*   – simple structure . . . . .complex structure
■ *Technological contingencies*   – simple tasks . . . . .complex tasks
■ *Labour market*   – cheap and plentiful labour . . . . .expensive and scarce labour
■ *State*   – weak legal constraints . . . . .strong legal constraints

■ *Social, cultural, political*
   – low unionisation . . . . .high unionisation
   – poorly educated labour . . . . .highly educated labour
   – female labour . . . . .male labour
   – migrant labour . . . . .non-migrant labour

The links made in Table 1.8 are intended simply to recognise that there are greater incentives or pressures on managements faced with circumstances to the right-hand side of these continuums to develop exchanges with their employees that give them high discretion and job security than if the prevailing circumstances are those at the opposite end. If a management is able to get work tasks done cheaply and efficiently by tightly supervising low-skilled workers who are readily hired and fired as circumstances demand, it is unlikely to invoke the costs and inconveniences of introducing HRM-style practices and high-commitment principles. An employer may thus pursue a deliberate strategy of *not embracing* new HRM-style practices.

The sort of 'fit' we have considered here is that often related to 'vertical integration'. But there is also the question of the degree of 'horizontal integration' to be pursued (cf. Marchington and Wilkinson, 1996). Whereas the *vertical integration* fit between contingencies and practices was a matter of consistency between external circumstances and internal behaviours, *horizontal integration* is a matter of consistency of approach within an organisation. If an employing organisation were to treat some of its employees in a significantly different way from others (and if these groups were ones prone to monitoring such 'differentials'), all sorts of disputes and conflicts would be likely to arise. A solution to this (and one reflected in the 'flexible firm' phenomenon discussed earlier) would be to separate such groups into core and peripheral categories (Table 1.9).

Table 1.9 The option of a single or a dual human resourcing strategy

A single human resourcing strategy	A dual human resourcing strategy
Allowing for variations across different levels in the hierarchy ('treating senior people better than juniors'), the approach to the major part of the workforce is consistently either a direct control/low-commitment one or an indirect-control/high-commitment one	The organisation's operations are divided into core and peripheral sectors, so enabling some of its human resourcing to be done within direct-control/low-commitment principles and other human resourcing to involve indirect controls and high-commitment relationships

Some of the circumstances that could lead to a choice of this kind can be seen in the O&V Joifel case study. But this is only one aspect of the messy process whereby a human resourcing strategy is emerging in this fast-growing business. Here we see an example of the ways in which different business circumstances, changing cultural values, labour market patterns, state policies, shifting employee expectations, managerial values, organisational contingencies, interpersonal conflicts and alliances, chance and personal ambitions all play their part in human resourcing strategy.

CASE STUDY 1.1

Seeing the wood for the trees: human resourcing in O&V Joifel

Oliver Joifel lived deep in the forest of Sherwood and was brought up regretting that this once deeply wooded area of England now included large areas totally devoid of trees. One night, in the best tradition of great entrepreneurs and business leaders, Oliver had a vision. He saw himself going to university where he would combine the study of forestry, genetics and business. He then envisaged himself (or 'envisioned' himself, as he learned to say on the management option of his degree course) setting up a business that would exploit the personal research work he would do on genetically engineered, fast-growing, multi-trunked trees.

Oliver soon found the brilliant teachers and researchers he needed in a university not too far from his home in the heart of Sherwood. And in the doctoral work he started immediately after obtaining a first-class degree, he not only discovered how to grow trees with three fat, parallel trunks that would shoot up from saplings to forest giants in only five years. He also found that he could get the trees to bear two types of fruit that, to all intents and purposes, were identical to coconuts and bananas.

The young Dr Joifel felt that he had found a business opportunity to surpass all business opportunities. Investors saw it this way too and money was soon found to set up the O&V Joifel company. The investors wanted the company to enter immediate production of the new type of tree and, at the same time, to engage in research to find ways of growing even bigger trees, even faster and with a greater variety of fruits. Oliver and his sister, Verity Joifel, who had studied HRM at a university on the other side of the forest and who was to take the title of human resources director, established a board of directors. This included two scientists, Bill Byng and Ben Byers, a finance director and company secretary, Arnold Beancounter, and a production director, Leonard Leaper. This small team was highly committed to building the business as fast as they could and to restoring the status of Sherwood as a true forest once again. Their strategy was to put as much of the land as they could acquire under the trees, to bring full employment to the forest and to make Sherwood the fruit garden of northern Europe. Not only this, but the tough hardwood that the trees yielded would transform the British building industry and delight new home owners with attractive wooden homes.

Very soon, trees were sprouting all over middle England and the workforce that Verity had recruited had grown to several hundred. Everything in the forest was sweetness and light (the trees produced only a thin canopy of leaves), but things were becoming very different in the boardroom of O&V Joifel (a wood-panelled boardroom, of course). All was darkness here, and the light-hearted camaraderie of early times had turned to sullen and bitter infighting. Employment matters played a key part in this. One reason the company had grown so fast was that there was a plentiful supply of cheap labour. Men who had previously toiled beneath the earth to produce coal were glad to leave the houses they had purchased with their redundancy settlements to work above ground in the fresh air, hewing timber for a modest wage. And the women who had previously been hunched over textile machines in factories and workshops thrived in the Sherwood fruit groves.

Verity Joifel had given little thought to it but, willy nilly, a complex pattern of part-time working had developed among the women as the flow of fruit was kept up over 24 hours for 50 weeks of the year and children of the forest were born and brought up. The men had preferred to work full time and a production pattern on the timber side had developed accordingly. However, unforeseen by Verity, the government had rather suddenly decided to bring in a law providing paid paternity leave. Men were also to be given the right to take regular, albeit unpaid, time off to help with child rearing. This fitted with the changing pattern of attitudes towards family life in the forest. A new pattern of task-sharing families was emerging among the workers. But this did not suit Leonard Leaper. He wanted to retain the tough, masculine, long-hours culture of the timber operation and the convenience of having his best people available whenever he wanted them. This meant a clash with Verity Joifel, who wanted the company to embrace a harmonious, family-friendly personnel mission with similar flexible working arrangements for men and women. And it meant an alliance between Leaper and Arnold Beancounter. Arnold was very worried about the financial implications of Verity's ambitions.

Leaper's strategic preference was to split off what he called the 'men's part of the business' from that which employed the 'fruit girls'. This was not only to make life easier for himself, as he saw it, by resisting the flexible hours policy. It also fitted with his personal gender politics and his concept of what a 'woman's place' and a 'man's place' should be in the scheme of things. But, probably more significantly, he saw the split as a career opportunity, one which could enable him to become the managing director of a separate timber business. His personal ambition here, however, clashed with that of Oliver who – supported by his sister – wanted the Joifel family name to be associated with a single, integrated business with common values, community commitments and a harmonised workforce. Verity, in part to demonstrate what a 'hard-headed businesswoman I am really', also argued that such an 'HR strategy' was important to avoid the emergence of a more assertive kind of trade unionism than the company had been used to. As the forest was now approaching full employment, the workers' union representatives felt themselves able to challenge the company for higher pay rates and shorter hours. Such a policy was attracting new members daily. Up to now there had been little collective bargaining. Verity found it very challenging to put clear proposals to the board on where the line was to be drawn between what would be settled by such bargaining and what should be kept to management discretion within the more developed consultative framework she wanted to develop.

All of these difficulties were compounded by the situation in the research and development part of O&V Joifel. Bill and Ben (known to all and sundry as 'the test-tube men') had recruited various scientists at various times on salaries that fell into no clear pattern. They would award bonuses or give increments to individuals who achieved technical or scientific breakthroughs, without regard to how this would be perceived by others. When challenged by Oliver, on his return from a seminar on 'HRM for chief executives', as to whether they were operating a performance-related (PRP) scheme, they did not know what to say. 'Do you have a pay strategy in the labs or not?', Verity asked them. This provoked blank incomprehension. And Leonard Leaper saw this as a chance to thrust himself into the fray. It was also about time they had a policy on working hours in the laboratories, he argued. Discipline in both the timber and the fruit operations was being undermined as manual workers noticed the 'long-haired lab types' coming into work mid-morning and 'sloping off whenever it suited them'. This set both Bill and Ben screaming about Leaper's ignorance of working in a 'creative culture' where people would often work night and day to solve a problem before 'sloping off for a well-deserved rest'. Leonard countered this with an attempt to show that he knew about labs and at the same time demonstrate his vigorous sense of humour by saying that all he ever saw in the laboratories were 'rotting cultures in dirty Petri dishes'.

Out of this clash of priorities, personalities and changing circumstances, Verity Joifel recognised that some kind of more coherent and consistent approach to human resourcing had to be shaped. There was no simple option of taking business strategy as a 'given' and working out what human resource strategy would be necessary to fulfil it, however. Human resourcing choices would influence the business direction as much as business direction would influence human resourcing. The choices to be made would involve fights and clashes of principle and there would be winners and losers. She remembered writing an essay back at the university about 'hard and soft HRM'. If she were to rewrite that essay now, she mused, she would entitle it: 'HRM is hard, hard, hard'.

Activity 1.2

Using Fig. 1.1 as a framework, note the variety of factors leading to the present human resourcing strategy at O&V Joifel:

■ First, consider what contextual trends, both political-economic and cultural, have emerged.

■ Second, note what contingent circumstances currently prevail.

■ Third, note the different interests and views existing within the decision-making group that will affect how these 'contingencies' are perceived and acted on.

■ And fourth, consider how these factors become mixed together in the conflicts, arguments and reactions to unexpected circumstances going on within O&V Joifel.

Activity 1.3

Imagine yourself in Verity Joifel's position as the company's HR director. You want to develop a more coherent and consistent human resourcing strategy to further the long-term development of the business. List all possible decisions that might help bring this about (recognising that these will be 'political' within the management group as well as straightforwardly 'rational' in business terms).

Activity 1.4

From the list of options listed in Activity 1.3, decide which you personally might take (or recommend to Oliver Joifel).

Conclusion

I have ended this chapter with a story about the human resourcing policies and practices of a particular organisation, and with an invitation to you to consider what might be done in such circumstances. The technology and the products that appear in this story might not seem to be very realistic. The same should not be said, however, of the managerial processes that we see unfolding. I would argue that the messiness and confusion that we see in this story are not at all untypical of the 'real world' of human resource strategy making. Nevertheless, as Verity Joifel herself recognises, one cannot simply accept whatever messiness comes about as human conflicts, changing business circumstances and chance events divert original intentions or compromise preferred policies. She cannot throw up her hands and say: 'This is just how the world is.' She and her colleagues have to manage this messiness. Her responsibility as human resources director is to work with the other directors to identify priorities and establish a sense of direction that can make human resourcing issues reasonably manageable.

A strategic direction needs to be identified in any employing organisation, one which can act as a guide to all of that organisation's managers across the range of their activities. As this chapter has tried to show, such a strategic direction is shaped by a whole variety of factors and is always a matter of compromise between different priorities and between different sectional interests. Human resourcing specialists trying to influence strategy do not succeed simply by sitting down in an office and drawing up big strategic plans derived from standard textbook principles. They have to engage in work that is essentially political and that requires the most sophisticated appreciation of all the economic, cultural, technological and moral factors that play a part. The present chapter, and those that follow, have been written in recognition of all of this and are intended to inform practitioners' decisions and activities and to sensitise them to all the nuances of the human resourcing dimension of the management of work.

Summary

In this chapter the following key points have been made:

- We need to avoid idealised and prescriptive approaches to human resource strategy making and, instead, look at the full range of factors and the various political, economic and cultural processes that operate in real practice in this field.

- Human resource strategy making is most usefully seen as a facet of the general management of an employing organisation.

- A human resourcing strategy is better viewed not as a 'plan to be implemented' but as the pattern to be seen over time in the way that organisational managements handle the human resources of effort, skill and capability that are needed for the organisation to continue in the long term.

- While mainstream approaches to human resource strategy making helpfully consider issues of *fit* between strategy and organisational circumstances (or *contingencies*), they nevertheless have serious limitations.

- The limitations of mainstream approaches can be overcome by a more *processual* style of thinking that sees contingent factors as *interpreted* by managers, who not only have to operate in a broad societal and cultural context of power, opportunity and inequality but also find themselves both competing and allying with other managers within the organisation.

- The fundamental choice that managers face – within the processes of contestation and managerial debate – is between strategies based on direct-control/low-commitment human resourcing principles and indirect-control/high-commitment principles. The latter principles imply adoption of 'HRM-style' management practices.

- The style of strategy adopted will be influenced by political-economic and cultural factors, but needs, to some extent, to fit with the organisation's circumstances – as these are understood by managers in the light of their own interests and values.

- Different styles of human resourcing strategy may be applied to different parts of an organisation (as in a 'flexible firm' approach, for instance).

- The actual processes that occur in organisations as strategies take shape are messy and confused. Human resourcing specialists have to come to terms with the politics, confusions and value disputes that inevitably arise in the process of strategy making. A human resourcing strategy that is coherent and consistent enough to help the organisation survive in the long term has to be forged out of shrewd analysis, effective advocacy and political adeptness.

Discussion questions

Take each of the above summary points and consider the extent to which they are help-ful to you when you try to make sense of what goes on with regard to human resource strategy making:

(a) *in general* – with reference for example to the sort of debates you come across in the academic and practitioner literature, and

(b) *specifically* – when you look at what happens in organisations of which you have some direct knowledge.

Further reading

The most appropriate further reading for this chapter is indicated in the text, where readers will follow up the citations that appear to fit best with their particular interests. General texts that deal helpfully and more broadly with matters of human resourcing strategies are those by Harrison (1993), Hendry (1995), Lundy and Cowling (1996) and Price (1997).

2

HUMAN RESOURCE PLANNING
Strategies, systems and processes

Carole Tansley

OBJECTIVES

Having completed this chapter and its associated activities, readers should be able to:

- provide a 'working' definition of human resource planning (HRP) and show how it has emerged historically from manpower planning;

- understand the debates about conceptualising the nature of organisations and the people who work in them as both *systems* adapting to environments and as social, political and economic *processes*;

- demonstrate ways in which aspects of HR planning connect to the concepts of *vertical integration* of corporate, business and HR strategies and *horizontal integration* of HR policies and practices;

- identify the role of budgeting in relation to HR planning;

- understand the difficulties inherent in the implementation of computerised HR information systems used for short- medium- and long-term planning.

Introduction

In this chapter, the notion of human resource (HR) planning is explored by considering its historical development and its relationship to corporate, business and HR strategy making and the utilisation of information technology (IT). Case-study scenarios from a medium-sized manufacturing company and a multinational employing organisation are used to reflect on the issues raised, and questions to enable further discussion are provided at the end of the chapter. It is important at this stage to provide definitions to be applied in the debates and activities in this chapter. First, we need a clear definition of HR planning. It is defined here as *the creation of explicit proposals by HR specialists, corporate and line managers (and sometimes other employees) using specific technologies to enable the supply or dispensation of the human resources necessary for the acceptable performance and long term survival of an organisation.*

Other relevant definitions are given in Table 2.1.

Table 2.1 Defining human resources and the HR task

Human resources	The human resourcing (HR) task
The efforts, skills or capabilities that people contribute to an employing organisation to enable it to continue in existence	Acquiring, selecting, supplying, shaping and sometimes dispensing with human resources in order to enable an organisation to survive and succeed in the long term

Because the historical context informing conceptual definitions is also important, let us consider the development of the notion of HR planning.

Manpower planning and/or human resource planning?

Activities related to 'putting the right people in the right place at the right time at the right price' (Bolton, 1997: 12) were formally developed in the 1960s and given the term 'manpower planning'. Manpower planning has been mainly concerned with forecasting, control and matching supply and demand of human resources and involves (Hendry, 1994: 191):

- analysing the current human resources;
- reviewing labour utilisation;
- forecasting the demand for labour;
- forecasting supply; and
- developing a (human resourcing) plan.

Manpower planning has generally been thought of as a tactical rather than a strategic activity, requiring a rational, utilitarian approach (Legge, 1995), where people tend to be regarded as *costs* to the organisation (Bramham, 1997: 162). Personnel specialists involved in manpower planning have traditionally been characterised as technically neutral, *systems* thinkers (Legge, 1995), involved in reconciling an organisation's need for labour with the available supply in local and national labour markets (O'Doherty, 1997: 120). Bramham claims that manpower planning should not be confused with what he calls HR planning. This, he argues, is more a strategic activity that emphasises employee commitment, creativity, motivation and development (Bramham, 1997: 168). Marchington and Wilkinson (1996: 88), on the other hand, argue that the adoption of 'new-style human resource management led merely to an *expansion* of the scope of what was previously called manpower planning'.

Marchington and Wilkinson (1996: 87–90) conceptually separate HR planning activity into two distinct parts, using the terms 'hard' and 'soft'. Some would see little difference in this from Bramham's 'separateness' argument, other than a name change from manpower planning to 'hard' HR planning. Table 2.2 shows how these essentially separate perspectives are generally conceptualised in the literature.

Table 2.2 Hard or soft human resource planning?

'Hard' human resource planning	'Soft' human resource planning
Characterised by 'direct' control of employees. Here, employees are viewed as just another factor in the input–output equation, to be managed as efficiently and tightly as any other resource. A unitarist view is taken, where it is assumed that employees will fall in line with the specified behaviours required by management.	*Characterised by 'indirect' control of employees.* Employees increasingly involved in deciding how tasks should be carried out, with teamworking becoming popular (Hendry, 1994). A pluralist assumption is made here, in that different people in the organisation are interested in different things and that these differences must be taken into account within management processes.
Akin to the notion of manpower planning, being essentially a statistical modelling activity related to management identifying required demand for human resources and identifying appropriate supplies of labour in an efficient and effective manner.	*Characterised by a widening of focus* to include the creation 'and shaping of the culture of the organisation so that there is a clear integration between corporate goals and employee values, beliefs and behaviours' (Marchington and Wilkinson, 1996: 89).
Undertaken by personnel specialists following discussion with line management	*Involves HR specialists and line managers and possibly other employees*
Related HR strategies are concerned with improving utilisation of human resources (the cost-effective approach), in effect, getting employees to accept that their interests coincide with those of the organisation – the principles of mutuality and commitment (Hendry, 1994).	*More emphasis on strategies and plans for gaining commitment* by informing employees about the company's mission, values, plans and trading conditions.
Critique: an outstanding weakness is 'the focus on stocks and flows of people, and the relative absence of any concept of skill as the basis for work performance' (Hendry, 1994: 190).	*Critique:* 'soft' HRP lacking in explicit practical application or specification and, if taking Bramham's (1997) definition, so synonymous with the concept of *human resource management* that it lacks a clear focus (Marchington and Wilkinson, 1996: 89).

The use of the terms 'hard' and 'soft' in this context is beset with problems. We can see that hard HR planning has been characterised as a more 'objective' approach, with an underlying image of *direct control* of human resources. Soft HR planning, on the other hand, is presented more in terms of *indirect control*, that is, as more of a 'shaping' activity involving attempts to control employees through the 'shaping' of organisational culture. Such strict separation of planning approaches assumes that an HR manager will only use one approach at any one time, when this is clearly not the case in most organisations. In order both to test out this point and to revisit our understanding of HR planning generally, let us consider the case of Electronic Instruments Limited.

CASE STUDY 2.1

Electronic Instruments Limited – 'hard' and 'soft' human resource planning?

When Electronic Instruments Limited (EIL) was taken over by a major computing conglomerate three years ago, initially there was general relief in the company. As manufacturers of electronic equipment for the computer manufacturing industry, the business had been seriously affected because of competition from other companies in both European and international markets. There were rumours circulating that the takeover would mean a major injection of capital for investment in the equipment necessary to maintain a competitive edge. However, it soon became clear that the takeover also meant massive organisational change that resulted in substantial job cuts.

The first major change was the replacement of over half the top management team. Then a business process reengineering exercise was undertaken by management consultants, and this showed several instances where work flows and processes were unnecessarily and expensively repeated in the company. Team working was introduced throughout the company, as well as setting up cross-functional project teams for special development projects. The installation of the promised advanced computerised production equipment also required many changes to the working methods in the design and development departments and on the shopfloor. Over the next three years, the workforce was gradually reduced from 1500 (including 1000 shopfloor workers) to 550. The remaining staff included:

- 25 directors and senior managers;
- 100 highly qualified research and development (R&D) staff, in disciplines such as electronics and IT;
- 25 marketing and sales staff;
- 100 administrative staff;
- 300 shopfloor technicians.

It was decided that, because of the mercurial nature of the industry, fixed-term contracts would be used as an alternative to permanent contracts. Attractive financial inducements were offered to current staff to change contracts, and new recruits were automatically placed on contracts ranging from three to five years.

The managing director complimented the human resource manager on the excellent way in which he had led the team on the management-of-change programme. A highly effective employee relations specialist, the HR manager had handled the negotiations with the three unions and two staff associations extremely well. He had also been adept at recognising the need for training and development. Unfortunately, he was headhunted by another company in the industry and a replacement was found. One of the first things the new HR manager did was to undertake an analysis of the different employment contracts in the company. She was extremely concerned to find that the fixed-term contracts of 30 of the 100 staff in R&D and 10 out of 25 in marketing and sales were due for renewal in the next eighteen months. She had already heard that many of these people had started to look for other jobs and she knew that this could be serious for the company. Unfortunately, although on temporary contracts, most of these staff were now key to the needs of the business. They all had specialist knowledge of the products, many had strong relationships with major clients and 70 per cent of each group were classed as excellent or good performers.

The managing director blamed the previous HR manager for the situation, saying that he had been obsessed with making the workforce more 'flexible'. The MD warned that this state of affairs had to be addressed with some urgency. Business was booming at present, but the company could soon return to the 'bad old days' because of a lack of suitably qualified and committed people in vital areas of the business. The MD then asked the HR manager to make plans to ensure that, at least over the next three years, top-quality human resources would be in place at the right time for the right price. His vision was that the company would not only survive but also grow with the level of potential business.

Activity 2.1

Using the different perspectives shown in Table 2.2, answer the following questions:

1 Briefly describe the changes that have occurred in EIL over the last three years.

2 Identify the factors that the HR manager needs to take into account in forecasting, control and matching supply of human resources for the future.

3 What further information might the HR manager collect, how she should collect it and for what purpose?

4 Given the current situation, what 'hard' and 'soft' planning options are open to the HR manager for the future effective utilisation of human resources?

5 Draw up a plan of action that shows which option(s) you would advise the HR manager to choose, and why, with specific plans of how that option might be achieved.

It can be seen from the case study described in Activity 2.1, that the use of the terms *soft* and *hard* in HR planning is not particularly useful, because the HR manager must use both *direct* and *indirect* methods of planning and control of human resources in her ongoing activities. Perhaps a more appropriate way to consider different ways of thinking about human resource planning would be to place that activity in the context of general organisational theory, using what will be called the *systems* and *processual* perspectives.

Systems and processual perspectives

Using the *systems* and *processual* analytic perspectives introduced in Chapter 1 (Table 1.3) can help us understand the relationship between organisations and the individuals who comprise them, and therefore assist us in conceptualising different approaches to

HR planning. When applying a *systems* perspective in HR planning, we would view the organisation as an *entity* with clearly specified boundaries, detailed structures and well-defined objectives in the form of shared goals and values. It has a concrete existence *separate from* the individuals who comprise it. In the systems perspective of the organisation, 'management' is viewed as responsible for rational decision making and design of organisational structures, and 'non-management' as restricted to executing orders. Management of change is seen in terms of technical problems, where the organisation needs to be changed to fit the environment, with 'an assumption that change is designed by only one class of person – managers' (Hosking and Morley, 1991).

The *processual* perspective, derived from criticisms of systems thinking, provides a more dynamic, interactional perspective than that characterised by the systems perspective. When taking a processual perspective on HR planning, we need to view the organisation as an emerging pattern of beliefs and behaviours, with *organising*, rather than *organisation*, given a key focus (Hosking and Morley, 1991). This perspective on the organisation works within an *action frame of reference* (Silverman, 1970), where people and their contexts can be characterised as being in a *relationship of mutual creation*. Out of this emerges human social order, as people try to agree a set of shared decisions to be used to monitor, control, interpret and justify their actions. The social order that emerges reflects the values, interests and commitments of the participants and the clashes and tensions that exist between these. This order is always changing; consequently, the social order is always *emergent* (Hosking and Morley, 1991: 32). With the processual perspective on the *individual*, individual differences are celebrated, with a view of the individual's 'self' as constantly emergent rather than as a static entity. Individuals are seen both to reshape and to be reshaped constantly by their contexts, 'particularly with and through their relationships with other people' (Hosking and Morley, 1991: xi). This perspective presents social exchange and negotiation as cognitive, social and political processes; the relationship of these processes to one another changes as the cognition of the individual changes.

So what does this mean for our understanding of HR planning? To answer this question, we have to put planning in the context of strategy making generally.

■ Systems and processual thinking mirrored in strategic management theory

We can see a shift from a systems to a processual way of thinking mirrored in the historical development of strategic management theory generally from the 1950s to the 1980s. Gluck *et al.* (1982) provide a useful four-stage map of the changes that have occurred. The first stage involved *basic financial planning*, a form of budgetary control where the key purpose of the organisation revolved around setting and meeting budgets. The second stage was *forecast-based planning*, where the use of long-range planning systems introduced an element of forecasting and future prediction. The third stage was *externally oriented planning*, a strategic planning activity where the implications of alternative courses of action were considered, thus resulting in a degree of strategic thinking. The fourth stage was *strategic management*, where managers seek through their current actions to alter and create the future.

Gluck *et al.*'s (1982) model shows that a systems perspective of strategy has dominated in the past and demonstrates how thinking on strategy has changed over time. In the early stages, a deliberate, profit-maximising motivation was assumed, with managers viewing strategic planning as a rational process of deliberate calculation and analysis. Perhaps the best-known of the 'rational' school of strategists is Michael Porter of Harvard Business School, whose work has been focused on how firms gain and maintain competitive advantage over their rivals. His influential concepts have included the five-forces framework, generic strategies and the value chain (Porter, 1980, 1985, 1990). However, the 'rational' approach, with its tightly coupled, systems perspective, can be restrictive because it requires us to see things in structural terms – 'regularities or patterns in social behaviour observed as "frozen in time"' (Watson, 1995b: 12).

Those taking a rational systems approach to strategy making have a tendency to produce checklists of activities (see De Wit and Meyer, 1994: 10; Tyson, 1995: 72; Harrison, 1997 for a historical perspective), such as:

1 Define and agree overall mission and values for the company.

2 Examine and validate proposals emerging from business and functional levels.

3 Identify and explore relationships between different business units.

4 Allocate resources with a sense of strategic priorities.

However, as Tyson argues, 'what happens in organisations is contingent upon a range of variables, and . . . explanations of the actions within organisations must take account of the variables within society which impinge upon the organisation as well as on the intra-organisational variables including relative power, and the dependency between organisational units or departments' (Tyson, 1995b: 115). In strategic management theory, a processual perspective has developed that encompasses Quinn's (1980) notion of *logical incrementalism*, viewing strategy as having emergent properties, and Mintzberg's (1973) thesis, where managers undertake *post hoc* rationalisation in the development of strategy. Here, we have the notion that strategic plans emerge in a fragmented and largely intuitive manner, evolving from a combination of internal decisions and external events (Quinn, 1980). Taking a processual perspective in relation to HR planning can therefore be useful, as this provides for the continual experimentation, revision and rethinking that occur among different managers and interest groups, where processes of argument, debate and conflict play a part.

With such a processual perspective, managers and others responsible for planning are seen to negotiate and trade within what Layder calls their *situated activities* (Layder, 1997: 85–6). By this he means the 'face-to-face' conduct between two or more people who are in each other's 'response' presence (the ability of each person to monitor the behaviour of the others present and to modify their own behaviour in the light of each other's responses). They are therefore attempting, through interpersonal transactions, to *shape their own projects* in terms of the development of their 'self'. This can be conceptualised as a linked series of evolutionary transitions or transformations in identity at various significant junctures in their life career (Hughes, 1937: 404–13). This shaping process is, in turn, dependent on the way in which other individuals in trading activities go about the process of shaping *their* life projects and self-identity. The manager 'trades' with others, while at the same time *playing an integral part* in the organisation (Watson, 1995a). Strategy makers and HR planners therefore need to take account of the notion that people and their contexts are in a constant process of interpersonal negotiation and the social and political processes that are inherent in this activity. Our next case study should enable us to consider the implications of this.

CASE STUDY 2.2

Cargill Inc.

Cargill Inc., the largest privately owned US multinational (Henkoff, 1992), was founded in 1865 in the Midwest United States. It is involved in international agricultural food processing and commodity trading. Over 75 000 people are employed in Cargill businesses operating in more than 60 countries with 40 product lines. The rate of business growth has remained high for most of its 130-year history, with a corporate strategy that anticipates that Cargill will double its net worth every five to seven years. Cargill's stated strategy makes a clear commitment to total quality, in both material and human resources. This stance required, as its European president put it, 'listening and responding to the requirements of our customers in the food, agricultural, trading and financial sectors and by investing in the development of our employees'.

Cargill Europe was established in 1955 and now supplies agricultural products, basic food ingredients and added-value food products. The company's European sector includes more than 100 offices and facilities in nearly 20 countries in eastern and western Europe, the former Soviet Union, the Middle East and Africa. Always family-owned, the appointment of Cargill's second non-family chief executive officer in August 1995 heralded significant systemic changes. These were not only changes to the corporate level of the organisation, but also for the European businesses, which constituted more than 20 per cent of Cargill's worldwide turnover.

Cargill's corporate strategy

In 1996, contrary to the actions of its competitors, many of whom had used rightsizing/downsizing strategies as a way of surviving, Cargill's senior management used business growth as the core thrust of its corporate strategy. Cargill's business performance outpaced the average return of the Fortune 500 companies and significantly outperformed its commodities industry competitors. As a 'global' organisation, it achieved early recognition of market forces to combat what was a difficult year for the commodity industry. This was done as a 'team effort', by managers working together towards organisational survival. As vice-chairman Bob Lumpkins said in the company newsletter, *Cargill News*.

> We worked as a team to capitalize on the market forces. That, more than any other factor, is what created our magnificent performance in 1996.

This comment demonstrates that relationship development is an important part of Cargill's strategy-making initiatives, including relationships with *all* Cargill's stakeholders:

- the family members who own the business (unusual in today's climate of conglomerates);
- the customers (1997 was declared 'The Year of the Customer' with Cargill's credo: 'Give the customers precisely what they want');
- the managers (benefiting from appropriate pay and benefits packages);
- the employees (another credo: 'If you want to beat your competition you need better thinking and better people – so listen to your employees');
- those who live in the poorer nations where Cargill operates (Cargill management is reported as

viewing the company's presence in countries like Brazil almost as a mission. The company president for Brazil stated: 'We want to fulfil a humanitarian function, to raise the standard of living.').

(Additional note: the state, pressure groups, trade unions, etc. are also stakeholders.)

Activity 2.2

From our previous discussion on the processual perspective, we see that human beings are both makers of social patterns and are made by them, with those patterns acting as both a constraint and an enabler. Within the case study:

1 In what ways might Cargill's strategy of corporate growth both constrain and enable the careers of managers in Cargill UK?

2 What initiatives could be undertaken in Cargill to encourage employees to contribute ideas about how to beat the competition? How might such initiatives enable or constrain employees?

Integration between strategy making and HR planning

A number of writers have used the joint notions of *vertical* and *horizontal* integration as an analytical device for theorising about the relationship between corporate strategies and human resourcing activities (Baird and Meshoulam, 1988; Legge, 1995; Tyson, 1995b). *Vertical integration* can be characterised as the links between environmental context, business strategy and human resourcing (after Marchington and Wilkinson, 1996: 359). *Horizontal integration* is a concept that relates to the degree to which different aspects of human resourcing are compatible with each other (Marchington and Wilkinson, 1996: 359). Let us first examine the notion of vertical integration and consider the implications for HR planning by returning to Cargill to see how a HR manager might conceptualise this idea in practice.

CASE STUDY 2.3

Vertical and horizontal integration at Cargill Europe

Dick Cross, Cargill's European training manager, was involved in the initial design of a change-management programme for Cargill Europe HR. His initial analysis of the current situation in Cargill Europe provides a useful example of how vertical integration can be conceptualised in practice. The model in Fig. 2.1 is Dick's characterisation of the changing nature of the HR environment, changes affecting the organisation and the HR strategy and planning responses required.

Three levels of change affecting Cargill's HR function

As Dick saw it, the first area of change was outside Cargill: social, economic, political and economic, legal-enforcing changes in the way people work and in what they want from work, in the economics of employment and in people management. Some effects of the changes he could see

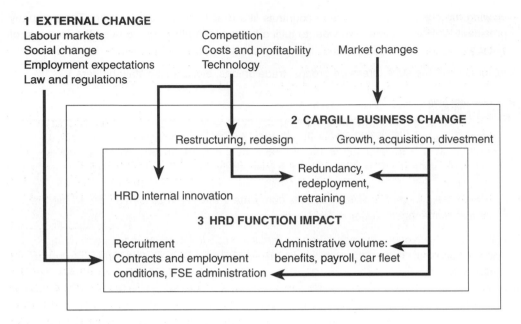

Fig. 2.1 Three levels of change in the HR function

working straight through to HR, others working via intermediate business changes. The second area of change was within Cargill but outside the HR department. The anticipated business changes included:

1 *Business growth*: doubling net worth every five to seven years will produce self-standing divisions increasingly able to provide their own HR services economically.

2 *Added value*: producing greater specialisation with resulting greater separation between divisions, greater difficulty in transferring staff and less apparent common ground in training and development.

3 *Acquisitions or divestment*: where Cargill has a strategic logic in purchase or sale, but is producing complex changes in benefits arrangements, salaries and grading, and in the volume of administrative effort.

4 *Efficiency/cost changes*: resulting partly from the competitive environment, partly from internal aims (business process reengineering programmes, for example).

The third area of change came from inside HR. The Cargill HR job family, as the members of the worldwide function are known, is managed by HR executive staff in the Minneapolis headquarters, overseeing HR activities in over 60 countries throughout the world. The corporate head of HR in Minneapolis is Nancy Siska, who has embraced the notion of strategic HRM in order to move away from a mode of traditional personnel management, characterised by bureaucracy and control. In Europe, technological innovations like the strategic HR information management project (nicknamed SHRIMP) incorporated a development programme for a global computerised HR information system, resulting from pressure to work more efficiently and from HR's own aspirations towards improvement. SHRIMP would enable managers to identify the key skills and competencies of their staff in a bid to attain effective competitive advantage in every market in which they were active.

Activity 2.3

1 Dick's 'systems' diagram shows clearly some of the entities and flows that constitute the notion of vertical integration between the external environment, the organisation and human resourcing. How does this compare with the situation in an organisation with which you are familiar?

2 Choose one of Dick's four anticipated business changes and consider the implications of that change in relation to human resource planning in Cargill Europe.

3 In Nancy Siska's move towards a strategic approach to human resourcing, she envisages that HR managers, line managers and possibly employees and their representatives will be involved in the HR planning process. What are the implications of such a shift in style?

A *resource-based view of the firm* is taken in Cargill's corporate strategy making, where the assertion is made that key human resources are a source of competitive advantage. Boxall advises that in order to gain *human resourcing advantage,* firms should combine their efforts towards generating both *human capital advantage* (by recruiting and retaining outstanding people) and *human process advantage* (instigating difficult-to-imitate, socially complex, historically evolved processes such as learning, co-operation and innovation) (Boxall, 1996: 66). This further attempt to 'mix' human resourcing activities inevitably presents HR planners with a major challenge. To help with this, we can turn to the notion of *horizontal integration*, which relates to the degree to which different aspects of human resourcing are compatible with each other. Let us return again to Cargill.

CASE STUDY 2.4

A strategic human resource plan?

At a meeting of Cargill Europe corporate, business and country HR management in Geneva in 1997, HR strategists from a number of countries devised the following human resources strategic plan.

Career development and the manpower planning process (MPP)

The development of talent is our goal. The identification of our key people, the tracking of their development and career, and the planning of potential developmental opportunities are essential elements of future business success. Employees must be aware of the actual career opportunities available in the company and their requirements. They must also be candid and honest in evaluating their capabilities and willingness to take the risks involved. Managers must be prepared to release and accept employees to/from other divisions/departments and coach their employees in this process.

Learning and development

The definition of competencies and skill requirements per job family and business and the correct assessment of the employee's skill gaps will facilitate the task to provide meaningful learning tools to fill in the training needs in sync with the business.

Compensation and benefits

Competitive compensation with regard to the market, the right job content and job value appraisal and the individual performance are the three main pillars of our compensation philosophy.

Improved transaction processing

The HR administration function involves a number of critical tasks for the whole workforce. It is our duty to ensure these tasks are performed accurately, timely and according to the law as well as to the Cargill Guiding Principles. Zero errors criterion is a must. The role of technology is key to responding effectively to the business needs.

Workforce performance management

Open communication, formal and informal feedback on performance and coaching are necessary elements of a continuously improved performance management process. These criteria must be pursued and promoted throughout our organisation.

Selection and diversity

In the diversity of our workforce lies its strength. The ability to create a working environment where everyone is empowered to succeed is our goal.

Foreign Service Employee (FSE) management

A mobile workforce allows us to grow and succeed. The management of our foreign service employees and their needs requires our particular focus.

Activity 2.4

1 Looking back at the definition of HR planning on page 40, consider the extent to which Cargill's planning statement can realistically be regarded as a plan.

2 To what extent do you think the designers of this HR strategic plan incorporated a balance between the needs of the business and the needs of Cargill employees?

3 Horizontal integration is a concept that relates to the degree to which different aspects of human resourcing are compatible with each other (Marchington and Wilkinson, 1996: 359). Apply the notion of horizontal integration by choosing two elements from the Cargill strategic HR plan shown above and indicate what factors would come into play when attempting compatibility between them.

4 When you have done this, choose a third element from the 'plan' and consider the difficulties of integrating it with the original two strategies chosen.

As both the external and internal environments of Cargill appear to be fairly unpredictable and dynamic, we can imagine that the production of 'static', rigid and highly formal plans could prove highly constraining for the managers involved. We can therefore usefully move to consider how managers undertake HR planning in such a context of 'action'.

HR planning in the context of action

With a *systems* view of HR planning, formal HR plans are theorised as *preceding* action, a position taken in many human resourcing texts. For example, Table 2.3 shows key points made by Schuler and Jackson (1996) about the different phases of HR planning.

Table 2.2 Five phases of HR planning

1 Identify the key business issues

2 Determine the human resource implications:
  ■ forecasting human resource demands (qualitative forecasting, using judgmental and estimation techniques such as the Delphi method, where managers meet to take turns at presenting their forecasts and assumptions to the others, who then make revisions in their own forecasts; quantitative forecasting, using statistical projections)
  ■ forecasting human resource supplies (internal and external).

3 Develop human resource objectives and goals (*what* to accomplish)
4 Design and implementation of HR policies, programmes and practices (i.e. *how* to accomplish objectives and goals)
5 Evaluation, revision and refocusing (linked to HR objectives and goals)

Source: Adapted from Schuler and Jackson, 1996: 137.

HR planning, it appears, should form the basis of pre-specified action plans. The objectives of these plans usually include the achievement of organisational change, the solving of anticipated human resource problems and the identification of new opportunities key to the success of the organisation (Marchington and Wilkinson, 1996: 89). However, one major issue which has to be faced by all managers is how specific and concrete these plans should be. Figure 2.2 shows two distinct positions on the relationship between planning and action.

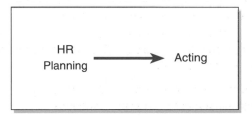

Fig. 2.2 A *systems* perspective of the HR planning process

In recent years, a growing critique has developed of attempts to seek long-term success through very 'tight', detailed and long-term planning (Mintzberg, 1994). In a systems perspective of HR planning, each stage is presented as a set of unproblematic sequences lacking political and cultural influences. However, three aspects can be said to have a significant impact on the generation of such plans. First, unforeseen circumstances and surprise contingencies can arise. Second, human independence of mind and the general human tendency to resist hierarchical authority in democratic cultures can subvert these plans as people seek their own ways of doing things and fulfil their own desire for choice and initiative making. Finally, there is often a discouragement of innovation, creativity and risk taking in human resourcing issues, all of which are important in an increasingly competitive global economy.

In light of this, then, rather than seeing the development of plans for human resourcing as *preceding* action (a *systems* perspective), as shown in Fig. 2.3, we need to see HR planning as a continual process of *action* (a *processual* perspective encompassing negotiation, revision and rethinking).

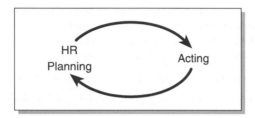

Fig. 2.3 A *processual* perspective of the HR planning process

To consider HR planning in this way does not mean that we have to reject completely the idea of the organisation as a system. Rather, we see the 'system' in a less static way, recognising that all organisations require resources to survive, but the human individuals who are involved with that organisation have a concern to further their own interests. HR planning therefore is seen as a continually negotiated, mutually creative process that is not the tightly controlled activity that the systems perspective makes it appear. One way in which this can be achieved is for the HR function to produce vision, mission and value statements. Let us consider the vision, mission and values statements that currently inform human resourcing practice in Cargill.

CASE STUDY 2.5

Cargill HR vision, mission and values statements

The HR vision for Cargill Europe

Human resources will be an effective customer and business focused division proactively participating in Cargill's success.

The HR mission for Cargill Europe

In Cargill, we know that the delivery of our key business strategies will only be achieved by capable and motivated people working together. Specifically, we commit to identifying business needs and sourcing, developing, rewarding and retaining high calibre employees for our businesses, thus creating an environment, culture and structure in which our people and our businesses can grow and prosper.

The Cargill Europe HR values

We in HR believe:

- that in our business, people make the difference,
- people deserve job satisfaction, personal growth, respect, safe working conditions,
- people are accountable for what they do,
- we should manage change to make it work for us,
- in a diverse workforce with equal opportunities,
- in open, honest, two way communication,
- that our people and organisation must learn continuously in order to thrive,
- in effective teamwork,
- in using simple language.

Activity 2.5

1 What difficulties might arise in the HR planning process when attempting to put these statements into practice?

2 What difficulties might face Cargill's director of HR when she attempts to gain the commitment of the staff in the HR function to the vision, mission and values statements?

3 In relation to the structure of HR, should it be a division like any other part of the business or should it be seen as a support function *to* the business divisions? What are the implications of each choice?

Vision, mission and value statements are not the only resources that management can utilise to encourage commitment and enable focused planning activities. One aspect of planning not often explored is that of budgets and the political processes involved in their control.

Budgetary control and HR planning

HR managers are continually pressured to focus on reducing overhead and labour costs in relation to personnel administration, training and development and reward packages. The budgetary process is therefore an important aspect in the HR activity. In *systems* terms, Hope and Hope (1997) see the budgeting ethos in organisations as impeding change and acting as a managerial 'glue' that holds the traditional organisation together. In *processual* terms, they argue that budgets define relationships, behaviours and power bases (Hope and Hope, 1997: 27). Let us consider an empirical example of a HR budget-planning process.

CASE STUDY 2.6

The Cargill HR budget-planning process

In a memo to those of her staff with responsibility for human resourcing tasks in the various countries in which Cargill Europe had a presence, Margaret Struder outlined the following structural requirements for their HR budgets:

> A HR manager in a country or business sector role will have prime responsibility for their area HR budget, which it is required will be agreed and 'signed off' by the various managers of product lines. Margaret Struder, as European sector HR head, has joint responsibility with those managers for setting strategies that define those budgets, working with each HR manager on obtaining agreement for their proposals. She then reports their numbers and plans to the European Management Team. HR managers have two key areas of relationships in the budget planning process. The first is with their functional head, Margaret, who will ensure that there is a cohesive budgeting strategy between different members of the HR function. The second is with the country/business managers. This structure of relationships and processes are in place to produce standardised systems for HR numbers and costs which can be presented to the businesses. Of particular interest here are the costs incurred on vendors across the function in order to negotiate better deals.
>
> The budget is divided into two parts. The first being the actual costs of the HR departments, such as HR employee compensation and benefits costs, departmental overheads and recharges from other services area inside the company. The second includes various service and provider costs for which HR have key responsibility and on which they have a positive influence. These areas include:

- professional services (tax advisers, salary survey providers, payroll vendors, etc.);
- recruitment (advertising, executive search and selection, graduate recruitment, etc.);
- training (internal, external and specific technical job training such as pension specific);
- foreign service employee costs (housing, removal, education, vendor, culture training, home leave, etc.);
- and European Work Council costs (travel and subsistence, materials and communications, etc.).

Cargill management clearly perceived a need for HR to develop annual budgets derived from financial and other resource plans and forecasts in order to support capital investment programmes.

Activity 2.6

1 Draw a model of the stakeholders in the HR budgetary process. Taking a processual perspective, identify possible areas of conflict between stakeholders in the process.

2 With reference to an organisation with which you are familiar, say how the HR budgetary process might influence relationships, behaviours and power bases.

By reflecting on the information produced by Activity 2.6, we can see how the HR budgetary situation can be viewed from the two perspectives, systems and processual, and note the value of each. Let us now move on to our final element of HR planning, the role of computerised information systems, an area that is often given scant attention by HR managers and academics alike.

The importance of computerised HR information systems in HR planning

Earlier in this chapter, we saw that there are a number of phases inherent in the HR planning process. In each of these phases, management information is required to facilitate decision making. HR specialists therefore need to ascertain what type of HR information the corporate centre needs, what HR information an autonomous unit needs to run as a business and how and in what form that information is to be received (Richards-Carpenter, 1993: 23). In an attempt in the last decade to achieve strategic objectives such as survival, competitiveness and profitability, organisations have been restructuring their operations. This invariably meant reducing the numbers of jobs ('downsizing') and 'releasing' staff from their employment contracts. Downsizing programmes therefore required that appropriate information be available to both HR and line managers to enable careful diagnosis of the current human resourcing situation and the development of plans to implement the changes.

In the late 1970s, 'manpower' planning in relation to the high level of unplanned redundancies in that era was an extremely difficult activity because of the lack of suitable HR systems (Richards-Carpenter, 1991: 24). Control of existing systems by data-processing managers, who tended to have a low priority for manpower planning systems and a high level of desire for in-house development, also made it difficult to utilise IT in employment management. The existence of limited applications of 'old' technology (the PC was not widely available), long development timescales and separate payroll systems that were difficult to integrate were just some of the difficulties to be accommodated. In the 1990s, a different picture gradually began to emerge.

Most texts on the subject of HR information systems (HRIS) mention the impact that organisational changes have had on approaches by HR specialists to the management of HR information (Kingsbury, 1997). From the systems perspective, the underlying essence of information management in HR planning is one of bureaucratic rationalisation and a search for technical efficiency by practitioners. In Activity 2.4, we saw the importance of HR information systems reflected in the list of Cargill's critical HR strategies (what it called 'improved transaction processing'). This commitment is underscored by the use of such statements as 'the role of technology is key to responding effectively to the business needs'. From a systems perspective, human resource information systems (HRIS) are seen as vital in the provision of the right information at the right time, so enabling managers to do their job effectively and efficiently. The HR specialist is presented as a collector, analyser and provider of information on human resources to enable an 'effective' response to corporate and business strategies for a number of stakeholders, not least the line manager.

Computerised information systems (databases and electronic network connections inside the organisation, and electronic connections externally, such as the World Wide Web via the Internet) are seen to play an increasingly vital part in the management of information for HR planning. Unfortunately, there are marked differences between organisations in relation to the provision and effective use of HRIS in both strategic and operational HR.

Research studies have highlighted the slowness of HR in utilising IT in comparison with other functions (Cerveny *et al.*, 1993; Dunivan, 1991; Kavanagh, *et al.*, 1990). Some HR managers argue that because of the high levels of uncertainty in HR tasks (Ceriello and Freeman, 1991), which involve subjective evaluation (Motowidlo, 1986), utilisation of IT in human resourcing work is insupportable. However, others argue that the use of computers in this area can actually assist what they deem to be a more 'objective' approach to HR decision making. The view that other functions, such as accounting, are 'advanced' in their use of IT is not always backed up by research (Powell and Xiao 1996). In addition, surveys have shown that over 90 per cent of HR departments are operating with some form of computerised HRIS (Kinnie and Arthurs, 1993; Louis, 1989; Neilson, 1994). In a survey undertaken by the (formerly named) Institute of Manpower Studies, a number of key changes were found to affect the use of HRIS (Richards-Carpenter, 1994: 55). These changes included the development of the HR function itself and the demise of many central IT functions, both used as a means of explaining the growth in the use of micro-based HRIS in support of the business unit, with the majority of micro applications now networked. However, as most respondents stated that their line managers did not know what information was available in their HRIS, this raised questions about the way in which HR was actually using its systems to 'add value' to the business.

The perception that HRIS are not 'adding value' is re-inforced by a number of writers who criticise the limited way in which they are utilised. HRIS are said to be poorly utilised because they are often slow and inflexible and the quality of the data input is frequently questionable (Hannon *et al.*, 1996: 245). Such systems are often used for operations such as record keeping and payroll administration (Kinnie and Arthurs, 1993; Louis, 1989; Meinhart and Davis, 1993; Richards-Carpenter, 1994) rather than for strategic management (Hall and Torrington, 1989: 30) or to reengineer the HR role (Richards-Carpenter, 1993: 55). In larger organisations, the trend for the dominance of the (often antiquated) payroll system rather than a complete management information system has been argued to have had a serious impact on the design and implementation of new systems to replace HRIS in home-country and global operations (Weitzner *et al.*, 1990).

Several authors have questioned the capability of the HR specialist to understand the HR information needs of the business, highlighting particularly the lack of commitment of HR managers to developing their interest or their skills in use of IT in HR decision making (Frantzeb, 1991; Kavanagh *et al.*, 1990; Kossek *et al.*, 1994; Lawler, 1992). Others have argued that in the UK the present education and training provision contributes to the failure of HR specialists fully to realise the benefits of HRIS (Beaumont *et al.*, 1992). They advised the professional institute of human resourcing specialists, the Institute of Personnel and Development (IPD), that it had a leading role to play in ensuring that HR practitioners have the appropriate attitudes, knowledge and skills to ensure that IT enables business benefits. In light of this, they recommended that the IPD needed to undertake a major educational initiative with different objectives for different target audiences, ranging from senior personnel practitioners to new recruits, and to consider fundamental changes to the design and delivery of its curriculum.

When we consider Hall and Torrington's (1989) research, we can see why better education and training might be required in the strategic use of IT in HR. They extracted one case-study organisation from a large-scale questionnaire study and interviewed 35 of its personnel managers who had introduced computerisation into the personnel function. They classified the managers into four categories: stars, radicals, plodders and beginners. 'Stars' (3) were those making full and imaginative use of the potential of 'leading-edge' computer applications to enhance the role and effectiveness of the function. In the other categories, 'radicals' (8) had begun with high aspirations, over-reached themselves, then had to start again after a failed first attempt. 'Plodders' (12) were making some use of the 'electronic filing cabinet', but the nature of personnel work remained unchanged and duplicate manual records were kept. 'Beginners' (12) were those departments where there was little leading-edge use of computers but there was evidence that such progress was beginning and in its early stages. The low number of 'stars' showed great potential for improvement. It is perhaps by considering such examples in more detail that we can learn valuable lessons in how to plan for the successful implementation of HRIS. Let us return to our Cargill case one last time.

CASE STUDY 2.7

Cargill Strategic Human Resource Information Management Project (SHRIMP)

Given that Cargill employs more than 75 000 people across the world, it was not surprising that the company felt it had a need for effective 'global' and 'local' HR information management systems. The Cargill managers found that they had:

- accelerated demand for information from the business;
- recurring communication problems in obtaining information for HR planning activities;
- a critical need to update, change and introduce new HR systems, as the majority of the present ones are outdated.

In the past, there had been a major system in the North American headquarters, but no cohesive computerised HR information system (HRIS) existed for company sites in the rest of the world. Europe, the Pacific Rim and South America were in need of HR systems to facilitate the strategy of corporate and business growth that had been announced in the mid-1990s.

Phase I

In late 1994, a group of Cargill HR and IT specialists from different countries worldwide met to discuss the possibility of creating a 'global data warehouse' where information on key individuals could be stored and subsequently consulted by both HR and management. Laurie Goche, a manager from corporate headquarters experienced in HR information systems development, facilitated the meeting. The intention of the meeting was to gather approximately 50 data elements on those key individuals that could be accessed by divisional and country management as required for human resourcing in Cargill. However, during this meeting, the following became clear:

- Information on all countries was not available to populate the database.
- In those countries where information was available, it was in a variety of formats (paper and computer) and languages.

- The information-reporting processes were not consistent among the various countries.
- There was no clear view of what was needed by the business (in fact, managers had quite a variety of views).

The conclusions of this four-day session were important in moving the group forward towards a global HRIS solution for the HR division. If they really wanted to have valuable, business-related information available for managers, then they had to make it as common and accessible as possible across the sectors, thus the idea of a common database was evolved. They all agreed on the necessity of a global data warehouse and that its contents needed to be defined up front in order to structure the local programmes. The global data warehouse was to be designed to:

- store critical, accurate HR information about employees,
- create an environment for Cargill's HR customers to utilise this on a timely basis,
- feed the data warehouse directly from local HR systems.

At the start of the meeting, the plan was to have a global data warehouse in place in six months. As people left the meeting, with a much better sense of reality, their goals had expanded considerable along with their timetable. The project was to be called SHRIMP (the Strategic Human Resource Information Management Project) and a vision statement was produced:

> *To have a common human resource information system that will meet human resource customer requirements and allow senior managers access to up-to-date and accurate information. This information will assist Cargill's management in making strategic personnel decisions that promote growth of the corporation as well as to effectively and efficiently manage employees' career development and manpower planning on an international basis.*

One urgently needed aspect was to review HR processes locally, by sector and on a worldwide basis, before any database (local or global) could be implemented. This was the basis for the formation of the CPD (core process definition) group. Core process definition was the first and most critical part of SHRIMP's success in each country. It is a methodology used to streamline and improve 'core' (critical) HR processes, HR organisation, HR supplier relationships and HR products. Basically, it is a set of reengineering techniques that allows a manager to step back and look at the HR operations and see how they can be designed to 'fit' with corporate and business strategies and HR customers' (managers, employers, etc.) needs.

CPD was undertaken in June 1995, with a European group looking at eight 'global' HR processes. They reviewed and recommended improvements to HR processes such as manpower planning, performance management, training, recruiting, foreign service employee administration and payroll. The next step was to undertake CPD in each country or product line. Cargill's employee population is continuing to expand, with this growth experienced mostly outside of North America. CPD was therefore seen as providing an opportunity to assess existing HR operations, assumptions and policies in preparation for major growth in Cargill's overall employee population.

Phase II – Research and development

Three groups were set the task of working on one of three project stages.

Group 1

Available databases provided by information systems suppliers were reviewed that would fit the specification the group had prepared in technical, practical and cost terms. Seven were initially chosen – two remained at the end of the research period.

The implementation strategy involved:

- Global and regional preparation:
  - data warehouse;
  - HRIS integration.
- Pilot in UK and Argentina.
- Rollout to:
  - Asia Pacific;
  - Europe;
  - Latin America.

In order to achieve common HR systems, Group 1 had to:

- deploy common HR systems in each country;
- support unique country issues, such as country/product line preparation, including:
  - allocate budget funds;
  - identify and train local implementation teams;
  - select payroll and benefit product solutions;
  - clean up existing HR information;
  - complete preparation checklist;
  - install the system;
  - establish local processes/structures;
  - train-end users;
  - load database;
  - test system and processes;
  - go 'live';
- manage data ('data centres');
- manage payroll/benefit systems separately in each country.

Group 2

This group reviewed Cargill HR global processes and mapped these in order to find efficiencies and improvements. In order to achieve common HR processes they had to:

- define common HR processes within Cargill;
- review, improve and reengineer those processes globally and locally;
- implement these processes in all countries;
- formulate a set of core HR processes to be used worldwide in the building of a common database. This process was also carried out locally as the implementation stage in each country was reached.

Group 3

This group finalised the key data elements forming the basis for the global data warehouse. They looked at the technical requirements needed to ensure that this data enters the warehouse in an efficient and timely manner. It is probable that each sector will also have a central data warehouse (e.g. London, Singapore) with information on that sector available to the businesses.

Phase III

The project was presented and approved at the January 1996 long-range planning committee meeting. Prior to the approval of the project by the committee, it was decided that the USA would not be included in the three-year roll-out plan. Its present system still had a reasonable 'shelf life' but unfortunately could not be considered in the vendor selection as it did not suit many of the requirements of a global system. Data from the US system will form part of the global data warehouse and the USA will be an integral part of the team as the HRIS product was 'rolled out'. Some parts of Asia were already using an earlier version of the HRIS product and they moved on to the new version that was adapted to Cargill's specifications.

The test site for the first roll-out was the UK. A new payroll product was chosen and the existing database 'cleaned up' in order to download valid and current information. In December 1996 the payroll system was completed with zero defects. This was an excellent exercise in planning for other roll-outs and one from which future sites benefited considerably. Problem areas were continually to be documented throughout the three-year programme in order to minimise difficulties. Some of the main challenges were seen to be: to ensure good links with local products; to test the language element (all non-English speaking sites will have an English and local-language version working in conjunction); ensuring a speedy roll-out; and eventually training managers to use the information available to them in order to improve business practices.

Activity 2.7

Taking a processual approach, identify why and in what ways a project like SHRIMP could fail.

We have seen from the case study that Cargill appeared to move very quickly (within three years) from what Hall and Torrington call 'beginners' mode towards becoming 'stars' in the utilisation of innovative HR information systems (Hall and Torrington, 1989). Its global and local integration was designed with vertical and horizontal integration of corporate, business and HR strategy making and also with HR planning in mind. Also implied in the case is that HR specialists in Cargill are being encouraged to see HR systems development as an integral part of their role. This has a bearing on the type of person being recruited into the function, one who needs to be intellectually able, a 'hybrid' who can use information systems to good effect but also provide ideas on how to manage information.

Also implicit in the case study are the complex changes that will occur at both environmental and interpersonal levels. As the number of businesses grow, in line with corporate strategy, this requires extensive employee population growth, which, in turn, has implications for HR planning and associated systems. The individuals responsible for the implementation of such systems therefore need to take account of macro patterns of human resources on a society-wide basis, as well as the interactional resources of organisational functioning, such as the role of culture and politics in decision making.

Summary

In this chapter we have built on the discussion in Chapter 1, where the focus was clearly on HR strategy making. In relation to HR planning, a number of arguments have been made:

- HR planning must always be seen within that strategy-making context.

- In particular, human resource (HR) planning can most usefully be defined as the relatively specific element of HR strategy making that proposes appropriate actions with regard to human resourcing.

- HR planning involves the creation of formal and explicit sets of proposals intended to achieve actions that will help achieve long-term organisational performance.

- The challenge for those undertaking HR planning is therefore to propose actions that contribute to long-term corporate success, not only by being prepared to take into account surprise circumstances, but also introducing new ways of thinking.

- This requires that there is sufficient openness or flexibility about the direction proposed.

- It also requires that there are opportunities for the variety of individuals and groups that make up an organisation to have an input into both the *thinking* and the *action* implicit in planning.

- The *systems* and *processual* perspectives provide two different ways of viewing the relationship between an organisation and the individuals who constitute that organisation.

- HR planning involves a combination of thinking and acting, so can usefully be seen in *process* terms. This involves the incorporation of continual experimentation, revision and rethinking in which processes of argument, debate and conflict between different managers and interest groups play a part.

Discussion questions

1 What are the characteristics of the two main perspectives on the relationship between organisations and people?

2 To what extent is it appropriate to distinguish between 'hard' and 'soft' HR planning?

3 In an organisation with which you are familiar, how would you characterise vertical integration between corporate strategy, human resourcing strategy and human resource planning?

4 Choose one of Cargill's stakeholders mentioned in Activity 2.2 and consider the nature of the relationship between those stakeholders and the HR planning process.

5 What importance does an HR vision statement have for HR planning?

6 What are the differences between HR planning in a large international organisation and a small family firm?

7 What are the issues of budgetary control in relation to HR planning?

8 Draw a diagram showing the stakeholders in the provision of computerised human resource information systems (HRIS). Choose two of these stakeholders and identify areas of conflict that might occur during the implementation of a HRIS.

Further reading

Bramham, J. (1997) *Human Resource Planning*, London: Institute of Personnel and Development. An up-dated version of Bramham's text on manpower planning which takes a more strategic approach to planning than that original text.

Hannon, J., Jelf, G. and Brandes, D. (1996) 'Human Resource information systems: operational issues and strategic considerations in a global environment', *The International Journal of Human Resource Management*, Vol. 7, No. 1, pp. 245–69. Describes the difficulties and issues related to the design and implementation of computerised global HR information systems and discusses implications for practitioners and researchers.

Hosking, D.M. and Morley, I.E. (1991) *A Social Psychology of Organising: People, Processes and Contexts*, Hemel Hempstead: Harvester Wheatsheaf. This text provides an excellent coverage of the basic processes involved in the creation and maintenance of organisations, with particular focus on the social and political activities that are performed individually and collectively. People are viewed as intelligent social actors who, in collaboration, competition and conflict with others, attempt to organise their lives by selecting and shaping their social settings in ways that will protect and promote their values and interests.

Layder, D. (1997) *Modern Social Theory. Key Debates and New Directions*, London: UCL Press. Whilst concentrating more on social theory than human resourcing, this text is well worth reading for a deeper understanding of some of the issues involved in the relationship between human agency and social structures.

Tyson, S. (1995) *Human Resource Strategy – Towards a General Theory of Human Resource Management*, London: Pitman Publishing. This text demonstrates the link between human resourcing and business strategy. It combines a review of the literatures relating to human resourcing with some excellent empirical examples of practice, with particular emphasis on the link between a company's success and its HR strategy.

3

MANAGING UNCERTAINTY OR MANAGING UNCERTAINLY?

Colin Bryson

'The best laid schemes o' mice an' men
Gang aft a-gley'

Robert Burns, 1786

OBJECTIVES

Having completed this chapter and its associated activities, readers should be able to:

- assess the choices available to the manager and HR practitioner in trying to balance requirements for human resources in a context of uncertainty;

- understand the issue of 'flexibility' and so-called flexible employment practices;

- evaluate which theoretical and conceptual frameworks may be appropriate in the analysis of this topic;

- systematically criticise a theory based on research evidence, using the example of the 'flexible firm';

- assess competing explanations about why flexible employment is introduced and practised at a national, sectoral and organisational level;

- understand several flexible employment practices with reference to empirical evidence of their use in the UK, the facilitating and constraining factors and apparent advantages and disadvantages to employers and employees;

- compare and contrast 'new' forms of employment practice with traditional approaches such as redundancy and overtime;

- assess the implications for using these approaches in detail within the organisation – issues of management, for HR strategies and outcomes for individuals;

- have some understanding of the implications external to the organisation, on labour markets, public policy and society.

Introduction

Predicting the future is not something at which human beings have been particularly successful. Even if we have some rough idea about likely trends, the plans we make to cope with them may not work out the way we intended. The more we learn about human resourcing in organisations, the more we understand how difficult it is to manage the present, far less the future. It is readily apparent that human resource planning has limitations. In the *laissez faire* markets of global capitalism, organisational survival is perceived to depend on two imperatives:

- alignment of outputs with demand;
- sufficient adaptability to cope with change.

Every organisation is subject to these imperatives. Even organisations in the public and voluntary sectors which, by tradition, were not exposed directly to market competition have been forced to comply. It is currently a norm and expectation of society that organisations must deliver services and products with maximum efficiency and at the lowest cost. Human resourcing has been at the forefront of this consumer- and market-oriented philosophy and great emphasis has been placed on the concept of *labour utilisation*.

The traditional approach has been stereotyped as *hire*, when additional labour or new skills are required, and *fire*, to shed workers when there is no longer demand for their labour or particular skills. Short-term increases in demand were met in the past by using overtime, paid at premium rates to workers already on the payroll. Most low-skill work was organised on Fordist and Taylorist principles with tasks broken down into simple steps performed by individuals requiring little training and development. Short-term decreases in demand were met by laying off part of the workforce. The laid-off workers, despite financial hardship because of loss of wages, more or less tolerated the situation as there was an almost certain guarantee of a return to work in the near future. Redundancy was more serious but, due to economic growth and social norms of full employment, finding another job was fairly straightforward. White-collar work was almost immune from lay-off or redundancy, with an even stronger expectation of a job for life.

Whether such a stereotype was generally applicable outside particular sectors and a fairly brief time period is moot. Temporary work was fairly common, indeed 25 per cent of the Civil Service, that bastion of secure employment, was made up of temporary workers in 1967. Nevertheless, it is notable that this was almost entirely confined to the lowest grades and that the work was available as long as individuals wished it. During this era, the 1950s and 1960s, female participation in the labour market showed a high degree of vertical and horizontal segregation and was substantially lower than today. Part-time work was starting to grow strongly, mainly through the demand from women.

However, major changes were unfolding. Without rehearsing debates about post-modernism and the crisis of capitalism (see Legge, 1995: 286–328), putative theories were proposed to explain both what was happening and how organisations were responding. A broad stream of the debate centred on the notion of *flexibility* as a response, even a solution, to the new era of uncertainty.

Conceptualising flexibility

Flexibility has many meanings. Every commentator tends to adopt a definition that is suited to the particular line of argument they propose. Boyer's (1987) comment that flexibility is 'a multiform and particularly ambiguous generic term' is very apt. Blyton and Morris (1991: 2) gave three reasons that the concept of flexibility has often been misused or misunderstood:

> it has been employed as a *summary* concept for a wide range of developments, the assumptions made about the *homogeneity* of the nature, pace, causes and consistency of these developments, and the tendency for it to be discussed as a *unitary* concept embodying no essential conflicts of interest.

Much of the debate concerning flexibility has been about the existence of new approaches at the level of industrial society. An example of this is *regulation theory*, which attempts to integrate the social, economic and political spheres and proposes that a new paradigm of capitalism has been created that is characterised by flexible production, differentiated and segmented consumption, a restructured welfare state and post-modernist cultural forms (Hyman, 1991). Another approach, but one that adopts a rather more narrow focus on production, is *flexible specialisation* (Piore and Sabel, 1984). The argument here is that mass-production techniques are no longer relevant and therefore have been replaced by flexible specialisation forms, e.g. adaptable, craft-based production utilising new technology. This theory drew on the development of 'industrial districts' in Northern Italy. Such new forms of production create changes in organisation and labour utilisation, e.g. from Taylorism to self-regulating work groups. For a much fuller explanation of these theories see Gilbert *et al.* (1992).

Other writers have suggested alternative explanations of what may be going on. Labour market theorists argue that changes in the nature of the *labour market* have led to more flexible utilisation of labour (Rubery and Wilkinson, 1994). A related explanation (Capelli, 1995), one more concerned with the changing nature of employment, contrasts the previous prevalence of internal labour markets, because of the pressure to internalise due to lower 'transactions costs' (Williamson, 1975), to the present emphasis on external labour markets due to changes in competition, markets, attitudes and public policy. In contrast to these explanations, labour process theorists (Braverman, 1974; Thompson, 1990) argue that 'crisis in capitalism' has been met by changes in the labour process, e.g. deskilling, commodification, increasing work intensity.

We are concerned, however, with human resourcing and our focus is at the level of organisation and particularly with management. Such macro-level frameworks as suggested above are useful in shedding light on changes in the nature of work and work organisation. They may help explain why there are some apparent differences between what is happening in different countries. However, they are less helpful in explaining what is going on in organisations and how managers may attempt to manage uncertainty. The approach we have taken in earlier chapters has been to be cautious of the orthodox approach to thinking about 'organisational strategy' and how this may be 'implemented'. Watson in Chapter 1 and Tansley in Chapter 2 have advocated a more processual approach to thinking about organisations. Understanding this type of thinking allows us to appreciate that different conceptual frameworks may all be useful, at least in part, because they tend to be reflections of different ways of looking at the issue rather than necessarily competing explanations. We will look at the next conceptual framework in some depth. Indeed, we may use this as an archetype for academic critique. Students may be familiar with the process of evaluating theories based on research evidence, but the example that follows demonstrates this process particularly well.

■ The flexible firm

Debates in the UK about whether managers in organisations have sought a new approach to managing and utilising labour have been dominated by the concept of the *flexible firm*. This concept was proposed by Atkinson at the Institute of Manpower Studies (now Employment Studies) (Atkinson, 1984; Atkinson and Meager, 1986).

The concept of the flexible firm was that of an ideal organisational design, promoted as the solution to the problems of the operating environment. Atkinson specifically argued that firms had been forced to change their strategy in the face of market stagnation, job loss, uncertainty, technological change and pressures to reduce working time. He suggested that the opportunity to move to the flexible firm model was facilitated at the time due to uncertainties resulting from turbulent markets and new technology, slack labour markets and the inability of weakened trade unions to resist change.

This introduced the notion of a *core* workforce enjoying employment security but subject to *functional flexibility* – the necessity for the individual to use a range of skills across a number of organisational tasks or roles. Workers may carry out multifunctional roles simultaneously or over the longer term through retraining and redeployment. This policy supposedly allows adaptation to new products and forms of production without requiring new staff.

In order to match the number employed to the exact demand for labour, another form of flexibility may be used. *Numerical flexibility* is applied to the *peripheral* workforce, e.g. those employed on a part-time or fixed-term basis, as well as casual workers and government-sponsored trainees. Therefore those workers enjoy less employment security. The periphery also includes *distancing*, the use of subcontracting and outsourcing.

Another form of flexibility that may be applied to both core and periphery is *financial flexibility* – the ability to adjust remuneration costs both up and down. This has two aspects: the necessity that the remuneration system for all groups is responsive to market forces and the introduction of more individualised rewards, particularly those that link pay to output, such as performance-related pay.

Therefore the core group is insulated in terms of job security from short- to medium-term changes in the marketplace, but the workers in the periphery are not. Atkinson identifies two separate peripheral groups. The first periphery group are full-time workers like the core but they show different features:

■ 'their jobs are "plug-in" ones, and not firm specific';

■ 'functional flexibility is not sought and, because these jobs tend to less skilled, little training or retraining is needed. A lack of career prospects, systematisation of job content around a narrow range of tasks, and a recruitment strategy directed particularly at women, all tend to encourage a relatively high level of labour turnover, which itself facilitates easy and rapid numerical adjustment to product market uncertainty' (Atkinson, 1984: 29).

Atkinson distinguishes a second peripheral group that has some functional flexibility if the numerical flexibility provided by the first peripheral group is not sufficient. The example he states as most appropriate for this group is part-time staff (especially for the purpose of creating more temporal flexibility), but he argues that job sharing, temporary and short-term staff and public subsidy trainees are all employed to fulfil a similar flexibility function and therefore also form part of the second peripheral group. Atkinson notes that none of these forms of flexibility is novel, but the innovation lay in combining all the forms in the dual model of core and periphery as a *deliberate strategy* to allow maximum labour flexibility and to optimise the organisation's response to changing market conditions. He argued that this model would operate at all levels and apply equally to all staff in the organisation (although the consequences for staff groups are clearly different depending on whether their jobs are deemed to be core or periphery). He even defined which staff roles would give 'core' status: 'managers, designers, technical sales staff, quality control staff, technicians and craftsman' (Atkinson, 1984: 29).

Atkinson predicted that the divergence between strategies to manage and control core and periphery workers would steadily widen and that the outlook for peripheral workers, whose numbers would significantly increase in his opinion, was bleak in terms of pay level, job security and career development.

The flexible firm model was derived from research on a small sample of organisations from the manufacturing sector. A wider survey (but limited to the retailing, financial services, engineering and food-manufacturing sectors) by Atkinson and Meager (1986) explored the extent of the use of flexibility. They did find evidence of change, but it was hardly conclusive. They found that:

- change tended to be *ad hoc* rather than strategic and purposeful;
- it was driven by short-term cost saving rather than long-term development;
- as a result there had been a large rise in cheap 'peripheral' labour.

■ Critiques

The model of the flexible firm has attracted an enormous volume of criticism from other commentators. In addition to criticisms of Atkinson's methodology and narrowness of sample (Penn, 1992), the evidence from other empirical studies has been contradictory. Several commentators found little empirical evidence of increases in flexible forms of employment in the 1980s. Most of these studies were based on large-scale samples (e.g. *Workplace Industrial Relations Survey, Employers' Labour Use Survey, Labour Force Survey, Warwick Company Level Survey, ESRC Social Change and Economic Life Research Initiative*). There was almost no evidence to show the use of functional flexibility, although this was difficult to measure (Blyton and Morris 1991). What evidence there was indicated minor increases in numerical flexibility although Marginson (1989) found that claims for numerical flexibility, were overstated. Penn (1992) found that the use of peripheral workers was associated with larger company size, but that the overall trend in company size was decreasing. MacInnes (1988) argued that the forms of flexibility proposed in the flexible form were merely 'reminiscent of older trends in British labour organisation'.

This criticism has been echoed elsewhere (Casey, 1988; Pollert, 1988), although Hakim (1990) noted that the pace of change had increased and Casey (1988) argued that there had been an increase in the proportion of peripheral workers whose status as temporary was involuntary rather than chosen by the employee.

Procter *et al.* (1994) took issue with this interpretation and argued that there was evidence of increasing flexible employment, particularly financial flexibility. More recently, Beatson (1995) argued that there was evidence from the *Labour Force Survey* supporting an increase in all forms of flexibility in the UK economy, although his evidence on functional flexibility was inferential at best.

Even if flexible forms of employment have increase, there are alternatives to the flexible firm as an explanation, such as changing demographics (Brewster *et al.*, 1994) and the number of women in the workforce (MacInnes, 1988). The degree of gender segmentation is indicated by over half of all women workers being in the periphery compared with fewer than a quarter of male workers in 1987 (Prowse, 1990).

A key problem, possibly the key problem, for the viability of the flexible firm has been the seeming lack of interest by organisations in it as a *strategic device*. For example, McGregor and Sproull (1991) found only a small minority of employers using a core/periphery model, with an even smaller minority using the model as a *deliberate* policy. They argued that: 'the prospects for changes in the extent and nature of non-standard employment are likely to depend for the most part on fairly traditional influences rather than decisions of personnel strategists' (McGregor and Sproull, 1991: 233).

This criticism has been echoed by others (Hakim, 1990; Hunter and MacInnes, 1991; Hunter *et al.*, 1993; Brewster *et al.*, 1994). O'Reilly (1992) found that employers developed strategies on flexibility in an '*ad hoc* and incremental manner'. She argued that it was not a matter of 'either/or choices'. However, Procter *et al.* (1994) have mounted a spirited defence of the model of the flexible firm by arguing for the *processual* view of strategy to be adopted.

There were also major criticisms of the flexible firm on other bases. MacInnes (1988) argued that the factors proposed by Atkinson to promote the use of the flexible firm did not have that effect, specifically that high unemployment and a consequent slack labour market had reduced labour flexibility rather than increased it. Penn (1992) found that unemployment was not very significant as a local parameter promoting flexibility. Walsh (1991) proposed that competition leads to promotion of an internal market, as firms do better by competing on product markets rather than labour markets. Rather than the reasons cited by Atkinson, studies have found that recession appears to the main causative factor in the use of temporary employment (Hakim, 1987; Prowse, 1990).

Pollert (1988, 1991) has been a leading critic of the whole concept of flexibility. She was particularly critical of the notion of 'static dualism' proposed by the flexible firm model. She argued that this ignored important aspects of class, gender and labour segmentation. Ambiguity between core and periphery has been shown to exist in several aspects: the nature and the skill level of jobs designated to core and periphery and which staff should be in which group. O'Reilly (1992) argued that skilled/professional temporary workers should not be categorised as periphery; and Walsh (1991) demonstrated that although temporary workers in the hotel sector had peripheral employment terms, the tasks they fulfil were neither peripheral in reality nor were thought of as such by their employers.

The rather prescriptive nature of the model has been attacked by Pollert (1991) and others. Atkinson did seem to imply that the flexible firm was the best strategic option under prevailing circumstances. Ursell (1991) demonstrated that there may be certain circumstances that could promote a flexible firm approach in a particular organisation, but subject to many constraints. For example, since functional flexibility may be severely limited for professional groups due to professionalisation (creating boundaries) and statutory regulations, alternative strategies such as decentralisation and team working were more appropriate strategies (Dastmalchian, 1991).

The debate about the flexible firm has receded, with little comment for several years. Paradoxically, stronger empirical evidence is beginning to emerge that seems to support both the notion that organisations are adopting a core/periphery dual structure and a host of flexible styles of employment. However, ambiguities remain and such organisations tend to be confined to a few sectors, with interestingly the public sector showing the strongest move towards this (Bryson, 1996). This perhaps shows that ideological imperatives have been more powerful promoting factors than those suggested by Atkinson (Farnham and Horton, 1996). There is a strong possibility that organisations that currently display a similar form to the flexible firm may still be in transition towards a total *peripheralisation* or casualisation of all their employees. Readers should seek to draw their own conclusions based on evidence presented later in this chapter.

Activity 3.1

From this review of the flexible firm, assess the evidence and arguments that support the model against the evidence and arguments that refute it.

1 Examine the empirical evidence. Were all commentators measuring the same thing?

2 Assess in which particular circumstances the model appears to be most viable.

3 Assuming that organisations do make use of the types of flexibility suggested by Atkinson, are there any alternative explanations to that of the flexible firm?

4 Does adopting a processual view of organisations lend more support to the model?

Factors promoting a different approach in human resourcing

The debate about the flexible firm gave us an insight into why some commentators suggested that organisations need to consider new or different approaches. Management gurus such as Handy (1994b) have for some time been preaching about the brave new world. Handy suggested a model of the *cloverleaf* organisation that is not dissimilar to the flexible firm. If anything, such commentators go much further than Atkinson in predicting the total demise of what is currently perceived as the standard employment situation of an employee working full time and for the same organisation until the age of retirement. These writers do no doubt have some influence on management thinking, not least because as politicians and the media begin to adopt these ideas they may gain momentum as a self-fulfilling prophecy. Despite the currency of these ideas, the realisation of the *virtual organisation* (Flood *et al.*, 1995) – a loose-knit aggregation of self-employed individuals joining together for a limited period to complete a project – still seems some way off, even in the unlikely event that it proves to be viable to more than a few, specialised sectors.

There is evidence from several countries that certain factors are combining to force change. Galin (1991) gave the following reasons for the growing international requirement for *non-standard* or *atypical work*:

1 To increase productivity and competitiveness. For most firms this creates pressure to cut labour costs and the size of the labour force – downsizing. This results in a need to seek optimal utilisation of human resources.

2 Adapting the organisation to accelerated technological changes. This requires continuous revision of skills and organisational structures, but enables new forms of organisation.

3 Increasing employment opportunities. There has been growing pressure from groups who find it hard to comply with a full-time, 9–5 routine. There has also been a reduction in working hours because of social developments.

4 Improving the ability of organisations to cope with peak workloads. Fluctuations may be seasonal or even daily.

5 Adapting to fluctuations in the availability of workers. Demographic trends have affected labour markets and social/legal changes have facilitated family and other leave.

6 To meet workers' aspirations. People now aspire to more interesting jobs and more leisure time.

Brewster *et al.* (1994) found evidence of increasing use of flexible employment in nine out of ten European countries (the exception was Sweden), although there was considerable diversity in the forms that were prevalent. Part-time work tended to be more common in Scandinavian countries (the incidence of part-time work has been strongly correlated to the participation rate of women in the workforce). Temporary work was much higher in Spain and also high in France and Italy. Studies comparing countries have offered competing explanations for such differences. Yeandle (1997) explained differences in the pattern of non-standard employment across five European countries as due to different historical social contexts, welfare regimes and gender dimensions.

Cousins (1997), in a similar study, emphasises the regulatory regime as paramount. More controversially, Robinson (1997) argues that greater labour market regulation creates more non-standard employment. He argues that the UK has not deregulated (in terms of employment) and in fact that the small rise in the number of non-standard employees is due to the influence of EU regulation. We shall examine constraining influences on the ability of management to exercise particular atypical employment options later in the chapter. A major problem for macro-level research and explanation is that it is based on aggregate measures and secondary data that may have been collected on different bases and using dissimilar definitions. In the next section we shall seek to adopt a coherent framework to use for analysis at organisational level.

A working definition of flexible employment and managing uncertainty

Although the debate about the flexible firm was almost entirely confined to the UK arena, it did give rise to some useful descriptive terms that are now shared between commentators more internationally. We shall use a working terminology as a basis here, developed from Atkinson's terms.

Our approach is to present the issues as a set of options from which managers may choose in the ways they both employ and utilise human resources. In some of these options there is no legal contract of employment, although there will always be some form of employment relationship.

Not all the forms suggested in Table 3.1 are clearly distinct from each other and it is important to remember that an individual worker may be subject to several forms that at the same time. Many of these forms are not new, indeed we have included forms are not even described in the literature as *flexible*. This highlights the nonsensical assertion of the flexibility debate that all aspects of flexible employment must be new and different.

We shall now examine some of these options to explore what they entail and why and to what extent they are used. There are far too many options to cover in detail – a whole book would hardly suffice to do so. Options will primarily be selected on the basis of representing the most innovative (or extreme – take your pick) forms drawn from each category together with a contrasting, more traditional form. We shall not examine the options under the category of reward flexibility because they are referred to in Chapter 7. Neither shall we examine in detail forms of locational flexibility, because neither outworking nor homeworking by itself is an option that gives management a tool to manage uncertainty; although such locational forms are often combined with more peripheral employment status of the numerical flexibility type, which does arguably give management such ability. In the section on further reading at the end of the chapter, reference is made to texts that examine all the forms in Table 3.1 in more detail. In addition, the reader is advised to refer regularly to publications such as *IDS Study*, *IDS Report*, *IRS Employment Trends* and *Labour Market Trends*. The later Workplace Employee Relations Survey (Cully *et al.*, 1998) will for the first time, provide detailed statistical evidence on the prevalence of non-standard employment in the UK.

Please note that although the discussion that follows treats each employment form in isolation, these options are not mutually exclusive. Employers often use many of these forms at the same time in combination, although use of some types may clearly preclude to some degree the use of other forms.

■ Functional flexibility – multiskilling

Boyer (1987) defined *polyvalence* as key to the multiskilling of employees. He argued that indicators of this would be:

■ an ability to occupy varied posts;
■ sufficiently broad general and technical training;

Table 3.1 Management options for flexibility

Type of flexibility	Focus	Form
Functional	Vary scope and range of tasks	Multiskilling Skill mix reprofiling Teleworking
Numerical	Vary size and structure of workforce	Dismissal Redundancy Lay-offs Fixed-term contracts Seasonal Agency temps Casual staff Outsource Subcontract Franchise Self-employment/freelancing Voluntary working
Temporal	Vary working hours and pattern	Unlimited Part-time Job sharing Overtime Short-time working Flexi-time Zero-hours contracts Relief/bank working Annualised hours Flexible rostering
Reward	Vary rate and composition of reward	Profit-related pay Performance-related pay Output-based pay Flexible benefits
Locational	Vary place of work	Outworking Homeworking

■ the involvement of workers in the maintenance of quality standards;

■ the lack of any insurmountable barrier between manual worker, supervisor and technician.

Gathering longitudinal evidence about this form of flexibility is difficult because until recently no systematic statistics are collected on its use. No survey with large-scale samples (e.g. *WIRS, ELUS, SCELI*) that had some focus on functional flexibility was conducted between 1990 and 1998. The earlier surveys yielded little evidence to show the use of functional flexibility (Blyton and Morris, 1991). Beatson (1995) sought to make inferences from the quarterly *Labour Force Survey* to show that multiskilling had significantly increased, but his methodology was highly dubious, as it was based on an extrapolation of data rather than any direct evidence. The preliminary results of the 1998 WERS show that in less than half of workplace is any formal training given so the workers are able to do jobs other than their own, and even so, this is hardly functional flexibility.

Legge (1995) reviews the evidence and draws heavily on Elger (1991). Virtually all of her evidence is from the manufacturing sector. She does find movement towards *task* flexibility, but with very modest progress. There was little evidence of *upskilling* – the enhancement or increase of skills – with an emphasis instead on job enlargement. Greenfield sites, which might have been expected to yield more innovation, were little different (Leopold and Hallier, 1996). Legge concludes that the outcomes of initiatives has been more about job enlargement and work intensification leading to enhanced management control.

Sparrow (1998) argues for a different perspective to be taken by widening the focus to *jobs-based flexibility*, which starts to bring in all the issues connected with design of work, jobs and even organisations, e.g. business process reengineering. Even so, he finds that the main approach in this has been downsizing. Within our framework of options, this would appear to be a numerical rather than a functional flexibility option.

An alternative source of evidence about multiskilling could be sought in all the research on processes such as team working, just-in-time (JIT) and total quality management (TQM). There is little space to do so here and one suspects that the conclusions would not be dissimilar to those of Legge (1995). Indeed, a fruitful source of such evidence – and similar conclusions – can be found in the literature on Japanisation (Watson, 1995b).

Some examples from non-manufacturing sectors may illustrate to what degree multiskilling is used (Table 3.2).

Table 3.2 Examples of multiskilling/functional flexibility

Retail and finance (Neathey and Hurstfield, 1995)
One supermarket expected staff to work in all departments rather than be limited to, for example, a bakery role – to move people in the store 'depending where the need is'. Another gave staff training as relief till operators.
Move to 'generic shop assistant' in department store.
A building society had moved towards generalisation of tasks so that a customer enquiry could be dealt with by anybody.
Banking (O'Reilly, 1992) – comparing UK and France
Found evidence in France that banks promoted functional flexibility in order to provide an integrated service policy facilitated by highly qualified staff using new technology. This strengthened the core position of such staff and increased job interest and career prospects.
In the UK, functional flexibility had been developed in an *ad hoc* way to meet staff shortages or to fill up slack times for staff.

Skill-mix reprofiling may best be shown by examples from the NHS. Within the ambulance service there has been separation between paramedics and 'drivers'. Paramedics are highly qualified and have incremental pay scales and the prospect of promotion and a career, whereas many former ambulance staff have been downgraded to 'driver' on a flat scale determined by local market conditions. Similarly, health care assistants (much cheaper to train and employ) have been introduced to take over the 'low-skill' aspects of nurses' jobs and some nurses have been allowed to take on a few duties previously restricted to doctors. We also find new generic grades for combined porter/cleaners. For a full discussion of this, see Bryson *et al.* (1993).

Facilitating factors promoting functional flexibility

1 Educational level of workers – more highly qualified workers should be more adaptable, particularly *knowledge workers* who may be expected to manage their tasks and take much of the responsibility for their own training and skills updating.

2 Decentralisation – acts against specialisation of function.

3 Fluctuations of workload – necessitates more efficient allocation of tasks to minimise 'idle' time.

4 New technology – enables a broader range of tasks to be carried out (although there are ambiguities in relation to upskilling and deskilling).

5 Ability of staff to resist – this is paradoxical, since the greatest use of multiskilling seems to be in highly unionised workplaces. Professionals are strongly opposed to *managerial* attempts to increase functional flexibility or to reprofile skills.

Barriers to functional flexibility (from Clark, 1993)

1 Most workers are more interested in some areas of work than in others.

2 Managers recognise that specialist knowledge is important and should be retained and used.

3 Commitment and achievement of high-quality work derive from a narrow 'ownership' of a particular area.

4 Cost and availability of training.

5 Skill retention – best maintained through regular use.

6 Tight staffing levels – staff could not be spared for training.

Note that the regulatory/legal regime in the UK neither facilitates nor constrains the use of functional flexibility – it is a 'voluntary' matter for the employer and employee to decide.

Advantages and disadvantages

Employers apparently gain more flexibility (for example it allows team working) and higher productivity, and they require fewer workers. The disadvantages could be through more and regular training (e.g. NVQs), more rewards (though either skill supplements or new grades) and in the cost of technology.

For employees, the situation is more ambiguous. Upskilling and empowerment may be illusory except for a small élite. For the others, work intensification is more likely.

Overview

Much of the hype around functional flexibility (Beatson, 1995; Dyson, 1991) promises a panacea to employer and employee. Wickens (1987) talks of a 'tripod of success', through flexibility, quality and team work. Legge (1995), drawing on Garrahan and Stewart (1992), presents an alternative 'tripod of subjugation', through work intensification, control and peer surveillance. The current evidence on functional flexibility hardly supports the post-Fordist paradigm or HRM notions of strong internal labour markets.

Numerical flexibility – fixed-term contracts

In theory, no employment contract is permanent – they are either indefinite or last until the age of retirement. The term 'temporary' is rather an ambiguous term. Casey (1988) has identified 11 often overlapping categories of temporary workers:

- consultants/freelancers;
- labour-only subcontractors;
- casual workers;
- seasonal workers;
- workers on fixed-term contracts;
- workers with a contract dischargeable by performance;
- workers on training contracts;
- temporary workers on indefinite contracts;
- agency workers;
- employees of works contractors;
- participants in special programmes for the unemployed.

Meager (1985: 11) avoids lists and focuses on *mutual recognition* by the employer and employee that the employment relationship is temporary:

> This applies irrespective of whether the individuals are employees of the organisation . . . and avoids the legal ambiguities surrounding the permanent or temporary nature of the employment contract.

The category of fixed-term contract has been chosen for coverage here because it is unambiguously temporary and involves a legal employment relationship (although there are examples of employees spending their entire career on fixed-term contracts for the same employer). In the UK, fixed-term contracts (FTCs) are the most common type of temporary employment, making up about 51 per cent of the temporary group, some 850 000 employees (DTI, 1998). FTCs have been one of the fastest-growing forms of temporary employment, growing by 39 per cent between 1992 and 1996 (IRS, 1997). Before this time, numbers of all types of temporary workers had been static for a decade or more. The use of FTCs is unevenly distributed (they are found in about 50 per cent of organisations claim Millward *et al.*, 1992); 3.9 per cent of the female labour force compared to 3 per cent of men (Beatson, 1995); particularly concentrated in the public sector where clerical and professional jobs were most likely to be subject to FTCs (Sly *et al.*, 1997), for example in higher education over 40 per cent of professional staff are on FTCs (Bryson and Barnes, 1997).

We may use higher education as representative of the sort of context in the public sector that has seen such an increase in FTCs (Bryson, 1996). The growth appears to stem from budgetary constraints and cuts made since 1980 and the unpredictable nature of future funding, leading to a very short-term cycle of planning. Universities have sought new sources of funding, but this is strictly time limited in nature, leading to a fourfold increase in the numbers of contract researchers. However, there has also been a sweeping casualisation of the core workforce, including academic teachers, technicians and support staff. Some institutions have even begun to recruit all new staff on FTCs, although there is little evidence that such moves are strategic, rather they are more *ad hoc* and opportunistic. This follows Hakim's (1990) view on the advance of numerical flexibility and contrasts with Atkinson's (1984) thesis, but does not mean that this form of flexibility may not be enduring.

Facilitating factors promoting use of fixed-term contracts

1 The need to cover short-term absence – this is the traditional reason and has been sharpened through decreased workforce size and loss of 'slack' capacity.

2 Staffing for short-term projects – this particularly applies to management and professional staff.

3 The need to bring in specialist skills for a particular project.

4 To reduce paybill/employment costs – by keeping the permanent headcount down and by offering temporary workers poorer terms and conditions and less staff development.

5 The need to deal with variations in workload – seen as increasingly important by organisations.

6 Uncertainties about the future – before local government reorganisation, for example.

Barriers to use of fixed-term contracts

The regulatory/legal regime in the UK offers little constraint on the use of FTCs. It even allows employers to require employees to sign contractual clauses waiving their right to claim redundancy pay or make an unfair dismissal claim at the end of their contract (currently under review). However, the ending of a fixed-term contract is a dismissal, and may be a redundancy, and therefore the employer may have to follow certain procedures (*see* redundancy section below). The weak UK regulatory regime is in stark contrast to the rest of the EU, where FTCs may normally only be used for 'legitimate' reasons (covering defined periods of absence) and must offer parity of terms and conditions to permanent contracts for similar jobs. An EU directive on temporary workers has become heavily bogged down in definitional issues. It is possible that EU-wide legislation on equal opportunities, particularly indirect discrimination and equal value aspects, might eventually allow temporary workers to gain parity through the same route as part-time workers in the UK.

Advantages and disadvantages

The advantages for employers are closely linked to the reasons noted above. To these we may add (Leighton and Syrett, 1989) the perception that staff on fixed-term contracts are cheaper, work harder (because of insecurity), are not unionised or included in collective agreements and are easy to dismiss. The disadvantages of FTCs are perceived to be that temporary workers are less reliable and less productive (Atkinson, 1996); that transaction costs (more recruitment, induction, redundancy) may be hidden, but much higher than expected (Bryson and Barnes, 1997); higher levels of absenteeism, lower commitment and loyalty, increased management problems (Leighton and Syrett, 1989). The latter also suggest that: 'Temporary work is most effective where professional and occupational loyalty is marked and therefore a powerful motivator overcoming ambiguous feelings of loyalty to the firm.'

There may also be issues of integration with HR policies and relationships with other employees (see later in the chapter).

For employees there appear to be few advantages, except that FTCs may offer a variety of experience or a foothold into a particular career; however, both of these can be gained through permanent posts in a fair labour market. FTCs may suit the present needs of some – student employment, probationary period, training or even higher earning potential (for example IT experts). Nevertheless, much of the actual evidence shows that most employees experience (Bryson, 1996, 1997; Bryson and Barnes, 1997) worse terms and conditions, lower status, exclusion from activities and governance, lack of career development and progress, insecurity and, particularly for women, segregation and discrimination.

Overview

There does appear to be a sharp increase and a fundamental change in the use of FTCs taking place in the UK, although there is some evidence that it is restricted to particular sectors. The 'new rationales' are associated with a strategy to deal with uncertainty. There would appear to be a polarisation of use to the most highly skilled, with the low skilled often being employed on an even more casual basis. The apparent advantages may be outweighed by the disadvantages. Although this type of *external* flexibility appears to provide a buffer against uncertainty, it greatly restricts the HR options available. The ability to recruit temporary employees relies heavily on a ready supply of appropriately skilled workers, and some organisations are now dependent on temporary workers for even core activities due to drastic pruning of the permanent workforce.

■ Numerical flexibility – redundancy

The traditional reason for making staff redundant was because there was no longer a requirement for their services. In the long period of economic growth after the Second World War, redundancies were comparatively uncommon. Indeed, there was considerable social and public policy pressure against making redundancies on any sort of large scale and generally a company would have to go the wall before jobs were lost. This all changed in the 1980s. There was to be no more government support for 'lame duck' industries and *downsizing, delayering* and the even more euphemistic *rightsizing* became fashionable. Waves of redundancy took place, in recessions and in economic boom. The basis of selection for redundancy changed from last in, first out (LIFO) to performance. Companies sought to 'cut out the dead wood' and sharply to raise productivity. In practise, resistance to involuntary redundancy led to severance schemes being put in place semi-permanently and also a swathe of early retirements. The latter policy has changed the whole age profile of the workforce, with many organisations now having no workers over the age of 50.

There were 786 000 redundancies in the UK in 1996. This seems to be about the current average for a non-recession year. The axe falls most heavily on men and on young and old workers, and construction and manufacturing sectors account for a disproportionate number of redundancies, with craftspeople, plant and machine operatives being at least twice as vulnerable as any other group (*Labour Force Survey*, November 1997). White-collar workers have become increasingly vulnerable to redundancy, especially in the business and financial sectors.

Two-thirds of redundancies were due to staffing cutbacks, i.e. downsizing (*Labour Market Trends*, April 1997). A survey by the Institute of Management (1995) showed that 67 per cent of organisations had downsized over the previous five years. The two sectors most likely to do so were plcs (83 per cent) and the public sector (84 per cent), although the former (61 per cent) were much more likely than the latter (4 per cent) to make involuntary redundancies.

Facilitating factors promoting use of redundancy

1 It is relatively easy to dismiss workers legally in the UK. An OECD study rated Britain at two on a 16-point scale of difficulty in dismissal, with most EU countries rated at over ten (Lehrman Brothers, 1994).

2 Workers and unions appear to have accepted that redundancy is a legitimate management tool.

3 Becoming more competitive. There is pressure to reduce headcount where staff costs are high.

Barriers to use of redundancy

1 There are a number of legal constraints. Once workers have two years' service they are entitled to a statutory minimum redundancy payment. If numbers of redundancies are over certain totals, individuals and unions must be consulted and alternatives to redundancy sought. A test of reasonableness in procedures must be met for dismissal to be fair.

2 Unions are very resistant to involuntary redundancies.

3 There may be strong pressure from the local community and public agencies against its use.

Advantages and disadvantages

Employers appear to be able to dismiss workers on permanent contracts with little difficulty and cost. The use of a broad-scale definition of performance as a selection indicator allows the dismissal of workers for all sorts of reasons consistent with maximising the use of human resources. It will certainly raise the profile of the HR function. There are many disadvantages: it is a fraught process to manage; it creates anger, distrust and industrial relations problems; it is inimical to 'soft' HR practices; it is highly damaging to the image of the HR function; and it leaves a legacy of problems among the 'survivors'.

For employees, voluntary redundancy may offer opportunities for early retirement or a new career (with a large deposit in the bank). However, the problems of involuntary redundancy are well known and the subject of a large volume of literature. There are many detrimental psychological and sociological effects. There is evidence of discrimination against ethnic minorities (Casey, 1995) and older workers (Arrowsmith and McGoldrick, 1997). Turnbull and Wass (1997) have described the 'lemon' syndrome, where a redundant worker becomes tainted and stigmatised. It is very difficult to get back to the same level of employment, with many former employees ending up in even more precarious jobs, particularly if they are older. For the 'survivors', insecurity is an ever-present threat.

Overview

Redundancies remain a very common form of numerical flexibility; virtually everyone is vulnerable. Although in a sense other forms of numerical flexibility have been introduced to replace redundancy, these workers are often made redundant too, in more than a legal sense. Redundancies create a paradox. They are ostensibly for the purpose of making the organisation more competitive, viable and secure. It is arguable whether this is delivered, but redundancies give exactly the opposite impression to the workforce

■ Temporal flexibility – zero-hours contracts versus overtime

With reference to working hours, there has been considerable pressure from both employers and employees to vary the length of the working week. Employees seek a reduction of hours and/or a pattern of hours to suit their personal needs – therefore flexi-time and part-time patterns have become more common, with a quarter of the UK workforce working part-time and 65 per cent of the new jobs created between 1992 and 1996 being part-time (LFS). Employers have traditionally responded to increased demand by using overtime. In response to the need to maximise use of plant or offer a round-the-clock service, they have increasingly moved to more, and more variable, shift working.

Overtime has traditionally attracted premium rates of pay and, in order to avoid this, a new form of temporal flexibility has emerged – zero-hours contracts. This is where the employee is not guaranteed any work at all but is required to be available as and when the employer requires them (unlike bank or relief workers who may choose whether to work). They are usually not paid any sort of retainer.

A recent survey by Cave (1997) showed that a quarter of organisations used zero-hours contracts (ZHCs). Most contracts were on an indefinite basis. Sectors with the most prevalent use were catering, health and local government. Although most workers on ZHCs were in unskilled or low-skilled work, the public-sector organisations also used ZHCs for professionals. There would appear to be an upward trend in the use of ZHCs (IRS, 1997). A recent estimate (DTI, 1998) of the number of ZHCs in the UK is 200 000.

Overtime appears to have increased as the base working time has decreased. A recent study (Casey *et al.*, 1997) found that this was the most common practice to increase output. It was frequently operated on an informal basis, in which case it was likely to be unpaid (particularly for managerial or professional staff). Over half of employees on fixed hours work overtime every week – a twofold increase over the last decade.

Table 3.3 Facilitating factors promoting use of zero-hours contracts versus overtime

Zero-hours contracts	Overtime
Little legal protection for workers	1 Simple to operate 2 Little legal restraint (but see below)

Table 3.4 Barriers to use of zero-hours contracts versus overtime

Zero-hours contracts	Overtime
1 Resistance from unions 2 The Fairness at Work White Paper (DTI, 1998) invites a review of the law on ZHCs	EU Working Time Directive sets a limit of a 48-hour week to be averaged throughout the year; the averaging aspect and the exclusion of many groups of workers mean it will have little effect on informal overtime

Table 3.5 Zero-hours contracts and overtime: advantages and disadvantages

Zero-hours contracts	Overtime
Employer advantages 1 Deal with fluctuations in work 2 Pool from which to choose employees 3 Cost saving, much poorer terms and conditions	1 Very flexible 2 Method of increasing output 3 Uses existing workforce 4 No recruitment, training or lay-off costs
Employer disadvantages 1 Poor morale and commitment 2 Ethical issues – negative publicity because of general public's poor opinion of ZHCs	1 Hard to control costs 2 Limited by employee willingness to do it – women seen as unwilling to do it 3 Lower productivity over a certain limit of hours
Employee advantages None	1 Ability to earn more 2 Seen as a perk
Employee disadvantages 1 Income uncertain 2 Few employee benefits 3 Problems associated with peripheral status (see fixed-term contracts)	1 No premium for part-timers 2 Workload and stress 3 Interference with outside life 4 Can be unpaid

Overview

Overtime (paid or unpaid) is the most common form of flexibility. Indeed, Casey *et al.*'s (1997) analysis of *Labour Force Survey* data shows that overtime exhibits the largest upward trend in the period 1984–94, with an increase in the number of workers with varying hours rising from 31 to 56 per cent. Despite the potential of temporal flexibility to balance the needs of both employer and employee, forms such as zero-hours contracts seem to be very one sided. Temporal flexibility is the one area that looks likely to be substantially affected by pending legislation.

Activity 3.2

Based on the example of an organisation for which you have worked or know about, consider the forms of employment that are used there. You may find multiple forms, in which case you should try to address the forms in combination. Assess the reasons that such forms of employment are used in this context, and the advantages and disadvantages they present. Consider:

- employers – particularly the issues that both HR and line managers face,

- employees – the issues for workers on these type of contracts or terms and their colleagues on standard contracts.

Implications and outcomes of different approaches to managing uncertainty

Our focus on particular forms oversimplifies the real picture. Unfortunately, this is not captured in national surveys or statistics, but case studies reveal that the pattern unfolding in many organisations is more complex. Several commentators have suggested that the pattern of labour utilisation is contingent on factors such as:

1 Labour costs and fluctuations in demand (Rothwell, 1986):
   - organisations with high labour costs and high fluctuations in demand employ a small core workforce (including homeworkers and part-timers) and meet fluctuations with agency workers and subcontractees;
   - organisations with low labour costs and high fluctuations in demand employ an average-sized core, using overtime and/or a pool of internal temporaries to meet fluctuations;
   - organisations with high labour costs and low fluctuations in demand employ an average-sized core using part-time and shift work; temporary workers may be used to meet seasonal peaks; they may need to respond to employee-driven demand for flexible work;
   - organisations with low labour costs and low fluctuations in demand have a large core, use overtime and part-time workers.

2 Historical precedent, product demand, labour supply considerations, the nature of the product, overall managerial approach, and the complementarity and substitutability of practices (Casey *et al.*, 1997):
  – fluctuations in product demand (which could be influenced by employer policy, e.g. using JIT or marketing approaches) create an unpredictable demand for labour;
  – labour supply is influenced by management stereotyping genders – assuming women will not work overtime but will tolerate part-time or temporary work, and vice versa with men. Employers tend to combine complementary forms of non-standard employment to manage working time, for example.

Smith *et al.* (1995) add technology to the equation. The findings of Casey *et al.* (1997) support the conclusion by Hunter *et al.* (1993) that employers prefer to use full-time permanent employees because they are the easiest to manage, the most committed and the least likely to leave.

Evidence of this type lends considerable weight to the *processual* view – managers enacting decisions based on their perception of organisational needs. A great deal of the debate around the flexible firm centred on whether organisations were adopting the model as a strategic choice. All the early evidence appeared to be against this, but that is unsurprising as strategy was viewed as top-down rationality. Interestingly, a recent study by Mayne *et al.* (1996) found evidence that high use of part-time/temporary workers correlated with explicit human resourcing strategies. The findings that it is the larger organisations that are increasing the use of flexible work forms and that many smaller firms are unaware of the types of option available (Casey *et al.*, 1997) lend credability to the notion that strategy has *emerged* and is now being taken up by senior management in organisations with sufficient resources to have a focus on HR.

However, there are still several constraints other than ignorance and traditional mind-sets. Regulations remain modest in the UK. Public policy remains firmly committed to flexible labour markets. The EU has also adopted such a view (EU Employment Guidelines, 1998, cited in *Employment Europe*), albeit from a much more regulated base. Part-time work and working time are coming into the regulation net and a directive on temporary work appears imminent (after eight years' discussion). The latest UK initiatives (DTI, 1998) do little directly to regulate any but the most extreme variants such as zero-hours contracts. However, the intention to ensure that individual employment rights are further extended to cover current grey areas and a boost to collective employment rights could allow trade unions to take a stronger initiative. Unions have been slow to respond to new employment forms, but could be the main champions of seeking to balance employer flexibility with the types of flexibility sought by employees. Individual resistance has been very weak in times of high unemployment. Despite the media reports fed by consultants and employment agencies about how many workers are both desiring and benefiting from flexibility, research shows that this is confined to a small minority.

There are clearly wider societal effects of flexible forms of employment. We do not have room here to discuss these in detail. The dual model of the core/periphery has been rejected by most commentators, who suggest a more complex interaction between internal and external labour markets (Rubery and Wilkinson, 1994) with several labour segments (Loveridge, 1983; Burchell and Rubery, 1990). Societal pressure may act as a constraint on employer policies such as redundancy or very insecure non-standard employment. There are major equal opportunities considerations in the widespread discrimination that currently takes place against women, ethnic minorities and the young and old – note the sort of stereotyping exhibited by employers above.

Are there indicators to help managers make more informed choices? Leighton and Syrett (1989) offer a checklist of advantages and disadvantages against almost every flexible employment option. However, what does research tell us? Studies that attempt to link organisational performance with one aspect, such as the use of outsourcing, from a minefield of complex factors occurring at the same time, are invariably fruitless. There are a host of studies focusing on the effect on the individual. An interesting debate has arisen around the concept of the psychological contract – the *implicit* contract between employee and employer. A group of commentators have stretched the concept to that of *new deals* (Herriott and Pemberton, 1995). This does not involve a relational contract of trust, commitment and security, but is much more transactional. Some (usually consultants and politicians) go so far as to argue that organisations should not offer any sort of career but, instead, the commodity of *employability*. It is dubious whether these new deals are what most employees seek and there may be serious resultant damage to the employment relationship. This could create both problems and costs for employers (Bryson and Barnes, 1997).

Watson in Chapter 1, Table 1.9, suggests that organisations may pursue dual human resourcing strategies. Empirical evidence suggests that this could be problematic. Geary (1992) examined three firms that used a dual strategy with permanent and temporary workers and noted that the managers were averse to this policy because of all the problems that arose. One of these was tension between temporary and permanent workers, which has been noted in other studies (Filipzcak, 1997). There are similar problems with freelancers (Lewis, 1995). Bryson and Barnes (1997) found problems that did not seem able to be 'managed' away. Indeed, when dual strategies are used, the problems in the 'direct-control, low-commitment' group seem to spill over into the 'indirect-control, high-commitment' group. It is difficult to assess if there are *managerial* solutions, because so often the peripheral groups are virtually ignored by HR policy makers and line managers seem just to be left to cope, often with reluctance and frequently without much success.

This raises another issue about 'new-style' HRM practices and flexibility. The rhetoric of HRM is full of references about the need to be flexible and adaptable. The problem is that the types of flexibility that are extensively used seem to be very far from the high-trust, high-commitment models; in fact, they undermine them. The rhetoric about new-style HRM practices and flexible employment shares similar contradictions and paradoxes (Blyton and Turnbull, 1992). Walby (1989) has pointed out, echoed by others (Geary, 1992; Legge, 1995) that many of the so-called flexible forms of employment actually create *rigidities*, the very thing that they are supposed to prevent. This occurs both within the organisation and in the labour market. There appears to be a considerable weight of evidence to support this.

One problem with the flexible firm is that it is a tight model, suggesting an optimal final configuration for organisations. This is somewhat paradoxical in a dynamic, uncertain world; surely adaptability entails being able to manage transitions, being in a permanent state of *transition*. However, the reasons that organisations are successful is that they are, at least to some extent, *organised*. They seek to provide some stability and predictability and a measure of control over uncertainty. An obsession with immediate responsiveness to markets is a recipe for chaos and confusion, but unfortunately reflects the patterns and policies that we observe.

Despite all the recent evidence that non-standard work forms are ever increasing – with populist predictions of a jobless future – we do observe considerable continuity from traditional approaches: Casey *et al.*'s (1997) finding that overtime was the most common form of flexibility), the continued use of redundancy, and recently Dex and McCulloch's (1997) claim that the tide has turned. The latter point to the fact that the most recent figures show that full-time standard employment is increasing and temporary work declining. However, it must be the private sector that is decreasing the use of non-standard forms, because in the public sector they are still on the increase. While the main ideological imperative may have decreased (although this is debatable), cost cutting and uncertainty remain very high in the public sector at the time of writing.

Conclusion

We have attempted to make some sense of the concept of managing flexibly by examining the sort of options that managers have available when conventional human resource planning fails to provide solutions. There would appear to be a whole host of flexible employment forms from which to choose. In practice, the choice is not so simple and managers would do well to avoid prescriptive advice and consider all the implications of their possible choices. They must be aware of the implications of integrating multiple forms of flexibility. We have introduced several theoretical frameworks that seek to analyse flexible employment and provide explanations; there was no over-arching conceptual framework that was adequate for the task. In order to gain a broader understanding, we need to synthesise concepts from diverse social science sources. Study at the individual level and in the context of case studies appears to be more useful than macro surveys and national statistics for understanding what is unfolding at organisational level, although the wider external environment is clearly important.

There may be evidence that managers are using flexible employment options as part of a strategic approach, at least from a processual perspective, but too often it reflects an expedient approach to make short-term cost savings – more 'muddling through' than managing and planning for long-term viability. Such cost savings might in fact be illusory. Very rarely do the choices exercised reflect a balance between the needs and imperatives of the employer and the needs and aspirations of the employee. This is not just about the absurdity of using overtime and making redundancies at the same time, but about a proactive response to workers in order to gain long-term productivity and quality. This is very unlikely to be based on numerical or reward flexibility, but rather on functional, temporal or locational forms. A few organisations appear to have achieved some stability by respecting and seeking this balance. None the less, the main conclusion is that management attempts to deal with uncertainty often do little to achieve this, and lead to unforeseen outcomes.

O&V Joifel – 10 years on

Please refer to the case study in Chapter 1, pp. 33–5, where you were introduced to O&V Joifel. Ten years have passed and there have been a number of developments. The company now has a number of rivals producing similar products. These rival companies were set up by entrepreneurs who have received the sort of training that Oliver had (how he wished that universities would not be so indiscriminate about training people for degrees, especially overseas students). There was stiff competition in lumber from a Scottish-based company that was reestablishing a new coniferous Caledonian forest. Several overseas companies had sprung up based on cheaper labour and warmer climes. The main customers, the big supermarkets, constantly drove down the wholesale price so that they could make bigger profits. To add to the company's woes, there had been a major climate change in the Midlands, with dry and wet seasons and constant hurricanes that entailed serious and unpredictable fluctuations in the crop. O&V Joifel's investors, despite all their earlier bountiful profits, had cut up rough and kept demanding a similar level of profit.

Against this context, the company had survived and even grown, but there had been a number of changes, some planned and some unplanned. Several years ago Verity had managed to introduce an overall HR policy. She sought to balance a family-friendly policy against organisational needs in a harmonised way. In order to get this past managerial opposition, the policy took the form of allowing employees to negotiate individually on terms and conditions with their line manager – who had considerable discretion within a harmonised overall framework. She had also hoped that this would exclude the trade unions. However, this policy had been distorted by local interpretation and a number of variants had formed.

Among the male timber growers and cutters, an unholy alliance had developed between Leonard Leaper and the particular trade union that the men had joined. In exchange for an arrangement that there would be no compulsory redundancies, the men agreed to do overtime at no extra premium. In addition to the permanent, full-time workforce, a large number of temporary workers had been taken on to cope with fluctuations such as replanting after hurricanes. They were on one-month contracts. This temporary workforce was recruited from the migrants who had flocked north after the great collapse of the City. There was considerable tension between the two workforces, the 'rednecks' and the 'suits'. The rednecks felt that the suits were far too compliant to management and undermined their position, even though management were as contemptuous of the suits as the rednecks were. The trade union refused to have anything to do with the suits.

Among the mainly female fruit pickers and processors, relationships were rather better and the situation more stable. There was a high degree of temporal flexibility, with most working part-time. There was one thorn in the fruit bed. One of the R&D boffins had produced a parasitic plant that lived on the trees and was capable of producing combinations of citrus-like fruits, but the process was rather random, sometimes resulting in poisonous varieties. This fruit was in great demand by the supermarkets as it was considered rare and exotic. Because of the uncertainty, a band of casual workers were employed on an *ad hoc* basis (hourly paid) specifically to pick this fruit. However, it was soon recognised that this work required considerable skill and many of these workers had now been employed off and on for several years. The trade union for the fruit pickers had recruited many of these workers and was pressing for them to be given better conditions and more security. The trade union was also becoming more vociferous about the lower level of pay that fruit staff receive compared to the tree staff.

The R&D department had seen great turbulence. Attempts to regularise and harmonise its contracts had caused outrage (rather fomented by Bill and Ben). Eventually, many of the staff had resigned and then returned on a freelance basis. At first Beancounter was delighted, as this seemed to be indicative of a performance-based culture. However, costs began to spiral out of control. This was countered by employing aspirant young scientists straight from university on low-paid, fixed-term contracts (anything looked better than a student loan). They soon became disgruntled as little training was offered and they just felt exploited. Turnover is very high among them. The flow of creative ideas is faltering and Bill and Ben have been pestering Verity Joifel with electronic complaints from their executive telecottage in Mauritius.

A recent strike by the rednecks has forced Verity to review the HR strategy. She must also address the imminent implementation of the new EU directives limiting the working week to 30 hours and allowing temporary workers to be employed for no more than three years.

Activity 3.3

1 Try to explain why the different forms of employment have arisen and been maintained within the company. Does this fit with the sort of factors driving flexible employment given in the chapter?

2 How well does the model of the flexible firm fit this example?

3 Do the flexible work forms present in this company actually deliver flexibility?

4 Verity is trying to establish a coherent and harmonised HR policy. Devise a framework addressing employment contracts that seeks to achieve this. Will this eliminate tensions within and between different groups?

5 Distinguish between the internal and external constraints that Verity faces.

6 Do any of the problems result from management styles or approaches (or lack of them)? Could these problems be solved by better management? In what way?

7 Do any of the other conceptual frameworks fit with this case study and explain any of the issues? You might consider labour-market segmentation, internal and external labour markets, psychological contracts or others not discussed in this chapter, such as motivation (for example equity theory) or the labour process.

Summary

In this chapter the following key points have been made:

■ We have suggested that organisations have struggled to cope with uncertainty due to the apparent inability of human resource planning to cope.

■ In addition to traditional methods of managing the size, costs and skills components of labour, we see the use of so-called new forms of employment flexibility.

■ We sought to conceptualise what flexibility actually means and looked at a number of theoretical frameworks. This included a detailed look at the critique of the model of the flexible firm.

- We looked at factors that arguably are combining to force changes in the way in which labour is utilised.

- We looked at evidence that non-standard employment is increasing internationally and why.

- We introduced a typology of employment and contract forms that employers could use, including those where is no legal employment contract.

- We analysed five contractual forms/strategies: multiskilling, fixed-term contracts, redundancy, zero-hours contracts and overtime. We looked at their context and prevalence of use, promoting and constraining factors and the pros and cons for employers and employees.

- We assessed the types of patterns emerging at organisational level.

- We assessed if there are management strategies of labour utilisation or whether it is *ad hoc*.

- We looked at the relationship between flexible employment and human resourcing.

- Finally, we assessed the implications of using such employment forms at the level of the individual, manager, organisation, labour market and society.

Discussion questions

1 Are flexible forms of labour utilisation genuinely new or just variants on old themes?

2 Discuss which conceptual frameworks may be used to analyse flexible employment and at what type of analysis they are most useful – for example national comparisons, impacts on society, impacts on the individual, employer strategy or the employment relationship.

3 To what extent are flexible forms of employment substitutable for each other?

4 To what extent is non-standard employment supplanting standard jobs, both currently and in the future?

5 Outline a form of flexible employment and discuss the advantages and disadvantages of its use to employers *and* employees.

6 Is the use of a dual strategy to utilise human resources consistent with new-style HRM practices?

7 What evidence is there to support the notion that managing uncertainty through labour utilisation is a strategic activity?

8 Have UK public policy and legal regulations had any influence over the use of non-standard employment?

9 Does flexible employment actually deliver flexibility and adaptability?

Further reading

The chapter has covered many issues in relation to flexible employment. Relevant references are given where appropriate, but the reader is referred to the following useful texts: Blyton and Morris (1991), Legge (1995), Leighton and Syrett (1989) and Sparrow and Marchington (1998).

4

INTERNATIONAL HUMAN RESOURCING

David Walsh

OBJECTIVES

Having completed this chapter and its associated activities, readers should be able to:

- make informed judgements on the management of human resources within different types of multinational organisation;

- understand the similarities and differences between national and international human resourcing;

- demonstrate an understanding of the process of globalisation and its significance for organisational approaches to international human resourcing;

- recognise the variety of factors that constrain and influence the operation of human resourcing in transnational companies in the context of different local cultures;

- address the organisational issues, tensions and contradictions associated with managing human resources across national boundaries;

- advise on key considerations for staffing the international organisation;

- appreciate the human resourcing implications of different approaches to staffing;

- analyse contingent factors for host-country employment arrangements.

Introduction

For some, a discussion of managing human resources across the globe invites exotic images of employees working in corporate outposts, where the customs, language, food, climate and laws are different from those of the parent company's national base. However, for those practitioners involved with international administration, the topic is more likely to suggest making travel and accommodation arrangements; intricate reward packages with tax and pension complications; and all manner of bureaucratic and legal formalities.

While these impressions do convey something about the nature of international human resourcing, they are plainly incomplete, and it is the aim of this chapter to provide a comprehensive framework for understanding the *essentials* of managing human resources across national boundaries. It will do so by concentrating on human resource strategy making from the viewpoint of the parent (home-based) company, and by seeking to apply Watson's proposition that 'strategic management processes involve both active management choice as well as the influence of various circumstances (or contingencies)' (Chapter 1, p. 18).

We will therefore need to explore the extent to which the choices and the circumstances associated with international human resourcing are different from those encountered by the human resourcing function of a domestic-only organisation. If we discover that the strategic management of human resources operates in much the same way, whether intranational or international, the practitioner will be able to build on what we already know about human resourcing in general and to focus more intently on any crucial characteristics of the international version of human resourcing that make it distinctive.

As this book has been written to help the reader make informed judgements on the practice of human resourcing, this particular chapter aims to concentrate on what might be distinctive about managing human resources internationally. In so doing, we may be able to discover principles that are likely to be *peculiar* to this area of work, and avoid replicating those that have a more general application. Our initial approach, however, is to identify the general features shared by national and international human resourcing in order to highlight differences that might be significant. This might then provide a way of thinking to help the practitioner tackle any *international* human resourcing issue, including the ability to assess the appropriateness and utility of human resourcing practices covered elsewhere in the book.

From domestic to international human resourcing

There can be few organisations that have not been affected to some extent by the increasing intensity of competition that comes from the globalisation of the economy. Business decisions taken by managers on behalf of their organisations are influenced by, for example, the exacting competition from companies from outside the UK and the relative value of sterling. Understandably, therefore, managers have placed greater emphasis on winning custom and growing or sustaining their business through attending to customer satisfaction via the provision of a quality service and product at an attractive price. In so doing, they have often sought to minimise costs by reducing the wage bill, typically through redundancy and restructuring exercises. However, pressure on costs seems unrelenting. In the late 1990s the rapid decline of the Japanese yen and the currencies of Asia's tiger economies, for example, and the relative strength of the pound posed a serious threat to those UK companies whose products became more expensive to export and that struggled to compete at home against a flood of cheaper imports. Such companies could readily suffer from falling profits and a loss of jobs. More extensively, the global nature of the foreign exchange and stock markets could perhaps mean that a Japanese economic crisis, as the world's second largest single economy, will halt western prosperity.

All managers ought to be aware that such is the level of integration in the global economy that most organisations, including their own, are not immune from the reverberations that accompany a collapse in business and consumer confidence, affecting both financial markets and trade with the rest of the world. Managers will perhaps have a greater awareness of such issues if they have contact with overseas customers or suppliers. But what are the implications of being actually engaged in employment relationships with foreign organisations, especially as part of a company with overseas subsidiaries and employees? Is human resourcing so very different when it is international and carried out across several nations compared with when it is conducted in a domestic setting and confined to one nation? The answer is that *in all essentials* human resourcing should be no different whether it is conducted in a domestic or international context. In either setting, human resourcing ought to be shaped by the same corporate imperative: to deliver the effective contribution of an organisation's human resources towards that organisation's long-term success. At the same time, however, we should also expect to find significant differences, but these might be considered more as differences of *degree* rather than of essence.

Indeed, the model outlined in Chapter 1 by Watson (Fig. 1.1) serves to demonstrate both the essential similarity and the differences between domestic and international human resourcing. On the one hand, the model can help to shape a human resourcing strategy for *any* organisation, whether national or international, but on the other it indicates that the management of an organisation encompassing business units or divisions in foreign countries is likely to encounter an increased range (and perhaps complexity) of political-economic contexts, cultural values, employment legislation and labour-market conditions compared with those operating in only a domestic environment.

■ Human resourcing in the domestic organisation

In order to expand on this view of similarity and difference, we will briefly explore the human resourcing issues associated with various forms of *domestic-only* (i.e. national) business organisations. Our aim is to develop a way of thinking about international human resourcing that builds on, rather than replaces, our understanding of its practice in a national UK context. We can assemble a picture made up of the essential similarities between domestic and international human resourcing together with those characteristics that are shared yet perhaps differ by degree. Through a process of filtering out similarities, we will be in a position to see whether there are any *additional* features that identify human resourcing in an international context as in any way distinctive.

The single-business organisation

It has already been established (Watson, Chapter 1) that an organisation, whether national or international in scope, relies on the skills and efforts that people contribute; and that a human resourcing strategy depicts how managers tackle the problems of securing, developing and dispensing with these human resources to enable the organisation to continue in the long term. In theory, and hence putting to one side issues of the relative power, status, influence and ambiguity of the human resourcing function, the process of human resource strategy making is at its simplest in the *single-business organisation*. As such, it will provide confirmation of the features of human resourcing that ought to be essential for any employing organisation, whether international or domestic.

The human resourcing function of a *single-site* organisation, whether it is a college, factory, hospital or software company, can operate as a centralised, corporate function that is mindful of the needs of the organisation and is also sensitive to local circumstances. Centrality and locality coincide. The function is thus well placed to adopt a human resourcing strategy that fits the organisational context and hence secures a level of *vertical integration* that promotes the organisation's goals. Being located on one site should also help the function deliver a co-ordinated and consistent approach within the organisation. In theory, then, there should also be fewer obstacles to *horizontal integration*, whereby human resourcing activities such as recruitment, selection, training and payment are managed in such a way that they are mutually supportive, compatible and consistent. In addition to the human resourcing function being centralised, employees are generally more accessible, so that communication is easier and change can more readily be instituted.

A human resourcing strategy exists to fulfil corporate goals, and management's choice of strategy for the single-business organisation can be a relatively straightforward application of Watson's model. In a medium-sized manufacturing company on Merseyside, for example, the management's direct-control/low-commitment strategy, exemplified through a no-nonsense macho-style of workplace supervision and the hegemony of quality control inspectors, fitted the situation of cheap and plentiful, non-union, female labour hired on low wages to carry out repetitive machining and assembly tasks. Following Watson's model, it is possible that a similar strategy would be appropriate in similar circumstances in another country. This suggests that this relatively uncomplicated model can operate in any country, and that one option for the management of a parent company is to adopt a *multidomestic* approach, where the human resourcing function of each foreign subsidiary adopts its own strategy in accordance with local circumstances (Hoecklin, 1995: 69). This *polycentric* approach may, however, rest uneasily with those responsible for advancing the merits of a *global* human resourcing strategy that can benefit from the expertise at the centre and across the company.

The multi-unit business organisation

It is clear that the nation-by-nation approach is only one option, and that we need to develop a comprehensive framework for understanding the essentials of managing human resources *across* national boundaries. To do so, we will continue with the process of filtering out similarities to human resourcing in the domestic arena by considering *multi-unit* business organisations. We aim to identify characteristics shared with international human resourcing, which clearly operates within a multi-unit business organisation, albeit one that is located in countries additional to its corporate home base.

Many domestic-only companies can be designated multi-unit or divisional business organisations. In addition to their corporate centre or head office, such companies may have several business units, each typically with its own location. Banks have branches, retailers have stores and supermarkets, leisure companies have hotel chains and clubs, logistics firms have warehouses and so on. In any multi-unit business organisation, management choice can be represented in the form of a continuum: from employing a centralised, corporate-level human resourcing function through to having a decentralised function that operates at the business-unit level. This approach is outlined more fully by Hall and Torrington, based on their UK research (1998: 73–95). As we explore the implications for domestic human resourcing, the similarities to its international counterpart should become clear.

One approach is for the human resourcing function to be *centralised*, with a manager given responsibility for several sites while being based at head office. This manager is able, therefore, to convey the human resourcing requirements of the parent company and to ensure a co-ordinated and consistent approach at each site. A centralised approach gives preeminence to the needs of the corporation and endeavours to deliver a cost-effective, standardised version of human resourcing based on expertise at the centre. As such, it is more likely to exist in companies where the product or service is uniform across the different business units and relies on the management of each business unit translating corporate objectives into workable local activities. In such a situation, however, communication is more problematic and the personnel specialist may need to make regular visits to individual sites for face-to-face meetings to solve problems, deliver training, evaluate events and promote change.

The focus on corporate control by a central human resourcing function can expose the organisation to difficulties associated with a lack of responsiveness to local issues. For example, a standardised corporate approach to recruitment, including wage rates and the psychological contract on issues of flexible working, can give rise to problems in the more affluent South compared with the North of England (*see* Walsh, 1992). In addition, centrally imposed demands that are perceived as out of touch with the situation can provoke local resistance or avoidance. One option for larger companies is to adopt a *regional* structure, a sort of halfway house for meeting corporate and divisional or business unit needs.

At the other end of the continuum is the decision by corporate management to adopt a *decentralised* structure, with the human resourcing function operating at business-unit level. This approach to human resourcing is more attractive where the business units have diverse products or services and there seems less need for standardisation across the group. Although there may be inconsistency between the business units in the way that employees are managed, local autonomy can ensure a speedy response to specific issues and the development of systems that are engineered to meet the needs of the business unit. This may, of course, be at the expense of meeting corporate requirements, but local decision taking can promote a feeling of ownership of tasks, which in turn can generate greater staff commitment.

In addition to the regionalised halfway house or its non-geographic variant of *clustering* related business units, what other measures can help to bridge the gap between the centre and the business unit in order to marry corporate co-ordination with local responsiveness? The simple answer is to ensure a two-way flow of communication, but in practice this is never straightforward, especially in larger organisations where centre and unit can seem far apart. Another solution is to propagate and cultivate a distinctive corporate culture that can engender a strong sense of identification with the organisation; evidence of this can be found in the fashionable statements of company vision, mission and shared values, indicative of new-style HRM practices. We should not be surprised to find, however, that 'attitudes are harder to change than behaviours' (Hall and Torrington, 1998: 32). The same authors then suggest that: 'In developing corporate culture we have to start with trying to change norms of behaviour; over time those changed behaviours may lead to a change in the more deeply-held beliefs of shared norms' (1998: 32). This alerts us to another possible answer to the problem: the use of company-wide human resourcing policies, procedures and systems that demand to be followed. Again, it should not surprise us to find local human resourcing units practising 'the art of keeping the centre happy whilst doing the right things by the business' (Hall and Torrington, 1998: 80).

Human resourcing in the international organisation

What can we draw from our analysis so far? It should already be clear that the international company is a type of multi-unit business organisation, one which has a corporate centre in its *home* country and its business units located in various *host* countries. We can also appreciate the added complication that a divisional or multi-unit structure creates for the strategic management of human resources of any international company. Parent company managers can, in theory, decide to operate somewhere on a continuum between two distinct choices: whether to manage human resources through a decentralised structure with an emphasis on *local* systems and methods appropriate and responsive to that area, region or nation – this also promotes a feeling of task ownership and the commitment of the staff to the local organisation – or to consider placing emphasis on the policies, systems and methods associated with the company's base or *home*. This advances the needs of the corporation worldwide and encourages a consistent, co-ordinated approach utilising the expertise established at the centre.

A local solution would be favoured by those who adopt a perspective of *cultural relativism* where cultural differences and societal diversity are considered preeminent. This strategy for managing cultural differences is that of leaving alone the culture of each business unit (Hoecklin, 1995: 56–70). For present purposes, a working definition of culture would refer to a community's shared values, attitudes and behaviour that are passed from one generation to the next. The corporate or global solution would appeal to those who are attracted to a *universal* outlook, where work is considered to be such a fundamental activity that its management (in the hands of experts) is viewed as having a general and uniform applicability. As previously suggested, this rather stark choice can be modified by efforts to combine the two approaches, though we have noted that this can be difficult to sustain even in a domestic context. How much greater the human resourcing challenge is likely to be in an international context, no matter how appealingly simple the often quoted edict of *think globally, act locally* may sound! The task of attaining vertical and horizontal integration of the human resourcing function across the companies of a global enterprise will always present difficulties, especially when managers believe that they have to pursue local diversity and corporate integration simultaneously (Torrington, 1994: 101).

How, then, can the balance between the centre and its subsidiaries be managed within the international organisation? How might it be possible to think globally yet act locally? Taking in turn the same solutions proposed for the domestic-only organisation: a two-way flow of communication between the centre and its foreign subsidiaries will present the same obstacles, but magnified by even greater differences of distance, time and perhaps linguistic expression. Great claims, however, are being made on behalf of electronic mail and video-conferencing, and certainly my observations of a leading UK transnational company reveal its staff's devoted use of these new media being supported by managers' regular visits to overseas subsidiaries. By contrast, the staff of a second leading UK multinational rely on postal and telephone systems and there is management concern about communication problems between headquarters and expatriate employees who are located around the globe.

Effective two-way communication is probably an essential but insufficient condition for achieving a combination of corporate and local effectiveness. It is the medium for the message. This leads us to the second possible strategy, one that is said to require relentless communication: to build a strong corporate culture internationally, to promote shared values and to reinforce consistent behaviour (Hall and Torrington, 1998: 41). *Building* a corporate culture that is distinctive almost always means a need to *change* the culture of its members. This is to amend the values, beliefs and attitudes of individuals as applied to their work. We have already asserted that it is not easy to transform a person's taken-for-granted view of their world, but it is debatable that it will always be more challenging to inculcate a distinctive corporate culture in a foreign location. My own observations tell me that the respective cultures of the Church of England and the British Army, for example, are probably more difficult to change than the work-related cultures of local staff employed by foreign-owned semiconductor manufacturers in Singapore and Malaysia. In this comparison, national culture is less significant for human resourcing decisions than organisational culture. The indigenous language and culture of the semiconductor staff are usually reserved for outside working hours, and those charged with changing the Army or the Church of England will need to be as discerning about cultural factors as any international manager (Welch, 1997; Overell, 1998).

Once again, we seem to reach the conclusion that international human resourcing differs little from its domestic counterpart, even in the apparently obvious area of culture. However, this is not to argue that culture, and especially national culture, is not a crucial factor in devising an appropriate human resourcing strategy. Work on multicultural teams reveals that the members' different nationalities (rather than their personalities) lie at the root of group tensions and misunderstandings (Adler, 1997). This should not be too surprising a revelation, since for most people our nationality or national identity can be said to define our *lifelong* culture (Billig, 1995). However, there is a danger of emphasising the employees' national culture at the expense of their subculture, which might be more significant. Variety exists within nations as well as between them; as visitors to multicultural societies, for example, can testify. In addition, a focus on national customs and rituals may divert attention away from that part of the society's culture that is concerned with work and employment. It is this particular dimension that a strong corporate culture should be seeking to change. Yet, just as work can come to dominate one's life, so can a company's work culture be perceived as omnipotent and not always welcome: *you bind me to a constancy that is not my way.*

This discussion of a cultural strategy to bind centre to subsidiary raises doubts about its efficacy, though the chiefs of companies such as Hewlett-Packard, IKEA and British Airways will no doubt attest to its part in their global successes. We have also confirmed the importance of taking into account relevant cultural factors when devising human resourcing strategies. This will apply equally to the design of human resourcing systems and procedures, which is our third possible way of bringing expertise, co-ordination and consistency from the centre to each local company. The thorough consideration of cultural and other contingent factors would seem to be a necessary component in shaping such procedures and systems if they are to work in each organisational context. However, this returns us to an earlier theme concerning the importance of the horizontal integration of human resourcing procedures and systems across each part of the global organisation, and the achievement of a high degree of internal 'fit' (Marchington and Wilkinson, 1996: 394–400). A contingent approach might appear not to deliver this outcome, and practitioners are often more attracted to models of so-called best practice. These would seem to offer a uniform collection of human resourcing practices that, in addition to qualities of integrity and consistency, claim to have universal application and the promise of delivering competitive advantage (Pfeffer, 1994).

However, actuality is almost certain to prove disappointing unless best-practice ideas can be incorporated into distinctly local solutions that ensure they are appropriate for the specific organisational context (Stopford *et al.*, 1994). This will apply to both domestic and international situations and a study of local cultures, including employee expectations, will help management formulate those recruitment, selection, employee development and reward practices that are the most likely to work, and to avoid those that won't. For example, an individual performance-related pay scheme may prove ineffective if the workforce has a collectivist or group-centred outlook. Similarly, a sophisticated approach to recruitment and selection may be at odds with a societal preference for personal recommendation. While this may sit uneasily with professional notions of propriety and impartiality, nepotism based on mutual obligation and respect as well as self-interest can offer the employer a guaranteed level of work performance that the recruit will feel personally obliged to honour. Finally, the case for a contingency approach to international human resourcing is demonstrated by the need to examine employment laws to determine which practices are permitted to work! This assumes, of course, that it is company policy to respect and operate within a country's laws, no matter how irksome or corrupt they may appear to be.

■ National and international human resourcing

The examples above illustrate our view that managers make human resourcing decisions based on their interpretation of societal and organisational factors: their choices are influenced by circumstances and their opportunities reined in by constraints. We have already seen that this process applies to national as well as international human resourcing; and both will be subject to a manager's *bounded rationality*, whereby interpretations are made and decisions reached on the basis of less than complete information or understanding (Simon, 1977). It would seem reasonable to presume, however, that human resourcing managers are more likely to perceive a foreign set of circumstances as more complex and indeterminate than those encountered in their home country. Consequently, managers with international responsibilities will perhaps be more conscious of the inadequacy of their knowledge and of the need to act on this by conducting investigations, taking expert advice, hiring a consultant and so on. It is ironic that a manager's assumption that they have sufficient knowledge about human resourcing issues in their national environment may lead to an inattention to detail and a neglect of significant factors.

Whatever the manager's level of awareness of the need to conduct a careful examination of contingent factors, the method of analysis outlined for human resource strategy making is identical for national and international contexts. This has to be so, since the contribution of the human resourcing function to the enterprise and the dilemmas associated with a multi-divisional organisation provide a common agenda for practitioners, whether within or across national boundaries. As such, the decision-making model emphasising management choice based on an evaluation of circumstances is valid for any context and calls for a sensitivity to those contingent factors that might have an impact on the management of the organisation's human resources. It is true that the choices and contingencies found in international human resourcing may provide the practitioner with a host of novel and different situations, but it is equally true that those features that might be thought to define an *international* dimension are essentially those found in all human resourcing situations.

Torrington assembled 'The seven Cs of international HRM': culture; cosmopolitans, i.e. staffing arrangements; compensation; communication; consultancy; competence; and co-ordination, 'to identify some activities that are different in nature when a business is international' (1994: 6). As will be evident from the preceding discussion, these seven activities are not exclusive to international companies, and the underlying principles of skilful human resourcing implicit in our analytical model should remain unaltered. However, we do need to acknowledge that these seven elements are likely to exhibit some differences in international companies. Though these are differences of *degree* and not of basic nature, they will visibly affect the tasks undertaken by those in the human resourcing function.

Furthermore, if our framework for understanding human resourcing across national boundaries is to be truly comprehensive, it will be necessary to incorporate any *additional* features that will complete our picture. In the next section, therefore, we will build on our way of thinking about international human resourcing and begin the process of providing more information on some of the choices and circumstances that practitioners may encounter. By focusing on the international dimension, we are acknowledging that other chapters in this book will be dealing with key human resourcing activities in more detail. As such, they represent a valuable information source that supplements and supports our approach to international human resource strategy making.

In general, management choice is restricted in effect by *constraints* that arise from the existing circumstances. Constraints such as those imposed by demands from the legal system are self-evident and likely to be observed out of necessity. Other constraints may offer a degree of choice for management decision makers who, in theory, will perceive their own self-interests as being best served by promoting the goals of the organisation. As an example, the technical skills required for a multinational company's foreign subsidiary may lead to the management decision to utilise those skills offered by an existing employee from the *home country*. These skills could then be allied to the willingness of a workforce from the *host country* to apply itself with an effort-bargain that surpasses any other and that is malleable and conveniently recruited, trained and retained (at least in the short term). Ideally, if successful, this human resourcing strategy ought to satisfy both the decision maker's self-interest and the goals of the organisation.

CASE STUDY 4.1

Going international?

Blakestone & Co. is a well-established family firm that employs 100 staff at its single site in the West Midlands, manufacturing a miniature machining tool designed for highly specialised precision work. Each machine can sell for up to £60 000 and, in spite of a strong pound, the company has carved out a niche export market against intense competition. While the USA is its main market, the firm has more than 20 distributors in the rest of the world and overseas sales teams attend regular meetings in the UK.

The company has so far been an assembly operation, buying components from various parts of the world. Mr Blakestone, the owner and managing director, is now considering opening his own manufacturing plant – not in the West Midlands, but in Mexico, where:

- costs are low;
- there is access to the whole North American market through the NAFTA trade agreement between the USA, Mexico and Canada;
- there would be a greater degree of security against movements in the US dollar.

Activity 4.1

1 What are the particular *human resourcing challenges* that will need to be addressed if the plans to establish a manufacturing plant in Mexico go ahead?

2 Blakestone & Co. managers already have considerable experience of overseas business through the company's connections with its sales distribution network and with its component suppliers in various parts of the world.

(a) To what extent can this experience be relied on to meet the human resourcing challenges to be addressed in Mexico?

(b) What further steps could be taken to ensure that the company meets these challenges?

Globalisation and organisational approaches to international human resourcing

Globalisation at a worldwide level refers to 'the growing economic interdependence among countries as reflected in increasing cross-border flows of goods, services, capital and know-how' (Govindarajan and Gupta, 1998a). At an organisational level, globalisation can refer historically to the extent to which a company has expanded its operations so that it engages in 'cross-border flows of capital, goods and know-how across subsidiaries' (Govindarajan and Gupta, 1998a). It can also be used to describe a corporate strategy, designed to reap the benefits of becoming a global company. Globalisation at all levels is, therefore, very much an outcome of corporate decision makers who perceive globalisation as an attractive and feasible proposition. As such, the process need not be an inexorable one. Economic uncertainties may drive national governments and corporate decision makers towards the protectionism of defending a home market and away from the free-market ideology that has been synonymous with globalisation. The downturn in East Asia and beyond has led to unresolved debates about what can be done to prevent global capitalism destroying itself. There is concern that 'global capitalism's blindness to anything but the bottom line and an apparent indifference to inequalities suffered in the poorest countries' makes the system unsustainable, which in turn places in jeopardy the living standards in the developed world (Elliott, 1998).

None the less, a global economy and global businesses remain very much a critical component of our existence. The best-known branded names – drinks, fast foods, sports equipment, motor cars, petroleum, computers, pharmaceuticals, electronics and other consumer products – can be found in the majority of the world's countries. Popular statistics can also reveal the dominance of multinational companies: 51 of the world's top 100 economies are not countries but companies. The largest 500 companies control 42 per cent of the world's wealth and conduct over half of its trade. The ten biggest companies together turn over more money than the world's smallest 100 countries, and the world's second largest multinational, Shell, owns or leases 400 million acres of land, which is larger than 146 countries put together ('Thinking Aloud', BBC Radio 4: 3.6.98).

We can sense the impelling force of globalisation ourselves. We can also appreciate that the economic liberalisation of the world's developing countries and the technological advances in telecommunications and transportation have made globalisation an enticing prospect for those corporations seeking to grow and survive. In the face of increasing international competition, multinational company chiefs have identified the opportunities afforded by the globalisation process as the means by which to meet the challenges. In turn, their business decisions help to sustain the process. These international opportunities include capturing new markets and realising great economies of scale; the creation of extensive networks for the transfer of new ideas and knowhow across the organisation; and the optimal allocation and relocation of resources. All of these set an agenda for an organisation's international human resourcing strategy. Attention to human resourcing activities and initiatives will be required to mobilise those resources that will best contribute towards growth and increased profits, leading ultimately to long-term corporate survival. In theory, a comparable agenda ought also to be present in a domestic organisation.

ILLUSTRATION 4.1

Jürgen Schrempp, Chief Executive of Daimler-Benz, explains his company's five-point globalisation plan

For a company like Daimler-Benz globalisation is not an optional strategy. It is the only one. In ten years time we want to be number one or two in each of our business areas. In some areas we are there already. For example we are the world leader in commercial vehicles, number one in rail systems through Adtranz and number two in aircraft through Airbus. And Mercedes-Benz is the leader in its segment in passenger cars. We want to double our turnover and be among the top quartile of global companies in performance. How will we achieve this? We have to do five things.

First, we have to be in the growth markets around the world. We have to have the right products and the right services in the right places. So we are building the M-class in Alabama, the A-class in Brazil, trucks and buses in many parts of the world and aircraft too, because we have to be near the markets we serve.

Second, we want to be a leader in innovation. Only companies which anticipate people's needs, translate great ideas into products and services, and get them into the market fast, will succeed. You only have to look at the transformation of the Mercedes-Benz and truck ranges in recent years to see what I mean.

The third thing is that it must be exciting and rewarding for our people. We know that globalisation creates jobs both in other countries and in our home market. We have been able to show our unions that for every three jobs we create abroad, we create one in Germany.

But we also have to have the right corporate culture. To be a successful global company we have to find exceptional executives – people who have industrial skills, but can also adapt to local communities and respond to their needs. So we have to be prepared to transfer people from one place to another and make sure nationality does not play any role. We are not there yet, but we are going in the right direction.

Somebody asked, what is the single most important thing about being a global company? I said being a good corporate citizen and that is the fourth thing. You have to put down roots and make a real contribution to the community – and that takes time.

Then, fifth, you have to have access to global capital. That means listing on the leading stock markets. And it means presenting your financial accounts to the standards of transparency demanded by investors. So these are the five things. But most of all, I believe globalisation is about creating value for people. Producing products they want, creating interesting jobs, and delivering excellent returns for our shareholders. That's the bottom line.

Source: http://www/ft/comhippocampus/v5aa8e.htm (visited 31 October 1997).

Herr Schrempp's pronouncement that 'For a company like Daimler-Benz globalisation is not an optional strategy. It is the only one' was to foreshadow an announcement in 1998 that Daimler-Benz was to join forces with Chrysler. As a result, 'DaimlerChrysler, the new US-German group, will become the biggest company on Germany's stock exchange' (*Financial Times*, 8.9.98). Such a merger is far from isolated, being part of an ongoing trend for major automobile companies to pool their assets. As a result, a decline in the number of corporations in the worldwide automobile industry would seem to be inevitable. A detailed account of this industry can be found in Chapter 15 by Towers.

Multinational companies are undoubtedly agencies for increasing global interdependence, but it would be wrong to assume that they are truly independent of any nation since, outside a handful of companies, the biggest corporations are owned by capitalists from a particular country and dominated by the culture of that country. 'Outside that handful, companies are very German, or very British, or very American' (Lowell Bryan, senior partner with McKinsey in New York, quoted by Jackson, 1998). Furthermore, most multinational companies remain firmly rooted in their native regions (Rugman, 1998). Indeed, 451 of the *Financial Times'* 1998 list of the world's top 500 companies based on market capitalisation are located in the 'triad' blocs of North America (235), the European Union (145) and Japan (71).

The UK has 51 companies in the top 500, behind the USA with 222 and Japan with 71, but ahead of Germany, France and Italy with 21, 19 and 5 respectively. The position occupied by the UK gives only a partial indication of its involvement in the global economy, since it also ranks as the most attractive European location for foreign investment. Indeed, inward corporate investment (mergers, acquisitions and strategic investments) reached a record $53 billion in 1997 compared with $59.8 billion spent in the USA and $19.8 billion for third-placed Germany (*Financial Times*, 19.1.98). Moreover, there is every chance that the UK will remain the most powerful magnet in Europe for the foreseeable future, having leapt from seventh to fourth place in a competitiveness league table (World Economic Forum, June 1998). The table aims to rank countries according to their capacity for medium-term economic growth. As the USA is ranked third behind the city-states of Singapore and Hong Kong, the UK can be regarded as the second most competitive of all the countries with large populations and diversified economies. By comparison, Germany, France and Italy are ranked 24th, 22nd and 41st respectively.

There is clear evidence of significant cross-border business activity involving the UK, and indeed 313 of the top 500 companies operating in the UK are foreign owned (Griffiths and Wall, 1996). It would be reasonable to conclude, therefore, that an examination of international human resourcing is especially relevant for UK practitioners, who will also have enhanced opportunities for networking both within and between international business organisations to add to their expertise in this area of work.

■ The structure of multinational companies

From the above analysis, we can also conclude that our model of a parent company controlled from its national home base and linked with its foreign subsidiaries remains an appropriate one for nearly all multinationals. We can also pursue our contention that a key consideration of global business is operating effectively across cultural boundaries and balancing organisational integration with responsiveness to local demands. The issue is how business units in several different countries are to be linked through human resourcing policies and practices. In theory, a strategic decision maker might select from among the several choices and alternatives that exist along a continuum of centralised and decentralised arrangements. However, practitioners need to be aware that the strategic choice that has been made or has emerged for their own employing organisation will constrain and guide the human resourcing activities that follow.

The first such constraint is defined by the *structural form* that the multinational company (my generic term for those companies operating in several countries, whatever their structural form) exhibits, whether by management design or not. Although individual multinational companies may display a set of arrangements that are specific to them, it is useful to employ a classification of the forms of organisation used to manage multinational companies. This will enable us to identify our own organisation's structure in relation to the alternatives. The most productive typology is probably that formulated by Bartlett and Ghoshal (1989), which shows multinational companies evolving from the 1960s to the present (Hendry, 1994: 72) and displays four distinctive organisational patterns, identified chronologically as:

- the multinational (1960/70s);
- the global (1980s);
- the international (1980/90s);
- the present-day transnational (1990s).

Multinational

The *multinational* pattern is predominantly a collection of decentralised and fairly autonomous operating units that are directed towards their own national markets. It displays relatively low company-wide integration and can be regarded as a multi-domestic organisation. The head of an operational unit is typically an expatriate, but one with a considerable degree of autonomy. Human resourcing focuses on the needs of the local operation and will usually be managed by a local national who will be familiar with local laws and employment practices. Control exercised from the centre may well be confined to financial targets and results.

Global

The *global* pattern is distinguished by a high degree of integration, managed from a corporate centre and designed to take advantage of the economies of scale from worldwide activities that are geared to distributing standardised products to global markets. The management of foreign operations is required to implement strategies determined at the centre, including decisions to switch resources between countries in the service of corporate goals. Consequently, in this structure human resourcing expertise and knowledge will reside at headquarters, where policies, systems and schemes are formulated and issued to those in the subsidiaries for implementation. Those at the centre may need to ask whether formalised policies and practices will be sufficient to ensure that local employees will carry out the directives or whether expatriate managers might be required to control the foreign units (Schuler *et al.*, 1993).

International

The *international* structure is best regarded as an intermediate type, combining the decentralised and centralised elements of the multinational and global types. This version is associated with managements' perceived need to be more responsive to distinctive local market needs, without losing the global integration that generates so many competitive advantages. The outcome is an arrangement that affords autonomy to the overseas units on some matters, while retaining central control over key areas like finance, product development and market development. The human resourcing expertise and knowledge developed at headquarters are transferred to the company's subsidiaries for local adaptation as appropriate. This requires the systematic development of umbrella policies and practices. However, where the foreign units exhibit considerable local differences, an all-embracing directive on, for example, compensation, recruitment or performance appraisal may prove fairly meaningless. There seems to be a presumption in this type that the predominant flow of information should be from the centre, which is assumed to be the repository of good human resourcing practice. This idea and its shortcomings are challenged in the latest organisational type, the transnational.

Transnational

The *transnational* structure provides an integrated network of highly interactive units that encourages all parts of the organisation, including the centre, to share and benefit from the expertise and knowledge that each possesses. As Hendry points out, it 'means transferring innovations from the centre to local markets, and from local markets to the centre and other localities' (1994: 74). It offers the synergies of co-operation with the autonomy needed for staff motivation and the best decisions for the local conditions (Schuler *et al.*, 1993: 429). It has been suggested that the transnational type is an ideal towards which multinational companies will need to develop for long-term competitive advantage. Multinational companies are faced by 'the need to manage globally, as if the world were one vast market, and simultaneously locally, as if the world were a vast number of separate and loosely connected markets' (Schuler, 1998: 138). This may render the ideal solution unattainable, since it means developing simultaneously the local responsiveness, the efficiency and the transfer of knowhow associated with the multinational, the global and the international types of organisation respectively (Bartlett and Ghoshal, 1989: 12).

However, one might envisage a transnational human resourcing function being managed so that the best ideas and systems were shared company-wide for consideration by managers with both local autonomy and an overall appreciation of corporate priorities. Understandably, this transnational approach is likely to entail particular attention to recruiting and developing a certain kind of manager. Management development programmes and events will be organised, co-ordinated normally by the corporate human resourcing unit, as a way of providing the glue that 'bonds together otherwise loose and disparate entities' (Schuler *et al.*, 1993: 433). One suggestion is the development of a *global mindset*, which places a high value on sharing information and skills across the whole organisation (Govindarajan and Gupta, 1998b).

Increasingly, it is the transnational type that receives attention from commentators, who assert that 'any structure must cope with what is likely to prove the 21st century's biggest management challenge: combining world-wide reach with the flexibility and speed of reaction of a local competitor' (Martin, 1998). The logic of this kind of thinking is that the success or failure of a multinational company will depend to a large extent on having an international human resourcing strategy that strikes the right balance between meeting corporate human resource needs and the particular local needs of its subsidiaries. We have now examined the first set of strategic choices on the *structural form* of the multinational company and how each can act as a major constraint on the subsequent operation of international human resourcing, which is shaped by the way in which the tension between central and local management is resolved.

◼ The dominant management orientation of multinational companies

The second major set of strategic choices, which in turn will significantly influence the practice of international human resourcing, is defined by the *dominant cultural viewpoint or approach* adopted by the multinational company's management at headquarters towards its foreign subsidiaries. As this contingent factor refers to top management's attitudes and values, it is not always the outcome of conscious choice but often the expression of a taken-for-granted view of the world held by individuals. As such, we are acknowledging that human resourcing priorities and practices can be circumscribed by the *Weltanschauung* or worldview of corporate decision makers, through which they seek to make sense of things. In our analysis we will be able to illustrate some of the implications of a dominant management orientation for human resourcing by looking at staffing decisions (Hendry, 1994: 79) and appraisal criteria (Tung, 1998: 384).

Heenan and Perlmutter (1979) have provided a fourfold classification of such an orientation:

- polycentric;
- ethnocentric;
- geocentric, with its regiocentric subset.

A particular orientation is identified through its *stance on different national cultures*. This is applicable to those at the helm of a multinational company, since their company is identified by its national home base in relation to foreign operations. It follows, therefore, that any orientation displayed by headquarters management towards their foreign operations may be heavily influenced by comparisons of national culture. In addition, it should soon become clear that, although the three main orientations have distinctive implications for human resourcing, they are also likely to correspond (though not precisely) to the forms of organisation, as follows: multinational-polycentric; global-ethnocentric; transnational-geocentric.

Polycentric

The *polycentric* orientation recognises the validity, at least for business reasons, of each foreign operation's national culture and as such replicates a multi-domestic view of the organisation's subsidiaries. As a consequence, each subsidiary is afforded considerable autonomy with regard to local human resourcing decisions and activities, although strategic decisions are controlled at headquarters. This means that subsidiaries are usually managed by local nationals, with the key headquarters' jobs going to staff from the parent company. There is a logical inclination to adopt local standards to evaluate staff performance, but this invites the problem of offering staff little incentive to adopt strategies that can maximise the firm's global position.

Ethnocentric

The *ethnocentric* orientation of the dominant management coalition sees the world, including foreign subsidiaries, from the viewpoint of its own particular culture, which in turn is regarded as superior to any other cultural background. Unlike *parochialism*, which assumes that the home culture is best because cultural differences are not acknowledged or recognised, *ethnocentrism* implies a conscious belief that the home culture is superior. This means that the organisational culture will mirror that of the home country and that little account is taken of the cultures of the host countries. It is not uncommon and quite understandable, therefore, for managers to see things from their own cultural perspective and to evaluate people in foreign subsidiaries against their own standards and expectations. The status of these home-country standards is then confirmed by the human resourcing systems and procedures that are devised by the experts at headquarters for transmission to each locality. This approach, when applied to appraisal, could lead to an unfavourable assessment of those managers who may be performing effectively in local circumstances that are not accorded sufficient consideration. Such a bias is further reinforced by a staffing structure that allocates key jobs at home and overseas to employees from headquarters. As Hendry notes, 'nationals from the parent country rule the organisation both at home and (as expatriates) abroad' (1994: 79).

Geocentric

A *geocentric* orientation, unlike the other two approaches, does not differentiate between employees on the basis of nationality. Instead, it endeavours to adopt a supranational view of the organisation, in which national cultures are regarded as a constraint on the global interests of the corporation as a whole. The only culture that matters is that embodied in the multinational company itself, which, in demoting nationality *per se*, will espouse the value of the diversity of skills and insights that national differences can bring. The development of multicultural teams sits easily with this orientation. Furthermore, ability rather than nationality provides the basis for staff selection, development and promotion, which means that the top management team must also be international in composition and global in outlook if this approach is to have credibility across the organisation. One manifestation of such an outlook is the creation of global standards for staff appraisal. The assessment of staff performance is gauged in relation to the organisation's global position. This may entail, for example, the rationalisation of production activities around the world. The opening of plants in one location may be accompanied by the closure of others elsewhere.

Regiocentric

A *regiocentric* orientation is best regarded as a subset of the geocentric orientation, replacing a global view with one restricted to the world's geographic regions. This means that a corporate region is perceived as a microcosm of the corporate world. The policy will be to promote the company's own regional culture and to appoint and develop staff from within the region to manage its operations. As with the geocentric view, this orientation is probably the result of a deliberate strategy related to the parent company's business operations. The definition of a *region* may differ between companies and the perceived coherence of a designated region will depend significantly on the approach of the human resourcing function towards issues such as staffing, training, rewards and career progression. The movement of staff across the geographic region promotes this orientation, but would be at odds with the continued domination of the very top jobs by managers from the parent country (Hendry, 1994: 79).

ILLUSTRATION 4.2

A multinational cadre of managers is the key, claims Percy Barnevik, chairman of ABB, the Swiss-Swedish engineering group

Too many people think you can succeed in the long run just by exporting from America or Europe. But you need to establish yourself locally and become, for example, a Chinese, Indonesian or Indian citizen.

You don't need to do this straight away but you need to start early because it takes a long time. It can take ten years. Globalisation is a long-lasting competitive advantage. If we build a new gas turbine, in 18 months our competitors also have one. But building a global company is not so easy to copy.

ABB has virtually finished building its global structure. The main task now is to bring more executives from emerging countries in eastern Europe and in Asia into the higher levels of the company. We have 82 000 employees in emerging economies. We have to bring the best of these to the top.

This takes time. Building a multinational cadre of international managers is the key. It is one thing for a chief executive himself to be a global manger. It is quite another to persuade other executives to think and act globally. At ABB we have about 25 000 managers. But not all of these need to be global managers. We have about 500. Very rarely would you get a global manager from outside.

Of course, companies such as Shell and International Business Machines have such people, but there are relatively few available to hire. Also it's better if people grow up with ABB values. It's difficult to digest our culture if you have spent 10 or 20 years in another company. The difficulty is that bosses tend to attract clusters of people from their own nationality around them.

They do this not because they are racists, but because they feel comfortable with people they know best. You get a German cluster or a Swedish cluster. So you must make sure that when a boss selects managers, he considers people from other countries. And you must make sure good people from other countries are available to him. Managers have to be asked to supply lists of potential candidates for work outside their countries.

Then, if a German manager selects four Germans for a task, you will be in a position to suggest an Italian or an American and ask him to think again. There's a disadvantage in doing this because you lose a little since maybe they will all have to speak in bad English instead of in German or whatever. But the advantage is that you get the best people in place. And you build a global company.

Source: http://www.ft.com.hippocampus/v4ef46.htm (visited 8 October 1997).

We have now examined the second set of strategic choices on the *dominant management orientation* of multinational companies and how each can act as a major constraint on the subsequent operation of international human resourcing, shaped by the way in which organisational decision makers approach national differences and cross-cultural issues. It is this latter dimension that distinguishes international human resourcing from its domestic counterpart. But in principle, the practice of human resourcing will be constrained by *dominant orientation* as well as *structural form* in both types of environment. However, in focusing on the international aspects of human resourcing, we can briefly consider the function's contribution to an organisation where the move towards becoming a transnational business is regarded as the best strategy for survival in the global economy.

■ Changing the mindset

As argued above, the transnational organisation model is perhaps one to which corporate decision makers are more likely to aspire than actually attain. Its attraction lies in its promise to deliver, to large and unwieldy multinational companies, organisational integration with local responsiveness: the capability of operating effectively across cultural boundaries without losing the essentials of good management within cultural boundaries. The slogan 'think globally, act locally' provides a simple lead; but how might those responsible for human resourcing assist in moving a company towards the transnational model?

One crucial ingredient appears to be the development of a *way of thinking* that will ensure that managers and other key employees operate in accordance with a geocentric organisational culture. This will embody a set of values, attitudes and behaviours that rests on a foundation of openness towards national cultures and 'operates on the premise that cultures can be different without being better or worse than one another' (Govindarajan and Gupta, 1998b). It then follows that staff should embrace the rationale and advantages of sharing ideas, information and work practices across the whole organisation and not just their small part of it. However, in practice multinational

Table 4.1 Human resourcing levers in the multinational firm

Staffing	A mix of nationalities, international experience and language skills in senior and other key positions
	The utilisation of cross-border business teams (multicultural project teams)
Development and training	Management development programmes with a mix of nationalities; international assignments
	Training programmes for cross-cultural awareness, language skills, IT applications and corporate information
Rewards	Career ladders that reward international experience and are open to employees worldwide
	Performance assessment and pay schemes that reflect global as well as local performance
Communications	The development of flexible networks of global relationships for the exchange of information
	Employing state-of-the-art communications media
The HR function	The corporate HR function will gain credibility to influence others only if it presents an example of how a transnational organisation: ■ recruits, develops and rewards people ■ makes decisions that integrate global and local perspectives ■ stimulates global networks

companies are much more likely to display an ethnocentric orientation (Govindarajan and Gupta, 1998b). So what are the human resourcing initiatives that might restructure this more closed worldview? How can the function help to create the new way of thinking that we have labelled geocentric and others have termed (perhaps confusingly, given the ethnocentric pedigree of the global structure) a *global mindset*? Assuming the adoption of an approach that is integrated by its reference to corporate goals and the need for mutually supportive practices, the human resourcing levers in Table 4.1 (Govindarajan and Gupta, 1998b; Pucik, 1998) may provide the basis for an answer.

It should be apparent that the task of managing change in a single-site domestic organisation is itself difficult; and that delivering cultural change will be even more difficult. The problems and barriers of doing the same for a multinational company with its conglomeration of national cultures and multitude of employees are bound to be immense. Not least, the levers identified above have to be enacted in a fairly coherent way in a very uncertain environment. It would appear that normative integration through the building of common perspectives, purposes and values is an attractive but complicated human resourcing strategy. Perhaps transnational co-ordination might be better achieved through bureaucratic control. Appealing to employees' self-interest through a consistent set of rules and procedures supported with straightforward messages may generate the behaviour and even the mindset desired.

ILLUSTRATION 4.3

I would like to illustrate this last point by reference to an analogy that affected me personally: a simple management decision that altered my behaviour and attitude towards what I had previously perceived as a trifling item, a five pence piece. The fare for my journey to work by bus was 70 pence, and my payment to the driver was constrained by the bus company's regulation that no change could be given to passengers. This meant that my energies were directed towards having the exact amount to give the driver for both the outward and return journeys. Consequently, gathering 50 pence and 20 pence coins became a priority, with a couple of 10 pence coins being considered an acceptable alternative. From my perspective, the five pence coin shared a low priority with the one and two pence coins in my pocket. At this point, such coins were not only insignificant to me, they were also an irritating nuisance.

Then the management of the bus company decided to raise its fare to 75 pence! My behaviour patterns and my attitude towards the much maligned five pence piece have been transformed. It now plays an important and obvious role in my travel arrangements; it appeals to my self-interest and operates within a very uncomplicated (exact fare) system. It would be simplistic to suggest that human resourcing systems can emulate such an approach, especially within a multinational company, since the control mechanism over the fare-paying passenger is face to face and immediate. However, it is worth postulating that the essence of effective human resourcing, international or otherwise, is one that has a direct impact on the perceived self-interest of the employee. The complication within a multinational environment arises because it is more challenging to establish how *self-interest* translates for and is perceived by employees of diverse cultural backgrounds. Self-interest can be viewed in our framework as a contingent factor for human resourcing managers to consider, and we will briefly address the issue of national culture as a contingent factor shortly.

Staffing for transnational companies

'Almost everything else in international HRM flows from the way the firm manages its movement of staff . . . the overall approach to staffing determines the degree of attention given to each of three groups of employee – parent-country nationals (PCNs), host-country nationals (HCNs) and third-country nationals (TCNs)' (Hendry, 1994: 79). PCNs come from the country where the multinational has its headquarters; HCNs are from a country where the subsidiary for which they work is located; and TCNs are from outside both.

Staffing policies represent our third set of strategic choices, as represented by the various combinations of PCNs, HCNs and TCNs who might be employed within the multinational company. In theory, staffing arrangements should be determined through a systematic human resource planning process. However, this activity can only come into play in conjunction with the organisation's staffing policies, which, as we noted above, are shaped both by the *structural form* and the company's *dominant management orientation*.

Most companies currently convey an ethnocentric approach to staffing, favouring PCNs for their headquarters staff and for the top jobs, whether in the parent country or a host country. PCNs are often used for foreign assignments for their technical expertise and product knowledge, and to ensure adherence to standards by local staff as well as allegiance to corporate goals. HCNs will figure more prominently in a polycentric approach, but predominantly in the host country where their local knowledge will be regarded as invaluable in dealing with local factors. Understandably, therefore, the human resourcing role, which needs to take account of employment laws and labour market conditions, is typically allocated to an HCN. Finally, TCNs are most likely to be employed by a geocentric, transnational organisation, which manifests a very pragmatic view in seeking to employ staff according to (suit)ability. Consequently, it does not differentiate between employees on the basis of nationality and a TCN can convey the international nature of the business

Activity 4.2

1 Draw up a brief job description and person specification for the post of Senior Human Resource Manager for a major multinational company, based on the following advertisement that appeared in the recruitment pages of a popular English-language daily in Malaysia.

2 In general, what are the likely advantages and the potential limitations of employing an HCN in this post?

3 What are the likely advantages and the potential limitations of employing a PCN in this post?

One of the world's largest suppliers of computers and information system solutions, telecommunications, semicondutor products, software and services has a vacancy for a suitably qualified Malaysian for the challenging position of:

SENIOR HUMAN RESOURCE MANAGER

As a Senior Human Resource Manager, you will be responsible for developing, directing and implementing comprehensive plans and programmes to ensure the most effective utilisation of human resources to support the achievement of corporate objectives. You will also be responsible for the formulation and implementation of human resourcing policies and procedures, manpower planning, performance appraisal, job evaluation and staff welfare. Other responsibilities include implementing an aggressive and effective recruitment strategy to attract candidates with the *right attitude to work*. You will also establish training and human resource development policies and programmes for all levels of employees for achieving staff excellence and to ensure total commitment in providing top-quality services to customers.

REQUIREMENTS

- Must possess a tertiary qualification, preferably a degree with relevant working experience of at least 4–5 years.
- Must be familiar with current human resource practices, which include labour laws, industrial relations, planning and job evaluation.
- Must have highly developed interpersonal and organisation skills, with good ability to interact with all levels of employees.
- Must be frank and give all necessary support to management to ensure that effective human resource programmes are implemented effectively.

REMUNERATION

The right candidate will be given a very attractive remuneration and benefits package. Interested candidates are requested to apply in confidence giving complete personal particulars, including age, career record, educational background, present position, current and expected salary and contact telephone number with a recent passport-sized photograph (n.r.) to:

The Advertiser
P.O. Box 1234 (Ref. 664)
Kuala Lumpur

Only shortlisted candidates will be notified

It is in the transnational company that a combination of all three groups of employee, PCN, HCN and TCN, is most likely to be evident. Furthermore, in tune with this approach to staffing is the quest for a *global mindset*. The logical outcome in the transnational organisation, therefore, is that all three groups of employee are unlikely to be limited to working in only one country. At various times during their employment, employees (as international transferees) might be classified as *expatriates* when working away from the company's parent country; *inpatriates* when working in the company's parent country but not their home; and perhaps *transpatriates* when operating in a country that is neither their home nor that of the parent company. For reasons of political correctness, the management of a transnational company might prefer to play down the significance of employee nationality implied in the above classifications. But for reasons of pragmatism, it is essential that the human resourcing function recognises and seeks to deal with issues associated with *employee relocation*.

■ International relocation

In addition to normative integration and bureaucratic control, *critical flows of staff* within and between the units of the organisation represent a third human resourcing strategy for achieving inter-unit co-ordination in the transnational (De Cieri and McGaughey, 1998: 631). The flow of people through staff transfers has an impact on the corporate culture by helping staff in all locations to develop a broader corporate perspective and increase identification with the global organisation. Transfers also promote networks for the exchange of knowledge and the sharing of ideas and skills.

According to De Cieri and McGaughey, relocation involves 'the transfer of employees – and often families – for work purposes between two locations and for a period of time that is deemed to require a change of address and some degree of semi-permanent adjustment to local conditions' (1998: 631). It is interesting that the prevalence of expatriate transfers reflecting the traditional multinational and global structures is gradually being rivalled by inpatriate transfers, which are associated with developments towards transnational structures. Evidence from the United States Immigration and Naturalisation Service indicates that over 80 000 foreign nationals annually are brought to the USA by their American employers. They come for development assignments, technical training, to manage project teams and to absorb the corporate culture. Many are being groomed to return in place of American expatriates. Human resourcing specialists in particular are trained so that they can use new skills on their return to their subsidiary unit.

The concept of international relocation draws our attention to the significance of the transfer to another country and the similarity of experience between the various types of international transferees. It seems reasonable, therefore, to confine this analysis to the expatriation scenario as a concise way to explore the relocation process. In so doing, we need to bear in mind that the UK may be as foreign and strange to international assignees as other countries are to the British.

The success of an international relocation can be gauged by the employee's work performance and contribution to the company's goals. All employee performance is clearly the remit of the human resourcing function and attention to human resource planning, recruitment, appraisal, development and reward activities, for example, can be found in other chapters. Work performance and staff retention also depend on adjustment to the new environment and culture, and establishing constructive relationships with new colleagues. Again, this will apply to all employees, domestic as well as international. The main difference in the expatriate's experience is that typically such adjustments are likely to be more demanding and may revolve around the family's inability to adapt. Furthermore, the cost of expatriate failure is very expensive in terms of lost investment. The direct cost of maintaining an expatriate overseas may exceed four times normal salary. Indirect costs may include lost sales, reduced productivity and competitive position, and damage to international networks. It is crucial, therefore, for the relocation process to be managed effectively in order to reduce labour turnover and to enhance the expatriate's work performance. This management of the process can be usefully divided into the pre-departure, expatriation and repatriation phases (De Cieri and McGaughey, 1998: 633).

The pre-departure phase

Building on the firm foundations of a systematic approach to human resourcing will help to ensure that the selection, remuneration and training processes utilised in a domestic environment are applied appropriately to the international situation. The selection criteria, including proficiency in the host-country language, can be constructed from an analysis of the job to be undertaken. Individual characteristics such as cultural tolerance and the ability to learn in an alien setting can be added, and many organisations also consider partner and family factors. One key reason for the resistance of employees to international mobility is the disruption of a partner's career or children's education. This leads us to the variable nature of the *inducement–contribution equilibrium*, which describes the calculation that an individual makes before deciding to take up a post or not. The individual will need to perceive that the contribution, effort and sacrifices required of them are balanced by the inducement or rewards on offer. This relates to another reason that employees are reluctant expatriates: the uncertainty surrounding their career on their return. Transnational companies, however, are less likely to invite this concern, since high office is often critically dependent on international experience.

The inducement–contribution equilibrium enables us to appreciate the significance of non-financial as well as financial rewards in the pre-departure phase. An expatriate remuneration package must attract the candidate in the first instance. Thereafter, it must motivate and retain the employee during the expatriation phase. It is important that the package is drawn up at an early stage, and the employee will probably be offered a package that includes base salary, expatriate premium, cost-of-living allowances and additional fringe benefits. Taxation advice is also of prime consideration (De Cieri and McGaughey, 1998: 635). However, a main issue will be that expatriate salaries may strain the organisational objective of fairness and equity for all categories of employees. Perceptions of inequity can demoralise employees. A home-based remuneration policy will ensure equity for the expatriate with colleagues at home, but will alert those in the host location who may be paid different amounts (Adams, 1965). The alternative host-based remuneration policy, however, may cause disquiet for the expatriate. It may well be that the incompatibility between the objectives of fairness and equity and motivation is insurmountable. However, it is perhaps the very complex structuring of expatriate remuneration that will enable a reward system to be designed so that it is perceived as respecting both host- and home-country relativities.

Pre-departure training and development can be equated to pre-assignment training in any domestic situation, and will therefore utilise the practices outlined elsewhere in this text on training needs analysis and programme design. Consequently, training interventions should enable managers to acquire the knowledge, understanding and skills to operate effectively in the host-country. In addition, training opportunities might sensibly be offered for family as well as expatriate orientation. The expatriate may be required to conduct business in the host country language and to develop cultural awareness and interpersonal skills. Both language and cross-cultural training typically entail a huge investment in time and energy, especially if field experience through an initial visit to the host country is considered desirable. Intercultural experiential workshops and sensitivity training are other methods used in cross-cultural training programmes, but it would appear that many companies limit their training to information briefings and the provision of reading material (De Cieri and McGaughey, 1998: 636), thus tempting expatriate failure.

The expatriation phase

Cross-cultural training in the pre-departure phase is designed to assist in the adjustment process during the expatriation phase, but further support mechanisms may also prove vital in ensuring that expatriates and their families can adjust to different organisational and societal cultures. This is important if the expatriate is to work effectively in the host environment, and introduces us to the possible detrimental repercussions associated with *culture shock*, which refers to 'the experience of psychological disorientation by people living and working in cultural environments radically different from that of their home' (De Cieri and McGaughey, 1998: 636). The springboard for these negative feelings is likely to be the way in which a seemingly alien culture challenges people's taken-for-granted assumptions.

Support through the appointment of capable and conscientious mentors at both the local and home sites, regular information from the parent company and social gatherings may help; but assistance with practical problems and building host-country networks will perhaps be more important as expatriates seek to establish a position in their new community. With appropriate support, the highs and lows of the initial 'honeymoon' and 'homesick' stages are more likely to lead to a realistic appraisal of the situation and acceptance of and adjustment to the new environment. The alternative is disenchantment and an inability to cope.

Culture shock and expatriate failure conjure up images of whisky-soused colonials from old black-and-white films. Yet this feature of the relocation process can also occur in a domestic environment. Adjustment can be painful when you are sapped by homesickness, whether or not you are 60 or 6000 miles from home.

The repatriation phase

In a transnational environment, a *repatriate* should be perceived as a valuable member of the parent company and settled into a new position that benefits the organisation because it calls on the knowledge, skills and contacts gained from overseas. In this example, human resource planning for career development has met the needs of both the company and the repatriate. In practice, however, insufficient attention is often paid to ensuring that the repatriate does not suffer from problems of readjustment (Forster, 1994). Having been away from the centre of activity for some time, the repatriate may find that they have been quietly forgotten, that there is no clear role for them. Things have moved on and no one is much interested in their tales from overseas. This can obviously lead to feelings of disillusionment with work and the company, which will not be helped if the repatriated employee and family find that they face similar problems at home.

A planned and positive approach to reentry is clearly preferable; and pre-departure training, repatriation planning, written job guarantees and mentoring may all have a role in sponsoring this approach (De Cieri and McGaughey, 1998: 639). In contrast, initiatives aimed at patching things up after the event, such as counselling, are tackling the symptoms and possibly focusing on the individual rather than the deficient relocation systems. Inadequate repatriation management in particular would have adverse implications for a transnational's human resourcing strategy. Potential expatriates within the company are unlikely to accept an international posting if they perceive the diminished career prospects of repatriates and their indifferent reception. Far better to create a virtuous cycle of a career structure that incorporates international postings. Effective human resourcing would ensure that such an approach would apply equally to host-country and third-country nationals as well. One outcome of this would be the creation of robust and purposeful international networks, which are the lifeblood of the transnational organisation.

Host country employment – contingent factors

In this chapter we have sought to establish a way of thinking about human resourcing and to use a framework for analysing any set of employment circumstances that will equip us in making decisions about the management of an organisation's human resources. We have asserted that the principles underlying this contingency approach hold for both domestic and multinational companies, though we have also identified additional features that strengthen our comprehension of an international version of human resourcing.

We have also seen the different ways in which a host country subsidiary can be viewed and the various implications of this for the employment of host-country nationals (HCNs). This depends partly on the degree to which any notice is taken of host-country conditions and circumstances. Our framework suggests that human resourcing decisions should always rest on a careful and sensitive analysis of contingent factors; but the role of the human resourcing function is neither to defend cultural traditions nor to ignore them. The decisions themselves are matters of human judgement and subject to bounded rationality. In balancing global business needs with local circumstances, human resourcing managers may have to decide 'where and how to push and where to give in to cultural differences' (Pucik, 1998).

The position taken in this chapter is that the analytical consideration of contingent factors is a process that applies equally to both domestic and international situations. It could well be, however, that domestic managers take for granted that their many assumptions about the local workforce are correct. They do not consider the need for 'careful and sensitive analysis of contingent factors'. International managers, on the other hand, may feel rather overwhelmed by the number of host-country factors that are not known or just cannot be taken for granted. This may lead to a concerted effort to conduct an analysis, possibly with the help of a fact file on the country and its ways, and perhaps through a specialist consultant. Unfortunately, much of this analysis starts and ends with environmental factors. These clearly are important influences on human resourcing activities, but can lead unhappily to a concern with national characteristics that detracts from the real focus of attention, the employee. By way of example, a traditional analysis of political and economic factors will examine the country's national systems and their influence on future business investment.

It is proposed, therefore, that human resourcing analysis concerns itself primarily with the employment relationship, since it is this reciprocal connection between employer and employee as buyer and seller of labour that is at the centre of all human resourcing activity.

■ The analysis of local conditions

The employment relationship

For students of the employment relationship, this starting point generates a collection of important variables that together provide a significant insight into the *choices* available to human resourcing decision makers (as outlined in Chapter 1).

The *legal* dimension of the employment relationship is in theory the most transparent of all factors, yet also the most elusive and complicated. Based on experience of the confusion and nuances surrounding British employment law, it is likely that even the least developed of societies will have regulations on contracts of employment and statutory rights that will warrant the advice of an expert. Decisions can then be made as to the level and nature of any legal constraints on the management of human resources.

The *economic* dimension of the employment relationship relates primarily to the terms and conditions of employment that prevail in the local labour market. A study of the financial and non-financial rewards on offer from other employers, and the productive endeavour that might be expected from the employees in return, may enable the subsidiary to recruit and retain suitable employees.

The *political* dimension refers to the balance or indeed the imbalance of power between management and the workforce. While this is likely to vary between organisations, several factors can contribute to the general balance of power in the host country. Those that would generally favour management include high levels of unemployment; low levels of trade union membership; and anti-strike legislation. A balance of power that works in management's favour will provide a greater range of options for human resource decision makers.

The *psychological* contract is defined by the unwritten, often unspoken, expectations that each side has of the other. For example, workers may be expected to give their employer loyalty and commitment in return for job security, recognition and mutual respect. An investigation into our host country may discover that the local workforce has relatively low expectations of the quality of working life and that management can, as a consequence, make greater demands.

The *social* dimension of the employment relationship concerns the actual relations between and within the parties: are they typically detached, affective, informal, deferential, collectivist or individualist? Analysis may detect patterns that identify our host society.

Finally, the *moral* aspects of the relationship define what is considered right and wrong. Some societies may exhibit very prohibitive outlooks on the use of child labour and sexist attitudes and behaviour; others may countenance both activities as acceptable. It is in such areas that those representing the company may be advised not to give in to cultural differences. Indeed, recent cases involving sweatshops and child labour in third-world countries have damaged the reputations of certain sportswear manufacturers. Hasty retreats have served to demonstrate that *ethical* human resourcing is often the best strategy.

Cultural factors

It will already be evident that our schematic analysis of the various dimensions of the employment relationship can help to inform corporate strategists on how a subsidiary's human resources might be managed. It will also be apparent that *all* of the above dimensions both define, and are informed by, the culture of the subsidiary's local community. This partly explains the interest, both academic and practitioner, in studies designed to identify the relevant attributes of national cultures and in comparative frameworks based on a considered view as to the *key* cultural dimensions (Hofstede, 1980, 1991; Laurent, 1983; Trompenaars, 1993; Hall and Hall, 1990). Our approach, however, would be to go beyond (though not to ignore) such broad characterisations of national cultures and to undertake a rigorous investigation into the actual situation affecting the host-country subsidiary. In so doing, we need to be sensitive to the particular values, beliefs, attitudes, expectations and patterns of behaviour as they relate to work and its management in a specific set of circumstances. Our aim, therefore, would be to unearth the relevant features of the host culture as it affects the employment relationship and hence the management of human resources.

→ As previously mentioned, human resourcing decision makers may find it useful to adopt a perspective that has at its centre employee self-interest as it relates to work performance and staff retention. The analysis of the local culture and the consequent design of human resourcing systems (in recruitment, training and rewards, for example) would then be concerned with how employee self-interest is interpreted within that particular culture. By way of illustration, individual self-interest in Asian and Middle Eastern countries is typically (and outwardly paradoxically) promoted through *collectivism*, where any personal success relies on and is gained through an allegiance and obligation to others and to one's circle. This contrasts with *individualism*, which is more obviously indicative of self-interest and is evident in some western societies. Self-interest can also be associated with *particularism:* a system that upholds the interests of friends and family. This is in contrast to one based on *universalism*, where there is a shared understanding that individuals will succeed on merit through a procedure that evaluates everyone according to the same impartial criteria.

In designing systems that enhance work performance and staff retention in an overseas subsidiary, the human resourcing strategist might well decide to amend or modify parent company systems and practices. Any different interpretation of employee self-interest ought therefore to be borne in mind. For example, where it is the local norm to recruit through personal or government connections, as in China, it may be prudent to reconsider the exclusive use of impersonal selection criteria. Similarly, a reward system linking pay to individual performance is unlikely to be effective in an Indonesian subsidiary where 'they manage their culture by a group process, and everybody is linked together as a team' (Vance, 1992: 323). Finally, that office with a window and the best view that we would expect to be earmarked for those with the highest status might not be welcomed in Japan. For a Japanese manager, a seat by the window could imply that 'you have been moved out of the mainstream, or sidelined' (Schneider and Barsoux, 1997: 23).

■ Determining host-country policies and practices

In recognising that the same policies will not produce 'the same effects in different cultural contexts' (Schneider and Barsoux, 1997: 128), we have suggested two broad approaches for human resourcing strategists to formulate policies and practices for host-country subsidiaries. They can do so *ab initio* on the basis of an analysis of the local circumstances impinging on the various dimensions of the employment relationship (see pages 115–16), or by a critical examination of central or corporate human resourcing policies and practices with a view to local modification. It is perhaps the second of the two options that is most likely to appeal to decision makers operating in a transnational organisation. Schneider and Barsoux envisage a management dialogue between headquarters and the subsidiary company, which would help to ensure 'a balance between global integration and local adaptation' (1997: 129). Needless to say, however, such a dialogue is in practice likely to be conducted within an inherently political relationship between the two parties, each with its own vested interests to pursue. Consider the following example of the efforts by the headquarters management of a major American multinational to hold sway over its subsidiary managements. While ostensibly inviting host-country managers to devise human resourcing practices suited to local conditions, there appears to be a clear steer in favour of adopting standards promoted by the centre.

CASE STUDY 4.2

Human resourcing in a major US multinational

Following the corporation's recent development of *best practices in leadership*, group management has sought to implement these globally by providing intensive training sessions around the world for the top managers of its subsidiary companies. The high-profile sessions are designed to promote the new *standards of leadership* by driving home the importance of best practice in leadership, and by demonstrating how they can be applied in business situations for the benefit of subsidiary operations. This executive-level training is complemented by another series of leadership programmes aimed at the next layer of management and devoted to guiding individual behaviour. All of these training interventions are supported by high-quality documentation and access to the various development guides on the company's intranet.

Promotional material for the initiative takes its lead from the group's worldwide house magazine, in which the corporation's group chairman notes that each business unit is being invited to take these best practices, comprising several competencies, and tailor them to fit its own needs. The aim is to weave the standards into each business unit and to implement appropriate managerial behaviours translated for different cultures. In the same article, however, executives operating in the Asia-Pacific region commented that although some of the behaviours were expressed in different ways, their managers had been able to apply them with no major changes. In addition, the corporation's decentralised structure had allowed host-country managements to apply the new standards to their recruitment and selection, succession planning, performance appraisal and culture training.

Activity 4.3

1 What evidence is there to suggest that this multinational company is more *international* than *transnational* in its structure (see pages 102–3)?

2 What conclusions can we draw about the likely effectiveness of this organisation's strategic approach to establishing host-country policies and practices?

■ Maintaining favourable employee relations

In transnational organisations, the intention is to ensure a satisfactory level of corporate consistency while avoiding the undesirable consequences of ill-considered or insufficiently modified human resourcing practices in the subsidiary company. This reflects an understandable management desire to attend to the quality of the employment relationship, so that it promotes rather than undermines the employee contribution that the human resourcing practices are designed to elicit.

From an employee relations standpoint, therefore, a human resourcing decision maker will be concerned with maintaining sufficient goodwill and co-operation within the subsidiary company. This is likely to mean not upsetting local employees through transgressing their cultural norms or expectations. A reading of some illuminating examples of such violations (Schneider and Barsoux, 1997) reveals a host of employee sentiments that are potentially harmful to a constructive employment relationship. Distress, discomfort, frustration, friction, exasperation, alienation, demotivation and disruption are some of the words used to convey the employees' adverse reactions to cultural infringements. Taken together, they indicate the significance of cultural factors in maintaining favourable employee relations within a host-country company. On the one hand, transgressions and misunderstandings ought to be avoided. On the other, management's sensitivity to a host country's work culture might usefully be developed and then harnessed to advance the goals of the organisation.

CASE STUDY 4.3

Saving face in Malaysia

The American manufacturing director of a multinational company in Kuala Lumpur continually affronts the sensibilities of his local Malaysian managers by his habit of putting his feet on the desk. This ignorance and transgression of a cultural taboo make the managers feel awkward and uneasy in the director's presence, and less inclined to act diligently on his instructions. They have also had to get used to his more direct, argumentative and less diplomatic behaviour in management meetings.

However, for reasons of perceived self-interest, employees *do* carry out his instructions and to some extent seem prepared eventually to reconcile themselves to his 'foreign ways'. After all, the director represents the power of management on behalf of the parent company. He retains the authority and legitimacy of his position in spite of his unacceptable behaviour. Not surprisingly, therefore, our American director seems to remain quite oblivious to his impact on employee relations, even though his direct and blunt approach to appraising staff continues to engender hidden resentment from those on the receiving end of any critical comment. In Asia in particular, 'confronting an employee with "failure" is considered to be very tactless and even dangerous' (Schneider and Barsoux, 1997: 141). This is related to the need to 'save face' and to maintain an individual's self-esteem and overall reputation.

By contrast, a previous director from the UK was so conscious of the need to 'save face' that his diplomatically delivered criticisms of staff were often misinterpreted as praise. This did wonders for individual morale, if not for work performance.

Activity 4.4

1 To what extent can we argue that, however inappropriate the behaviour of the American director, its consequences for the subsidiary company are likely to be negligible?

2 What kind of measures would you recommend for ensuring that both types of expatriate director manage their staff effectively?

3 This multinational company is the same as that featured in Case study 4.2. In view of the shortcomings outlined above, what further conclusions can we draw about this organisation's strategic approach to establishing host-country policies and practices?

■ Cross-cultural comparisons – the work of Hofstede

Case study 4.3 helps to illustrate our approach and preoccupation with:

- identifying local organisational conditions, including relevant cultural factors; and
- establishing human resourcing practices for the host-country environment.

As indicated previously (page 116), our investigations and analysis would aim to go beyond those broader studies and typologies that seek to generalise comparatively about national cultures. However, such studies ought not to be disregarded. At the very least, they are likely to increase our awareness of possible cultural dimensions, providing our own organisational research with a convenient starting point and a general guide as to what we might find.

In order to explore the nature and utility of these typologies, we will briefly consider the work of Hofstede (1980, 1991), a Dutch psychologist who has earned a considerable reputation as an international management scholar. By conducting a worldwide survey involving 116 000 employees of IBM, the giant US multinational company, Hofstede was able to show the enduring significance of national cultures in shaping employees' work-related values. Although IBM was renowned for having its own strong corporate culture, there remained 'substantial differences in work-related attitudes and values from country to country, revealed by his extensive and unique sample' (Barsoux and Lawrence, 1990: 8). The underlying national values espoused by the survey's respondents appeared to persist and the implication for management was clear: differences of national culture could not be ignored.

The four dimensions of culture

Through careful analysis based on the values held by people from different countries, Hofstede was able to characterise the differences by reference to just *four key dimensions of culture*: power distance, uncertainty avoidance, individualism/collectivism and masculinity/femininity. Furthermore, he was able to score and rank order each of 53 countries against each of these key dimensions. This simplification of a potentially overwhelming number of cultural differences, combined with the quantitative reassurance of league tables featuring many different countries, might help to explain the attraction for management of Hofstede's typology. In addition, his value survey model appears to offer information that is sufficiently systematic, comprehensive and relevant for a managerial audience keen to make use of demanding yet accessible ideas. 'From a practical perspective, the cultural variables described by the model are intuitively appealing because of their apparent relationship to the management process' (Punnett, 1998: 20).

Through the work of Hofstede, the human resourcing decision maker can seek to locate a particular host country on each of the four cultural dimensions with a view to establishing the implications for management practices. A clearer indication is more likely where a country scores at the extreme end of a continuum, though it has to be acknowledged that most countries score neither very high nor very low on these indices.

Power distance indicates the extent to which people in a particular culture accept and expect the existence of power differences within organisations and institutions. In a country ranked high on this dimension (Malaysia is ranked highest), organisations are likely to have more levels of hierarchy and greater centralised control, with little reference to employees for decision making. Status and power would be viewed as appropriate reward mechanisms, since those in authority are treated with the deference that is considered their due. At the other end of the spectrum (Austria followed by Israel), power differences in organisations are minimised and employees are more likely to participate in management decision making.

Uncertainty avoidance refers to the extent to which people feel uncomfortable with uncertainty and ambiguity. In a country where this sentiment is generally high (Greece is ranked highest, closely followed by Portugal), people look for certainty and predictability in their lives. In work organisations, these might be secured through the precision of written rules and procedures; a reliance on specialist expertise; and a preference for planning to minimise risk taking. In terms of work motivation, staff are likely to be especially interested in stability and security (Schneider and Barsoux, 1997: 79). By contrast, in a host country where uncertainty is seen as inevitable (Singapore exhibits the lowest levels of uncertainty avoidance, followed by Jamaica and Denmark), opportunities for innovation and change are typically welcomed and there is a greater acceptance of individual decision making and risk taking.

Individualism relates to the degree to which people in a particular country accept the pursuit of individual self-interest and value the effort and initiative associated with taking personal responsibility for decision making and task completion. This contrasts with *collectivism*, at the other end of the continuum, where the emphasis is on group co-operation and decision making and where group consensus and loyalty are valued. As an example, such cultural differences have clear implications for reward management. Rewards based on individual effort should be more effective in the most individualist societies (the USA is closely followed by Australia and the UK). Those based on team effort should prove more appropriate for the most collectivist societies (Guatemala, Equador, Panama and Venezuela). At the same time, however, this particular cultural dimension is likely to affect most if not all facets of the human resourcing armoury.

Masculinity serves to describe a bias towards the values of assertiveness, competitiveness, performance, ambition, achievement and materialism. In Japan, which is ranked highest on this dimension, we might expect to find work organisations dominated by these task-centred characteristics and an emphasis on organisational success. *Femininity* refers to the opposite end of this continuum. It portrays those values that give priority to the quality of life, relationships and the environment; and it expresses a concern for those people considered less fortunate. Sweden, Norway, The Netherlands and Denmark (in that order) are ranked highest on this dimension, and managements in these countries might be expected to devote some of their attention to 'satisfaction with work and [the] development of a congenial and nurturing work environment' (Punnett, 1998: 21).

Using Hofstede's value survey model

Where the human resourcing decision maker is most interested in a particular host-country culture, this will be represented by a specific combination of its ranking and score on each of the four dimensions. Consequently, any interpretation of Hofstede's results may need to be more holistic than his model perhaps permits. Nevertheless, some conclusions can be drawn, as the following example of Singaporean culture indicates:

> Singapore as a society is collectivist, does not avoid uncertainty, believes in power distinctions and is relatively low in masculinity. This suggests a paternalistic leadership system, with the leader expressing concern for subordinates and the quality of life, but without undue concern for job security. (Punnett, 1998: 19)

While this type of national portrait is helpful in alerting us to possible cultural similarities and differences between host and parent countries, the human resourcing strategist would be well advised to assume that this represents no more than a general guide and a convenient starting point for further organisational research and analysis. This makes allowance for the cultural diversity that may reside in a single nation and recognises that 'any culture is far more complex than such models would suggest' (Punnett, 1998: 21). In just the same way that an organisation based in Nottingham, for example, might be characterised as *feminine*, so another Nottingham company in a different industry could quite accurately be labelled as *masculine*.

The question can also be raised of how representative and accurate are the model's descriptions of national culture as a whole. Since the study involved only IBM employees, there is a strong possibility that the scores reported by Hofstede for these particular respondents are 'an indication of the similarities and differences that one might expect to find among employees in this type of organisation in different countries' (Punnett, 1998: 19). Furthermore, any attempt to encapsulate all national cultures within just four key dimensions raises concern about whether important cultural variables might have been overlooked.

Notwithstanding these concerns, Hofstede's work should offer the discerning practitioner some useful concepts and insights. Furthermore, its focus on national cultures might well provide an appropriate *beginning* for the kind of organisational research that we have been advocating, leading to the comprehensive analysis of contingent factors and the subsequent establishment of host-country employment arrangements. However, our approach should not be restricted to host countries. As we have argued, domestic and international human resourcing are the same in all fundamentals. They also share the same essential methodologies and have access to the same portfolio of methods, techniques, systems and procedures – many of which can be gleaned from this book. It is on this basis that this chapter has directed its attention to those *international* aspects of human resourcing that might be considered as in some way distinctive.

CASE STUDY 4.4

The Bee-K-Gee Corporation

As recently as five years ago, the Bee-K-Gee Corporation, a well-known American confectionery manufacturer, was managed as a US company with overseas operations. The USA was the main market for Bee-K-Gee's range of chocolate bars, accounting for 75 per cent of the company's sales income. As a consequence, its overseas companies in some 60 countries were managed in an American way. Since then, however, the corporation has strenuously sought to promote its global presence, especially through expansion into emerging markets in Asia, Africa, Latin America and Eastern Europe. The corporation now operates in over 80 countries, which account for almost half of its sales income; and the present strategy emanating from its Baltimore headquarters is for Bee-K-Gee to be seen as a truly global enterprise. With over 16 000 employees based overseas from a total headcount of 35 000, a US-centric attitude has been adjudged to be no longer appropriate for a corporation with such global intentions.

Today, Bee-K-Gee is organised into six regional groups: North America, the European Union, Asia-Pacific, the Middle East, Africa and Latin America. Each region is seen as an autonomous entity though part of the global corporation. The aim is to link the regions and their business units by a corporate mindset to think globally and act locally. By being more sensitive to host-country differences while following corporate values, headquarters management intends to combine global integration with local responsiveness and to banish any trace of its US-centric approach. Its new emphasis is to allow the managers of its foreign subsidiaries to act in keeping with local conditions, including local laws and local cultures.

One aim, therefore, is to employ as many *host-country nationals* as possible, as they are considered to be generally better equipped to operate in their home locations. However, with the ongoing expansion there has been a significant need for *parent-country nationals* to oversee the new start-up operations. This includes recruiting and training suitable local employees, ensuring that they adhere to the corporate mindset and delivering a competitive business operation within two years. Expatriate Americans might also be relocated to a foreign subsidiary for their own development. International exposure is increasingly being regarded as a prerequisite for senior management responsibility in the company. Currently, half of the company's top executives have been expatriates at one time or another, but only the head of human resourcing is not an American national. Furthermore, Bee-K-Gee employs very few *third-country nationals* and there is little evidence as yet of host-country nationals being developed for high-level corporate jobs. Corporate management sees this as very much a legacy of the company's 'US-centricity', a situation it is seeking to remedy through, for example, a global succession planning initiative.

Over the past four years the corporation has recruited nearly 4000 additional overseas employees. This expansion, involving numerous start-up operations, has made heavy demands on the corporate human resourcing function in Baltimore; directly through staff secondments and indirectly through the appointment and support of expatriate managers. In addition, the role of the central function has been to offer *all* of the company's subsidiaries ongoing support. Guided by the doctrine of respecting local cultures while staying true to the corporate culture and vision, headquarters HR provides subsidiary managements with the following:

1 A clear direction on corporate human resourcing policies and principles, encouraging and enabling host-country managers to act locally while thinking globally.

2 A set of 'best-practice' human resourcing procedures and methods so that local managers do not need to 'reinvent the wheel' and which they can adopt and adapt as they see fit.

3 Expert advice, hands-on assistance and decisions on issues needing corporate consistency on the treatment of employees.

The headquarters human resourcing function is assisted in these aspects of its role by the following:

1 Regional human resourcing specialists who provide a link between local operations and head-quarters and often undertake the support activities outlined above. These specialists have been trained to ensure horizontal integration of activities in a way that reinforces the global–local philosophy.

2 A two-week orientation programme for human resourcing practitioners and managers worldwide who have recently joined the corporation. Held at headquarters at considerable expense, this training and development event is designed to cover all of the above human resourcing arrange-ments. Attendance is restricted to 100 at a time and interactive delivery methods are favoured, as these also help to build up an international network of contacts.

3 Additional communication through the company's worldwide newsletter and a newly installed intranet system.

4 Efforts within the function itself to think more globally and to be taken seriously within the com-pany. The function has been helped considerably by the influence of its executive head, Charles Barthes. A Frenchman with excellent international credentials, it is quite usual for Barthes to visit up to 10 countries a year to offer support and direction. He is also a close asso-ciate of Dan Levy, Bee-K-Gee's chairman and chief executive officer, and is accorded immense respect at executive meetings where discussion on global strategy takes centre stage.

Perhaps more than anyone, Barthes understands that the human resourcing task has much fur-ther to go if the function is to attain his ideal global–local balance. In his view, the initial move from a US-centric approach to a decentralised structure had to be a radical one. Future initiatives, how-ever, will need to redress the balance towards the global dimension in order to deliver greater corporate consistency and fairness, and to take better advantage of pooled resources and exper-tise. Global approaches to staff development, succession planning and competencies are all being proposed as possible corporate initiatives. Barthes contends that all of these need not be incompatible with a continuation of local management autonomy in the host-country subsidiaries.

Activity 4.5

1 Using concepts from the chapter, analyse and explain the rationale behind the present and proposed human resourcing approaches adopted at Bee-K-Gee.

2 In your view, to what extent has the human resourcing function mastered the balance between global integration and local responsiveness? What advice would you offer Charles Barthes at this point?

3 One year on and Bee-K-Gee is set to announce the closure of its well-established Scottish subsidiary, which employs nearly 300 (non-unionised) staff. This follows the decision to centre production in its Belgian plant, arising from reduced demand in Europe's highly aggressive product market. What damage might this do to the Bee-K-Gee Corporation? How might the human resourcing function minimise any unfavourable repercussions?

Summary

In this chapter the following key points have been made:

- The globalisation of the world's business economy has been particularly significant for the UK, resulting in an increase in the importance of, and interest in, international human resourcing.

- A comparative analysis of international and national human resourcing indicates that in all essentials they share the same characteristics. Consequently, a grasp of international human resourcing builds on, rather than replaces, our understanding of the practice of human resourcing in the UK.

- Our framework suggests that human resourcing decisions should rest on a careful analysis of contingent factors, with the implication that any differences between international and national human resourcing will be a matter of degree only.

- Those responsible for managing across national boundaries are likely to encounter a greater range and a less familiar set of contingent factors. It is this particular aspect that gives the *impression* that the international version of human resourcing is in some way distinctive.

- International human resourcing is conducted within a multi-unit business organisation that operates in several countries, giving rise to conflicts and tensions associated with the inherently political relationship between managements of the parent company and its overseas subsidiaries.

- Parent-company strategy makers can decide to manage human resources somewhere on a continuum between two distinct choices: either through a decentralised structure with an emphasis on local autonomy and responsiveness; or through a centralised human resourcing function with its emphasis on global integration.

- Human resourcing strategists are showing more interest in securing the advantages of combining both of the above approaches by 'thinking globally and acting locally'.

- Measures that might contribute to a global–local approach include: ensuring a two-way flow of communication between the centre and its foreign subsidiaries; building a distinctive corporate culture; and the design of human resourcing systems and procedures by the centre for consideration by each subsidiary.

- International human resourcing practitioners will be constrained and guided in their operational activities by the strategic choice that has been made or has emerged for their own multinational company.

- A contingency model suggests three sets of strategic choices in relation to the multinational company: its structural form; the dominant management orientation; and staffing arrangements.

- A useful fourfold typology of the structure of multinational companies shows a development from a decentralised *multinational* pattern to a centralised *global* pattern. Subsequent efforts to achieve a global–local structure are seen in the *international* form, which has been superseded as the 'ideal solution' by the *transnational* structure.

■ An analysis of the dominant management orientation towards different national cultures has produced a fourfold classification comprising the following orientations: *polycentric*, which recognises the validity of each national culture; *ethnocentric*, which regards the culture of the home country as superior; *geocentric*, which does not differentiate between employees on the basis of national culture and which recognises the value of cultural diversity; and *regiocentric*, which views national cultures in terms of the company's worldwide regions.

■ The human resourcing function can help develop a geocentric way of thinking or *global mindset* across the multinational company through a mix of human resourcing levers that include initiatives in training, rewards and staffing. Attention to the horizontal integration of these activities is essential.

■ The overall approach to staffing the multinational company determines the degree of attention given to parent-country nationals (PCNs), host-country nationals (HCNs) and third-country nationals (TCNs); and to the flows of staff within and between the units of the company.

■ In the ideal transnational organisation, all three groups of employee are likely to work in more than their own home country and will be subject to international transfers, as *expatriates*, *inpatriates* or *transpatriates*.

■ The process of employee relocation must be effectively managed throughout the pre-departure, 'patriation' and repatriation phases in order to minimise problems of adjustment to changing circumstances and to enhance work performance.

■ A careful investigation of host-country conditions and circumstances will help determine how a subsidiary's human resources might be effectively managed.

■ Human resourcing policies and practices can be formulated *ab initio* on the basis of an examination of the local employment relationship in terms of its legal, economic, political, psychological, social and moral dimensions. A second approach is to amend or modify parent-company practices in the light of contingent factors. Both approaches will need to be informed by an understanding of the local culture as it relates to work and its management.

■ Attention to cultural factors will help maintain favourable employee relations and avoid those negative employee sentiments and actions that can arise from transgressing local norms and expectations.

■ Comparative studies and typologies of national cultures, such as that by Hofstede, are understandably appealing to a management audience. However, the human resourcing decision maker would be well advised to treat these studies with caution.

■ Hofstede's work may be useful as a general guide, but should ideally be no more than a starting point for a comprehensive analysis of specific factors and circumstances affecting the foreign subsidiary.

Discussion questions

1 How can we account for the increasing significance of international human resourcing in the UK?

2 To what extent can it be argued that there are no essential differences between the international and national forms of human resourcing when the actual experience of working overseas is so obviously different?

3 What conflicts and tensions are likely to exist between the managements of a parent company and its overseas subsidiaries? How might they be successfully managed?

4 What is the attraction for a human resourcing strategist of working towards a transnational-geocentric approach for their multinational company? What practical measures can be taken to ensure that this approach is not just an unattainable idea?

5 How useful is the concept of the inducement–contribution equilibrium for human resourcing practitioners faced with identifying and posting staff to Australia and Cambodia respectively?

6 Employing a cost–benefit analysis, what assistance would you recommend for a group of design engineers who are scheduled to be 'inpatriated' to their UK parent company from the USA for up to two years?

7 How useful is Hofstede's fourfold classification for establishing the employment arrangements in an overseas subsidiary?

Further reading

This chapter sets out to provide a framework and methodology to help practitioners understand and tackle international human resourcing issues, including the ability to assess the appropriateness and utility of human resourcing practices that are covered elsewhere in the book. The reader is encouraged, therefore, to refer to those chapters that deal with any pertinent human resourcing activities. These chapters represent a valuable and convenient source of information to supplement and support the contingency approach advocated for international human resource strategy making.

A concise but informative text that covers the major human resourcing activities from an international perspective is that by Dowling *et al.* (1994). A comprehensive account of the personnel issues posed by internationalisation can be found in the text edited by Harzing and Ruysseveldt (1995). A thematic approach is taken by Torrington (1994), which the author supplements with organisational case studies.

Finally, two books that focus on cultural issues and their management are Adler (1997) and Schneider and Barsoux (1997).

Part II

HUMAN RESOURCING POLICIES IN PRACTICE

5

ASSESSMENT, SELECTION AND EVALUATION
Problems and pitfalls
Sue Newell and Chris Rice

6

PERFORMANCE MANAGEMENT AND PERFORMING MANAGEMENT
Colin Fisher

7

PERFORMANCE PAY AND PERFORMING FOR PAY
Lynette Harris

ASSESSMENT, SELECTION AND EVALUATION
Problems and pitfalls

Sue Newell and Chris Rice

OBJECTIVES

Having completed this chapter and its associated activities, readers should be able to:

- emphasise the centrality of assessment, selection and evaluation processes to management in general, and human resourcing in particular;

- see assessment, selection and evaluation as a learning process, which is inherently emergent and subjective;

- review, briefly, epistemological options in the field of behavioural science;

- critically consider the importance of the validity of different methods of selection;

- consider the importance of different levels of criteria in assessment;

- emphasise the importance of individual perceptions and constructs in all assessment processes;

- develop a 'healthy scepticism' regarding both management theory and received HR wisdom.

Selection is about making choices between different alternatives. We have to make selections continuously in our lives. This evening you may well have to select what to eat for dinner, select whether to go out or stay in, select what time to go to bed and so on. These selections will be made on the basis of our assessment of the likely outcomes of each potential choice. Many of the selections that we make on a daily basis involve selecting between people – whom to date, whom to go to lunch with, whom to ask help from etc. Therefore, we have to make assessments about other people – which of these potential 'others' will be friendly, interesting, sympathetic, fun and so on. The problem of *assessing* people, their actions, motivations and satisfactions, is fundamental to the behavioural sciences. As we will see in this chapter, it is full of problems and potential pitfalls. Moreover, once we have made a decision (selected a particular person for a date, for example), there is also the issue of *evaluating* how effective that decision was – was the person we thought would be fun and interesting actually like that on the date? Again, however, as we will see, evaluation is often very difficult if we are going to do it effectively. The aim of this chapter, then, is to enlarge the horizon of those readers who have not been subjected to extensive training in the behavioural sciences. This is done by raising issues and questions, which should encourage critical questioning of many of the assumptions implicit in current managerial teaching in relation to assessment, selection and evaluation.

Introduction

Management is about making decisions and in this book it is proposed that these decisions may be the fundamental element, or underlying building block, of strategy making. Assessment, selection and evaluation are fundamental aspects within any decision-making process, permeating all stages of the process – we *assess* a number of books we might read, *select* one that looks good, and then *evaluate* our selection on the basis of the enjoyment we had in reading the book. This chapter concentrates on assessment and evaluation in relation to personnel selection decisions. That is, decisions about whom to employ, whom to promote, whom to reassign, whom to train, and sometimes even whom to dismiss, for example when a company is going through a redundancy programme. While this chapter tends to focus on selection decisions in respect to the employment of new personnel, many of the issues discussed are relevant to the other types of personnel selection decisions, and indeed to assessment, selection and evaluation in the broader management domain.

There is an extensive literature on the subject of 'personnel selection', but before exploring this literature *per se* let us look at the field through two different lenses. This provides an introduction to alternative ways of examining the bundle of techniques that we commonly think of as personnel selection.

Two different perspectives on selection

The 'normal' human resourcing position regarding recruitment and selection is to assert that it is perhaps the most basic of personnel activities – if we get the wrong people in the organisation, we will get problems. The symptoms of these problems may emerge as high labour turnover, absenteeism, disciplinary problems, disputes and low productivity. Having the 'right' people in the organisation is crucial. The notion of the 'right' people, by inference, means that there are 'wrong' people, and this indicates that differences between people are relevant for organisations. Indeed, our daily observations of others provide us with ample evidence of the many ways in which individuals differ. At the most obvious level, people differ in their physical appearance, but we also recognise psychological differences – in terms of personality, abilities, motivation, emotion and so on. It is also very obvious that jobs and organisations differ and that therefore some individuals will be more suited to some jobs/organisations than others. The traditional view was that, given these differences in individuals and jobs/organisations, recruitment and selection should be thought of as a process by which the organisation (or at least its managers) matched the individual to the job.

The objective of the selection system is, then, to get the right people into particular jobs. The emphasis here is usually on the word *right* – 'too good' may pose as many problems as 'not good enough'. It is generally accepted that the process can be made more systematic by adopting the following sequence of activities:

1 Define the job – in terms of tasks and responsibilities.

2 Define the ideal candidate – in terms of the type of person most likely to be able to carry out the defined tasks and responsibilities effectively.

3 Attract good applicants.

4 Measure applicants – using a variety of measures that provide data that can be used to assess differences between applicants (these measures of relevant individual differences are referred to as the *predictors*).

5 Selection decision – choose those candidate(s) who have the personal profile most similar to the defined ideal candidate profile.

6 Evaluation – measure selected employees' performance on the job and decide whether the predictors that have been used are in fact related to job performance (this measure of job performance is referred to as the criterion).

Throughout this systematic approach we are describing a choosing process. Basically, the idea is that it is possible to define an 'ideal candidate' profile, based on a systematic analysis of the job demands, and then to measure potential employees in order to choose that candidate who most closely 'fits' this ideal profile. Selection thus involves a number of logical steps, with objective assessments being made at each step, which results in a rational decision where the 'best candidate' is offered the job.

In this chapter it is argued that this systematic or systemic approach to selection provides an inaccurate view of what really happens, because assessment of people and jobs can never be entirely objective. Instead, a processual perspective of selection is presented. It is argued that adopting a processual perspective not only provides a more accurate picture of the true nature of selection, but that this perspective can also increase our understanding so that selection decisions are improved (for a fuller comparison of a systems and processual perspective, see Chapter 2). Next, the systemic and the processual perspectives on selection are examined in more detail.

■ The traditional, systems approach to selection

In this traditional, systemic approach, the focus is very much on the 'job', which is portrayed as a set of discrete tasks. Job performance on these tasks is the criterion, that we are attempting to predict. Prediction is based on identifying individual attributes of various kinds that are considered likely to influence this criterion behaviour. Another term for this traditional approach to selection is the criteria-related predictive validity approach, because the goal is to achieve a high correlation between the predictors (the measures of individual attributes) and the criteria (the measures of job performance).

In metaphorical terms, the systemic approach attempts to select a square peg (the 'right' individual) from a set of non-square, multi-shaped pegs (the 'wrong' individuals) to fit a square hole (the job) (*see* Fig. 5.1). Taking this approach, jobs are defined in terms of their tasks (job description) and, then, the characteristics of the person who will be able to carry out these tasks successfully are specified (person specification). Recruitment is a process of attracting individuals who might meet this specification. Selection is the process of measuring differences between these attracted candidates to find the person who has the profile that best matches the person specification as indicated by the job profile – in Fig. 5.1, Candidate C would be chosen, being the best match.

Another way of thinking about this approach is to visualise it as a hurdles race between the candidates. The organisation that is 'doing the selecting' puts up increasingly high hurdles over which the candidates must jump. Each hurdle represents a competence that is deemed necessary for the job incumbent. The first, lower hurdles, are those competencies that are deemed essential for the person to have. If you can jump these, you are assessed on other competencies that are less central but still seen as useful. The individual who can demonstrate the greatest number of competencies that are deemed essential or useful (that is, can jump the most hurdles with the greatest clearance) is given the job. Thus, if the job involves gathering numerical data from various Internet sources and manipulating these in complex mathematical ways to arrive at business forecasts, the 'right' individual is likely to have high numerical ability, to have computing expertise through previous experience or education, and to be a fairly introverted personality (as there will be little personal contact in that particular job). Assessment will focus on measuring candidates in terms of these desired characteristics.

The problem with this view of selection is that it assumes that there is 'one best way' to do a particular job – hence the person specification. Just because the previous job incumbent did the particular job in a certain way, the assumption will typically be that

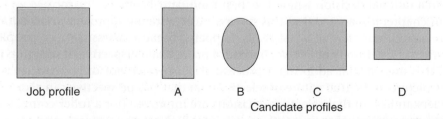

Job profile A B C D

Candidate profiles

Fig. 5.1 The traditional, 'psychometric' view of the selection process: fitting a square peg to a square hole

it is necessary to find a similar 'square peg' to replace them. This can result in unfair discrimination. So recruitment and selection are about discriminating between individuals, but based on relevant and so fair criteria like ability, rather than irrelevant criteria like sex, race or disability. However, given the 'one best way' assumption, unfair discrimination and prejudice can be the result even when focusing on seemingly relevant criteria like ability. To take the example above, the job involved forecasting but whether this had to be done, or was indeed best done, in the way described is problematic. Recruiting a less numerically biased, more extroverted individual might lead to a very different way of carrying out the tasks – for example, talking to people about what they predict will happen rather than basing their decisions on the manipulation of remotely accessed published data. Using the systemic approach to selection, the tendency is to perpetuate the status quo, which restricts certain groups who have been previously under-represented in particular jobs, for example black women in senior management positions.

This systemic view of selection also presents a very static picture of the job. It underestimates the degree of change within organisations (Atkinson, 1984). Jobs change continuously in response to changes in the environment, so that the 'square hole' today may well be a 'round hole' next year, requiring very different knowledge, skills and attitudes. Moreover, this view also presents a static view of the individual. It overestimates the personal criteria that influence job performance and underestimates the role or situational demands. Thus in many jobs role expectations are so strong that individuals have limited flexibility in how they behave. Moreover, individuals can and do change as a result of job experiences (Illes and Robertson, 1997). Finally, this approach assumes that it is possible to measure relevant differences between individuals in the same kind of objective way as physical differences between individuals can be assessed. Thus, I can measure my height accurately with a tape measure and the assumption is that I can also measure my verbal or numerical ability or my personality accurately with a test of some kind. All of these assumptions can be questioned and this is precisely what adopting a processual perspective achieves.

■ The exchange, processual approach to selection

The assumptions of the traditional, systemic approach to selection are therefore no longer appropriate (if indeed they ever were) and a different approach is required. Herriot (1984) has long been arguing the need for change. His view of selection presents a very different metaphor of the process – an exchange or negotiation between two parties, the employing organisation and the potential recruit. Both of these parties have a set of expectations related to their current and future needs and values. Selection is portrayed as a series of episodes in which increasing amounts of information are exchanged to determine whether there is indeed compatibility between the organisation and the individual. Negotiation is possible because neither the organisation nor the individual is seen as having fixed characteristics, although the underlying values and needs of both sides are seen to be more stable. The outcome of this process, if successful, is that a viable psychological contract is negotiated that encapsulates congruence between the expectations of both parties. However, if the process of negotiation breaks down because the parties are unable to develop this sense of congruence, this can also be construed as

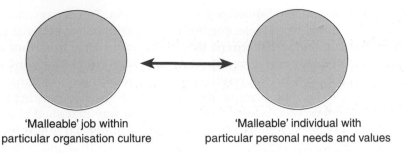

'Malleable' job within
particular organisation culture

'Malleable' individual with
particular personal needs and values

Fig. 5.2 Recruitment and selection as a process of exchange and negotiation

positive – or, in Herriot's terms, 'valid negative' – because in this way the organisation avoids employing someone who will not fit within the organisation and the candidate avoids taking on a new job for which they are not suited.

So both the systemic and the processual approaches emphasise 'fit' between the person and the job environment (Schneider *et al.*, 1997). However, in the former, systems case it is based on fixed dimensions of both the job and the person, with the organisation's management having the sole prerogative to determine the 'fit'; while from the latter, processual perspective, 'fit' is the outcome of a process of exchange and negotiation in which both parties make decisions. Moreover, in the former case, 'fit' is assumed between the personal characteristics of the individual and the technical demands of the particular job (person–job fit). In the latter, 'fit' relates to the matching of expectations and needs of the individual with the values, climate and goals of the organisation (person–organisation fit) (Ostroff and Rothausen, 1996).

This contrast between the systemic and processual views of selection is directly analogous to the contrast between the mainstream and processual views of strategy making presented by Watson in Chapter 1. There the metaphors used to contrast these two views of strategy making were of architecture (very similar to the square peg, square hole metaphor used in this chapter) versus crafting (very similar to the negotiation metaphor used here). Thus, the mainstream view of strategy making is that it involves producing plans that are subsequently implemented. In exactly the same way, the systemic view of selection is that it involves producing specific job specifications (the plans) and then finding the person to 'fit' this specification. On the other hand, the processual view of strategy making outlined by Watson is clearly aligned to the exchange view of selection. Thus, the exchange view sees selection decisions as emerging from complex processes of interaction between the candidate and the organisation. Indeed, we could use the same words to describe the processes. Thus, exchanging the word 'strategies' for 'selection decisions' we could write: '*selection decisions* are outcomes of human interpretations, conflicts, confusions, guesses and rationalisations rather then clear pictures unambiguously traced out on an engineer's drawing board'.

Reviewing the systematic approach to selection

In general, the route to successful selection is held to lie in following a systematic approach such as that outlined and, where humanly possible, avoiding 'hunches'.

1 How adequate is this systematic approach?

2 Think of a job with which you are familiar – are there alternative ways of carrying out this job that might be equally effective?

Selection and learning

One way of looking at the exchange approach to selection is to consider it as a learning process. This also helps us to understand the limitations of the traditional, systems model of selection. This section begins by adopting the traditional, systems view of selection and identifying the problems associated with this approach using the lens of learning.

When a manager assesses somebody in order to make a decision about, for example, their suitability for a particular job, the manager is, in effect, attempting to learn something about this other person – their attitudes, abilities, personality, motivation etc. The manager then uses this information to decide whether they fit the job requirements. Perhaps the most influential idea in the field of learning theory as applied to management is the contribution of Kolb *et al.* (1974). Kolb developed the 'experiential learning cycle' to describe the learning process. This sees learning as a perpetual process in that the output of one cycle (testing or experimentation) provides the experience that begins the cycle again. This approach is generally referred to as 'experiential learning' and is based on a learning cycle as shown in Fig. 5.3.

The core idea here is that people are cognitive beings who are learning from experience and making assumptions regarding the world in which they operate. Learning is

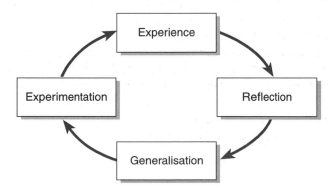

Fig. 5.3 Kolb's learning cycle

thus seen as an incremental process. This model can be applied to the learning that takes place during the selection process:

■ *Concrete experience*: This refers to any experience, either planned or unplanned. In selection it could be applied to the experience (either direct or indirect) that the manager has of the job to be filled and of candidates during the various selection episodes (which will be discussed in more detail later). Examples are reading about candidates from application forms, listening to their responses in interviews, reviewing their responses to psychometric tests, observing their behaviour during group exercises and so on.

■ *Reflective observation*: This stage refers to the cognitive process of thinking about or reflecting on the experience – trying to make sense of the experience. This will involve attempting to understand the causes of what was observed. In selection, it relates to the reflection by the assessors on the assessees' behaviour during the various selection episodes.

■ *Abstract conceptualisation and generalisation*: This stage relates to the conclusions that are drawn from the review process. The assessor will generalise from their reflections about each of the candidates involved as to their suitability for the particular job and then make the selection decision.

■ *Experimentation and evaluation*: This involves transferring the experience to other situations. In selection, this stage could be seen as the evaluation of the decision made – that is, evaluating whether the person actually chosen for the job has indeed been successful in the job. To the extent that the person has not been successful, a new cycle will be activated, perhaps using different selection methods, so that a different range of experience is provided about the candidates.

Kolb's learning cycle is perhaps overly simplistic (Rice, 1993), but it provides a useful vehicle for considering the problems involved in assessment, selection and evaluation. First and foremost, considering assessment, selection and evaluation as a learning process reminds us that there are two parties involved, both making decisions – the manager and the candidate. So the candidate is also gaining experience about the job and the organisation from the different selection episodes; reflecting on what that experience means in terms of what the job will be like and the culture of the organisation; generalising as to whether they feel that this meets their own expectations for a job or career; and then subsequently testing out how far their expectations have actually been met on the job. To the extent that the systemic approach to selection ignores the learning process of the candidate, it presents a limiting view of the whole process. Thus candidates make decisions throughout the selection process – choosing whether to apply for a job, choosing whether to turn up to an interview to which they have been invited, choosing whether to take up a job that they have been offered. Ignoring this side of the learning process is therefore problematic. However, there are also additional limitations in the traditional, systemic approach to selection, which can be considered by looking at each step in the learning cycle in more detail.

■ Experience and impression management

Decisions made about candidates during selection depend on the concrete experiences that are provided. These experiences of the 'target person' (i.e. the candidate) may be indirect (e.g. information from an application form or a personality test) or direct (e.g. behaviour exhibited during an interview or a group exercise). The assumption of the traditional view of selection is that this 'experience' should be systematically designed so that it provides an accurate reflection of *the* person being assessed. That is, the various recruitment and selection methods employed need to be specifically designed to gather the information about the target person that will be relevant to the particular job. Thus if the candidate does not make much of a contribution to a group discussion, it is assumed that this is typical behaviour. The problem with this approach is that it assumes that the target person is passive. In reality, candidates are active, attempting to create a certain image of themselves. This is particularly the case during selection, when it is so obviously a situation in which the candidates' performance is being assessed. The candidates will attempt to create and maintain a particular impression of themselves which coincides with what they believe the assessor is looking for. Thus, to some extent at least, the assessor only sees what the target person wants them to see. This is referred to as impression management (Rosenfeld *et al.*, 1995). A variety of techniques can be used to convey a particular impression, such as ingratiation ('I have always wanted to work for this organisation'), selective description of events (candidate ignoring details of failed assignments in which they have been involved and only giving information on the positive ones), positive descriptions of self ('I am a very self-motivated person') (Arnold *et al.*, 1997).

Not surprisingly, the 'high stakes' nature of the selection situation makes it a setting particularly ripe for impression management (Rosenfeld, 1997). Moreover, it is the selector as well as the candidate who engages in this behaviour – the candidate because they believe it will help them get the job, and the selector because they want to attract the best applicants. For example, Fletcher (1989) found that 25 per cent of survey respondents admitted that they had lied during a job interview.

Research has demonstrated that impression management tactics can influence the perceptions of the selector. For example, Gilmore and Ferris (1989) had interviewers view a videotape in which a female applicant either engaged in impression management tactics (e.g. smiled and complimented the interviewer) or did not. In addition, half the interviewers were given the information that she was well qualified for the job as customer representative, half that she was less qualified. Where the woman engaged in impression management tactics, she was rated as having performed better in the interview than where she had not used these tactics. Ratings were not significantly different dependent on her qualifications. Other research has found that impression management tactics can be overused (e.g. Baron, 1989). This alerts us to the fact that using impression management is not easy during selection, because the applicant must balance being 'confident but not brash, polite but not sycophantic, lively and interested but not voluble and manic, sufficiently nervous to show an appreciation of the importance of the occasion but not visibly anxious throughout' (Fletcher, 1989: 273).

However, individuals differ in their use of these impression management techniques. Snyder (1974) distinguished between high and low 'self-monitors' to reflect the extent to which individuals use cues from the situation to guide their own self-presentation. High self-monitors are those individuals who can more readily adapt their own behaviour to suit the particular situation. On the other hand, low self-monitors tend to behave in ways that coincide with how they feel.

Impression management is inevitable in selection situations. What perhaps is problematic is that some people, perhaps because they are high self-monitors, may have an unfair advantage because of their ability to use these tactics (of course, whether or not it is unfair depends, to some extent at least, on how far impression management is an important requirement for the job). Rather than trying to eliminate, or at least minimise, impression management, as the systemic approach might advocate, the alternative is to recognise it as inevitable. The processual perspective recognises the inevitability of impression management, because selection is viewed as an inherently subjective process of interaction. This perspective would then advocate that attempts are made to level the playing field by providing all candidates with more information about how they are expected to present themselves at the various selection episodes (Herriot, 1984; Fletcher, 1990). Then high self-monitors will be at less of an advantage. This means accepting a processual approach, recognising and trying to understand how both parties (candidates and managers) are interacting to influence the process.

■ Reflection and attribution theory

Once the manager or assessor has some kind of concrete experience of the candidates, they then use this information, reflecting on that experience to form a view of the candidates. This obviously involves a cognitive process of thinking about the experience. While structured checklists can help here so that all candidates are assessed using the same criteria, the process is, by definition, subjective. One way of considering this process of reflection is to consider it in terms of attribution theory (for a good overview of the usefulness of considering attributional processes during selection, see Herriot, 1989b). Attribution theorists begin from the premise that we naturally try and look for the causes of either our own or other people's behaviour. These theorists (dating back to the work of Heider, 1958) have sought to uncover the principles we use in deciding the causes of what happens. Basically, these causes can be narrowed down to two kinds:

1 *Internal causes*: where the outcome is explained in terms of the individual's own behaviour, which may be either in terms of something the individual can control (e.g. effort) or in terms of something the individual cannot control (e.g. ability).

2 *External causes*: where the outcome is explained in terms of something outside the individual him/herself.

For example, suppose that mathematical ability is considered to be an important predictor of job success and a candidate provides information that he failed his maths A level the first time it was attempted. The assessor then looks for explanations of this. She can decide that the failure was due to internal factors, which might be either because the candidate lacked ability or because he did not try hard enough. Or she may decide that it was due to external factors, for example the candidate's teacher was not very good. The type of attribution made will significantly effect what the selector feels she has learnt about the candidate. The external attribution excuses the failure because it was 'not his fault' and so does not reflect on his abilities. The internal, controllable attribution (that it was due to a lack of effort) is not taken as an indication of underlying mathematical ability, although it may still reflect negatively on the overall impression if self-motivation is considered to be a key predictor of job success. The internal uncontrollable attribution (that it reflects a lack of mathematical ability) will lead to the conclusion that this candidate is deficient in a required ability, thereby probably meaning that he will be rejected. So the same information (experience) can lead to very different assessments, depending on the cognitive process of attribution.

The problem is that research evidence demonstrates that there are regular biases in the ways in which we attribute causation. *The fundamental attribution error* refers to the strong tendency to attribute responsibility to the actor – i.e. to infer an internal attribution. We tend to ignore situational factors that influenced the behaviour, at least in western society with its strong emphasis on individual responsibility (Morris and Peng, 1994). The one exception to this is when we are looking at our own behaviour, when we are likely to make the *self-serving error*. That is, when things go well, we accept personal responsibility, but when things go badly, we find 'excuses' in the external environment. So if I do well in my exams it is because of my own effort and ability, but if I do badly it is because of the bad teacher, the lousy textbook, the poor library facilities, the fact that the teacher does not like me etc., etc. . . .

In terms of reflecting on candidate information, it is the fundamental attribution error that is more pertinent. Assessors will tend to assume that the 'data' they have about an individual candidate can be attributed to personal qualities of the individual, rather than seeing it as a reflection of his/her situation. Thus, candidates may wrongfully get the credit for successful performance, either during the selection episodes themselves or from previous history, or may wrongfully get the blame for failures. For example, in an interview situation, the candidate's behaviour is strongly influenced by the behaviour of the interviewer, so that the same interviewee can behave very differently with different interviewers (Dougherty *et al.*, 1994). Or in a group discussion exercise, a normally fairly shy person can appear to dominate because they are working with others who are even more shy, while a fairly dominate person may appear reticent because he is working with a group who are all high on assertiveness.

These biases in perception clearly, therefore, influence what we believe we learn about candidates in a selection situation. There are also other biases in perception, for example the halo effect. This is where we decide we like a person because, for example, they attended the same school as we did, and then view all other information about them through 'rose-tinted spectacles'. The opposite, the horn effect, is also possible, where we decide we dislike someone and then view all subsequent information about them through 'muddy spectacles'. This led Dipboye (1997: 459) to conclude that 'the outcome of these biases in the conduct of the (interview) session is that the information gathered reflects more on interviewer behaviour in the session than the applicant's knowledge, skills, and attitudes.' These biases can never be totally eliminated, but if we acknowledge them as part of the inevitable, subjective process of assessment, we can attempt to minimise the extent to which they have an unfair discriminatory impact on decisions. One way of doing this is to consciously build into the selection process a consideration of the attributions that are being made (Herriot, 1989b).

◼ Generalisation and personal construct theory

Once we have obtained information about candidates and reflected on its meaning, we make the actual decision, generalising from the specific selection situation to predict future job behaviour. The systemic approach assumes that past and present behaviour will predict future behaviour. The processual approach assumes more flexibility on the part of the individual and the job. We can contrast these two approaches by considering the difference between the nomothetic and idiographic views of personality.

The *nomothetic* approach to personality (e.g. Eysenck, 1953; Cattell, 1965) seeks to identify the core characteristics of personality. There are two main approaches here, the type and the trait approach. The trait approach uses bipolar trait continuums, with individuals fitted somewhere along each continuum, e.g. somewhere between extreme introversion and extreme extroversion (Cattell, 1965). The type approach uses 'pigeonholes' into which individuals are fitted, e.g. you are either 'an introvert' or 'an extrovert' (Eysenck, 1953). There is not scope here to compare these two approaches (*see* as an introduction McKenna, 1994). Rather, we are interested in the underlying assumptions of this nomothetic approach. In addition to the assumption that we can all be characterised using the same basic dimensions, the nomothetic approach makes the following assumptions:

1 Personality is relatively fixed, being determined at least in part by hereditary, so that we are born more or less aggressive.

2 Behaviour is a reflection of underlying personality, so we behave in an aggressive way typically because we have an aggressive personality. Obviously, it is recognised that the situation will influence the display of this trait, but if we are comparing two people in the same situation, e.g. a board meeting, differences in aggressive behaviour are seen to be the result of underlying personality.

3 It is therefore possible to predict future behaviour on the basis of past behaviour, given assumptions one and two. So, if we have tended to exhibit aggressive behaviour in the past, then it can be assumed that we will demonstrate these again in the future in situations that encourage this trait to be exhibited. If the organisation is looking for an aggressive manager, it can infer this on the basis both of behaviours exhibited during the selection episodes and from accounts of past behaviour.

Cattell's trait theory of personality is perhaps the best exemplar of this method, and his 16PF is still used to measure people's personality during selection. Cattell used statistical analysis (specifically factor analysis) to reduce the hundreds of trait words that we use in everyday language to a small number of what he called 'source traits'. He believed that these source traits affect the pattern of behaviour that is observable in day-to-day activities. He developed the 16PF to measure the 16 most important source traits. This is a questionnaire that asks a number ($n = 187$) of questions (e.g. 'People don't often get the better of me in an argument') where the respondent has to reply to each question on a Likert-type scale with 'agree', 'uncertain' and 'disagree'. Administration produces a 'sten' (standard ten) score, which places the subject in relation to a normal distribution of respondents. Interpretation is relatively complex (although computer programs are now available that reduce the time and effort involved) and training and proven competence to British Psychological Society (BPS) standards is a requirement for using personality instruments.

Each trait is assessed depending on answers to a number of questions, which indicate the extremity of that particular trait dimension for the individual. In Table 5.1 are the 16 traits as measured by the 16 PF.

Table 5.1 16PF traits

Low score description	1	2	3	4	5	6	7	High score description
Reserved, detached, critical								Outgoing, warm hearted
Less intelligent, concrete thinking								More intelligent, abstract thinking
Affected by feelings, easily upset								Emotionally stable, faces reality
Humble, mild, accommodating								Assertive, aggressive, stubborn
Sober, prudent, serious								Happy-go-lucky, impulsive, lively
Expedient, disregards rules								Conscientious, persevering
Shy, restrained, timid								Venturesome, socially bold
Tough minded, self-reliant								Tender minded, clinging
Trusting, adaptable								Suspicious, self-opinionated
Practical, careful								Imaginative
Forthright, natural								Shrewd, calculating
Self-assured, confident								Apprehensive, self-reproaching
Conservative								Experimenting, liberal
Group dependent								Self-sufficient
Undisciplined, self-conflict								Controlled, socially precise
Relaxed, tranquil								Tense, frustrated

While it is not possible here to reproduce the 16PF questionnaire, you might still find it useful to reflect on how you see your own personality profile by completing the grid in Table 5.1 for yourself.

Activity 5.2

Completing a personality profile

1 Complete the personality grid in Table 5.1 for yourself. If you see yourself as 'reserved' rather than 'outgoing', you might place a cross in box 2 or 3 on the first trait.

2 You could ask someone who knows you well to complete the grid as they see you. Then you can compare the difference. Where there are differences, especially where these place you on a different side of the continuum, why do you think this happened?

3 Now ask someone who knows you in a different context to complete the profile for you (e.g. a parent as opposed to a friend). Again, where there are differences, why do you think this happened?

In reflecting on your experience with the 16PF and the questions it hopefully raised, it is helpful to consider the alternative approach to personality. The *idiographic* approach starts from the premise that the assumptions of the nomothetic approach are unfounded. Personality is not fixed, certainly not fixed from birth. Rather, personality is the outcome of our interactions with other people. So it is the way in which people treat us and respond to us that leads us to develop a particular self-image (Mead, 1934, reproduced in Clark *et al.*, 1994; Rogers, 1970). We then strive to behave in accordance with this self-image. But as our interactions change, so the possibility of our self-image changing is clear. Moreover, as our interactions differ in different situations, so our 'personality' can be expected to differ. So, for example, just imagine what your parents would think if they caught you in certain situations! They may be shocked because your personality at home is somewhat different to your personality when out with a group of friends. An example is the English football hooligans who behaved so badly at the 1998 World Cup in France but who were portrayed as 'upstanding members of the community' back home! The idiographic approach attempts to capture the wholeness and uniqueness of the personality as it functions in a diverse range of situations. An example of this idiographic approach is Kelly's personal construct theory.

Kelly (1955) proposed a useful way of considering both psychology and the processes of perception. His starting point is that people are fundamentally inquisitive and wish to make sense of their world. He suggests that we all conduct our lives rather like scientists – exploring, hypothesising, experimenting, explaining our experiences and predicting the future by developing strategies and procedures (very similar to the ideas underlying management and this book). The term that Kelly uses to describe the units of meaning we develop in order to make sense of the world is *personal constructs*. He suggests that we have personal constructs about all aspects of our lives (including ourselves). These constructs essentially define and make sense of our existence and, once formed, they will be the basis from which we interpret events, experiences and future possibilities.

The emphasis of the idiographic approach is on how we construct our own meaning from our experiences (Spinelli, 1989). The basic insight to emerge from this approach is that no individuals ever share an identical construct, and so their experiences of 'reality' will be unique and separate. For example, if I use the word 'father', this will immediately trigger the reader's unique personal construct of 'father', a construct that will have been formed over a long period of time based on the reader's experience of fathers. If they have a good, positive relationship with their own parents their construct would be very different to that of a person who had been regularly beaten and abused by their father, which in turn may be very different from that of a person who was orphaned at an early age. In other words, your construct of 'father' is uniquely your own, and this will influence your perceptions, reactions and responses every time that word is used.

To explore constructs, Kelly devised what is called the repertory grid technique. In the original format, he would make a series of cards that related, for example, to occupations. These he referred to as the elements; so there would be cards with job titles written on them such as barperson, teacher, accountant, doctor, librarian and so forth. The experimenter chooses three of these at random, shows them to the subject whose constructs are being elicited and asks: 'Which one is different?' When the subject has identified the 'different' one, the next question is: 'In what way is that occupation different to the other two?', thus eliciting a personal construct about occupations. A personal construct always has two poles (or is bipolar), which refer to the way in which two elements are the same (e.g. teacher and nurse are both 'caring') and different from the third element (e.g. as opposed to an accountant who is 'uncaring'). Next, another three cards are chosen at random and the process repeated, with the sole proviso that the same construct cannot be used a second time – in other words, an alternative way of recognising 'difference' between jobs has to be found.

Once the jobs have all been compared and the constructs elicited, they can be placed in a matrix of elements (jobs) against the bipolar constructs. Each job can then be assessed in terms of each of the constructs. In this way, a grid can be developed that allows examination of the ways in which constructs relate or overlap, or of the similarities and differences in perceptions between elements. Clearly, such a technique could be used to establish the dimensions (constructs) that managers use to assess applicants for jobs (or assess existing staff) and the extent to which competing candidates are similar or different.

Doing this exercise has hopefully encouraged you to understand how your interpretation of 'reality' is different from others, which is the essence of the idiographic approach to personality. The idiographic approach is obviously fundamentally different to the nomothetic approach, since the latter assumes that there is a fixed reality that can be measured using systematically developed psychometric 'tests'.

Another way of considering these differences between the idiographic and nomothetic approaches is to consider them in terms of more underlying assumptions about ontology and the associated epistemological perspective. *Ontology* refers to our understanding of 'the nature of being', while *epistemology* refers to our understanding of how we 'can know the world'. Objectivist epistemology rests on the idea that we can know something through independent observation, because it assumes that the world exists independently of our knowledge of it. For the subjectivist, on the other hand, all knowledge is filtered through the knower, whose 'knowing' depends on social and cultural forces that shape the process of interpretation. The objectivist assumes that, as there is a specific reality 'out there', we need to develop theories and test these objectively against that reality. So there is a 'real person', with specific traits that determine how

Activity 5.3

Repgrid exercise: developing personal constructs

It is useful to try an exercise to look at your own constructs regarding different people:

1 Across the top of the grid opposite you see a number of 'people types' – yourself, your partner, your parent, your boss, a colleague you like, a colleague you dislike, yourself as you would like to be. Pencil in the space provided the names of the real people who fit those descriptions in your life.

2 You will see that three boxes have been picked out in bold type in the first horizontal row – corresponding to the characters 'yourself', 'your partner', 'your parent'.

3 Think of the three people you have identified in these boxes – which one is different?

4 Write in the left-hand column the characteristic that makes that person different from the other two.

5 Write in the right-hand space what you perceive as being the opposite of that characteristic. It will help if you avoid using 'closed' constructs such as male, female, bald, etc. wherever possible and use more open, personality-type adjectives.

6 Now work along the next three people (partner, parent, boss) that you have identified and again think about which one is different and identify the characteristic on which they differ from the other two – complete the bipolar construct.

7 Complete the rest of the grid, row by row, following the same procedure – the only limitation is that you should not use the same construct more than once.

8 To score the grid, imagine a rating scale between each bipolar construct from –3 at one end (how one person was different) to +3 at the other end (how the two 'other' people were the same). Go through each bipolar construct for yourself and give yourself a score from –3 to +3 on each construct.

9 Repeat the exercise for the other people in the grid.

10 Now you can look at the grid and see the relationship between the different constructs that you use to describe other people.

Questions

1 What do the relationships look like in your grid?

2 What does that tell you about the way you perceive other people?

3 What might the implications be for your selection processes?

How one is different	Yourself	Your partner	Your parent	Your boss	A colleague you like	A colleague you dislike	Your ideal self	How two are the same

they behave and through the various episodes of selection we must attempt to 'uncover' that real person and assess their fit to the pre-specified job requirements. The subjectivist makes no claims about whether a specific reality exists, because they assume that this can never be known since all knowledge is mediated by experience, i.e. knowledge is socially constructed. So selection is a *process of sense making*. For example, the assessor looks at the candidate not as an object to be measured but as a subject whose meaning is to be appreciated and understood, while simultaneously the candidate needs to make sense of the organisation and the job. Such a view of selection is very different to the 'square peg, square hole' traditional, systemic approach.

■ Experimentation and validity

The final step in the learning cycle is to test out the conclusions from the earlier steps. In terms of selection, what we are interested in at this stage is to see whether the people whom we have selected are indeed the competent employees that we anticipated. The traditional approach saw this very much in terms of job-related (or criteria-related) validity. In other words, were the measures (the predictors) that we used able to predict accurately who would be successful in the job (the criteria)? This is referred to as *predictive validity*. So does our assessment of people during the interview as either potentially 'good' or 'poor' employees actually match (or correlate) with their subsequent performance on the job? The difficulty with this is the length of time that might need to elapse before such studies could be undertaken. We would need to measure applicants, but then ignore this evidence so that a follow-up study could be conducted at a later point to establish whether initial ratings on the selection methods (the predictors) accurately predicted future work performance (the criteria). Ideally, we should employ people randomly so that we have a normal distribution, from those predicted to be 'no hopers' right through to those predicted to be 'stars'. If we only employ those predicted to be 'stars', we can never know for certain whether those predicted to be 'no hopers' would actually fail on the job. However, managers are, understandably, very reluctant to employ people who have been predicted to fail. As a result, predictive validity, although of great importance, is rarely established in practice. The exceptions are in those jobs where large numbers are recruited, such as the armed forces or the Civil Service.

A cheaper and more common approach is to establish *concurrent validity*, which involves establishing the relationship between the predictor measure (e.g. an in-basket test) and some criterion of job training or performance that may be obtained at the same time. Concurrent validity is usually established using current employees, who are asked to complete the proposed in-basket exercise (the new selection method) and then some measure of their job performance is obtained. If there is found to be a relationship between performance on the new selection method and job performance for current employees, then it is assumed that this will also be the case for prospective employees. Thus, if those people who score highly on the in-basket test also obtain high job performance ratings, while those who score poorly on the in-basket test get lower performance ratings, then the test can be considered to have concurrent validity. Establishing concurrent validity is obviously more attractive to organisations, as it allows judgements as to the validity of a measure to be established relatively quickly. Its weakness is the assumption that an existing relationship will predict accurately for the future. It also ignores the fact that current employees do not represent a full cross-section of potential employees, since they have already been selected using past methods. Establishing concurrent validity may, therefore, create a more homogeneous group of employees than is necessary for effective performance. Moreover, given the increasing emphasis on team work within organisations, which depends, at least to some extent, on heterogeneity, this may stifle effective team work and so reduce innovation and creativity (Wiersema and Bantel,1992).

There are other types of validity that can be established (Reber, 1985), but the one that is most important for contrasting the systems and processual views of selection is *face validity*. This refers to whether a measure 'looks right'. The systemic approach would not really consider this important, so under this approach it does not matter whether candidates believe that a particular selection method can (or cannot) predict future performance. The only real question is whether or not it does (i.e. whether it has criteria-related validity). However, from the exchange perspective face validity is important, because it will determine how candidates respond to the various selection methods. For example, graphology (analysing handwriting to assess personality) is a popular selection method in France but is very uncommon in the UK (Shackleton and Newell, 1994). A British candidate asked to provide some handwriting for personality analysis may well find this rather strange. More importantly, this may influence her view of the organisation she is applying, perhaps encouraging her to develop a less positive view of the organisation. The point is not about whether or not graphology can be used as an accurate measure of personality (in fact, the evidence about the predictive validity of graphology is that it is no better than chance). Rather, it is about how candidates' perceptions of a selection method can influence their interpretation of the job and the organisation. As has been seen, this is considered essential from the processual perspective. Indeed, there is now a literature on *impact validity*, which considers how far a measuring instrument has an effect on candidates' psychological characteristics (Robertson and Smith, 1989). Thus, candidates' reactions to a particular method of selection can affect their commitment to the organisation and their personal self-esteem (Illes and Robertson, 1997). From the exchange perspective, therefore, the narrow focus on predictive (or concurrent) validity is restrictive because it ignores how selection methods themselves influence the process of interaction between the candidate and the organisation.

The other problem stemming from adopting the narrow, criteria-related predictive validity approach relates to the issue of the criteria used. Thus, much research on selection has focused on establishing the validity of various selection methods, and there is now a wealth of information about the relative validity of different methods (these will be considered when we look more specifically at the different methods of selection). However, the other issue that is important when we are attempting to evaluate the selection decisions that have been made is to consider the criteria we are using to determine the effectiveness of our measures (Guion, 1997). One evaluation model that is helpful here is that developed by Kirkpatrick (1967). This model distinguishes between different levels of outcomes, including evaluations of 'behaviour' and of 'ultimate outcomes'. That is, Kirkpatrick argued that we need to distinguish between what people do in their particular jobs and how this affects organisational performance. The problem is that the criteria-related predictive validity model (the systemic approach to selection) tends to focus almost exclusively on predicting job performance. However, we might select someone who can carry out the individual tasks of the job very effectively (job performance criteria or 'behaviour'), but who does this in such a way that they antagonise or disturb people in other jobs, who therefore perform less effectively, so that overall organisational performance is inhibited (organisational performance criteria or 'ultimate outcomes').

The reality is that evaluating something is very difficult to do, partly because the criteria we choose can affect the evaluation at which we arrive (Ibbeston and Newell, 1998).

Activity 5.4

Evaluating an academic course

If you were asked to evaluate your course:

1 What criteria would you use?

2 Is it likely that students will all have the same objectives?

3 Are your objectives the same as your tutor's objectives?

4 Are they the same as the university's objectives?

Normally there is a wide divergence between responses to an exercise such as Activity 5.4. It becomes clear that the criteria used in any evaluation are likely to determine the outcome to a large extent, i.e. tutors' and students' evaluations of the course may often be at variance. For example, students may use the criterion of whether the course leads to a good job, while tutors may use the criterion of whether the students can write what is judged to be a good dissertation. Which evaluation do we accept? Similarly, in looking at selection validity, we also need to think about different levels of evaluation.

Smith (1994) distinguished between three types of individual characteristics that relate to job performance: 'universals', which refer to characteristics that are relevant to all jobs; 'occupationals', which refer to characteristics relevant to particular jobs or occupations; and 'relationals', which refer to characteristics relevant in a particular work setting. This typology suggests that it is important to match people's characteristics with the characteristics of particular work settings, and not just with the characteristics of the particular job to be undertaken,. Research has indeed shown that people who 'fit' the work setting are more satisfied and committed compared to people who do not feel they fit (O'Reilly *et al.*, 1991).

Schneider (1987) proposed his attraction–selection–attrition (ASA) model to consider the process through which this fit between personality and organisational environment is established. People with similar personalities will be attracted to particular types of organisation. During the selection process, individuals with characteristics that are similar to those existing in the organisation will be more likely to be chosen. And finally, individuals with individual characteristics that are different to the dominant characteristics will be more likely to leave. Thus, according to Schneider *et al.* (1995), there is considerable empirical evidence that organisations will tend towards personality homogeneity of their employees. However, in a study of the relation between organisational climate and recruiters' perceptions of the 'ideal' personality of new recruits, Van Vianen and Kmieciak (1998) found very little evidence to support the idea that recruitment and selection created homogeneity of personality. Rather, they conclude that:

> Organisational climate is mainly created by homogeneity of behaviour and not homogeneity of personalities. People with different personalities enter the organisation. These people are socialised into the existing organisational climate, which will result in homogeneity of their behaviour. A comfortable fit between the person and the environment (i.e. a successful socialisation) is probably more dependent on the fit between the needs of the person and the fulfilment of these needs by the environment and less on the fit between the person's personality and the environment. (163)

Therefore, 'assessment of person–environment fit in selection should not be based primarily on personality–climate fit but on the fit between the person's needs and organisational practices'. Such a view of selection fits much more easily within an exchange view of the process than within the traditional view.

From the exchange or processual perspective, therefore, the focus on criteria-related validity is too narrow because it treats selection and job performance as discrete entities. Yet it might well be the case that a very competent individual was selected for a position but that their subsequent treatment within the organisation, because it did not meet expectations, has left them feeling demotivated in the job and uncommitted to the organisation. Their performance is therefore likely, to be judged as poor. Focusing on narrow, criteria-related validity may obscure the reasons for the poor performance and lead to the assumption that the methods used to select the individual were not valid. In recognition of this, a growing body of literature is considering selection and performance in a more holistic sense, using the concept of *socialisation* to understand the entire process.

'Selection as socialisation' is the title of a chapter by Anderson and Ostroff (1997), where they argue for an integrative approach: 'We contend that selection and socialisation are facets of essentially the same overarching process – the screening and integration of newcomers into an organisation and their learning of specific knowledge relevant for work role performance' (413). That is, both are stages in a longitudinal process of 'newcomer integration' into both the job and the organisation. They argue that adopting this perspective takes the focus away from narrow job performance prediction to the establishment of a set of congruent expectations between the parties. In this sense, the concern is not so much about how far a particular selection method predicts job performance, but how far this method affects the attitudes and behaviours of candidates (Illes and Robertson, 1997). Anderson and Ostroff developed a typology of selection methods, not dependent on their predictive validity but on the accuracy of the information they convey (Fig. 5.4).

It is only in Quadrant 1 that selection methods actually allow candidates to determine if the organisational context is an appropriate fit, because they are able to develop realistic expectations about the job and the organisation. So while a selection method such as the unstructured interview may have a low predictive validity in the traditional

Organisational message

	Accurate	Inaccurate
Accurate	Quadrant 1 Realistic – correctly construed	Quadrant 2 Unrealistic – correctly construed
Inaccurate	Quadrant 4 Realistic – misconstrued	Quadrant 3 Unrealistic – misconstrued

Candidate perception

Fig. 5.4 Typology of selection methods

sense, it may encourage the beginnings of a negotiation that leads to the development of commitment and adjustment to the organisation. On the other hand, a selection method with a very high predictive validity, for example a structured interview, may actually present a misleading picture of the organisation or even the job so that expectations are encouraged that are not realistic. The person selected may then possess the narrow competencies for the job, but because of unmet expectations may leave the organisation in any case.

This is not as far-fetched as it may seem. For example, it is estimated that up to 50 per cent of graduates leave their first job within five years, despite the fact that they form are perhaps the most rigorously selected group within many organisations. The most common reason for leaving is because of unfulfilled expectations. They typically do not leave because they are not competent at the job, but because they do not feel committed to an organisation that they feel has misled them. So companies spend vast amounts of money ensuring that their selection methods have good predictive validity, ignoring the fact that such predictive validity (especially if measured in terms of narrow job performance criteria or 'behaviour') does not necessarily translate into long-term commitment to the organisation. Considering selection as part of the whole socialisation process provides a better understanding and a more holistic way to view the evaluation of the selection process itself.

A good example of the limitations of focusing in isolation on the selection process is provided by BellSouth (Leopold and Hallier, 1998). BellSouth was a new telecommunications company in New Zealand. As with many greenfield sites at the start-up phase, it had loose management structures and so wanted to recruit employees who could work in an uncertain, ambiguous, fluid environment. It used a very rigorous selection process in order to select people who were intelligent, flexible and high on energy. Employees who had been selected viewed the selection approach adopted very positively, as it had made them feel 'special individuals on whom a lot of time and effort had been extended'. The problem was that nearly 25 per cent of new staff left the company within six months and 50 per cent in the first year. Analysis of why this was occurring demonstrated that it was because the job had not turned out as expected. So although they had been made to feel 'very special' during the selection process, they reported that thereafter they had received much less individual attention and support. In other words, the socialisation that had begun during selection was not carried through to their initial experiences on the job, where they felt they were 'thrown in at the deep end'.

Nearly 20 years ago, Wanous (1980) criticised recruitment practice based on *attracting* applicants on the grounds that it was often at the expense of honesty about the position to be filled. Recruiters, he argued, regularly painted a rosy picture of the job that raised unrealistic expectations in applicants – and, perhaps even more significantly, the successful individual then faced disappointment when taking up the position. Wanous argues for *realistic job previews* and this is very much in line with Herriot's (1989a) case for making the process both realistic and two way. It is a depressing observation that these criticisms would still appear relevant to much current practice.

Activity 5.5

Reassessment of the O&V Joifel case

Go back to the O&V Joifel case study in Chapter 1 (pages 33–5) and reflect on the ways in which you assessed the evidence in the light of the above discussions. How confident are you with the recommendations you made to Oliver?

A critical exploration of 'normal' practice

Having considered selection as a learning process, it is now possible to consider how selection is generally carried out within organisations and the problems associated with this, again comparing the systemic and processual approaches.

■ Defining the job and the ideal candidate

It was argued in the earlier part of the chapter that 'best practice' from the systems perspective begins with a thorough job analysis. This seeks to identify the knowledge, skills, abilities and other characteristics required to carry out the defined tasks involved in a particular job. If this stage is carried out superficially, then any subsequent judgements and decisions could well be flawed (Algera and Greuter, 1993). So the demanding and time-consuming process called job analysis is used to identify functions, tasks and subtasks (the job description) that, in turn, determine the characteristics of the ideal candidate (the job specification).

Traditional methods of job analysis focused on collecting documents (e.g. from training analyses), interviewing the job holder or the line supervisor about the job, observation of someone in the job and, sometimes, attempts to do the job by the analyser. Other methods include using group interviews (a form of job-based focus group), holding a technical conference with 'experts', or asking job holders to keep a diary record. The critical incidents method can be used in an attempt to focus interviews or observations on those aspects of the job that are critical, as opposed to those aspects that are more mundane (Flanagan, 1954). There have also been attempts to develop questionnaires and checklists that simplify the job analysis process. Examples include the Position Analysis Questionnaire (PAQ) (McCormick *et al.*, 1972) and Saville and Holdsworth's Work Profiling System (WPS) (Saville and Holdsworth, 1995).

Once there is clarification of what the job entails, the person specification (ideal) is drawn up. This identifies such issues as attainments, aptitudes, physical requirements, personality characteristics and any possible external constraints such as the need to travel away from base or work shifts. The model developed by Rodger (1970) has been a popular framework for considering these personal characteristics (Mackay and Torrington, 1986). Rodger's Seven Point Plan groups these personal characteristics under seven headings:

1 Physical make-up.

2 Attainments.

3 General intelligence.

4 Special aptitudes.

5 Interests.

6 Disposition.

7 Circumstances.

Under each heading, those characteristics considered to be essential and desirable are identified, along with any disqualifiers – characteristics, that would make it difficult for the person to do the job effectively. More recently, the focus has been on competencies, what the person can do, rather than characteristics or attributes, what the person is like (Sparrow, 1997).

When developing a person specification, it is worth considering employing a variation on the repertory grid technique discussed earlier in the chapter. In this situation, it can be illuminating to compare 'stars' and 'failures' in the role to attempt to isolate and clarify the factors that lead to stardom or its opposite. This may sharpen the specification by avoiding bland and trite statements and focusing on the real discriminators between good and less good performers. This is more likely to lead to the identification of specific behaviours or competencies that are relevant for effective job performance.

It might be argued that as the nature of work changes from predominantly physical work to an increasing emphasis on knowledge or conceptual work, the job analysis process becomes very much harder, as less of what makes people effective in the job can be seen by external assessors if much of the activity goes on inside the job holder's head. Moreover, with the increasing emphasis on team work, there is a need to incorporate a broader analysis of competencies than those directly related to the particular job. Even more significant is the move towards flexibility and continuous change. All these factors suggest a need to broaden the scope of traditional job analysis. It needs to be done at different levels:

1 Person–job fit (job analysis), the traditional approach, which considers the competencies necessary to fulfil the specific job.

2 Person–team fit (team analysis), which considers the competencies necessary to work within a multi-disciplinary team (West and Allen, 1997).

3 Person–organisation fit (organisational analysis), which considers the competencies necessary to work effectively within the particular organisational culture (Schneider, 1987).

4 Person–environment fit (environmental analysis), which considers what kinds of competencies will be needed in the future, given the changes in society generally and in markets in particular.

Once these different levels of analysis are undertaken, they might well highlight contradictions between what is required at different levels (Herriot and Anderson, 1997). For example, at the job level there may be a requirement for an aggressive approach, but this may conflict with an organisational culture that values compromise and discussion. Or the environmental analysis may demonstrate a need for creativity and innovation, while the current organisational culture rewards caution and little risk taking. The traditional, criteria-related validity approach misses these contradictions because it focuses exclusively on job analysis. While this appears neater and more systematic, it ignores the real-world complexity where such contradictions are commonplace.

Adopting a processual perspective must involve the recognition of this complexity and, therefore, the need to go beyond an overly simplistic focus on job analysis. Perfect 'fit' is unlikely at all levels, but in the processual perspective this is considered to be inevitable. The focus will be on negotiation, in order to arrive at some kind of compromise that can allow both the organisation and the individual to grow and develop. This may mean purposively employing individuals who are not the best 'fit' for the job, but who are brought in because they have good team-working skills. Or it may mean employing a person for a particular job who is more creative than most others within the organisation, because this is felt to be particularly necessary for the future. But there would be open discussion about these 'misfits' during the selection process, so that individuals are aware that they are going to be seen as different and do not start with unrealistic expectations.

■ Measuring candidates

Once the analysis has been completed and there is an understanding of the requirements (which, as has been seen, may involve recognition of contradictory requirements), the next step is to decide how individuals are going to be measured or assessed against these requirements. There are a variety of methods that can be used here and research provides an indication of their predictive validity. This predictive validity has been established on the basis of meta-analysis, which brings together the results from a number of individual studies in order to provide a more robust calculation (Hunter and Schmidt, 1990). However, from a processual perspective it is also necessary to consider how these methods are used in practice and how they are seen by candidates. In this section we consider different methods, concentrating on those that are used most commonly, at least in the UK.

Application forms and biodata

Application forms and biodata are both methods that are used to screen out unsuitable applicants and so leave a pool of applicants for further investigation. Such pre-screening is especially necessary where there are a large number of people applying for a limited number of jobs. Application forms ask candidates to provide information on a range of topics. Some of this information is, at least in principle, verifiable, e.g. last salary or qualifications obtained, while other information requested is non-verifiable, e.g. the reasons for wanting to apply to the company. As Marchington and Wilkinson (1996) state: 'the most effective application forms ensure that the information provided ties in with the person specification and core competencies required for the job.' However, research has demonstrated that this is, in practice, not in fact the case. For example, Keenan (1995) found that very few of the 536 organisations in the UK included in a study of recruitment practice actually designed their application forms around selection criteria, with over half relying on off-the-shelf products. It has also been shown that the information on application forms is not used in a systematic way, so for example different individuals within the same organisation may use different information on which to base their decisions (Knights and Raffo, 1990). This occurs despite the fact that the information on application forms appears significantly to influence selection outcomes, at least in graduate recruitment (Keenan, 1997). Such random pre-screening cannot be considered ideal from either a systemic or a processual perspective.

Biodata is a highly structured and detailed form of the application blank and consists of demographic and lifestyle questions that have been found to be sound predictors of job performance. For example, if past data demonstrates that first-born children do better than those who have older siblings, then this question is asked and those who are first-born score points for this fact. If data also demonstrates that those with a first-class honours degree do better than those with poorer degrees then points will be awarded to those with this qualification. A whole series of data is collected about candidates where this has been shown to link to performance criteria. The items are weighted appropriately and scored according to the strength of the link with performance. Armstrong (1995) observes that the approach is most useful when large numbers of applications are received for a limited number of posts.

The predictive power of biodata is comparatively high. However, by its very nature it is particularly vulnerable to charges of unfair discrimination. If we have an organisation where successful managers are predominantly white, male, middle aged and middle class and then we construct our criteria based on their responses to demographic and lifestyle questions, it seems highly probable that we will select even more white, middle-class, middle-aged males. To overcome this, Cook (1993) suggests that cross-validation with independent assessment is necessary and goes so far as to assert that 'an inventory that has not been cross-validated should not be used for selection'.

Biodata is not widely used despite the good predictive validities that can be achieved (Shackleton and Newell, 1997). Application forms are much more common and are generally used as a pre-screening device, leading to the direct elimination of candidates. However, as has been seen, application forms are often used unsystematically. What is also interesting in comparing the systemic and processual perspectives is to consider candidates' reactions to the different methods of pre-screening. On application forms, especially on the free-format, unverifiable questions, both potential candidates and recruiters assume that candidates will 'fake' answers (e.g. to a question about the reasons they have chosen that particular company to apply to). Even on biodata questions, Stokes *et al.* (1993) found that job incumbents responded differently to items compared to actual job applicants, with the latter responding in more socially desirable ways. In other words, real applicants were using impression management tactics to respond to the questions, especially those questions where answers were non-verifiable. Moreover, biodata has been found to engender negative reactions (Robertson *et al.*, 1991), especially among candidates rejected by this procedure. These rejected candidates expressed doubts about its accuracy, validity and usefulness.

Perhaps one key point in terms of this pre-selection stage is for organisations to be more open and honest about the likely opportunities available. At present, this early stage in selection is little more than a ritual dance, with organisations presenting limited 'real' information that allows candidates to select out. Instead, glamorous or glossy information is presented that would attract almost anyone. This encourages potential candidates, in turn, to present themselves in unrealistic ways, trying to preempt what they think the organisation is looking for. Research has indeed shown that offering potential candidates a realistic preview of the job does lower expectations to a more realistic level. Moreover, realistic information also means that those candidates who continue to pursue the application and are successful demonstrate a greater level of commitment to the organisation, higher job satisfaction, better performance and longer tenure (Wanous, 1980).

Psychometric measures

There are a variety of different psychometric measures, although the two most commonly used in the context of selection are ability tests and personality questionnaires.

Ability tests

Intelligence testing has a long history, from the initial work of Alfred Binet and Theodore Simon in the early years of the twentieth century onwards. Reber (1985) observes that 'few concepts in psychology have received more devoted attention and few have resisted clarification so thoroughly' as intelligence. Thus, it was defined as 'that which is measured by intelligence tests' by the delightfully named Boring (1923). Nevertheless, there is general agreement that intelligence involves an ability to adapt to a variety of situations; an ability to learn; and an ability to employ abstract concepts (Phares, 1987). However, it is also a concept that may include quite different aspects of intellectual activity, particularly logic and creativity – roughly equivalent to ideas such as convergent and divergent thinking. This is not the place to rehearse the work of Binet, Guilford, Spearman, de Bono, etc.; suffice it to observe that there are a number of tests that purport to measure these qualities.

Aptitude tests are also measures of ability, but are concerned with more specific abilities. They commonly measure specific areas such as:

- verbal;
- numerical;
- perceptual or diagrammatic;

- spatial;
- mechanical;
- clerical;
- sensory or motor aptitudes.

It is common to administer batteries of aptitude tests, such as those published by Saville & Holdsworth, ASE, The Psychological Corporation, EITS (Educational and Industrial Test Services) and Oxford Psychologists Press. These tests are designed to measure an individual's propensity to acquire a particular skill or set of skills at some future point.

Both general intelligence and specific ability tests are typically presented as multiple-choice questions with right/wrong answers. In both cases it is essential that the tests are administered consistently (e.g. with exact time limits) and scored and interpreted by qualified individuals (in the UK this means being BPS accredited). These kinds of tests will provide standardised norms for the relevant population, e.g. if a test is being used for graduates then graduate norms will be used. Individuals are given a percentile score, which compares their result against this population norm. For example, if someone scores at the 10th percentile this means that 90 per cent of the comparative population score higher than this.

The key issue from the systemic perspective is predictive validity with respect to the job being filled. Here intelligence tests and aptitude tests do very well, having a relatively high predictive validity across a range of jobs. They also have high face validity and are relatively easy to use when setting up predictive validity studies and correlations with work performance. However, there is a question about how much additional information intelligence test results provide, over and above that obtained from already accessible information such as qualifications obtained.

Personality questionnaires

Personality testing is becoming increasingly popular in the UK (Shackleton and Newell, 1994). For example, Keenan (1995) found that personality inventories were used by up to 80 per cent of all organisations in the recruitment of graduates and managers. The two alternative approaches to personality have already been briefly reviewed – the idiographic and the nomothetic. There is not space here to revisit specific theories of personality. Suffice it to say that the majority of personality questionnaires used during selection come from the nomothetic tradition, at least in the UK. Thus they are concerned with a stable element of people, which could be thought of as dispositions of behaviour.

The measures in use currently are self-report instruments. This raises immediate issues of faking (sometimes referred to as motivational distortion or the social desirability effect) or, alternatively, self-delusion. We may safely assume that in work situations of selection, promotion, etc., faking will be a probable occurrence and this must be borne in mind when contemplating the use of personality questionnaires. We can relate this back to our earlier discussion of impression management. So we immediately have validity issues surrounding assumptions about personality predicting work performance and the reliability of the measures. This is confirmed by research demonstrating that personality questionnaires generally have very low predictive validity.

Aside from these validity issues, there is also a more fundamental problem. The systemic approach to selection would begin from the assumption that there is a particular type of personality or ability required for a particular job. Individuals would then be chosen who demonstrated that particular profile. It is to be hoped that the reader, having read the rest of this chapter, can begin to think through for themselves what the limitations of this approach might be. Specifically, it does not allow for the fact that someone with a different personality or a different range of aptitudes might do the job equally effectively but in a very different way. Nor does it allow for individuals to change and 'grow' into their jobs.

From a processual perspective, ability tests and personality measures might still be used during selection but in a rather different way. Rather than looking for individuals with the 'ideal profile' and rejecting those who have different abilities and personalities, the results might be used as the basis of discussion. Thus, if I apply for a job as an operations planning manager and a personality measure demonstrates that I am a relatively 'unconscientious' person, this could be used during an interview to discuss whether I am in fact suited to this position, given that the previous incumbent took a very methodical and conscientious approach to the job. This discussion might well encourage me to decide that I am not in fact suited. On the other hand, I might feel that I could do the job effectively and with personal satisfaction, because I recognise that I am not that thorough but have developed coping strategies for dealing with this. Moreover, I may convince the interviewer that actually this is a benefit, because the manager who is relatively disorganised means that the subordinates will have to plan more for themselves so that they will develop valued skills and experience. Meanwhile, my high level of creativity can be used to bring in new ideas to solve some of the routing problems within the department. In other words, I might do the job very differently from the last incumbent but be equally, if not more, effective. Such negotiation during employee selection is likely to lead to a much more heterogeneous workforce. However, given the importance of innovation and change in contemporary organisations, this should be viewed as a benefit rather than a cost (Bantel, 1993).

Performance tests

These are of particular value when specific job activities can be set up as tests of performance. Keyboard or driving skills could be assessed relatively easily and, for some occupations such as musicians and actors, they are well established as 'auditions'. In academia, for example, candidates are often asked to present a lecture as part of the selection process. Performance tests are relevant when we are seeking persons who already possess a skill or competence. Trainability testing (attempting to measure an applicant's ability to *develop* the required skills) could be considered a subset of this type of measure. It is also possible to attempt to design exercises such as the 'in-tray' that seek to replicate job skills and allows measures to be taken at the selection stage. The 'in-tray' exercise involves giving candidates a range of different correspondence (e.g. memos, faxes, letters, minutes of meetings, etc.). Candidates must then respond to these different items, typically having to state what action they would take and why and with what level of priority.

It would appear that such work-sampling approaches are less prone to accusations of unfair discrimination (*see* Cook, 1993). These types of tests can have high levels of predictive validity, but most importantly they can provide candidates with a realistic understanding of what the job involves. Clearly, the closer to 'real life' the exercise is, the greater this level of understanding will be and therefore the more likely candidates are to develop realistic expectations. However, while it is possible to emulate job tasks in this way, it is much more difficult to provide candidates with an insight into the organisational culture. Probation periods and/or short-term contracts can serve as extended performance selection tests and provide an increased feel for the organisation. Unfortunately, in most cases short-term contracts, in particular, are used more to enable organisational flexibility than to encourage an extended period of negotiation.

Group selection methods

Group selection exercises are used in an attempt to assess subjects' social, interactive and influencing skills. Typically the group is given a task to tackle – this may be a business problem such as budget allocation, devising strategy, generating ideas for marketing initiatives, designing structures to achieve some goal with limited material or forming a specified structure with building blocks. The exercises may involve candidates being given roles to play (managing director, sales manager, accountant, etc.); alternatively, the task may be set to the group without any roles either being assigned or indicated. The participants are observed and assessed while tackling the group exercise. The assumption is that the behaviours seen in a group setting will be typical of 'real-life' responses. However, validity tests have not yet confirmed how effective these measures are. This is at least partly because this would depend on establishing team-level criteria against which to judge the outcome from these exercises. Such criteria have rarely been used. Nevertheless, these exercises may still be useful if they involve activities that bear some resemblance to the team working that will be expected on the job. The problem may be that, given that few organisations undertake any team-level analysis in identifying the requirements for the job, the actual tasks involved in these activities may bear little relation to the actual team-working environment.

References

Requesting references is very common in the UK (Shackleton and Newell, 1994). They may be used to check on the accuracy of factual details given by the applicant and/or they may seek opinions to predict success in the job. However, predictive validity is low. There are a number of factors that influence this:

- The stage in the process at which they are sought. Commonly in the world of education, references are demanded as part of a short-listing process (i.e. before interview). However, it is more common for references to be taken up after a job has been offered, simply to check that there is nothing in the individual's history to suggest that they are not suitable, e.g. a criminal record.

- Referees are normally asked to comment on generalities of personality such as honesty, co-operativeness and social adjustment. Such vague personality constructs are likely to be interpreted very differently, so the basis of comparison is limited. Work on more structured approaches to collecting references has shown that this can improve their validity (Dobson, 1989).

■ Who chooses the referee. If it is the applicant who defines the respondent, we should not be surprised if the result is a favourable observation. The alternative, which is only practicable if it occurs later in the process, is for the assessor to determine what information is required and then ask the applicant a question such as: 'Who, in your current organisation, could we contact in order to get a realistic opinion of . . .?'

■ The specificity of the question asked of the referee. Generalised questions are likely to get generalised replies. This generality, together with a reluctance of many people to be critical, can lead to a very unhealthy practice of 'reading what is not included' in the reference.

Interviews

Interviews are almost always used in selection in the UK (Shackleton and Newell, 1994), but their predictive power is depressingly low. Much of the difficulty arises from issues of interpersonal perception (Eder and Ferris, 1989). The traditional interview suffers from being unstructured, self-reporting and open to bias. The subsequent rating of applicants is bedevilled by halo and horn effects, leniency (an unwillingness to give poor ratings) and central tendency (using the middle of the scale). The low validity and openness to bias have led to criticism in relation to equal opportunities. The response has been to attempt to make the interview more structured by using standard questions with scaled pre-rated responses.

There are several different types of structured interviews, but the two most common are:

1 The 'situational interview', which poses hypothetical situations to candidates and asks them how they would react to this situation – i.e. what they would do. These hypothetical situations are based on a critical incident job analysis (Latham *et al.*, 1980). In the interview itself, interviewers ask each question in turn, using exactly the same words for each candidate, with no follow-up or variation allowed. The applicant is then rated on each question according to a pre determined set of dimensions that were identified from the original critical incident job analysis. Each of the dimensions is anchored with behavioural rating scales that depict what are good, mediocre and poor answers,

2. The 'behavioural interview', which is where applicants are asked to identify situations where they have experienced certain job-relevant situations. The interviewer then probes to establish what the applicant actually did in that situation. So rather than ask the candidate 'What would you do if . . .?', the candidate is asked 'What did you do when . . .?' (Janz *et al.*, 1986). The questions asked are, as with situational interviews, related to those job dimensions considered important in the particular job. The assumption here is that past behaviour predicts future behaviour. During the interview, the interviewer is encouraged to take concise notes and to use follow-up questions to probe answers. After the end of the interview, the interviewer rates the candidate on pre-defined rating scales, again derived from the job analysis.

Both these approaches have been shown to improve criteria-related validity through increasing job relatedness, providing limited access to ancillary data that may bias interviewers' impressions (interviewers do not view data from the application form prior to the interview) and standardising questions (Dipboye, 1997). That is, these techniques limit questions to those that have direct relevance to the knowledge, skills and attitudes required for the particular job. Yet despite the clear evidence that structured interviews have a higher predictive validity than unstructured interviews (Heffcutt and Arthur, 1994), evidence of actual use suggests that the unstructured (or at best semi-structured) interview remains the norm. There are a number of reasons for this:

1 The flexibility of the unstructured interview allows the interviewer to shift from assessment to recruitment when it is clear that the candidate is well suited to the job (Dipboye, 1997).

2 Unstructured interviews are preferred both by candidates, possibly because this gives them more control over the situation (Schuler, 1993), and by interviewers (Meehl, 1986).

3 While structured interviews may encourage a good fit with the particular job, they may be less effective at selecting for the organisational context (Bowen *et al.*, 1991). As Judge and Ferris (1992: 23) comment: 'Calls for structured interviews as a way to improve the validity of the interview may be misplaced if the true goal, and utility, of the interview lies not in selecting the most technically qualified, but the individual most likely to fit into the organisation'. Similarly, the unstructured interview may allow more scope for the candidate to explore, through the interviewer, more about the job and the organisation, thus allowing them also to make a better assessment of fit.

What this suggests is that the interview has multiple functions, only one of which is to assess the direct fit to the job. In addition, it can be used as a basis for negotiating a mutually agreeable psychological contract and it can serve as a preliminary socialisation tactic (Anderson and Ostroff, 1997). A structured interview will be severely restricted in facilitating this negotiation. This does not mean that good practice should abandon all the evidence of the last 50 years and revert to totally unstructured interviews, which are not based on any understanding of the job to be done or its context. Rather, it should adopt a processual perspective that recognises the multiple functions of an interview, with job prediction being only one of these. A semi-structured interview, which allows exploration and negotiation on both sides, can meet these multiple functions and be satisfying to both parties.

Assessment centres

Assessment centres (AC) are not a method *per se*. Rather, they are an amalgam of previously discussed selection methods and operate on a multi-trait, multi-method basis. ACs have been shown to have high criterion-related validity (Gaugler *et al.*, 1987) and face validity (Macan *et al.*, 1994). Fundamental to the design of an AC is the notion of a matrix of dimensions against which candidates are assessed in a variety of exercises/methods. The AC allows a group of candidates to be assessed at the same time – this has a number of advantages, particularly in terms of the cost effectiveness of test administration. It also allows group dynamics to be examined via group exercises etc. On the other hand, it is also expensive and time consuming, demanding trained (and expensive) observer/assessors for a period that may be as long as three days. The predictive power of ACs is impressive, but there is an irony in that, as Cook (1993) observes, 'the fact is that psychologists don't know why ACs work so well'. Thus, despite the good overall validity, the actual ratings of candidates on the individual dimensions across exercises within an AC is more problematic. Numerous studies have shown that ratings on different dimensions within a particular exercise correlate highly with each other (thus demonstrating low discriminant validity), while measures of the same dimension across different exercises do not correlate very highly (low convergent validity) (Kauffman *et al.*, 1993). Part of the problem here concerns the design of ACs; it is now clear that there are a number of things that can be done to improve AC construct validity (Lievens, 1998). In particular, it is advocated that:

- a small number of dimensions are used – say three or four;
- dimensions are used which are conceptually distinct;
- dimensions are defined in concrete and job-related ways;
- training is given to familiarise assessors with the dimensions;
- dimensions are revealed to the candidates so that they know what they are being assessed against – this will reduce the advantages to high self-monitors (Snyder, 1974).

Most importantly, not only do ACs demonstrate good predictive validity, it is also clear that they are generally favourably regarded by candidates and perceived to measure job-related qualities accurately and fairly (Dulewicz *et al.*, 1983; Robertson *et al.*, 1991). Interestingly, therefore, ACs fulfil both the systemic requirements for good predictive validity and the processual requirements for good opportunities to develop realistic expectations and to begin the process of organisational socialisation. However, it should always be remembered that ACs are only as good as their designers make them. While research has demonstrated good predictive and face validity, this can only be achieved through a careful design process. The AC design should be specific to the job being filled and to the organisation – it is not satisfactory to throw together a rag-bag of tests and exercises, often borrowed or taken off the shelf. Each element should be purposeful and there should be plenty of scope for candidates to find out more about the organisation as well as for the organisation to find out about the candidates. ACs should also be evaluated to establish how far the people actually selected are in fact effective at the various levels that may be relevant – effective in the job, in the team, in the organisation and in relation to the changing environment.

◾ Selection decisions

Once the selection methods have been completed, decisions are made – the organisation decides to whom to offer jobs and the candidates decide whether to take any job that is offered. From the point of view of the organisation, one would hope that decisions are based on a careful weighing of the evidence. However, the organisational literature is replete with studies that have shown that decision making in organisations typically deviates from this rational model (Pfeffer, 1981; Hickson *et al.*, 1971). Beach (1990: 13) suggested that most decisions are made 'quickly and simply on the basis of "fittingness", and only in particular circumstances are they made on the basis of anything like the weighing and balancing of gains and losses that is prescribed by classical decision theory'. This is consistent with the finding that interviewers typically make their decision well before the end of the interview and sometimes very early in the process (Tullar *et al.*, 1979).

Activity 5.6

Here are three characteristics of a person. They

■ love music – Mozart in particular;

■ are vegetarian;

■ like animals, especially dogs.

1 What sort of person are they?

2 What car would you expect them to drive?

3 What paper would they read?

4 Of what political party might they be a member?

There is usually considerable agreement among people who have not come across Activity 5.6 before as to the kind of individual we are considering. It therefore comes as something of a shock to discover that all three characteristics were, allegedly, shared by Adolf Hitler. The problem is that people generally seek to find simple 'boxes' in which to place others, rather than recognising that behaviour is affected by a number of factors such as motivation, personality, values and expectancies, which may not all be consistent. However, consistency is typically assumed and so is often found because of stereotyping and selective perception. We like things to be easy and clear cut, we want the 'goodies' to wear white hats and to be generally saintlike! This means that, despite efforts to make selection 'objective' and 'scientific', decision processes are inevitably effected by human subjectivities, as exemplified by the anecdote in Illustration 5.1.

ILLUSTRATION 5.1

One of the authors had been involved in designing an assessment centre for graduate trainees for an internationally famous organisation. Analyses were conducted, competencies identified, exercises designed and matrices justified. Managers and staff underwent the experience for themselves and were trained in interviewing and assessing behaviours. Finally, the great day arrived and the first set of applicants who had survived the short-listing process were invited to central London.

No expense was spared – the chief executive greeted them, videos of organisational plans were shown, the HR director wished everybody well. The assessment centre progressed with exercises, tests and interviews.

At lunch, the high and mighty returned to mingle with the troops. On arrival, the HR director sidled up and inquired, *sotto voce*, 'How is the girl in the red coat getting on? – I really like the look of her.'!

CASE STUDY 5.1

Monks Brewery

Monks Brewery is a significant UK player in the beer and alcohol market. It has a full range of management functions from market research and advertising, through HR and operations, to accounting and auditing.

It has plans for expansion and, due to the competition and the limitations on significantly increasing its existing markets and market share, the major new expansion is hoped to be in linked areas such as hotels, health clubs, bingo, cybercafés, etc.

As an investment for the future, Monks has decided to recruit 24 graduate trainees to ensure a suitable pool of talent for this future growth.

Activity 5.7

Design and justify the recruitment and selection procedures you would recommend.

Conclusion

There is a great deal of literature and research on selection. However, it has been dominated by a particular perspective, which we have called the systemic or criteria-related validity approach. While this appears very objective and scientific, the reality is that in selection we are dealing with human judgements, which are inherently subjective – judgements by managers as to the suitability of candidates and judgements by candidates as to whether they would like to work for a particular organisation. To try to overcome or minimise this subjectivity is to ignore its inevitability. Instead, we have advocated adopting an exchange or processual perspective, which recognises the subjectivity.

Selection is thus a process of two-way negotiation (Herriot, 1989a) in which both parties attempt to make sense of the other (Dachler, 1994) to determine whether there is any mutually beneficial fit or accommodation (Hesketh and Robertson, 1993). This processual approach therefore recognises that applicants are also making decisions (Wanous, 1992) and that the impact of the selection process on these individuals may have a significant bearing on their future involvement with the organisation (Illes and Robertson, 1997). Adopting this processual perspective does not necessarily change the selection methods used, but it certainly changes the ways in which they are used.

Summary

This chapter leads to the following conclusions in relation to adopting a processual view of selection:

■ Understanding and theorising from the processual perspective requires an approach that captures dynamic processes through time, as the individual and the organisation negotiate the 'messy web of reality' (Newell, 1998).

■ The focus needs to be on how individuals create their own environments through the processes of interaction, rather than simply studying individuals as if they were determined by their biological trait structures. Adopting the processual perspective therefore requires a move away from the positivist epistemology that has dominated to date.

■ Adopting a processual perspective, however, does not mean abandoning all that we have learnt from past research on selection, but it means building on this base.

■ Understanding predictive validity is important, but we need to expand this to focus beyond the individual job level, to think also about the team, the organisation and the environment.

■ Recognising these different levels of analysis will highlight inconsistencies within organisations. Selection is then seen as the process through which such contradictions are openly negotiated with prospective candidates.

■ In particular, we need to move from the current situation where prospective candidates are wooed to work for an organisation by promises that cannot be fulfilled, so leading to disillusionment when they confront the often less than glamorous reality.

■ Instead, prospective candidates should be encouraged to develop realistic expectations so they can begin the process of organisational socialisation 'up front'.

Discussion questions

1 In what ways might the traditional or systemic approach to selection result in decisions that discriminate against minority groups?

2 How far, if at all, does the processual or exchange view of selection overcome the problem of unfair discrimination?

3 Can managers make informed selection decisions, given the subjectivist view that sees 'knowing' as dependent on social and cultural forces that shape the process of interpretation?

4 Adopting the systems and processual perspectives in turn, what might be the respective roles of personnel/HRM specialists versus line managers in assessment, selection and evaluation?

5 Consider any two selection methods and compare and contrast how they might affect a candidate's view of the organisation using them.

6 In your view, what makes an effective selection method? Consider your answer in relation to a small family firm and then a large multinational firm.

Further reading

For a comprehensive general overview of issues to do with assessment, selection and evaluation, *see* either Anderson and Herriot (1997) or Cooper and Robertson (1995). For a more detailed discussion of the role of personality testing in selection decisions, *see* Blinkhorn and Johnstone (1990) and, as a counter to this viewpoint, O'Reilly *et al.* (1991).

PERFORMANCE MANAGEMENT AND PERFORMING MANAGEMENT

Colin Fisher

OBJECTIVES

Having completed this chapter and its associated activities, readers should be able to:

■ describe various approaches and techniques of performance management so that the practices followed in its name are clearly understood;

■ analyse some of the difficulties and criticisms attached to the practice of performance management;

■ describe the possible benefits and advantages of the techniques.

Introduction

Walters (1995) defines performance management as the process of improving the quality and quantity of work done and bringing all activity in line with an organisation's objectives. In this chapter the following methods of performance management will be reviewed:

- clarifying and publishing programme structures that attempt to show the links between staff's activities and the objectives of the organisation;
- the use of performance measurement and performance indicators;
- target setting and monitoring;
- 360° appraisal;
- personal development planning;
- dealing with problem staff;
- staff appraisal interviews – very often the arena in which all the above activities are played out.

For a discussion of performance-related pay as part of performance management, see Chapter 7.

■ Performance management as managerial folklore

Insecurity is a common phenomenon in organisations. Senior managers, for example, may be concerned about their lack of grip on what is happening in the organisation and on what it is achieving, or team leaders and middle managers might be told by management trainers that their role is to 'achieve things through others' while they are unsure about how this can be done. People in personnel and HR departments argue that their function is critical to the performance of the organisation but worry about whether they have instituted enough programmes and policies to convince others of their work's worth. Staff at all levels worry about whether they can prove to their bosses that they have met, or exceeded, the organisation's expectations of them.

Performance management can be seen as a corpus of folk prescriptions and recipes. The purpose of folk remedies is to reduce people's anxieties about their problems by giving them something to do. In seventeenth-century England, for example, people would visit the local cunning woman or man for help in finding a missing belonging or for a charm against ill luck or curses (Thomas, 1973). In similar fashion, the models, homilies, procedures and techniques of performance management help people feel that they are doing all that can be done to do their job well. Managers may be assured that they are meeting their targets by checking the monthly metrics (the performance-measurement information that their organisation produces). Team leaders can bring forward, as evidence of competence, their exemplary records in conducting staff appraisals and in mentoring the personal development plans of their staff. Personnel and HRM staff may reinforce their perception of their worth to the organisation by redesigning the staff appraisal scheme. Staff attend at cascade or team briefings to understand their role in the organisation. Performance management therefore incorporates a wide range of activities that are linked by the common aim of giving form, purpose and structure to the otherwise chaotic experience of working in organisations.

Performance management is an important issue to many organisations. In its latest survey, of 562 companies, the IPD reported that two-thirds of the sample reported that they had performance-management systems. There were changes, between the IPD's 1992 survey and the one conducted in 1997, in the popularity of the techniques listed above. Highly bureaucratic systems have lost favour, while the development-oriented approach, 360° appraisal and personal development plans have increased in organisational popularity (Donkin, 1997).

The body of performance-management methods and folklore, like any heap of ideas, will contain things of value and things of doubtful provenance and utility. Some of the remedies and prescriptions will be based on rigorous research and sound theory, such as expectancy theory and goal setting theory (Mabey and Salaman, 1995: 90). Goal setting theory argues that people work better when they have clear, realisable and significant goals. Expectancy theory takes a more sophisticated tack and argues that people will put more 'E' (energy, effort, enthusiasm, excitement and so on) into their work if they believe that their efforts will result in tangible achievements that will help them fulfil their personal needs.) Some ideas will be commonly held beliefs that have developed, through the accretion of anecdote and experience, until they finally emerge in a textbook and acquire authority. Many prescriptions will be the result of cumulative plagiarism, as when, for example, a purloined copy of one company's 360° appraisal questionnaire is used as a starting point by someone with the task of designing such a scheme in another organisation. Some of the prescriptions are communicated by myths (case studies, pub stories, corporate and training videos and newspaper stories) of organisations that have, as the story goes, increased turnover by 200 per cent by introducing target setting. Within this matter there is also an undercurrent of contrary stories and theories that challenge the validity of performance-management methods. Some of these emerge in the proceedings of academic conferences and others are found in the office ephemera that people put on their pinboards at work.

ILLUSTRATION 6.1

The canoe race

Once upon a time it was resolved to have a boat race between a Japanese team and a team representing an NHS trust. Both teams practised long and hard to reach their peak performance. On the big day they were as ready as they could be. The Japanese won by a mile.

Afterwards, the trust team became very discouraged by the result and morale sagged. Senior management decided that the reason for the crushing defeat had to be found and a working party was set up to investigate the problem and recommend appropriate action. Their conclusion was that the Japanese team had eight people rowing and one person steering, whereas the trust team had eight people steering and one person rowing.

Senior management immediately hired a consultancy company to do a study on the team's structure. Millions of pounds and several months later they concluded that 'too many people were steering and not enough rowing'.

To prevent the team losing to the Japanese next year, its structure was changed to three assistant steering managers, three steering managers, one executive steering manager and a director of steering services. A performance and appraisal system was set up to give the person rowing the boat more incentive to work harder.

The next year the Japanese won by two miles. The trust laid off the rower for poor performance, sold off all the paddles, cancelled all capital investment for new equipment and halted development of a new canoe. The money saved was used to give higher than average pay awards to senior management.

Source: Various versions of this story exist, naming specific companies.

In case you are inclined to dismiss the story in Illustration 6.1 as a piece of unrepresentative mischief making, it is worth noting that in its 1997 survey the IPD reported that a third of respondents believed that performance management was time consuming and bureaucratic and had little or no impact on performance (Donkin, 1997).

■ The uses and abuses of performance management

Folk remedies should not be trivialised or dismissed because of their apparent irrationalism. In the context of the processual approach taken in this book, folk remedies can be seen as part of the process by which pattern is identified in, or imposed on, the flow of organisational activity (cf. Chapter 1). Folk myths are a resource for the *enactment* of contingencies by organisational actors. In other words, it may be argued that the corpus of performance management is important because of the rhetorical and practical resources that it provides for the performing of management. For example, the stories about the benefits of macho target setting, which originated in the private sector, appear to have affected how ministers in the Labour government have understood and enacted their understanding of social problems. In education, for example, all problems have to be tackled by setting targets, such as the amount of time to be spent teaching phonics in primary schools or the level of truancy that is acceptable.

It is not necessarily the case that the corpus has to be justified by claims that its use produces optimal managerial performance. Such a claim would be hard to substantiate. All performance-management techniques can be challenged. We might ask, for example:

■ Do performance-measurement systems measure the right things and are managers sufficiently skilled at interpreting the statistics?

■ Why is it that most staff appraisal schemes fall into disuse within three years and need to be relaunched? (This is my contribution to the folklore of performance management. At an anecdotal level the claim seems true, but I have no systematic evidence to support it. Bowles and Coates (1993: 9) suggest that appraisal schemes are long lived, but their survey did not investigate the frequency of relaunches of companies' performance-management schemes.)

■ Are personal development plans seen by staff as a genuine aid to growth; or are they part of a developmental liturgy that people first acquire at schools, preparing their records of achievement, and that they then repeat by rote as they proceed to the production of continuous professional development portfolios?

■ Why is it that most staff seem to dislike appraisal, or do they?

The methods of performance management are intended to clarify managers' roles but, from a processual perspective, this is a vain task because organisations are ineluctable and messy. The tension between clarity and ambiguity can be illustrated by discussing a common problem of performance management, the level at which performance management should operate. Should the focus be on the whole department or organisation, on teams, on individuals or on a combination of all three? In a hierarchical structure, it should be possible to specify targets for the organisation as a whole and then disaggregate these into targets for subunits, teams and individuals. In practice, this can be difficult. A survey from Saville and Holdsworth (1997) reported that less than 40 per cent of the sample used appraisal to set team objectives and only 11 per cent thought that the process was effective. There can be overlap between targets. It may be that an individual is charged with a target that can only be achieved through a team effort, or that a senior manager's targets are achieved when all their subordinates have achieved their goals so that it is uncertain wherein lies the particular contribution of the senior person. In such circumstances, a traditional view of organisations and management cannot explain the situation. A processual view is needed because it emphasises the adjustments and negotiations that are required to deal with the consequences of the overlap of responsibility for targets. These accommodations would include, when targets are reviewed for example, much retrospective rationalisation to explain why, in the illustrations just given, it was a lack of co-operation from team colleagues that led to a failure to meet the target, and why the senior manager should be rated highly because their staff have done their jobs. In the appraisal interview, the appraisee will create stories to convince themselves and their interviewer of a favourable interpretation of their performance against the targets. Jacques (1992) argued that an appraisal is an occasion when appraiser and appraisee make sense of their organisational experience by creating stories that interpret and justify their actions.

If the reader has detected a sceptical (some may say a cynical) tone in this chapter, they may be assured that the intention is not to advise people to avoid performance management because it is ungrounded and uncertain and to cultivate their gardens instead. Rather, the objective is to help the reader towards an understanding of the purposes of the remedies and recipes discussed and to learn how to use them in an exploratory and experimental way.

Clarifying and publishing objectives

It is a common view among managers that staff will perform better if they understand the contribution that their work makes to meeting the written objectives and goals of the organisation (Hackman and Oldham, 1976). It follows, therefore, that anything that makes this connection clearer to staff should enhance performance. This insight encouraged organisations to publish documents that showed, through the medium of a programme structure, how all the myriad jobs undertaken contributed to meeting the organisation's objectives. An example, based on the work of a district council, is shown in Illustration 6.2. By studying this document, a person who was employed to survey drainage and assess the risk of flooding could see in the programme structure how their work contributed to the council's wider purposes.

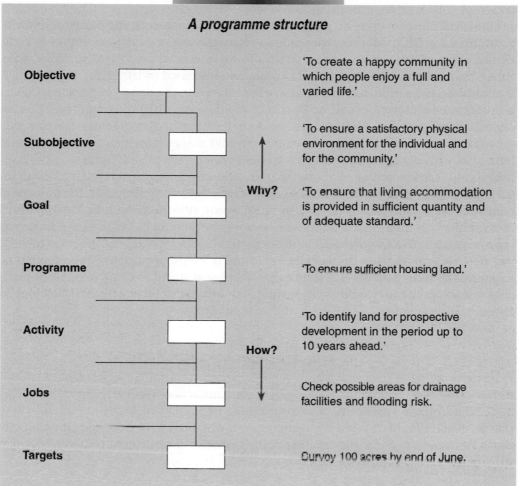

ILLUSTRATION 6.2

A programme structure

Objective	'To create a happy community in which people enjoy a full and varied life.'
Subobjective	'To ensure a satisfactory physical environment for the individual and for the community.'
Goal	'To ensure that living accommodation is provided in sufficient quantity and of adequate standard.'
Programme	'To ensure sufficient housing land.'
Activity	'To identify land for prospective development in the period up to 10 years ahead.'
Jobs	Check possible areas for drainage facilities and flooding risk.
Targets	Survey 100 acres by end of June.

Why?

How?

Programme structures, like the one in Illustration 6.2, are often at the core of performance-management schemes (Lowson and Boyce, 1990). It is worth noting that the example illustrates the uncertainty of performance-management jargon. In many textbooks (Walters, 1995: 9), unlike Illustration 6.2, a goal would be higher than an objective in the programme structure. Similar methods have been used in private-sector organisations. One proprietary package, for example (CALM, n.d.), suggests that managers should first identify intent objectives. These are general and woolly statements that describe the purpose or focus of an organisation. Once this generality is stated, managers should identify their direction objectives. These state, by using active verbs such as improve, decrease and increase, the broad direction in which the managers should go. Direction objectives, like the intent objectives, are not measurable. At the next level down in the structure, managers are required to produce measurable result objectives. These state a precise result measured against at least two of the following criteria – quantity, quality, time and money. The achievement of these result objectives is dependent on fulfilling task objectives, the lowest element in the structure, which specify which jobs have to be done and by when.

The hierarchical nature of programme structures, including the CALM approach, gives them a mythic value to organisational management. It locates employees at a particular place and status in a great chain of organisational being and so reduces the threat that individuality might pose to organisational good order (Legge, 1995: 115). It is allowable that, within a skilfully conducted interview, discussion of objectives, using a programme structure, could tie staff into compliance with, or commitment to, an organisational purpose. It is perhaps more doubtful whether a programme structure, presented in a thick, closely printed, document, would make a convincing story that could bind staff with silken cords of rhetoric to senior management's purposes.

The value of programme structures to performance management is less in their motivational impact than in the encouragement they give to questioning the value and contribution of particular activities. In other words, it is the process of constructing a programme structure that is important because, in creating it, people have to review whether each activity undertaken in the organisation does make a contribution towards its objectives or whether the activity could safely be dropped. Once the programme structure has been published as a final document and stored in filing cabinets, it probably reinforces the inevitability of existing activities rather than acts as a challenge to them.

Performance measurement

In Hackman and Oldham's (1976) model of job satisfaction, feedback is as important as understanding the significance and contribution of one's work. Many managers believe that feedback should be based on measurement (Watson, 1994a: 136) and consequently much of the effort under the heading of performance management is used to develop systems for measuring performance.

■ Identifying appropriate measures

Most measurement methods are based on a systems model that attempts to measure the input to an organisation, the uses to which those resources are put and the services and benefits that arise from that activity. In Table 6.1, two examples are given that show how such a model might be applied in public- and private-sector organisations.

Performance measures only have value, as information rather than data, if they are constructed as ratios that put one piece of statistical data into the context of another. All of the performance measures in Table 6.1 meet this criterion. But more information can be obtained by comparing one level in the systems model with another. If a final output measure is divided by a measure of input, then the result is a cost-effectiveness figure that purports to show how much good was achieved per unit of resource. If an activity statistic is compared with an input statistic, the result is a measure of efficiency.

Table 6.1 A systems approach to performance measurement

Stages in a systems model	Public sector example: hospital physiotherapists	Private sector example: pharmaceutical salesperson
Inputs	Unit costs of staff and materials Conformance and variance on cost budgets	Unit costs of staff and materials Conformance and variance to cost budgets
Activity	Number of patients treated per month Quality of treatment judged against professional standards	Number of GPs visited per month Number of conferences and exhibitions attended per month
Intermediate output	Patient satisfaction with service as measured by questionnaire compared with the same time period in the previous year Improvement in patients' clinical condition assessed on a rating scale	Orders taken as a percentage of orders for the same time period the previous year. Percentage change in market share for each category of product compared with the same period in the previous year
Final output or outcome	Improvement in patient's quality of life (in terms of relief of distress and improved mobility [Gudex, 1986]) and expectations of longevity.	Company growth rate Profitability as a percentage of capital employed

■ The complexities of performance measurement

There are a number of issues that arise out of the use of performance measures. They can be expressed as a syllogism, a form of argument in which a conclusion is drawn from two premises. The first premise is that important things about an organisation's performance are more difficult to measure than the less important things. The second premise is that managers and staff will only give their effort to achieving those things for which they have been set targets and objectives. Therefore, the conclusion can be drawn that performance-measurement systems can undermine the achievement of an organisation's objectives. This argument is clearly a generalisation and it needs to be covered in more detail.

The problem of devising valid measures of the important issues is considered first. In the public sector, for example, the objective of a service is often to bring about an improvement in the state of society. This normally means studying the impact of a service on individuals and aggregating the results to arrive at an overall assessment of the service's impact. This is a technically difficult trick. In the case of social services, for example, an improvement in a person's state of well-being can normally be measured against several dimensions and so there is the immediate problem of the weightings to be used to integrate all the different aspects (Challis, 1981; Smith, 1995). A further problem is that it would be impracticable to assess the benefit to all clients and so sophisticated sampling procedures would have to be used. If equity were to be taken into account, then it is arguable that the disutility of people who need services, but do not receive them, should be discounted against the benefits to those who do.

The mismatch between the desirability and the practicability of performance measures is well expressed in the results of a small survey of hospital consultants (Table 6.2). Pollitt (1985: 4) also attests to the difficulty of defining measures of the effectiveness of medical (clinical) interventions.

Table 6.2 The desirability and practicability of performance indicators in hospitals

Indicators of clinical outcome			
	%		%
Very desirable	88.6	Reasonably practical	11.5
Fairly desirable	11.4	Difficult but possible	81.4
Undesirable	0	Impractical	7.1
$n = 113$			
Indicators of patient satisfaction			
	%		%
Very desirable	57.5	Reasonably practical	23.7
Fairly desirable	38.1	Difficult but possible	50.9
Undesirable	4.4	Impractical	25.4
$n = 113$		$n = 114$	

It is normally reckoned that, because the important objectives of a private company relate to growth and financial returns, they are easier to measure. But even in private companies, many common performance measures are of doubtful validity because of the discretion available in calculating them. An example is given in Case study 6.1.

CASE STUDY 6.1

The validity of financial measures in the private sector

The public utilities in the UK work under a regulatory regime that controls the rate of price rises. A formula is used, RPI −*x*, which states that for a given time period prices may only rise by the rate of inflation minus a figure for *x* that is determined by the regulator. The utilities therefore attempt to maximise their costs and minimise their profits in ways that will ensure that the regulator's price controls are lenient. This tendency can be illustrated by a joint cost-allocation exercise undertaken by British Gas and the regulator (Price, 1994: 151) in 1986. British Gas's markets could be divided into three categories: the regulated domestic market for consumers using fewer than 2500 therms per annum, the unregulated firm market for large industrial users and the interruptible market for very large users. It was advantageous to British Gas to allocate as much of its costs on to the regulated market to show that its rate of return was low and so ensure a lax value for *x*. But it also wanted to load costs on to the firm market because there were suspicions abroad that excessive profits were being made. If costs were being charged against the domestic and the firm markets, then fewer could be allocated to the interruptible market, and British Gas argued that the onshore costs of supplying the interruptible market were negative, i.e. it claimed that it made savings by supplying the interruptible market. The justification was that, as interruptible customers could have their supply halted when there was pressure on the network, this market gave British Gas flexibility in balancing the pipeline system at times of peak demand and so made it possible to enter into contracts in the firm market that would otherwise be too risky to take on. Price (1994) rather curtly commented that, while she could believe that the cost of supplying the interruptible market was low, she found it hard to accept that it was negative.

Another illustration of the tendency to maximise the reporting of costs in the accounts occurred in the case of British Gas Transco's calculation of the value of its capital assets (Vass, 1996: 159). Transco wished to value its assets at current replacement cost, higher than a valuation closer to the costs that the shareholders paid for the assets, which the regulator wished to use. The advantage of a higher capital valuation was that the company's rate of return would appear lower and its costs higher and the figures could be used to justify a lower value for x. At various stages during the negotiations between the regulator Claire Spottiswoode and British Gas, the regulator argued that British Gas had valued its assets at £17 billion when a figure of between £9 billion and £11 billion would have been more appropriate, that its forecasts of capital expenditure were too high and that its depreciation mechanisms were excessive (Barnett, 1996; Beavis and Barrie, 1996). British Gas countered by saying that if it had to cut its prices at the rate demanded by the regulator, it would have to make up to half its workforce redundant. The two sides could not agree. The issue went to the Mergers and Monopolies Commission which found, in 1997, in favour of the regulator.

Activity 6.1

1 How much do accounting practices affect the validity of financial performance indicators?

2 Can you find in press reports examples of similar accountancy manipulation in non-regulated or public-sector organisations?

■ The balanced scorecard and a stakeholder approach to performance measurement

The second term of the syllogism is characterised by the work of Kaplan and Norton (1992: 71). They argued that 'what you measure is what you get'. This suggests that performance-measurement systems distort managerial effort by privileging the achievement of financial targets. In particular, Kaplan and Norton argued, it is important for organisations to maintain their competitive advantage in the marketplace by encouraging innovation and continuous improvement. But, when there is a premium on achieving a measurable rate of financial return, it is tempting to achieve it by squeezing out of the system the time and resource necessary for innovation and experimentation. In local government, for example, there was an anxiety, which actually turned out to be unjustified, that the introduction of the Citizen's Charter performance indicators, which focused on input costs and the speed with which phones were answered (Audit Commission, 1993), would drive out interest in the measurement of more important aspects of local government services (Ball and Monaghan, 1996). Performance measurement can lead to suboptimisation, which means that one goal is achieved but only at the expense of another.

Kaplan and Norton's solution to this problem was the balanced scorecard. This was a proposal that companies should collate performance information from four viewpoints:

- the financial perspective;
- the customer perspective;
- the internal business perspective;
- the innovation and learning perspective.

The ability to inspect trends and developments in all four areas would make it easy to spot whether achievement in one area was at the cost of a worsening in another.

The notion that it is possible to identify some measures as more important than others, which has been central to the argument so far, is a problematic one. In an evaluation study of a psycho-geriatric day hospital, Smith and Cantley (1985) developed a pluralistic approach to service evaluation and performance management. In the investigation, the perceptions of different groups about how well the service met their needs, as they interpreted them, became the key information in deciding whether the hospital was doing a good job and how services needed to be developed. A number of interest groups concerned with the hospital were identified, such as doctors, nurses, social workers, patients, patients' relatives, administrators and so on. Then six different criteria of success used by the interest groups were isolated. They were:

1 Free patient flow – preventing blocked beds and 'silting up'.
2 Clinical care – improving the patients' clinical condition.
3 Integrated service – good communication and liaison with other related services.
4 Impact on related services – provision of support to other agencies concerned with this client group,
5 Support of relatives – the relief of the strain put on relatives who have to care for older people.
6 Quality of service – concern for ethos and excellence in the way the service is actually delivered.

The criteria have been simplified. However, within the developing argument, the important fact is that the different interest groups viewed the six criteria differently:

> Some groups of staff and relatives employ some criteria and some others. Some employ several criteria and some adopt a more single-minded stance . . . In practice different criteria are used in different ways by different groups at different times in different contexts for different purposes with different effects. (Smith and Cantley, 1985: 44)

In short, the researchers found disagreement about the relative weighting of the six criteria. They could produce a very useful evaluative analysis of the hospital, but could not produce an overall evaluative judgement about it. It all depended on who you were within the system. This perspective places a significant limitation on the usefulness of performance measurement.

■ Manipulating metrics

It would be useful at this juncture to return to the theme of performance management as folklore and myth. Part of the function of myth is to palliate conflicts and contradictions (Kirk, 1976), such as those revealed by a pluralistic or post-modern view of organisational evaluation, which challenges as illusory any hope of an ultimate purpose for organisations. The use of management metrics creates an appearance of measurable and fixed purpose, while the difficulties implicit in performance measurement and prioritisation create opportunities for employees to manipulate the measurement system. Most examples of manipulation are, of course, anecdotal. My example relates to an occasion when someone tried to steal my car from my drive. The policeman who came to register the crime complained that, because of new regulations, the incident would no longer be registered as a crime. The thieves had set off the alarm when they broke open the car door and had run away before they could steal it. As the car had not been taken from my property, no recordable crime had been committed. The policeman expected that there would be a noticeable drop in recorded car crime within the coming year.

The folklore of the manipulation of metrics suggest that managers are highly skilled at using and abusing statistical information. But there is also a contrary theme in the literature that suggests either that managers are insufficiently numerate to understand and benefit from performance information, or that they are provided with information that is so poorly presented that it is impossible to discover the patterns and trends skilfully buried in the spreadsheet or the half-inch-thick, A3-sized, blue-ruled computer printout (Meekings, 1995).

Target setting

Performance measurement can provide the basis for target setting. Once it is possible to measure an activity or outcome, it is a small step to set or agree a point or level on the measure that an employee must achieve. There are three issues that need consideration in judging the usefulness of target setting. The first is the motivational impact of target setting: does it encourage staff to perform better than they otherwise would? Second, how equal and open is the process of agreeing targets when a member of staff and their boss meet to discuss these things? Third, how skilled are people at judging appropriate targets?

■ Targets and motivation

Intuitively, it might seem that setting targets increases the standard of people's performance. The chances of my finishing the writing of this chapter were much improved by the knowledge of a deadline drawing ever nearer. Hofstede (1984: 148–50) analysed research about the motivational effect of targets within the context of budget management. Building on experimental and survey research, he considered the impact of loose and tight budget targets. There must, in his analysis, be an equilibrium point where the amount of the budget is perfectly balanced with the level of resource needed to do the job. A loose budget is one that provides the budget holder with more resources than they could possibly need to do the job. Hofstede argued that when a very loose target is set, the budget holder is aware of the fact and plans to spend rather less money (their aspiration level) than is available. When the budget is in balance with resource needs, the budget holder will be relaxed and probably spend up to the budget limit but not beyond. When the budget is tight (i.e. the budget is below the equilibrium point), there will be a significant motivational effect and the budget holder will both aspire to, and probably achieve, a level of expenditure lower than that defined by the equilibrium point. As the budget becomes tighter, the budget holder will try to reduce their costs to the budget level, but the chances are that the task is not possible and they will over-spend on budget but probably still spend less than the equilibrium level. A point will be reached, however, when the budget is so tight that the budget holder recognises it as impossible and not only ceases to try to restrict expenditure but, in a glorious cocking a snook at the situation, will spend money with abandon. The conclusions of Hofstede's own reflections and research are that tight targets can produce better than expected per-formances, but targets that are too tight or too loose do not.

A further finding of Hofstede's work is that where there is good upward communica-tion, where a boss is open to the ideas of their subordinates, people are less likely to see the targets as tight. Departmental meetings are also useful in helping budget holders internalise external targets into personal aspirations. The implication of these findings is that effective targets are arrived at by an open and consensual process. This is not always the case in organisations, either because of the temperaments of the people involved or because of the systems of the organisation. In one organisation, in which the author was involved in setting up a performance-management system, staff appraisals were held in March, when it was expected that the appraisees would negotiate and agree their targets for the coming financial year. But in practice, the planners in the finance department had been working on their budgets for the coming year since October and November the pre-vious year. By the time of the appraisals, a detailed sales and revenue budget had been constructed for the whole organisation and, in effect, appraisees were presented with their targets as a *fait accompli* at their appraisal. To have adjusted the targets at that late point in the year would have caused too much disruption to the organisation's plans.

■ The skills of target setting

Setting targets involves forecasting and judgement. This is a difficult craft and people often make mistakes in their forecasting. The error can be compounded by poor cali-bration. A well-calibrated person knows what they know and are conscious of their limitations (Wright, 1984). A poorly calibrated person is either over-confident (they think their targets are fair and sensible when they are not) or under-confident (they are so uncertain that they find the act of fixing a target intimidating). To make an assess-ment of your target-setting skills, try the exercise in Activity 6.2.

Activity 6.2

Setting time deadlines and targets

Your appraisee's task is to put a specified number of staff through a customer care programme. The first stage towards this goal is to get top management support for the idea and to obtain their agreement to fund it. This will probably take three weeks of lobbying and persuading, but if their luck is in it could be done in two weeks. If their luck is bad it could take twelve weeks. The second stage in the task, which can only be started when formal approval has been obtained, is to research existing customer care practices. This will take a minimum of four weeks, a maximum of nine, but will probably be completed in six weeks. The other stages of the project are listed in Table 6.3 with their time estimates.

Table 6.3 Customer care programme

Phase of project	Most likely time estimate	Pessimistic time estimate	Optimistic time estimate
3 Identify a training provider organisation	4	10	2
4 Design the programme	2	5	1
5 Run the programme	6	10	5

1 How many weeks would you give the appraisee to complete this project?

2 How certain are you that this target is fair?

By using a critical path network and the PERT technique, it can be calculated that the probability of the task being completed in 24 weeks or less is 50 per cent. To set a target of less than 24 weeks is therefore tough. But when this exercise is used in training programmes, people commonly set targets that are less than 24 weeks. The distortions to which judgement are prone do not always favour the boss. Anchoring and adjustment, which is a well researched heuristic of judgement, can favour the appraisee (Hogarth, 1980).

■ Target setting and management control

From a critical perspective, the purpose of target setting is to make employees visible to the panoptic gaze of management. Jeremy Bentham's panopticon (a design for a round prison where it would be easy to keep all prisoners under surveillance from a central point) is a metaphor, much discussed in management literature, which had a physical existence for example in the Victorian circular wards of Nottingham General Hospital. Under the gaze of the nurses at the centre of the circle, the Victorian patients would, as would staff in modern organisations who have to meet their performance targets, be obliged to conform, albeit reluctantly, to expected standards of behaviour. This process can be evident in conflicts between management and professional staff. In a solicitors' practice in which the author and others acted as consultants, there was a partner who had used his professional autonomy to develop a specialism in Spanish conveyancing law. This subject was of great interest to the partner, but it detracted from his ability to meet the billing targets that were imposed on him by the performance-management system we installed. Targets were the mechanism used to distract him from his professional interests towards the interests of the management of the partnership (of which he, of course, was a part). If he had given priority to his professional interest his status in the firm, as well as his personal share of the partnership's profits, would have diminished. As Townley argues, performance management systems allow management to 'measure in quantitative terms and to hierachise in terms of values the abilities, level and the nature of individuals' (Townley, 1993: 533–4). The visibility of individuals that comes from performance management is not always contrary to the perceived self-interest of staff. An insurance broker, for whom we devised an appraisal scheme, differentiated between 'inside staff' who did all the backroom work and 'outside staff' who did the selling and had the contacts with clients. In response to feedback, an appraisal scheme was designed that focused on development for the inside staff, but that also incorporated target setting and monitoring for outside staff. However, there was a provision that any inside staff who wished to agree targets for themselves could do so. A few took the opportunity because they were ambitious for promotion and valued the increased visibility that came from target setting. They thought that it improved their promotion prospects.

360° appraisal

Interest in and application of 360° appraisal as a performance-management practice are increasing. It is sometimes called multi-rater assessment and that perhaps is a more accurate name for the activity. The term appraisal evokes the image of an interview between appraisee and appraiser. However, face-to-face contact is a rarity in 360° appraisal, which is mostly conducted through the use of questionnaires (Ward, 1995). The questionnaires are normally designed around a competency framework or a psychological instrument (such as Leadership Impact [Human Synergistics, n.d.]). A range of people are asked to assess an individual against the competency framework. The feedback can be from the subject's staff (90° appraisal), from their bosses (180° appraisal) and from colleagues and clients or customers (the full 360° appraisal).

In summary, to design a 360° appraisal scheme, you would construct a questionnaire that asked people to rate the subject of the appraisal on certain dimensions. The questions might, for example, be based on a list of competencies that are essential to the subject's job and ask the respondent to say whether the subject is incompetent, has basic competence or is highly competent on each listed competency. The questionnaires would be gathered together and the replies abstracted and formed into a report to the subject, which would say such things as (and here I caricature such feedback): 'Your staff believe you are a competent teamworker but your peers believe you to be incompetent.'

There may well be an interview in which a member of personnel or HRM explains the results of the opinion poll (which is what 360° appraisal essentially is) to the subject and helps formulate development plans to improve the subject's competency.

The questionnaires can be large and cumbersome because their designers are too anxious to obtain feedback on every aspect of managerial performance. In a scheme used in a factory in Soviet Leningrad, for example, a large number of questions were asked. The largest bank of questions in the questionnaire concerned political consciousness (Redman and Snape, 1992: 39). The intention of 360° appraisal is to give a broader and more objective assessment of people's competence, although from another angle these systems must multiply the biases and distortions of judgement to which all appraisal is prone. As Stewart (1998) points out, much assessment procedure in organisations accepts a logical fallacy that the sum of many subjective judgements is an objective one.

Managers are often willing to accept multi-rater appraisal within certain constraints (Redman and Snape, 1992: 40–1). They accept its use for development purposes, but are less willing to see it used as a basis for judgements concerning pay, performance or promotion. Multi-rater feedback is often only used when a manager has, in different cases, four, five or eight people reporting to them. With small numbers it may be difficult to maintain the raters' anonymity and the judgements made may be sweetened to avoid any danger of reprisals. In a full 360° system, there is also a problem of the weighting to be given to the various perspectives: should the views of subordinates have the same value as those of senior colleagues and how seriously should the assessments of customers or clients be taken? It can be argued that upward appraisal (if not the full 360°) is an appropriate balancing of the power relations between management and non-management staff. Appraisees may see their appraisal as an occasion when they have to accept what their appraiser gives out and it can take them a long time to get over the experience (Kay *et al.*, 1965). Upward appraisal can be an attempt to empower appraisees to reciprocate by judging their appraisers. It can certainly be a painful experience for the subjects. Edwards (1995) mentions the (apocryphal?) case of a senior manager who unwittingly upset people by standing too close to them and by spraying them when speaking words containing sibilants. Upward appraisal, together with a backward step and a visit to the dentist, made him a more effective manager. Another manager was observed coming out of his office, having received his appraisal feedback, and loudly proclaiming: 'I'm a bastard. I know I'm a bastard. You know I'm a bastard. So why should I change?' (Brewerton, 1997).

Personal development plans

The personal development plan (PDP) is a document and a process that encourages employees to:

■ undertake a systematic diagnosis of their development needs;

■ present their needs to the training managers and their line managers in a way that should get them the training resources they need;

■ keep a record of their learning achievements against their learning targets;

■ provide others with a systematic profile of their competencies and achievements.

In organisations that are following this path, there is an explicit recognition that PDPs, although they are individually driven, need to be positioned within organisational processes of performance management (Floodgate and Nixon, 1994). In many organisations PDPs are introduced as a discretionary task. Staff are encouraged to keep them but this is not insisted upon. However, in many professions, such as nursing, PDPs have become obligatory as part of the process of continuous professional development that practitioners have to undertake in order to maintain their professional registrations (UKCC, 1996; Jones and Fear, 1994). Children are introduced to the critical aspects of PDP, self-analysis and action planning in their primary education and the processes are continually in use in education up to and including the completion of the national records of achievement. The ubiquity, and relentless nature, of the action plan and the portfolio can convert them from personally significant learning activities to bureaucratic hoops to be leapt through.

The impact of both 360° appraisal and personal development plans is to individualise the employment relationship. They focus responsibility for personal development on the employee and remove responsibility from the organisation. In TSB, the PDP was presented to staff as their personal business plan that would make them more employable in the labour market.

> As with any product, if they [the staff] became out of date, no longer met their customers' requirements or ceased to offer a competitive product they would lose their share of the market and their ability to attract customer interest. Learning logs were also encouraged in this way – 'Who would buy a second-hand car without the service history and the logbook?'. (Floodgate and Nixon, 1994)

A dialectical tension can emerge. Multi-rater appraisal and PDPs make an individual confront, and take responsibility for, their own limitations, but the limitations are defined by comparison with a competency framework designed to express the needs of the organisation. In developing themselves to conform with this framework, the individuals might be distorting or denying their own ethical values and positions. The formal benefits of appraisal and PDPs – the right to personal growth and development – can be contradicted by the manifold and contingent organisational demands placed on the competency frameworks by their corporate designers. In the policy document of one organisation, staff were given a 'right' to receive feedback on their work performance; but if they chose not to exercise this right they would be subject to disciplinary proceedings.

Managing problem staff

Managers may consider that their staff present problem behaviours and some feel that they have problem staff. If the key question of whether labelling people or behaviours as a problem is in itself problematic can be put aside, it is clear that there is a management development market for providing managers with packaged solutions to supervisory difficulties. Management 'how to do it' books and seminars try to give puzzled managers bullet-pointed techniques. Very often these devices draw their inspiration from the clinical psychology technique of behaviour modification (Honey, 1980; Miller, 1989) or counselling. Many training videos (Gower, n.d.) on appraisal skills tell appraisers to use a counselling approach: not to jump in with solutions to the problems presented by the appraisees, but to encourage the appraisees to recognise and articulate their own problems and to identify their own solutions. The two sources of technique carry very different implications for the relationship between superior and subordinate. Behaviour modification places the responsibility for change on the appraiser, whereas a counselling approach places it on the appraisee. Only, it is suggested, if these techniques bear no fruit should recourse be made to the disciplinary procedure.

Staff appraisal

The appraisal interview is the occasion when, and the forum in which, many of the practices already discussed are acted out. Judgement of employees' abilities and contribution, as assessed through performance measures, personal development plans or whatever, is the central act of appraisal. But judgement is suspect. As well as the possibility of an appraiser responding to malice or prejudice when they make an assessment, there is the possibility of more insidious distortions of judgement. An assessor may, for example, give more credence to a recent failure than to a whole string of successes in the more distant past. The halo and horns effect, well known to personnel practitioners, may still cause someone to be given a better or worse assessment than their performance might justify. The horns effect is a variety of bias in which an assessor's exception to one aspect of someone (they have a moustache or they wear blue suede shoes) is generalised into the belief that everything about the person and their work must be bad. The halo effect is the reverse, when one good feature leads to the conclusion that the person must in all respects be good. How to minimise the consequence of inaccurate or biased judgements is central to the task of designing appraisal systems.

Designers of appraisal schemes have many options from which to choose. The first choice concerns the purposes of appraisal, the varieties of which are shown in Fig. 6.1. The first of the two dimensions shown in Fig. 6.1 concerns whether the intention of appraisal is accountability or development. The former is concerned with results achieved and resources expended, whereas the latter focuses on behaviour, competence and knowledge. The second dimension concerns the person who conducts the appraisal and whether they are the appraisee's line manager or a peer. These dimensions lead to the identification of four purposes of appraisal. The purpose of the first type of appraisal, peer review and development, is to give supportive feedback to the appraisee and help them plan their self-development. It focuses on helping a person make sense of their work experience and it does not give any priority to the needs of the organisation. As a commentator on one such scheme reported: 'It [the interview] was not seen as a management exercise but as a personal opportunity to reflect and plan' (Oxford Polytechnic Educational Methods Unit, n.d.).

Competence assessment and development appraisals are also focused on development, but they are designed to integrate the individual's development with the

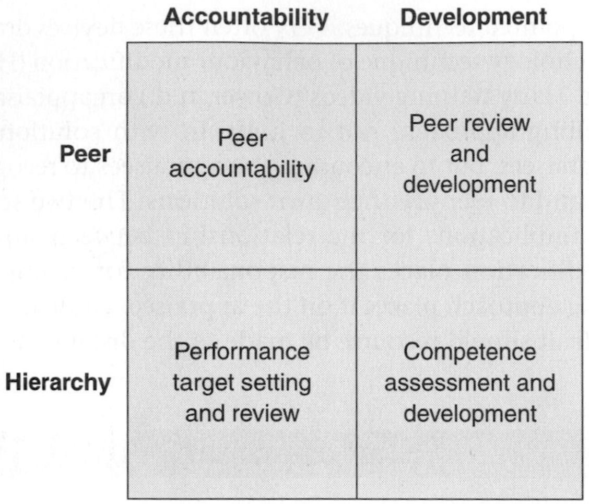

	Accountability	Development
Peer	Peer accountability	Peer review and development
Hierarchy	Performance target setting and review	Competence assessment and development

Fig. 6.1 The purposes of staff appraisal

competency requirements of the organisation. It follows, therefore, that the organisation requires appraisers to make ratings of the appraisee's knowledge, competency and qualities against an organisational framework. The framework may be purpose designed for the organisation (Glaze, 1989) or use generic standards such as lead body occupational standards. The assessments are entered into an organisational database to give management an inventory of the skills available to them. The next form of appraisal is peer accountability and it is often found in professional contexts. Medical audit of clinically significant events (Marinker, 1990: 120), in which clinicians conduct 'a systematic, critical analysis of the quality of medical care', is a good example of the genre. Such appraisals take place within the context of external professional standards rather the imperatives of the organisation. In some cases, such as the hospital consultant's merit scheme, peer review is the mechanism used to allocate financial awards (Department of Health, 1989). The final type of appraisal is concerned with setting and monitoring targets. Within this approach, appraisal becomes a cascade process in which targets are set for the whole organisation and are then disaggregated and allocated to people throughout the organisation.

The designers of appraisal schemes also have a range of design features that they can choose to include in their schemes. The main choices are shown in Fig. 6.2. They are not disconnected. A choice of one option may affect or limit the designers' choices in other areas, but it will be helpful to describe the choices separately. The first issue is whether appraisal should be linked with performance-related pay. This subject is discussed in more detail in Chapter 7. The next choice is whether the scheme should include arrangements for dealing with appeals against the ratings or decisions made during appraisal and the degree to which legal or formal process should be used in any appeal mechanism.

The next three areas of choice all concern the degree of formalisation of a scheme. The most important issue here concerns appraisal documentation. One option is to have no pro-formas and to let the participants write reports on appraisals in any way that seems suitable to them. Another possibility is to have an appraisal form, such as that used in

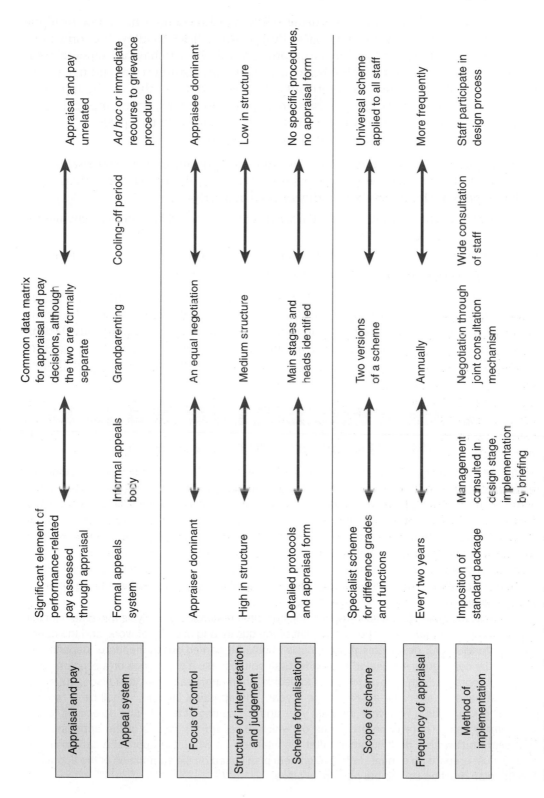

Fig. 6.2 Design options for designers of appraisal schemes

the NHS Individual Performance Scheme (NHSTA, 1987), which has a few headline questions to guide discussion but a great deal of white space to allow the form to be completed in a variety of ways. The most formal possibility is to have an appraisal form entirely composed of rating scales, behaviorally anchored rating scales and tick boxes. There are also different degrees of formality and standardisation that can be applied to the procedure for conducting appraisals. In some organisations, for example, the procedure might specify the time of year when the appraisal has to take place.

The last three areas of choice listed in Fig. 6.2 concerns:

- the frequency of appraisal (some people argue that preparing for an appraisal is such a major task that once every two years is more than sufficient, whereas others argue that appraisals should be six monthly or even quarterly);

- whether one scheme should suit all or whether there should be different schemes for different categories of staff;

- the method of design and implementation. This last issue concerns the degree to which staff should be involved in the design of the scheme.

The success of an appraisal scheme will, in part, reflect the contingent fit (as negotiated by managers and staff) between, to use Mohrman *et al.*'s (1989) terms, appraisal schemes and organisational realities. The notion of fit in this context refers, not to some technically correct, or necessary, solution to the design problem, but to the degree of acceptability that a scheme has among all the parties with an interest in it (Fisher, 1995).

CASE STUDY 6.2

Designing an appraisal scheme for a university

Skegmouth University introduced its appraisal policy in 1993. It began by proclaiming: 'Appraisal is the process by which as accurate a picture as possible of staff performance and staff professional needs is obtained. It is concerned, therefore, with developing the abilities, strengths and aspirations of all staff and working positively with them to fulfil their needs. Skegmouth University appraisal scheme is focused on staff development. The whole emphasis of the scheme will be to offer positive opportunities to staff.'

The university has performance-related pay for managerial staff, but the operation of this scheme is formally separate from the appraisal scheme, which applies to management grades, the 800 academic staff and the 1600 support staff.

Appraisal, according to the policy document, has three features: the analysis and determination of objectives; the measurement or judgement of the quality and quantity of work; and the operation of effective staff development. Appraisals should be carried out by heads of departments (HoD) or by colleagues nominated by heads. Staff can express a preference or a concern about who may appraise them. It is up to heads to decide when appraisals shall take place, but everyone must have an interview at least once a year. The appraisal interview 'shall be a two-way process' and include a review of the past year and the setting of targets and objectives for the forthcoming year. There is no pro forma on which to record the results of the appraisal. The appraiser must write a draft summary after the interview on which the appraisee can comment. Heads must prepare an annual staff development plan based on the summaries of the appraisals and the plan must be sent to the personnel office.

Staff were wary of the scheme. Many of the manual staff found the scheme's obsession with setting targets irritatingly irrelevant to their jobs. They pointed out that, when they had achieved competence in their jobs, it was only required of them that they maintain the standard. The setting of annual targets, such as 'to maintain last year's error rate at 0.25 per cent', would become monotonous. The scheme also implied a fixation on personal growth that seemed almost insulting given the narrowness of their job roles.

Academic staff tended to harbour suspicions about the real purpose of the scheme. Academics value their professional autonomy (although as Skegmouth is a new university the idea of academic tenure has no contractual validity) and they saw the appraisal scheme as an attempt by management to replace collegial relations between staff with a hierarchical and managerial line relationship. The chain of argument leading to this conclusion was byzantine. Until the introduction of appraisal, it was assumed that all academic staff reported directly to their HoD. Such a large span of control gave lecturers a good deal of freedom from managerial interference. It was also practically difficult for HoDs to interview all their staff and many appraisals were conducted by principal lecturers (PLs), a post which in the past had not been seen as a line managerial post. In some departments, an appraisal conducted by a PL was seen as a peer appraisal. But a difficulty could arise. Appraisals, under this scheme, involved setting targets and agreeing expenditure on staff development; as these could be seen as managerial functions, the fact that they were being carried out by PLs could be seen as, *de facto*, converting the PL post into a line management or team leader post. The argument could then be developed that appraisal was a device for undermining professional autonomy and replacing it with a centralised and hierarchical chain of command. Indeed, some academics, from other institutions, had written academic papers on the role of appraisal in the proletarianisation of the academic labour force (e.g. Wilson, 1991; Townley, 1990).

If PLs were not seen as line managers, they had the problem, when conducting appraisals, of not having any managerial discretion with which to agree or finance staff development activities.

Other issues were raised. A substantial lobby argued that the lack of formality in the appraisal reports and procedures meant that the scheme could easily allow discrimination and prejudice to seep into the system. There is much opportunity for people to be treated unequally and there was certainly no standardised documentation that could be used to prove otherwise. Many staff were afraid of biased or incompetent appraisers; and the trainers who carried out the appraisal training were surprised at how many of the latter there were. A further problem emerged when the university failed in its first attempt to become accredited as an Investor in People. The reason given by the assessors was that there were parts of the organisation, especially among the support staff, where appraisals were not being carried out.

The Appraisal Steering Group is charged with monitoring the workings of the appraisal scheme and it is meeting to consider changes to the scheme.

Activity 6.3

1 What are the expectations and anxieties of staff and management concerning the existing appraisal scheme and any changes that might be made?

2 How might these anxieties and expectations be assuaged or met by changing the existing appraisal scheme?

3 What changes would you recommend and why?

Conclusion – does performance management work?

If performance management is seen as a body of lore, then the task of deciding whether it works is a difficult one. The answer would depend on what function the lore fulfils. The Saville and Holdsworth (1997) report argued that the problem with performance appraisal is that there are too many stakeholders who want it to do contradictory things. Most schemes therefore fall between several stools. Some might see performance management as a way of creating a false consciousness among staff that blinds employees to the ways in which they are being manipulated and exploited (Buglear, 1986). Bowles and Coates (1993: 15) argued that, as organisations experience difficulties with their performance-management schemes, they try to create good impressions of them: 'those actions they take [in relation to the schemes] appear to be aimed at maintaining an idealised view of PA [performance appraisal] in their organisation, and not at the actual realities of the problems involved'. The implication is that management is in danger of believing its own propaganda. But staff are not necessarily convinced by impression management and can deliberately use schemes to manipulate their bosses into having a good impression of them (Wayne and Ferris, 1990).

Some people would argue that the value of the lore of performance management lies in its effectiveness in helping organisations achieve their goals. This conclusion is not supported by research evidence. The IPM (1992) surveyed 500 high-performing private companies (with a consistent profits performance over five years), 750 private companies selected at random and 538 public-sector organisations. It reported:

> The most important conclusion is that organisational performance is not associated with the pursuit of formal performance management programmes. Such programmes are as likely to be introduced by poor performers (in relative terms) as high performers and even more likely to be adopted if the organisation is in the public sector (where performance measures are difficult to compare). (IPD, 1992: 17)

In a subsequent, interview-based survey of a smaller sample of organisations, only two company managements claimed, without any evidence, that performance management had improved their company's overall performance. But many managers in the sample did claim that it had made a difference at individual and team level. In particular, respondents in public-sector organisations claimed that it had made staff 'output conscious' (IPD, 1992: 98).

It can, finally, be argued that the function of performance management lore is to provide people with the rhetorical raw material from which they can craft personally relevant interpretations of their organisational and personal roles. There is much evidence that, even when people are critical of aspects of their organisation's schemes, they can still find value in them. In one confidential survey of a PM scheme in a county council, 67 per cent of the respondents agreed (strongly or slightly) that the process of reviewing their accountabilities and assessing their performance helped to clarify their sense of purpose and the direction of their job, even though they had many detailed criticisms of the scheme. It is as if staff want performance appraisal to work even when they are worried about the fairness of the assessments made and the amount, and usefulness, of the training and development that will emerge from the process.

Summary

In this chapter the following key points have been made:

■ Performance management can be seen as a body of lore and recipes, some based on good research and theory, some based on symbolic resonance and workplace myths.

■ The main elements in the corpus are programme structures, performance measurement, target setting, 360° appraisal, personal development plans, performance-related pay and techniques for dealing with 'problem' staff. These activities wax and wane in popularity.

■ The key issue concerning programme structures is the maintenance of their currency and accessibility.

■ The main managerial concern in performance measurement is designing schemes that do not lead to organisational suboptimisation

■ Pitching targets at an appropriate level is the main area of difficulty in target setting.

■ The problem of the sensitivity of managers' egos, especially in relation to evaluative, as opposed to developmental, multi-rater feedback (McEvoy, 1990), and the difficulty of weighting the feedback from different groups, are critical issues in designing 360° appraisal schemes.

■ Personal development plans can be a powerful tool for individual learning, but they can degenerate into bureaucratic chores.

■ Appraisal schemes need to be carefully designed to be broadly acceptable to both appraisees and appraisers.

■ There is no solid evidence that performance management improves an organisation's performance, but there is evidence that people can find it helpful in interpreting and evaluating their organisational roles.

Discussion questions

1 In what ways do people in your organisation attempt to manipulate, sabotage or avoid performance measures and indicators? How might this situation be changed?

2 Should performance management focus primarily on the organisation/department, the team or the individual?

3 Compare the advantages and disadvantages of peer and hierarchical staff appraisal.

4 How useful is staff appraisal when dealing with 'problem' staff?

5 Is 360° appraisal a necessary counterweight to staff appraisal?

Further reading

Articles by Fisher (1994, 1995) go into much more detail on designing acceptable appraisal schemes. Mohrman *et al.* (1989) is a key book on designing appraisal schemes and particularly valuable on the use and design of rating scales and behaviourally anchored rating scales. Walters (1995) is a good introductory book on the subject with a strong emphasis on measurement.

7

PERFORMANCE PAY AND PERFORMING FOR PAY

Lynette Harris

OBJECTIVES

Having completed this chapter and its associated activities, readers should be able to:

■ demonstrate an understanding of the centrality of performance-related rewards in organisational approaches to performance management and human resourcing strategies;

■ explain the growth in performance-related pay (PRP) in the UK;

■ identify the issues, tensions and contradictions associated with the practice of performance-related pay;

■ evaluate the effectiveness of performance-related pay as a means of improving 'employee performance';

■ identify the responsibilities of the line manager and the personnel specialist for the design and application of performance-related pay;

■ recognise the variety of factors that can influence the implementation and operation of performance-related pay.

Introduction – PRP in context

The growth in performance-related pay (PRP) has been one of the most significant developments in human resourcing practices in recent years. This chapter will consider the principles, growth and experience of PRP within the context of organisational approaches to performance management as discussed in Chapter 6. Performance management, described by Bevan and Thompson as 'how to harness employee performance for the good of an organisation as a whole' (1992: 7), is a relatively contemporary term for a concern that is as 'old as the hills' for employers. The roots of current approaches to managing performance can be found in the merit ratings and management-by-objectives schemes of the past (Fowler, 1990). If a key purpose of management has always been to strive for improvements in employee performance as a means of getting better organisational results, is there really anything new about contemporary approaches to performance management and performance-related pay? Armstrong (1994: 21) suggests that well-developed performance-management strategies of the 1990s differ from past practice in that they:

- are an integrative process, reflecting corporate, functional, team and individual objectives and linking these to human resourcing practices;

- are treated as part of the normal line management process, not an administrative chore imposed by personnel departments;

- focus on improving performance by developing competence and releasing potential;

- provide a basis for performance-related pay decisions where such schemes exist.

It is this last defining characteristic that is the concern of this chapter, the increasing propensity of organisations across all occupational sectors to seek ways of linking pay to employee performance (IPD, 1998). The focus will be on individual performance-related pay (IPRP), as this is the area where the growth of systems designed to measure and reward performance has been the most significant. It is a trend in employment practice that has captured the attention of both the practitioner and academic commentator, possibly due to the difficulties of developing pay policies that focus on improving future performance and rewarding past achievements in the same process. The role of incentivised pay in rewards strategy has always been particularly complex. The tendency is that in solving the dominant issue of allocating pay according to individual contribution, a host of other problems are created.

Recognising reward systems as one of the most influential of all human resourcing strategies on employee behaviour (Lawler, 1973), performance-related pay is a demonstrable means of identifying and reinforcing corporate objectives. To quote Hendry *et al.* (1997: 23), 'rewards are one of the main ways in which organisations structure their relationship with employees and PRP is an overt attempt to realign this relationship'. Yet the very significance of pay as a means of pursuing various managerial objectives has 'led to the design and implementation of systems facilitating short-term achievement of managerial objectives which have often given way to goal distortion and displacement' (Kessler and Purcell, 1992: 17).

The process of achieving the desired alignment is widely recognised as complex and 'reward management can be seen as indicative of the contradictions that exist within the discipline labelled human resource management' (Kelly and Monks, 1998: 113). In part, this is due to the tangible nature of pay compared with many other human resourcing practices, which may explain why PRP is so frequently selected to illustrate the distinction between 'hard' and 'soft' human resource management (Storey, 1992: 27). The contradictions observed in so many reward policies certainly provide plentiful examples of the conflicts that exist in human resourcing strategies, designed to elicit commitment through the development of employee potential (Walton, 1985) at the same time as optimising the use of human resources just 'as any other economic factor' (Storey, 1987: 6).

What do we mean by performance related pay?

Performance-related pay can be used as a generic term to describe a variety of payment systems that link employee pay to some measurement of performance of individuals, work groups or the organisation to which they belong. It is, however, most commonly used to describe individual appraisal-related performance pay. Based on the typology developed by Bevan and Thompson (1992) for the Institute of Personnel Management/Institute of Manpower Studies research into performance management in the UK, PRP schemes can be broadly defined as follows:

1 *Individual payment related to performance.* Traditionally, these were the outcome of payment by results schemes or piecework for hourly paid employees where an individual's earnings are totally or partially based on individual performance in terms of output against set targets. In the past 20 years, the emphasis has been on 'individual performance-related pay' (IPRP), predominantly for salaried employees. In IPRP schemes the assessment of individual performance is linked to a level of bonus or an element of basic pay through a performance-review process. In most organisations this review process is conducted via a formal appraisal system.

2 *Merit payment* with no links to formal appraisal.

3 *Team or group performance payment*, where pay is divided between a work team or work group according to measures of team performance.

4 *Financial participation*, where the employee receives rewards in terms of cash or an option of shares related to company profits over a fixed period. To some degree the profit-related pay schemes approved under favourable taxation arrangements due to end in January 2000 fall into this category, although they have provided for an element of basic pay to be directly related to profits. For a discussion of financial participation schemes, *see* Chapter 13.

The growth in performance-related pay

Bevan and Thompson (1992: 41) reported in the IPM/IMS survey that: 'Performance pay has become increasingly central to the personnel agenda in recent years. There is some growing evidence that performance related pay (in some form) is being more widely introduced in both private and public sector.' The study found that appraisal-related pay was used by 54 per cent of organisations for senior managers, dropping to 44 per cent for other managers; 31 per cent used it for other white-collar staff but only 7 per cent for manual workers. Cannell and Wood's research (1992) for the IPM and the National Economic Development Office (NEDO) similarly established that 47 per cent of the 390 organisations surveyed used PRP for managers and other salaried staff. Its usage was less in the public sector, with very limited occupational application. A Local Authority Conditions of Service Advisory Board survey (LACSAB, 1990) reported 40 per cent of Authorities using IPRP, but only for some 4 per cent of employees.

Manual employees have been largely excluded from the growth of PRP schemes (ACAS, 1988; Kessler, 1994: 471), despite some examples of organisations that have introduced pay-related appraisal schemes for manual workers as part of integrated pay structures (Kinnie and Lowe, 1990). The focus in rewards has moved away from incentive schemes for manual employees. This is in sharp contrast to the first three decades after the Second World War, when payment by results schemes for manual workers, which were predominantly output driven and based on traditional piecework principles, were the main preoccupation in remuneration. By the end of the 1970s, many of the wage and salary systems in the UK were in a depressingly chaotic state, which Smith (1983: 53) argued was due to 'ad hoc adjustments to pay in response to immediate pressures'. The market-based ideology of the 1980s, combined with economic, societal and technical changes, altered the context for organisational reward policies and led to employers' interest in performance-related pay. Its growth can be particularly attributed to:

- the search for human resourcing strategies that link the efforts of individuals to the corporate objectives of organisations;

- the most frequently quoted organisational rationale (IDS, 1988) for PRP – attracting, retaining and motivating key staff;

- attempts to improve a sense of company and commercial awareness by offering a share in success through forms of financial participation;

- the philosophy of the enterprise culture and the prevailing political ideology of an unfettered market economy, which emphasised the importance of pay systems that were sufficiently flexible to take account of market forces rather than retaining payment systems whose primary concern was maintaining a demonstrable internal equity;

- a belief that linking rewards more closely linked to individual performance is more motivating and equitable than providing identical rewards for dissimilar levels of contribution and standards of performance;

- decentralisation and a focus on making managers manage by discriminating between different levels of performance for the allocation of rewards, by recognising good performance (Cannell and Wood, 1992) and sending out signals about under-performance;

- a weakening of trade union-dominated pay bargaining, with a shift away from collectivism towards individualism in reward policy, combined with a reassertion of managerial control in employment matters (Kessler and Purcell, 1992);

- a perception that rewarding the 'right' behaviours would assist cultural change and reinforce the desired organisational values by providing a tangible means of recognising achievements that were supportive of organisational goals.

The increasingly competitive environment of an open market economy demanded human resourcing strategies based on principles that contributed to the maximisation of business performance. Until the 1980s, in larger organisations there was all too often a lack of association between wages and organisational performance, which insulated employment from competition and external labour markets. As Capelli (1995: 585) argues, this resulted in a psychological contract based on exchanging *employee commitment, loyalty and adequate performance* for *job security and predictable improvements*. Armstrong (1988) describes this as the 'old orthodoxy' on pay, concerned with internal rather than external relativities and establishing system and order based on a collective view of the allocation of rewards. The approach still prevails in areas of the public sector where long incremental salary scales operate within grades and an employee's position on a scale reflects length of service rather than the quality of individual contribution. The search for more flexible reward strategies linked to business performance grew out of a rejection of the rigidities associated with traditional approaches to pay.

As the degree of integration between human resourcing strategies and business strategy is increasingly identified as a vital ingredient in organisational success, the relationship between pay and organisational performance has grown in importance.

PRP and the employee commitment agenda

Promoting the link between organisational performance and employee commitment is a key concept in the literature on human resource management (Walton, 1985; Guest, 1987). For Kessler (1995: 260), the search for greater employee commitment to the organisation has explicitly informed the more recent use of various long-established systems linking pay to indicators of company performance. Increasing commitment has been a frequently stated reason for the introduction of individual performance-related pay schemes from the mid-1980s onwards (ACAS, 1990). Establishing individual targets against corporate goals as part of a cascading-down process is a visible means of demonstrating the relationship between an organisation's objectives and individual contribution – reinforced by financial rewards for the types of behaviours that employers are seeking to encourage (Scott, 1993).

Wood's study (1995) of employment practices suggests that a distinction can be made in organisational approaches to human resourcing between the commitment system and the performance management approach (*see* Watson, Chapter 1). The first approach focuses on progression, training and development and internal forms of flexibility, which Hendry observes (1995: 432) is similar to the traditional 'internal labour market', although lower on job security. By comparison, the performance-management approach is dominated by the concept of increasing commitment bought through pay incentives and an emphasis on achieving high performance tied into the strategic objectives of the organisation. Many of the difficulties associated with using PRP as a vehicle for gaining greater commitment are related to the fact that its effectiveness is so highly contingent on the prevailing organisational context. Under-estimating this, combined with a visible lack of congruence between employment practices that use the language of development yet apply hard measures when it comes to the allocation of rewards, can erode rather than improve levels of commitment.

A move to IPRP, away from centrally based collective bargaining, has been one of a number of human resourcing initiatives that have driven culture-change programmes in organisations. This has been particularly evident in the public sector and the privatisation programmes of the public utilities. Dismantling the bureaucratic controls that supported the operation of internal labour markets (Edwards, 1979) led to an early focus in the newly privatised companies on rewards policy as an immediate way of signalling a break with past practice. In the author's own study (Harris, 1998) into middle management's perceptions of performance-management processes, the significance of IPRP in changing employee attitudes, for better or for worse, was widely acknowledged. An experienced personnel manager who had been highly involved in the implementation of IPRP in the electrical supply industry observed:

> For the first couple of years it was chaos. Managers just didn't have the skills to appraise and make decisions on individual pay. Every one felt the new system was unfair but to be honest it really did change attitudes. Things weren't taken for granted any more.'

Yet the line managers in the same study challenged the wisdom of implementing incentivised pay systems that were ill thought out as a vehicle for change, even if they altered employee behaviour. As one network operations manager working in the same industry put it:

> the new pay system has been very successful in changing the culture, but the thousand dollar question is whether it has actually taken us to where we want to be.

Motivational principles and PRP

A fundamental assumption in support of PRP is that monetary incentives linked to performance will act as a motivator and increase performance. Mabey and Salaman (1995: 190–2) suggest that the two motivational theories particularly pertinent to any discussion of performance management are expectancy theory (Vroom, 1964) and goal-setting theory (Locke *et al.*, 1981; Locke and Latham, 1984, 1990). In terms of its application to performance-related pay, expectancy theory's linked concepts of expectancy, instrumentality and valence suggest that only if rewards are valued will individuals adjust their behaviours to attain them. Put another way, unless the financial rewards available are perceived by the individual to be sufficiently attractive and worth the effort needed to achieve them, they will not spur an individual on to try to achieve a higher level of performance.

Activity 7.1

The Christmas bonus at Robinsons

Robinsons is a small, high-quality wood manufacturer with just over 100 employees. After several difficult trading years, the company had a better year in 1998 so the managing director, James Simpson, decided to pay a Christmas bonus to all employees. He announced his intention to express his appreciation for the staff's contribution in this way at a meeting with the four employee representatives in early November. As a result, the pay slips to staff circulated the Friday before the Christmas break revealed that everyone had received an extra £50 in their pay packet. Much to the managing director's dismay, his gesture was not received with the universal approbation he had expected. Most employees appeared to be disappointed with the amount they had received and James Simpson began to wish he had not bothered with the bonus at all but put the £5000 to a more productive use.

1 To what extent does what we know about motivational theory explain the staff's reaction to their Christmas bonus?

2 What lessons can be learnt about rewarding performance from James Simpson's unfortunate experience?

3 What do you think James Simpson should do about a Christmas bonus next year?

The basis of goal-setting theory is that the goals that employees pursue are a significant factor in achieving superior performance, but for these to be motivating in the organisational context the empirical evidence (Mento *et al.*, 1987) suggests that these have to be specific, demanding but realistic, accepted as desirable and the subject of subsequent feedback. Looking at these requirements, it is not difficult to see where the SMART (specific, measurable, agreed, realistic and timed) targets in evidence in so many organisational performance-management schemes stem from. The following extract from British Gas's 20-page employee guide *Rewarding Performance* (1998) illustrates how these concepts can be applied to rewarding individual/team performance. It also reveals how, in the effort to broaden the basis for evaluation, schemes grow in complexity.

Porter and Lawler's motivational model (1968) recognises that individual abilities and role perception have to be taken into account in the wage/effort bargain. The essential argument is that what individuals believe they are required to do or believe they should be doing plays a crucial part in the process of establishing mutual expectations and goal setting. This is a dimension that is easily under-estimated in the application of performance-related pay, particularly in the public sector where the beliefs of individuals may be at odds with the growing influence of the marketplace in the provision of public services. If the job itself is the true source of motivation (Herzberg, 1966), then offering incentives to do it better may at best be regarded as an irrelevance to occupational groups whose loyalties are more closely linked to the attainment of high professional standards than to specific organisational objectives. Such a response was exemplified by the reported case of the Hampshire police constable who declined a Home Office appointment because it included an element of IPRP, on the grounds that 'the notion I will work harder or more effectively because of PRP is absurd and objectionable, if not insulting' (Hogg, 1998).

ILLUSTRATION 7.1

How the performance management scheme works

- At the beginning of each year, you will discuss and agree your targets for the year ahead with your line manager.
- Your manager will ask you to agree two kinds of objectives: *smart* and *stretch*.
- Your *smart* objectives will be the standard performance that is expected of you over the year.
- Your *stretch* objectives will be stretched versions of each of your smart objectives. These stretch objectives will represent a higher level of achievement, and you will earn a maximum bonus of 4% of your salary if you achieve all of them.
- If you exceed your smart objectives but do not meet all your stretch objectives, your bonus will be calculated on a pro-rata basis up to 4%.

Source: Rewarding Performance – What it means for you, British Gas Trading Ltd, January 1998.

Goss (1994: 85) points out that the design of payment systems can result in outcomes that are quite different from 'those expected or desired by those designing or implementing the system'. Kerr (1991: 485) argues that this can actually lead to certain behaviours being rewarded that the organisation may be seeking to discourage. He provides the example of US university teachers who it is *hoped* will not neglect their teaching responsibilities although they are *rewarded* for their research and publications. This tension is very familiar to lecturers in UK universities, where it is increasingly rational for staff seeking promotion to concentrate on research activities rather than teaching. An even more extreme example is found in the bonuses paid out to hospital consultants under a performance pay system implemented in the mid-1970s (*Guardian*, 25 March 1998: 2). Under the scheme there is the potential for doctors in certain clinical disciplines to double their annual salaries, but there are growing concerns that the system rewards the publication of research and conference attendance rather than treating patients in an NHS facing rising waiting lists due to lack of money.

The amount of money available for performance-related pay emerges as a critical factor in its motivational effectiveness. Expectancy theory highlights the requirement for the rewards offered to have a positive valence. When the size of the 'compensation pot' for the performance element is overly small due to financial constraints, or considered insignificant by the occupational group, then its motivational impact will be considerably reduced and even eradicated completely as Marsden and Richardson found in their study of Inland Revenue staff (1992). For employees on lower pay, the amount of PRP needed to make a 'noticeable difference' can be smaller to have an impact on employee behaviour (Heneman, 1992). In recent years, low inflation has reduced pay awards and has similarly reduced the amounts payable for IPRP. Smaller awards are likely to encourage managers to revert to a traditional collective approach to pay (Harris, 1998), in line with the perceived wisdom expressed by one departmental head in the Civil Service '*If there isn't much for anyone then it is better to share it as evenly as possible – it makes for less trouble in the long run*'. Individuals are likely to receive more performance-related pay in the early stages in a role than when they are fully experienced and it is more difficult to demonstrate improvements in job performance. This can raise organisational reward issues for experienced employees performing well in a job, but who are unlikely to progress beyond their current position.

Spending the incentive pay budget on rectifying anomalies created by market rates leads to problems if it results in employees' expectations that IPRP was to be based on individual contribution not being met. This was recently observed in one major UK engineering company that was experiencing problems in attracting and retaining recruits on its graduate training scheme. Managers who had been given considerable autonomy in their pay budgets used them to resolve retention problems, resulting in considerable dissatisfaction among other grades of staff who felt that their efforts had been overlooked and even devalued.

The felt-fair concept

Torrington argues (1998: 627) that 'the growth in performance-related pay undoubtedly owes as much to the appearance of fairness as to its supposed incentive effects'. At face value, the concepts underlying performance-related pay would appear to be self-evidently fairer than paying the same rewards to everyone regardless of their performance. The logic that it is only right to pay more to those who make the greatest contribution, or, to reverse the argument, less to those who contribute the least, seems intuitively right. Yet the application of this principle is repeatedly shown to be problematic and its outcomes even dysfunctional in practice. One explanation for this may lie in the inadequate attention paid in the design, implementation and operation of performance-related pay schemes to equity theory (Adams, 1965), which is concerned with *how* individuals perceive they are being treated in comparison to others. It reinforces the importance of the 'felt-fair' principle in reward systems (Jacques, 1961), which suggests that the concept of fairness in pay systems depends to a very considerable extent on whether or not they are seen as equitable by the individuals who have to apply them and experience their outcomes.

Lewis (1991) suggests that the concept of 'rewarding the goodies and punishing the baddies' through the use of PRP presents dilemmas for most managers and HR specialists. The argument is that, while the application of IPRP to reward the high performer is an approach with which most managers are happy, there is discomfort about its use essentially to punish the poor performer. The intention is that the results-oriented approach of many schemes will make such issues clearer for the manager, even if uncomfortable. The reality is likely to be far less straightforward, as Activity 7.2 demonstrates. The rating systems of many schemes are quite unequivocal about the link between performance and annual pay increases, as the rating system of one publicly funded research organisation reveals. Managers are required to rate individual performance against five boxes of achievement, as in Table 7.1.

Yet the questionable effectiveness of IPRP as both 'carrot and stick' is borne out by the findings of the latest IPD survey (1998). Respondents felt that their IPRP schemes had the most positive impact on high performers, but over half felt that it had not resulted in behavioural changes among poor performers (*see* Table 7.3 on p. 205).

Table 7.1 Rating of individual performance

Box 1	Outstanding
Box 2	Significantly exceeds
Box 3	Fully acceptable
Box 4	Incomplete – no annual pay award or bonus unless the interim report is at Box level 3 or above
Box 5	Unacceptable – no annual pay increase or bonus

Activity 7.2

Applying the 'felt-fair' principle

Sue and George are two shipping clerks working in a busy agricultural machinery export office. Sue is tireless. She works demonstrably harder than George, is more punctual, extremely helpful and is always observed as giving of her best effort, frequently staying late in the office for no additional payment. George, on the other hand, achieves just as much as Sue and is actually more accurate, but is nowhere near as hard working, never stays beyond finishing time, is regarded generally as having a rather unco-operative manner and as getting away with the minimum of effort. This poses a problem for their supervisor, Helen, when it comes to deciding the performance-related element of pay appropriate for the two staff. In all her training sessions on the new performance-management scheme, it was emphasised that achieving the set goals was the crucial measure she must apply in assessing individual levels of performance.

1 To which shipping clerk should Helen award the higher level of performance-related pay?

2 Taking account of the 'felt-fair' principle in pay, what would be the implications of your answer to Question 1 in terms of improving both Sue and George's performance?

3 What measures of performance would you apply in this case?

The continuing use of PRP

Despite something of a backlash against the heady enthusiasm of employers in the 1980s for IPRP and a greater emphasis on development than performance-related pay (*see* Fisher, Chapter 6; Donkin, 1997: 13), the evidence is that it is being used for a wider number of employees within organisations. The 1998 IPD survey into performance pay reported that 40 per cent of employers operated IPRP for management employees and 25 per cent for non-management employees. The extent of PRP schemes revealed by the survey is illustrated in Table 7.2. Although IPRP continues to be the most frequently adopted form of performance-related pay, other approaches to performance pay have grown in recent years. Over half of the initiatives in the other three main types of schemes (excluding share ownership) had been implemented in the previous two years.

A brief glance through the managerial remuneration packages offered in the appointment pages of the national press confirms IPRP's enduring popularity for managerial posts. An examination of the jobs in just one edition of the *Sunday Times* (18 February 1998) revealed that 60 per cent offered a performance bonus payable in addition to basic salary. In a competitive labour market, IPRP is clearly an aid to recruitment for certain types of appointment. It can also lock individuals into organisations where an attractive bundle of performance pay arrangements, particularly share options payouts, can be hard to match.

The IPD survey (1998) found that 23 per cent of respondents who currently used none of the forms of performance-related pay set out in Table 7.2 had discontinued them after 1990. This represents an average cessation rate of 3 per cent which, although it is far smaller than the growth in schemes, does highlight that organisations may have become more reflective about the sort of reward strategy appropriate to their requirements. Although a quarter of local authorities introduced IPRP in the late 1980s and early 1990s the most widely publicised incidences of PRP schemes that have been abandoned have been in local government. For example, Lewisham Borough Council axed its scheme in 1994 on the grounds that 'it demotivated more people than it motivated' and Brent phased out its scheme in 1996, along with Cambridgeshire County Council. The general consensus was that many schemes were introduced too hastily and were not appropriate to the type of services that the sector provides (Littlefield, 1996: 15).

Table 7.2 The extent of performance pay schemes, October 1997

Performance pay scheme	Management employees %		Non-management employees %	
	Yes	No	Yes	No
Individual performance-related pay	40	60	25	75
Team-based pay	8	92	8	92
Skill/competency pay	6	94	11	89
Profit-related pay	35	65	34	66
Employee share ownership	17	83	15	85

Source: Institute of Personnel and Development (IPD) *1998 Performance Pay Survey*, Executive Summary.

Measuring and rating

IPRP is governed by measurements and ratings that may take account of inputs such as skills and competencies as well as outputs against measurable targets. Although it has been generally applied to individuals, there is increasing interest in team-based pay schemes, although as Armstrong puts it 'they are not always easy to design or manage' (1996: 313). IPRP is frequently linked to graded pay structures, broad-banded pay scales, individual job ranges and pay curves that allow for different rates of individual progression and maximum flexibility for organisations. One fundamental difference between IPRP and collectively bargained pay is the greater dependency on the assessment of individual managers in the allocation of rewards for performance. As Kessler and Purcell observe, it provides 'opportunities for the greater exercise of managerial control' (1992: 23) and herein lies one of its central problems.

To allocate performance-related pay there has to be a rating, whether this is used to calculate a performance element increasing base pay or a non-consolidated bonus. This is frequently achieved through the use of a performance scale of four to five points and accompanied by guidelines to managers from the HR function on the allocation and distribution of ratings in each category (IDS, 1997). Imposing parameters can be a source of frustration for line managers, who see it as negating the principles of IPRP schemes. One production manager in a pharmaceutical company in the author's own study (1998) complained:

> We are constantly told to make decisions and manage the performance of our staff by recognising their individual contributions but then we are told by our personnel function to follow a prescribed formula for allocating individual pay. It just seems to make the whole process a total waste of time.

United Distillers recognised that a pay matrix was perceived as supporting a 'control from the centre culture' (IDS, 1997), so it no longer uses a pay matrix but leaves the responsibility for individual pay awards with the line manager. Although a minimum rise is specified for different performance bands, no maximum is determined centrally, an approach likely to be easier for a company whose total budget is not overly dominated by labour costs. Similarly, Scottish Amicable abandoned its company-wide pay matrix and fixed distribution across the company in 1996 to try to overcome the forced ratings that had resulted in a lack of faith in the system. Local managers are now allocated a budget and expected to distribute their allocation as pay awards based on their ratings of an employee's performance.

A distinguishing feature of PRP is that it operates largely outside collectively agreed procedures. One perspective is that it has been actively developed within organisations to reduce union involvement in pay bargaining (Procter *et al.*, 1993). Certainly, its operation reduces transparency in pay decisions and encourages secrecy, heightened by decreasing the trade union involvement previously relied on to provide procedural checks and balances. The lack of a developed or independent appeals process can aggravate feelings of mistrust about the process. Standard practice for appeals arising from IPRP decisions is for these to be dealt with outside existing grievance procedures, with one stage of appeal to the next level of management; an approach that hardly encourages perceptions of impartiality.

If 'correctability' of decisions is taken as an essential measure of fairness (Sheppard *et al.*, 1992), then most PRP schemes fail to encourage employee optimism in their neutrality. Demonstrating equality of opportunity is also difficult in a process that focuses on the person rather than the job, and schemes can mask indirect discrimination (IDS, 1998). The lack of demonstrable internal measurement systems other than the use of appraisal leads to the key criticisms levied at IPRP by employees – that it is overly subjective and relies too heavily on the judgements of individual managers.

Measures to overcome the 'twin vices of subjectivity and inconsistency' (Kessler,

1994: 485) are evident in the use of the balanced scorecard (Kaplan and Norton, 1992) to appraise employee performance and the development of 360° appraisal (see Chapter 6). This 360° appraisal is an attempt to widen the circle of sources used for performance assessments to include peers, subordinates and customers. Hewlett-Packard and Shell (IDS, 1997) both use 360° techniques, although at Shell it is an optional development tool and at Hewlett-Packard the use of feedback obtained through 360° is optional for performance evaluation. In practice, its potential for assessing performance for pay purposes appears limited. The following correspondence in the *Financial Times* suggests that it could actually make matters worse by further heightening the tensions between pay and development objectives.

ILLUSTRATION 7.2

360° feedback and pay

Dear Professor Hunt,

I have been asked to look at whether we could improve the effectiveness of our managers by introducing 360° feedback. The idea sounds fraught with danger to me. Don't you think it is asking for trouble to encourage subordinates to criticise their managers? I'd be certainly nervous about taking part – though I have to admit I'd be intrigued to hear what my department had to say about me.

Yours,

A. Sceptic

Professor Hunt replies:

You are right to be concerned: done badly 360° feedback is potentially lethal. But handled carefully these surveys can provide a powerful lever for change . . . I am often asked whether 360° feedback should be used to determine people's pay. One obvious criterion for assessing managers should be managerial competence. The 360° survey could, it is argued, be used to provide measures of this competence. But this simple logic breaks down when objectives become muddled. Most 360° feedback is intended for personal development. Extending that to include an annual assessment of managerial competence as a basis for reward is risky. Managers will begin to manipulate the process by selecting those people who will give them good results. We have even seen cases where it was clear that the managers had filled in all the questionnaires themselves.

Source: *Financial Times*, 8 December 1997, p. 14.

PRP in practice

The actual process of introducing IPRP, how it is communicated and managed, can be as significant as the amounts paid out in terms of employee perceptions of its acceptability and fairness. Dowling and Richardson's (1997: 360) survey of performance-related pay for managers in the National Health Service revealed that the money available was less important as a motivator than the clarification of objectives that the scheme could offer, They concluded that the degree of success of the NHS scheme 'revolved mostly around the way in which work objectives were set'. Getting the implementation process right has long been recognised as a vital success factor in payment schemes (Bowey *et al.*, 1982). The demotivating effects reported in studies of PRP schemes in the 1980s (Gallie and White, 1992; Marsden and Richardson, 1992; Geary, 1992) may well have reflected the 'quick-fix' nature of their implementation. One danger is that PRP is regarded by employees as just another 'fashionable fad', leading to cynicism about its value from the outset (Harris, 1998) that is very hard to overcome however carefully a scheme is designed and implemented.

Although the fundamental assumptions underlying IPRP appear eminently rational, there are constant tensions about what individual contributions should be and how these are to be measured. The key question for organisations investing time and effort in its operation is to what extent it improves organisational performance. Even in contexts where its application seems highly appropriate and it is popular with the workforce, it can have unforeseen consequences, as illustrated by the following brief case study.

CASE STUDY 7.1

The Mutual Alliance Bank

The Mutual Alliance Bank has a long and successful history of retail banking. It has two tele-banking centres that provide a 24-hour telephone banking service to its customers. One of these is based in Scotland and the other in the South West. The volume of work processed has expanded significantly since the centres opened three years ago. At present, staff are paid unconsolidated bonuses set against regularly reviewed numerical targets. After trying a number of different approaches, pay incentives linked to individual performance have been found to be the most effective in encouraging productivity.

To ensure that other aspects of employee behaviour are taken into account as well as sheer output, each employee is rated against a competency matrix of four main headings. These are accuracy, attendance levels, co-operation (which includes team work) and communication skills. Employees are rated every three months by their team leader against these criteria and a joint action plan is agreed with identified development needs. These quarterly reviews form the basis of the annual pay review, which decides the rate of individual progression through a broad-banded salary scale. The financial incentives for achieving or exceeding target figures are currently paid as an unconsolidated bonus every three months, which, for top performers, can amount to as much as £800. The bonuses are not consolidated with basic salary. They are regarded as a positive aid to recruitment in a competitive labour market and are very popular with the call centre employees.

The concern of the HR director is that other problems are now beginning to emerge and she has been set the task of reviewing the present incentivised pay arrangements. Staff turnover has increased at both centres, but is most severe at the Glasgow centre where it has grown to 50 per cent in the last year. Existing employees are reluctant to take time away from their own work to assist and train new staff in case it adversely affects their quarterly bonuses. Team leaders are reporting increasing difficulties in obtaining cover for holidays and other absences. Absenteeism is rising and is currently running at an average of three days a month per employee.

Activity 7.3

1 What explanations are there for the problems now being reported among the telebanking staff at the Mutual Assurance Bank?

2 As the HR director, what changes would you recommend to the current performance-related pay scheme for the call centre staff?

The reported experiences of PRP from the evidence of the 1996 Industrial Society and the 1992 IPD studies found no correlation between the use of PRP and higher organisational performance. The latest IPD survey (1998) considered the effect of IPRP on the behaviour of different groups of employees in the private and public sector. Table 7.3 summarises its findings.

Table 7.3 The impact of IPRP on employee behaviour in the private and public sector

Percentage responses – private sector v public sector (public sector in italics)									
	A large improvement		A small improvement		No real change		A small deterioration		A large deterioration	
High performers	27	8	44	30	28	62	1	1	0	0
Average performers	6	1	56	45	35	52	3	2	0	0
Poor performers	4	2	38	30	46	62	10	3	2	3

Source: Institute of Personnel and Development (IPD) 1998 Performance Pay Survey, Executive Summary.

Table 7.3 illustrates a striking difference between the private and public sector's perception of IPRP's impact. The public sector consistently views IPRP as less effective than the private sector in improving performance and over a range of 10 indicators 51 per cent of public-sector respondents saw IPRP as presenting problems to some degree, compared to 34 per cent in the private sector. Yet both sectors identify IPRP as having the least effect on the behaviour of poor performers.

PRP and line management

In applying PRP (other than company, divisional or plant-wide bonuses), the individual line manager plays a vital role in transmitting the desired corporate messages about pay to the workforce. Trends towards decentralisation and the greater empowerment of managers combined with changing approaches to rewards appear, at least theoretically, to have devolved more responsibility to line management in pay decisions. The difficulty is that the manager is invariably identified as the weak link in the application of performance-management systems (Hendry *et al.*, 1997). In the pursuit of personal goals and objectives, they can undermine the organisational objectives of the process.

The author's own research revealed managers who were widely supportive of the need for change, but their practical experience made them cautious and concerned at what the new approaches would actually achieve (Watson, 1994a). As Fig. 7.1 (Harris, 1998) illustrates, the managers identified an unofficial agenda as well as the officially stated objectives for the introduction of IPRP. The majority of respondents viewed the reported dysfunctional outcomes illustrated in Box C as fairly predictable in view of the *hidden* agenda identified as frequently containing the dominant reasons for changing reward policies.

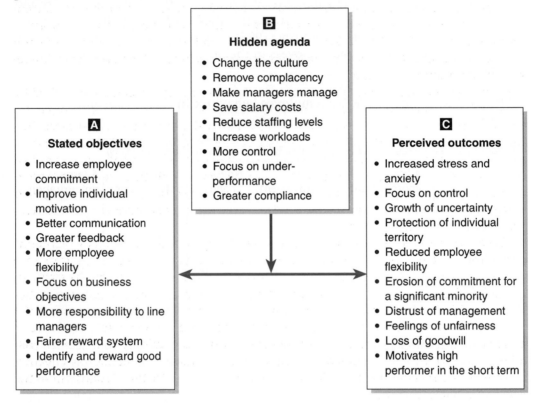

Fig. 7.1 Middle managers' perceptions of organisational initiatives on appraisal-related pay

The hidden agenda identified by the managers emphasised the control aspects of performance-management systems far more than the 'party line'. An unwillingness to deal with under-performance problems of a long-standing and frequently complex nature was held to have led to an over-willingness to abandon pay based on uniform annual pay rises or incremental scales, in favour of systems linked to individual performance. Earlier research by the author (Beaver and Harris, 1996a) revealed a tendency to adopt performance-related pay as a form of 'abdication management', on the misplaced premise that a system could address what had not been rectified due to a lack of managerial skills.

Performance-related pay was dismissed by one Civil Service manager as 'a joke, it's simply a sneaky way of saving on the salaries budget'. Exhorting individuals to work harder and longer to maintain or further reduce staff levels was seen as a major objective which led one building society branch manager to observe: 'It was naïve to think [this] would go unnoticed by employees consistently required to "out perform" their contracts.' It was viewed as overly simplistic to interpret 'changing the pay culture' as merely encouraging greater flexibility, when it was equally concerned with removing complacencies about automatic pay increases and security of employment if performance standards were not achieved. Creating a climate where the old securities had gone and reinforcing a message that continued employment was contingent on individual contribution was designed to bring a level of anxiety, and even fear, into working relationships. To Stiles *et al.* (1997: 65) the emphasis on linking pay to performance and short-term pressures has made 'the employment relationship more transactional' despite a 'company rhetoric' stressing commitment.

From the managers' standpoint, the effectiveness of the new systems was limited by increased individualism. Employees prone to feelings of insecurity created by organisational 'survival anxiety' (Boxall, 1996) resorted to defensive tactics, showed less initiative, became isolated and even territorial. Where team work and close co-operation were fundamental to the effective working of a section or department, the managers had developed coping strategies reflecting their own concepts of distributive justice (Miller, 1996) rather than the principles on which the systems were based (*see* p. 199. Using their own interpretation certain managers, within their delegated discretionary powers, allocated rewards as evenly as they could.

This collective approach adopted by a number of the managers in the study highlights one of the fundamental tensions in adopting a contingency approach to performance and related rewards. On the one hand, as a survival mechanism for managers trying to achieve high levels of trust and reciprocity it is a justifiable means of achieving what Watson (1994b: 32) describes as 'productive co-operation'. On the other hand, if the system is based on a fundamental principle of distinguishing between different levels of performance, then it can increase the levels of distrust that employees have about a relatively closed system of performance measurement and evaluation. Managers frequently revealed a value system that made it difficult for them to exercise their judgement in the way that a scheme intended.

Running a team that was as united as possible was the main preoccupation for one health service manager, who saw attempts to incentivise pay as: 'Demotivating for the majority – I just try to keep my lot happy and cope as best we can with the mounting pressures of work.' This was not a deliberate attempt by the individual to sabotage new initiatives, but in common with the majority of other managers she saw her prime responsibility as concentrating her efforts on making the process as workable as possible both for all concerned. If this meant mitigating the risk to the individual to reduce internal friction and anxiety, then this was believed to be an essential part of the managerial role. Achieving and sustaining predictability in the employment relationship is an under-estimated but central objective of management (Osterman, 1987). The driving force 'to get the job done' by whatever means at their disposal was a dominant one for the respondents, reinforced by a belief that their ability to do so would be the measure of their own success.

Whose responsibility?

The study found little apparent sense of ownership among the managers of their performance-management systems and related PRP schemes. These were regarded very much as the 'brainchild of the HR function', driven by senior management and the board despite the trend to devolve pay decisions away from the centre to line managers. While many line managers welcome the opportunity to make pay decisions about their own staff, for some being in the spotlight is too uncomfortable. In organisations where managers have been ill prepared, or there is an inadequate level of skills, being asked to discriminate between different levels of performance is potentially threatening aspect of the process, resulting in excessive 'middling' when rating performance (Beaver and Harris, 1994).

Devolving pay decisions to local management is an interesting, and possibly questionable, development in view of the frequent criticisms of the subjective and arbitrary nature of IPRP. As Armstrong (1996: 244) observes, it can 'create the problem of ensuring that such decisions are equitable, fair and consistent'. The dilemma is that *in* resolving the problems of too much policing of IPRP schemes by the HR function the scope for inconsistencies is heightened. For the HR specialist the tensions can be particularly acute. Exhorted to ensure that human resourcing decisions are made by line managers, they still carry a wider organisational responsibility when things go wrong, for example a claim of sex discrimination in an IPRP decision. For a fuller discussion of the challenges this can present for the HR function, *see* Chapter 11.

The received wisdom at present is for the HR function to play an active role in developing and supporting managers so that they are equipped to handle the processes involved; a familiar facilitating role that can consume large tracts of HR practitioners' time but produces no measurable outcomes for the assessment of their own contribution. The challenge for the HR function is how to achieve some consistency of application across the organisation while playing no active part in pay decisions.

Activity 7.4

1 What role should the line manager and the HR specialist play in the design and operation of performance-related pay systems?

2 Who decides individual pay levels in your own organisation or an organisation with which you are familiar?

3 What are the advantages/disadvantages of these arrangements for deciding individual or team pay?

Developments in paying for performance

Recent studies (IDS, 1997, 1998; IPD, 1998) indicate that although performance-related pay has remained high on the human resourcing agenda, employers are increasingly evaluating and revisiting their systems. The IPD study (1998: 5) found that four out of ten employers of doing so had modified their schemes since 1995 and a large number were in the process or about to do so; 30 per cent described the changes they had made as radical. The most frequently cited reason for modifying schemes was that 'IPRP did not link pay closely enough to key organisational objectives'. Greater diversity and an emphasis on development issues are reflected in the new approaches to PRP as employers become more reflective about the appropriateness and relevance of systems to their particular organisational context. Pay related to assessments of individual or team performance still shows minimal growth among manual workers. Where it has been introduced, it has often been as part of programmes to harmonise conditions of service. One of the obstacles to its wider usage is that for manual employees paid according to hours worked, payments for overtime, unsocial hours and other shift premiums are likely to offer better and more assured financial rewards.

Pay matrices within broad-banded pay scales emerge as a common solution to issues of progression and pay flexibility to cope with labour-market pressures. Ratings are increasingly linked to behavioural competencies as well as achieving targets. This approach is identified by many employers as the way forward (IDS, 1997), but cannot be adequately considered within the scope of this chapter. Problems of definition hinder a quick treatment of the topic, so for the purpose of establishing a shared understanding, *competence* is defined as referring to the knowledge, skills and behaviours required 'to meet performance expectations in a role' (Armstrong, 1996: 291). The rationale in linking pay progression to competence is that it encourages continuous improvement and offers greater integration between pay and development. Nevertheless, the emphasis is still on delivered performance and it is difficult to see real distinctions in application between competence-based pay progression and most other approaches to IPRP.

Due to the concerns that IPRP can erode co-operation and team work, there has been a growing interest in team-based PRP as an alternative, although its application is limited because it is so driven by the organisational context. As Fig. 7.1 reveals, the IPD research found that its take-up was low, but 45 per cent of initiatives have taken place in the past two years. In terms of its effect on employee performance and commitment, it was not perceived to be as effective as competence-based pay, but schemes where it was in operation were seen to be having a useful impact on the effectiveness of team working. A well-established example of a team bonus scheme operates at the Bradford & Bingley Building Society, where payments are awarded as fixed cash sums rather than as a percentage of salary. All staff, including branch managers, receive the same amount and receipt of payment does not depend on individual performance but on branch performance to foster team contribution. To address the role that managers play, branch managers are eligible for additional bonus payments linked to other targets (IRS, 1997: 7–8).

An IDS study (1998b) reported a wider use of non-consolidated bonus payments to overcome some of the problems created by the relatively small amounts available for IPRP due to low inflation. Such payments limited recurring costs while increasing the visibility of the payment to the employee.

The Eastward Housing Association

The Eastward Housing Association has experienced significant growth in its operations during the past 10 years. There has been an increasing emphasis on generating income from private housing developments to reduce dependency on government funding. The Association has, in general, responded well to these new challenges and three of its sheltered housing schemes for the elderly have received national acclaim. During the same period, the Association's own workforce has doubled to 185 staff, although there has been a growing trend to appoint people on one- or two-year contracts who work alongside staff in permanent posts because of uncertainty over funding. This has been accompanied by a far greater use of subcontractors to meet the fluctuating demands of building programmes. The workforce is represented by Unison as the recognised trade union and membership is currently 70 per cent but is continuing to grow.

Despite the significant changes in the nature and organisation of its work, many of the Association's employment practices have not altered to any great extent. Nowhere is this more apparent than in its rewards system, which has become a real source of dissatisfaction for the staff and senior management. The present approach is highly informal but also quite rigid. Salary scales are largely based on local authority rates of pay and there are 12 pay grades. These range from grade A for trainees and junior clerical/secretarial staff to Grade K for senior architects and quantity surveyors with a final Grade L for certain managerial roles. The six members of the senior management team who head up the different functional areas are on separate individual pay rates, again modelled on the scales for chief officers in local government. There are 48 points on the salary scale and each grade contains, on average, seven incremental points, but in the middle range some of the grades are longer with greater overlaps between the grades, whereas the top three grades only contain six points with an overlap of only one increment. An added complication is that the pay scales cover a diverse range of occupations, from routine administrators, wardens and rent collectors to highly qualified professional roles and technical posts – all requiring very different levels of skills, qualifications and experience.

An employee's initial salary point is at the discretion of the manager responsible for the appointment or promotion and a job's grade is essentially based on precedent and the decision of the chief executive. There is no formal system for grading jobs or regrading existing jobs where the content has changed or the responsibilities have grown. Grade changes are entirely dependent on the recommendation of the departmental head and ultimately decided by the management team, who have a tendency to safeguard the interests of their own functional areas. Annual pay increases are established through collective bargaining and there are no mechanisms for rewarding the above-average performer other than with a promotion should the opportunity occur. There is no culture of dealing with under-performance issues, although it was intended that the appraisal scheme introduced two years ago would encourage managers to identify particular performance problems as well as development needs.

The Association's six senior officers and the chief executive are very aware of the limitations of the present approaches to pay. They are anxious to encourage greater awareness of the more commercially focused environment in which the Association is operating, as well as increasing employee commitment to its key objectives. The performance of all Housing Associations is externally monitored. For the past four years, external performance indicators have been set for all Associations by the Housing Corporation and future funding is highly dependent on demonstrating that these are achieved. A reward system that reflects the required standards of achievement is increasingly required. In addition, there have been persistent problems in recruiting staff with specialist computer skills, to work in finance or on special projects. There is no means of recognising market rates within the present pay system, which can result in staff being recruited on to a higher grade, subsequently causing a pay relativity problem with existing staff doing the same work.

Employees have complained formally through their staff representatives about the inequity of the present pay arrangements. They have the impression that there are inconsistencies in pay rates and too much subjectivity in the way in which they are applied. There is a general feeling that recognition through rewards is part of a 'blue-eyed' syndrome and only comes if you are one of the senior manager's favourites. Even the relative informality of the place, which staff recognise makes it an enjoyable place to work, is seen to have its downside. There are real frustrations for hard-working staff who see colleagues, as they put it 'getting away with it', while they are working very hard or shouldering increased responsibilities compared to someone with longer service who is paid more for less onerous work. As one senior manager points out: 'We are very lucky here. It is a lovely atmosphere but in fact it may be a bit too relaxed. You see people do take advantage.'

Staff turnover is low and many of the workforce have long service, which means that they are at the top of their grades and no longer receive annual increments. The formal appraisal scheme is theoretically linked to individual development plans, but it has been very patchy in its application. Several senior managers see it as something of a time-wasting exercise that has led to a degree of cynicism among the staff. The truth is that not all the senior management team have been appraised themselves and at least one-third of them were unable to attend the 'in-house' training sessions on the appraisal process due to work pressures.

The majority of staff are hard working and very dedicated to Eastward Housing, but there are tensions between different functions. This is particularly evident among the surveyors and the architects, who tend to be very protective and even defensive of their own areas of professional expertise. As a result, the multi-functional teams essential to project development do not always function as well as they could, although the problems seem to be rather greater at a senior level than among the staff on lower grades.

The chief executive has made it clear that he wants to introduce a payment system that recognises individual attainments and encourages greater flexibility and team working particularly between functional areas. He is also anxious to attract and retain the right staff so is seeking a system that can be more responsive to the external labour market. Although a personnel officer was appointed three years ago, there is no one of sufficient experience or expertise to review the present reward system or recommend alternatives. None of the senior managers has any managerial training, as they have all been appointed to their posts on account of their particular professional experience and abilities, with the possible exception of the housing managers where the supervisory element is a particularly dominant feature of the role. In the circumstances, the management team decides to appoint a consultant.

Activity 7.5

You have been appointed as the consultant for the Eastward Housing Association. Your brief is to evaluate the current pay arrangements and make recommendations for a more flexible reward strategy that is more closely linked to employee performance.

1 What are the key issues for a reward strategy at the Eastward Housing Association?

2 What further information would you seek to find out and from whom?

211

---

3 Based on the information already provided, identify the advantages and disadvantages of introducing performance-related pay into this organisation.

4 What changes would you recommend to the present reward system and why?

5 How should these be implemented and what do you see as the main obstacles to their effectiveness within the Eastward Housing Association?

6 Suggest ways in which these could be overcome.

7 Compare the factors to take into account in paying for performance at the Eastward Housing Association with those at the Mutual Alliance Bank, Case study 7.1.

Conclusion

Despite the early optimism about the benefits of PRP, it has not provided the panacea to that most elusive of human resourcing issues – how to develop pay systems that improve employee motivation, productivity and commitment. The debate about its effectiveness in improving the contribution that employees make to organisational performance looks set to continue. There are worrying messages (Fletcher and Williams, 1992) that PRP can actually be demotivating if expectations are not met. Pfeffer (1999a), writing in the *Harvard Business Review*, points to the absence of evidence that PRP schemes improve productivity despite absorbing significant amounts of management time and creating employee discontent. Kohn (1993: 55) argues that three decades of research studies in the US reveal that people who expect to receive a reward for doing a task successfully perform less well than people who expect no reward.

Faced with such arguments, it is difficult to explain why performance-related pay has proved to be quite so enduring or so widespread in its application for managerial and other white-collar workers. Yet employers who have invested heavily of their time and effort in developing performance-related pay as part of their performance-management systems are showing a marked reluctance to abandon the concept, despite the fact that a belief in its effectiveness is something of an 'act of faith'. The principle of paying people according to their contribution appeals to a sense of fairness in most of us, but as we have seen the problem lies in establishing what should be rewarded and the perceived equity of the assessment process.

Summary

In this chapter the following key points have been made:

■ Although the relationship between pay and performance is complex and problematic, PRP remains of central interest to employers in their attempts to develop human resourcing strategies that improve organisational performance through greater employee contribution and commitment.

- PRP continues to evolve as part of performance-management schemes within organisations, but the experience of the schemes introduced in the 1980s has reduced the reliance on pre-packaged solutions. PRP is increasingly being tailored to fit organisational requirements.

- The tension between developing the individual and rewarding past achievement is ever present in IPRP. Pay is a dominant influence and it can result in reduced flexibility, increase individualism and reduced co-operation within and between work groups.

- From the limited evidence available, PRP's impact as a motivator is highly questionable. It has more impact on high performers, little impact on the average performer and virtually none on the under-performer.

- Measurement and rating processes are full of contradictions about how to reward fairly and what constitutes a good performance.

- Individuals develop their own strategies for coping with PRP, which can result in behaviours that employers were not seeking to reward.

- The trend towards increased autonomy in pay decisions to line managers is seemingly at odds with attempts to reduce criticisms of IPRP's subjectivity and its heavy reliance on individual managerial judgement.

- As the interpreters of IPRP schemes, managers are vital to their success or failure but need to play an active role in their development if they are to develop a sense of ownership. Most managers will ultimately resort to a collective approach if they feel that it will reduce friction and 'get the job done'.

- HR specialists have a particularly difficult role in the development of reward policies and practices that are linked to performance. While decentralisation is diminishing certain aspects of their role, they are still expected to oversee PRP processes in terms of problem avoidance and ensuring some consistency of approach.

- an increased emphasis on the link between pay and performance makes the employment relationship more transactional, focusing on short-term achievements at the cost of longer-term commitment.

Discussion questions

1 Taking into account these summary points, why do you think performance-related pay has an enduring interest for employers despite its unproven motivational qualities?

2 Why is it frequently difficult to establish what constitutes good performance and what should be rewarded?

3 How effectively has this been achieved in any work roles that you have undertaken?

4 To what extent can the tensions between rewarding past performance and encouraging future development be resolved?

Further reading

Discussions on performance-related pay appear in most textbooks on human resource management. In addition to the references provided in this book, there are a number of texts that are practitioner oriented and describe in more depth the processes and systems of performance management and PR. Two texts that address such issues are that by Walters (1995), suggested as additional reading in Chapter 7, and Armstrong (1994).

Part III

TRAINING AND DEVELOPMENT

8

EMPLOYEE TRAINING AND DEVELOPMENT
Jim Stewart, Eileen Manhire and Rachael Hall

9

MANAGEMENT DEVELOPMENT
Jim Stewart

8

EMPLOYEE TRAINING AND DEVELOPMENT

Jim Stewart, Eileen Manhire and Rachael Hall

OBJECTIVES

Having completed this chapter and its associated activities, readers should be able to:

- articulate an understanding of employee training and development;

- analyse approaches to and roles of employee training and development in organisational contexts;

- critically evaluate potential and actual contributions of employee development processes in organisational contexts;

- critically analyse the role of employee training and development in managing organisational change;

- locate the role and contribution of employee training and development in wider human resourcing strategies.

Introduction

This chapter examines the specialist function and processes of employee training and development. As the first main section makes clear, confusion and debate can and do arise over the meaning of particular terms. For example, Harrison (1997) titles her book *Employee Development* to comply with the term preferred by her publisher, but quickly makes clear her own preference for the term human resource development (HRD). While the chapter is concerned with meanings and definitions, it does not claim to provide definitive answers. Different terms can, arguably, be associated with different approaches and roles adopted by professional practitioners. This argument provides a focus for the chapter in exploring the research and writing of a number of leading authorities in the field of employee training and development.

Most if not all individuals have some experience of employee training and development, if only as formally defined 'learners', 'trainees', 'delegates' or 'participants'. This may help to explain a widely held perception that training and development are straightforward and relatively unproblematic in the functioning of work organisations, since they can be seen as consisting only of direct instruction. The overall and main purpose of the chapter is to question such a perception. A number of conceptual and empirical analyses are presented and explored. These are utilised to support an argument that employee training and development poses a number of critical questions and options for organisational decision makers, whether specialist HR or non-specialist managers. Such questions are perhaps more sharply focused when considering organisational change and responses to the argued shifts in the conditions of external operating environments. Organisational change will therefore provide a particular focus of interest in the chapter. In summary, the chapter is intended to enable readers to reflect critically on current organisational practices related to employee training and development, and to demonstrate achievement of the objectives listed above.

Employee development is seen by many as the 'poor relation' to more mainstream personnel activities, due perhaps to the perception that the key task of training is 'instructing'. Recent years have seen the introduction of the terms 'development' and human resource development (HRD) to the vocabulary and, while this may not have changed the perceptions of some, there is a growing recognition that training and development can develop individuals and, more significantly, organisations. But this can only be achieved when training and development, and their practitioners, are able – and enabled – to contribute to human resource strategy making in the organisation (Harrison, 1997).

It is probably useful to start the chapter by reviewing the terms 'training' and 'development' and by considering a model of what training and development are undertaken in organisations and why they are done.

Training or development – a matter of perception?

Training is sometimes viewed as that which happens to junior and operative members of an organisation and may still be epitomised by the definition from the 1971 *Glossary of Training Terms* as 'the systematic development of the knowledge, skills and attitudes required by an individual to perform adequately a given task or job' (Department of Employment, 1971). Implicit within this definition are the notions of present needs and structured or mechanistic processes designed to meet specific job performance standards. In many ways, the organisational world has changed significantly since this was written. However, this definition is still held by many – one only needs to ask a group of managers for their definition of training for confirmation of this traditional view. In contrast to the more junior members of the organisation, managers were not 'trained' *per se*, they were 'developed'. Such development focused on the longer term, met wider organisational and personal needs and was not specific to the current job, but rather related to the potential of the individual and their future role in the workplace. (Detailed discussion of management and manager development is to be found in the next chapter.) Baum (1995) identified some key differences between training and development, characterising development as a process that can take place at any time and is not constrained by formal parameters or at specified points within an individual's life cycle. Development is not confined to the classroom or the coaching situation, nor is it a situational term restricted to planned or formalised group sessions. There has to be considerable diversity in terms of where, when and how development occurs (Garavan, 1997: 40; see also Chapter 9).

However, traditional definitions and perceptions of training and development have had to be reconsidered to some extent over the last decade, given the nature and pace of change. Managers *do* need to be trained to acquire the new skills demanded in their fast-changing environments and all employees should be developed to their maximum potential and therefore be regarded as a significant resource to the organisation (Garavan, 1997: 45).

Activity 8.1

1 Identify the training and development that are undertaken in an organisation with which you are familiar for both managers and other staff

2 Are managers developed or trained – or both?

3 Are other staff trained or developed – or both?

4 What differentiates the provision of training and development for managers and that for others?

■ Defining training and development

Learning may be considered a key theme of all training and development. Training can be thought of as helping people to learn:

- for the present and future health of the organisation;
- for personal fulfilment within the organisation;
- and in helping the organisation to learn, to cope better with its fast-changing environment.

Three definitions of training and development illustrate this notion of individual and organisational learning:

- First, training and development are 'the planned learning and development of people as individuals and as groups, to the benefit of the business as well as themselves' (Garavan *et al.*, 1995: 4).

- Second, it may be seen as 'any organizationally initiated procedures which are intended to foster learning among organizational members in a direction contributing towards organizational effectiveness' (Hinrichs, 1976).

- A third definition comes from the American Society for Training and Development (ASTD): 'the integrated use of training and development, career development and organization development to improve individual, group and organizational effectiveness' (Nijhof and De Rijk, 1997: 247).

Of course, learning is often unplanned, haphazard and accidental, and this can be successful in unwittingly meeting individual and organisational goals. However, if learning can help to harness the organisational resources to benefit all, as the definitions suggest, it perhaps needs to be viewed as a manageable concept and to be considered with some degree of planning.

◼ Approaches to training and development

A useful model from Bennett and Leduchowicz (1983) can help readers to plot why their organisations train and the predominant ways in which they train. The model (Fig. 8.1) may be seen better as two continuums, rather than as exclusive segments. On the vertical axis, concerned with *why* organisations train, training activities are seen as maintenance – maintaining systems, processes and standards – but also reactive in that they respond to situations, often crises, to solve problems or fire-fight. Training and development can also be proactive, ensuring that the organisation has the skills it needs

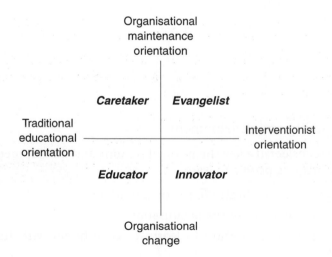

Fig. 8.1 Why and how organisations train

to deal with change and therefore to adopt a change rather than a maintenance orientation. On the horizontal axis – in response to *how* organisations train – the continuum moves from an 'educational' approach towards an 'interventionist' one. The former can be equated to the traditional approach to training – trainer led and didactic. The latter is more associated with the language of 'development' – less structured, more evolutionary and with the trainer having a supporting and guiding role. As can be seen from the model, this framework creates four quadrants:

- 'Caretakers' view training as a mechanism for maintaining and controlling the current systems through a traditional course approach.
- 'Educators' recognise that training can contribute to organisational change, but also use a traditional approach.
- 'Evangelists' want to maintain the status quo but prefer to use a range of interventionist approaches, which will be learner-centred and will often take place within the working environment, rather than on courses.
- 'Innovators' innovate – both in terms of the role they see for training (to encourage and support change) and the innovative training and development activities they use to enable this.

It may be useful to consider this model to debate:

- whether there is compatibility between the espoused approaches to training and development and the actual practices in one's organisation;
- the extent to which the organisation accepts and allows training and development to contribute to its human resourcing strategy. This model reinforces Mabey and Salaman's view that 'training and development can be conceived as different things by different organisations, sometimes as an ad hoc activity, sometimes as a response to a complex and changing environment, sometimes as a strategic device for changing that environment' (Mabey and Salaman, 1995: 176).

Activity 8.2

Use the Bennett and Leduchowicz model (Fig. 8.1) to identify the following:

1 For what purposes does an organisation with which you are familiar invest in training? (Thinking about what training and development is carried out, and why, should help you to plot the organisation on the vertical axis.)

2 What are the preferred training strategies used?

3 Where does training take place and how is it undertaken?

4 What mechanisms are used to determine what training and development are done?

Employee development roles

How important are training and development to the organisation? Finding evidence to answer this question can be difficult and the perception of such difficulties often prevents training practitioners from making serious attempts to evaluate the worth of their activities in achieving organisational goals. So, while practitioners seek greater recognition (and perhaps a seat on the board), they may not be able to prove their case to the key decision makers in the organisation. Two of the key issues surrounding the status of training and development in many organisations are: who these organisational trainers are and what they do, and how the effectiveness of their activities can be 'proved'.

There has long been a view that trainers 'run courses', that they 'instruct' – and many of them do – but this is certainly far from the potential of the majority and the reality of most training practitioners. Working away from the 'line', with their highest visibility to much of the workforce being in 'running courses', has encouraged this view. In our experience, we have met career trainers who have failed to see their wider organisational role and have pursued their own agenda, resulting in an increase in the separateness of the function. Watson, in Chapter 1, emphasises the importance of managers bringing their specialist expertise to influence the overall performance of the organisation, rather than operating in isolation, being 'in charge' of a particular department or function. Should not the practice of trainers, whether managers or not, be seen as influencing organisational performance?

The roles of trainers do appear to be shifting. In their research in the chemical industry in 1982, Pettigrew and his colleagues identified five key roles for what might be termed the 'career trainer' – whether this is a long-term notion of a career, or a developmental task for a limited period (Pettigrew *et al.*, 1982). Two roles related to 'providing' training: the provider and the passive provider. All trainers are 'providers' to some degree, at different levels in the organisation, although the term is occasionally used dismissively, particularly in relation to the passive provider. Pettigrew found this an apt label for some, depending on the culture of the organisation and the lack of personal and influencing skills of some trainers. There is a significant difference between trainers involved in induction sessions or running routine health and safety courses for operative members of staff, and trainers who are facilitating weekend workshops for the senior management team on the values and philosophy of the organisation. Of course, the latter may not perceive themselves as 'providing training' and may not even have the word 'trainer' in their job title!

Pettigrew's third role is that of the training manager, particularly to be found in larger organisations where there is a well-established training and development function with a number of specialist trainers. This role was often viewed as the same as any other departmental manager and it was not found necessary that the role incumbent necessarily had any training expertise.

Pettigrew's research identified that for many their role was 'in transition', normally relating to the transitional period when the organisation recognises a need for an agent of change rather than a training provider, so his final role is that of the change agent.

Trainers as change agents

In recent years, training has been seen as a significant cornerstone of any planned change interventions and, in 1982, Pettigrew observed that increasingly trainers had these change agent roles. More recently, in their comparative research of HRD practitioners in four European countries, Nijhof and de Rijk found that in the UK the role of change agent was chosen by the largest number of respondents as their most important role (1997: 251). Keep suggests that the increasing forces for change have served 'to convince some senior British managers of the need to lay far greater stress upon the importance of HRD activities within their companies' (Keep, 1992: 323). A 1994 survey showed that two of the key influences triggering training in organisations were organisational restructuring (59 per cent) and technological change (50 per cent). (Saggers, 1994: 443). In using an organisational development (OD) approach to facilitate change, the success of change often rests on the qualities and capabilities of those who act as facilitators of change. While it is important that line or functional managers 'own' such change processes, they often do not possess the knowledge and skills required to implement them effectively. The 'change agents' may be sufficiently removed from the day-to-day issues and problems, so that they are able to stand back from the current situation to see how things might be and how they might be achieved. Increasingly, these change agents are trainers who are critical in the wider focus of organisational change and who possess the skills and competences to help others through the process of change.

Stewart (1996: 208) identified several contributions that the training function can make to the management of change:

- ensuring that the people implications of change are raised and understood by the organisational decision makers;
- helping individuals, especially managers, to develop their ability to cope with change;
- developing managers to manage the required learning;
- providing the knowledge and skills to utilise in the change process;
- helping in the development of an outward-looking and future-oriented approach to managing the organisation.

Another key change of trainer roles is the move to 'advising and consulting', which was first recognised in the significant work done in the UK on trainer roles by the Manpower Services Commission in 1978, when a framework of trainer competencies was identified. Implicit in the notion of trainers advising and consulting is that managers – the trainers' clients – do indeed consult them and seek their advice. The process of service departments having to submit themselves to tender for the right to continue to provide their service – which was largely started in local authorities and subsequently spread to many other organisations – has affected training departments, among others. This customer focus has led to these departments reviewing the purpose of their organisational task and recognising that they *can* provide solutions to organisational problems or, at the very least, can contribute to discussions on the more effective use of people. There is an increasing number of consultancies on the outside only too willing to provide advice, and this competition has undoubtedly sharpened the competencies of training practitioners internally. A more recent typology of trainer roles would add the internal consultant to Pettigrew's framework (Sloman, 1994: 25). It would appear that much of the language of training activities echoes the language of marketing and it could be argued that it is perhaps timely for an organisation's training and development function to consider what lessons can be learned by adopting such a marketing perspective.

ILLUSTRATION 8.1

Sarah is HRD manager for a regional brewery. The rationalisation and intensive competition being experienced in that industry have led to Sarah's company increasingly emphasising customer service in the way it operates. 'Customer Charters' have been developed for both manufacturing and retail operations. The same notion is also being applied internally, with each department and function in the company identifying its internal 'customers' and developing and agreeing service standards. As well as leading the development of these standards for the development function, Sarah and her staff have worked closely with the managing director and other members of the board in developing the concept of 'customer service' and devising and implementing employee development activities to support required changes in individual and organisational behaviour. These have included facilitating cross-function and hierarchy project groups examining operating procedures and standards. It has also included working with departmental managers and their staff to examine, review and improve team working. Sarah can clearly identify a shift in the role of the development function since she joined the company 10 years ago. In those days, the function provided standard courses. Sarah estimates that the amount of time spent delivering such courses has shifted from 80 per cent to 20 per cent over the 10 years.

Another useful trainer role framework was developed in the USA by McLagan and McCullough (1983) for the American Society for Training and Development and is presented in Table 8.1.

The evidence of all these analyses presented would suggest that 'instructing' is only a small, though important, part of the role of the 'professional' or career trainer and the status of trainers is slowly improving in many organisations. The whole issue of an organisation's culture will also have an influence on the roles and status of trainers.

Activity 8.3

1 What roles do the trainers perform in an organisation with which you are familiar?

2 How do the trainers fit into Pettigrew's – or any other – framework?

3 What evidence do you have that shows the effect of the organisation's culture on trainer roles and status?

■ Training responsibilities of line managers

Training and development appear to be changing and the roles of training practitioners are likewise changing. This question from Galagan – 'has your company fired the trainers, but added training?' – suggests that, rather than this causing a decrease in training,

Table 8.1 Roles within HRD work

Job title	Roles
Administrator	Provide co-ordination and support services for the delivery of HRD programmes and services
Career development adviser	Help individuals to assess personal competencies, values and goals and to identify, plan and implement development and career actions
Evaluator	Identify the impact of an intervention on individual or organisational effectiveness
HRD manager	Support and lead a group's work and integrate that work within the total organisation
HRD materials developer	Produce written or electronically mediated instructional material
Instructor/facilitator	Present information, directing structured learning experiences and managing group discussions and group processes
Marketer	Market and contract for HRD viewpoints, programmes and services
Needs analyst	Identify real and actual performance and performance conditions and determine causes of discrepancies
Organisational change agent	Influence and support changes in organisational behaviour
Programme designer	Prepare objectives, define content and select and sequence activities for a specific intervention
Researcher	Identify, develop or test new information (theory, concepts, technology, models, etc.) and translate the information into its implications for improved individual or organisational performance

Source: McLagan and McCullough, 1983.

it has in fact led to an increase. If there is more, not less, training, with fewer trainers, it is likely that line managers are taking more of this responsibility (1994: 22). It would appear that 'on-the-job training' is increasing, that is, training taking place within the work environment and facilitated and managed by the supervisor or manager of the department. This is supported by Saggers' research that indicated that on-the-job training had increased by 56 per cent over the previous two years, along with a rise in the use of managerial coaching (Saggers, 1994: 45). As one manager is quoted as saying, 'We are moving towards line managers becoming enablers, facilitators and coaches. The training department acts as a support service to managers, providing guidance and help to allow managers to achieve and fulfil their responsibilities' (Saggers, 1994: 41).

This raises issues about the respective and changing roles of the line manager and the trainer. It also suggests that training does not equal courses, but rather, in returning to the definitions earlier, the key concept of learning – which happens probably even more within the job as outside it – ought to be recognised more. Training courses have their strengths and purposes and their cessation is not proposed, although evidence shows that off-the-shelf courses are declining in favour of tailored courses (Saggers, 1994: 45). However, trainers and managers are both likely to benefit from considering the most appropriate vehicles for learning in particular circumstances. An alternative to training courses is perhaps a shift to where training and development focus on the process of 'natural learning', learning taking place on the job and not always planned. A focus on this kind of learning is supported by interest in high-performing and learning organisations in which managers are challenged to take more responsibility for training: their own and that of subordinates, the teams they lead and the organisation's learning (Marsick and Watkins, 1997: 295). Gunnigle and Flood comment that personnel responsibilities, particularly for training and development, are increasingly being 'delegated' to line management – from the managing director at the top of the organisation to the line supervisor (1990). And unless the line owns it, training and development will always be seen as something that occurs outside the mainstream activity of organisations (Webster, 1990: 46).

Within the concept of a human resourcing strategy, the implication is that the responsibilities are vested in line managers who, as business managers, are responsible for co-ordinating and directing all resources in the business unit in pursuit of bottom-line results, as discussed by Watson in Chapter 1 (*see also* Legge, 1991: 28). Personnel policies are not passively integrated with business strategy in the sense of flowing from it, but are an integral part of strategy in the sense that they underlie and facilitate the pursuit of a desired strategy. It may be useful to consider the iterative process of policy and strategy making in the organisation and the mechanisms through which managers are involved – or could be involved. Managers are beginning to demand that managing human resources be approached in an integrated, proactive and strategic way, one relevant to their business and management problems (Heraty and Morley, 1995: 31). This 'demand' may lead managers and trainers to consider how it will be achieved and by whom, in other words, within the training sphere, to consider the range of training and development activities and roles. However, devolving the prime responsibility to the line managers is seen as engendering problems such as the lack of appropriate skills in the manager (at the same time as losing the skills of the specialist); lack of confidence; poor attitudes towards training and development, influenced by the relatively low level of their own education and development (Storey, 1991; Garavan, 1991); or such attitudes stemming from an increasing workload and pressures for greater output. The concept proposed by Jones, of a shift in the 'partnership arrangements' from a strong relationship between trainer and trainee to a stronger relationship between the trainer and the organisation, through its managers, is a useful one to review who is driving the training process and the possible effectiveness of the relationship between the partners (Jones, 1991). Rather than *devolving* responsibility, it may be that *involving* the line more – or there being a stronger partnership as described by Jones, between the training and development specialist and the line manager – is a possible solution.

Whatever roles are undertaken by whichever people to enable the training and development function to make its best contribution to organisational effectiveness, it undoubtedly needs to have a higher profile in many organisations. A key concern is being able to convince the key decision makers, who will prove to be particularly influential not only in securing the financial resources needed for training, but more importantly in determining the perceived value of training and development to the stakeholders of the organisation.

Activity 8.4

1 What training and development activities do the line and functional managers undertake in an organisation with which you are familiar?

2 What involvement do they have with the organisation's trainers?

The state of flux and change that most organisations are experiencing has already been mentioned. The capability of people to cope and manage within such an environment is a vital element in the success of any business and ultimately a determinant in national economic performance (Garavan *et al.*, 1995: 4). If an organisation does not recognise the significant contribution that training and development can make to improving people's capabilities, the effectiveness of its planned change may be significantly hampered. When considering some of the factors that are driving change, it becomes clear what contribution training and development can make to helping organisations achieve successful change. Very little in the external environment has not been the subject of change and, in turn, this affects the internal environment of the organisation (*see* Watson, Chapter 1, Fig. 1.1). The notion of the 'learning organisation' suggests that it is the people throughout the organisation who need to be equipped to manage these organisational and environmental changes, to operate within new constraints and to have the skills and attitudes required to cope with constant change. Some suggest that it is only those organisations that are best equipped through their people to change that will survive (Pedler *et al.*, 1991). In recent years, the concept of learning has been accepted 'as a fundamental organisational process which has come to be viewed as integral to the effectiveness, adaptability and success of an organization' (French and Bazalgette, 1996: 15). Indeed, Stewart argues that, without a conscious, well-planned and professionally delivered training and development component, any strategy for managing change is likely to be deficient (Stewart, 1996: 4).

Few managers or chief executives would disagree with this need for organisational and employee development. However, it is a long way from training and development practitioners being deliberately involved in human resource strategy making, or even in determining how the strategic plans can be achieved. It may be that this is unlikely to happen until senior people in organisations see the benefits and potential of employee development. If trainers were more skilful in demonstrating that training and development can improve organisational capability, and that organisational learning results, then the attitudes of many senior managers would be likely to be more positive. In principle, this seems straightforward and indeed it may be. But in practice, evidence suggests that rarely are sufficient resources given to evaluating the benefits of training activities in organisational terms. Neither are some practitioners prepared to examine what they are doing and why, and to put their expertise – and maybe their livelihood – under such scrutiny, so evaluation is infrequently done and, when it is, it is often inadequate and ineffective. In their reluctance to evaluate, there is perhaps an understandable degree of self-protection against the threat of trainers having to justify their existence (*see also* Stewart, 1999).

ILLUSTRATION 8.2

Ashok is head of training and development in a financial services company. The business is geographically dispersed, with the main employees, known as financial planning advisers (FPAs), operating from the branches of the parent high street bank. Six regional managers, each with on average six district managers reporting to them, manage the field salesforce. Ashok has among his ten staff, six regional training managers who are located in each of the six regions. The sales performance of districts and regions is clearly seen as the responsibility of the district and regional managers. Thus, in Ashok's company, responsibility for the development of FPAs equally clearly resides with the district and regional managers. The role of Ashok and his staff is to provide advice and support in the form of devising procedures and materials, as well as in facilitating district and regional conferences and workshops in response to local and regional issues. While reporting to Ashok, the regional training managers work very closely with 'their' regional and district managers. Ashok enjoys a similarly close relationship with the chief executive and sales director of the company. Their joint concern is the implementation of 'cultural values' intended by the chief executive to govern the way the company conducts its business.

■ Evaluating training activities

Practitioners and writers alike would strongly argue that evaluation is one key to promoting the organisational value of training and development. Evaluation of training can be defined as judging the value of the training/development activity, in other words, 'any attempts to obtain information (feedback) on the effects of training and to assess its value' (Hamblin, 1974). But who makes the judgement? Who determines its value? All too often the answer to both these questions is the training practitioners, who are typically more concerned with their performance and job security than with the wider issues of the validity of their interventions. Who should make the judgements leads to the concept of the stakeholder, where each stakeholder is likely to have different objectives and will place different values and interpretations on the outcomes – all of which are likely to be valid and which ought to be addressed.

Our experience of working with a large number of organisational trainers has confirmed that it is the end-of-course questionnaires that are used by the majority as 'evaluation'. Many simply do not have the time, the resources or the expertise to evaluate further. These gather the immediate reactions of the participants and are often left to gather dust in some filing cabinet – or now more usefully recycled through the office paper bank! The traditional training cycle of planning, implementing and reviewing has perhaps been responsible for evaluation being viewed as a task to be undertaken at the *end* of the training intervention, rather than recognising its role both *before* and *during* it. In addition to the reactions of the trainees to their training, evaluation includes what they have learned; what changes there are in their job behaviour; and what are the ultimate changes in organisational effectiveness (Kirkpatrick, 1971: 88). After reaction-level evaluation, the next most frequently undertaken activity is to evaluate learning – did the participants learn what the training was designed for them to learn? This can be a relatively easy activity when people are learning psychomotor skills or factual information, but it is maybe less so when the subject is to do with their attitudes, social or intellectual skills. Again, one can question whether this learning-level evaluation is sufficient if judgements are being made about the contribution of training and development to the organisation. Of greater value, and more difficult to do, is to determine whether the job behaviour of people is changed and whether this makes a difference to the achievement of organisational goals. There seems to be a hierarchy of complexity in the evaluation of training and the more complex it is, and the less the link can be demonstrated, the less likely such evaluation is to be undertaken (McMahon and Carter, 1990).

One needs only look in the HR practitioner journals to realise that a great deal of the training and development activity that goes on in organisations is driven by what is currently popular ('flavour of the month' fads and fashions); or by things that are readily available; or things that are deemed to be important (or, even worse, preferred) by the training and development practitioners – rather than by the needs of the organisation to achieve its goals through the effective development of its people. In these cases, it is hardly surprising that training and development activities are seen to have low priority, when they are not based on clear business needs or seen to contribute to business goals. In support of the importance of setting objectives and evaluating changes in workplace behaviour, Galagan believes:

> Simply depositing information into worker's heads will no longer be sufficient justification for trainers to maintain their positions. The *application* of knowledge within the context of the work environment – to help the organization achieve its goals – will become the thrust for people who want to maintain their role, particularly if they want to have any influence in the organization of the future. (Galagan, 1994: 27)

Chickens and eggs spring to mind! Without rigorous and wide-ranging evaluation, it would seem that trainers are unlikely to convince top management to support them. Without this support, they will have a difficult task to prove that training and development activities make a difference. In order to break out of the negative cycle, there perhaps needs to be a managerial supporter and a training practitioner, both with commitment and the belief that such practice *can* make a difference to organisational goals, the belief preferably stemming from some evaluation evidence.

The importance of evaluation has long been recognised, not just by trainers. The CBI recommended that its organisations' managers seek to evaluate the business benefits of training and development (CBI, 1989). In researching trainers' activities across several European countries, Nijhof and de Rijk found that, while their respondents recognised evaluation as a core output, only two out of over 400 identified it as their most important role – below tasks such as developing materials, marketing, career development adviser, needs analyst, etc. (1997: 251). One could argue that evaluation should be considered of greater importance, in order for many of these other roles to be carried out effectively.

Our experience of working in a range of organisations shows that many still afford training and development a relatively low status; however, the strides made by other organisations towards a growing recognition of the value of training and development are encouraging. This is supported by a survey of training strategies by IDS in 1990 that showed some common trends:

- Training was becoming more related to business objectives.

- Line managers were playing an increasing role in training and staff development through the introduction of performance-appraisal schemes.

- A greater variety of 'delivery' methods were being used.

- Training was beginning to be perceived as a long-term investment rather than a short-term cost (IDS, 1990: 1).

Similarly, in his review of several major UK companies, Keep identified that the integration of training and development into wider business planning had been crucial to their development. Training and development activities were no longer peripheral to the achievement of corporate objectives, but were recognised as making an important contribution to the achievement of business objectives (Keep, 1991: 114). It would seem that there is a growing awareness of the importance of employee development in enhancing competitive capability (Harrison, 1997: 149). This is supported by Sloman's final training role, that of the strategic facilitator, who is able to 'express and ensure the implementation of a clear training strategy with clear targets, clear control and clear accountabilities' (Sloman ,1994: 27).

We have commented on the challenges facing training and development professionals in raising their profile in the organisation. However, the contention remains that in an increasingly turbulent business environment, training and development activities in an organisation are vital and must be integrated with business planning, therefore moving from the traditional view of training to *support* the organisation, operating on the *periphery,* towards an emphasis where the training and development of employees is a *core* activity. With the aim of raising their profile, training and development professionals need to take into account the bases of organisational power and the impact these may have on the internal stakeholders' perceptions of the training and development activities within the organisation.

Garavan comments that 'the relative power of the different stakeholders is fundamental and the HRD function may sometimes trade one off against the other' (1995: 11). If we accept that this is the case, it may often be the stakeholders with the greatest degree of power (more than often senior management) who will drive HRD activities within the organisation. This will be powerful if the organisational vision is shared by the internal stakeholders. However, if the senior managers seek to impose their views on HRD activities without gaining the commitment of all internal stakeholders, then it may be the case that learning is seen as 'a politicised process, where new knowledge, systems and techniques are viewed suspiciously even rejected because they are seen to represent the priorities of others, whose priorities are distinct and possibly opposed' (Mabey and Salaman, 1995: 151).

If it is intended that HRD activities should contribute to achieving long-term benefits and the commitment of all internal stakeholders, 'each stakeholder group . . . should therefore participate in determining the future direction of human resource development activities within the organisation' (Garavan, 1995: 11).

Employee training and development and organisational change

To explore the discussions surrounding the role of stakeholders in HRD activities, the currently popular 'culture change programmes' can be considered. It would be difficult to dispute the contention that to facilitate an effective change initiative, senior managers must lead and support culture change from the top. However, what implications does this have for the training initiatives in organisations? 'If senior managers ignore or misread the cultural centre of gravity themselves, the training initiatives they launch are likely to avail little in the long term and possibly meet with indifference and cynicism in the short term' (Mabey and Salaman, 1995: 154).

Those involved in training should, it seems, consider all stakeholders in the organisation. While it is crucial that in change programmes senior management play the role of 'cultural conductors' (Mabey and Salaman, 1995: 151), organisations cannot afford to ignore the 'orchestra'. It is only when support can be secured from all that employee development professionals can even attempt to play a successful role in any organisational change programme.

While we suggest that training can and should play a key part in any 'change' initiative, this will only be effective if it is operating at the core of the organisation. If the role of training and development is seen as supporting change from the periphery, operating in isolation and not as part of any strategic plan, therefore delivering 'bolt-on' training programmes, it may be that 'the excitement engendered in a good corporate training programme frequently leads to increased frustration when employees get back on the job only to see their new skills go unused in an organisation in which nothing else has changed' (Beer *et al.*, 1993: 100). Such programmes that operate in isolation cannot hope to effect change, 'at their best they are irrelevant . . . at their worst they actually inhibit change . . . by promoting scepticism and cynicism. . . . and can inoculate companies against the real thing' (Beer *et al.*, 1993: 101).

Culture change programmes are often aimed at challenging people's ingrained beliefs, by encouraging their commitment to a new vision, delivered through training initiatives (see Goodstein and Burke, 1993; Lauermann, 1997). Stewart (1996) suggests that the balance between developing an individual's knowledge, skills and attitudes is likely to reflect the nature of the change being sought. In turn, this influences whether the training and development function will be delivering training programmes (probably traditional activities adopting didactic methods) if the change is relatively minor, or development programmes, which are more appropriate to achieve personal development required in major change situations.

This introduces a further perspective of the significant role that employee development can play in an organisation: the role of training and development in enabling and supporting the personal development of employees so that they are continually developing their skills to achieve both personal growth and task flexibility.

■ Self-development

Self-development initiatives reflect a growing approach to training and development. Stewart provides an overview of the reasons for such growth (1996: 171):

■ an increasing recognition of its value in managing change;

■ a recognition of the need to manage change;

■ unwillingness of managers to accept traditional approaches to management development;

■ a growth in supporting infrastructure to facilitate such interventions, i.e. open learning, distance learning materials.

Self-development produces a new challenge to the training and development function, with activities moving away from traditional and formalised training into a new arena, offering new opportunities to the function in encouraging and facilitating a learning climate that promotes flexibility and independence. Certain conditions are required to facilitate and support successful integration. The obvious resource that often springs to mind is financial support; however, self-development programmes require far more significant resources. Individuals will require time to pursue their development and organisations should make access to such opportunities readily available. A critical requirement is a management style that demonstrates commitment and support to the concept of self-development. Stewart suggests that what is needed is a style of management 'which encourages participation, questioning conventional wisdom, innovation and risk taking' (1991: 173).

If this is the style of management required, what support will be required from the training function? The training activities that are required move away from traditional didactic and structured training, towards those aimed at encouraging and developing the personal growth of self-developers. In addition, the function needs to work with managers to facilitate the organisational conditions required to support such learning. This may be achieved through helping managers to develop the necessary style of participative and facilitative leadership.

While we acknowledge that self-development can develop individuals within an organisation who have the ability to learn and be more adaptable to change, we cannot ignore the tensions. Self-development promotes individual learning towards individual objectives and by nature tends to lack structure. Therefore any learning achieved is not always transferred into the organisation, which may make it difficult to elicit senior management commitment.

To develop the discussion surrounding tensions relating to gaining senior management commitment, action learning can be considered. This is an approach to management development introduced by Revans (1976, 1980, 1982) with underlying principles that can be said to mirror self-development (Stewart, 1996). Action learning requires managers to take responsibility for their own learning, which in turn enables them not only to develop their ability to learn and manage but also to manage learning. This approach to development is widely believed to lead to a 'radical questioning process . . . shaking the cage of entrenched attitudes and mindsets' (Harrison, 1997: 404). If this is the intention, the question that must be posed is: how willing will senior managers be to encourage such questioning and how far will they be willing to have employees 'shaking the cage'? This is a tension that the training function must take into account.

■ The concept of the learning organisation

The idea of learning autonomy can be associated with the concept of the learning organisation. As Stewart suggests, 'an organisation peopled by self developers is, in part at least, almost by definition a learning organisation' (1996: 177). Starkey (1996: 2) depicts the learning organisation as a 'metaphor, with its roots in the vision of and search for strategy to promote individual self-development within a continuously transforming organisation' and suggests that 'in the learning organisation human resource development is central to strategic management'.

Learning in the learning organisation has to be facilitated at two levels by the training and development function. At a formal level, learning needs to be encouraged that can be directly transferred to the organisation; at an informal level, opportunities need to be available for individual development, which may or may not be transferred to the organisation. The concept of the learning organisation therefore requires organisations to support individual learning, with an additional aim to 'draw upon the integration of the sum of individuals' learning to create a whole that is greater than the sum of its parts' (Starkey, 1996: 2). Harrison questions the ability of organisations to provide such requirements:

> Such a skilful balance between formal systems and informal features, presupposes an approach to knowledge development and human relationships in an organisation that does not fit easily with the lack of expertise and awareness about Human Resource Development and learning, the organisational research repeatedly shows to prevail. (1997: 405)

Even if such expertise exists in the training and development function, the issue remains of promoting such learning and development initiatives that may not have direct 'payback' to the organisation.

As suggested earlier, this links to the concept of power within the organisation. Coopey (1995) suggested that often the concept of a learning organisation ignores the question of control within the organisation and how new learning will be used. In considering this view, the question arises of who will decide that an organisation is to become a 'learning organisation'. Does the concept of a learning organisation really represent a new approach to management and learning in organisations? Coopey argues that 'senior managers within enterprises where the principles of a learning organisation are put into practice will be able to bolster and safeguard their prerogatives by articulating aspects of the ideology implicit in the literature of the learning organisation' (1996: 365). Such sceptical comments illustrate how crucial it is that real commitment is visible and demonstrated from senior management and that all internal stakeholders have a shared clarity regarding the concept of a learning organisation. If this is not the case, we could consider the cynical view that 'those who propagate the principles of a learning organisation, risk opening the latest phase of a long history of metaphors which have been used manipulatively (Giddens, 1979) by managers, with a long pedigree of instrumental interest in social science as a means of solving industrial problems (Pfeffer, 1981)' (Coopey, 1996: 365).

However, while taking into account the above argument, we would suggest that 'The Learning Organisation has evolved over time, to the point where it now represents a coherent approach to maximising human potential in the service of organisational effectiveness' (Roderick, 1993: 13). The challenge facing training and development is to be able to convince senior management that an individual's ability to learn is an asset to the organisation. As Jones and Hendry comment, 'the paradox and dilemma for organisations is how to relax their control over the learning process while channelling benefits from it' (1994: 160).

Even if organisations cannot relax their control over the learning process, Harrison (1993, 1997) suggests that individuals should be encouraged to take personal responsibility for their own learning. As Harrison stated, 'Self-directed learning and self-development are increasingly important for everyone whether in or out of employment' (1993: 131). Changes that are occurring within the employment sector, including fixed and temporary contracts, delayering of organisational structures and technological advances, among others, emphasise the need for individual flexibility and reflect the requirement for individuals to take responsibility for their own learning and continual development.

So what of the future of training and development? With evidence such as the increase in drives to encourage individuals to take responsibility for their own development, will the organisation and its training and development function increasingly be seen as incidental to an individual's growth? This is a question that has, for now at least, to be left open.

ILLUSTRATION 8.3

Diane is employee and management development manager of a medium-sized trust hospital. Since achieving trust status, the hospital has restructured into a series of strategic business units with devolved accountability for resource utilisation and management. This reorganisation brought together staff responsible for employee development, professional nurse development and management development into one unit, which Diane manages. The unit is part of the HR directorate, a central SBU created at the time of the restructuring. Diane's unit is quite small in terms of staff and budgets relative to the size of the total organisation. Diane is aware of a concern at the top level of the trust that the creation and operation of SBUs are having the effect of diluting corporate identity and are encouraging unhelpful internal competition. Diane believes that becoming a 'learning organisation' will help to overcome these problems and will represent the best use of her limited resources. Having gained approval for establishing a steering group with representatives from across the hospital to work on this idea, Diane is beginning to learn that different groups, e.g. medical staff, nurses, professions allied to medicine and non-medical staff, have very different ideas about what a 'learning organisation' might be.

CASE STUDY 8.1

Bainbridge NHS Trust Hospital

The NHS has been through many changes in its relatively short history. Change is now perhaps truly considered the norm rather than the exception. However, this does not mean that change is any more or less welcome or any more or less easy to implement.

Heather Walton ponders these factors as she attempts to get to grips with the potential implications of the proposed merger of her current employer, Bainbridge NHS Trust Hospital, with another NHS trust hospital, known locally as the 'General'. Both hospitals provide similar services, in that they deal with general, acute and emergency services to their local populations. Part of the rationale for the proposed merger is that there is overlap in the populations served by the two hospitals, as well as in their respective services and specialisms. Bainbridge is the larger of the two, employing 1500 staff across all grades and types of staff, while the General employs 950 staff. There has in the past been an element of competition between the two hospitals, since both bid for contracts and funds from the same main purchaser, the Bainbridge and District Health Authority. While Heather considers that this will create its own problems in facilitating the merger, she accepts the logic of potential cost savings arising from this reduction in the need to 'compete'.

Heather is aware that the impetus for a merger came about as a result of the policies of the recently elected government. These policies in turn are only part of a national scene that includes the never-ending discovery and application of new treatments, the continuing emphasis on preventive medicine and community-based care, and changes in the training, development and qualifications of professional staff and associated changes to their contracts. Local pressures, including financial constraints experienced by Bainbridge and District Health Authority as well as difficulties experienced by both hospitals in devoting enough resources to develop their services, have also been instrumental in making the case for the merger.

As organisation development manager at Bainbridge, Heather is aware of current and recent research that emphasises the importance of culture and HR issues in achieving successful mergers. Heather is, naturally, even more familiar with studies of mergers within the NHS. These tend to support the general findings on culture and HR issues, as well as highlighting the support of key stakeholders and agreement on future business and direction as being critical factors influencing success or failure. While both trust boards and all directors of both hospitals have confirmed their support for a merger, Heather is unsure of the level of support among the varying staff groups. Equally, Heather is not at all certain that powerful groups such as consultants do, or will, agree on priorities for developing clinical services in the new trust to be created by the merger.

Actions taken so far to facilitate planning and implementation of the merger included a 'trust strategy group' meeting held over a weekend in a local hotel. The event was organised jointly by the two current chief executives and included all directors, senior managers, senior nurses and consultants from both trusts as participants. Heather was actively involved, along with the director of human resources from the General and the two chief executives, in designing and facilitating the event. A number of workshops were held with mixed groups of staff from both hospitals to examine various questions surrounding the merger, and to produce an overall action plan to be implemented by a number of cross-functional and cross-hospital project groups also formed at the event. However, Heather came away with the feeling that staff from the General felt that they were being 'taken over' rather than merged, and that such a view was shared by some staff at Bainbridge, especially consultants. A major focus of concern, especially among staff from the General, was the range and number of redundancies to arise from the merger.

Heather has personal concerns about her own future. No structure has yet been proposed for the new trust. However, her current work on advising the merger steering group on facilitating the required changes will continue for six months at least. At the moment, Heather is faced with the task of writing a paper for the steering group to examine the training and development implications of the merger. Her brief requires a particular focus on the contribution that training and development can make to making the merger a success, once the new trust exists and a new organisational structure is in place, and what role therefore the function should adopt in the new organisation. Heather is encouraged that the request for the paper suggests that training and development is seen by the steering group as an important part in the merger and the new organisation. However, she also recognises the importance of the paper, not only for her own future but for all employees of both hospitals and in establishing an appropriate training and development function in the planned new trust.

Activity 8.5

1 What role and contribution can employee training and development play in managing organisational change?

2 What are the key factors influencing change in the form of the merger of the two existing NHS trusts?

3 What options might Heather consider and present to the steering group as possible roles for employee training and development?

4 Given the circumstances of the case, what contribution can you see for employee training and development in achieving a successful merger?

5 Based on your response to Question 4, what role for employee training and development would you suggest is the most appropriate for Heather to recommend?

Conclusion

We have suggested that 'training' can be associated with highly structured processes intended to produce predictable and prescribed performances in tightly defined jobs and tasks. The primary purpose being pursued in such circumstances is 'control'. However, the focus of control is not simply job performance, it is also, through structured and didactic training methods, control over and of individual learning processes. An alternative focus is possible on 'development', both individual and organisational development, especially when seeking to achieve managed organisational change in response to changed operating conditions. It is possible to characterise these two approaches as falling within the 'direct-control/low-commitment' or 'indirect-control/high-commitment' human resourcing strategies detailed in Chapter 1. Thus, an approach to employee training and development that emphasises 'training' at the expense of 'development' will be consistent with the principles of the 'indirect-control/high-commitment' strategy (*see* Table 1.6 and Chapter 1). To the extent that such principles are applied consciously and deliberately in developing human resourcing strategy, horizontal integration can be achieved for employee training and development simply by placing an emphasis on either 'training' or 'development'.

Following the arguments of Chapter 1, a human resourcing strategy seeking to adopt and apply HRM-style practices would therefore give greater attention to 'development'. It is of course possible, and may be considered desirable by decision makers, to adopt a 'dual human resourcing strategy' where 'training' is emphasised for some groups of employees and 'development' for others. This may in fact reflect the traditional use of the term 'development' for managers and 'training' for non-managerial staff mentioned earlier in the chapter. It may also be applied within the notion of 'core and peripheral workers'.

It is possible to relate these arguments to the model given in Fig. 8.1. Innovators in employee development can be argued to be pursuing the principles of indirect control/high commitment and applying HRM-style practices. Conversely, caretakers can be argued to be adopting an approach consistent with direct-control/low-commitment principles. Educators and evangelists adopt intermediate positions. As argued in Chapter 1, the two sets of principles do not necessarily represent a simple dichotomy, and therefore the educator and evangelist approaches in the Bennett and Leduchowicz model can be argued to apply different combinations of the two sets of principles.

Two conclusions can be offered. First, choices in relation to human resourcing strategy necessarily involve issues and choices to do with employee training and development. This also implies that, to the extent that human resourcing strategy making represents a complex and problematic process, so too does employee training and development. Second, to the extent that HRM-style practices can be argued to be relevant to and consistent with the current demands of complex and changing operating environments, so an emphasis on development as opposed to 'training' can be argued to be of increasing relevance and importance in work organisations. As we have seen in this chapter, however, this will in turn create new roles for and demands on the specialist function and professional practice of employee training and development.

Summary

In this chapter the following key points have been made:

- Employee development is concerned with more than direct instruction and is more complex than is sometimes assumed.

- Definitions of employee development vary, but a common focus on learning can be suggested.

- A number of frameworks or typologies have been created to categorise varying approaches to employee development and associated roles adopted by professional practitioners, and these can be seen to represent choices for practitioners and decision makers.

- There appears to be increasing evidence of a shift in role to that of 'change agent'.

- Employee development is increasingly argued to be central to achievement of organisational goals and objectives, with a related need for practitioners to operate at the 'core' rather than on the 'periphery'.

■ Attention to evaluation does not seem to be increasing, but its importance to achieving a 'core' rather than a 'peripheral' role seems to be increasingly recognised.

■ Employee development can be important and significant in attempts to achieve organisational change.

■ While the concept of the 'learning organisation' is often associated with organisational change, many formulations of the concept fail to address the issue of power relations in organisations.

■ Employee development can form part of a coherent human resourcing strategy and be consistent with selected or preferred human resourcing principles.

Discussion questions

1 What do the terms 'training' and 'development' mean to you and how do you distinguish between them?

2 In what ways can the employee training and development function gain influence and power in organisations?

3 What are the potential benefits to each set of stakeholders, e.g. senior managers, line managers, non-managerial employees, customers/clients, shareholders, etc., of each of the approaches in Fig. 8.1 being adopted?

4 How can employee training and development practices achieve *horizontal* and *vertical* integration?

5 What are the potential advantages and disadvantages for practitioners arising from an emphasis on 'training' and from an emphasis on 'development'?

Further reading

Harrison (1997), published by the Institute of Personnel and Development, is considered by many to be the standard text on the subject. It does provide comprehensive and accessible treatment of the main concepts. Also published by the IPD is Reid and Barrington (1997). Now in its fifth edition, this book has much to commend it, especially for readers new to the subject. Stewart (1999) is a new book that provides a more academic and less mainstream analysis of the subject. His 1996 book focuses specifically on the relationships and connections between employee development and organisational change, and provides an accessible exposition of many important concepts. The IPD publishes a series under the general title of 'Training Essentials'. This contains short books on specific topics and is a useful resource for examining particular concepts, for example that of 'training need', in more detail.

9

MANAGEMENT DEVELOPMENT

Jim Stewart

OBJECTIVES

Having completed this chapter and its associated activities, readers should be able to:

- articulate a range of perspectives on and definitions of management development;

- critically evaluate varying approaches to management development;

- describe the role and contribution of management development programmes and activities in wider human resourcing strategies;

- formulate and argue a position on the value of investment in management development;

- produce, justify and defend proposals for investment in management development.

Introduction

The purpose of this chapter is to examine critically the concept and practice of management development. This will necessarily entail a consideration of the meaning of the terms 'management' and 'development', and the results of joining them together to construct the concept of 'management development'. Expressed in this way, the task can be said to be both ambitious and complex. Such ambition and complexity are perhaps beyond the scope of a single chapter if full justice is to be done to the task. However, certain important arguments can be discerned from existing research and writing on the subject, and these arguments are critical to any serious consideration of the theory and practice of management development. The aim therefore is to identify and examine the important arguments and debates surrounding management development, and to locate these in the wider context of what are referred to in this book as human resourcing strategies.

Locating management development in the wider context of human resourcing strategies suggests a concern with application. Application in turn raises questions to do with 'how'. Such questions can take at least three forms. First, how *is* management development done? Second, how *could* management development be done? Third, how *should* management development be done? Answering this last question requires a prescription of what is 'right', or 'correct' or 'best'. In line with the philosophy of the book, such prescriptions are not possible, even if they might be desirable or desired. Some perspectives and approaches can, however, have more utility than others. The concern here therefore in dealing with each of the 'how' questions is to provide the responses that will be most useful and helpful in informing decisions on and in practice. The primary concern will be with the first two formulations of 'how'.

These opening points set the scope and limitations of the chapter. The focus will be on examining *what* constitutes management development and *how* it is and might be practised. By the end of the chapter, you can expect to be able to achieve the objectives listed above.

Management development – an overview

The view adopted here is that management development (MD) is both complex and problematic. In part, this arises from the fact that the term has no single or definitive meaning. Definitions and meanings vary according to the perspectives adopted by different writers (Storey, 1989; Harrison, 1997). Related to this is the fact that MD can and does pursue various agendas (Lees, 1992). In other words, investment in MD can be undertaken to serve different purposes. Mabey and Salaman (1995) suggest four possible purposes, each with distinct characteristics and problems and derived from different assumptions. Their four purposes, or 'agendas', are summarised in Table 9.1.

Each of these purposes can be pursued by any and all organisations. However, it is probable that 'political reinforcement' and 'psychic defence' are more likely to be found in times of planned change. The privatisation of public utilities undertaken in the 1980s would be an example of the former, while mergers and takeovers are an example where the latter might occur. The purposes of 'functional performance' and

Table 9.1 Management development agendas

Type	Description
Functional performance	Focuses on knowledge, skills and attitudes of individual managers. Assumes unproblematic link between MD and performance.
Political reinforcement	Focuses on reinforcing and propagating skills and attitude valued by top managers. Assumes top managers are correct in their diagnosis and prescription.
Compensation	MD is seen as part of the reward system for managers. Assumes development is motivational and encourages commitment.
Psychic defence	MD provides a 'safety value' for managerial anxieties. Assumes competitive careers and associated anxieties.

Source: Based on Mabey and Salaman, 1995.

'compensation' are more likely to be pursued in times of stability, with the former being found in large organisations and the latter in professional partnerships such as accountancy or legal consultancies.

A second problem is that, notwithstanding variation in meaning, much research and writing, and therefore common usage of the term, assumes or implies formalised and structured systems within work organisations for the provision of MD (Mumford, 1997; Harrison, 1997). Such research and writing, more or less explicitly, further assumes medium- to large-scale enterprises that can afford the investment required to operate, for example, sophisticated approaches to performance management. Indeed, each of the agendas included in Mabey and Salamon's typology in Table 9.1 seems to assume MD as a formalised and structured system, and thus the typology as a whole is limited to MD being defined and constituted by such approaches. There are two weaknesses with this perspective. First, the small firms sector is both a significant and growing feature of the UK economy (DfEE, 1995). Perspectives that assume formalised and structured MD systems will have little relevance or application in this important sector. Second, an assumption of MD as a formal system excludes, literally by definition, the role and contribution of what is variously referred to as 'accidental', 'informal' or 'situated' learning and development (*see* Fox, 1997; Mumford, 1997).

The analysis so far suggests that disagreement exists about what constitutes MD and that, within the context of that disagreement, common usage of the term tends to exclude both important contexts of application and a range of potentially significant, if informal, learning and development opportunities. This confused and confusing situation is complicated even further by examining the concepts of 'management' and 'managing'.

■ The nature of managerial work

Formalised and structured approaches to MD assume, to some extent, that *managing* is a formal and structured activity. Perhaps more accurately, perspectives on MD that emphasise formalised and systemised approaches assume the possibility and actuality of clear and unambiguous specifications of managerial tasks and managerial behaviour. However, the processual view of managing argued in Chapter 1 raises doubts about this conventional view of managing as a rational and technical activity. The processual view finds support in recent work focused directly on management learning (Chia, 1997). Doubts about conventional views on management are supported and confirmed by empirical research. The works of, for example, Stewart (1982), Mintzberg (1973), Kotter (1982) and Watson (1994a) all suggest that what managers actually do is far removed from the rationalist and ordered specifications found in many textbooks. The pictures revealed by these studies stand in contrast to the logical, ordered and rational portraits contained in universalist prescriptions of management and associated MD programmes.

Two significant implications arise from this argument. First, management as process encompasses a wider range of individuals than might be included in more conventional approaches to MD. As was argued in Chapter 1, *all* managers are inextricably bound up in strategy making, and thus in contributing to managing the organisation. This argument is taken further by Chia (1997), who suggests that every individual is part of the process of managing. By implication, therefore, we can say that all employees are engaged in managing the organisations who employ them. Such a view finds support, from different perspectives and for different reasons, in the work of Fredericks and Stewart (1996) and that of Harrison (1997, especially Chapter 19). So it is arguable that management development could, perhaps should, encompass wider constituencies than conventional treatments normally suggest.

The second implication concerns both the content and methods of MD. It is often argued that MD needs to be located in, and to support the achievement of, business or organisational imperatives (Harrison, 1997; Mumford, 1997; Jones and Woodcock, 1985). This prescription is not though as simple as it may appear, for two reasons. First, it assumes that those imperatives will be clear, unambiguous and pre-determined. However, deciding business or organisational imperatives is part of the managing process. And selecting particular imperatives rather than others is, in part, the result of a political process, itself involving the interests, values and power bases of varying and, sometimes, competing groups (*see* Watson, 1994a, Alvesson and Willmott, 1996). Second, if managing is indeed confusing and uncertain, as suggested by the studies referred to earlier, it is by no means clear how business imperatives can or will or should be achieved. Thus, if MD is truly to reflect the requirements of organisational imperatives, the content cannot be universally prescribed and methods need to recognise and work with the informal, unsystematic and political nature of managerial processes.

■ The nature of development

The concept of 'development' raises additional problems for thinking about what constitutes MD and how it could or should be practised. One problem is to consider whether and how development is distinct from education and training. In other words, is MD different from management education and management training? Mumford (1997) suggests that the words 'education' and 'training' tend to focus attention on inputs, while the terms 'learning' and 'development' focus attention on results or outputs. From that perspective, education and training become ways of achieving development and, therefore, they contribute to, but do not constitute, management development. This can be a useful formulation, since it suggests that MD does not necessarily require education or training and, relatedly, that alternative or additional approaches and methods are possible. A similar argument is advanced by Stewart (1999). Here, the case is made that attempts to distinguish between education and training lead to sterile debates that overlook the more important common feature that both represent deliberate interventions in learning processes. This first problem can be disposed of by concluding that education and training programmes represent two ways of practising MD, which may or may not form part of the design of MD schemes and activities.

According to Mumford (1997), development focuses on outcomes. However, this view can be problematic. It raises questions concerning the nature of those outcomes and how and when they are, or become, known. For example, should, or even can, the outcomes of MD be specified in advance of any planned activity? The earlier analysis of the nature of managerial work would suggest that knowing what outcomes are needed or desirable in advance would be difficult, at least with any degree of specificity or confidence. The processual view of managing questions the idea, let alone the possibility, of 'fixed' or 'end' states that are capable of specification (Chia, 1997). Development itself is defined by some (e.g. Pedler and Boydell, 1985) as transformational change towards a different, but unknown, state of being. So each of these varying perspectives would question the notion of specifiable outcomes. This is not to say, however, that development is not concerned with outcomes. The point is to question conventional wisdom on MD, which would suggest that outcomes can and should be specified in advance (*see* next section).

A very useful analysis of the concept of development, especially as it applies to management learning and development, has been provided by Lee (1997). Four different conceptions, or ways of understanding development, are suggested. Each conception varies in the assumptions and beliefs that are implicitly or explicitly applied to two factors. The first factor is the nature of the 'individual', which, according to varying perspectives, consists of either a unitary or co-regulated identity. The basic distinction here is the degree of involvement of others in creating and constructing the 'individual'. In other words, the extent to which 'I' and who and what 'I am' exist independently of the perceptions, actions and behaviours of others and the social experience that 'I' share with others. The second factor concerns the 'end point' of development. This can be assumed to be either known or unknown. This now gives four broad possibilities: co-regulated identity and known end point, co-regulated identity and unknown end point; unitary identity and known end point; and unitary identity and unknown end point. These combinations are used by Lee to suggest four broad approaches to development, summarised in Table 9.2.

Lee argues that these conceptions of development can be and are applied to individuals, groups and organisations. She also attempts to highlight dilemmas associated with each approach, including those for professional developers. The value of her work here is to support the argument that the concept of development is complex and problematic and also it provides a useful framework for examining definitions of MD and the place of varying, and perhaps competing, methods.

To close this discussion of development, it is possible to conclude that the concept is concerned with change and movement. These characteristics seem to be inherent in

Table 9.2 Approaches to management development

Approach	Characteristics
Maturation	Assumes a unitary identity and known end point. Development involves passing through known and pre-determined stages.
Shaping	This approach combines a co-regulated identity and known end point. The basic difference to 'maturation' is that the end point is not determined by some inevitable process but is open to choice and decision. It is, however, known.
Voyage	Assumes unknown end point and unitary identity. Development represents a journey 'into the self'.
Emergent	Combines co-regulated identity and unknown end point. This approach, in simple terms, applies the idea of 'voyage' to the social system of which the individual is a part, and development therefore becomes a joint, interactive and interdependent process.

Source: Based on Lee (1997).

each of Lee's approaches and are in line with the arguments of Mumford (1977), Harrison (1997) and Pedler and Boydell (1985), among others. They are also, especially the notion of movement, congruent with the processual analysis central to this book (Chapter 1 and Chia, 1997). The conclusion of this section is that the status of the two central concepts of 'management development' is problematic, and that that status is important to any examination of MD as an area of professional practice.

Activity 9.1

1 Consider the implications for management development practice arising out of analyses suggesting that managerial work is ambiguous and uncertain.

2 Consider the implications for management development practice if outcomes cannot be specified in advance.

3 Discuss your responses to Questions 1 and 2 with a colleague and debate the consequences for designing and providing management development programmes.

Management development – definitions and meanings

As was suggested earlier, MD can have a number of different meanings. One factor that provides a common distinction between different conceptions of MD is the focus, or emphasis, on *manager* as opposed to *management* development (Harrison, 1997). The former implies a primary concern with *individual* learning and development and a purpose for MD associated with improving individual ability and performance. In contrast, the latter implies a primary concern with collective learning and development and a purpose for MD associated with producing shared values and consistency in management style and approach. The focus in this conception of MD is then the organisation as an entity rather than the individual manager. There are therefore two possible and different focuses for MD practices: the organisation or the individual.

While the two possible focuses suggest varying specific purposes, the broader purpose of MD programmes can also be said to vary, and there are again two broad possibilities. The first possibility is primarily concerned with changing behaviour, either of individual managers or of the organisation as a whole, as a means of maintaining or improving current performance. The second possibility is primarily concerned with ensuring availability of skills and experience to meet future demands. This purpose can be applied to individual managers in the sense of preparing them for future promotion opportunities, or to the organisation as an entity in the sense of ensuring a supply of managerial ability to fill senior management positions as they become vacant. In both cases, the purpose represents an attempt to manage internal labour markets through interventions in 'career progression'. Of course, some recent works might question the possibility or advisability of 'managed careers' in the current and future employment context (*see*, for example, Handy, 1994b; Hirsch and Jackson, 1995; Pemberton, 1995). Others suggest individual responses to this changing context (Bridges, 1995; Crainer, 1995). The argument here is that some conceptions of MD assume a purpose concerned with managed career progression.

The analysis in this section so far suggests a possible framework for categorising varying conceptions and definitions of MD. The framework categorises definitions according to whether individuals or organisations provide the primary *focus*, and according to whether changed behaviour or career progression provides the primary *purpose*. The resulting framework is given in Fig. 9.1. The suggestion is that most conceptions or definitions of MD can be accommodated by one of the four boxes in the framework. As will be shown later, the same framework can also be useful in categorising varying approaches and methods, since these do have logical connections to varying conceptions and definitions.

The value and utility of the framework in Fig. 9.1 can be examined and evaluated by analysing two formal definitions of MD. The first is that offered by Mumford (1997: 6): 'an attempt to improve managerial effectiveness through a learning process'.

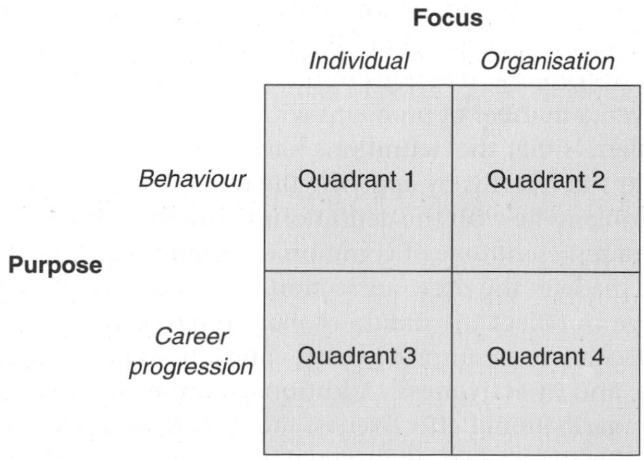

Fig. 9.1 Dimensions of management development

It seems clear from the definition that the purpose of MD in this conception is improving current performance, and therefore is associated more with behaviour than career progression. The question of focus is, however, a little less clear. Nevertheless, Mumford explains a shift in his thinking, and therefore his definition, between the second and third editions of his book (Mumford, 1993, 1997). This shift has taken out the words 'planned and deliberate' as adjectives attached to 'learning process' to accommodate the significant contribution of accidental, incidental and informal learning. This shift and explanation make clear a concern with the learning of individual managers. Therefore, it seems appropriate to place Mumford's definition in Quadrant 1 of the framework.

The second definition is taken from Harrison (1997). In distinguishing between 'manager' and 'management development', Harrison offers the following definition of the latter:

> Building a shared culture across the whole management group and enhancing management capability throughout the organisation in order to improve the organisation's capability to survive and prosper. (Harrison, 1997: 356)

There is little room for doubt that Harrison, in this definition, sees MD as having a primary focus on the organisation, rather than on managers as *individuals*. The dimension of purpose is less clear or certain. However, use of the term capability suggests a future orientation, as does the concern with survival. It seems reasonable therefore to argue that in terms of purpose, there is greater emphasis on career progression than on current performance. This argument is strengthened if a view is adopted that ensuring a supply of appropriately developed managers to fill senior positions is significant in achieving organisational survival in the medium and long term. It is appropriate, therefore, to say that Harrison's definition of MD can be placed in Quadrant 4 of the framework.

■ Discussion

The examination of two formal definitions of MD has demonstrated that the framework in Fig. 9.1 is capable of accommodating variations in academic conceptions of MD. Each of the selected definitions has been shown to be capable of classification within the framework. The framework will therefore have practical value in aiding understanding of the various meanings and purposes of MD. Such understanding will have additional value in informing decisions and actions in professional practice.

There are, however, a number of problems with this argument. The first and perhaps most obvious problem is that the definitions have been deliberately selected. It will be instructive for readers to test this by applying the framework to alternative definitions. More significant problems lie with the definitions themselves. While they can be said to be 'mainstream' and representative of common conceptions of MD, they do not reflect some of the points made in the previous section. They do not, for example, directly or overtly acknowledge or reflect the nature of managerial work. Each seems to assume, implicitly at least, that there are unproblematic connections between managerial behaviour, performance and effectiveness. Additional connections between managerial effectiveness and organisational effectiveness are further assumed. There is an overall sense that desired, effective or 'best' managerial behaviour can be determined and specified. The earlier analysis of managerial work suggests otherwise.

Activity 9.2

1 Through research, find three more definitions of management development. Journal articles as well as books will provide some examples.

2 Analyse the definitions and allocate each to one of the quadrants in Fig. 9.1.

3 Evaluate the utility of the framework based on the results of Questions 1 and 2. Is it capable of categorising a variety of definitions?

4 Consider how the framework can be used to inform decisions on practice.

The work of Lee (1997) on conceptions of development described earlier suggests additional problems. The definitions examined here seem to assume known end points for development, represented by concepts such as 'effectiveness' or 'capability'. They perhaps vary more in terms of whether identity is unitary or co-regulated according to the emphasis they give to the individual manager or the organisation. Harrison's (1997) definition of MD, for example, with its concern with a 'shared culture', could arguably reflect a co-regulated perspective. However, this still limits the definitions to only two conceptions of development in Lee's analysis: either development as maturation or development as shaping. The two remaining conceptions of development, as voyage or emergent (*see* Table 9.2), are not therefore represented in conventional and mainstream definitions of MD.

The definitions also seem to reflect a 'unitary' conception of organisations. Such a conception assumes an unproblematic formulation of specifiable and specific organisational goals and objectives. There are, of course, alternative conceptions of organisations (*see* Alvesson and Deetz, 1996; Morgan, 1997). In a recent application of institutional theory to the field of management learning, Burgoyne and Jackson (1997) argue what they term the 'arena thesis'. This analysis, in essence, proposes a greater validity and utility for pluralist conceptions of organisations, and a role for management development in providing a 'meeting point' where 'conflicting purposes and values can meet to be reinforced, reconciled or proliferated' (Burgoyne and Jackson, 1997: 68). The implication here for conventional definitions of MD is that if the assumed unproblematic nature of organisations, and organisational goals, is questionable, then the conceptions of MD drawn from those assumptions are also questionable. In defence of the originators of the definitions, it is fair to say that the analyses of MD provided by Mumford (1997) and Harrison (1997) do in fact reflect, take account of and apply many of the points discussed so far. Single-sentence definitions cannot accommodate every factor or detail examined in the analyses from which they are derived. The potential failings and weaknesses discussed are much more fully recognised and acknowledged by the writers concerned than their definitions might otherwise suggest. However, there is one final problem with the definitions where this is arguably less the case.

Processual perspectives on and analyses of organising and managing both question and challenge the reification implicit in more conventional treatments. The language form of the preceding sentence makes the point. Conventional analyses treat 'organisations' as independent, objective entities; in other words, an 'organisation' is a 'thing' or an 'it'. They therefore suffer from what Chia (1996) refers to as 'misplaced concreteness' in their analyses. From a processual perspective, 'organisations' do not have entitative status. They are not 'things' or 'its'. Rather, organising is a process, with more or less regularity and patterning, that produces and reproduces the shared experience that we label an, or the, 'organisation'. 'Organisations', as entities, are created by our shared experience and the language we use to make sense of that experience, and therefore 'they' do not have an independent, objective existence (*see* Chia, 1996, 1997; Watson, 1994a). The same arguments can be applied to 'management' and 'managing', and indeed to individuals.

What this means for definitions of MD is clear. They do not, as they might claim and we might assume, provide accurate descriptions of a given reality. They represent attempts to make sense of an ongoing process of reality construction. It can be useful to conceive of organisations as objective entities, and to relate professional practices that we label 'management development' to such conceptions (*see* Stewart, 1999). However, as argued in Chapter 1, it is also useful and instructive to think about organising, managing and professional practice from a processual perspective. It is perhaps particularly important to emphasise this point when leading and influential writers on MD continue to apply more traditional perspectives.

The arguments in this section lead to a number of significant conclusions. First, influential analyses of the meaning of MD continue to apply what might be labelled conventional perspectives within organisation and management theory. Second, within that context, and partly because of it, variations in meaning can be related to a small number of factors. Third, the framework in Fig. 9.1 is capable of categorising varying conceptions of MD arising from conventional, though influential, analyses. Fourth, while what is termed conventional analyses remain influential and helpful, the processual perspective has utility in providing an alternative way of thinking about MD, which both allows and encourages new insights to inform and influence professional practice. Readers may wish to adopt that way of thinking at this point as an individual, or perhaps group, activity, to explore what insights might be generated by a processual analysis of MD. The results of such an activity will be useful in examining approaches and methods within MD.

Management development approaches and methods

It will be clear that the approaches and methods to MD adopted will be influenced by and related to the conception, or definition, being applied. For example, a conception of MD fitting Quadrant 1 in Fig. 9.1 is likely to lead to the use of methods different from those utilised if a conception fitting the requirements of Quadrant 4 is applied. According to some writers (e.g. Jones and Woodcock, 1985; Harrison, 1997), various other factors will also be influential in decisions on what approach and methods to adopt. These factors are associated with what Jones and Woodcock term 'organisation readiness'. This concept suggests that particular approaches will be more appropriate than others, depending on particular organisational circumstances. A different way of framing this argument is to say that particular circumstances make it more likely that one approach rather than another will be adopted. The first formulation suggests a normative theory, i.e. one in which prescriptions are provided on how to practise MD to meet the requirements of varying circumstances; while the second formulation implies a descriptive theory, i.e. one which provides an analysis of how MD is practised in varying circumstances. In either case, MD is assumed to be constituted by deliberate and formalised activities. An indicative list of what circumstances, or contingencies, might be significant is given below:

- level of top management commitment to MD;
- organisation/business priorities;
- intended organisation and business strategies;
- the level of resources available and/or allocated to MD;
- clarity and specificity of managerial roles;
- size of organisation/numbers of managers.

These factors are unlikely to operate independently, since they have clear connections and interrelationships. For example, resources allocated to MD will be influenced by the level of top management commitment which, in turn, is likely to be influenced by their perception of the relevance of MD to their intended business strategy. Taking potential connections and relationships further, an intended strategy of expansion may lead to increasing numbers of managers being employed. The content and objectives of MD activities for these managers will, however, be influenced by the degree of clarity on their expected and intended roles.

One factor not included in the indicative list is the application or otherwise of HRM-style practices, and indeed the nature of human resourcing strategy apparent in a particular context. The connections between this and MD will be examined in a later section. A further point on the indicative list needs to be made. It is simply that the factors listed do not operate independently in an additional and important sense. The factors are examples of 'organisational contingencies' mentioned in Fig. 1.1 (p. 31). The spirit of a processual analysis suggests that such contingencies, and their consequences, are mediated by the interpretations and meanings assigned to them by decision makers. This is also indicated in Fig. 1.1. It is not the case, therefore, that particular factors either should or will produce particular approaches to MD, since the meaning and associated significance of each is not 'given' or 'pre-determined' and will vary between different managers and over time.

■ Approaches to MD

The argument advanced so far suggests that approaches adopted to MD will relate in some respects to variation in conceptions of MD and particular organisational contingencies, both mediated by individual and collective interpretations and, following Chapter 1 and Fig. 1.1, by conflicting and competing values and interests. Within that context, the available and possible approaches to MD are argued to be capable of categorisation. The typology provided by Mabey and Salaman in Table 9.1 is one example. Two further typologies are of value and interest since, in more or less explicit ways, they can be related to the indicative organisational contingencies.

The first typology is that first suggested by Burgoyne in 1988 (Mumford, 1997).

Which approach is adopted within Burgoyne's broad categories will be a function, in part, of what Jones and Woodcock (1985) refer to as 'organisation readiness' which, in turn, will be a function, in part, of organisational contingencies. Burgoyne uses the term 'organisation maturity' (Mumford, 1997) in a similar fashion to 'organisation readiness', and argues similar connections between level, or degree, of maturity and organisational contingencies. His six possible approaches to MD are therefore distinguished and categorised according to the degree of 'organisation maturity'. The approaches are as follows:

1 No systematic management development.

2 Isolated tactical management development.

3 Integrated and co-ordinated structural and development tactics.

4 A management development strategy to implement corporate policy.

5 Management development strategy input to corporate policy formulation.

6 Strategic development of the management of corporate policy.

Approach number one is, according to Burgoyne, most likely to be evident in young and small organisations. Approaches one and two are probably those most widely adopted across all organisations, and approaches three and four represent what might currently constitute 'best practice'. 'Best practice' is most likely to be found in large, well-established organisations operating in large and well-established industries. Examples of these will include process industries, financial services and retailing. Public-sector organisations, such as local government and those in the health service, are also likely to adopt approaches three and four. The final two approaches are only occasionally encountered and are rarely sustained (*see* Mumford, 1997). It seems clear from the first point that size is seen by Burgoyne as a key contingency initiating formal approaches to MD. The descriptions of the remaining approaches explicitly suggest that intended business strategy is a further critical contingency in influencing the approach adopted. Finally, and related to this point, it seems reasonable to argue that the descriptions implicitly rely on top management commitment as an important contingency influencing the approach adopted.

As Mumford (1987) argues, one problem with Burgoyne's typology is that it assumes, and is therefore built on, a conception of MD as deliberate, formalised and planned programmes. While Burgoyne recognises the occurrence and potential value of informal learning and development, which accounts for the totality of MD in the first approach, his descriptions of approaches two to six rely on planned and programmed activities. This analysis is confirmed and partly explained by Burgoyne's definition of MD, which is 'the management of managerial careers in an organisational context' (Mumford, 1997: 47). (Readers may wish to apply the framework in Fig. 9.1 to this definition as a further test of its utility.) A potential weakness therefore with this typology is its failure overtly and directly to accommodate informal processes of learning and development. Additional potential weaknesses will be examined later in this section.

An alternative typology is that provided by Mumford himself (1993, 1997). This classification has two possible strengths. First, it overcomes the potential weakness of not dealing directly with informal processes. This is particularly important in applying a processual perspective to organisational analysis. Second, it is limited to three categories or approaches. This makes the typology less conceptually complex and therefore easier to apply to inform practice. However, ease of application should not be associated with lack of rigour. The three approaches suggested by Mumford are described in Table 9.3. They have some similarity and resonance with those suggested by Storey and his colleagues (Storey *et al.*, 1997) and therefore can be said to be supported by recent research.

Table 9.3 Typologies of management development

Type	Description
Type 1	Informal managerial – accidental processes
Type 2	Integrated managerial – opportunistic processes
Type 3	Formal management development – planned processes

Source: Based on Mumford, 1997.

Each of the three types has particular characteristics that, according to Mumford, will have implications and consequences for their effectiveness as approaches to MD. Type 1 has the strength and advantage of focusing on and occurring in 'real' work. However, learning is usually unconscious, undirected and insufficient. Type 3 overcomes these disadvantages by being planned and therefore directed. The disadvantages of Type 3 are fairly obvious, however. The two problems of relevance and transferability are common criticisms of learning and development that form the focus of formal programmes. According to Mumford, the Type 2 approach has the potential to maximise the advantages and minimise the disadvantages of each of the other two types. This argument in part relies on Mumford's contention that the either/or choice of formal or informal approaches is in fact a false dichotomy. This view, while not directly connected, has resonance with analyses associated with a processual perspective (*see* Chia, 1996). Mumford's argument on the falseness of the dichotomy is a little weakened by his stated view that naturally occurring learning opportunities in and at work can be, and perhaps should be, planned and directed. However, his overall analysis is valuable in emphasising the actual and potential learning inherent in the everyday experience of carrying out work tasks and activities.

One further factor arising from Mumford's typology is of particular interest. Mumford suggests that a characteristic of both Type 1 and Type 2 approaches is that 'ownership' of MD processes and activities remains with managers themselves. Type 3 approaches, by contrast, imply ownership by professional practitioners. There is therefore in Mumford's typology a clear choice to be made in terms of the relative roles and contributions of professional developers and other managers. Type 3 approaches provide professional practitioners with control and ownership; the other approaches do not. Control and ownership in Types 1 and 2 can operate in the sense of individual managers' control both over their own development and over the development of their employees. This issue of control and ownership is one of the main reasons, though not the only one, for Mumford advocating Type 2 approaches as producing the most effective management development.

Applying Mumford's typology to current practice, it is likely that Type 1 approaches will be more commonly found in small to medium-sized enterprises. There is likely to be some variation in this generalisation, nevertheless. For example, Type 1 is more likely to be associated with small-scale manufacturing companies in traditional industries such as engineering. Small-scale service companies such as information technology or management consultancies are perhaps more likely to practise MD in line with a Type 2 approach. Type 3 approaches are commonly associated with large-scale bureaucracies across all sectors of the economy. One factor that may help to explain this being the case is the existence of specialised and professional MD functions in such organisations.

It was indicated earlier that Burgoyne's typology has additional potential weaknesses. These relate to the processual analysis advocated and advanced in this book. The levels of 'maturity' described in Burgoyne's six approaches explicitly rest on a notion of separation of corporate strategy and human resourcing strategy. Perhaps more implicitly, they also assume that corporate strategy is exclusively associated with the plans and intentions of top and senior managers. In other words, Burgoyne's typology seems to reflect what was termed 'mainstream thinking' in Chapter 1 of this book. The view argued in Chapter 1, and throughout this book, would in fact see Burgoyne's sixth approach as more closely reflecting the actuality of strategic processes in organisations, and therefore the remaining approaches as arguably false choices since they rely on less useful premises. This is not to say, however, that the varying degree of formality and planning implicit in Burgoyne's typology is without value. It does in fact have significant utility in making judgements concerning which approach or approaches to adopt to MD. For example, in circumstances where time, resources and attention are devoted to producing detailed strategic plans for an organisation, it would be literally nonsensical to refuse to undertake similar processes in relation to MD, or not to contribute the views and ambitions of MD to the corporate planning process, or indeed not to take account of formal business plans, where they exist, in formulating MD plans and programmes. However, it is arguable that more informed and, in that sense, 'better' decisions on MD approaches will arise when the actuality of organisation strategies as realised outcomes is recognised. Such a recognition is likely to lead to greater focus on and attention to the informal processes of managerial actions and behaviour and, following the arguments of Chapter 1, will have implications for the content of any formal MD programmes. For these reasons, Mumford's typology offers greater utility in understanding and making decisions on approaches to management development. In addition, his Type 2 represents a commendable overall approach. It is fair to say also that Burgoyne's more recent work (e.g. Burgoyne and Jackson, 1997; Pedler *et al.*, 1996) would support a similar conclusion.

Activity 9.3

1 Identify some possible relationships and connections between organisation contingencies and the idea of 'organisation maturity'. Think about how a 'mature' and an 'immature' organisation might differ in relation to these contingencies.

2 Consider the likely implications for management development practice arising from changes in organisation contingencies.

3 Research and access some examples of management development practice from published cases in journals such as *People Management*.

4 Analyse the descriptions provided and categorise the approach adopted in each case according to the Burgoyne (1998) and Mumford (1997) frameworks.

5 Evaluate the utility of both frameworks and decide which is most effective, and for what reasons, in categorising varying approaches.

■ Methods

There are obvious connections between approaches to and methods of management development. A simple example would be that Type 3 approaches in Mumford's typology are likely to be associated with programmes of management education and training, while Type 2 approaches are likely to emphasise work- and job-based methods such as action learning, coaching and mentoring (*see* Mumford, 1997; Stewart, 1996). There is as well a vast array of methods available and advocated for use by professional developers (Huczynski, 1983) and by managers themselves (Pedler *et al.*, 1994). It is therefore necessary to be selective here. The choices are guided by the conceptual frameworks described so far in this chapter, and by some additional classifications focusing on methods.

One commonly applied method of MD is to produce frameworks of management competence (Thomson *et al.*, 1997). This concept is more complex than is sometimes allowed and is not without controversy or criticism (Devine, 1990; Bates, 1995; Stewart and Sambrook, 1995). It is at the heart of national policy on vocational qualifications, however, and has been applied by the Management Charter Initiative (MCI) to produce occupational standards for managers (Harrison, 1997; Reid and Barrington, 1997). These standards provide a specification of 'competencies', or abilities, that managers in various roles and at various levels are argued to require. They can therefore provide a starting point in determining development needs and can be used to inform the design of development programmes. The nature of assessment for MCI qualifications also provides the opportunity of applying a Type 2 approach, since award of the qualifications requires evidence of demonstrated competence in and at work. MCI specifications of competence do not of course have to be utilised and many organisations have produced their own frameworks (*see* Tate, 1995). Alternative generic frameworks are also available (*see*, for example, Jones and Woodcock, 1985; Boyatzis, 1982).

Mumford (1993, 1997) criticises the MCI framework and the processes that led to its production. However, he does support the value of producing some framework or model of competence. Such models, he argues, need to focus on 'effectiveness' as well as competence and to take account of the vagaries and ambiguities of managerial work. Using these two criteria, Mumford also suggests a range of methods which, since they focus on combining learning and working and working and learning, reflect the benefits of a Type 2 approach. The methods are categorised into three sets, as follows:

- *Changes in the job*
  - promotion;
  - job rotation;
  - secondments.

- *Changes in job content*
  - additional responsibility and tasks;
  - specific projects;
  - membership of committees or task groups;
  - junior boards.

- *Within the job*
  - coaching;
  - counselling;
  - monitoring and feedback;
  - mentoring.

This list of MD methods explicitly focuses on what might be described as informal methods, which nevertheless are capable of, and perhaps would benefit from, some degree of formalisation and planning. It does, however, exclude off-the-job and other methods that are normally associated with more formalised and systematic approaches. Alternative classifications are offered by Reid and Barrington (1994) and by Jones and Woodcock (1985). These classifications add the following methods:

- group-based methods, e.g. managerial grid;

- in-house courses;

- planned experience outside of the organisation;

- external courses, qualification or non-qualification based;

- role analysis;

- seminars;

- exchange consulting;

- performance review;

- development centres;

- career management and development.

The latter three methods have links and connections with succession planning, discussed by Harrison (1997) as a method of MD. The two lists need not be seen as mutually exclusive, nor indeed need individual methods on each list. Combinations of methods from both lists will in fact support and enable application of Mumford's Type 2 approach. Expressed another way, adopting a Type 2 approach is likely to lead to use of methods from both lists. It also needs to be recognised that the methods included are not exhaustive.

This discussion of methods illustrates a further application of the framework in Fig. 9.1. As well as being useful for categorising and comparing meanings and definitions, the framework can also be useful in categorising methods. Fig. 9.2 shows this by placing some methods in each of the quadrants. The placing of the managerial grid (*see* Stewart,

Focus

	Individual	*Organisation*
Behaviour	Coaching Competence Specifications	Promotion Managerial grid
Career progression	Secondments Mentoring	Succession planning Career management

Purpose

Fig. 9.2 Classification of management development methods

1996) in Quadrant 2 follows the argument that MD is centrally concerned with shared values (Harrison, 1997).

In closing this section, readers may find it useful to test this application of the framework further by allocating the remaining methods from the two lists, and any others with which they are familiar to one of the four quadrants.

Activity 9.4

1 Allocate each method on the two lists to one of the quadrants in Fig. 9.2.

2 Evaluate the utility of the framework in Fig. 9.2 as a means of categorising MD methods.

3 Allocate each method on the two lists to one of Mumford's three types of MD.

4 Select a combination of methods from either or both lists that could be combined to produce a coherent MD programme.

5 Discuss the results of 4 with a colleague.

Management development and human resourcing strategy

This final substantive section is concerned with examining the relationships between MD and human resourcing strategy. The focus is therefore with matters of *horizontal integration*. The section will draw on some recent empirical research, as well as applying some of the conceptual frameworks introduced in Chapter 1.

A useful starting point is always 'first principles'. Table 1.6 (p. 29), suggests two key alternatives, while Table 1.9 (p. 33) argues that these alternatives can be applied singly or in combination. The latter table allows for variation across organisational hierarchies within a single human resourcing strategy. This might be expected to be common, with arrangements for managers being quite different from those for other employees.

Certainly in terms of MD, conceptually at least, it is reasonable to expect approaches and methods to both assume, and to be intended to encourage, the principle of indirect control/high commitment in their design. To the extent that this is the case, and that development arrangements for 'non-managerial' employees are likely to be different, this could be said to represent an alternative dual human resourcing strategy that does not rely on the distinction between core and peripheral sectors.

However, the picture is a little more complicated. For example, it is arguable that competence-based designs are in effect intended to exercise control through precise specifications of desired behaviours. When such specifications are linked to MD through activities such as development or assessment centres and performance appraisal and/or reward systems, an intention and attempt at direct control seem apparent. Approaches such as these seem to reflect what Mabey and Salaman (1995) describe as a 'political reinforcement' agenda for MD, perhaps with elements of 'functional performance' (*see* Table 9.1). If the distinction between 'direct control/low commitment' and 'indirect control/high commitment' is accepted as a matter of degree, rather than a straightforward either/or choice, then it is possible to argue that competence-based methods of MD *tend more* towards 'direct control'. Precise specifications of behaviour will provide little discretion for managers, and application of those specifications to rewards and promotion through appraisal and assessment/development centres will provide opportunities for close supervision and monitoring. Therefore, both broad principles suggested in Table 1.6 are available to, and can be applied in, approaches to MD. That being the case, a single human resourcing strategy does not necessarily have to accommodate variations across different hierarchical levels, except perhaps at the very top.

Competence-based approaches then provide an example of 'direct-control/low-commitment' principles being applied within MD. Applying Mumford's (1997) arguments on 'ownership' will enable identification of approaches that reflect the principles of 'indirect control/high commitment'. The reasoning here is that the latter principles encourage and provide a higher degree of discretion to managers. It would be incongruous to adopt approaches and methods within MD that provide a high degree of discretion to managers themselves in a situation where such discretion was not available in their jobs. This argument does, of course, associate 'ownership' with 'discretion'. It does seem reasonable to say, however, that high degrees of management ownership of MD will be more likely in circumstances where high levels of discretion exist or are encouraged in relation to job performance. So application of Mumford's Type 2 approach can be argued to be most appropriate as a means of integrating MD with an 'indirect-control/high-commitment' human resourcing strategy.

Methods such as action learning and self and peer assessment (*see* Stewart, 1996), or indeed managerial self-development (*see* Pedler *et al.*, 1994) provide the degree of ownership, and the explicit connections between learning and work and work and learning, necessary to meet the characteristics that Mumford associates with Type 2 approaches to MD. Such methods will therefore both reflect and promote 'indirect-control/high-commitment' human resourcing principles. The methods will also reflect at least four of the HRM-style practices detailed in Table 1.7. MD becomes the concern of all managers rather than development specialists only; activities include and directly influence strategic deliberations; they promote trust, teamwork and co-operation and, finally, they stress continuous personal development. To the extent that HRM-style practices are associated with 'indirect-control/high-commitment' principles, as argued in Chapter 1, this connection of Type 2 methods with HRM-style practices further supports the contention that Type 2 MD is congruent with an 'indirect-control/high-commitment' human resourcing strategy. To return to the earlier point, to the extent that this is limited exclusively to managers or to certain level managers only, there may be a case for arguing a second form of dual human resourcing strategy.

Turning now to empirical sources, some evidence suggests a growing prevalence of programmes of culture change being attempted and implemented in UK work organisations (IRS, 1997). It has to be recognised that the IRS report on culture change suggests that 80 per cent of programmes fail to meet their intended objectives. However, what is of particular interest here is that development activities and a focus on management development are, according to the same report, common components of change programmes. The focus on management development is, again commonly, intended to promote 'empowerment' and devolution of authority and thus can be associated with 'indirect-control/high-commitment' human resourcing principles. The IRS report notes, however, that increased levels of participation do not apply to decisions concerning culture change programmes themselves, which are often initiated and directed by senior managers. There may be possible relationships between this factor and the suggested failure rates. This research seems to suggest that culture change cannot be achieved solely through MD activities aimed at promoting new or different styles of managing. To the extent that explicit and intended culture change can be associated with implementation of HRM-style practices, it can be further suggested that attempting to achieve such practices through MD alone is unlikely to be successful.

A major survey of MD carried out by the Institute of Management (Thomson *et al.*, 1997) suggests that the priority given to MD in UK organisations continues to grow and is expected to increase further in the future. There is, however, no expected change in approaches or methods and therefore those described in this chapter, and in other texts, can be expected to form the basis of MD activities into the next millennium. The Thomson report also suggests that there exists a balance of responsibility for MD between the individual and the employer in the majority of organisations. Taken together with the finding that most employers do not expect managers to stay for a career, there is perhaps a shift away from associating MD with career progression. These two points from the report also suggest a growing relevance and recognition of Mumford's Type 2 approaches. This is further supported by the finding of a balance of formal and informal approaches and methods being applied in MD practice. Two additional conclusions of this research are of interest. The first is that the majority of employers are satisfied with the achievements and impact of management development. It is possible to argue that 'they would say that, wouldn't they?'. However, the conclusion does suggest some empirical support for the value of MD. The second conclusion is that investment in MD is a matter of policy and therefore of choice. Based on statistical analysis of the relationship between a number of variables, Thomson *et al.* (1997) conclude that the existence or extent of investment in MD is not determined by external or structural factors, and that investment or not arises out of the choices made by decision makers. Such choices do seem to have some relationship to decision makers' views on 'strategic issues'. The research therefore supports the position taken in this book. It is also the case that the findings on 'satisfaction' and 'impact' could have significance in influencing the perception of decision makers of the strategic importance of investment in MD.

A recent book comparing MD in the UK and Japan (Storey *et al.*, 1997) is relevant here. The authors argue that 'as market competition intensifies and as firms have to rely on making the most of their people the importance of the topic [MD] can only increase' (1997: 229). However, they also recognise that management development may be a necessary but insufficient condition for success. While having a different focus, this argument appears similar to the conclusions of the IRS study on culture change. Storey and his colleagues warn against the possibility of universal approaches to and solutions for MD. They do, however, also argue that a relative weakness of UK practice compared to Japan is a propensity in the UK to change MD systems too much and too quickly, especially without well-thought-out reasons. Their research also leads them to conclude that career planning remains a useful lynchpin of management development and that MD systems should respond to managers' expectations by providing more direction and control. This seems to rely on a restricted and restrictive conception of MD, which reinforces established ideas related to formal programmes in large organisations. Perhaps the most comforting conclusion of the research is that Japanese practices, and the satisfaction of the recipients, are by no means universally superior to those found in the UK. However, some of the implications and suggestions arising from the research – especially in relation to integration of MD, career planning, objective and target setting, performance appraisal and so on – would seem to support 'direct-control/low-commitment' HR strategies being applied to managers. They also imply more control for HR development specialists and a consequent reduction in managerial autonomy in relation to their development.

Management development can be argued to be a significant lever in achieving change in relation to issues concerning equal opportunities and managing diversity, since some models of managing and development applied to MD can propagate and legitimate, for example, stereotypical and ethnocentric conceptions of organisations and management (*see* Lee, 1996; Wilson, 1996; Chapter 4). Leaving aside programmes specifically intended to redress the effects of such models, the empirical picture is not encouraging. Research conducted for the then Employment Department and the CRE (Cheung-Judge, 1993) found that fewer than 40 per cent of management programmes provided by educational institutions included equal opportunities (EO) issues in their content. The same research also found that, where employers provided development related to EO and diversity issues, such development was not, in the majority of cases, linked to or integrated with management development policy and practice. It is perhaps instructive on this point that the survey by Thomson *et al.* did not directly address the EO implications and applications of MD. Therefore, the conclusion seems to be that there remains a great deal of scope for articulating those implications and applications.

CASE STUDY 9.1

Highfield College of FE

Highfield College of FE is located in a medium-sized Midlands city. It has recently experienced its third reorganisation following the appointment of its third principal and chief executive since incorporation. Hilda Emanuel has retained her position as chief administrative officer for the College in the new structure. Her position is third tier, i.e. she reports to the deputy principal (resources), who in turn reports to the chief executive. Hilda's responsibilities encompass finance, personnel and schools administrative support, and her level equates to the academic heads of school. Other positions at the centre of the college include a registrar and chief estates officer, both of whom report to Peter West, the deputy principal (resources).

Designated managers in the college include heads of school, subject co-ordinators and course leaders among academic staff, and departmental heads, supervisors and team leaders among non-academic staff. Hilda herself has direct responsibility for 65 staff, including three departmental heads, one of whom is head of personnel. The new principal and chief executive is Samantha Hall, an energetic, authoritative and innovative leader who has persuaded the college board of governors that the future survival and success of the college depends on 'going for growth' which, in turn, depends on devising new products and creating new markets. Samantha's appointment was in part a response to the failure of the previous principal to address and resolve pressing financial problems, which are still there. However, Samantha believes that expansion and growth cannot be achieved without some speculative expenditure. This nevertheless has to be linked to securing the long-term survival and prosperity of the college.

Samantha Hall, with the support of the chair of governors, Jack Golding, has instituted a strategic working group to produce new policies and working practices to support and encourage her plans for growth. Membership of this group is as follows:

- Jack Golding (chair of the board of governors);
- Samantha Hall (principal and chief executive);
- Peter West (deputy principal, resources);
- Ruth Kitchen (deputy principal, academic affairs);
- Hilda Emanuel (chief administrative officer).

Management development is currently very *ad hoc* and is primarily provided in response to individual requests and constituted by qualification-based courses such as the DMS provided by a local university. Hilda has persuaded Peter West that the new organisational structure, and the intended strategy of growth, are unlikely to succeed without some improvement in managerial ability and performance. Both Peter and Hilda are aware, however, that Mike Newell, head of finance, believes the college cannot afford to spend money that it doesn't have to or that cannot guarantee some return. They also believe that Samantha Hall, while open minded, is not a natural supporter of MD and that, if resources are allocated, Ruth Kitchen will argue that priority should be given to academic staff. They also know that Jack Golding will take a close interest in the financial implications of any proposals considered by the group. Hilda and Peter have agreed to present a joint paper to the group on the need for and potential benefits of investment in MD in support of the intended business strategy. They are aware that Mike Newell, as head of finance, will need to make some contribution to the paper on any financial implications. As a starting point, however, they have agreed to request the head of personnel, one of Hilda's staff, to prepare an initial draft.

Activity 9.5

Imagine that you are head of personnel for the college and consider the following questions:

1 What factors would you take into account in preparing your paper and how might these influence the content?

2 What will be the main issues that you address in your paper?

3 What approach or approaches to MD will you advocate and why?

4 What preparatory steps will you take before giving your paper to Hilda, e.g. consulting on its contents with others?

5 What advice will you give to Peter and Hilda for dealing with possible responses from members of the working group?

Conclusion

This chapter has argued that management development can and does have multiple meanings. A range of approaches to and methods of management development have also been described. It has been further argued that the conceptions and definitions of MD adopted will influence the approach and methods applied in practice. Other influencing factors will include 'organisation contingencies' such as size and top management commitment. In the end, however, the levels of investment and approaches adopted are a matter of managerial choice rather than the result of independent forces. Management development policy and practice can be congruent with human resourcing principles and are capable of integration with other human resourcing practices to form a coherent strategy. Competence-based methods have been suggested to be more congruent with a 'direct-control/low-commitment' strategy, and Mumford's Type 2 approaches as being congruent with an 'indirect-control/high-commitment strategy'. The latter is argued to reflect the characteristics associated with adoption of HRM-style practices. It has been further suggested that this choice in relation to MD may form the basis of an alternative form of a 'dual human resourcing strategy'. Some empirical evidence has been included that suggests that MD is often associated with formal attempts to change organisational culture, although other research suggests that this is not the case in relation to implementation of policies related to EO and managing diversity. However, a recent and major survey provides some evidence to support an argument that investment in MD produces valued outcomes.

Summary

In this chapter the following key points have been made:

- Both 'management' and 'development' are complex and problematic concepts.

- This complexity in part explains the variations in meaning attached to the term 'management development'.

- Management development can focus on managers as individuals or as a collective resource, and can have a purpose related to developing skills and abilities or to developing consistency in values in support of 'corporate culture'.

- A number of attempts have been made to categorise various approaches to and methods of management development.

- The categorisation produced by Mumford (1997) that suggests three 'types' of MD is useful and his arguments in favour of Type 2 – 'integrated approaches' are persuasive.

- Alternative approaches to MD allow integration of MD with alternative human resourcing strategies, including those associated with application of HRM-style practices.

- Recent research suggests that investment in MD is growing and that organisations perceive value and benefit from that investment.

- Research also suggests that relying on MD to produce culture change is unwise, and that redressing inequalities in organisations requires closer links between MD and EO initiatives.

Discussion questions

1 Examine and determine what conception of MD is currently being applied in an organisation with which you are familiar.

2 What factors do you think account for this being the case?

3 To what extent do you think that MD policy and practice are congruent with a coherent and integrating human resourcing principle in this organisation?

4 What alternative conceptions of MD, in your judgement, might be more appropriate for the organisation and why?

5 How would current approaches and methods need to change to accommodate this shift?

Further reading

As with other chapters, the sources referenced in the text provide a rich variety of research and writing on MD. The text by Mumford (1997) is obviously a 'must' for MD specialists, as is the collection edited by Burgoyne and Reynolds (1997). More general texts on development such as Harrison (1997) and Reid and Barrington (1997) are also valuable. New perspectives on the nature of organising and managing are important in considering MD, and the texts by Watson (1994) and by Alvesson and Wilmott (1996) provide exemplary treatments. Connections and relationships between MD and human resource development (HRD), especially in relation to diversity and EO issues, can be explored in the collection of papers edited by Stewart and McGoldrick (1996). The book by Storey and his colleagues (1997) provides an interesting overview and the results of a comparative analysis of UK and Japanese practices. Both elements of the book offer valuable reading. Finally, the book by Woodall and Winstanley (1998) is a very useful analysis of theory and practice which draws on a wide range of case examples.

Part IV

LAW, ETHICS AND EQUALITY

10
EMPLOYMENT LAW AND HUMAN RESOURCING
Challenges and constraints
Lynette Harris

11
ACHIEVING EQUALITY OF OPPORTUNITY?
Mary Crow

12
MANAGING MESSY MORAL MATTERS
Ethics and HRM
Colin Fisher and Chris Rice

EMPLOYMENT LAW AND HUMAN RESOURCING
Challenges and constraints

Lynette Harris

OBJECTIVES

Having completed this chapter and its associated activities, readers should be able to:

- demonstrate an understanding of how the legislative framework is a factor in human resource strategy making;

- recognise how the degree of employment regulation affects the specialist human resourcing function's organisational role;

- identify the respective responsibilities of the human resource (HR) specialist and the line manager for the interpretation and application of employment law to operational practice;

- assess the impact that increasing regulation may have on human resourcing strategies and the relationship between line management and the specialist HR function.

Introduction

The key theme of this chapter is to examine the impact that external employment regulation has on the role of the human resource function, the focus of its activities and the perceptions that other managerial groups have about its organisational contribution. It considers the responsibilities of line managers *vis-à-vis* those of the human resource specialist for interpreting and implementing employment legislation. Although developments in employment law and the growing influence that European Court of Justice (ECJ) decisions are having on the UK will be considered, it is not within the scope of this chapter to explore the detailed content of the legislation. Taking a historical perspective, it will be argued that a growth in employment regulation has implications for human resourcing strategies and the respective roles of line management and the specialist HR function.

The role that the law should play in the workplace is a topical issue for UK employers as they prepare for new European legislation. Reports of an escalation in employment litigation in the American workplace for reasons similar to those frequently cited in the UK are hardly reassuring (Olsen, 1997). A US study of HR professionals (Overell, 1997) revealed that the majority of organisations had experienced litigation and 23 per cent of the HR respondents had been personally sued over an employment issue in the past five years. The demands made by this growth in litigation were seen by the HR specialists as detracting from their ability to undertake more proactive and developmental work. The need for more centralised HR processes to cope with the pressures of the legislation appears to be back on the agenda in the USA, despite the prevailing trend for increasingly devolving levels of responsibility for personnel matters to line management.

As Jefferson (1997) observes, employment law has been one of the most important areas of conflicting economic, political and social theories over the past 30 years and its effectiveness is highly reflective of prevailing labour-market conditions. The level of legal intervention in the workplace plays a significant part in how approaches to human resourcing develop and change over time. It can be a critical factor in strategic HR planning and can lead to radical shifts in practice. One example of this in the past 20 years has been the growth in the 'core/periphery' approach to employment (Atkinson, 1987) in sectors such as local government previously characterised by a large permanent core with a minimal peripheral workforce. Differing perceptions about the part that employment regulation plays in creating labour-market rigidities are at the heart of the flexibility debates among European member states (Hakim, 1990; Chapter 3). In the UK, successive Conservative administrations argued that the freedoms of employers in the labour market are central to cost-effective human resourcing strategies, and the present Labour government continues to identify the danger of excessive regulation impeding the development of workforce flexibility.

Leaving political perspectives aside, the evidence that legislation acts a deterrent to flexibility in employment practice is far from conclusive. Research by Brewster *et al.* (1996) into working time and contract flexibility in the EU does not support the assumption that the UK, as the most deregulated country in the EU, demonstrates the greatest flexibility. Sparrow and Marchington (1998: 19) suggest that the frequently stated view that the UK has more flexible employment practices than elsewhere in the EU may be explained by the relative ease with which its employers can carry out dismissals.

Whatever the impact of the UK's relatively low levels of regulation has been on the development of flexible employment practices, it is argued that:

- the volume of employment legislation and related case law is already extensive in the UK and will continue to expand;

- employers driven by competitive pressures will seek out those human resourcing strategies that minimise labour costs. The resultant HR practices will be heavily influenced by prevailing labour-market conditions, government policies and levels of labour law and social protection.

In large part due to a climate of economic uncertainty, the trend since the 1980s has been for HR policies to focus on adaptability and responsiveness to change rather than stability and continuity (Blyton and Turnbull, 1992). The two alternative resourcing principles of direct control/low commitment and indirect control/high commitment, described by Watson in Chapter 1, are reflected in the nature of the employment contract. An uncertain external environment has led organisations to 'hedge their bets' when formulating the terms of individual appointments by offering a variety of employment contracts other than full-time, permanent positions. As discussed elsewhere (Beaver and Harris, 1996b), using the legal contract to limit employer commitment can easily result in its becoming the means of control, serving as a substitute for effective performance management and eroding any durable employment relationship.

An illustration of this approach is the frequent use of short-term contracts or part-time lecturing appointments in higher education, where there is high control over the type of work that the employee is required to do but low long-term commitment from the employer. Individuals seeking more hours or permanency tend to leave as soon greater security is offered by another institution. The use of the law to reduce the contractual commitment of employers to individual employees has flourished in an environment where the risk of business fluctuations has increasingly been transferred from employer to employee. Examples of this risk transference in operation are:

- the currently legally permissible but questionably fair practice of offering fixed-term contracts of under two years to avoid termination costs, even when this is not required by the short-term nature of the work or related funding;

- the development of the 'zero'-hours contract, particularly popular in the retail sector, where the employee has no guaranteed hours or income.

ILLUSTRATION 10.1

Zero hours in high street banking

High street banks have been criticised by the bank workers' union BIFU for the use of Burger King-style contracts. BIFU claimed that using employment contracts with no guaranteed hours and paying only when there is work denied people employment rights. The banking industry responded that most temporary staff are former employees who have chosen to become flexible register employees because it offers them the choice of working when they choose to do so.

Source: People Management, 11 September 1997: 16

Activity 10.1

What legal protection, if any, should employees who work under zero-hours contracts enjoy?

To trace how the UK's legislative framework has influenced human resourcing practices and the nature of the HR specialist's organisational contribution requires an examination of the key phases in its development during the post-war period. Table 10.1 sets out the principal labour law statutes enacted from 1960 to the present time to illustrate the expansion of employment law during this period.

Table 10.1 Key developments in legislation relating to employment from 1960 onwards

1963	Contracts of Employment Act	1986	Wages Act
1965	Redundancy Payments Act	1986	Employment Act
1965	Trades Disputes Act	1988	Access to Medical Records Act
1970	Equal Pay Act	1989	Employment Act
1971	Industrial Relations Act	1990	Employment Act
1974	Health & Safety at Work Act	1992	Trade Union & Labour Relations (Consolidation) Act
1974	Rehabilitation of Offenders Act	1993	Trade Union Reform & Employment Rights Act
1975	Employment Protection Act		
1975	Sex Discrimination Act	1994	Sunday Trading Act
1976	Race Relations Act	1995	Collective Redundancies and Transfer of Undertakings (Protection of Employment) (Amendment) Regulations
1977	Safety Representatives & Safety Committees Regulations		
1978	Employment Protection (Consolidation) Act	1995	Employment Protection (Part-time Employees) Regulations
1980	Employment Act	1995	Disability Discrimination Act
1981	Transfer of Undertakings (Protection of Employment) Regulations	1996	Employment Rights Act
1982	Employment Act	1998	The Employment Rights (Disputes Resolution) Act
1984	Trade Union Act		
1986	Sex Discrimination Act		

In considering the thrust and direction of employment law developments, Kahn-Freund's (1972) broad categorisation of *auxiliary law*, *regulative law* and *restrictive law* is helpful. These distinctions can become blurred in practice, but do provide an initial structural framework for classifying developments in this area of the law (see Table 10.2).

Table 10.2 A framework for categorising labour law

Auxiliary law – Provides support and a framework for collective bargaining
Regulative law – Provides employment rights
Restrictive law – Specifies what is allowable in the conduct of collective bargaining

Activity 10.2

1 Research into the main developments in UK employment law in any 10-year period from 1970 onwards.

2 Identify the prevailing trends during the period you have selected using the categories of auxiliary, regulative and restrictive law outlined in Table 10.2.

The development of employment law in the post-war period

■ Minimal intervention

Until the 1960s in the UK there was very little in the way of legal intervention in the relationship between employer and employee. Wedderburn suggests that the prevailing view across British industrial relations at the time was that 'most workers want nothing more of the law than it should leave them alone. A secure job is preferable to a claim to a redundancy payment; a grievance settled in the plant or the office is better than going to a court or to an industrial tribunal' (1986: 1). This preference for non-intervention by a third party contrasts sharply with the growing propensity of UK workers to seek redress through the Employment Tribunal system. During the era of full employment in the 1950s, there was a continuance of the approach taken since the First World War, namely broad support for pluralism with statutory support in those sectors where collective bargaining was insufficiently developed. These took the form of 'props' such as Wages Councils and the Fair Wages Resolution, which enabled government to ensure contract compliance among its contractors.

The 1960s saw the beginnings of a minimum floor of individual rights for all employees regardless of the existence of workplace collective bargaining with the

Contracts of Employment Act 1963 and the Redundancy Payments Act 1965. State intervention was further evident in the Industrial Training Act 1964, aimed at encouraging employers to train through a grant/levy system operated by Industrial Training Boards for the different occupational sectors. A growing concern about the impact of the country's high levels of industrial stoppages on the UK's economic performance led to the setting up of the Donovan Commission to investigate the country's industrial relations problems. While the Commission's report in 1968 supported the continuance of the voluntary system of bargaining, it recommended reform based on 'properly conducted, collective bargaining' with 'a greater formalisation of the process at company level', which was to include the professionalisation of personnel specialists.

An election defeat for Labour heralded a radical change in direction with the new Conservative government's Industrial Relations Act in 1971. Based on American collective bargaining models, key concepts introduced by the Act were legally enforceable collective agreements and 'unfair industrial practices'. These met with resistance and failure because, as Hepple observes (1995: 308), the act tried to bring about too drastic a change in behaviour by means of law. It was repealed by an incoming Labour government, although the provisions on individual rights to seek redress for unfair dismissal were reenacted in the 1974 Trade Union and Labour Relations Act. The almost universal unpopularity of this piece of legislation makes for an interesting comparison with the popular support given only a decade later to a 'step-by-step' approach to legislation aimed at reducing trade union powers.

■ The social contract

The period from 1974 to 1979 saw a rapid expansion of employee rights in the workplace, the majority of which are still on the statute book today. Compared to the present growth in regulation stemming from the EU, the impact of EC law was minimal at this time, although the Equal Pay Act of 1970 was intended to reflect the provisions of Article 119 of the Treaty of Rome. The basic purpose of the new legislation was to restore and extend the legal base for voluntary collective bargaining together with an improved 'floor of rights' (Wedderburn, 1986: 6) for workers and unions. This period has been labelled the 'social contract' because it was based on trade union co-operation with government's policies on wage restraint in return for an expansion of employment rights. The Employment Protection Act 1975 promoted and expanded collective bargaining and included new rights to time off for maternity, trade union activities and public duties. Further interventions were introduced by the Sex Discrimination Act 1975 and the Race Discrimination Act of 1976. The social contract finally came to an end with the widespread pay disputes in the public sector in 1979, known as the 'winter of discontent', which culminated in the election of a Conservative administration with a very different ideology about the role of state regulation than previous post-war governments.

■ The market rules

For a government committed to a monetarist, free-market ideology, deregulation was a key means of achieving the low-cost and highly flexible workforce seen as essential to increased competitiveness and lower unemployment (Deakin and Wilkinson, 1996).

This heralded the beginning of a 'watershed' in UK labour law policies with the passing of successive Acts to reduce what were seen as unnecessary restrictions on business. There was a steady dismantling of trade union immunities in the Employment Acts of 1980 and 1982, the Trade Union Act of 1984 and the Employment Act of 1988. The immunity for acts in contemplation or furtherance of a trade dispute, known as the golden formula, was limited to direct disputes between workers and their employers, and picketing became lawful only at the place of work of those engaged in the industrial action. Secondary action was restricted to lawful picket sites and the closed shop was finally rendered illegal in 1990. The freedoms of trade unions in conducting their internal affairs were constrained by provisions on balloting, union elections and the rights of members against their union.

The changes did not stop at reducing the power of the trade unions. There was also a reduction of certain individual rights that increased the freedoms of UK employers in the processes of 'hiring and firing' (Beatson, 1995: 31). The qualifying period for unfair dismissal claims was again increased from one year to two years in 1985 and protections for certain groups of workers disappeared with the dismantling of Wages Councils in 1993. By the late 1980s there appeared to a growing gap between the level of regulative law experienced by UK employers in their employment practices and their EU counterparts (Emerson, 1988; Grubb and Wells, 1993), with the UK having the least stringent employment laws. Yet as Fredman (1997) observes, in the period since 1979 there have been two different forces moving within the law, the one driven by the prevailing ideology of a free market with minimal restrictions and the other from the European Community based on reducing divisions and inequalities through protective legislation.

The impact of the EU

After a period of low activity in the 1980s (Hepple, 1995), EU labour and social policy laws have had a growing impact on domestic legal development in the 1990s. Bercusson, commenting (1995: 3–6) on the symbiotic relationship between national and EC labour laws, observes that 'it is not merely that UK labour law is required to incorporate EC norms. EC norms are themselves the reflection of the national labour laws of member states.' To date, the greatest impact on employment matters in the UK has been in the areas of equal treatment and the transfer of undertakings under the Acquired Rights Directive. Table 10.3 (see p. 272) illustrates those EU directives (both implemented and pending) that apply to just one aspect of human resourcing in the UK-equal opportunities.

Alongside the unchanging rhetoric advocating workforce flexibility, recent statements from the European Commission reveal a growing concern with the lack of employment rights for marginal workers reflected in the provisions on social policy contained in the 1997 Amsterdam Treaty. Despite the UK's opt-outs from the Social Chapter, European law has increasingly challenged and curtailed its deregulatory approach, particularly in the public sector (McMullen, 1994).

The involuntary changes made in British employment law stem mostly from the EU's different perception of equal treatment and the rights of individual employees in redundancies and business transfers. For example, as a result of an ECJ ruling,

Table 10.3 EU legislation and equal opportunities

Directive and reference	UK implementation
	All five EU Directives implemented in UK by the:
■ Equal Pay 75/117 ■ Equal Treatment 76/207 ■ Equal Treatment (State Social Security) 79/7 ■ Equal Treatment (Occupational Social Security) 86/378 ■ Equal treatment (Self Employed) 86/613	■ Equal Pay Act 1970 as amended ■ Equal Pay (Amendment) Regulations 1983 ■ Sex Discrimination Acts 1976 and 1986 ■ Employment Act 1989 ■ Employment Protection (Part Time Employees) Regulations 1995 ■ Occupational Pensions (Equal Treatment Regulations) 1996
■ Part-Time Work (Extension to UK) 97/81 ■ Parental Leave (Extension to UK) 97/75 ■ Burden of Proof in Sex Discrimination Cases (Extension to UK) 97/80 ■ Equal Treatment revision (in progress, COM (96) 93)	■ April 2000 ■ December 1999 ■ June 2001 ■ To be agreed

Source: Adapted from *European Update July 1998*, Institute of Personnel and Development (IPD).

regulations were introduced in the UK in February 1995 that provided for all part timers to have the same legal entitlements to redundancy pay and claim unfair dismissal as full-time employees regardless of the hours worked. Organisations employing large numbers of part timers in preference to full-time employees to reduce labour costs have had to reassess their human resourcing practices and will need to do so again when the draft directive on part timers becomes law.

The employment of full-time female employees on temporary contracts currently carries with it an element of legal uncertainty. The outcome of the referral to the ECJ of the *Seymour Smith and Perez* case (IRLR 464 CA) could result in women with less than two years' but more than 12 months' service having an entitlement to claim unfair dismissal if they were dismissed during the period from 1986 to 1991. The validity of the two-year qualifying service period for claims of unfair dismissal will then be open to further challenge, but this will be limited by proposals in the government's white paper on

Activity 10.3

1 What impact could the introduction of the right to claims for unfair dismissal from (a) after one year's service or (b) from day one of employment have on organisational employment strategies in different occupational sectors?

2 What are the implications for organisational employment practices of removing the limits on awards for unfair dismissal?

'Fairness at Work' to reduce the qualifying period for claiming unfair dismissal to one year and removing the limits on compensation for unfair dismissal.

The transfer of undertakings provisions of the Acquired Rights Directive (ARD) continues to be dominated by decisions of the ECJ. The controversial decision in *Süzen* v *Zehnacker Gebäudering* (1997) (IRLR 255 ECJ), called for all transfers to second-generation contractors to be considered on a 'case-by-case' basis. This challenges the UK's widely held belief that transfers to second-generation contractors automatically fall within the scope of the ARD. Proposed revisions to the ARD are under consideration by the Commission at the time of writing. More stringent requirements to notify, consult and inform employees' representatives in advance were introduced as a result of an ECJ judgment that ruled the UK in contravention of the Collective Redundancies Directive (75/129) and the Acquired Rights Directive (77/187). Employers of more than 20 employees in large redundancy situations and in transfers of undertakings are now obliged to consult with the elected employee representatives even when there is no recognised trade union.

Waiting in the wings are changes that will add to the volume of regulation in the workplace. Despite the opposition of the UK government at the time, the Working Time Directive (WTD) was passed as health and safety legislation under Article 118(A) of the EC Treaty, so only required qualified majority voting. The key provisions of the UK's draft regulations due for implementation on 1 October 1998 reflect the provisions of the EC directive and are set out in Table 10.4.

Table 10.4 The Working Time Directive

- Maximum weekly working time 48 hours over a 17-week reference period, which can be extended to 26 or 52 weeks

- An average eight-hour shift per 24 hours for night workers over a 17-week reference period

- Free health assessments for night staff

- A rest break after six consecutive hours of work of 20 minutes

- A rest period of 11 consecutive hours per 24-hour period

- A minimum uninterrupted rest period of 24 hours in addition to the 11 hours daily rest, resulting in a minimum of 35 hours consecutive rest per seven-day period, which can be averaged over 14 days

- A minimum of three weeks' annual leave rising to four weeks after 23 November 1999

The EC directive provides for wide-ranging derogations except over annual leave but the only employees not covered by the 48-hour week are certain 'independent' employees, including managing executives, family workers and ministers of religion. The government's draft regulations allow for employers and employees to enter into agreements (which may or may not involve trade unions) about alternative arrangements for rest periods, shifts and the length of night work, as long as there are equivalent compensatory rest periods, but the maximum working week will still apply. The directive does not apply:

- to those sectors of activity concerned with air, rail, road, sea, inland waterway and lake transport, sea fishing, other work at sea, doctors in training;

- where characteristics peculiar to certain public-service activities such as the armed forces or the police conflict with it, provided due regard is paid to the general principles of health and safety.

Without doubt, the WTD will place the spotlight on working time in the UK, where working long hours is very much part of the present employment culture. UK workers undertake the greatest amounts of overtime in the EU and their patterns of work differ significantly from other European countries (ILO, 1997) due to fewer constraints on the structuring of working time (*Labour Market Trends*, 1995; Grubb and Wells, 1993). Traditionally, the hours of work an employee is required to work in the UK have been governed by the contract of employment and collective agreements and the adverse effects of the long hours culture emerged as a key message in the IPD's research into the state of the psychological contact in Britain (Guest *et al.*, 1996). An IRS survey in 1996 on holiday entitlement and working time in UK firms indicated that, whereas employers do not have much to fear from the directive, all organisations, large and small, will have to look closely at patterns of work, break and rest provisions, with particular attention to existing shift patterns.

Activity 10.4

Working Time Directive

1 What impact do you think the European Working Time Directive will have on the UK's long hours culture?

2 Identify the implications of the Working Time Directive's main provisions on the working time arrangements in two organisations with which you are familiar. If adjustments are needed to take account of the Directive, how are the selected organisations likely to alter their current employment practices?

The Posted Workers Directive was adopted in September 1996, although it will not come into force across member states until 1999. It will affect workers who are temporarily subcontracted or seconded by their employer to work elsewhere in the EU. Under this Directive, the employment laws, collective agreements and regulations of the host country will apply for the period in question.

■ The end of the UK's Social Chapter opt-out

The UK government agreed to the removal of its social chapter opt-out in the Amsterdam Treaty revisions in June 1997. At the European Council of Ministers' meeting in December 1997, the UK agreed to proceed with Directives dealing with the burden of proof in sex discrimination cases, sexual harassment and the rights of part-time workers to the same level of pension, sick pay, holiday, staff discounts and share-option benefits as full timers. In addition, there is a commitment to the implementation of the two Directives on European Works Councils (EWC) and Parental

Leave. For a fuller discussion of worker participation and Works Councils, *see* Chapter 13.

Owing to transitional provisions, the UK has been granted an extended implementation date of 15 December 1999 for both the EWC and Parental Leave Directives, although the latter which grants all employees an individual right to three months' unpaid leave on the birth or adoption of a child, will require UK organisations to undertake an early review of their existing leave arrangements. Multinational employers operating in the other EU states have already had to implement the EWC Directive from September 1996. One effect of this deferred implementation is that special dispensation will apply to the composition, procedure and functions of Works Councils set up before December 1999 – a strong argument for proactivity where employers facing a request from employee representatives would prefer to exercise more influence in the form that any initiative should take. This provision has not been overlooked by a number of UK multinationals as Illustration 10.2 shows.

ILLUSTRATION 10.2

Works Councils at Sun Chemical Europe

Sun Chemical Europe chose to set up local agreements rather than have a centralised European Works Council as it felt that designing its own arrangements would fit in better with its structure and culture. It agreed with its employees to make use where possible of its existing system of domestic works councils and employee representation. The company made 56 agreements with its 4500 employees covering 60 locations in Europe. Each agreement is virtually identical and covers the requirements of the EU directive.

Source: People Management, 12 June 1997, p. 27.

The EU adopted a new major Directive on the protection of individuals in the processing of personal data in October 1995. New legislation is required in the UK, amending the Data Protection Act of 1984, which will have significant implications for certain manual as well as computerised personnel records maintained within organisations. Elements of the new law were due to come into effect in October 1998 to comply with the EC Directive, but due to the large amount of work involved, the government now expects to give effect to the directive in early 1999.

The UK's new agenda

Although Labour's overwhelming election victory in May 1997 placed the new government in a very strong position to make radical changes to legislation in the field of employment, every indication is that its approach will be a cautious one. On the immediate horizon lies minimum wage legislation which the government will seek to set at a level that makes sense of its 'welfare to work' policy. The Low Pay Commission set up to consider the level of a national minimum wage has recommended a minimum of £3.70 per hour from June 2000, with an initial rate of £3.60 per hour from April 1999, while the TUC wanted a rate set at £4.62. The recommended rate for 18–20-year-olds is £3.30 per hour from June 2000. An estimated two million people should receive higher earnings if the Low Pay Commission's proposed minimum wage levels are adopted (IDS, 1998). There is evidence that some employers have already increased wages to avoid an excessive increase when the minimum wage is introduced, for example McDonald's has raised its basic rate to £3.50 per hour for staff outside London and to £4.00 an hour in the city (*Management Today*, April 1998: 12).

Activity 10.5

Minimum wage

1 Which sectors and types of organisations are likely to be most affected by a minimum wage?

2 Which groups of employees are likely to benefit most from the implementation of a minimum wage?

3 Using two different organisations known to you, identify the strategies they are likely to adopt to contain any additional labour costs created by a minimum wage.

4 What are the arguments for and against including commission payments and other gratuities towards compliance with the minimum wage?

The government's white paper on 'Fairness at Work' aims to provide a legislative framework for partnership between employers and employees. It is intended to complement the minimum wage proposals and the Working Time Directive. The proposals are divided into three sections: individual employment matters; collective law and particularly trade union recognition; and 'family-friendly policies', including a simplification and extension of maternity leave to 18 weeks and a framework for compliance with the Parental Leave Directive. New proposed individual rights include changes to the qualifying period for unfair dismissal claims and levels of compensation already referred to, and views have been invited on increased protection for employees on fixed-term and zero-hours contracts. The centrepiece of the paper is concerned with the enactment of a manifesto commitment to a statutory right to trade union recognition. Key proposals on collective rights are:

- for trade union recognition where the majority of the relevant workforce want it, with statutory procedures for both recognition and derecognition;

- a change in the law so that those taking part in lawfully organised official industrial action can claim unfair dismissal;

- a legal right for employees to be represented by a fellow employee or union representative of their choice during grievance and disciplinary procedures;

- prohibition of the black listing of trade unionists.

In the area of equal opportunities, the Labour Party's manifesto promised to address discrimination at work, because age and some form of anti-age discrimination legislation is anticipated. The Employment Rights (Disputes Resolution) Act, described as a 'jumble sale of reforms' (Inman, 1998: 11), came into force in April 1998 with the aim of over-hauling the 30-year-old Industrial Tribunal system (renamed Employment Tribunals in 1998). The growing complexity and volume of cases referred to Employmentl Tribunals have changed them out of all recognition in relation to what they were intended to be – an informal, speedy and cost-effective means of deciding justice in employment disputes. The new legislation is an attempt to revert to the initial concept and reduce the current overloading of the Tribunal system, and a key provision of the new Act is an arbitration alternative to Tribunal hearings for unfair dismissal claims.

The government published its Human Rights Bill in October 1997. Its main effect is to incorporate the European Convention on Human Rights into domestic UK law, which will address one of the main problems in the UK's current legal framework – that its courts cannot decide on rights under the convention as they can in most other member states. At present, such cases have to be referred to the European Court of Human Rights in Strasbourg, a laborious process that also results in decisions being made by non-UK judges not necessarily familiar with the national context.

A common feature of all the developments described above is the uncertainty related to how changes in the law will apply to different organisational contexts and their employment practices. Not only will there be a demand for local interpretation, but the dynamic nature of employment law requires the HR professional to be familiar with new legislative requirements, anticipate forthcoming changes and be aware of potential cost implications. Increased regulation will lead to a reassessment of current approaches to human resourcing. While employment may become relatively more secure, capital–labour substitution (Hammermesh, 1987) will increase if labour costs escalate.

ILLUSTRATION 10.3

Hiring industrial robots

When it comes to hiring industrial robots the UK lags behind its competitors, ranking 16th after Spain, Norway and Australia according to statistics produced by the British Robots Association (BRA). Those manufacturing firms that have installed industrial robots, such as Perlos, a Finnish plastic component moulder and toolmaker group, claim that competitiveness requires investment in robots to stay competitive with cheap labour countries and to provide a more consistent quality than manual labour. As the UK managing director of Perlos puts it: 'Robots don't have bad days.' Why then has most of the UK's manufacturing industry been slow to invest in robotics? The president of the BRA blames UK employers' propensity to hire and fire, making manual labour relatively more flexible alternative at comparatively low wages reducing the incentive to use robots to save labour costs.

Source: Financial Times, 6 March 1998, p. 10.

Activity 10.6

1 What changes in labour law are likely to encourage UK employers in manufacturing industry to invest more heavily in robot installation?

2 How might a wider use of robotics affect flexible working practices in UK workplaces?

The impact of employment law on the specialist function

An examination of the development of personnel management since the 1960s provides insights into the impacts that internal and external regulation have had on the nature of its specialist contribution. Although it can only claim to show a general trend, Fig. 10.1 illustrates how the focus of the personnel specialist has reflected the prevailing level and nature of legislation regulating employment in the UK and questions what the impact of increasing EC legislation could be on its future role. Examining developments within the context of each decade runs the risk of being overly simplistic, but key landmarks in each period discussed earlier in the chapter provide a rationale for this approach.

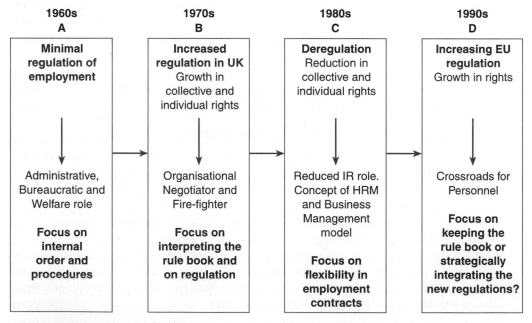

Fig. 10.1 Levels of employment law and the HR specialist's role

■ The value of expert knowledge

It can be argued that the relationship between levels of regulation and the focus of specialist functions' activities goes to the heart of some of the tensions long identified as inherent in professional personnel management. The difficulty of demonstrating its value and the specialist nature of its contribution to other managers is a theme that permeates the literature on personnel work (Watson, 1977). Legge (1995: 24–6) observes that the development of the occupation as a distinctive specialism was, and continues to be, characterised by the search for a source of unique expertise, which Guest (1991: 165) suggests explains the function's 'introspective neurosis' about its organisational role and influence.

One outcome of the propensity of personnel managers compared with other managerial groups to 'agonise about their lack of effectiveness and influence' (Torrington, 1998: 24) has been the ever-changing focus of the specialist function. The post-war period of full employment led to the development of a balancing role for the personnel function. This was reflected in the 1963 Institute of Personnel Management's definition of its role as one of administering and internally regulating the employment contract, which stressed the dual responsibility of achieving 'both efficiency and justice'. Due to the demanding industrial relations climate of the 1960s and 1970s, its specialism or expertise was seen to lie in the area of industrial relations. The earlier ideal of professional neutrality was increasingly compromised by the need to represent the organisational position and prevent industrial disruption.

Despite initiatives to 'professionalise' the function, it was still difficult to identify a specialism that distinguished the occupation from other managerial groups until the expansion of labour law in the mid-1970s. A knowledge of the new legislation potentially offered to the personnel function a source of influence and a power base more self-evident and transparent that anything that had gone before (Harris and Bott, 1996). It also complemented the industrial relations expertise still seen as the function's key contribution. Furthermore, the new legislation was not apparently a body of knowledge in which other managers actively sought to become involved. Most line managers appeared to be far too daunted by the perceived complexity of the legislation to become engaged in its intricacies through choice.

For the majority of organisations, the solution was to identify a named person with a specific responsibility for interpreting the new legal requirements in the workplace. Membership of the Institute of Personnel Management (renamed the Institute of Personnel and Development following its merger with the Institute of Training and Development in 1994) grew in membership by 59 per cent between 1971 and 1981. The Warwick IRRU survey of 1978/79 (Brown, 1981) reported that personnel specialists attributed the increase in the importance of the industrial relations function over the previous five years as overwhelmingly due to the growth in employment legislation. On the face of it, this model of personnel as 'specialist adviser' (Fowler, 1994) appeared to resolve many of the problems associated with the occupation's lack of an obvious body of specialist knowledge. Leopold and Beaumont (1985), in their study of personnel officers in the health service, saw the legislative changes of the 1970s as providing a welcome opportunity to prove their value to both line managers and the organisation as a whole.

The value of this expertise is, however, diminished by a double bind (Watson, 1986; Legge, 1995). If line managers are persuaded of the need to pass complex employment issues with legal implications on to HR practitioners then, as the 'acclaimed specialists', they will constantly be faced with the most problematic employee relations situations to resolve and run the risk of being scapegoated when there are no quick or acceptable solutions. A specialist function intent on demonstrating its indispensability may do so at the risk of being constantly overloaded with problems which line management is better placed to deal with. The function also faces the danger of being identified by other managerial groups as undertaking an essentially policing role due to a preoccupation with regulation and the judicial element of its role.

The expansion of the rights of employees and trade unions in the 1970s led to a period that Torrington and Hall (1987) describes as dominated by 'legal wrangling'. The interpretation of collective agreements and individual contracts could subsume a personnel practitioner's working week, leading to the function having little scope to be proactive as the need for fire-fighting skills and the 'quick fix' to keep production or services going was the order of the day. As Purcell argues in Marginson *et al.* (1988: 76), personnel's heavy involvement with the trade unions isolated the function so that it was seen as having an 'operational responsibility unconnected with strategic management. It has primarily a gatekeeper function: the act of divorcing trade unions from strategic management consideration is undertaken at the cost of personnel itself being excluded from, or seen as having little contribution to make to strategic management.'

The call for a different approach

The recessionary times of the early 1980s led to pressure to reduce overheads and a closer examination of personnel management's specialist contribution (Guest, 1982; Tyson and Fell, 1986). A new mood among employers in relation to human resourcing issues was reinforced by the policies of a Conservative government committed to reducing the power of the trade unions and increasing the freedoms of individual employers in the labour market. While the other member states in the European Community faced a steady growth in the regulation of work, in the UK there was a step-by-step approach to reducing trade union immunities, the end of incomes policies and a significant reduction in employment rights in cases of dismissal.

This radical change in the external environment led to a realignment of the work of personnel practitioners. The ACAS report of 1982 commented on the general movement 'to return as much responsibility as possible to the line manager and in particular to the first line supervisor'. Millward and Stevens (1986) reported that without its high-profile crisis-management role, even if it had no involvement in the planning process, the function was in danger of becoming increasingly isolated along with the trade unions with which it had been so involved. Potentially, the function faced a future of acting largely in an administrative capacity without a clear contribution to make to business outcomes unless it could redefine its organisational purpose and refocus its activities.

The concept of human resource management, originating in the USA (Beer *et al.*, 1984) and claiming to offer an approach to the employment relationship that was radically different from traditional personnel management, had begun to receive attention in the UK by the mid-1980s. A radical realignment of the personnel function was advocated. The emphasis was to be on the greater integration of human resource policies with business objectives and between different human resourcing practices. Personnel managers could no longer rely on their previous mediating and arbitral role to justify 'fence sitting' in employment matters. The new agenda was that they had be clearly recognised as part of management, even as business managers in their own right, who were making an identifiable and measurable organisational contribution (Tyson and Fell, 1986).

How this was to be achieved was left largely unclarified and the mixed messages of the time were frequently confusing for the personnel practitioner. By implication, accepting the argument that human resourcing issues were the concern of all managers and too crucial to be left to the specialist function meant giving away certain responsibilities previously associated with that function. The difficulty was that the specialist contribution that the function was then expected to make to the development of human resourcing strategies was largely left undefined. The trend towards multi-divisionalisation and decentralisation tended to reinforce personnel work as a generalist activity (Ferner, 1990).

Despite the dangers of losing core responsibilities hitherto regarded as the justification for the existence of a specialist function, Hope-Hailey *et al.* (1997) argue that the exhortation to move away from the bureaucracy of personnel management to the apparent flexibility and responsiveness of HRM was not without its attractions. A certain optimism prevailed that a move away from the dominance of the rule book and a policing role provided an escape route from the vicious circle that Legge (1978) had identified in personnel work of a heavy involvement in crisis management and no involvement in the planning process.

Deregulation and a reduction in industrial relations issues theoretically provided personnel practitioners with a real opportunity to be more proactive and take an active role in making strategic inputs to the development of new working practices. In the event, a plentiful labour supply during much of the ensuing period, with the exception of predicted shortages of young people in the late 1980s, led to little demand for a specialist input on human resource planning. The reduction in internal industrial relations issues did, however, lead to a refocusing of the practitioner's activities. Handling reductions in the workforce, redundancies and the growth of new employment patterns tended to focus attention on individual rather than collective rights.

Using the continuing decline in industrial action as a key indicator of an improvement in employee relations looks increasingly inappropriate as a measure of the state of the employment relationship in the less unionised environment of the 1990s. Individual conciliation cases referred to ACAS and Employment Tribunal statistics tell another story, with an escalating number of annual potential and actual claims reported to ACAS (ACAS annual reports 1987–97). In 1990, ACAS received a total of 52 071 cases for individual conciliation, with 26 per cent of these proceeding to Tribunal, compared to 106 912 cases in 1997 with just over 30 per cent proceeding to Tribunal, the main increase being in claims of unfair dismissal. The HR specialist may well have found that the time-consuming negotiations of the annual pay awards were replaced by ensuring that the organisation's documentation and personnel policies would stand scrutiny before an Employment Tribunal.

Enter the line manager

The devolvement of personnel activities to line management has been identified as a key characteristic of human resource management (Guest, 1987; Storey, 1992). The central argument is that for employment matters to receive the attention that it has been widely stated they deserve, line managers have to be the key players in operational personnel issues. As different models of decentralisation and related processes of delayering have emerged, it is worth examining how line managers and HR specialists view their organisational responsibilities for the interpretation and application of employment law.

Findings from a five-year longitudinal study conducted by Hope-Hailey *et al.* (1997) into the changing nature of the HR practice revealed that ideas about what personnel responsibilities should and could be devolved were often based on ill-defined assumptions. Not unsurprisingly, contextual variables were found to play a major part in influencing different roles and HR practices.

A survey conducted by the author (Harris, 1997) as part of the research for this chapter asked 50 line managers and personnel specialists about their perceived responsibilities for different human resourcing activities within their organisations. While there was increasing devolution to the line in activities associated with recruitment and selection, appraisal, rewards and HR planning, any related employment law issues and the handling of dismissals were identified as the domain of the HR function. A considerable consensus emerged that the responsibility of the line manager lay in the implementation of policies developed by the specialist function to ensure adherence to external regulatory requirements. The absence of such 'in-house expertise' was identified as a weakness by respondents working in smaller organisations, who felt that this rendered them particularly vulnerable to litigation, an issue that is illustrated in the case study at the end of this chapter. The option of buying in legal advice was widely regarded as an expensive and not ideal solution when only routine advice was required but familiarity with the organisational context was all important.

Although the HR function appears to have retained its role as 'interpreter of the rules', devolvement had sharpened individual managers' sense of accountability in an area described by several of them as a 'minefield'. Seeking advice and guidance from the specialist working in the business unit or in a central function on the potential legal implications of any employment issue emerged as routine practice. This was not without its problems in terms of the relationship between the line and specialist. While a key motivation for line managers seeking advice was personal insurance, particularly if mistakes could lead to an adverse assessment of their performance, they were frequently critical of the advice provided. It was often regarded as less than helpful and even as an obstacle to operational effectiveness. A typical comment about the advice received from the specialist function was:

> I always phone up our central HR Department to find out what I can do and then they tell why I can't do it which leaves me trying to find a way round the immediate problem. (Unit manager, privatised electricity company)

The growing complexity of the law and a recognition that their success would be measured on achieving operational targets left most line managers taking the pragmatic view that they had neither the skills nor the time to devote to the intricacies of legislative requirements. Although the complexity of the law was recognised, there was a view that the procedures it demanded ignored operational reality. As one production manager observed:

> Our personnel department does a good job but I don't think they always appreciate the operational pressures I am facing while they are trying to sort things out. At the end of the month I'll be judged on my production figures – dragging their feet on just a couple of long term sickness cases really does affect the bottom line. (Production manager, engineering company)

Activity 10.7

Managing absence

According to the Confederation of British Industry's annual survey (1996) absenteeism costs UK employers an estimated £12 billion a year. The average time lost per employee is 3.7 per cent or about eight and a half days per year. A frequent criticism from line managers of the specialist HR function is the length of time taken to resolve cases of persistent absenteeism or long-term sickness cases.

1 What is your understanding of the legal framework to be taken into account in handling absence cases?

2 What distinctions, if any should be made between handling persistent short-term absence and long-term sickness?

3 Why do line managers frequently see handling absence as a specialist HR responsibility?

4 Identify the responsibilities of the line manager for handling absence in your own organisation. Compare these to the responsibilities of your HR function.

5 What do you think the respective responsibilities should be of the line manager and the HR specialist for a constructive approach to absenteeism in the workplace?

While the key responsibility for keeping the organisation 'out of trouble' and away from Employment Tribunals lies in the hands of the specialist, line managers have the freedom to complain about the extra burdens imposed by selection or dismissal procedures that demand detailed records, written evidence of a systematic approach and the application of personnel processes demonstrably free of bias. The real value of such an approach was questioned. There were concerns, particularly in the public sector, that the driving force in much HR practice was the ability to defend potential claims of sex and race discrimination, which did not result in identifiable benefits and even detracted attention from the formulation of more effective HR practices. This is particularly evident in developments in public-sector recruitment and selection processes (Williams, 1991; Harris, 1997), illustrated by the following comment:

> We have check lists and procedures for every stage of our selection process designed to make sure we can defend our case if legally challenged. The trouble is that the whole process is now so tram lined that we end up appointing the person who is best at coping

with our processes but who may not be the best person for the job. (Deputy treasurer, local authority)

Activity 10.8

Equality of opportunity in recruitment and selection

How do you design recruitment and selection processes that demonstrate equality of opportunity and provide a defence in law against claims of unequal treatment with the needs of applicants seeking to demonstrate their distinctiveness and individuality?

Some propositions to focus on are:

1 Whether the same application form should be used for all applications and the use of CVs discouraged.

2 The selection decision should only consider performance in the actual selection process. The past performance of internal candidates should not be taken into account to avoid discriminating against external candidates.

3 Following the principles for highly structured interviews to avoid discrimination put forward by Campion, *et al.* (1988), interviewers should ask all interviewees the same questions with no follow-ups or variations.

4 The final judgement is reached by a simple averaging of the panel members' ratings of the candidate's performance.

5 Only the current essential requirements of the job should be taken into account when drawing up the person specification.

The dilemma for HR specialists lies in identifying on what their own performance is likely to be judged. One interpretation is that senior executives may adopt quite negative measures of success for the function, for example avoiding litigation and any accompanying publicity, which reinforces the need to check that the organisation's HR actions are fully defensible and recorded at every stage as a priority activity. This emphasis leads to criticisms by operational managers of the HR department's bureaucracy, inflexibility, long-windedness and lack of appreciation of the immediacy of their operational problems. In return, HR specialists perceive that line managers' judgements about their efficacy are all too often based on the speed and favourability of response to administrative issues. One HR director described her credibility with other senior managers in the following terms:

> I often feel I am really judged by the speed with which I can deal with a manager's immediate question about holiday entitlement or find a temporary replacement for an absent secretary rather than any wider contribution I make to the business. (HR director, leisure industry)

This observation lends support to Fowler's hypothesis (1994) that the increased involvement of managers in HR activities could lead to the specialist function's essentially becoming an administrative support to the line rather than gaining influence through greater strategic involvement. Fowler's alternative hypothesis was that a role could develop that was concerned with setting and monitoring standards that would lead to inputs in the strategic planning process. Specialist knowledge such as employment law is an essential ingredient of such a role and there is evidence that HR specialists recognise the importance of studying the law. Short courses in the law aimed at the HR profession are a growth industry and employment law is the most popular specialist elective on the IPD's professional qualification scheme. The IPD national examiner for employment law (Bone, 1997) explains its popularity as stemming from the high value placed on it by employers, who want their HR professionals to act as the first-line adviser to management on a constantly evolving subject reflecting changes in the working environment.

ILLUSTRATION 10.4

New technology – new areas for litigation

Recent cases in the USA and the UK indicate that e-mail brings with it not only instant communication but also potential legal problems. Two test cases in the UK took the view that e-mail was a form of publication and as such libel laws apply.

Activity 10.9

Should human resource managers start developing e-mail policies to reduce the risks of litigation?

Different directions for the specialist function

The perceptions that line managers have of the specialist function's regulatory role raise all too familiar dilemmas for practitioners facing growing levels of legislation. As Keenoy suggests (1990), there are inherent tensions and conflicts between the imperatives of the market, external levels of regulation, organisational demands for the control of employees and the needs of individuals at work. The balance is a delicate one that alters quite quickly whenever the level of influence of these recognised regulators of the employment relationship changes. The combination of more legislation and an emergent skills shortages (DfEE, 1997) in an increasing number of occupational sectors may, while a favourable economic climate prevails, reduce the focus on organisational control and freedom.

The challenge for HR specialists is how to combine their responsibilities as the frontline providers of legal services while at the same time developing the integrated strategic role advocated as essential if the function is to have any form of influence over organisational events. This is not to suggest that the possession of specialist knowledge and expertise erodes the function's ability to contribute strategically. Rather it is argued that it is the very possession of technical expertise such as legal knowledge that can provide the function with the credibility and authority necessary to make its inputs to the strategic decision making process valuable (Torrington and Hall, 1998). The risk, however, is that the heavier the reliance on the rule book in employment practice, the greater the emphasis on the regulatory aspects of the specialist role, which reinforces negative perceptions about its contribution.

If UK employers operating in a deregulated labour market have shown little innovation in their use of flexible working practices (Brewster, 1998), one positive outcome of increased regulation could be more imaginative HR approaches to flexibility in the workplace. Where there is an environment conducive to a genuine consideration of more innovative and creative approaches to employing people at work, the personnel specialist may have the opportunity to act as a catalyst for change. It can be argued that changes in levels of employment protection provide an ideal opportunity to reconsider past practice and develop what Edwards (1979) identifies as 'enlightened managerialism', with organisational policies reflecting and reinforcing a genuine concern for employee commitment and involvement.

To the older, experienced HR manager, this analysis has overtones reminiscent of the aims of 'good old-fashioned' personnel management (Torrington and Hall, 1991), seeking to retain humanity in the relationship between employer and employee and relying on both internal and external regulation to construct and support a moral order for the organisation. Indeed, the advent of legal decisions that have begun to readdress the balance of power between employer and employee, after a period in which the employment deal has appeared strongly weighted against the employee (Herriot and Pemberton, 1995), may well be welcomed on the grounds that it gives real support in circumstances where the HR specialist may have been a lone voice for more socially responsible practices.

Connock and Johns (1995) identify a real danger for the personnel function if it is the only part of the organisation advocating a more ethical approach to human resource practice. The HR specialist can be perceived as presenting obstacles to change by raising legal impediments to proposed courses of action and taking the moral high ground, despite the immediacy of business pressure. Once HR professionals become labelled as the organisation's 'oddballs', it becomes difficult for them to exert influence in the change process, with the result that they become isolated and removed from mainstream problem solving and decision making. In such circumstances, a more comfortable, less threatening option for the personnel specialist is to assume from the outset the role of a distanced professional adviser, augmenting management resources as and when required. Fowler (1994: 34–7) suggests that this 'consultant' model stems directly from the market concept of the separation of the roles of purchaser and supplier. The 'in-house' personnel function in essence becomes an internal contractor providing a support service in line with management requirements.

At its simplest, such a role is unlikely to have a direct strategic input, but depending on the quality and status of the provider, the potential is there to make a contribution to organisational strategy at the request of core management. Yet again, the biggest obstacle to personnel's ability to influence events lies in establishing its own credibility (Pickard, 1995). The attraction of the consultant model is that it removes many of the tensions identified earlier, although it renders the function vulnerable to total disbandment and replacement by external sources providing the same type of services for a fee rather than a salary. In spite of such vulnerability, it is a model that may sit more comfortably with the values and beliefs of many HR professionals.

If influence and power (Johnson, 1977) are seen to stem from expert knowledge as they do for the traditional professions, then this may be a direction worthy of real consideration for the HR specialist. As the conventional wisdoms on strategy making in organisations are under challenge (Mintzberg, 1987), the specialist function may be better advised to concentrate on acquiring, honing and sharpening its own areas of technical expertise, rather than seeking an elusive and questionable strategic role (Torrington, 1998).

CASE STUDY 10.1

The Arctel Company Ltd – conflict in the maintenance section

The Arctel Company Ltd is a small gas burner manufacturer employing 110 people consisting of 74 hourly paid employees and 36 staff on weekly or monthly pay. The Transport and General Workers' Union represents the hourly paid staff and enjoys a good relationship with the company. In February 1998, Philip Walters, the production director, had to deal with a severe breakdown in the relationship between the factory's maintenance supervisor, Rob Edwards, and one of his two maintenance fitters, Jim Clarke. For some time the relationship between these two employees had been a growing cause of concern, as it was beginning to adversely affect the operation of the company's small maintenance section, which consists of a supervisor, two fitters, three maintenance operatives and one general labourer. The section regularly works long hours both during the week and at weekends and is absolutely vital to the smooth running operation of the plant.

Jim Clarke, aged 38, joined the company nine years ago, initially as a brazier/welder until joining the maintenance department as a fitter in 1996. Jim is widely regarded as a resourceful and hard-working employee who is particularly skilled at resolving technical problems. The position in maintenance provided a real opportunity for him to work in an environment better suited to his abilities than routine production work. Although the standard of Jim's work was excellent, there had been some complaints about his attitude to supervision and his working relationships with other employees just before his move to maintenance. At the time, the production director felt that this was probably due to boredom, which more challenging and varied work would resolve. For the first 18 months, both in terms of skill and working relationships, Jim progressed very well in maintenance, becoming the section's weekly paid chargehand in 1997. In this role he continued to report to Rob Edwards, who was five years his junior and had joined the company 12 years ago as a maintenance fitter before his promotion to the role of maintenance supervisor in 1993 when the previous incumbent retired.

After a year and a half, the relationship between the two employees started to deteriorate. Rob complained regularly that Jim would not tell him where he was going to be working and would come into work but not start straightaway, but just sit there drinking coffee and reading the newspaper. Matters took a turn for the worse when Rob Edwards decided to clear out some old jigs that were no longer needed while Jim was on his summer holiday. In the process, a treasured examination test piece belonging to Jim Clarke was thrown away, which he immediately interpreted as a deliberately provocative act, although Rob was adamant that it had been a complete accident. After this incident, Jim's general attitude became so unco-operative in the eyes of his supervisor that he told Philip Walters he could no longer work with him in the section.

At the time, Jim was experiencing the break-up of his marriage. In view of these personal circumstances, the production director decided to take a low-key, informal counselling approach and Jim admitted that he was under a great deal of strain. The outcome of discussions with both employees was that Jim was given a week's paid leave to try to sort out some of his personal difficulties, and on his return the relationship appeared to be more harmonious. This improvement was to be short lived. Only a few weeks later, Rob Edwards was complaining that his chargehand was acting obstructively again and repeatedly challenging his authority. The production director once more intervened and told Jim that he would now have to be transferred to the only remaining production department, the press shop. Jim, supported by his supervisor who was sympathetic to his chargehand's personal problems, appealed for one last chance. This was agreed, although Jim was told that there would be no further reprieves if his behaviour did not improve.

On 20 February 1998, events came to a head over the heating of the maintenance workshop. When the gas heater used to heat the workshop was in operation, the maintenance supervisor liked the window to be kept closed, whereas Jim preferred it to be open. To prevent the window being opened, Rob had wrapped electric trunking firmly round the window rod. When Jim saw this he was so enraged that he retaliated by immediately cutting the plug off the heater with a pair of pliers. The exchange that followed resulted in Rob's physically evicting Jim from the workshop, along with his coat, shoes and lunch box that he was permitted to keep in the supervisor's office. Despite Jim's repeated efforts to regain entry to the workshop, his supervisor barred his access and in the process Jim alleged that Rob tore his shirt.

The production director interviewed both men that day and decided to suspend Jim on full pay to allow tempers to cool down, pending a fuller investigation and the examination of witnesses. Owing to the operational needs of the factory, he did not to suspend the maintenance supervisor. As a result of his investigations, Philip Walters decided that the only solution was to move Jim Clarke out of the maintenance section and transfer him with immediate effect to work in the press shop as press operative on an hourly rate of pay. This meant a reduction in Jim's basic pay of £40 per week and a significant loss in overtime earnings as no overtime was being worked in the press shop. Although overtime in the maintenance department was not guaranteed, Jim had worked an average of 12 hours a week since he had joined the section, payable at the agreed premium overtime rates.

After his considerable efforts to find a solution that kept Jim in employment, Philip Walters was extremely concerned and annoyed to receive a letter from him one week later tendering his resignation. On the advice of his union, Jim wrote that he was claiming constructive dismissal on the grounds of his loss of earnings, demotion and the disparate treatment that he had received in comparison to his supervisor who had received no penalty whatsoever.

Activity 10.10

1 What are the key arguments that can be put forward in support of:
(a) management's actions;
(b) Jim Clarke's claim of constructive dismissal?

2 On the basis of the information provided, how likely is Jim Clarke to win his case if it proceeds to an Employment Tribunal? Please give reasons for your answer.

3 Identify what you would have advised the production director to do differently and why from the perspective of *both* an operational line manager and a personnel specialist.

4 What particular issues may have arisen for Philip Walters in handling this problem because Arctel is a small company?

5 What initiatives can be taken to reduce the reoccurrence of such a situation in the future?

Conclusion

There are various roles that HR practitioners can adopt as the first-line provider of legal services. It is suggested that in reality the role will drift between that of rule keeper, business manager, organisational catalyst and consultant, with the emphasis being highly contingent on the organisational context. Changes in the law could present the opportunity for human resource practitioners to act as the 'deviant innovators' identified by Legge (1978: 85) to promote new values in the organisation. The pressures of competition, devolvement and a focus on measurable performance objectives suggest that their contribution is more likely to be what Legge terms 'conformist innovation', where the emphasis is on demonstrating the contribution that human resourcing practices can make to organisational success (1978: 79). The organisational management style, type of workforce, the nature of the product or service, the commitment of chief executives to HR issues as well as the skills and personality of the personnel practitioners will all be influencing factors.

Based on the evidence of the past 30 years, the level of external regulation, combined with the prevailing economic climate, emerges as a major influence on the focus of the function's activities and the contribution it makes to the strategic process. As the function becomes increasingly fragmented (Sisson, 1995) claiming ownership of a specialist activity left unclaimed by other managers is attractive, but it is important for practitioners to evaluate where this may lead. If it signals a return to the dominance of a policing role, it is questionable how this will strengthen relationships with line management and a joint commitment to proactive HR practices. The demands of greater regulation need to be recognised and planned for to avoid the all too familiar circle of reaction, crisis management and short termism, which detracts from opportunities to develop approaches to human resourcing that maximise the collective and individual contributions of employees.

Summary

In this chapter the following key points have been made:

- Employment law is heavily influenced by the prevailing political, economic and social factors. The past 30 years have reflected different ideological perspectives on the role of the state in regulating the employment relationship.

- The legal framework is a key factor in developing human resourcing strategies and in changing the focus of the specialist function's activities.

- Despite increasing decentralisation and devolvement to line management, HR practitioners are still essentially regarded as the 'guardians of the rule book' acting as 'general practitioners' (Torrington, 1989: 65), responsible for an initial diagnosis when it comes to the provision of legal services on employment issues.

- The absence of an 'in-house' personnel specialism leaves smaller organisations particularly vulnerable to procedural lapses and litigation.

- HR processes created primarily to ensure that there is an identifiable organisational defence against litigation and claims for compensation can result in line managers abdicating their responsibility for decision making in employment matters.

- Knowledge of the law provides a valuable specialism and a potential source of influence attractive to an occupation uncertain of its organisational contribution, but it has its disadvantages. It can 'handcuff the HR function into a policing role' – creating or reinforcing negative perceptions about its contribution as bureaucratic and 'rules driven'.

- An expansion of employment legislation is likely to exacerbate these perceptions by refocusing the work of the function on to regulatory and procedural issues, which is likely to have implications for the relationship between the line and the specialist.

- Increasing employment regulation could result in a reassessment of the nature of devolved HR activities and where accountability lies in handling complex employment matters.

- Human resource specialists need to develop their legal knowledge so that they can apply it in an innovative and constructive way when developing human resourcing policies and practice.

Discussion questions

1 What are the arguments for and against greater regulation of employment practices?

2 How much specialist knowledge of employment law does a line manager need compared to an HR specialist? Would it be better simply to refer all legal matters to do with employment to a qualified legal practitioner?

3 In any organisation with which you are familiar, how much influence has legislation appeared to have on its employment processes?

Further reading

The sources in the text will provide readers with the appropriate further reading depending on the particular aspect of the law they wish to follow up. Two general texts that offer guides to this increasingly complex area of legislation are Jefferson (1997) and Lewis (1997).

ACHIEVING EQUALITY OF OPPORTUNITY?

Mary Crow

OBJECTIVES

Having completed this chapter and its associated activities, readers should be able to:

- demonstrate that equality of opportunity issues are relevant to all areas of human resource management and the managing of the employment relationship;

- highlight the legal, socio-economic and political context within which equal opportunities issues arise;

- discuss why it can be argued that employers feel it necessary to take action to remove obstacles to equal opportunity;

- evaluate critically the 'liberal' approach to equality of opportunity and provide alternative analytical perspectives;

- assess the effectiveness of equal opportunity initiatives in changing discriminatory practices within organisations, in light of the evidence that shows the ways in which discrimination against members of certain social groups (women, ethnic minorities, disabled) continues to be embedded in the formal and informal rules and regulations that govern employment;

- clarify the distinctions between equality of opportunity and 'managing diversity'.

Introduction

The promotion of equality of opportunity has long been justified on grounds of moral or legal fairness. More recently, there has been much discussion of the ways in which demographic trends, skill shortages and increased competitiveness are increasing employers' interest in untapping the under-utilised potential of their human resources. It has been argued that successful organisations will be those that anticipate and design human resource strategies that recognise the positive value to be gained from equal opportunity policies and practices:

> Good equal opportunities is about good management practice: about recruiting, developing and retaining the skills and creative ideas we all so badly need in our organisations. It is about the way we manage our most precious resource – the women and men in our workforce. About the way we interview and assess, the way we train, the way we promote, the way we recognise performance and about the sort of conditions we offer. It is also about the sort of culture and ethos we nurture. (Foster, 1989)

For various reasons (see below), the 'business case' for realising the full potential of employees has placed equal opportunities on management agendas in a number of organisations. A range of initiatives have been taken and equality legislation has given the added weight of official government policy to the principle that discrimination is wrong. However, there is continuing discrimination in the labour market on grounds of sex, race, disability and other factors such as age, class, sexual orientation and a lack of equality of opportunity in employment (*Equal Opportunities Review*, 1998a, b, c). This co-existence of anti-discrimination and equal opportunities, with differential experiences of the employment relation on the basis of social group membership suggests that there are problems with the approaches that have been used to counter inequality.

A main concern of this chapter is to highlight the contradictions and paradoxes inherent in approaches to 'equality management'. In adopting this approach, the chapter does not attempt to provide an equal opportunities prescription; rather, it takes a 'critical-evaluative' approach (Legge, 1995). Discussion begins by exploring the reasons for employers being concerned with equality issues and moves on to evaluate initiatives that have been introduced in organisations to bring about equality of opportunity. Differing analytical approaches to discrimination are discussed in the following section and different types of equality are identified that inform both governmental and organisational policies and initiatives. The problems associated with translating espoused equal opportunity models into practice (operational models) are given in the next section, and it is then argued that even best-practice models do not necessarily produce equal distributional outcomes. Finally, it will be assessed whether managing diversity is the way to proceed along the pathway to achieving equality.

Reasons for taking equality initiatives

While initiatives to promote greater employment equality can arise from a sense of social justice or moral responsibility, Dickens (1994) maintains that there are two distinct, pragmatic reasons that employers might want to take action to remove obstacles to equal opportunity: penalty avoidance through compliance and the positive pursuit of organisational benefits. We can examine each of these below.

■ Compliance and penalty avoidance

The main external factor influencing the *compliance* and *penalty avoidance* approach is equality legislation. A summary of the relevant equality legislation is provided in Table 11.1.

Table 11.1 Legislative developments in the UK concerned with equal opportunities

---

- Sex Discrimination Act 1975 (amended and extended 1986)

- Race Relations Act 1976

- The Equal Pay Act 1970 (amended by Equal Value (Amendment) Regulations 1983)

- Disabled Persons (Employment) Act 1944 (amended 1958, 1981, repealed 1996)

- Disability Discrimination Act 1995

- Fair Employment (Northern Ireland) Acts 1976 and 1989

Individuals have statutory rights to complain of discrimination on grounds covered by the legislation and can seek to enforce these rights through the Industrial Tribunal system. The Equal Opportunity Commission (EOC) and Commission for Racial Equality (CRE) have statutory investigative powers as well as a role in aiding individual complainants. They also advise and give guidance on the legislative requirements and the promotion of equal opportunities (EO).

The legislative threat to employers' interests centres on the adverse publicity and the direct and indirect costs that a tribunal claim or commission investigation would involve. Threatened or actual investigations by the EOC/CRE have helped stimulate progress in a number of sectors of employment. In 1983, for example, the possibility of an investigation by the EOC led Barclays Bank to reform its recruitment and selection practices.

The threat of industrial tribunal claims has been a significant factor in persuading employers such as J Sainsbury, Co-operative Retail Societies, Asda and Marks & Spencer to review grading structures in relation to equal value cases. Moreover, the threat of numerous individual claims for equal pay has been a tactic used by some unions to persuade employers to review grading structures (Dickens, 1994).

While legislation can lead to organisational reform, 'avoidance tactics' have also been well documented. Without actually breaking the law, employers have pursued strategies that have minimised their obligations under equality legislation. Between 1970 when the Equal Pay Act was passed and 1975 when it came into force, many companies took care to ensure that whenever possible women and men did not do the same jobs. Research carried out by the London School of Economics between 1974 and 1977 on the effects of the Equal Pay and Sex Discrimination Acts and a later study for the Department of Employment outline ways in which employers avoided the full cost of

ILLUSTRATION 11.1

Recruitment and selection practices at Barclays Bank

After receiving a formal complaint regarding recruitment and selection practices at Barclays Bank, the Equal Opportunities Commission proposed to undertake a formal investigation. As a result of this, the bank examined its recruitment practices and it discovered that of the A-level applicants (the entry level for potential managers), a higher proportion of males were successful than females and the situation was reversed for applicants with O levels (the requisite qualification for clerks). An agreement was reached between Barclays and the Equal Opportunities Commission that stipulated that new recruitment practices would be implemented, recruiters would receive more training and the bank would provide the commission with statistics for the next four years on applications, interviews and job offers. In view of this, the formal investigation was deferred.

Source: Boyden and Paddison (1986).

equal pay. These included job-evaluation schemes, job segregation and unisex pay scales (Snell *et al.*, 1981). There is also evidence of direct discrimination being replaced by covert indirect discrimination. Collinson *et al.* (1990) provide research case studies illustrating that a substantial number of employers are 'managing to discriminate' covertly through a variety of recruitment practices (an area that will be discussed later in this chapter).

It becomes apparent that a fundamental change in attitudes and behaviour regarding EO is unlikely if organisations subscribe to the compliance and penalty-avoidance route. It may even result in a line of 'avoidance rather than compliance, with organisations seeking to minimise the likely impact of the law' (Dickens, 1994: 272).

■ Organisational interest

Factors such as competition in the labour market, concern with more efficient management of human resources, better employee relations, positive company image and gaining from diversity have encouraged employers to take an interest in equality initiatives (Dickens, 1994).

Competition in the labour market

In the late 1980s, concern arose in relation to the 'demographic timebomb' (fewer young people entering the labour market) and skills shortages that led employers to look outside the traditional pool of recruits. Women, ethnic minorities and differently abled people were seen to constitute an untapped or under-utilised labour supply. The link to equal opportunities here is that 'atypical' workers or 'non-traditional' recruits were being encouraged to apply for jobs, and interest in initiatives such as employer nursery provision, flexible working and career breaks was seen as a way of holding on to valued employees. Illustration 11.2 discusses the rationale behind Midland Bank's decision to provide workplace nurseries for employees' children.

ILLUSTRATION 11.2

Workplace nursery provision at Midland Bank

Midland Bank was one of the forerunners in piloting workplace nursery provision in the late 1980s. Concerned with predicted labour shortages, Midland's philosophy was: 'once you have people with experience, you don't want them to disappear into oblivion'. It spent £350 000 on initial costs in setting up two pilot nurseries. Given the costs of approximately £10 000 to train each member of staff, Midland argued that the investment in workplace nurseries would be recouped by retaining its highly trained and qualified workforce. Anne Watts, the equal opportunities director, maintained that 'well run nurseries free parents from worries about whether their children are being well cared for, allowing them to concentrate on their work, so increasing productivity and commitment to the company'. She also argued that individuals with childcare responsibilities bring additional attributes into the business arena: 'women or men who return to work after looking after children have a different sense of priorities than before, they are more mature and do not get upset about trivial things'.

Source: Hall (1988).

In the early 1990s, economic recession led to many organisations putting such initiatives on the 'back burner' as the effect of demographic trends was being masked by high levels of unemployment. The underlying features remain, however, and skill shortages are predicted to emerge when there is an upturn in the economy (Dickens, 1994: 262).

Efficient management of human resources

Employers who implement equal opportunities policies and practices often wish to be viewed as having professional management practices that encourage the efficient use of human resources. This is questioned by assertions that discriminatory practices are part and parcel of poor personnel procedures and bad management policies (Seear, 1981: 295). Nevertheless, equal opportunities can be seen to reinforce a professional image for personnel/HR functions.

Better employee relations

It is sometimes claimed that equal opportunities policies and practices help to increase the motivation and performance of employees, resulting in reduced turnover levels and a more productive atmosphere and creating a better quality of working life (EOC, 1986: 1).

Image

In addition to wishing to avoid a bad press (as seen earlier in compliance and penalty avoidance), employers can use EO to present themselves as a 'good employer' to attract and retain quality employees and also present a positive image to their customers and the local community.

Gaining from diversity

Having employees from a wide range of backgrounds (women, ethnic minorities, differently abled) can be seen to 'add value' to organisations. Benefits are said to include gains from multi-culturalism (wider ranges of ideas), but also from challenging stereotypical views and assumptions.

Dickens (1994: 269) argues that the existence of *compliance* and *organisational interest* pressures of the kind previously discussed may produce action for equality, but are not necessarily adequate or sufficient. Compliance with the equality laws does not require employers actively to promote equality; the main concern of the legislation is with ending discrimination. Organisational interest considerations will be experienced differently by different organisations. Indeed, the pursuit of organisational interest may run counter to, rather than support, EO initiatives.

Equal opportunity policies and initiatives

If employers wish to take action to enhance the opportunities of previously disadvantaged groups, there is a wealth of guidance on ways in which discrimination can be avoided and suggestions for promoting equality (CRE, 1983; EOC, 1986).

The centrepiece of the guidance concerns the adoption of an equal opportunities policy (EOP). Illustration 11.3 provides an example.

ILLUSTRATION 11.3

Equal opportunities policy at MacGowan plc

MacGowan plc actively works to implement equality of opportunity for all staff. An equal opportunities policy statement has been accepted and supporting documents and policies have been developed and implemented in the following areas:

- recruitment and selection;
- harassment;
- assessment;
- HIV/Aids.

The equal opportunities mission statement currently reads:

> MacGowan plc aims to foster a community with an atmosphere of trust, harmony and respect. It is committed to the elimination of both direct and indirect discrimination, and will take appropriate action wherever possible to enforce its Equal Opportunities Policy.
>
> The company will actively implement positive policies to promote equality of opportunity for all present and potential staff, regardless of race, ethnic or national origin, sex, sexual orientation, age, political or religious beliefs, membership of professional associations or trade unions, disability, marital status, family responsibility and social class.
>
> All staff will be informed of the Equal Opportunities policy, and its operation will be subject to regular monitoring and review.

In a survey of 285 organisations, 94 per cent had a policy on equal opportunities (Kandola and Fullerton, 1994). Initiatives associated with these can include equal opportunities monitoring, fair selection training for recruiters, making buildings accessible to those with disabilities, an explicit policy on harassment, flexible working hours, time off to care for dependants and the elimination of age criteria from selection decisions. The 1998 WERS (Cully *et al.*, 1998: 13) found that two-thirds of workplaces (64 per cent) have formal EOPs. The areas covered include sex (98 per cent), race (98 per cent) and disability (93 per cent). Religion (84 per cent), marital status (73 per cent) and age (67 per cent) also featured strongly. The area which featured least often was trade union membership (51 per cent). Half of the workplaces without a formal policy claimed to have informed EO initiatives or an unwritten policy. However, in a third of the workplaces without a policy, managers saw them as unnecessary, and a further 2 per cent said 'that they did not need a policy as their workplace employed few or no people from disadvantaged groups!'

It is possible to establish targets for increasing the proportion of particular groups within certain occupational areas. An example of this is *Opportunity 2000*, which was launched with government backing in 1991 to increase the proportion of women in the labour market. Such initiatives are not the same as the US approach of setting quotas, which is illegal in the UK. Instead, the intention is to indicate what is being aimed at and to have some measure of progress. The intention of these initiatives is to allow women to combine careers with other commitments, but research into 75 *Opportunity 2000* employers suggests that the initiatives adopted tend to be relatively low cost, such as flexible working, career breaks and extended maternity leave, rather than the more costly benefits like workplace nurseries (*PM Plus*, November 1992). The problem is whether such a campaign addresses the barriers to equality in the workplace for all women or for only a few.

Training can contribute to the success of an equal opportunities programme. This can happen in three complementary ways. There are training courses that are developed to assist the *policy implementation* discussed earlier. The purpose of this training is to provide managers with the skills to implement EO and HR policies effectively. *Awareness training* focuses on changing (rather than merely suppressing) hostile attitudes towards under-represented groups. A third area is related to *positive action* training, which targets groups that are statistically in the minority. Here training helps prepare minorities to compete for opportunities on equal terms with the majority.

Positive action training has mainly been directed at women. At one level, it could simply involve imparting new skills. More often, however, it is focused on helping women progress up the hierarchy. The provision of single-gender training courses is probably one of the most contentious issues in EO and Table 11.2 outlines the arguments for and against such provision.

Activity 11.1

You have been asked, in your capacity as training manager, to provide evidence to support your claims that the training department should continue to provide women-only training courses. You should take the arguments in Table 11.2 into account, consult additional sources (texts, journals) and provide illustrations or examples from your organisation or an organisation with which you are familiar.

Table 11.2 Women-only training

A significant number of organisations have developed women-only courses. Three major arguments are typically put forward against the provision of women-only training courses (Colwill and Vinnicombe, 1991: 42; Vinnicombe and Colwill, 1995: 81):

1 This mode of training serves only to highlight further the differences between women and men, thus making integration in the workplace even more problematic.

2 Training that takes place in single-sex groupings is artificial and out of touch with organisational realities whereby women have to interact with men, either in teams or on an individual basis.

3 Men's perceptions of the courses – the view that the training is seen as frivolous and of low status precisely because it involves women and not men.

There are also three broad arguments in favour of women-only training courses (Limerick and Heywood, 1993: 26):

1 Women have a different set of experiences from men and it is only through separate sessions that these can be discussed. Their preferred styles of managing are likely to be different, with a much greater emphasis on co-operation and teamwork than men, with the latter tending to be more competitive and individualistic.

2 Women-only training courses can be run in a way that is more suitable for women than is the case with mixed sessions. Research indicates that mixed courses tend to be dominated by men, with sessions focusing on issues that are derived from existing organisational cultures – principally male issues. A women-only course can allow for consideration of issues that have traditionally been more important to women – such as balancing work and childcare commitments, or dealing with aggressive or sexist male behaviour.

3 Attendance at a women-only course can act as a stimulant for further activities back at the workplace, through networking, women's support groups, mentoring arrangements and the opportunity to identify role models.

In promoting equality initiatives such as those discussed above, EO enthusiasts have sought consistent treatment, encouraging procedural approaches. One of the pitfalls, however, in adopting an approach that relies heavily on adherence to bureaucractic procedures is that the outcome is likely to be 'a destructive spiral of ever greater checks and controls followed by more sophisticated avoidance tactics' (Liff, 1989: 32).

Perspectives on the promotion of equality

Whether employers seek actively to promote equality, comply with legislation or adopt a business case approach depends on the type of equality for which such policies are aiming. Are policies formulated to achieve a 'liberal' type of equality that emphasises the elimination of direct and indirect discrimination, or do they have 'radical' aims, i.e. seeking changes in employment outcomes?

■ Liberal and radical approaches

Jewson and Mason (1986) characterise the approach outlined in 'codes of practice' as 'liberal'. Here equality is seen as treating everyone the same. The aim of the liberal perspective is to ensure that rules and procedures are fair so that justice is seen to be done. It is the liberal perspective that has informed UK legislation and, while this legal framework sets some boundaries, it would be misleading to suggest that it establishes fair rules.

Jewson and Mason contrast the liberal with a 'radical' approach. In this, equality revolves around the goal of equal outcomes. They argue that this involves a commitment to achieving fair distributions of under-represented groups within the workforce.

ILLUSTRATION 11.4

Liberal or radical approach?

Imagine a 100 yard dash in which one of the two runners has his legs shackled together. He has progressed 10 yards, while the unshackled runner has gone 50 yards. At that point the judges decide that the race is unfair. How do they rectify the situation? Do they merely remove the shackles and allow the race to proceed? Then they could say that 'equal opportunity' now prevailed. But one of the runners would still be forty yards ahead of the other. Would it not be the better part of justice to allow the previously shackled runner to make up the forty yard gap; or to start the race all over again? (US President Lyndon Johnson, 1965)

From the liberal perspective, it would be enough to remove the shackles and ensure that henceforth there is no unfair advantage. However, as President Johnson pointed out, this does not actually do anything to rectify the existing inequality. A more radical approach suggests that policy makers should be concerned with the outcome, rather than the process, and should therefore be seeking to ensure a fair distribution of rewards.

Source: Adapted from Noon and Blyton (1997: 182).

From the radical perspective, there is a requirement to intervene directly through policies of *positive discrimination* or *affirmative action*. The most typical example of this is setting quotas for disadvantaged groups, which organisations must achieve or face penalties. The policy of positive discrimination is by no means without its critics. First, there are those who argue that it merely shifts the unfairness from one group to another. In particular, it means that white, able-bodied, heterosexual men may find themselves victims of discrimination and this has led to a backlash in the USA (Woodall, 1996: 334). A second group of critics of affirmative action are members of disadvantaged groups themselves, who condemn the policy because it devalues their achievements by raising the suspicion that they did not really deserve the job or promotion (Chacko, 1982). In the UK, positive discrimination is unlawful, and policy suggestions towards it have been condemned by the Institute of Personnel and Development, which labels it 'reverse discrimination'. Neither the Commission for Racial Equality nor the Equal Opportunities Commission believes it to be an appropriate way forward.

Critics of both of the above perspectives argue that these approaches are based on an acceptance of jobs and organisations as they are currently constructed (Webb and Liff, 1988). In seeking to ensure a fair distribution of rewards, the allegedly 'radical' approach focuses on gaining power, not changing it. Attempts are made to advance disadvantaged groups within existing organisational structures whereas, as Cockburn (1989) identifies, it is the organisational structures themselves that need to be changed to 'better accommodate all'.

The extent to which equal opportunities concerns are integrated into organisational practice or used as a vehicle to transform organisational structures is likely to depend on differing 'agendas'. Cockburn (1989) describes the ways in which equal opportunities can be located within *long* or *short* agendas.

■ The long and short agendas

The 'short agenda' is concerned merely with those policy measures that are necessary to ensure compliance with legal requirements and is similar to Jewson and Mason's 'liberal approach' and Dickens' 'compliance and penalty avoidance route'. However, where economic expediency becomes an issue, e.g. a shortage of 'conventional' employees (the demographic time bomb), this may translate into a 'token' agenda to relieve immediate labour requirements (*see* Goss, 1994: 157).

Despite the prevalence of short-agenda approaches, it is possible to identify in some areas, especially in the public sector and in larger businesses, the development of what may be the beginnings of a 'long agenda' (Cockburn, 1991). The basis of the long agenda is an approach to equal opportunities that is both broad in its coverage and geared towards positive action to equalise employment opportunities. In terms of coverage, therefore, the long agenda is likely to include not only inequalities based on sex, race (and derivatives of these, such as nationality and marital status) and disability, but also those associated with, for example, age and sexual orientation. The approach to these issues is not one of 'equal chance' but 'equal share' (Straw, 1989).

Cockburn advocates a 'transformative EO strategy', with the transformation of the organisation in terms of equality being considered as part of the long agenda, the short agenda focusing on 'cleaning up' personnel practices. While the long agenda is concerned with the nature, culture, relations and purpose of the organisation, this should not be taken as an argument against attempting the kind of EO initiatives indicated earlier, as these can produce gains for members of disadvantaged groups.

ILLUSTRATION 11.5

The cement roof

The boardrooms of Britain's companies are alive with the sound of ethnic voices, but only before six in the morning. For these are the army of early risers who clean, dust and vacuum the executive suites. (Pandya, 1997)

One study has identified that ethnic minorities, and in particular black people, are virtually excluded from the boardroom (Pandya, 1996). Even in sectors where relatively large numbers of ethnic minorities are employed, such as transport and health, they are still unable to progress to the boardroom. The authors of this report have concluded that the career progression of ethnic minorities is blocked by a 'cement roof'.

Activity 11.2

Drawing on the work of Cockburn (1989) (long and short agendas) develop a human resourcing strategy that deals with the 'cement roof' problem identified above.

Espoused EO policies and operational practices

Officially espoused EO policies can be neutralised through operational procedures being neglected or through being followed in letter but not in spirit (Jenkins, 1986). The failure to translate declared equal opportunity policies into practice can in part be explained by looking at the distribution of power within organisations. As Dickens (1994: 279) points out, 'procedures operate within an organisational context and power in decision making may not be in the hands of the guardians of good practice, namely the personnel managers, who are likely to have developed the espoused model'. Personnel managers, for example, are often marginal to selection decisions, with real power being vested in line managers (Collinson *et al.*, 1990; Jenkins, 1986). Line managers may resist the formalisation, accountability and monitoring required by EOPs viewing such practices as interference with their discretion in decision making. Change *per se* can be threatening and unwelcome, but in the case of EO this threat can be exacerbated because it may be seen as a challenge to personal attitudes and traditional local norms or values. In particular, EO may be experienced as a criticism of those in power: managers can resent the ways in which elements of equal opportunities policies imply that they might act in a discriminatory way (Collinson, 1987b). Jones (1988: 43) found that even fairly low-key initiatives, such as the redesign of application forms, 'implicitly and overtly cast aspersions on and criticise management'.

Research indicates that the personnel/human resource function is frequently viewed as 'external' or 'interfering' by line managers (Watson, 1977, 1994a; Legge, 1978). Personnel professionals acting as the 'guardians of good practice' can lead to EO initiatives becoming seen as an external imposition and dismissed as not relevant. In view of this, operational procedures are likely to be neglected or manipulated, with decision makers using their discretionary powers to continue as before.

It is important to recognise a possible tension between centralised equal opportunity policies and decentralised, more flexible management, seen by many to be a desirable characteristic of human resource strategy making. The general trend towards expansion of the line manager's role by devolving many of the functions that were previously seen as the concern of personnel specialists means that their awareness of equality issues and commitment to them become even more crucial to the process of change:

> Effective equal opportunity policy and, more importantly, practice will result when we achieve line management 'ownership'. This can only occur by integrating equal opportunity ethos into every aspect of human resource strategy and its local application. (Mahon, 1989: 79)

Reflecting on reasons for espoused models not being adequately translated into operational procedures can suggest that adequate implementation might produce desired outcomes. However, this is not the case. Fair procedures do not necessarily produce fair outcomes, as can be seen in the following discussion.

■ Problems with prescriptive approaches

The 'prescriptive model' of recruitment and selection embodies EO considerations focusing on unbiased assessment: assessing individuals against relevant, job-related criteria rather than according to their membership of a particular social group (*see* discussion in Chapter 5). The emphasis is thus on *suitability criteria* (technical ability to do the job) rather than *acceptability criteria* (attitudinal, behavioural, personality factors), a distinction made by Jenkins (1986). Since acceptability criteria are less easy to quantify than suitability criteria, it is here where the operation of covert discrimination is most likely to occur. Through the use of criteria of acceptability, such as manner, attitude, appearance, maturity and personality, Jenkins argues that white male hegemony is sustained.

Jenkins shows how 'age and married status' can be used as criteria of acceptability by recruiters in order to select stereotypical male breadwinners, whose stability, maturity and motivation were believed to be assured by their family and financial responsibilities. Conversely, in relation to women applicants, young family dependants were viewed as a 'definite handicap'. This suggests that domestic responsibilities are viewed positively for men because they are believed to indicate stability and motivation, but negatively for women since they suggest divided loyalties between home and work. It has also been found that managers use different (gender-based) criteria to assess whether applicants were able to meet the job requirements. For example, the same type of behaviour was described in a male applicant as 'showing initiative' and assessed as desirable, and in a woman applicant as 'pushy' and undesirable (Collinson *et al.*, 1990).

Although many personnel managers have a role to play in recruitment and selection, it does not follow that they will always strictly adhere to the professional EO model. Local personnel managers 'often contribute to the reproduction of both highly vague and informal selection criteria, channels and procedures, and sex discriminatory practices' (Collinson, 1991: 58). This is in part due to the fact that many local personnel managers are 'poachers turned gamekeepers', transferred line managers with 'no allegiance to those principles and ideals of the personnel profession that could conflict with the more immediate and short-term managerial priorities or profit and production' (Collinson, 1991: 59).

As Lovenduski (1985: 15) points out, a key implementation problem in respect of EO 'is that support for taking action designed to improve prospects for women, ethnic minorities and the disabled must come from an overwhelmingly white, male and "non-disabled" dominant group who may well regard equal opportunities as a threat'. The threat comes in part from the fact that white men's characteristic career paths are implicitly predicated on the existence of 'unpromotable' categories, including women and blacks (Crompton and Jones, 1984: 248).

ILLUSTRATION 11.6

Unpromotable categories

Crompton and Jones (1984: 145), having researched careers among staff at a major clearing bank, found that 'young women were actively discouraged from taking bank examinations which . . . were regarded as virtually automatic for young male recruits'. Of the women interviewed, 46 per cent said that they had been actively dissuaded from taking the Institute of Bankers exams. Men were encouraged to progress and women were not. The possibility of career progress from junior to senior jobs for the male career was premised on the fact that large amounts of routine work were carried out by women who were not eligible for promotion, so allowing the prospects of these men in routine jobs to be enhanced.

Resistance to EO initiatives does not come only from white, non-disabled men. In striving for 'equality', organisations could well have to contend with resistance from within the disadvantaged groups that an EOP is designed to help. We have already seen that it is possible for organisations to adopt different approaches to equality and follow different equality agendas, so that the term itself can mask multiple and conflicting meanings that result in conflicting expectations from disadvantaged groups. According to Dickens (1994: 285), the assumption of shared interest implicit in much universalistic EO prescription is misplaced. She highlights how seniority rules may advantage ethnic minority men in an organisation where there is low turnover, but may not be of advantage necessarily to women with interrupted employment patterns. There are also cases where certain disadvantaged groups may have an interest in the EO prescription not being followed. In their study, Jewson and Mason (1986) found that formalising recruitment and selection in the name of EO resulted in existing informal channels of communication valued by the ethnic minorities being severed. The refusal of a new personnel manager to recognise traditional links with an Asian broker, for example, resulted in resentment.

A further complication is that divisions also exist within any one disadvantaged group. For example, women are not a homogeneous group. They are divided by class, ethnicity, age, occupation and status. Within 'ethnic minorities' not only are there different groups (Asians, Africans, Caribbeans, Greeks and so on), but the situation and experience of men and women within these diverse groups also differs, for example 70 per cent of black Caribbean women are economically active, compared to only 20 per cent of Bangladeshi women (Faichnie, 1997: 5). Among people with disabilities there is great diversity depending on the nature of disability, as well as other factors such as their gender, ethnicity etc. What all these diverse groups do have in common, however, is that they 'do not conform to the standard which informs and shapes formal and informal organisational structures and norms in Britain, namely, the white, non-disabled male' (Dickens, 1994: 286).

Managing diversity

When describing their programmes, some employers are beginning to use the term *managing diversity* instead of *equal opportunities*. The concept of diversity has been hailed as a move beyond equality issues covered by the law and has been described by Sir Michael Bett, when President of the Institute of Personnel and Development, as adding 'new impetus to the development of equal opportunities and the creation of an environment in which enhanced contributions from all employees will work to the advantage of business, people themselves and society more generally' (IPD, 1997).

According to Kandola and Fullerton (1994: 49), the key differences between equal opportunities and managing diversity are as follows:

- *Equal opportunities* concentrates on removing discrimination, is seen as an issue for disadvantaged groups, is primarily an issue for personnel practitioners and relies on positive action.

- *Managing diversity* focuses on maximising employee potential, is seen as relevant to all employees, is an issue that involves all managers and does not rely on positive action.

It is not yet clear whether this signals a significant change of approach. It remains to be seen whether as a result of diversity management 'all shall win and all shall have prizes' (Woodall, 1996: 334). Where 'diversity' could prove a positive way forward would be if it led to an increased questioning of the skilled white man as the archetypal worker against whom all other workers are judged. Equal opportunities could then be less about adjusting the rest of us to rules based on his abilities and behaviour and more about restructuring the rules to reflect the reality of the current British workforce.

Moves towards a greater recognition of *individual differences* shift the debate away from the recognition of disadvantages shared by different groups (a collective focus) to an emphasis on the unique attributes and requirements of each employee (individual focus), recognising that there are many dimensions of inequality at work. This has contradictory implications. On the one hand it could signal a recognition of different needs and interests within the workforce – a positive development for equal opportunities. But, carried further, it could lead to a denial of collective basis for disadvantage. The danger is that unfair discrimination at work would no longer be acknowledged as the 'common experience of disadvantaged groups of people, but the private experience of isolated individuals' (Noon and Blyton, 1997: 186).

Conclusions

This chapter has provided evidence of the ways in which EO has been placed firmly on management agendas in a number of organisations and the range of initiatives that are undertaken. Despite these initiatives, changes in the representation and distribution of various disadvantaged groups within organisations are less easy to identify (*Equal Opportunities Review*, 1998a, b, c). It can therefore be concluded that EOPs and initiatives have had only limited success in 'achieving equality' in the workplace.

The fundamental question is whether the practices consonant with the liberal perspective are the best way to proceed along the EO pathway. As we have seen, the focus here is on adopting a more effective approach to policy implementation as the best way forward. This entails doing the same things in a more committed manner, as can be found in the prescriptive management literature (*see* Coussey and Jackson, 1991; Ross and Schneider, 1992). What is missing from the liberal perspective is any analysis of the structures and dynamics that characterise the social relations and practices of organisations and labour markets and that make the implementation of EO difficult. This chapter has discussed the problems associated with stereotyping and bias in recruitment and selection, the precarious relationships between line and personnel managers, inherent conflicts between EO and other priorities facing managers and even resistance from disadvantaged groups themselves. In so far as the liberal perspective negates these issues, then the principle of EO is in danger of being reduced merely to a legitimatory ideology, characterised by assumptions that have the effect of reinforcing the status quo.

A more critical approach to EO highlights the ways in which present initiatives usually consist of 'special measures' to help individuals in minority groups compete for jobs designed with only white, non-disabled men in mind. That is to say, there is a template for employment shaped around white, non-disabled men against which those seeking to get into and progress up organisation hierarchies are measured. As Dickens (1994: 288) states, 'rather than adopting this Procrustian approach, with its focus on changing individuals to fit the template in order to obtain distributive justice, the template should be abandoned'. There is no theoretical reason why radical restructuring associated with cutbacks and mergers should not provide an opportunity to rethink occupational boundaries in a way that breaks down social group divisions. However, there is no evidence of this happening in practice (Liff, 1995).

The 'valuing diversity' approach has the potential to open the way for different formal and informal organisational cultures and structures, reflective of diverse contributions, needs and attributes. Managing diversity appears to be about a more positive valuing of difference. Crompton (1996: 125) warns, however, that while white masculine characteristics continue to be associated with material success, the celebration of 'difference' may result in the intensification of material inequalities. (For a useful discussion of sameness or difference in the context of EO, *see* Liff & Wajcman, 1996.)

It has been implied that 'new-style human resource management practices' represent a potential advance for equality. Sisson's model of the 'HRM organisation' (1994: 8), for example, cites equal opportunities as a key personnel policy. However, Dickens (1998) shows how the implementation of human resource policies may have different implications for men and women at work: 'demonstrating how the implementation of HR concepts and policies perpetuates rather than challenges . . . inequality'. Thus, if advocates of 'new-style human resource management practices' are to be serious in their commitment to the development of all human resources, they need to face the challenge of wider patterns of social inequality. This means not only looking at disadvantage, but also addressing the issue of who benefits from the status quo. Such a recognition means that equal opportunities initiatives are 'essentially a political project, as much concerned with deep organisational change as with simple personnel administration' (Goss, 1994: 173).

CASE STUDY 11.1

Developing equal opportunities at Star Entertainment Ltd

Graham Biggs joined Star Entertainment Ltd as the Company Personnel Manager just over a year ago for a considerable increase in salary having previously spent most of his career as an HR specialist in the electricity supply industry. Star Entertainment specialises in the provision of entertainment equipment to leisure outlets and a major part of its work is the supply and maintenance of fruit machines to public houses throughout the UK. It had been a demanding year, Graham had not fully appreciated just how competitive and prone to fluctuations in customer demand the leisure industry would be.

Graham is concerned, he has just completed his first audit of the composition of the five thousand strong work force and it contains some worrying statistics. Less than three percent of the workforce are of African/Caribbean or Asian origin even though the Company is a long established employer in locations where these ethnic groups are well represented in the local population. Graham's analysis has also revealed that there is currently only one woman senior manager and fifteen women working jobs of a managerial nature even though thirty percent of the total workforce is female (calculated on the basis of full time equivalents). It was difficult to establish how many of these worked on a part time basis although Graham is aware that this is common practice for administrative female staff working in the depots which provide the machine hire and service in the different geographical regions. Women in the company, as Graham anticipated are almost entirely employed in lower paid clerical roles but it did rather surprise him that the collectors of fruit machine rents from public houses are all female. He knows the collector's role can be a hazardous one. In the past twelve months alone two men have been attacked in the course of their duties but the audit revealed that the only male rent collector left after six months service. The termination form completed by the employee just stated that the reason for leaving was '*unsuitable job*'.

In contrast the Company's service engineers are all male and there was no evidence of any women having been recruited as engineers. Admittedly the job could involve high levels of overtime, which had the effect of boosting the engineers' monthly earnings but it did seem strange that the job attracted no female applicants. When it came to considering the company's record on employing people with disabilities Graham could reach no conclusions, the records were just not available so something clearly had to be done. Out of curiosity Graham had used his newly acquired HR software package to obtain an age disperson chart for the employees in the different salary grades which had added to his concerns. The impact of removing levels of management and supervision, largely through successive phases of early retirements, was clearly evident. The organisation's new flatter structure revealed a white male management who were, with the exception of the senior management team, virtually all under forty five years of age with seventy percent in the thirty to forty year old age bracket.

The company's policies all stressed its policy of providing equality of opportunity but it had experienced several claims of sex and race discrimination although only two had proceeded to an Industrial Tribunal hearing in the past five years. Graham had been involved in the last of these as a company representative. The case had been one of alleged sex discrimination bought by a Mrs Hughes, an application turned down for promotion to the position of General Manager. She had claimed that her lack of success was due to her domestic circumstances as a recent divorcee with two children aged seven and eleven being well known to her employer as she had at one stage had to take leave to resolve some personal problems. Although the Company had won the case the eventual outcome had been far from predictable. Mrs Hughes had alleged that at her interview for promotion she had been directly asked if she would be able to offer the mobility and the hours the job demanded because of her family commitments which had not been a concern explored with other applicants. In fact the person appointed had been a married man with even younger children than she had with less years of experience. The Company had been able to demonstrate at the hearing that work based performance factors had been the criteria for selection but Graham knew it had been 'touch and go' in view of the way the selection interview had been handled. One positive outcome of the case was that Graham had been strongly supported by the Managing Director in running a series of two-day interview training courses to be attended by all staff in the company with recruitment responsibilities. Graham was sharing the delivery of these courses with an external HR Training Consultant to try and find out more about existing working practices and the views of operational management but he wasn't very reassured by what he learnt.

Asking groups directly about the under representation of Asians and African/Caribbeans in the work force he was told that the company just failed to attract applicants from these ethnic groups which certainly seemed to be borne out by the evidence. Trying to establish why all the rent collectors were currently female the managers were adamant that the answer lay in the nature of the work. It was acknowledged that number of male applicants for collectors' posts was increasing and across the different regions probably now formed a quarter of all applications, but experience had shown that male collectors were not as efficient or as quick to learn the job as women. The fact was they never stayed for long, which could possibly be explained by the level of pay. Certainly publicans said they preferred female collectors and their preferences counted in a customer driven industry. Based on this past recruitment experience it was unusual for male applicants to be asked to attend for interview.

When the question was about the lack of female service engineers the problem was again identified as the job. Machines were heavy, the hours were long, the job was technical and it was not difficult to get good male applicants with the right experience in the electronics industry when vacancies occurred. An added consideration for managers was that they thought it would be difficult for a woman working with a close knit team of service engineers most of whom had long service with the company. Graham is beginning to see that he has a major task ahead if there is to be a real commitment within the company to developing greater diversity in the work force and promoting equality of opportunity.

© Lynette Harris

Activity 11.3

1 What are the equal opportunity priority areas which Graham Biggs needs to address?

2 Identify the issues which should be seen as 'short' and 'long' agenda equal opportunity priorities for Star Entertainment.

3 Which legal, socio-economic and political factors influence the management of equal opportunities within this organisation?

Summary

In this chapter the following key points have been made:

- Although a number of organisations have taken equal opportunities initiatives and governments have passed legislation outlining some forms of discrimination, discrimination in the labour market still persists on a number of grounds.

- Companies pursue equal opportunities measures either to achieve compliance and penalty avoidance or out of organisational interests.

- Legislation has led to both organisational reform and 'avoidance tactics'.

- Organisational interest includes the impact of competition in the labour market, the efficient management of human resources, better employee relations, image and gaining from diversity.

- Equal opportunities policies often form the centrepiece of company initiatives, but there are a number of difficulties in pursuing these in practice.

- Liberal-type equality is based on treating everyone the same and involves establishing fair rules and procedures.

- The radical approach revolves around the goal of equal outcomes and utilises positive discrimination or affirmative action.

- The 'long agenda' (Cockburn, 1989) implies a 'transformative EO strategy'.

- Translation of espoused equal opportunities into practice can be hindered or obstructed by tensions between personnel and line managers, inherent conflicts between EO and other priorities and conflicting expectations from disadvantaged groups.

- The differences between an equal opportunities and managing diversity policy are explained and discussed.

- Managing diversity appears to be about a more positive valuing of difference, but this could result in the intensification of material inequalities (Crompton, 1996).

Discussion questions

1 Are equal opportunities different from diversity, or are they the same thing repackaged under a new name?

2 How do organisations that promote diversity reconcile it with having group aims, such as getting women into management?

3 Should we abandon activities and initiatives such as positive action training that were established under the equal opportunities banner?

Further reading

Dickens (1998) provides an account of ways in which new-style HRM practices contribute to the gendering process in organisations.

Liff and Wajcman (1996) argue that a clearer recognition of different types of initiatives and their potential strengths and weaknesses can contribute to a more sophisticated understanding of the theory and practice of equal opportunities.

Bagilhole (1997) incorporates an examination of three key areas, gender, race and disability, as both separate oppressions and as integral to the concept of equal opportunities. While this text draws on practice and research within the area of social policy, it is also of use to human resource practitioners in both public and private organisations interested in introducing or developing equal opportunities.

Cockburn (1985) provides important insights into the ways in which jobs came to be seen as appropriate for men and women.

MANAGING MESSY MORAL MATTERS
Ethics and HRM

Colin Fisher and Chris Rice

OBJECTIVES

Having completed this chapter and its associated activities, readers should be able to:

- identify the type of ethical issues that HR professionals and managers have to face at work;

- identify the main ethical principles appropriate for organisational and HR contexts;

- understand the function of ethical and professional codes of conduct;

- understand the styles of ethical thinking and how these are affected by social and organisational processes.

Organisation, management, strategy and ethics

Ethics is about what is right – but this chapter will not tell you what is right and wrong in organisational and managerial life. Instead, it aims to help you become clearer and more rigorous in the way you think about ethical issues at work. Like many issues of peripheral interest to organisations, it is often the formal responsibility of people in the HRM function. Or, as others (Connock and Johns, 1996: 159) put it, HRM managers claim ethical leadership because they believe they are best placed to do so. This claim gives HR people access to organisational strategy processes. Strategy involves setting missions and visions and defining core organisational values. As these things cannot be done without considering ethical questions, anyone who has a legitimate role concerning organisational ethics becomes part of the strategy process. Other HR managers argue that, to the contrary, the claim to ethical leadership diminishes the strategic role of HR because it associates the function with soft welfare issues rather than with a hard, business achievement orientation.

The focus of this chapter, however, is not on ethical leadership, at least in the sense of writing statements of value and codes of conduct, but on the ways in which people in organisations think and act on ethical issues. The reasons for this emphasis need to be explained. Corporate bodies cannot be made to act ethically by mission statements, ethical audits and codes of ethics alone. Partly this is because, although such things have their purposes, they cannot anticipate and pre-empt every possible ethical difficulty. A further cause is that organisations are characterised by value plurality, and mission statements and core values are part of that plurality rather than the means of overcoming it. If you need to be convinced of this, consider the O&V Joifel case study in Chapter 1. Analyse the variety of values and ethical positions that the characters in the case study present, ask whether these values clash and whether a mission statement or a code of organisational ethics would serve to resolve the conflicts. If senior management does wish to use a code to enforce ethical uniformity, it would have to require employees, as some companies do (Connock and Johns 1996: 217), to sign an annual certificate that they have complied with the code and that they know of no other staff members who have transgressed against it.

Corporations, as legal fictions without consciences, will only act ethically when the people who are part of them are skilled at thinking about, and coping with, ethical issues and are supported by an organisational culture that encourages ethical awareness and debate. This approach is sometimes labelled virtue ethics (Dobson and Armstrong, 1995). The approach assumes that if people develop their virtues – honesty, perseverance, fairness and so on (you can make your own list) – then rules, which tell people how to behave ethically, are unnecessary because people will be able to work it out for themselves. But virtues can only be developed if people are in a organisation or community that nurtures the virtues and if there are good people who can act as role models. The idea of a virtue incorporates the Aristotelian notion of a golden mean. A virtue is a midway position between two unwanted extremes. Sometimes, for instance, too much honesty can be as bad as too little and so virtue is the ability to get the appropriate balance between the two extremes. This perspective allows HRM a contribution to ethical leadership through its training and development role, particularly its role in developing ethical awareness, tolerance of ambiguity and debating skill among staff.

There follow in Activity 12.1 some examples of ethical difficulties that may be found in organisational life. The vignettes are designed to map out the breadth of questions in which HR staff may become involved, either as result of their role of ethical leadership or in carrying out their managerial responsibilities. These mini case studies are not simply designed for you to say what you personally believe is right and wrong. It may be that we use values and ethics at work that are different to those we hold personally.

Activity 12.1

Consider what the people in the following case studies should do.

Life at the top (who wants to be a decision maker?)

THINK – The head of research of a major producer of instant coffee goes to see the chief executive. He says that he has discovered a highly addictive (but not banned) substance that is tasteless and appears to have no side effects. They realise that adding a little of ingredient X to the coffee could ensure immediate product loyalty – they can even imagine the slogan: 'New, improved Chriscafé, with added oomph! One taste and you'll never drink anything else!'

1 Is this ethical? Is the maximisation of profit within the law the only guideline to which companies need to pay attention?

2 If the company manufactured pet food, would it be more acceptable/less acceptable/different?

3 If you were the HR manager, how should you respond when an employee, who feels strongly that this is wrong, goes to the local media with the story?

Life in the middle – problems, problems, problems

THINK – The company has a rule in its rule book (of which every employee gets a copy at induction) stating that private telephone calls should be paid for. The organisation has never enforced this rule. The new itemised billing from the telephone company has allowed the accounts manager to identify patterns of calls. One of the emergent patterns is regular calls to Australia. It is known that one of the marketing department staff has a close friend in Australia and has in fact spoken of the possibility of emigrating and getting married out there. The accounts manager presumes guilt and comes to the personnel manager for advice on what to do.

1 What should the personnel manager advise/do?

2 In what ways would your answer differ if the 'accused' were the finance director?

Life in the middle – the postman always rings twice

THINK – Approximately a year ago a medium-sized company appointed a marketing specialist to revitalise that side of the business. The person appointed has been very successful and is looked on as a key (and rising) member of the management team. He

---

lives some 25 miles away from the plant and has seemed happy commuting to and from work. Little is known about his private life. The personnel manager receives, anonymously, a cutting from the local newspaper referring to a court case in which the marketing specialist was found guilty of domestic violence against his wife. He was fined £500.

1 What action, if any, should the personnel manager propose?

2 In what way would the decision differ if the offence was importuning young men in a public place?

3 Identify offences that might be 'acceptable' and those you feel to be 'unacceptable'.

THINK – A manager joined her present employer, a medium-sized manufacturing organisation, some two months ago. She was rather surprised to discover that the general manager's secretary was married to the senior shop steward. When she expressed her surprise, she was told that both had been long-term employees and that their romance and subsequent marriage had been a matter of general interest, knowledge and general good-natured badinage for a long while. She has also just heard strong rumours that an affair is going on between the general manager and his secretary.

1 What should the new manager do?

2 Why?

Life at the bottom – it's hell

THINK – The organisation is in the process of being inspected for ISO9000 and to help out the personnel assistant/administrator has been temporarily transferred to the chief executive's office. The assistant/administrator is looking forward to returning to personnel in a few days time when the chief executive himself comes up to her and, *sotto voce*, asks her to 'type this memo quickly, date it three months ago, crumple it up a bit and put it in the file in the "right" place'.

1 What should the assistant/administrator do?

2 If you were the personnel manager to whom the administrator comes for advice, what would you say?

Most of the examples in Activity 12.1 do not involve illegality at work. The one case that does, using work phones for private calls, would probably make criminals of everybody if the law were severely enforced. Ethical difficulty arises in the uncharted gaps and overlaps between morality and legality. These are confusing terrains in which things may be legal but wrong or, conversely, right but illegal. To find a sure path through such territory people need ethical principles to guide them. Activity 12.2 gives you an opportunity to reflect on the principles you may have used when thinking about the incidents in Activity 12.1.

Activity 12.2

Prioritising your ethical principles

Below are a number of principles commonly discussed in the literature on business ethics. Identify your top three and rank them 1, 2 and 3 in order of importance/relevance to you and your decision making. Then mark your least relevant 9, 10 and 11.

Principle	Description	Rank
Categorical imperative	You should not adopt principles of action unless they can, without inconsistency, be adopted by everyone else	
Conventionist ethic	Individuals should act to further their self-interests so long as they do not violate the law	
Golden rule	Do unto others as you would have them do unto you	
Hedonistic ethic	If it feels good, do it	
Disclosure rule	If you are comfortable with an action or decision after asking yourself whether you should mind if all your associates, friends and family were aware of it, then you should act or decide	
Intuition ethic	You do what your 'gut feeling' tells you to do	
Means–ends ethic	If the end justifies the means, then you should act	
Might equals right ethic	You should take whatever advantage you are strong enough and powerful enough to take without respect for ordinary social conventions and laws	
Organisation ethic	This is an age of large-scale organisations – be loyal to the organisation	
Professional ethic	You should only do that which can be explained before a committee of your professional peers	
Utilitarian ethic	You should follow the principle of 'the greatest good for the greatest number'	

Source: Carrol, 1990.

Carrol (1990) used the above list as the basis of a research project and found that the golden rule was the principle given the highest ranking by his respondents. No ethical principle is ever straightforward, however. If the key to the golden rule lies in the notion that, if we wish to be treated well, we need to treat others well, it could be seen as a form of self-interest. Altruism, as Kanungo and Mendonca (1996: 39) pointed out, can either be self-seeking or genuine. The disclosure rule came second in the study.

Perceptions of ethical issues

■ Categorising moral questions

Having mapped out the range of ethical issues and the types of ethical responses possible, the next question to be considered is how people decide what principles should be brought to bear on any particular issue. In this section, the question will be answered by developing a framework of differing perceptions of ethical issues. The framework is based on the assumption that when managers are faced with an ethical question they seek to categorise it as a particular kind of issue. It can be helpful to recognise the range of different categories of ethical concern; eight are defined in this chapter. They are listed here and are discussed in more detail later in the chapter:

- ethical neutrality;
- ethical awareness and reaction;
- ethical convention;
- ethical puzzle;
- ethical problem;
- ethical dilemma;
- ethical cynicism and caprice;
- ethical negotiation.

The process of classification has a functional value because, it will be argued, each type of issue has associated with it a range of appropriate responses and ways of thinking.

Categorisation is a tool for thinking that helps us deal with complex moral issues. But categorisation has to be placed within the context of the rhetorical and cognitive tension, as discussed by Billig (1996: 148–85), between it and particularisation. If categorisation alone were the main tool used in thinking, then all thought would be either bureaucratic or bigoted. By way of illustration, categorisation is the process used by a doctor's receptionist when they point out that, under the rules, you have to wait two days for a repeat prescription; particularisation underlies their willingness, under the circumstances that you are out of tablets and have asked nicely, to provide your prescription today. Particularisation is the cognitive process of separating things out from a general category and treating them as a special case. It allows people to modify their categorisation of ethical issues, as new particulars come to their attention, and it can prevent thinking from becoming inflexible. People need to be able to place events into categories to deal with the otherwise overwhelming mass of information confronting them; but the category to which they assign an event or issue will depend on the particulars of the case.

The particulars that we use to categorise issues facing us can be drawn from a number of sources. One will be the nature of the issue itself. For example, one study (Couch *et al.*, 1995) reported that managers made choices of lesser ethical worth when dealing with questions concerning the survival of their company than they did when dealing with issues concerning profit maximisation. Another study (Weber, 1996) indicated that the nature of the harm (whether physical, economic or psychological) involved in an issue, and the magnitude of its consequences, influenced the moral rationales given by managers.

The way in which the ethical question under consideration is presented by others will also influence a person's view of it. If that presentation alters as new material or evidence becomes available, then the person's categorisation may change. Others may include:

- family and friends;
- the organisation and work colleagues;
- professional associations and their codes of conduct;
- society and the legal system.

The views, opinions and reactions of these groups may act as triggers or cues for categorisation of an issue. There is no reason for it to be thought that all these influences would suggest the same categorisation. It is more likely that they would lead to different classifications. The question of which cues, and which groups, an individual may respond to in their categorisation of an issue will depend, in turn, on many factors, including the importance and power of each group in relation to the individual. A person's self-image will also play a part in their responses to demands and pressures from others.

■ Dependency theory and strategic exchange

Dependency theory, proposed by McGregor (1960), provides a mechanism for explaining the influence that a group or organisation may have on an individual. The theory suggests that there is a relationship between the amount of authority or power that someone can exert over another person or an organisation and the degree to which that person or organisation is dependent on them. He illustrated the relationship diagrammatically (*see* Fig. 12.1). The theory can be applied globally, nationally or individually.

Using the ideas from dependency theory, we could predict that the influence of the

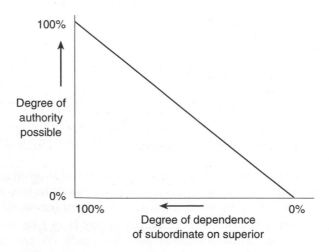

Fig. 12.1 Dependency theory

different groups *at any point in time* will be a function of the degree to which the organisation (or the management/decision makers) is seen as dependent on that particular group. As we observed earlier, we can sometimes respond to one dependency to satisfy another. Examples could be organisations adopting 'green' policies and products due to a dependency on the environmental groups and (perhaps) the government – thus keeping their market share, producing profit and satisfying another primary stakeholder, the owners/shareholders. Dependency theory can be seen as an example of strategic exchange (cf. Chapter 1) in which a readiness to be influenced is exchanged for real or rhetorical resources.

■ A framework for categorising ethical questions

The categories of ethical perception, listed on p. 315, can be defined in relation to two dimensions that are shown in Fig. 12.2. The first dimension concerns ethical integrity, by which is meant the extent to which an individual's values are mutually consistent and whole or the degree to which they are plural and fragmented. There is no suggestion of preference in this dichotomy: it should not be assumed that the former state is preferable to the latter. The second dimension describes a dialectic (which will be explained shortly) of ethical purpose within which the contradictions of behaving ethically are played out. The explanation of the framework in Fig. 12.2 is necessarily complicated and, to simplify the task, it will be done step by step under a number of headings.

Ethical integrity, the horizontal axis in Fig. 12.2

The dimension of ethical integrity will be described first. The position at the extreme left of the horizontal axis in Fig. 12.2 represents clarity and certainty about values. A person

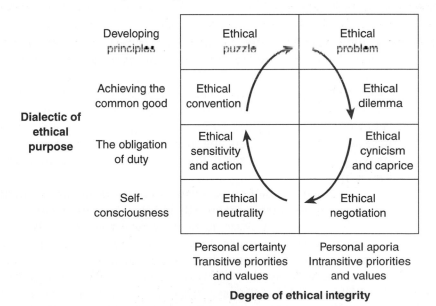

Fig. 12.2 Managers' perceptions of ethical issues – a framework

at this point on the scale sees moral issues in a straightforward way, which helps them to know what should be done in a situation or how an issue should be analysed and resolved. A person at the extreme right of the dimension, however, is more likely to be confused or even aporetic. Aporia is a state in which a person is unsure what to do or think because of the complexity of something. A person in this condition will find the plurality of views and positions on an issue difficult to reconcile and they will think that a simple resolution of the issue would be difficult to achieve.

One aspect of the distinction between these two positions on the scale concerns the psychological concept of transitivity (Wright, 1984: 16). A person is transitive in the values they hold if their values can be ranked in a consistent and hierarchical manner. If a person with transitive values, for instance, believes that Jane would make a better director of corporate ethics than, say, John, and that John would be better at the job than Peter, then they must also believe that Jane is a better candidate than Peter. A person whose values were intransitive, however, could agree with the first two statements concerning Jane and John but also happen to believe that Peter would do the job better than Jane. The transitive person has a single basis for their value judgements, whereas the intransitive person has various value bases.

The dialectic of ethical purpose, the vertical axis in Fig. 12.2

The vertical axis of Fig. 12.2 represents a dialectical movement as awareness of ethical purpose emerges from the contradictions inherent in moral reasoning. Dialectical progress is represented by a series of steps and is not a continuous scale such as the one used to represent ethical integrity. A dialectic is a method of argument or analysis in which an initial formal idea (thesis) is challenged by practical contradictions contained within it (antithesis) until a synthesis is formed that overcomes or transcends the tensions between thesis and antithesis. In each row of Fig. 12.2 the thesis is on the left-hand side of the diagram and the antithesis is on the right. The synthesis for each pair is found on the left-hand side of the next row up in the diagram.

The origin of the dimension is called self-awareness, because people at this point want to keep themselves to themselves and are troubled by the expectations of others. They are aware of the moral demands that others try to impose on them, but they are unhappy about accepting the impositions because it would threaten their tranquillity. These demands are normally such that, if they were accepted, the person would have to take action or stand out against a perceived moral wrong. The self-conscious person seeks to avoid these demands either by refusing to accept that the issue is an ethical one or by going along with the demands of the majority or the powerful without articulating their own viewpoint.

The instability of the phase of self-consciousness comes from the contradiction between a person's sense of their own moral worth and their defensive refusal to take a moral position on an issue. The next phase in the dialectic is therefore duty, the negation of self-consciousness. At this stage, people are required to do their duty, to family, friends, organisations and so on. In the preceding stage of self-consciousness, obligations to act are hypothetical. That is to say, they are based on a hypothesis that says that a particular action will achieve an end that the agent desires. In this aspect of the dialectic the end is nearly always prudential – to keep out of trouble. In the phase of duty, in contrast, people act according to their obligations because they feel they have to, not because it will bring about a wished-for conclusion. Indeed, following the dictates of conscience may well be uncomfortable and difficult. Duty relates to an obligation beyond the self and derives, unbidden and unanalysed, from people's consciences.

If duty is intuitive, then there will be a multiplicity of ideas of duty as people are led in different directions by their consciences. A dutiful approach to ethics leads to confusion and arbitrariness because it is impossible to differentiate between various conceptions of duty:

> Unreflective duty can take its imperatives from the dooms of Zeus, from priest or parent, from the custom of a tribe or city, and act in peace and faith. But the first conflict unveils an Antigone and the question 'Whose standard?' soon brings down all standards. (Mabbott, 1967: 44)

(Antigone, in Greek myth, followed her own conscience by giving a ritual burial, against custom and the decree of king Creon, to her brother Polyneices who had tried to usurp the throne.)

The revelation of the instability of duty can lead to cynicism and claims that it is of no value to take action, or a stand, on an issue because such things are always insincere and the outcomes always the worst.

The next thesis in the dialectic of ethical purpose develops the idea of the common good as a way of overcoming the fragmentation of the previous phase. Duty, which up to this point has been seen as independent of the ends being pursued, becomes associated with the idea of doing good for the whole of an organisation or society and not just for particular interests within it. In this phase, things are done because they are to the benefit of all. People follow the conventional rules and norms of a society or organisation because doing so maintains good order. In the jargon of the philosophers, this phase of the dialectic is consequentialist. That is to say, the existence, in organisations, of statements of values, policies and procedures is justified because they help the achievement of organisational goals (Mackie, 1977: 149).

This stage of the dialectic strains the ability of a society or of an organisation to make decisions, because it assumes that everyone within and outside the organisation agrees with the organisation's norms. Particular dilemmas emerge when one set of rules and conventions clashes with another. For managers and professionals, these problems often emerge as conflicts between personal and organisational norms. A few years ago, by way of illustration, a company tried to introduce chewing tobacco as an exciting new product into the UK (Stuttaford, 1990). The company saw a market niche that it could profitably fill and as long as the product wasn't banned, which it was eventually, there was no reason that it shouldn't be marketed. This proposal must have caused anxieties for people who worked in the firm as their obligation to the firm was perhaps challenged by personal doubts about the propriety of introducing a carcinogenic product to the market. Contradictions such as these cause individuals to move beyond the competing norms of different groups and to work out their own positions on the issues. This is the next step in the dialectic.

The final position, represented by the point at the top of the vertical axis in Fig. 12.2, is the development of ethical principles. The difficulty of defining a common good, and the route to it, causes people to think about their own values and to work out for themselves a set of principles that are personally significant for them and that they can use to make their own ethical judgements. These values are not the intuitive ones of the stage of duty but precepts that have been achieved by difficult self-reflection and thought. Some argue that the realisation of such an ethical self-consciousness is the purpose of higher education (Reeves, 1988: 14–16). This phase is deontological in the simplest definition of the term – the study of moral obligations – and it is the apogee of the dialectic, because it can go no higher. It necessarily includes within itself constant review and reconsideration of values.

These self-validated principles could include, *inter alia*, as Snell (1993: 31) suggests, utilitarianism (*see* Activity 12.2), which is consequentialist, or the golden rule, which is deontological in its more restricted sense, concerning precepts or virtues of innate worth that are not justified by their consequences. At this level in the dialectic, consequentialism takes the form of a technique for decision making rather than a generalised justification for following conventional norms. Utilitarianism opens up the possibility of calculating the amount of good that would flow from taking various decisions and identify the one that would produce the most good or happiness. The Rawlsian (Rawls, 1972) principle, of only admitting those inequalities between people which benefit those who are worst off, also listed by Snell, is not easy to allocate to either the consequentialist or the deontological category of ethical thought.

■ The eight categories of ethical concern

Now that the dimensions in Fig. 12.2 have been described, the eight categories of ethical issue can be defined in relation to them. These categories are important because they define how a person reacts to a moral issue. The example of redundancy will be used to illustrate these differences, which often explain the arguments about ethical issues that occur at work.

Ethical neutrality

People have put an issue into this category when they argue that there is no ethical aspect to the question – that there are no issues of conscience to be argued over and that the question is simply a pragmatic one. By regarding the issue as technical and managerial, people can isolate themselves from any anguish that might be associated with admitting an ethical dimension to it. It has long been a complaint of academics who study public administration, for example, that values are seen by public officials only as a source of irritation and that, as such, officials try to avoid them (Hart and Scott, 1973). In the case of redundancy decisions, a person working from this perspective would refuse to accept that there was a moral dimension to the issue and see it simply as a pragmatic and managerial question.

Ethical awareness and action

This is a category of ethical issues that causes a person to feel uncomfortable because the issue offends against their instinctively held values. At this stage, the individual has an intuitive knowledge of what their duty is. As Mabbott (1967: 45) argues:

> everyone knows what in any particular set of circumstances his duty is . . . I know my duty in each particular case and that I can give no reasons, nor are there any, why I should assert this act or that to be my duty, except the self-evidence of every particular instance.

In the stage of duty, a person knows what it is right to do but cannot say why. These people will often instinctively feel that redundancy is an unethical act. Their reaction to this issue may only involve making their feelings known, but it may extend to active opposition to the proposal under consideration.

Ethical convention

An issue is allocated to this category when particulars of its description suggest that it can best be resolved by applying conventional rules and norms to it. They may be social norms, laws, organisational policies, professional codes of ethics or schemes of arbitration and conciliation. A manager who has categorised an issue as a conventional one will seek to know from their organisation what is the policy or procedure to be used for dealing with it. If it is a question of redundancy, for example, they will want to know if there is any policy or joint agreement about compulsory redundancy or for the use of the criterion of 'last in, first out' and will be content to apply whatever rules the conventions provide.

Ethical puzzle

A puzzle is a conundrum, such as a mathematical teaser or a crossword puzzle, to which there is a technically correct or best answer. Arriving at the correct solution may be no easy matter, involving much hard thought and work, but the effort is justifiable because a best answer can be obtained. A puzzle can only exist in a clear moral context in which there is little argument about the values appropriate to its resolution. The wish to transform ethical difficulties into puzzles can be illustrated by those who argue that if only we had, for example in the NHS, better information (on clinical effectiveness, public views on medical priorities, costs and hospital activity rates) and better decision-making software to process the data, then questions of medical priorities could be settled technically, optimally, without recourse to messy political arguments about competing values in which the loudest arguer gets the most resources.

The most famous of the attempts to rationalise health-care priorities (by clarifying the values to be applied) was the Öregon experiment. This was a study that tried to put medical treatments into rank order, so that the health authority could decide where to draw the line between what it would and would not finance. Community meetings were called to elicit the priorities given to various categories of diseases and the various benefits that could be gained from medical intervention (Klein *et al.*, 1996: 110–11). The hope behind these methods was that the findings could be used to enable a more calculative approach to the determination of health priorities and budgets.

A decision to see an issue as a puzzle requires the puzzle solver to place the issue within a coherent moral framework and to ignore the demands of contrary values and perspectives. A puzzle-solving manager who has to decide who is to be made redundant will choose one criterion (for example length of service) and apply it, to the exclusion of others, when making their decision.

Ethical problems

A problem is a conundrum to which there is no optimum solution. It may be necessary to take action on a problem, but the action will not resolve the difficulty; a problem may be ameliorated or modified, but it is unlikely to be abolished. Problems are complicated entities that form, develop and disappear according to their own dynamics. An issue is likely to be categorised as a problem because it involves many different values and principles which, when taken in isolation, make perfect sense, but which, when taken together, fall into conflict. In these situations there has to be a debate between the differing conceptions of value and part of the difficulty, for people who see issues as ethical dilemmas, is to ensure that the arguments in the debate are conducted rigorously and fairly (Fischer, 1983; Thouless, 1953; Schreier and Groeber, 1996). Problems involve rhetoric as much as analysis. The reappearance of the same problems, in one form or another, on the agendas of meetings gives opportunities for rhetorical ploys to become well honed. The use of rhetorical figures such as 'hard' and 'soft' HRM in the continuous debates that managers have about balancing the need for downsizing with the equal requirement to empower staff is an example of the phenomenon.

Ethical dilemma

A dilemma is a perplexing state involving difficult or unpleasant choices. The choices presented by a dilemma are often unpleasant because they demand a choice between conventions. If the person decides to act according to one set of conventional norms or rules, then they will break another set of expectations. As conventions are social constructs, it follows that dilemmas are essentially social and political issues. Breaking out of a dilemma necessitates choosing to support one group, by accepting their rules and values, but annoying another group by offending against theirs. It is not unsurprising, therefore, that categorising an issue as a dilemma can lead to aporia, inaction and indecision.

Ethical cynicism and caprice

Cynicism emerges when ethical duty turns bitter. In the category of ethical sensitivity and action, a person tries to do what their conscience tells them is right. The cynical person, however, has given up on this aim and become, in the original definition of the word, like a surly dog. The cynic believes that all ethical issues will be resolved in ways that primarily meet the personal and private interests of those involved. Sometimes, the cynic thinks, it would be better to leave matters to capricious chance than to try and improve things. The cynics' aim, apart from maintaining their safely detached position, is to cast blame on those who are trying to deal with an issue. Some old satirical advice on how to behave in meetings, quoted by Citrine (1952: 231), illustrates the point. When in meetings:

- never accept office as it is easier to criticise than to do things;
- if asked to give your opinion, tell the Chairman you have nothing to say. After the meeting, tell everyone how things should be done;
- do nothing more than is absolutely necessary, but when others willingly and unselfishly use their ability to help matters along, howl that the meetings are run by a clique.

Managers are prone to become cynical, that is to say, they gripe about the situation but do nothing, when they have been through too many cycles of downsizing.

Ethical negotiation

Ethical negotiation is the process followed when someone is seeking to protect their self-interest (by keeping their head down and getting on with their work) by remaining ethically neutral, but find themselves caught between powerful groups with different views and values. Ethical negotiation is therefore a search for consensus or compromise between differing ethical positions. This category is not concerned with the rightness of a decision but with the correctness of the process used to arrive at it. Put another way, the transcendent morality of an action is ignored; only a broad acceptability of the action, as determined by voting, opinion polling, consensus seeking, deal cutting and negotiation, is required. Responding to opinion becomes more important than doing the right thing, which was a barb frequently thrown at the Labour Party during the 1997 election campaign as they responded to feedback from focus groups. This category involves defending oneself by responding to the demands of competing interest groups. In the case of redundancy decisions, a person thinking in this way will take great care to find the views of all the parties and assess their capacity to create problems for themselves. They will do what those with the greatest weight require them to do while keeping their own views private.

■ Transition between the ethical categories

The final element in Fig. 12.2 to be explained is the circular movement, represented by the arrows in the diagram, that connect the various categories of ethical issues. This suggests that the movement up the left-hand side of the diagram signifies an increasingly sophisticated and self-aware understanding of an ethical question. But as the understanding of an issue becomes ever more complex, and analysts become aware of the plurality and incommensurability of the values involved, they travel down the right-hand side of the diagram that is characterised by confusion and, eventually, abdication. (Incommensurability means that there are no objective grounds according to which one person's values can be measured or judged against another's. It is a post-modern or relativist philosophical position that denies the existence of eternally and universally true moral standards.) The top row of the diagram represents attempts to develop personal principles for dealing with ethical questions, but increasing complexity causes people to be less sanguine about the prospect of achieving ethical resolutions.

The circle of arrows in Fig. 12.2 represents one logical and dialectical movement through the eight categories of ethical perception. This is not the only possible route. People may move backwards, as well as forwards, around the circle or become stuck with a particular categorisation. Different dialectics may also come into play, which means that individuals move in different sequences from one category to another. However, results from a research instrument that has been developed to study people's perceptions of ethical issues (Fisher *et al.*, 1998) suggests that the route plotted in Fig. 12.2 is feasible. In particular, these preliminary results suggest that people can change their categorisation of a single issue over time as they think more about it, discuss it with others and become involved in arguments about it.

Moral reasoning

The process of ethical categorisation is important to moral and ethical reasoning because each category has its characteristic modes of thought and action. In this section, various approaches to moral reasoning are discussed. The most famous model of ethical reasoning was developed by Kohlberg (1969, 1984).

■ Kohlberg's model of moral reasoning

Kohlberg argued that a person can develop, over a long period, ever more robust ways of thinking about moral issues. Although an individual may become more sophisticated in their moral thinking, this does not mean that they cannot, on occasion, regress to earlier and cruder forms of thought. The theory is described here because it is frequently used in studies of organisational and managerial ethics (for example Mason and Mudrack, 1997 and Trevino and Youngblood, 1990) and it helps people to understand the varieties of moral reasoning available to them. It also underwrites an interesting technique, identified by Snell, that will be discussed later (Activity 12.4).

The model has three broad stages, pre-conventional, conventional and post-conventional. Each of these divides in turn into two substages. The model is shown in Fig. 12.3. A brief description will be given of each of the stages and they will be mapped on to the framework of ethical categorisation in Fig. 12.4.

The first approach to moral reasoning is one in which the agent guides their actions by a concern to maintain their peace of mind by avoiding punishment and retribution from those more powerful than themselves. At this level, people do what their bosses

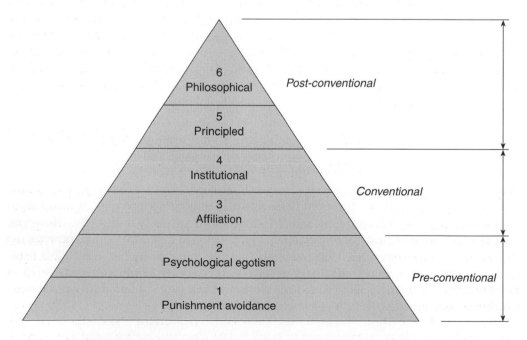

Fig. 12.3 Kohlberg's stages in the development of moral reasoning

want them to do because they are afraid of upsetting them. This form of reasoning is appropriate to the category of ethical negotiation. The next stage involves thinking about one's immediate self-interest. Ethical thinking takes the form of a series of calculations about what is best for the individual. It is a form of hedonism that is not concerned about others or about the long term. This form of thinking is appropriate to the ethical neutrality category.

With the third form of moral reasoning, social affiliation, the model moves into the conventional phase. At this stage, moral reasoning considers the expectations placed on an individual by friends, family, colleagues and neighbours. At its most banal, it is washing your car on a Sunday morning because that is what is expected in the nice, middle-class estate you live in. This form of thought is appropriate to the category of ethical awareness and action. Stage four in Kohlberg's model is adherence to the rules, regulations and laws of the society, associations and institutions of which one is a member. Ethical issues are resolved by following the rules. This style of moral reasoning is appropriate to ethical convention.

In the post-conventional phase, the forms of moral reasoning become more difficult to describe. Stage five is defined as principled because it involves the individual in thinking through, and determining for themselves, a set of principles that will guide their actions. However, these principles are set within a social context and often take the form of an implied social contract. A social contract is an unwritten agreement between members of a society to behave with reciprocal responsibility (Bullock and Stallybrass, 1977: 578). Some philosophers held that this contract existed before the state and so could form a basis on which the state (i.e. the conventional rules) could be challenged. This is the mode of thought that people bring to bear on ethical puzzles because treating an issue as a puzzle means determining which value, from a set of competing values, should be chosen and using it as a basis for solving the problem. At stage six, the emphasis is still on personally developed principles but at this philosophical stage the agent is developing universal principles based on notions of justice. People who reason at stage six may challenge conventional rules that break the higher requirements of justice. This can lead to the highest form of principled whistle blowing. Stage six thought is appropriate to issues that can be categorised as problems.

CASE STUDY 12.1

Whistleblowing: the Graham Pink case

Graham Pink was a senior charge nurse working the night shift in three hospital wards for elderly and ill patients. He came to the conclusion that staffing levels were not sufficient to provide proper nursing care. Based on the dossier of incidents he kept, he felt that the administration of drugs was an area of risk and that the needs of patients (relating to toileting, incontinence, terminal care and the care of the confused) were not being met. He complained about the situation to his managers and, when there was an inadequate response in which it was claimed that the situation was as good as it could be in the light of financial constraints and better than it was in comparable hospitals, he wrote to the chair of the health authority. Pink claimed that he was following the ethical code published by the UKCC (the body responsible for the professional registration of nurses), which requires nurses to make known any situation that threatens the quality of care given to patients. He started making his complaints to senior managers in the NHS and to politicians. But in most cases he either received no response or dismissive replies. He felt that his campaign was on behalf of all nurses who cared about patients and about proper professional standards. The pension he had from his previous career as a teacher, and the fact that he had no dependants or financial liabilities, made it possible for him to speak out where others might be more cautious.

After seven months of consideration, he went public by writing to the newspapers. He told one story to a local newspaper concerning a terminally ill man who could not be assisted because other patients had to be seen to first. Because there were not enough staff, the patient was left alone and crying, lying in a pool of urine. The name of the patient was not given to the paper, which published the story none the less. The patient's relatives recognised him as the man in the story and complained to the hospital that patient confidentiality (which is a very important principle in medical and nursing care) had been broken. Pink had not intended to break confidentiality, but he realised it was a danger when he involved the press. The risk was justified, he argued, because he was working for the interests of all patients and was seeking to prevent further human tragedy. He was suspended from duty for breaking nurse/patient confidentiality.

Pink had never been a union member. Concern for his propriety during his campaign caused him not to join a union because he did not want the issue to be seen as a political one. After being suspended he did join the union. There was a disciplinary hearing that found him guilty of various items of misconduct. The health authority, however, offered to retrain him and transfer him to a community nursing job. Pink refused this offer and went to appeal, which he lost. The case eventually went to an Industrial Tribunal and the health authority came to an out-of-court settlement with Pink.

Source: Lovell, 1992.

Activity 12.3

Use Kohlberg's model to identify the level of moral reasoning that you think Graham Pink was using:

1 Was Pink right to go to the press? How might this be justified in terms of Kohlberg's model?

2 Some employers have clauses in their employment contracts that prevent employees from discussing their employer's business with the media, or even with anyone outside of the organisation. What are the arguments for and against such clauses?

3 Would you consider Graham Pink to be a good role model or moral exemplar?

Kjonstad and Willmott (1995: 444) have identified hints in Kohlberg's work of the existence of two other stages. The first is stage 0, at which individuals do not see themselves as subjects capable of changing the world. When, at this stage, their view of a benign commonality of interest among people is challenged by the squabbles and conflicts of organisational life, cynicism is a frequent response. A seventh stage is also identified in which the individual loses the sense of being an observer and becomes one with the thing being observed. At this stage, ethical stances are governed by a sense of oneness with the world and by care and compassion for us/it. The nature of stage seven resonates with Kjonstad and Willmott's Buddhist beliefs and is a suitable form of moral reasoning for confronting ethical dilemmas. Only a search for universal oneness holds out the possibility of overcoming the deep oppositions that characterise the horns of a dilemma.

At this stage, a conflict between Kohlberg's model and the one presented in Figs 12.2 and 12.4 may have become apparent. Kohlberg's model is teleological (which means proceeding to a predetermined final purpose), because each stage is an improvement on the preceding one until the point is reached when the thinker has reached the highest level of ethical perfection and spiritual oneness. The model in Figs 12.2 and 12.4, however, is circular. In this model, as a person moves along the circumference of the circle into the right-hand side of the diagram, the categories of ethical issues become rebarbative, that is to say, irritating and repellent (because of the plurality of perspectives and values that have to be considered) and so they move first into uncertainty, second into cynicism and eventually into ethical abdication.

This can be expressed more formally. As the arrows progress down the right-hand side of the model, a reverse dialectic takes place. When a decision maker who views an issue as a problem looks at the relative simplicity of a puzzle-solving perspective, their disdain for its barbaric reductionism has an equal but opposite reaction and moves them into the state of confusion associated with ethical dilemmas. When, in turn, a dilemma perspective makes the ease of application of ethical conventions look naïve and illusory, the agent retreats into cynicism. At the next stage of the dialectic, the inactivity caused by cynicism is shamed by the perspective of ethical action (and particularly the freedom it gives to respond to the dictates of one's own conscience) and agents move into the ethical negotiation category which, by focusing on the process of decision making rather than on the rightness of the decision, provides a means of action while still accepting the cynics' belief that all action serves the interest of the powerful. And so the dialectic continues around the circle.

The tension between Kohlberg's model and the framework in Figs 12.2 and 12.4 can be explained in terms of a particular criticism that has been made of Kohlberg's work

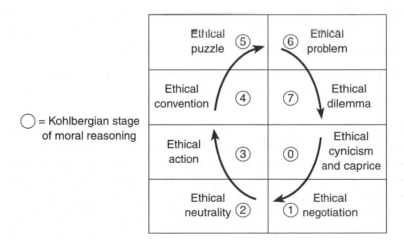

Fig. 12.4 Mapping Kohlberg's stages of moral reasoning on to the framework of ethical categorisation

(Fisher *et al.*, 1987). This challenges the model from a post-modernist perspective (which doubts whether we can derive from reason an authoritative and definitive moral code) by arguing that:

> the highest stages of ethical reasoning [should] entail a capacity for sophisticated relativism (a love for principled questioning and endless dialogue, along with the celebration of doubt and paradox, and a playful sense of irony), rather than the somewhat more dour Kohlbergian progressive liberalism, with its concern for universal justice, dignity and emancipation. (Snell, 1993: 20)

In response to these criticisms, Snell adapted Kohlberg's framework (at stages five and six) so that these stages are:

- less expressive of a personally developed ethical certainty;
- defined by ethical uncertainty and humility;
- concerned with constant self-questioning;
- challenges to the gaps between espoused values and those practised;
- based on rigorous self-reflection.

This interpretation of stage six in particular fits better than the original into the model in Fig. 12.4.

The choice between Kohlberg's framework, which implies a possibility of ethical advance and the creation of a universally valid ethic by a process of debate unfettered by power imbalances (Lovell, 1995: 70), and the post-modern version, which implies ethical struggle without any guarantee of improvement, must be an issue for everyone to wrestle with.

Thinking through ethical issues

In this section, three ways of improving our awareness of, and the quality of our analysis of, ethical issues will be considered. They are:

- raising levels of moral reasoning;
- understanding the roles of values and heuristics;
- understanding the role of codes of ethics and behaviour.

Raising levels of moral reasoning

Snell makes the intriguing suggestion that we should identify the Kohlbergian stage of moral reasoning that is causing difficulty in resolving an ethical issue and then move our thinking up through the stages of Kohlberg's hierarchy (Fig. 12.3) until a solution can be found (Snell, 1993: 62). An illustration is given in Activity 12.4.

Activity 12.4

Moving through the ethical levels

Jane was leaving the company restaurant after lunch and found that a college assignment for an MBA course had been left behind on a chair. She picked it up and saw it had been written by a managerial colleague who had been causing her difficulties by blocking a project that could prove very beneficial for the company. Jane read the assignment with increasing interest when she saw that it was angrily critical of the managing director (which is why it said on the cover 'Not to be distributed outside of Skegmouth College of HE'). Jane saw that this document could be of great value to her, but she was unsure how best to proceed. She could contact her colleague and offer to return the document in return for a little more support when the new projects committee next met, or she could let the managing director see it and discredit her colleague.

Jane was thinking about the problem at stage two in the Kohlberg model, self-interest, but she was stuck because she could not see along which route her best interest lay. The issue could only be resolved if she moved her thinking up one stage (at least). The next stage up is the affiliation stage, in which the disclosure rule is the main ethical guideline. This requires people to do only those things that they would admit doing to colleagues and friends. When Jane applied this rule, she decided to return the assignment anonymously to the colleague who had written it.

1 Do you think Jane was right?

2 Would it make a difference if Jane's proposal could save the company from collapse and the colleague's objection to it was based on personal dislike of Jane?

■ The role of values and heuristics

Much ethical thinking, especially at the conventional stage, is habitual and unselfconscious. Values play an important part at this level of thinking. They act as heuristics, tools for thinking, by helping to identify what is 'relevant' to an issue and what can be excluded. Once it has been adopted, a value can be used as a machete to cut through the thickets of moral confusion. In a study of resource allocation in the public sector, Fisher (1998) identified six value/heuristics (concerned with the proper ways of sharing out scarce resources) that people use to help them with difficult decisions. They are:

1 *Deservingness* – moral worthiness.

2 *Individual need* – assessments of individuals' needs in relation to the concept of a 'normal life'.

3 *Utility* – maximising contribution, maximising a function.

4 *Fairness* – equal opportunity and the application of arbitrary methods.

5 *Ecology* – minimising threats to the group and meeting the legitimate expectations of others.

6 *Personal satisfaction and gain.*

As was argued earlier, each category of ethical perception has its own characteristic ways of thinking. Different heuristics can be triggered by different categories. The ecology heuristic, for example, would be appropriate to ethical negotiation, and utility is often favoured by those who are thinking within a puzzle-solving perspective.

The workings of these heuristics can be illustrated by the process of deciding who should be made redundant when an organisation is shedding staff. Deservingness is the idea that people can be divided into the deserving and the undeserving. The latter can be identified by their unhelpfulness, their grumbling and the fact that whenever bad things happen to them it is normally their own fault. If this heuristic is being used to decide whom to make redundant, then the decision maker will reflect on the candidates' moral worth and make redundant those lowest on the scale. Individual need is a criterion that focuses on individuals and benefits those with greatest need. In the case of redundancy decisions, the younger members of staff, who have not yet established themselves in their careers and who have heavy family responsibilities, will be less likely to lose their job than the older staff members who have paid off their mortgages and have 'had a good innings'.

The heuristic of utility is concerned with maximising an objective. In an organisational setting, this is likely to be either minimising costs or maximising achievement against corporate objectives. In this case, the decision makers will ignore all information except the pay rates and work performances of the staff. Those who cost most and/or contribute least will be the ones who go. Fairness, as a heuristic, is blind to such considerations. Fairness is the requirement that all people are treated equally. The only fair way to decide who is to lose their jobs is to draw lots (or use some other arbitrary means), since this will give all staff the same probability of losing or keeping their jobs.

Ecology is a more complex heuristic. Stewart (1984) provides an interesting redundancy case study that uses this approach. She identified three groups who tried to influence the criterion for choosing who was to be made redundant. They were the senior management, the equal opportunities lobby and the trade unions. Under the operation of the ecology heuristic, the views of all the interested parties are sought and a decision is arrived at that meets the requirements of the most significant groups. In the UK, until recently, the criterion that met the wishes of two of the most significant groups, unions and management, was 'last in, first out' – LIFO. The final heuristic is personal satisfaction and gain. This may be no more than a wish to do a proper job. Many people, for example, might object to making the decision by lots because it would offend their belief about how such things should be settled. But it could be that private factors are involved, such as in a decision not to sack your partner's brother who happens to work in the organisation. Heuristics provide decision makers with a straightforward decision rule and in many cases they are adopted and applied as a matter of course. There can be occasions, however, when individuals have an internal conflict about which of the heuristics they should apply.

■ Ethical codes

Professional bodies and organisations may develop codes of practice that are, in part, designed to help members or employees resolve ethical difficulties. Examples of codes can be found on the World Wide Web site of the Center for the Study of Ethics in the Professions (1998). Texas Instruments' (1998) *Ethics Quick Test* is a particularly interesting example. The idea of professional ethical codes is an old one. The Hippocratic oath (MacLean Center for Clinical Medical Ethics, 1998) taken by medical doctors originated in ancient Greece. It is worth noting that only half of the medical schools in the UK require newly qualifying doctors to take the oath (Catholic Online, 1998). Codes of ethics perform an important function because they inform employees, or members of the professional body, of the minimum ethical standards expected of them and provide a basis for disciplinary action when someone contravenes the code. The bulk of the IPD (n.d.) code, for example, is given over to a description of its disciplinary procedures.

Codes can also be a resource that people bring into play to support their ethical arguments. The use of the Hippocratic oath as a rhetorical flourish in the arguments about euthanasia and abortion is an example (Catholic Online, 1998). Codes therefore can have a principled, post-conventional role, as well as a conventional regulatory role in ethical issues.

There is a strand of academic criticism of such codes arguing that they are of limited use because, in Kohlbergian terms, they restrain people from moving beyond stage three moral reasoning into post-conventional awareness. Kjonstad and Willmott (1995: 448–50) argue that codes:

- are restrictive rather than empowering, aimed at avoiding negative acts rather than promoting positive ones;
- are instructions that demand compliance rather than involvement and understanding;
- tend to be drafted by senior management and professionals and are composed in anodyne and commonsensical terms that imply no ethical challenge to staff. Staff's level of commitment to the codes is consequently low;
- provide people with an excuse for not thinking through ethical issues for themselves.

Lovell (1995: 71) argues that the ethical codes of professions 'are a defensive strategy necessary to assuage public fears that a state granted trade monopoly and self-governance will not be abused in favour of a profession's members'. In summary, it would seem that codes are a necessary, but not sufficient, requirement of ethical thought and action.

Conclusions

The tools for ethical analysis that have been reviewed are all aids to thinking; and ethical analysis is not the same as ethical action. An important factor, which mediates between thinking and action, is the culture or moral ethos, to use Snell's (1993: 70) term, of an organisation. Some organisations have a moral ethos that encourages a high level of ethical action and others have an ethos that discourages it.

There are a number of ways in which, it is suggested, organisations can improve their moral ethos. The first is to have forums and rigorous rules of debate that allow people, even when they are in a minority of one, to present their arguments. The idea of using the mechanisms of advocacy and debate as a means for evaluating policy options has a long pedigree in public-sector management (Fischer, 1983: 18). A linked suggestion is to increase the openness of organisational decision making to internal and external scrutiny; although in an age in which employment contracts often prohibit people from discussing organisational affairs with outsiders this would be difficult. A third method would be to provide training and development in organisational ethics. Some researchers have found that the more MBA-type management development managers have, the higher will be their propensity for corporate criminality (Daboub *et al.*, 1995). This suggests that ethical training has been neglected in most management development and that more effective ways of delivering it need to be identified and tested. Another suggestion (Donaldson, 1989: 189) is that organisations, or professional bodies, should find ways of preventing (legitimate) whistle blowers from suffering for their honesty.

The final suggestion often made is that organisations ought to be led by ethical leaders. Kanungo and Mendonca (1996: 35) argued that only altruistic organisational leaders can be effective. However, they (1996: 81) recognised that the socio-cultural forces in the western world favour egotism rather than altruism; and that this is not the best basis on which to create a strong moral ethos in organisations. Cornford's biting analysis of academic politics in Cambridge University (published in 1908) suggests that, although unethical behaviour is common, it may not be as deeply rooted as is usually supposed:

> The number of rogues is about equal to the number of men who always act honestly; and it is very small. The great majority would sooner behave honestly than not. The reason why they do not give way to this natural preference of humanity is that they are afraid that others will not; and others do not because they are afraid that *they* will not. Thus it comes about that behaviour which looks dishonest is fairly common, sincere dishonesty is about as rare as the courage to evoke good faith in your neighbours by showing that you trust them. (Cornford, 1908)

Ethical leadership would have to focus on creating an organisational moral ethos in which people would be less afraid and more likely to act ethically. On this view, codes of ethics will not produce ethical organisations. This can only be achieved by filling organisations with virtuous people (Solomon, 1993) who can use their moral judgement to decide what it is right to do. The relative roles of codes and judgement are explored in the following case study.

CASE STUDY 12.2

Reverse headhunting – Part I

A new activity, called reverse headhunting, is appearing in the recruitment consultancy industry. When a company decides that one of its employees is a square peg in a round hole, it asks a recruitment agency to find a new job for the ill-fitting employee. The employee is unaware this is happening until they receive a flattering phone call from the agency telling them that another company wants to employ them.

You work for a recruitment agency and one of your major clients, Fice plc, for which you do a great deal of bread-and-butter business of clerical and technical recruiting, has asked you to reverse headhunt for one of its senior managers, let's call him Tom. The HR people in Fice argue that reverse headhunting benefits everyone:

■ The person being reversed headhunted is offered a new job, probably at a higher salary, and probably avoids being made redundant by their original employer.

■ The employing company loses an employee who is not suitable and saves the substantial cost and hassle involved in the use of redundancy (not being able to recruit to exactly the same job description, for example).

■ The agency earns a fee from the company that is paying for the reverse redundancy and from the company that appoints the reverse headhunted person.

■ the recruiting company has a new member of staff.

Fice managers point out that the company works in a competitive marketplace and it is driven by the need to hit tough financial targets. To survive in this business environment and maintain the jobs of all its employees, the company needs to ensure that its management team is young and dynamic. The management wishes to avoid the downsizing that has characterised the company's recent history. The company is not so much dissatisfied with Tom's performance as of the opinion that a younger person would be better suited to the role. Tom is 55 and has been with the company for 15 years.

The recruitment industry association, of which your agency is a member, has a code of conduct that states that member companies must:

■ conduct their business professionally and lawfully;

■ declare potential conflicts of interest;

■ agree 'off-limits' rules with clients;

■ supply the client with a statement of the methods used to carry out the assignment;

■ maintain client and candidate confidentiality;

■ encourage equal opportunities.

Under this code, the agency would have to declare to any company thinking about employing Tom, in order to avoid a conflict of interests, that it was receiving a fee for reverse headhunting him. But the industry's code was not drafted with reverse headhunting in mind and there is nothing in it which suggests that it is improper. If you accept the commission, Fice would insist that Tom was not informed about what was happening. It sees it as a kind way of avoiding a redundancy situation.

You have to decide whether to accept the commission. On the one hand, you know perfectly well that if you do not accept it one of your competitors will. On the other hand, you have a balanced portfolio of clients and the loss of Fice as a client would not be a disaster.

Activity 12.5

1 What would you do and why?

2 Is the maximisation of profit the only proper goal for private organisations?

Reverse headhunting – Part II

Below are extracts from the IPD (n.d.) code of professional conduct.

IPD members:

4.1.4 must within their own or any client organisation and in whatever capacity they are working, seek to adopt in the most appropriate way, the most appropriate people management processes and structures to enable the organisation to best achieve its present and future objectives

4.1.5 must promote and themselves maintain fair and reasonable standards in the treatment of people who are operating within scope of their influence

4.1.7 must respect legitimate needs and requirements for confidentiality.

Source: Material provided by G. Franklin.

Activity 12.6

1 Assume that you are a member bound by this code. Would it help to decide on what, in the case-study situation, it is right to do?

2 Compare the usefulness of moral judgement and codes of conduct to the consideration of ethical questions at work.

In a chapter on ethics, it should not be unexpected if it ends with a sermon. Organisations will not become ethical by publishing codes of ethics or by appointing professional ethicists (Seedhouse, 1994). The idea of having official moralists in organisations is particularly unattractive (Seligman, 1997). As Elias Cannetti pointed out: 'The word "moralist" sounds like a perversion, one wouldn't be surprised at finding it suddenly in Krafft-Ebbing' (Gross, 1987: 197). (Krafft-Ebbing (1924) wrote the first clinical study of sexual deviancy in the nineteenth century and introduced the terms sadism and masochism.) Ethical organisations only emerge when they have members who are skilled at thinking morally for themselves and who are able to act on their thoughts.

Summary

In this chapter the following key points have been made:

■ Human resource managers and professionals face a range of ethical issues, both in their claimed role as ethical leaders in organisations and in carrying out their job roles.

■ How people think about ethical issues is affected by whether they categorise the issue as one requiring negotiation, cynicism, neutrality, awareness, knowledge of appropriate conventions, or as a puzzle, a problem, a dilemma.

- Differing categorisations of ethical issues can trigger the application of different levels of moral reasoning; or different value heuristics; or cause people to use professional and organisational codes in different ways.

- Ethical reasoning is not the same as ethical action and the extent to which the former guides the latter will, in part, depend on the level of moral ethos and ethical leadership in the organisation.

Discussion questions

1 Is the framework of ethical categorisation presented in Fig. 12.2 helpful in explaining your own reactions to ethical questions?

2 A circular route through the categories is suggested in Fig. 12.2. What other route through the categories could be suggested (could it, for example, be a zigzag or a ∩ rather than a 0)?

3 What arrangements could be put in place to ensure that whistle blowers do not always suffer for their honesty?

4 Is it possible to provide development and training that would improve the ethical level of behaviour in organisations, and if so, how?

5 Is ethical and/or altruistic leadership possible?

Further reading

Bowie and Duska (1990) is a good introductory book for the study of ethical issues in an organisational setting. It introduces the reader to the main jargon terms in a relatively painless way.

Connock and Johns (1996) is a useful introductory book on corporate ethics and ethical leadership in the context of human resource management.

Fisher (1998), in Chapter 2, provides more discussion of the role of value heuristics and provides some questionnaires from which you can assess your own value preferences.

Snell (1993) provides a very thought-provoking analysis of how to improve people's capacity for moral reasoning through management development approaches. The analysis of the idea of moral ethos is particularly valuable.

Solomon (1993) is an account of the virtues approach to organisational ethics, in which the relentless search for profits is replaced by organisations' role in helping staff develop their virtues and live the good life.

Part V

EMPLOYMENT RELATIONS

13
EMPLOYEE PARTICIPATION, INVOLVEMENT AND COMMUNICATION
John Leopold and Susan Kirk

14
CONFLICT AND CO-OPERATION IN EMPLOYMENT RELATIONS
Tony Watson, John Leopold and Kirsty Newsome

15
CONFLICT, CHANGE AND COMPROMISE
Comparative industrial relations and
the world automobile industry
Brian Towers

EMPLOYEE PARTICIPATION, INVOLVEMENT AND COMMUNICATION

John Leopold and Susan Kirk

OBJECTIVES

Having completed this chapter and its associated activities, readers should be able to:

- differentiate between industrial democracy, employee participation and employee involvement;

- explore different objectives held by managers, employees and trade unions, in terms of employee participation involvement;

- consider these in terms of a participation continuum;

- review movements in employee participation in terms of waves or cycles;

- examine forms of representative participation;

- review a number of forms of employee involvement;

- assess the potential impact of European Union policy and practice;

- show, through a case study, ways in which potentially conflicting objectives of participation and involvement schemes might be related to an organisation's overall human resourcing strategy.

Industrial democracy, employee participation and employee involvement

Hyman and Mason (1995) offer a clear differentiation between three approaches to the employment relationship, related to the radical, pluralist or unitarist frame of reference. Industrial democracy flows from the radical frame of reference and involves a profound reordering of work relations that would allow workers to secure access to control over the means of production. This approach focuses on democratic control of the organisation and, while current at various points earlier in the twentieth century, is a concept that has disintegrated as a set of ideas and practice. The term 'industrial democracy' is not to be confused with the approach adopted by British unions in the 1970s in advocating worker representation at board level through statutory rights (Bullock, 1977). This approach is an example of Hyman and Mason's pluralist-based employee participation, in that through the state, procedures are advocated or introduced to regulate potential conflict between employers and labour. It is state supported, union initiated, usually based on indirect participation of union (rather than employee) representatives in joint union management decision making such as for collective bargaining purposes or as part of works councils.

By contrast, employee involvement is seen as management initiated, attempting to secure the direct involvement of individual employees in various schemes designed to secure employee commitment, motivation and loyalty so as to contribute to the achievement of organisational goals and objectives. Unitarist in essence, this approach usually by-passes or ignores trade union presence and, while becoming the dominant approach in the 1980s and into the 1990s, can in some organisations be found sitting alongside forms of the employee participation approach (Hyman and Mason, 1995; Millward *et al.*, 1992).

The key points of contrast between employee involvement and employee participation are presented in Table 13.1. We will draw up these points of distinction as we examine in detail some of the possible institutional forms of employee participation and involvement. The essential point to establish is that the two approaches are distinct in their origin, advocacy and intended outcomes, and therefore we must avoid using the terms interdependently. The distinctions may be highlighted by considering the potential range of form of employee participation and involvement in terms of a participation continuum, as in Table 13.2.

By use of this continuum, we can differentiate clearly those institutional forms of participation and involvement that are management inspired or controlled, such as financial involvement or communication schemes, and those that are more likely to be workers and/or trade union inspired and controlled, such as collective bargaining or the election of worker directors.

Table 13.1 Employee involvement and participation compared

Employee involvement	Employee participation
Management inspired and controlled	Government or workforce inspired; some control delegated to workforce
Geared to stimulating individual employee contributions under strong market conditions	Aims to harness collective employee inputs through market regulation
Directed to responsibilities of individual employees	Collective representation
Management structures flatter, but hierarchies undisturbed	Management hierarchy chain broken
Employees often passive recipients	Employee representatives actively involved
Tends to be task based	Decision making at higher organisational levels
Assumes common interests between employer and employees	Plurality of interests recognised and machinery for their resolution provided
Aims to concentrate strategic influence among management	Aims to distribute strategic influence beyond management

Source: Hyman and Mason, 1995: 25.

Activity 13.1

Use Table 13.1 to relate to your experience of employee participation and involvement:

1 Which approach is currently dominant in an organisation known to you?

2 Offer specific examples to support your analysis.

Table 13.2 Employee participation and involvement continuum

Management inspired and controlled schemes ←						→ Worker/union inspired and controlled schemes	
No participation	Financial involvement	Communications	Employee involvement	Consultation	Collective bargaining	Worker representation on final decision-taking bodies	Self-management
Job roles	Profit sharing	Briefing groups	Job enlargement Quality circles	Joint consultative committee	Joint negotiating committee	Worker directors	Worker co-operatives

Within the continuum, there is an area where management and union aspirations overlap so that there are possibilities of areas of joint consultation and decision making. On the other hand, managers are unlikely to advocate or actively support worker self-management, while unions are unlikely to be comfortable with a management that insists that the organisation has no participation, or only forms that are totally management controlled.

Two other points of distinction will be explored throughout this chapter. The first is the distinction between direct involvement/participation of individual employees and of employees being represented indirectly by representatives. The other is the distinction between participation/involvement on task- or job-related issues, and business-related levels of decision making. First, it is necessary to trace the origins and trajectories of the various approaches.

◼ Waves or cycles?

Study of the movements in the incidence of various possible forms of employee participation and involvement has centred around the debate on whether fluctuations in the incidence of various forms is best characterised by the metaphor of cycles or waves. Ramsey (1977, 1983, 1990) is the main advocate of the theory that the incidence of employee participation moves in waves; in particular, that management is forced to introduce concessions of employee participation in periods when a strong, organised labour movement presents a challenge to management control, so that management can regain control by appearing to share it and incorporate the threat from trade unions. The converse of this argument is that when the pressure ebbs, so too does the practice of participation. The 'cycles approach' stands in contrast to the evolutionary view, which suggests that factors such as more educated employees, an erosion of deferential attitudes and managers being more willing to treat their staff as 'resourceful humans' mean that, from the 1970s, employee participation, and joint consultation in particular, are here to stay (Marchington, 1994).

Empirical evidence suggests that the incidence of forms of employee participation neither remains constant nor follows an even, onward and upward path. However, the precise nature of the ebbs and flows remains disputed between cycles (Poole, 1986; Ramsey, 1977), a ratchet movement (Brannen, 1983) and waves (Marchington, 1992). The waves metaphor allows for varying degrees of intensity in the incidence of particular forms of participation or involvement, for the movement to be differently paced and timed in different organisations and for the various forms to have separate rhythms. Marchington (1992) argues that the wave metaphor allows for management simultaneously supporting various forms of participation, even if the objectives of these initiatives contradict. The mix of institutional forms being practised in any organisation is related to managerial choice and organisational context, not just to broader movements in the relationship between employers and trade unions (Marchington *et al.*, 1993).

This in turn reminds us of a central point of this book, namely the creation and development of strategic human resourcing and the need to consider the broad goals being pursued and how the specific tools of employee participation and involvement might contribute to them. This cannot be done by considering management alone, but requires consideration of potential differences within management, as well as the interplay of tensions and commonalities between employees and unions.

We have already identified that in the 1970s indirect representation schemes such as joint consultation and moves towards worker directors were dominant (Hyman and Mason, 1995: 29–30). These debates were union led, but through the 1980s the focus shifted to management-led initiatives. Marchington (1995, 187) quotes a manager in a food factory who summarises the dynamics of the change in emphasis and position along the participation and involvement continuum: 'It's pushing negotiations down to consultation, and consultation down to communication.'

Now we will examine the use of representative participation within the workplace.

Representative participation

Joint consultative committees (JCCs) are the most commonly found form of representative participation where management and employee representatives, usually but not always trade union based, meet on a regular basis to discuss issues of mutual concern. JCCs have waxed and waned in terms of popularity, which can be interpreted in terms of cycles (Ramsey, 1977). In the 1960s, it was argued that they would fade away as workers would prefer to have issues pursued through strong shop steward organisations (Clegg, 1985). But JCCs went through a resurgence in the 1970s, before declining to being present in only 30 per cent of workplaces by the end of the 1980s (Millward *et al.*, 1992). This can be partially attributed to the fall in the number of larger workplaces, where they were more likely to be found. This finding was confirmed by the *1998 Workplace Employee Relations Survey*, which revealed that 28 per cent of workplaces had a JCC (Cully *et al.*, 1998). However, like other surveys, the WERS study showed that formal JCCs were more likely in unionised than non-union companies, in larger companies and in the public sector. This appears to confirm the duality of representative participation identified by Hyman and Mason (1995: 127) of formal approaches in large manufacturing companies and the public sector, but informal and loose structures in smaller organisations and the service sector.

Beyond the debate on the rise and fall of JCCs in practice is the question of the significance of those committees where they continue to exist. Marchington (1988) offers four models of joint consultative committees that might exist and these are presented in Table 13.3.

These alternatives are presented as ideal types, but they serve to stress that joint consultation is not monolithic and that it can vary between organisations as well as within the same organisation over time (Marchington, 1992, 1994).

Activity 13.2

1 Does the experience of organisations with which you are familiar fit into any of these ideal types?

2 If not, why not?

3 Has there been any attempt to change the focus of these JCCs in recent years?

Table 13.3 Models of consultation

	1 Non-union	2 Competitive	3 Adjunct	4 Marginalistic
Purpose	Prevent unions	Reduce union influence	Problem solving, co-operative	Symbolic, keep representatives busy
Subject matter	'Hard' and 'soft' information	'Hard', high-level information	'Hard', high-level information	'Soft' information and trivia
Representation	Employees Line or personnel manager	Shop stewards and other employees Line manager	Shop stewards Line manager	Union and non-union union representatives Personnel manager
Process	Educative Grievance procedure Chaired by management	Educative Advance information Chaired by management	Mutual influence Advance information Pre-meetings for reps Rotating chair	Fire-fighting
Levels/layers	Establishment level and no links	Establishment level and below	Multi-tiered clear links	Establishment level, no links

Source: Marchington, 1988.

Employee involvement

The change from employee participation to employee involvement highlights a number of points of contrast. As Hyman and Mason (1995) argue (*see* Table 13.1 on p. 341), there are different supporting mechanisms, trajectories and objectives underpinning employee participation and employee involvement. The objectives of management-initiated employee involvement include educating employees about the realities of the business; gaining employee commitment to corporate goals; developing employee contributions to increased efficiency; improving productivity and customer service. The term empowerment is sometimes used interchangeably with involvement. Wilkinson (1998) argues that empowerment should be applied properly to information sharing, upward problem solving, task autonomy, attitudinal shaping and self-management. What all these schemes have in common is that they are based on the unitarist frame of reference and 'take place within the context of a strict management agenda' (Wilkinson, 1998: 40). Marchington and Wilkinson (1996) identify four categories of employee involvement:

- downward communication;
- upward problem solving;
- task participation;
- financial involvement.

Each of these will be considered in turn.

Downward communication

The principle objective of such schemes is for managers to inform and educate employees directly so that they accept management plans. A variety of techniques are available that vary in their degree of formality/informality, their regularity and in whether they rely on oral or written communication, and whether they are face to face or indirect. They include formal written communication such as employee reports, house journals or company newspapers, videos and increasingly e-mail, informal and non-routinised communication between managers and their staff, formal team briefings based on a cascade system, and larger meetings of groups of employees, representing of all the employees in the organisation (IDS, 1997).

Townley (1994), drawing on a number of surveys conducted in the 1980s and early 1990s, reveals that while management uses a number of different methods of communication, oral rather than written methods of communication are preferred. Larger companies preferred management chain meetings with all employees and newsletters, whereas small and medium-sized companies were more likely to use face-to-face communication and staff meetings. The 1990 *Workplace Industrial Relations Survey* (Millward *et al.*, 1992) revealed that just under half of companies surveys used team briefing, while the ACAS survey of the same year found just over half, a figure that had risen to 61 per cent of workplaces in 1998 (Cully *et al.*, 1998: 10). Two further points are of note from this survey evidence. First, use of multiple channels of communication was more common in unionised than non-unionised workplaces, which suggests that unionised workers have greater opportunities to explore their views with management than do non-unionised workers (Gennard and Judge, 1997: 128). This view was confirmed by the TUC report on human resource management (1994). The second point is that while around half of organisations in surveys are using a mix of communication techniques, it also follows that half are not and that therefore the move to increase direct communication with employees is far from universal.

Moreover, reports on the operation of direct communication in practice, and team briefing in particular, indicate that there are a number of problems that may well inhibit the achievement of senior management objectives (Townley, 1994). Prime among these is the lack of commitment of middle managers to implement the briefing system, combined with a lack of appropriate skills to enable them to do this. Thus a device designed to demonstrate management dominance and control may in practice highlight weaknesses such as management incompetence or lack of commitment.

Team briefing also faces problems of maintaining regularity. It is often set aside to meet pressures of output or customer service, to maintain flows of relevant and detailed information to deal with changing staff working patterns. Managers also need to overcome deep-seated employee cynicism and suspicion (Townley, 1994). Attempts to resolve some of these problems include the use of 'communicators' to reach part-time staff at Sainsbury's and company intranets at ICL to update staff regularly (IDS, 1997).

Managers themselves may perceive the increased dissemination of information to subordinates as threatening and undermining (Marchington *et al.*, 1992). Finally, introduction of new downward communication schemes in a unionised organisation may be seen by the union as a threat and challenge to established means of communication through the union and its representatives. Attempts to go over the head of the union and communicate directly with employees can be met by union attempts to resist and undermine the new system. A more common response is for unions to improve their own communication network to their members, as a counter to any views that management is communicating through the briefing system.

■ Upward problem solving

The principal objective of participation schemes that come under this subheading is to permit management to draw on employees' knowledge of their jobs. This can be either at an individual level through attitude surveys or suggestion schemes, or at a group level through quality circles or total quality management (TQM). Marchington and Wilkinson (1996: 262) argue that these managers wish 'to increase the stock of ideas within the organisation, to encourage co-operative relations at work, and to legitimate change' and increasingly such schemes are part of an overall continuous improvement approach.

Survey evidence reveals that two-way communication systems are used in a minority of companies. Attitude surveys have a long history (Townley, 1994: 604), but WIRS 3 found that only 17 per cent of organisations used them (Millward *et al.*, 1992), while the ACAS (1991) survey on consultation and communication put the level at 31 per cent. A more recent survey confined to the South West of England found that less than a fifth of organisations used them (Tailby and Pearson, 1998). These same surveys found the use of suggestion schemes slightly higher (28 per cent, WIRS 3; 36 per cent ACAS, 37 per cent Tailby and Pearson, 1998). Although there is also evidence that larger organisations are more likely to use such schemes, they none the less remain a minority practice in British companies; indeed, their use is more likely in foreign-owned establishments (Townley, 1994: 605). One final point from this survey evidence is that unionised workplaces were more likely to utilise the full range of communication methods than non-union ones.

At first sight, this low usage of attitude surveys and suggestion schemes seem puzzling. There are a number of high-profile accounts of companies saving large sums of money from suggestions made and of employees receiving financial rewards for their suggestions. A UK Association of Suggestion Schemes survey found savings to companies of almost £40 million, including as much as £2.75 million at British Airways, and payments to employees of nearly £2 million (IDS, 1997). The IPM (1988) believed that in addition to the financial returns, there are also benefits in that the climate of employee relations can improve, as can two-way communications because employees feel that management is prepared to ask for their views. Finally, some organisations believe that knowledge of a successful suggestion scheme enhances their position with both customers and potential employees.

These schemes may not be so universal because in practice such formality may not be necessary in smaller organisations. But Marchington (1992: 185) has pointed out three drawbacks that may make organisations wary of adopting them. First, while some employees may feel good about the payout from the scheme, others may be resentful of the amount, or of the amount relative to the size of savings made. Second, supervisors may feel that their position is threatened or undermined by senior management going directly to employees rather than through the line. Finally, and this relates to other upward problem-solving approaches such as quality circles and TQM, why should some staff be specifically rewarded for good suggestions, when the alternative approach requires a constant search for continuous improvement by all staff?

Quality circles and total quality management

Quality circles and total quality management (TQM) may be considered together. Tuckman (1994, 1995) has pointed out that British companies' interest in quality management practices began in the late 1970s with some experimentation with quality circles, but by the mid-1980s, as these showed signs of failure, the focus shifted to TQM. Hill (1991: 15) accounts for the failure of quality circles in Britain primarily because they were implemented as a grafted-on technique and often without management training, whereas TQM was expected to have a greater potential for success precisely because it is total rather than partial.

Wilkinson *et al.* (1992) offer a framework to compare quality circles with TQM (Table 13.4).

Table 13.4 The differences between quality circles and TQM

Factor	Quality circles	TQM
Choice	Voluntary	Compulsory
Structure	Bolt on	Integrated quality system
Direction	Bottom up	Top down
Score	Within departments/units	Company wide
Aims	Employee relations improvements	Quality improvements

Source: Wilkinson *et al.*, 1992.

From this we can examine areas where the operation of quality circles may run into difficulties. Quality circles are groups of volunteers, usually between four and eight in number, who meet regularly to identify, analyse and solve job-related problems, generally under the guidance of a supervisor. They present their solutions for management to decide whether to implement them or not. Researchers (Collard and Dale, 1989; Hill, 1991) have identified two distinct, although related, management objectives for quality circles to enhance organisational performance and to improve employee relations. WIRS 3 (Millward *et al.*, 1992) found that only 5 per cent of manufacturing organisations operated quality circles, whereas the 1990 ACAS survey found them in 27 per cent of its sample (ACAS, 1991). The general view is that they grew rapidly in the mid-1980s, but then declined rapidly (Geary, 1994: 640; Gennard and Judge, 1997: 131). Even where they exist in an organisation, the number of employees actually participating is often fewer than 10 per cent of those eligible to join (Black and Ackers, 1988; Hill, 1991). Moreover, there is a clearly identified susceptibility of quality circles to fall into disuse over time; Bradley and Hill (1987: 73) found that only 20% per cent of circles were still in operation three years after the inception of the programme.

A number of reasons have been put forward to account for quality circles' lack of success. One major area concerns the position of management. Quality circles can threaten the position of middle managers and supervisors, partly because they are tackling problems that they might have been expected to identify and solve, partly because they change the relationship between the managers and the workforce in ways that they perceive as being 'soft' and because quality circles add to their workloads for comparatively small returns (Bradley and Hill, 1987: 75–6).

The evidence of the impact of quality circles on employees is mixed. Evidence from the USA suggests that involvement in them can have a positive impact on attitudes and performance (Griffin, 1988). This is supported by research in the UK (Webb, 1989: 23), but this and other research (Bradley and Hill, 1983: 303; Marchington and Parker, 1990: 199) suggests that any such improvement may not be sustained over time and that there can be differences between members and non-members of circles that can have an overall disadvantageous impact.

Quality circles can be perceived by unions as being a threat to their position, in that established working practices and agreements may be undermined by decisions of quality circles without reference to established procedures, or that employees will come to identify more closely with the employer to the detriment of the relationship with the union. In reviewing the evidence of the influence that unions can have over the success or failure of quality circles, Marchington (1992: 90) concludes:

> In situations where circles are an integral part of union-based EI schemes, unions may have little to fear from their introduction. Conversely, where quality circles are implemented in an attempt to reform industrial relations in a climate of mistrust, the end-result is likely to depend more upon the relative balance of power in the workplace.

Tuckman's (1994) analysis of the situation following the fizzling out of quality circles was that management turned to TQM because it appeared to offer a solution based on the notion of a *total* management system. Drawing on the contrasts in Table 13.4, TQM was to become everyone's concern and responsibility, not just the small minority who volunteered to participate; it would be company wide rather than confined to departments that opted in; and be led by senior management. The aim of the approach shifted from improving employee relations to improving quality in order for the organisation to remain competitive. In the later 1980s, these concepts spread from manufacturing to the service sector in the guise of customer care (Tuckman, 1995). In approaching this, however, TQM necessitated a workforce willingly co-operating in continuous improvement rather than merely complying with existing approaches and methods. Or, as Geary (1994: 643) put it:

> TQM places considerable emphasis on enlarging employees' responsibilities, reorganising work and increasing employees' involvement in problem-solving activities. The search for continuous improvement is the responsibility of all employees, management and manager

alike, and all functions. TQM requires quality to be 'built in' to the product and not 'inspected in' by a separate quality department. Where employees are not in direct contact with the organisation's customers they are encouraged to see their colleagues at successive stages of the production process as internal customers. Thus, a central part of TQM is the internalization of the rigours of the marketplace within the enterprise.

Marchington (1992: 93–5) distinguishes a 'hard' and 'soft' approach to TQM in practice. On the one hand are those advocates, following the 'excellence school of management', who call for open management styles, delegated responsibility and increased autonomy to staff. This 'soft' approach is contrasted with the 'hard' operations management view, which stresses measurement and arguably leads to less discretion for employees. The third, 'mixed' approach borrows from both the other approaches but in a unitarist fashion. Putting TQM into practice means balancing the production-oriented and employee relations-oriented elements which, as Marchington clearly identifies, means managing 'the tensions between, on the one hand, following clearly laid-down instructions while, on the other, encouraging employee influence over the management process' (Marchington, 1992: 94).

Work by Wilkinson et al. (1998) allows us to assess how these tensions have been played out in the 1990s, as the authors put it, between the promise of TQM and its principles of continuous improvement, or TQM as a slightly longer-lived management fad. The evidence appears to be mixed. Wilkinson et al. review a number of studies from the UK and the USA as well as presenting their own survey and case-study results. They conclude that TQM has become more widespread in both countries, is usually implemented in response to perceived competition, and represents an attempt to win and sustain competitive advantage. But 'whilst there is evidence of successful implementation with a significant impact an organisational performance, the results are disappointing for the proponents of TQM in a large number of cases' (Wilkinson et al., 1998: 86). Problems in implementing TQM included severe resource limitations, costs constraints, an emphasis on short-term goals, the impact of the reduction on staff morale and difficulties in the measurement of quality and lack of commitment within the organisation, including top management (Wilkinson et al., 1998: 181). There was, however, little evidence of union resistance to quality management despite the suspicions that unions may have about the implicit unitarism of TQM.

However, unitarism can give rise to contradictions. For example, TQM is based on high trust, building employee commitment to the need for service quality and continuous improvement, but in Wilkinson et al.'s food retailing case 'mystery shoppers' were used to check that predicted norms of customer care behaviour were being implemented. This low-trust compliance approach could backfire when set aside the commitment approach. The fundamental unresolved tension is between 'the call for empowerment and individual innovation on the one hand and the requirement for conformance to tight behavioural specifications on the other' (Wilkinson et al., 1998: 179).

Wilkinson et al. examine the views expressed by some (Hammer and Champy, 1994) that TQM is not capable of effecting the transformational change that is believed necessary to regain competitive advantage because it is based too much on incremental change. Thus TQM is seen as a fad whose time is gone and is being replaced by business process reengineering (BPR) and stretch management. Wilkinson et al. (1998: 188) dispute this view and suggest that 'while the high tide of the TQM movement may have receded, this does not mean that its impact has been negligible or insignificant; it has left its mark on British management'. But they do concede that TQM is often reinterpreted by managers who are reluctant to give up power and are driven by short-term considerations. Thus they suggest that what exists in the UK is partial quality management. BPR is also criticised as a management fad (Peltu, 1996) and indeed transformational or radical BPR has given way to revisionist BPR. But both BPR approaches and TQM exhibit the contradiction between employee empowerment and management control discussed above (Valentine and Knights, 1998).

■ Task participation

Task participation is a form of direct employee involvement in which employees are encouraged or expected to extend the range and type of tasks undertaken at work (Marchington and Wilkinson, 1996: 262). Here we consider three examples of task participation – job redesign, job enrichment and teamworking. Marchington (1992) identifies three separate, but potentially overlapping, reasons for employers introducing task participation: as a counter to work alienation; as an attempt to increase employee commitment; and as a contribution to competitive advantage. These three reasons may be linked to Buchanan's (1994) contention that historically there has been a periodisation of approaches to work design: scientific management (1900–50); quality of working life (1950–80); and high-performance work systems (1980–?).

Task participation as a counter to work alienation was in effect a reversal of scientific management and emphasised job redesign and job enrichment. While these approaches were meant to satisfy employee needs for more interesting and satisfying work, they also addressed management needs to reduce absenteeism and labour turnover and increase productivity. There is, however, a tension between satisfying employer and employee needs simultaneously (Kelly, 1982). Recent work in this area has highlighted management responses to a highly competitive and unpredictable operating environment, which has turned attention to ways of improving flexibility and performance through work and organisational design (Buchanan, 1994: 106), hence a greater emphasis on commitment and competitive advantage and less emphasis on the needs of workers.

The restructuring of jobs

Other methods designed to increase employee commitment within the workplace include job redesign and job-enrichment programmes. This work restructuring can range from horizontal job redesign to vertical job enrichment. The former involves only changes in what Goss (1994) called the *content* of the work, i.e. changes in the number or variety of operations that an individual performs at the same skill level (Marchington, 1992). It is task- rather than decision-based participation and can result in job-rotation programmes that do little to alleviate the stress and monotony of boring, repetitive jobs.

Job-enrichment schemes, on the other hand, may either offer employees' increased task responsibility or, more radically, are intended to alter the *form* of participation and provide workers with increased discretion over decision making. Derived from Herzberg's two-factor theory of motivation developed in the 1950s, this type of participation is also reflected in so-called 'empowerment' initiatives such as the 'Whatever it Takes' programme in Marriott Hotels, which sought to empower staff to satisfy customer needs (Lashley, 1997: 49–50).

Herzberg's work has been criticised in terms of the research methods employed but also methodologically on the grounds of psychological universalism (Hackman *et al.*, 1975). In other words, every employee may not share the need, for example, for increased responsibility within the workplace. In short, even though employers may find the notion of obtaining functional flexibility through multi-skilling beguiling, to some workers (and indeed managers) these types of programmes may be an increased source of stress and demotivation (Marchington, 1992: 113–14).

Team working

The concern about flexibility is reflected in the use of team working as the 1990s manifestation of job redesign. In its ultimate form it has been labelled high-performance work design (Buchanan, 1994) and involves a group of multi-capable workers who switch between tasks, organise and allocate work, and are responsible for all aspects of production, including quality. Buchanan (1994: 100) sees this approach as being quite different from the QWL (quality of working life) approaches of earlier decades, in that 'management motives are therefore strategic rather than operational, concerned with competition and customer satisfaction rather than with employment costs'.

As Geary (1994: 441) notes, team working is a term used in a variety of different ways, a unitarist rousing cry for all employees to work together, not least as forms of team working range from groups of individuals simply sharing skills and knowledge to more or less self-managing work units. He suggests that this latter, more sophisticated form is largely confined to a small number of well-publicised companies, many of which were originally established on greenfield sites, and indeed often incoming Japanese companies. (Geary, 1994: 642). Marchington (1992: 116) suggests that the chemicals and vehicle-production industries are the predominant location of team working in practice and cites a number of examples. These approaches require a heavy involvement in training, rotation of tasks, delegated responsibility for meeting production targets and a markedly changed role for supervisors. Buchanan (1994: 101—3) cites the example of the Digital Equipment Corporation plant in Ayr, where 'the high performance teams were clearly seen as fundamental to the plant's competitive strategy, and they were supported by extensive training, a re-definition and eventual elimination of the role of first line supervision, and changes to management structure and style'.

This may be due to the fact that team working can face similar problems to those in experienced job restructuring programmes. It can be stressful (Berggren, 1989; Black and Ackers, 1990) for workers and managers alike. In addition, it can be viewed by the workforce as an attempt to increase control over the labour process and intensify work (Parker and Slaughter, 1988).

■ Financial involvement

A number of different schemes exist aimed at linking part of an individual employee's rewards to the success of the unit and/or of the organisation as a whole. These include profit sharing, employee share-ownership schemes and ESOPS (employee share-ownership plans). These schemes have been encouraged by successive governments since 1978 and although there have been many changes in the detail, the essence of state support is through tax relief that benefits both the individual employee and the organisation offering the scheme.

There are a number of objectives behind the introduction of such schemes and, while these may be overlapping, they can also be competing and contradictory. Baddon *et al.* (1989), in a survey of 1000 companies and detailed case-study work in five organisations, discovered five main management objectives behind the introduction of profit-sharing and employee share-ownership schemes:

- encouraging the co-operation and involvement of all employees in improving the performance of the business;
- giving employees a sense of identification with the company;
- rewarding employees for past performance;
- generating a sense of business awareness among employees.

One rationale for management introduction of profit sharing not prevalent in Baddon *et al.*'s or other recent surveys, but found historically (Bristow, 1974; Ramsey, 1977), was a union deterrence motive. The Baddon *et al.* survey did show that financial involvement schemes were almost invariably introduced without negotiation or consultation with a trade union where one was recognised, but also that the union attitude towards them was one of 'bored hostility'. This was because they were not a threat to mainstream pay determination through collective bargaining but were seen as a bonus or an add-on. However, where financial participation is conceived as replacing or substituting part of normal pay, such as with profit-related pay, then union opposition is stronger (Duncan, 1988).

Perhaps one of the reasons that union opposition to financial involvement schemes is so muted is that, despite government facilitation and encouragement, the take-up has not been extensive. In Table 13.5 we can see the extent of these schemes.

Table 13.5 Use of Inland Revenue-approved profit-sharing and share-ownership schemes

April 1996	Schemes	Employees covered	Tax relief cost (£ million)
ADST	855	740 000	110
SAYE	1 305	610 000	270
Discretionary and company	4 486		
PRP	14 553	4 000 000 +	1.5 billion

Source: Inland Revenue Statistics, 1997.

A number of points can be made about these figures. First, after 20 years of tax relief, ADST (Approved Deferred Share Trust) and SAYE (Save as you Earn) schemes are not widespread. The 1998 WERS Survey confirmed this view, revealing that only 30 per cent of workplaces had any form of profit-sharing scheme for non-managerial employees and half of these had employee share-ownership schemes (Cully *et al.*, 1998: 10). The smaller number of employees interested in SAYE schemes suggests that the requirement of the employee to contribute some of their own money and to commit to a medium-term savings plan is a barrier to employees expressing their commitment to their employing organisation through purchasing shares in it. Indeed, the Baddon *et al.* (1989) study suggested that rather than share schemes being a vehicle for eliciting employee commitment, it was only already committed and loyal employees, personal finances permitting, who took up share schemes. Moreover, this was more likely to be white-collar workers and managers than blue-collar workers. In other words, those employees whom management would most like to build a commitment relationship with are the very ones who are least likely to take up financial involvement.

A second point is that the number of what were called discretionary or executive share-option schemes, but are now company share-option plans, vastly outweigh the all-employee ADST or SAYE schemes. In other words, while there may be some rhetoric about ending 'them and us' and building employee commitment and loyalty, the practice of most companies has been to offer share-option schemes to senior executives only. This may have been driven by the need to recruit and retain such staff and/or to establish a vehicle to encourage and reward short-term performance. Such schemes were criticised by the Greenbury Committee, which the government established to investigate the remuneration of directors and which recommended that profits should be taxed as income rather than as capital gains. This led to revisions to the tax status of these schemes – the 1996 Finance Act resulted in the creation of company share-option plans with less favourable tax relief than the previous scheme. However, they remain discretionary and most schemes in existence are still limited to senior executives. Two notable exceptions to this are the all-employee schemes at Asda and Kingfisher (IDS, 1998a).

Finally under this heading we must consider profit-related pay (PRP), although the tax relief on this scheme is due to be phased out by January 2000. Based on the ideas of Weitzman (1984) that postulated a link between aggregate levels of unemployment and variable pay, legislation in 1987 permitted and encouraged companies to introduce schemes that would convert part of existing guaranteed pay to variable pay. Thus, if the company was profitable, the payout would be more than would have been the case with conventional pay and tax, but if the company made a loss pay bills would be able to be reduced without necessarily losing jobs. In practice, however, most PRP schemes only related PRP to pay increases rather than total pay and its early impact, especially during the 1990/91 recession, was limited. However, there was an upsurge in the mid-1990s so that by March 1997 some 14 553 schemes were in existence, covering over four million employees. At this point the Conservative government announced that PRP schemes would be phased out as the cost of tax relief (£1.5 billion) was too great. The tax relief is due to end by January 2000 and some two years before this the majority of companies had not formulated a PRP exit strategy (IDS, 1998a: 2).

A final tax beneficial scheme, employee share-ownership plans, was introduced in 1989. These schemes permit the participation of employees in the ownership of companies; but use in Britain has largely been confined to the privatised bus industry (Pendleton, 1997). Even here, the subsequent takeover of these companies by larger companies has meant that employee owners have, like many non-employee owners, preferred capital gains to long-term ownership of the firm for which they work.

Impact of financial involvement

A number of studies have been conducted that have tried to assess the impact that the various forms of financial involvement have had. An early attempt, admittedly from two strong advocates of such schemes, was from Bell and Hanson (1984), who argued that financial involvement schemes are warmly welcomed by employees and that they are seen as 'good for the company and its employees'. While this research might suggest that such schemes do have an impact on employee commitment and loyalty, a number of other more detailed research studies cast doubt on this. Work by Baddon *et al.* (1989) reveals that profit sharing and employee share ownership are seen by employees in very instrumental ways. They conclude that:

> The benefits of most schemes are generally too small to have much prospect of making the kind of impact management would wish. The benefits tend not to be seen by employees as an essential element of pay which would generate commitment but are more typically regarded as 'just another kind of bonus'. (Baddon *et al.*, 1989: 274)

The emphasis on an instrumental approach is confirmed by other research. Poole and Jenkins (1990) conclude that the impact of profit sharing on company performance is likely to be minor, as both profits and share price are affected by a number of factors such as exchange rate movements or cost of materials that are beyond the day-to-day influence of employees. However, once a financial participation scheme is in place, failure to maintain the benefits may actually have an adverse impact on employee commitment and on employee perceptions of the competence of top management. Currently, management will have to be wary of the impact of the withdrawal of PRP schemes and need to find new ways of maintaining their economic value to employees.

A long-standing trade union objection to share ownership is that of 'double jeopardy', i.e. that employees should not have both their jobs and their capital tied up in the same company, because redundancies would lead to a loss of income and savings simultaneously. From the employees' perspective, two further potential drawbacks about financial participation exist. First, none of these schemes, with the exception perhaps of ESOPs, offers employees any increased participation in decision making. At best, they may elicit an orientation towards an appreciation of the marketplace and an understanding of business priorities as seen by top management, but they do not permit employees to exercise a voice in decision making, even in their role as share owners. Nor with many of the schemes is there a direct link between the scheme and the effort expected of the employee on a day-to-day basis, nor is the payout regular enough to act as a motivator. Other payment and motivation systems would be necessary to provide such links. Moreover, the existence of share-ownership schemes that focus on the parent plc may not sit comfortably with other involvement schemes that focus on the work team or the subsidiary company.

The spectre of Europe

A central theme of this chapter has been the marked shift along the participation continuum from worker/trade union-inspired and controlled schemes towards management-inspired and controlled schemes over the period from the 1970s to the

1990s. Our discussion of particular forms of employee participation and involvement has borne this out, revealing that a variety of forms, best described as employee involvement, are prevalent. The dominance of involvement mechanisms in the 1980s and 1990s has been assisted by enabling legislation (such as that for financial involvement); government exhortation (on flexibility and efficiency); through the example of inward investing industry, particularly Japanese and American; and because of the focus on competitive advantage through efficiency and quality.

However, throughout this period the spectre of Europe has haunted the former Conservative government and many British managers. The practice of employee participation in much of continental Europe – with worker directors, Work Councils and consultation, often with statutory backing, and attempts to generalise this throughout the European Union via Directives – has horrified both government and many managers in Britain (Burchill, 1997: 197; Department of Employment, 1989; Hyman and Mason, 1995: 30). Based on the employee participation approach, such measures and practice rub against the grain of experience and policy in Britain. Above all, the previous Conservative government and most British employers were opposed to the idea of legislation to require companies to adopt these practices. Rather, the Conservative government implemented legislation that deregulated the labour market, while at the same time weakening the position of trade unions. The government took a voluntarist approach to participation in an attempt to demonstrate to Europe that the statutory alternatives were neither required nor helpful in pursuing competitive advantage. At the same time, it blocked progress on measures under consideration in the European Union that might have enhanced worker and trade union rights. These included the draft Fifth Directive on employee directors, the Vredeling proposals on information and consultation in multinational companies, and the European Company Statute with its implication for employee participation. This policy culminated in the optout from the Social Chapter at the Maastricht agreement in 1991 (Hall, 1992).

However, in 1997 the newly elected Labour government reversed these policies and it has been agreed that the European Works Council Directive will be implemented in Britain by 15 December 1999. This Directive provides for a pan-European information and consultation system to be set up in all organisations with at least 1000 employees in the states covered by the Directive (the EU member states plus Iceland, Liechtenstein and Norway) and 150 employees in at least two of these countries. Affected companies had until 22 September 1996 to agree a customised system under Article 13 before the special negotiating body procedure laid down in the Directive took effect. Many British companies were in any case covered by the Directive, notwithstanding the previous government's optout, by virtue of their European Union subsidiaries. After the government opted in, some 130 British companies and a further 170 non-UK owned but UK-based companies now have a new date to agree a voluntary package. A further issue that companies have to consider is whether to include employees from eastern European states in anticipation of the widening of EU membership and coverage of the Directive (IDS, 1997).

Many British companies, such as BT, ICI and United Biscuits, had established voluntary agreements at an early stage (Cressey, 1998). By negotiating voluntary agreements, companies were able to influence the tone, approach and constitution of the European Works Councils. Management could seek to use it as a vehicle to project management plans, demonstrate management expertise and seek to elicit trade union and employee commitment to the espoused strategy. Moreover, through early agreement management could seek to influence whether worker representation would be employee, or trade union based, and whether any trade union representation would include full-time officials or be confined to lay representatives working in the company (Cressey, 1998; IDS, 1997). From the experience of the establishment of EWCs involving British firms, Marchington and Wilkinson (1995: 266) concluded that 'despite the generally negative response from employers and the Conservative government to these proposals, organisations which already have workable structures for multi-level consultative committees have little to fear from EWCs'.

Conclusion

In this chapter we have stressed the differences between employee participation and employee involvement and demonstrated the prevalence of employee involvement forms in the 1980s and 1990s. We have related this to a concern by management to elicit employee commitment and identification as part of an overall strategy to gain and retain competitive advantage. At the same time, we have shown that although employee involvement approaches may be dominant over employee participation ones, neither is a majority practice. In many cases, employee involvement initiatives are more likely to be found in foreign-owned companies and in large organisations, and by no means are the practices widespread and dominant. Indeed the 1998 WERS Survey discovered only three practices (employees working in formally designated teams, team briefing and performance appraisal) present in more than 50 per cent of workplaces and one of these, team working, fell to only 5 per cent when a more rigorous definition was used. (Cully *et al.*, 1998: 10–11).

We now turn to consider the extent to which the various forms of employee involvement and participation that we have identified and considered fit together, either with each other or with the organisation's overall human resourcing strategy. Wilkinson (1998: 50) argues that empowerment needs to be situated within the whole work environment within which it operates and not be an isolated initiative. Here we need to consider the extent to which various forms of employee involvement are merely management fads and fashions that come and go. We have already suggested that some approaches might be contradictory. For example, a share-ownership scheme that focuses on the parent company might not sit comfortably with a team-working initiative that focuses on the immediate work group. Similarly, a communications approach that emphasises line management's position and authority might not be compatible with a task participation approach that seeks to eliminate immediate supervision and emphasise autonomous work groups. At a higher level, there is a tension between the recent emphasis on an employee involvement approach and earlier approaches based on employee participation. This is often common in public-sector organisations, where union-based joint consultative committees operate alongside team briefing and other communication schemes based on direct involvement between management and employees.

McCabe and Wilkinson's (1998) account of TQM at Medbank offers an example of a

unitarist based employee involvement initiative failing, partly because of poor implementation, but more significantly due to its unitarist-vision not being shared by all staff,
nor even by all managers. Moreover, concurrent restructuring and consequent redundancies emphasised the contradiction between a unitarist TQM vision based on
customer service, and recessionary and competitive pressures forcing large-scale redundancies. Here the strategy behind the TQM initiative was overtaken and overwhelmed
by that of restructuring and redundancies.

Marchington *et al.* (1993) provide a useful device that allows us to make sense of the
dynamics of schemes and their interrelationship that we have explored in detail earlier
(*see* Fig. 13.1). In this, the dynamics of EI are graphically represented as a series of
waves, thus capturing the ebbs and flows of a particular technique over time and in
comparison with each other. This diagram can be replicated for any organisation.

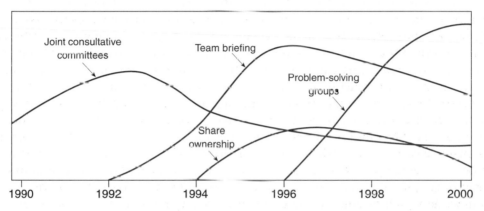

**Fig. 13.1 Movements of employee involvement and participation schemes within
an organisation over time**

Source: Adapted from Marchington *et al*; 1993.

Activity 13.3

Draw the equivalent diagram for an organisation with which you are familiar. Consider the
trajectories of each form and why they declined or continue to (co)exist.

It is also suggested by Marchington *et al.*, 1993, that the confused and confusing pattern that emerges can be further complicated by inter-departmental rivalries over the
ownership and objectives of particular initiatives. Figure 13.1 implies that there is no
guarantee of success for employee involvement initiatives. We have stressed that one of
their distinguishing features is that they are management led. Yet the practices we have
examined here suggest that employee involvement can fail or move into decline because
of the action of managers. The messages can be contradictory and competing, the penetration of the initiatives can be weak, and first-line managers, on whom much depends,
can feel threatened or by-passed by initiatives and may not actually implement them.
Moreover, there is evidence that the training of managers to implement schemes is often

inadequate and that when faced with the dilemma of spending time and money on developing initiatives and the rigours of meeting production or service demands, the latter take priority.

We have stressed that employee involvement is based on a unitarist view of the organisation; that there is an identity of interest between employee and employer. Yet many of the initiatives we have examined are designed to create the very commitment and identity that is presumed already to exist. Marchington (1995: 290), on the basis of a review of survey evidence, concludes that employees are attracted to the general concept of involvement and participation, but somewhat cynically points out that this is unremarkable since the alternative is an autocratic and non-communicative management style. But often, as we have shown above, their support is based on instrumentalism, a share bonus or time off monotonous work, rather than signs of commitment and loyalty. Many schemes, such as team briefing and quality circles, only involve a minority of employees for a minority of their working time and therefore their potential to transform the total employment relationship must be limited. That is why approaches such as TQM, which are intended to form an employment relationship rather than build on one, might be expected to be more successful (Hill, 1991). Even here, the evidence from Wilkinson *et al.* (1998) suggests that it is only partial quality management that is practised in the UK at the end of the 1990s.

The final point of contrast between participation and involvement is to consider the role and position of trade unionism. Participation is seen as being union led, whereas not only is involvement management led, it is often designed to undermine or by-pass union organisation (Kelly, 1988; Smith and Morton, 1993). The biggest threat to unions is that management may attempt to weaken collective bargaining, where unions effectively have a right of veto, to channel more issues through joint consultation and to increase direct communication to employees so as to reinforce the management message. On the other hand, union responses to some specific involvement initiatives have tended to be more in the 'bored hostility' camp than outright opposition.

While there is some evidence of non-union firms using a combination of employee involvement techniques to maintain a non-union presence, the survey evidence indicates that non-union firms as a whole are less likely than their union counterparts to operate them (Sisson, 1993). In many cases, employee involvement and collective bargaining run in parallel (Storey, 1992). A more recent trade union approach (Monks, 1998) is to take the rhetoric of employee involvement and turn it into a trade union demand for greater involvement in the management operation of the workplace. Combined with the window of opportunity offered by the European Works Council Directive, this may allow unions in workplaces in which they are still strong to put the employee participation approach back on the agenda. But for many employers operating in the 'black hole' of neither traditional industrial relations nor HRM, employee involvement is alien. Here we might let Marchington have the final say by repeating his words of 1995 (302):

> It could be argued that the haphazard, uneven and piecemeal way in which EI has been introduced into most employing organisations so far many not provide a fair indication of what it can achieve under a regime of 'soft' HRM.

Ragtime Textiles

Background

Ragtime Textiles is a subsidiary company of Fabrico plc, which manufactures lingerie, sports and swimwear on six sites concentrated in the East Midlands. Each of these sites employs approximately 200 people, with a further 25 at the head office in Nottingham. Eighty per cent of its business is with one customer, a major retailer. The organisational structure is very hierarchical. There are five directors in charge of the main functional areas. The managing director is in poor health and is considering early retirement. Relationships between senior management levels are strained and there is a sense of 'empire building'. Approximately 60 per cent of employees are members of the Hosiery and Knitwear Workers' Union. Machinists work in production lines and are paid on a piece-work scheme based on industry-wide negotiated rates, while office staff's salaries are determined by management on an individual basis. Issues covered by collective bargaining centred on pay and hours, despite unsuccessful attempts by the union to introduce wider issues. In 1988, a consultancy firm recommended lowering the piecework rates. This was done without negotiation or consultation and led to a five-day strike and a return to work on the old rates. In the offices it is common knowledge that no two people's wage packets are the same, even if they are carrying out identical tasks, and managers urge their subordinates to keep their salaries secret.

Participation and involvement schemes

Within Ragtime Textiles a joint consultative committee had operated since the mid-1970s. At this the production manager and personnel manager at each site met with union representatives to discuss issues around production, health and safety, and welfare. A JCC was meant to exist at each manufacturing site, but in practice only three of these still met and even then not on a regular basis. There was a high turnover of union stewards on some sites, which meant that their membership varied. On another site the production director did not see regular meetings as a high priority given the pressures of meeting the retailer's demands for high quality at a fixed price.

On two sites, under the influence of enthusiastic new personnel managers, a team-briefing system had been introduced. This was designed to convey company information to all employees, not just those who were union members, and was an attempt to gain employee commitment to the production changes necessary to meet customer demands. Team briefing had started in a blaze of glory, but after about 18 months had ground to a halt, largely because there was little enthusiasm from line managers and supervisors to implement it and because briefings took place in the evenings after work, with the result that employees were reluctant to stay long, if at all.

Being part of a larger plc, employees were part of a group profit-sharing scheme that paid out shares in the Fabrico plc. This scheme was based on the plc profits and had on two occasions in the recent past led to a bonus payout of £250 of shares, even though Ragtime Textiles was actually making a loss in those financial years. Ragtime is currently back in profit.

New relationships with customers

The production director had led the introduction of total quality management in the company. This was designed by senior management to bring about quality improvements that would reduce the percentage of garments rejected by the main customer. As part of this process, the number of inspectors on each site was reduced and machinists were given the responsibility for the quality of their own output. This system was introduced without any consultation through the JCCs where they existed, nor was it an issue communicated through the team-briefing system. Faced with the increased responsibility for quality, combined with pressure to increase output, many experienced machinists had left the company to work for rival firms. Replacement machinists were less experienced and after a number of months of operation the company had to reinstate the inspectors. During this period, relationships with the prime customer deteriorated as lead times and delivery of finished goods were unsatisfactory and the company complained of the difficulty of obtaining accurate information regarding the progress of their orders from the sales team.

In response to this, the newly appointed financial director, on the advice of a consultancy firm but contrary to the views of a significant number of line managers, decided to introduce a fully integrated, computerised business system. The financial director also decided that the best way to introduce this was through cross-functional task forces, project teams and user groups to design and implement changes to improve operating efficiency. Under this approach, machinists would be empowered to make changes to production and design to achieve the desired level of quality and output.

Activity 13.4

1 How has employee participation and employee involvement at Ragtime Textiles evolved? You might like to consider this in relation to Fig. 13.1.

2 Identify and account for the use of specific forms of participation and involvement related to the employee participation and employee involvement approaches summarised in Table 13.1.

3 What are the prospects of the financial director's approach to introducing change being accepted and implemented successfully?

4 What does this case tell us about the development of human resourcing strategies?

Summary

In this chapter the following key points have been made:

- A differentiation can be made between industrial democracy, employee participation and employee involvement.

- An employee participation and involvement continuum can be used to distinguish between those initiatives that are management led and those that are worker/union controlled.

- The changing form and content of employee involvement and participation in organisations can be explained in terms of cycle, ratchet or wave metaphors.

- During the 1980s to the 1990s, the dominant approaches in organisations have largely been management inspired and controlled.

- Managers have sought to use employee involvement techniques in an attempt to gain employee commitment to organisational goals.

- Legislation from the European Union, together with the more pro-European stance of the Labour government, may see a movement towards employee participation.

- Four models of joint consultative committee can be identified.

- Four main approaches of involvement can be seen: downward communication, upward problem solving, task participation and financial involvement.

- A framework can be used to understand the movement of particular forms of employee participation and involvement within an organisation over time, the relationship between different forms and between these and HR strategy.

Discussion questions

1 How would you differentiate between industrial democracy, employee participation and employee involvement?

2 In your view, which metaphor best describes movements in the incidence of forms of employee participation and involvement, waves or cycles?

3 Examine ways in which European Union policy and practice have influenced the policies of UK governments and/or the practices of UK companies.

Further reading

Employee participation, involvement and communication issues appear in most HRM and Industrial Relations textbooks. Appropriate references for specific topics have appeared in the text and are listed in the bibliography. Two key texts that address all the issues covered in this chapter are Hyman and Mason (1995) and Marchington (1992).

CONFLICT AND CO-OPERATION IN EMPLOYMENT RELATIONS

Tony Watson, John Leopold and Kirsty Newsome

OBJECTIVES

Having completed this chapter and its associated activities, readers should be able to:

- recognise that alongside the co-operative activities that managers have to bring about in work organisations, there will always and inevitably be conflicts and differences in interest;

- understand that conflicts in work organisations take a variety of forms – and that some aspects of conflict are more visible than others;

- appreciate that conflict is as much a phenomenon that has to be managed as is co-operation and that formalised arrangements like bargaining arrangements with trade unions are one possible facet of this;

- see some pattern in the changes that are occurring in employer–union relationships and note the strategic human resourcing options that relate to these;

- understand the nature of *new workplace regimes*, which combine a focus on the individual with new production concepts, and their route to achieving managerial control;

- observe that moves towards *indirect control* (and 'HRM-style practices') in new workplace regimes do not lead to the removing of conflicts and the dawning of an era of workplace consensus;

- analyse different and contradictory meanings of partnership in the employment relationship.

Introduction

Once upon a time, two young people sat in the waiting room outside the office of the chief executive of a business that they both hoped to join. They were applicants for the new post of human resource manager. Let us call them Unity Fairweather and Polly Politick. Both candidates had management studies qualifications and had worked for several years in human resourcing jobs. They were discussing how they would handle the question that they had been told would be put to them by the interviewers: 'How would you contribute to taking the business forward as the HR manager?'

Many of the issues that are to be addressed in this chapter are raised in the following dialogue, which one can imagine taking place between these two *reflective practitioners* (Schon, 1983) of human resource management.

ILLUSTRATION 14.1

Unity Fairweather The main thing I'll stress is the need to get everybody to 'sign on' to the business's key objectives. I know this isn't a simple matter, but I believe that if we clearly communicate to all employees what needs to be done to ensure a prosperous future for everybody then we really can move forward. Do you think that'll go down well, Polly?

Polly Politick Yes, I rather expect it will. It's the sort of thing the top managers who will be interviewing us like to hear.

UF Great. So you'll be saying something similar then, I take it.

PP Well, I have a bit of a dilemma there. It would probably put me in a good light with the interview panel. But I am not sure that it's a realistic way of thinking.

UF But surely it's very realistic. Don't you think that a key part of the top manager's job, supported and guided by HR experts, is to persuade people in an organisation that they are all in the same boat and need to pull together so that everybody gets what they want in the long run?

PP Oh, indeed. I agree that this is what you have to *try* to do. But I think that you are simply heading for disappointment, disillusion and failure if you convince yourself that you will ever achieve anything like this. You can only go so far. Managers must work at persuading people to 'pull together'. This is vital, because without co-operation between people there is no organisation, let alone a successful organisation. But what you have to come to terms with is that this 'pulling together' can only come about if you recognise that you are dealing with people who are bringing a whole lot of different needs, wants or interests to the workplace. To get them to co-operate, you have got to work all the time to persuade people with different interests to compromise. Conflicts are always there and . . .

UF Yes, I agree: conflict, conflict, conflict. But one of the reasons I want to change my job is because I am sick of all the conflict that I've put up with in my previous companies. It's sick. Don't you agree that we HR experts have got to find ways of getting rid of these artificial conflicts?

PP No, I don't, Unity. And I think I can put my finger on where we differ. You talk about these conflicts being artificial. I think that they are anything but artificial. They are real and inevitable.

At the most basic level, for example, the employer is trying to get the most they can out of their employees at the best cost they can achieve, while the employees, not unreasonably, want to get the most they can out of the job for the best return they can get.

UF Polly, this is so depressing. If it really is like that, then there's no point in having 'people experts' like you and me trying to make things better.

PP Oh, but there is, Unity. I shall talk in my interview about trying to makes things better, as you put it, but I shall make my pitch in terms of 'managing conflict' – not getting rid of it. I'm happy to use rhetoric like 'we are all in the same boat', but I'm not stupid enough to believe my own propaganda. When I try persuading the union people that we are all really on the same side, I am – in reality – trying to achieve a *management win*. I'm not daft enough to think that there really is no difference of interests between employers and employees. Our job is to get some co-operative work done, within the realistic recognition that underlying differences between people and between groups are regularly going to come back up to the surface and will continually need to be dealt with.

UF I see what you are getting at. I probably talk about the same things as you but in a different language. I like to talk about putting in place a strong and healthy culture that has clear and agreed values that people use to guide them in the right direction for the future of the business and for meeting their personal goals. I also talk about setting up effective appraisal systems and employee development schemes that enable business needs and personal aspirations to be matched.

PP I go along with that – up to a point, Unity. These culture and system things you talk about play a part in what I have called managing conflict. Perhaps you mean the same thing as I do when you talk about 'matching business needs and personal aspirations'. What I would say, though, is that you are never in any conclusive and settled way going to 'match' these different aims and wants. You get them to coincide as much as you can, to get things done. But things never settle. Management is not a matter of designing systems that sort everything out. It is a process whereby you are all the time negotiating and renegotiating compromises and achieving working agreements. Management is best seen as a process that . . .

With mention of this word 'process', we leave the discussion between Unity Fairweather and Polly Politick for the moment.

We might well infer that Polly Politick read Chapter 1 of the present book at some time in her studies of human resourcing. The emphasis there on looking at what goes on in managing and organising in *processual* rather than *systems* terms is clearly relevant to the concerns of the present chapter. But Polly Politick not only analyses organisational activities in processual terms. She also operates within what Fox (1966, 1974) calls a *pluralist* perspective – always taking into account the fact that there is a plurality of interests, goals, wants and priorities among the variety of people involved in any given organisation. And note that pluralism does not necessarily imply an equality of power among the plurality of interest groups (Fox, 1979). Unity Fairweather, in contrast, sees organisations and employment relations from what Fox calls a *unitary perspective*. This assumes the predominance of common interests and shared priorities across the organisation. Conflict is not an inevitable part of social life. It is pathological – a sickness to be cured, as Unity sees it. This perspective is one that the writers of the present chapter, along with Polly Politick, feel to be unrealistic. And it takes managers towards the danger to which Polly refers – that of believing their own propaganda. The wise manager, we could say, may well try to persuade people that they are all 'on the same side', to encourage them to act co-operatively. The foolish manager is the one who assumes that this is actually the way the world is or that something close to complete harmony is, in fact, achievable.

Activity 14.1

Briefly look back to Chapter 1 and remind yourself of the 'processual' way of thinking about human resource strategy making. Then come back to what Polly Politick is arguing and make a note of:

- things she says about employment relationships that have some of these 'processual' characteristics;

- things she says that indicate that she is working within a 'pluralist perspective'.

Whether we are focusing on human resource strategy making or on employment relations, the main advantage of looking at organisations as ongoing processes rather than as fixed systems is that it keeps us aware that nothing in organisational life ever settles into a steady state. Organisations are not big machines that when once designed and 'put in place' will smoothly and harmoniously harness human energies to meet a set of clear 'organisational objectives'. Many managers aspire to making their organisation into this kind of smoothly functioning, perfectly designed set of goal-fulfilling systems and subsystems. But this is not realistic. Organisations are made up of the activities of human beings – and every single one of these people (and every grouping of people) has their own interests, priorities or agenda. Also, organisations have to deal with numerous interests and pressures outside their boundaries. This means that there is continual adjustment, negotiation, balancing and rebalancing to ensure that sufficient productive co-operation comes about for the organisation to continue in existence.

The handling of conflict is central to these processes. But what do we mean by conflict? To answer this question we have to establish, first, that it is not simply the opposite of co-operation or an absence of co-operation. Conflict and co-operation are intimately related and typically co-exist. Once this point has been made, we can go on to look at the two-sided nature of conflict itself – its darker or less visible side and its more visible or overt side. Having noted the very varied ways in which conflicts manifest themselves in organisations, we will then concentrate on the management–union relationship as an area in which strategic human resourcing options exist with regard to managing co-operation–conflict issues. After this, we will look at some of the forms in which underlying conflicts continue to come to the surface in employing organisations adopting *new workplace regime* styles of human resourcing strategy. Finally, we consider notions of 'partnership' and their relationship to our understanding of the interplay between conflict and co-operation.

The interplay of conflict and co-operation

A processual view of organisational life is one that fully recognises the existence of differences of interest, value and orientation in organisations. It thus incorporates the insights of the 'pluralist perspective' on employment relations. In practical terms, it draws to our attention the continuous need for people to *manage their differences* so that they might co-operate sufficiently well to make it possible for them to stand any chance of achieving any of their different purposes. Conflict, we might say, is a facet of co-operation, and co-operation is a facet of conflict. To explain this apparent paradox, we can take the simple example of a football match. There is conflict – each side wants to win by getting more goals than the other. Yet for this conflict to occur, there has to be co-operation. This is not just about following the same set of rules. It involves such matters as turning up on time at the same venue. Here we could say that co-operation was a means to conflict being expressed (the teams co-operate to enable one of them to defeat the other). But we could equally well say that the conflict was a means to co-operation (the teams engage in a conflict in order to achieve the co-operative outcome of an entertaining football match). Indeed, the point is illustrated by the example of the World Cup qualifying match in Tallinn when Scotland was due to play Estonia, but Estonia did not turn up and the 'match' was abandoned after three seconds. There can be no conflict without co-operation.

Note that even in what might at first look like a historical case of out-and-out conflict – a world war – there has to be co-operation over rules about prisoners of war or about which weapons are acceptable and which are not. Each side presumably recognises that without some degree of co-operation, there would be no victory worth having. And this is precisely the case in the employment context. In even the bitterest dispute between a capitalist employer and unionised employees, for example, there has to be co-operation in the handling of that dispute. This is vital to avoid a situation where the employing organisation completely collapses, with the effect there is neither work for the employees nor profits for the employer.

This co-existence and, indeed, interplay of conflict and co-operation in the work situation is something we all experience every day. As a departmental manager, for example, one might come into conflict with the staff in the department over the amount or quality of work they are producing. It is in the manager's interest to get as much 'output' as possible within a wage bill that is kept as low as is reasonably possible. And it is in the interests of the staff to avoid coming under too much workload pressure while obtaining the best wage they can. There is clearly an underlying conflict of interest here. And co-operative activities of consultation and negotiation between managers and staff would be one way of dealing with this – one way of 'managing' this basic conflict of interest. This would be a fairly normal way of proceeding. But the interplay of conflict and co-operation might go beyond this, as we see in the Dogger Bank loans department case.

CASE STUDY 14.1

Conflict and co-operation in the Dogger Bank loans department – Part I

Bill Borrack was the manager of the department of the Dogger Bank that processed loan applications. Constant complaints were made in the bank about how long it was taking his staff to deal with applications and Bill was told that he had to do something about this. At the same time, the accountants were telling him that his salary costs were unreasonably high. Bill felt that to keep his job – and his annual performance-related bonus – he would have to push his staff harder. But as he was coming to recognise this, Sandy Gate, the staff's elected union representative, was developing a claim to management for a salary improvement. This was said to be about bringing pay up to what was seen as equivalent to that paid by competing local financial services providers. And there was also a claim for reduced hours. This was based on observations about increasing stress levels in the department.

After a number of fairly heated arguments between Bill and Sandy, and following a refusal by staff to do overtime at weekends, a crisis arose. The department developed a serious backlog of loan applications and Bill's annual appraisal review was approaching. The staff were increasingly unco-operative, both with managers and with other departments in the bank. Arguments and outbursts of ill temper became more and more frequent. A higher number of resignations than usual started to come Bill's way.

Bill had no idea how to proceed. He decided to telephone a member of the human resources department to seek advice about what to do.

Pause here in your reading and ask yourself what you might say to Bill if you were that HR person.

As it happened, the HR person concerned saw it as part of their job to keep informed about what was going on throughout the bank building and was aware of the frustration of the staff in the loans department. The suggestion was therefore made that Bill invite Sandy to help him form a 'working party' to examine how the work across the department was organised. This was an informal group whose brief excluded issues of pay or working hours. These would be dealt with in formal negotiations organised by the HR department and the trade union. The working party spoke to every member of the department about how they did their jobs and ended up recommending a team-based reorganisation of the department along lines that the staff themselves felt would be more efficient and, at the same time, more satisfying.

Following the reorganisation, the tensions reduced in the department. There were fewer arguments and complaints became a rarity. The goodwill that was created enabled Sandy to strike a very good bargain with the bank over pay – one that involved dropping the claim for reduced working hours.

Everything, Bill found himself boasting, was now sweetness and light.

What we see here is an increase or improvement in the co-operative work done in the bank's loan department. But it has arisen out of a pattern of conflict that was growing in the department. The case illustrates that we cannot straightforwardly see conflict as a 'bad thing' (as 'dysfunctional', in the social science jargon). It produced better outcomes for both the employer and the employees. The conflicts – given skilled conflict-management work by both managers and employee representatives – led to generally beneficial changes.

The 'sweetness and light' that Bill Borrack was so pleased about is something that we might expect to warm the heart of Unity Fairweather. In her terms, common objectives had come to be shared by everyone and new 'systems of working' had been put in place that ensured that those objectives continued to be fulfilled. Polly Politick, however, might see things a little differently. In her processual perspective, nothing is ever finally settled, you will remember. However effectively people at work might be persuaded to co-operate and might negotiate solutions to problems, underlying differences remain and conflict is always prone to return to the surface. Managing conflict, in Polly's terms, is an ongoing process. Differences between parties to the employment relationship are never resolved. They are simply handled better or worse at any given time. Let us return to the Dogger Bank loans department to see what occurred 12 months later.

Activity 14.2

Can you think of any situation (real or imagined) where conflicts, tensions or rivalries between individuals or groups have led to improved outcomes for all parties concerned?

CASE STUDY 14.1 (continued)

Conflict and co-operation in the Dogger Bank loans department – Part II

Twelve months after Bill Borrack had concluded that his problems were over and all was 'sweetness and light' in the Dogger Bank loans department, the staff put in a claim for a large salary rise. They argued that the department was so successful because they were working at a much higher skill level than previously and that this should be reflected in considerably enhanced pay levels. The bank's management argued in response that it could not afford such a rise because of the heavy competition for loans business that Dogger was experiencing. The trade union would not accept this and threatened strike action. The management at this stage, as part of a broader 'cost-reduction programme', made two of the staff in the department redundant. Bitterness increased. The quality of work fell. A backlog of work built up.

Bill did not know what to do. He telephoned the HR department . . .

In the processual way of looking at conflict and co-operation, these two facets of human existence and behaviour are constantly in dynamic tension. And part of this dynamic tension is understood as involving deeper or 'underlying' differences of interest 'rising to the surface'. To make sense of processes of conflict and co-operation in organisations, we need a framework that distinguishes between aspects of conflict, which can be said to exist at two levels.

Two levels of conflict and its variety of expressions

We often associate conflict with aggressive or argumentative *behaviour*. In terms of formal employment relations, we think of strikes and other forms of so-called industrial action. We would all readily label the bickering and arguing that occurred at the worst times in the bank loans department as 'conflict', as we would the staff's threat to go on strike in support of their pay claim. However, social scientists typically see these behaviours as just one facet of conflict – it is the overt or *manifest* face of conflict. Behind the visible face – the fight or argument we see going on – there is always some issue, some *difference* that exists between the protagonists. And this difference of interest does not necessarily lead to overt conflicts. It may stay buried or *latent* (where the two parties with different interests have not yet found an occasion to fall out overtly as a result of their different concerns). Or it might be handled or managed in a relatively peaceful way. To help us here, we can make a distinction between conflict at the level of interests and conflict at the level of behaviour (Table 14.1).

Table 14.1 Two levels at which conflict exists in employment relations

Conflict at the level of interests	Conflict at the level of behaviour
Exists where there is a difference between employer/managers and employees over desired outcomes – a difference that is not necessarily stated or immediately obvious	Exists where parties desiring different outcomes either: (a) directly and overtly clash over those differences and engage in open dispute, perhaps applying formal sanctions (such as one party stopping pay or locking people out or the other party going on strike); or (b) express their differences indirectly through such gestures as withdrawal of co-operation, generalised belligerence, destructive behaviour

Polly Politick expressed very clearly one of the most significant ways in which there is a conflict of interest at the heart of the employment relationship that is typical in the industrial capitalist type of economic and cultural order. She argued that:

> at the most basic level, the employer is trying to get the most they can out of their employees at the best cost they can achieve, while the employees, not unreasonably, want to get the most they can out of the job for the best return they can get.

Polly recognises that the economic system is set up this way: that there is the basic economic conflict of interest that exists between any buyer and seller (be they buyers or sellers of fish, bread or labour). In recognition that these conflicts are an inherent part of the way in which industrial capitalist society and economy is structured, Edwards (1986) provides us with the useful notion of *structured antagonism*. This conflict does not necessarily take a destructive form (although Marxist analysis suggests that, in the long run, it is bound to lead to the collapse of the economic order of which it is a part). We saw how, for example, the way the conflict was managed in the bank led to benefits for everyone concerned – for a certain period of time at least. But the banking case study also illustrates the other side of conflict represented in Table 14.1. The basic or underlying economic conflict of interest was expressed behaviourally in both the ways indicated on the right-hand side of the table. The 'industrial relations' dispute over pay and hours, the arguments between the manager and the union representative and the threat of 'industrial action' are all overt and direct manifestations of the conflict 'at the level of interest'. And the bickering, the unco-operative behaviour and the increased level of resignations from the department all illustrate how less obviously interest-based behaviours can be understood as related to such deeper differences.

If we think about the growing dissatisfaction that was developing in the loans department of the Dogger Bank as the staff came to believe that their higher performance warranted a higher level of pay, we can see the logic of their threatening to withdraw their labour. But further thought might suggest that the strike threat was only one way in which this grievance might have been expressed. If the staff had not been relatively well organised as union members – and if Sandy Gate had not been there to articulate their dissatisfactions – we might well have seen alternative expressions of the underlying conflict coming to the surface. It could have meant a return to the awkwardness and bickering of the year before. It might have meant an increased rate of resignations or more absenteeism. It could have led to staff's being less polite to customers or even to their sabotaging aspects of the loan operation. Yet again, it might have resulted in staff's slowing their work down by meticulously observing every detail of the official rules and procedures ('working to rule'). It could even have led to their refusing to comply fully with the Dogger Bank uniform requirements (a type of protest observed among airline cabin crew by Hochschild, 1983).

It has always been a key insight of industrial sociologists that underlying differences of interest or orientation between employers (or their managerial agents) and employees can be expressed in a range of interchangeable ways – including and going beyond those we have mentioned (Edwards and Scullion, 1982; Edwards and Whitson, 1989; Hyman, 1989; Turnbull and Sapsford, 1992; Watson, 1995b). This is an insight to which we will return later in the chapter, when we note evidence of employees adopting a range of conflict expressions within so-called new workplace regimes. For the moment, however, we should note that several of these types of behaviour often appear together, the one reinforcing the other. At other times, however, they may shift from one form to another – high absenteeism disappearing, for example, as a group of workers move towards taking more concerted, union-organised action to express dissatisfaction. And this example gives us some insight into the reasons for employers often choosing to set up institutionalised conflict-management procedures in the form of bargaining and consultative arrangements with trade unions. But such a strategic direction is not the only one open to employers, as we shall now see.

Strategic human resourcing options in management–union relations

One of the main ways in which employing organisations can manage conflicts and handle many of the potential differences that can arise between employer and employee has been through institutionalised arrangements of collective bargaining and consultation with trade unions. A key human resourcing strategic decision for the managers of any employing organisation is whether or not they are going to recognise, or continue to recognise, a trade union (or several unions) as a legitimate vehicle for the expression of employee interests. While ultimately this decision is for the management of each organisation to decide in the light of all the contingent factors influencing human resourcing strategy decisions identified in Chapter 1, the decision is likely to be framed by two critical factors in the macro environment. On the one hand, managers will be aware of the decline of union membership and representation in the two decades since the peak of union density in 1979 and of the consequent decline in the proportion of employees having their pay and conditions determined through collective bargaining. On the other, they need to operate in the context of statutory support given to union recognition by the proposals in *Fairness at Work* (DTI, 1998) and their subsequent implementation. We shall examine each of these contexts in turn.

■ Patterns of change in union membership, collective bargaining and strike activity

The overall position of union membership in the UK is set out in Table 14.2.

Table 14.2 Changing levels of union membership

Year	Unions	Number	Working population %	Employees in employment %
1979	453	13 289	50	57
1982	408	11 503	44	54
1987	330	10 475	37	49
1989	309	10 158	39	34
1992	268	9 048	36	32
1995	247	8 031	32	29
1996	245	7 938	31	28

Sources: Employment Gazette and Labour Force Trends (various).

The overall picture is that union membership has fallen dramatically since its peak in 1979, both in absolute terms and as a percentage of the working population. A number of competing explanations have been put forward to account for these dramatic changes – the impact of the business cycle (Disney, 1990); the changing composition of employment, with the loss of jobs in traditionally heavily unionised sectors of the economy and the growth of new jobs in traditionally less well-organised sectors (Millward and Stevens, 1986; Booth, 1989); changes in the legislation governing unions and their relations with employers (Freeman and Pelletier, 1990); the ways in which employers responded to the changed context by either pursing high-commitment policies or operating in an aggressive anti-union manner (Blyton and Turnbull, 1998); and ways in which unions sought to respond to continuing decline and the relative success or failure of approaches such as 'new realism', recruitment campaigns among hitherto weakly organised areas and mergers to remain viable organisations (Bassett, 1986; Mason and Bain, 1991; Willman, 1996).

Two important points need to be made about this analysis. First, the decline should not be attributed to any single cause, but rather to the interplay and interaction of all five (Metcalf, 1991). Second, in changed economic and political circumstances it may be possible for unions to exert greater influence on their position and therefore employers may need to assess the circumstances and context in which they respond to employee and union demands differently from those that might have prevailed in the 1980s and early 1990s. After all, 44 of the UK's largest firms continue to recognise and operate with trade unions. Moreover, the overall decline in trade union membership masks some continuing pockets of strength, notably in the public sector, in banking and among professional employees. Of course, the corollary of this is that there are areas of trade union weakness such as in small firms, in private services and among young workers. The WERS 1998 Survey (Cully *et al.*, 1998) revealed a strong association between management attitudes towards union membership and the presence of unions in the workplace. Where management was in favour of unions, nearly two-thirds of the workforce were members and unions were recognised in 94 per cent of these workplaces. But where management was opposed to unions only 7 per cent of the workforce were members and only 9 per cent of such workplaces had union recognition.

We also need to consider union membership from the employee's point of view. Kochan (1980) has provided a useful model to enable us to consider the line of thinking that most employees may go through in considering whether to join a trade union or not. This is presented in Fig. 14.1.

The first stage in the employee's consideration is how they perceive the work environment. If it is a well-paid job, in excellent working conditions, with supportive

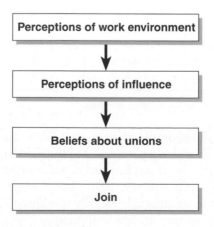

Fig. 14.1 Why individuals join unions

Source: Adapted from Kochan (1980): 144.

managers and prospects of career advancement, then individual employees may not feel any need to seek to change this state of affairs. On the other hand, if pay is absolutely or relatively poor, if physical working conditions are inadequate, if managers are authoritarian and oppressive and future prospects are limited, then the employee may see a need to do something about the situation. However, it is not automatic that this will lead to joining a union and seeking a collective solution to collective problems. In some circumstances, the employer may be known to be aggressively anti-union, or the situation may seem so desperate that a more immediate solution is sought. This is likely to be the individual one of seeking employment elsewhere rather than collectively seeking to improve the present employment. However, in some cases it may be perceived that unions might be able to negotiate changes, and certainly combined with union attempts at recruitment this may lead to workers joining and seeking recognition. But even at this stage, some employees may not support the principle of collective action and seek alternative solutions. At all of these stages in the process, employers may seek to intervene by unilaterally altering pay and conditions of employment, by changing management style or by making senior management's views about unions known. Similarly, unions may seek to influence this process by emphasising the areas where they believe they can positively influence outcomes. We will return to these considerations when reviewing strategic options later in this chapter, but first we go back to other changes to the environment that need to be borne in mind.

Related to the decline in trade union membership has been a decline in the coverage of collective bargaining and the decentralisation of the locus of bargaining where it continues to exist. Evidence from the third *Workplace Industrial Relations Survey* showed that the overall proportion of employees covered by collective bargaining fell from 71 per cent in 1984 to 54 per cent in 1990 (Millward *et al.*, 1992). This decline occurred in every sector of the economy, even in the highly unionised public sector where more groups of workers came under the remit of pay review bodies. National pay determination remains important in the public sector, but in most other parts of the economy where collective bargaining continues it has been decentralised from the multi-employer industry level to single-employer bargaining at either company or plant level. Jackson *et al.* (1993) relate these changes to a desire by employers to relate bargaining strategy to business strategy, and to link bargaining over market relations to bargaining over managerial relations.

A final change in the macro environment of employee relations of which managers may wish to take account has been the decline in an overt manifestation of conflict, namely strikes. In Table 14.3 we present figures on the UK's strike record since the end of the Second World War.

From this information it can be seen that the number of strikes has declined since the peak decade of the 1970s and especially in the 1990s. The numbers of workers involved and the number of working days lost have also fallen, but not as markedly as the number of strikes because these figures are influenced by large strikes that can affect the figures upwards and downwards. Thus the number of working days lost increased sharply in 1996 with large strikes in the railways, London Underground and the Royal Mail. Significantly, these were all in the public sector and it is here, where national pay determination has remained, that large national strikes have also remained a feature (Kessler and Bayliss, 1995). However, we should not conclude that the decline in strike

Table 14.3 The UK's strike record post WW2

Period	Number of strikes	Workers involved (000s)	Working days lost
1950–59	2119	663	3252
1960–69	2446	1357	3554
1970–79	2601	1615	12 870
1980–89	1129	1040	7213
1990–95	318	208	748

Source: *Employment Gazette* and *Labour Market* Trends (various).

activity should be equated with or indicative of a decline in industrial conflict, nor of the demise of trade union power (Blyton and Turnbull, 1998). As most commentators agree, both union and management negotiators have absorbed changes in the law regarding the conduct of strikes, especially those on balloting, into their practice (Kessler and Bayliss, 1995). Unions win the vast majority of pre-strike ballots, but in most cases strikes do not occur because further negotiations to reach a final settlement occur (Labour Research Department, 1993). The *1998 Workplace Employee Relations Survey* revealed that while, in the year preceding the survey, 7 per cent of workplaces had seen ballots of union members, in only 2 per cent of cases was there industrial action and in only half of these had that taken the form of a strike (Cully, *et al.*, 1998: 25). Thus Blyton and Turnbull (1998: 301) conclude that strikes may be viewed as a sign of union weakness, not strength, because a strong union is able to achieve a negotiated settlement through the *threat* of strike action backed by membership support in a ballot rather than actually conducting a strike.

One final point needs to be made about the decline of strikes in the UK. This has not been a uniquely British phenomenon and, notwithstanding the acknowledged difficulties of comparing like with like, the incidence of strikes fell considerably in almost all industrial countries. Indeed, it was only in the 1990s rather than the 1980s that the UK's position in any international league table changed to show relatively less incidence. Thus it is not possible to attribute the lessening of strikes in the UK solely, or even primarily, to changes in legislation under previous Conservative governments. Edwards (1995), for example, examines the interplay of five explanations for the decline in strike rates – economic conditions, the changing structure of employment, legal restrictions, improved means of dispute resolution and 'better industrial relations'. Like our examination of the reasons for union decline, it is safer to conclude that all of these factors played a part rather than to attribute monocausal explanations to any one of them. It is better to follow the conclusions of Blyton and Turnbull (1998: 303) that 'over the long run, strikes have tended to occur in waves' and that an analogy of a spiral can capture the interplay of continuity and change in the wavelike movements. In other parts of this chapter we examine ways in which industrial conflict might be manifested other than through the single measure of strikes.

Faced with demands from a trade union for recognition, managers may adopt one of three broad strategies:

1 They could agree to the principle of recognition and seek to negotiate a recognition

agreement with the trade union or trade unions that would establish the procedural parameters of the relationship.

2 They could seek to avoid employee demands for recognition by managing the employment relationship in such a way that employees feel no desire or need to seek union representation, but believe that the way the organisation is managed takes account of employee views and offers satisfactory rewards and working conditions that compare well in any comparison that may be made with similar organisations, whether unionised or not.

3 They could seek to avoid recognition at all costs and may operate in what has become known as the 'black hole' of neither high-commitment work practices nor traditional, pluralist industrial relations.

Let us examine each of these possibilities – or strategic options – in turn.

■ A union recognition strategic option

Recognition of one or more trade unions for collective bargaining implies that the employer is willing to reach joint agreements over certain areas of decision making about the employment relationship and that consequently these will no longer be areas of unilateral management decision making. Some might see this as a loss of management prerogative; others that joint decision making is more likely to be acceptable to employees and therefore more likely to be adhered to and operated in practice than decisions solely made by managers. We have already discussed various ways in which employees can resist management decisions that are perceived as being contrary to their interests. Although employers may be faced with demands for union recognition, the process of reaching agreement with the union(s) is likely to lead to a clarification and codification of a number of key issues. One would be the establishment of the bargaining unit – which group of employees is to be covered. Management may be willing to bargain over the pay and conditions of production workers, but not those of supervisors or support staff. The union may only have organised production workers and therefore only seek recognition for that group, or it may seek wider recognition covering all employees up to managerial grades.

Negotiations over recognition are also likely to confront a key issue that is seen by many managers to be at the heart of policy, that is, whether there will be more than one union or just a single union covering all the employees in the agreed bargaining unit. In the UK unions emerged as *trade* unions representing employees in particular trades and therefore their multiplicity in any workplace was the norm. In the 1960s and 1970s in particular, it was alleged that the multi-union nature of unionised workplaces caused particular difficulties for British managers, especially over demarcation disputes, that were not faced by managers in the then West Germany where a smaller number of industry-based unions had been created after the Second World War. In subsequent years, inward-investing companies that were prepared to recognise unions preferred to do so on a single-union basis or not at all. This was not an option for already unionised workplaces, but the 1990s saw moves towards the establishment of single-table bargaining, where all the recognised unions in an organisation negotiated common pay and conditions agreements together rather than a series of separate agreements (Gall, 1994).

The final area of decision making in a recognition agreement is over which issues are to be part of the substantive agreements, that is, which areas of decision making are to be subject to joint decision making. These are likely to include basic pay and conditions of employment such as hours of work and holidays, but when unions are strong they seek to extend the scope of collective bargaining into other areas such as pensions or training, whereas management might seek to restrict the areas covered when they feel that bargaining power is in their favour. Finally, a recognition agreement would also contain provisions for the resolution of disputes through conciliation or arbitration. Clauses would probably exclude the use of strikes or lockouts until these procedures had been exhausted, thus providing one of the key benefits to management of formal recognition – the avoidance of informal or wild-cat strikes while disputes are considered through the formal procedures.

In the event of statutory recognition rights, a parallel derecognition procedure would also exist that employers could follow. There is evidence of both derecognition and marginalisation of unions in the 1980s and 1990s. Gall and McKay (1994) estimate that 200 000 employees were affected by explicit derecognition strategies, but there is evidence of specific industries being greatly influenced by such an approach, for example provincial newspapers (Smith and Morton, 1990) and docks (Turnbull and Weston, 1993). It is important not to over-exaggerate the position, but Marchington and Wilkinson, (1996: 241) conclude that it 'seems to be a small but increasingly significant practice across Britain'. Some employers have sought to marginalise unions by reducing the numbers of shop stewards, reducing union organising facilities and increasing direct communication to individual employees and reducing the scope of collective bargaining. In both derecognition and marginalisation managers have to determine whether they are going to pursue a union-substitution or a union-avoidance policy, and we consider different possible approaches to this in the next section.

Activity 14.3

In the *Fairness at Work* white paper published by the British government in May 1998, the following proposals were made on union recognition:

Recognition should be granted where the union can demonstrate 50 per cent plus one membership among the proposed bargaining unit or where in a ballot 40 per cent of employees eligible to vote, vote for recognition.

- Recognition will cover pay, hours and holidays.
- The procedures will not apply to firms with 20 or fewer employees.

1 Find out the details of the final proposals which became legislation.

2 List the differences between the Act and the white paper.

3 Account for these differences.

Proposals were also made for derecognition procedures. Obtain a copy of the final procedures. Consider whether they could ever be implemented in a workplace with which you are familiar.

■ A substitution strategic option

Beaumont (1987) distinguishes between union substitution and union avoidance as approaches to staying or becoming non-union. In the context of union-substitution approaches, it might be useful to consider what unions have to offer employees and relate this to the chain of thought through which employees might go in deciding to join or not, which was discussed above. The implication is that if management can intervene to influence any of these decisions, then the outcome may be that employees do not perceive any need to join a union, as they do not believe that it would be able to improve the terms and condition of employment or the nature of the employment relationship.

Essentially, trade unions have three broad claims to make in order to attract employees into membership – that they can:

- improve pay and conditions of employment through the strength of collective bargaining;
- provide individual employees with 'insurance' and protection against arbitrary management decisions;
- provide membership services such as cheaper car insurance and holidays.

The vulnerabilities of unions are therefore that employers are leading payers and providers of good working conditions in an industry or geographic area, so that employees do not think that these can be improved substantially through collective bargaining. Employers could seek to provide alternative channels of 'employee voice' through such devices as open-door systems, employee-based Works Councils and individual-based employee-participation mechanisms (*see* Chapter 13), so that again employees do not feel that union channels of representation would significantly improve their situation at work. Finally, many alternative providers of membership services exist through other membership and commercial organisations, so that this is not likely to be the prime route into union membership for non-members (Whitston and Waddington, 1994). The essence of Beaumont's argument is therefore that employers can seek to introduce policies and practices that substitute for those that might follow from union membership and recognition. Employers can actively pursue such policies, and in Chapter 1 we have characterised such an approach as being a high-commitment indirect-control one. Beaumont (1987) refers to 'household name' non-union companies such as IBM, Marks & Spencer and Hewlett-Packard and they are presented as being distinctive from the traditional, sweatshop, non-union employer that we consider next. However, subsequent to Beaumont's analysis, even the employment relations practices of his 'household name' companies have come under fire as they have reduced employment levels and evidence has emerged that their purchasing power forces poor employment practices on to their small suppliers (Blyton and Turnbull, 1998: Chapter 9; Marchington and Wilkinson, 1996: 242–4). We examine this practice further in the Data-Cables case study on pages 382–4.

■ A 'black hole' strategic option

To the above categories of employer–employee relationships may be added the 'black hole' approach of operating with neither a high-commitment indirect-control approach nor industrial relations. The location of such an approach can be seen in Guest's (1995) fourfold classification of options for managing the employment relationship, as displayed in Fig 14.2.

Beardwell (1997) has researched the characteristics of companies operating in this sphere. While there is no direct union recognition and consequent collective bargaining, there is evidence of a wide variety of pay-determination mechanisms being used. The largest single category in his study was non-bargained collective pay rather than the emphasis on individualised pay that being non-union might at first sight imply. Moreover, there were companies in his study that derived their pay structures, either wholly or in part, from collective bargaining mechanisms in the industry to which the firm belonged. The main conclusion was that pay-settlement mechanisms were often unsystematic and this in turn reflected the absence of a clear overall strategy towards the management of the employment relationship. It is therefore no surprise to learn that not only did these firms lack unions, they also lacked personnel specialists, had patchy information flows and weak information channels. Or, as Brown (1994) put it, 'we are not witnessing the emergence of a brave new world of non-union HRM but a tired old world of unrepresented labour'.

HRM priority

	High	Low
High (IR priority)	**New realism** High emphasis on HRM and IR	**Traditional collectivism** Priority to IR without HRM
Low	**Individualised HRM** High priority to HRM No IR	**The black hole** No HRM No IR

Fig. 14.2 Options for managing the employment relationship identified by Guest

CASE STUDY 14.2

Union recognition in Kleensweep

Kleensweep is a UK-based company that distributes hardware goods and garden supplies to a chain of retail shops throughout the country. Up until now, the company has operated what might best be called a dual human resourcing strategy. The 50 staff at head office in the Midlands are relatively well paid compared to other companies in the distribution industry. Other terms and conditions are perceived as being good, including a non-contributory pension scheme, share options and open access to senior managers. Most of these staff have been with the company a long time and willingly work long hours, especially at times of peak seasonal demand.

The 100 distribution drivers based at 10 depots throughout the UK, on the other hand, are paid around the average for the industry, have quite high levels of turnover and work long overtime hours to supplement their low basic pay. The company has successfully resisted two attempts by the Transport and General Workers' Union (TGWU) to gain recognition for this group of employees.

Kleensweep has recently acquired a further distribution company in order to complete the national network of depots. This is likely to lead to redundancies in three areas where there is an overlap of depots, but potential expansion of employment in the South West of England and Scotland where the company only had a limited presence. The newly acquired company has a recognition agreement for drivers, although not for its head office staff. Although an annual wage agreement is negotiated, depot managers believe that less than half of the 60 drivers are members of the union.

Future policy

The board of directors has asked for an assessment of what the company's future policy on union recognition should be. They are particularly concerned about complying with new legislation on union recognition, but have an underlying preference to remain non-union as the parent company always has been. The board has asked for a report setting out three alternative strategies.

Strategy A

To adopt a hostile anti-union approach throughout the merged company and to derecognise the TGWU in the newly acquired company.

Strategy B

To seek to develop and extend the high-commitment approach adopted for head office staff, which has not led to any interest in union membership or demands for union recognition, to the rest of the company.

Strategy C

To consider extending union recognition in the company, given the inheritance of this among drivers in the newly acquired company. In reviewing the options here you should consider bargaining units, level and scope.

Activity 14.4

What do you see as the advantages and disadvantages of attempting to follow each of these possible strategic directions?

New workplace regimes and the suppression of conflict

Those arrangements that have been characterised as following a 'black hole' approach to managing employment relations are said not have an explicit or deliberate strategic focus to them. Nevertheless, they can still usefully be seen as a type of strategy – if we think of strategy in the processual sense discussed in Chapter 1, a pattern of activities that develops over time. This is indeed what has happened in 'black hole' organisations and we need to recognise that 'black holes' are unlikely simply to have emerged randomly and 'out of the blue'. In fact, many of their characteristics can be seen to be associated in some organisations with deliberate innovations involving practices that, at first sight, we would tend to associate with indirect-control/high-commitment strategic styles. The term *new workplace regimes* has emerged to characterise approaches that combine the 'HRM-style' focus on the individual efforts of employees (as opposed to dealing with labour collectively) with new production concepts such as just in Time (JIT), lean production and total quality management (Elger and Smith, 1994; Keeney and Florida, 1993; Legge, 1995).

It is vital to give these some consideration to the new workplace regimes because they remind us that indirect-control, high-commitment or 'HRM-style' practices – however 'progressive' or 'enlightened' they might appear to be – are still dedicated to achieving managerial *control*. Not only this, but they demonstrate that managerial choices between direct-control/high-commitment practices (and HRM-style innovations) and indirect-control/low-commitment approaches are not straightforward 'either/or' decisions. Certain employers are combining elements of the two; and this is being done in the context of competitive pressures on strategic direction. As Edwards and his colleagues observe: 'New forms of work organisation are being introduced throughout advanced capitalist countries and along with them goes a managerial emphasis on the point of production, as distinct from legal regulation or an industry-wide collective agreement, as the key site for generating competitive advantage' (Edwards *et al.*, 1995: 284).

How does all of this relate to our concern with conflict and co-operation? Various analyses of new workplace regimes suggest that they can be understood as attempts to contain, if not to deny, the opportunity for employees to display the more overt forms of conflict. These regimes can be viewed as attempts to camouflage the emergence of conflict by denying it legitimacy, coupled with managerial attempts to create a workplace apparatus concerned with harnessing employee contribution and reshaping notions of identity more directly into the competitive struggle of the organisation (Gee *et al.*, 1996). Indeed, it can be argued that the regimes provide employers with an unprecedented opportunity to reshape and recast battles over the frontier of control. Elger (1996) argues that new workplace regimes can best be seen as attempts by management to match the direct worker effort with the exigencies of production, whereby opportunities to question, and to participate, are drastically reduced.

We have to be careful not to imply that all of this is part of a fully deliberate strategic shift on the part of employers. The mechanics of workplace regulation are always complex and multi-faceted. Nevertheless, the impact of new workplace regimes has been such that the nature of work and working for many people may have changed, as we witness what has been referred to as a trend towards 'broadening the ideological remit of work' (Martinez Lucio and Simpson, 1992). Such a shift is bound to precipitate a change in the manifestations of conflict seen in workplaces, as employers seek to create an inclusive culture in which workers are prepared to offer that 'little bit more' in the cause of matching customer requirements, meeting competition and ensuring continued company survival. Many innovations, such as increased team working, continuous improvement schemes and quality awareness programmes, can be seen, in effect, as attempts directly to tie employee interests into those of the employer.

It is possible, then, that we may be witnessing some redefinition of expected workplace behaviours and employee contributions coupled with attempts to 'police' this work behaviour more closely (Geary, 1995). There is in fact increasing evidence pointing to an intensification of the work process within new workplace regimes. Much of the research regarding the impact of JIT innovations on the work process, for example, points to increased and intensified workloads prompting a significant invasion of the 'spaces for freedom' that workers find within the working day. Delbridge and Turnbull (1992), for example, exploring the impact of JIT, with its emphasis on the removal of idle capital and idle labour from the immediate work process, refer to this process as human resource maximisation based on the restriction of worker autonomy, discretion and democratic representation. The current prescriptive interest in 'lean production', sometimes characterised by critics as 'management by stress', tends to exaggerate claims of worker participation and involvement. More significantly, it involves increased workloads and intensified flexibility pressures alongside narrow job roles and increased stress levels (Babson, 1995; Parker and Slaughter, 1995). We return to lean production in Chapter 15 but, for the moment, note the tendency for opportunities for employees to resist managerial initiatives or to engage in direct conflict behaviours to be increasingly driven out – however legitimate they might be in basic human welfare terms.

The critical literature on these innovations not only notes the intensification of work efforts and the denial of channels for conflict expression, it also highlights the relative exposure of employees to increased levels of surveillance and monitoring. Some research evidence points to the 'Panoptic gaze' use of information systems (where people are constantly observed and checked on by what amounts to a set of managerial prison warders). Others speak of the power of the 'cult of the customer' and some researchers show how more direct surveillance can be accompanied by the use of assembly line and peer pressure. Sewell and Wilkinson (1992), for example, look at the traffic light system in a UK Japanese electronics plant, whereby operators who made incorrect insertions of equipment had their mistakes paraded to the rest of the factory through a series of traffic lights displaying the level of the misdemeanour. Research by Du Gay and Salaman (1992) points to the role of the customer in reinforcing managerial pressures and the monitoring of the work process. And other accounts note how workers' own perceptions of the customer and the perceived relationship between their own work effort and the meeting of customer demands acts as a particularly powerful disciplinary mechanism in the work process (Danford, 1997).

Studies of the growing number of telephone call centres provide pictures of white-collar workplaces that are highly monitored, tightly controlled and, additionally, demand a direct 'emotional engagement' with the work process and the satisfaction of customer demands (Taylor, 1998; Baldry *et al.*, 1998). The implication of all of this is that under new workplace regimes the opportunity to resist, to escape the demands of the work process, are increasingly denied. Consequently, the workplace becomes more exposed, accountable and quantifiable, with the impact of bringing a disciplinary gaze into the heart of the work process effectively limiting resistance and suppressing conflict. The emphasis is on cultivating compliance. The ambiguities and complexities that arise here are shown in the following research-based case study (Newsome, 1996).

CASE STUDY 14.3

Co-operation and conflict in Data-Cables

Data-Cables is a small cable and harness assembly supplier to a large multinational company, Photo-Tech, based in the South of England. It employs about 15 people, mainly women engaged in predominantly labour-intensive assembly work. The company has an annual turnover of approximately £900 000k and has supplied Photo-Tech with cables and harnesses for five years. It is not the only suppliers of these components. The value of this supply to Photo-Tech is £350 000k per year, representing 38 per cent of Data-Cables' total business. This figure highlights the crucial importance of ensuring a continued good relationship with the customer.

Conditions affecting the organisation of production

For Data-Cables, the relationship with Photo-Tech can be viewed as one of increasing domination and dependency and one that creates a precarious existence. It was highly apparent within Data-Cables that the continued survival of the company depended on maintaining effective supply relations with Photo-Tech , which had recently shifted to just-in-time production. The new supply relationship was thus predicated on factors other than purely price. As a result of Photo-Tech's shift to JIT production, it became imperative to ensure the reliability and dependability of Data-Cable's supply to Photo-Tech.

An additional response to the need to secure the continued supply relationship with Photo-Tech was a concern to be seen to offer something beyond reliability and dependability. This manifested itself as an attempt to 'entice' Photo-Tech with a supply relationship beyond the technical requirements of the product itself. The MD argued: 'We like to try to promote the idea of us as an extension to Photo-Tech's workshop . . . They used to make cables in-house, and now they put the cables out we are just part of their workshop. If you like, we just do the work for them and make sure that it is there for them on time . . . The advantage for them is that they have none of the hassle of buying bits, they don't have to make them and they don't have to control staff. It's cheaper for them in the end.'

Despite the apparent advantages this gave Photo-Tech in terms of being able to ensure the reliability of its supply from Data-Cables, it was acknowledged that this didn't give Data-Cables any bargaining strength in being able to influence the nature and terms of the supply relationship. This lack of bargaining power, coupled with the dependence on a continuation of supply relations, was compounded by an inability to object to changes in the nature of the demand for supply coming from Photo-Tech. The shift to JIT production within Photo-Tech was both chaotic and erratic; as a result, the call for goods from suppliers, including Data-Cables, was highly unpredictable. This unpredictable demand for cables from Photo-Tech came in a number of forms. A provisional schedule for supply was sent every two months and this covered the provisional requirement for that two-month period. Following this, the actual 'call-off' for goods required on this schedule came in every week. While this was meant to correspond to the provisional schedule, in many cases it bore very little resemblance to it. The 'call-off' could and often did differ dramatically from the provisional schedule. This schedule and weekly call-off could also be supplemented at any time by additional 'one-offs' that were not on either the schedule or indeed the 'call-off'.

The ability of Data-Cables to cope with these fluctuating requirements depended on a number of factors. First it was dependent on relations with its own suppliers which carried stock for it and, second, it was forced to stockpile components itself. Other options for coping with the unpredictable nature of demand involved what was referred to as 'juggling the work schedule'. Consequently, the use of overtime, often at very little notice, was commonplace. In certain circumstances the company was forced to employ agency staff to ensure that the product got to Photo-Tech in time. Ultimately, however, the whole of the work process was restructured in order to reduce lead times to ensure that the supply requirements of Photo-Tech could be satisfied almost immediately.

'The red card monitors the whole thing'

The precarious nature of Data-Cables' existence, allied to the unpredictable nature of the scheduling coming from Photo-Tech, inevitably led to changes in the organisation of work. The influence of and domination of supply relations at Photo-Tech were such that a completely separate workroom, an upstairs room with no natural light, was dedicated to producing the requirements of Photo-Tech. The allocation of work came directly from the scheduler at Photo-Tech. Once the requirement for a product came in, orders were transferred to a red card. Operators were required to fill in the red card with their name and the times when they started and finished the job. All the tools and cables were colour coded to correspond to the exact job, giving very little room for any misunderstanding of the precise requirements. The MD stated commented that 'the red card monitors the whole thing from the beginning to the end . . . the whole thing is controlled through a red card'.

The MD similarly recognised that the impact of the red card system emanating from the requirements of JIT was to push responsibility on to operators not only for quality, but also for dealing with, and reacting to, the unpredictable supply requirements. This sense of urgency in matching supply requirements was met with a corresponding increase in the intensity of the work process. 'What JIT is doing,' commented the MD, 'is making people responsible for their own job.' He explained his philosophy here: 'Once you are paid to do a job, you get a rate of pay per hour and I expect so much back. If you waste time, then you won't pay me the money back, will you?' And when the question was directly put to him of whether he was trying to 'get more out of people per hour', he responded: 'Correct, they have to be aware of what is wanted, where to get it all from, all the bits and pieces. Before, people made excuses. So you take away the excuses.'

This concern about balancing meeting the supply requirements to Photo-Tech on time with the security of jobs within Data-Cables was echoed by shopfloor workers. The direct relationship between individual workers' efforts and satisfying the supply requirements of a large, dominant multinational company was evident. As one operator argued, 'We work dinner hours and work through tea breaks. That was done last week. I worked through to get the cables out . . . I did hours of overtime just so they could get them up the road – so Photo-Tech's could get them . . . Once they phone up for an urgent job, everything has to run through properly at the same time.'

Using quality to smack people

Data-Cable workers also spoke of the ways in which they were made responsible for quality. Photo-Tech pressured the Data-Cables managers who, in turn, pressured the employees. 'If it goes out of here not right it is rejected,' explained one manager. 'The thing is that their quality knows what is going on. They can monitor us. We very rarely get a reject. It is our responsibility to make sure that what goes out here is right.'

In effect, the requirements of quality were used by management as a form of discipline at the heart of the employment relationship. 'I've used quality to smack people across the head with, putting it bluntly,' said the MD. The result for the women assemblers was that they operated within a climate of fear and apprehension and a feeling of increasing vulnerability and pressure.

'If a union came here they would ruin it all'

Despite the precarious nature of the company's existence, the intensification of the work process and rigorous quality procedures, any articulation of overt resistance or oppositional force within the organisation was limited. This was apparent with the very clear hostility towards the possibility of any union presence within the company. The management was vehemently anti-union, suggesting that was not an issue. Unions were spoken of as 'nothing but trouble'. This attitude was equally prevalent on the shopfloor. It was suggested that unions were not needed 'because we are all out for the same thing – we all want this firm to carry on and get better deals. After all, if they get better deals it is better for us.'

   There was a managerial perception that a union presence would directly hamper the workers' ability to get the product out to Photo-Tech. The direct relationship between workers' effort and satisfying external supply requirements would be, it seemed, polluted and violated by the influence of a union presence. A shopfloor worker endorsed such a view: 'I would imagine that if a union came here they would ruin it all, like working the half-hour lunch break, you can imagine the union coming here and saying, "Come on, you are entitled to that." Little things that we don't mind doing – they would come in and ruin . . . If somebody comes here with that sort of attitude, if you are on a rush job, Photo-Tech might want it tonight and you could do it by working your half-hour break . . . but if a union came here they would say, "No you are not working." If that job doesn't go out at the end of the day Photo-Tech could come along and say, "Sod that, we'll go and find somebody else to do it for us."'

Activity 14.5

1 In the light of the earlier analysis of the variety of ways in which conflicts of interest can be expressed in work organisations, what expressions of conflict might Data-Cables come to face in the longer run?

2 Consider the factors, both external and internal to Data-Cables, that operate to suppress these expressions of conflict.

Evidence of continuing conflict in new workplace regimes

In the Data-Cables case study we saw how management had cultivated the notion that the destiny of the predominantly female workforce was directly tied up with the destiny of the organisation and its ability to satisfy the supply requirements of Photo-Tech. This, together with the avoidance of trade union representation, helped suppress conflicts of interest between employer and employees. However, as Edwards *et al.* (1995) argue, new workplace regimes like that in Data-Cables may carry costs for employers, particularly when 'voice' mechanisms become closed off to employees. All sorts of costs could arise if the company found itself facing unanticipated problems of repressed discontent. And research on employment relationships in these restructured work organisations in increasingly providing evidence of conflict expressions. Thompson and Ackroyd (1995: 629) argue that, 'the essential conditions for resistance and misbehaviour are still present' and we need research that is sensitive to this, recognising that 'innovatory employee practices and informal organisation will continue to subvert managerial regimes'.

   This kind of sensitivity has perhaps been most notably absent from studies of Japanese enterprises in the UK. One exception is the study by Palmer (1996) of three Japanese manufacturing companies. This was concerned to shift emphasis away from providing descriptive accounts of the intentions and prescriptive possibilities of new management rhetorics to a consideration of *the actual outcome* of these initiatives. The research provides evidence of high levels of absenteeism and labour turnover in the three organisations, coupled with the emergence of a host of defiant shopfloor behaviours, such as writing graffiti on the toilet walls, showing reluctance to join voluntary groups and chatting about personal issues instead of focusing on work tasks. All these activities demonstrate the continuing interest of employees in pursuing their own agendas and not devoting themselves to those of the employer. In fact, managers in each of the companies were 'faced with unwanted and unforeseen outcomes of policy measures. Policies have had to be amended, either officially or informally, or in some cases reversed in order to discipline or placate the workforce' (Palmer, 1996: 141). Co-operation had to 'won back' out of conflict, we might say.

In a similar type of study of an allegedly archetypal 'HRM organisation', 'Phone Co', McKinlay and Taylor (1996) report on the introduction of new forms of working designed to harness worker commitment. 'Self-managed teams' were introduced with both a productive and an organisational function. Yet employees within an experimental team-working group found themselves in highly stressful situations, juggling responsibilities and training newcomers as well as appointing new recruits. Moreover, as the pressure to maintain production tightened and the work process intensified, the teams increasingly withdrew from their disciplinary, peer-review role. Consequently, management was forced to intervene, undermining any notion of worker autonomy and returning to more traditional direct control styles of managing.

Successful opposition to management pressures is also demonstrated in Stephenson's (1996) account of trade unionism in a Japanese transplant. In a way that contrasts with the relentlessness of the Data-Cables situation, she shows how the women workers at relatively high-skilled jobs were able to oppose the implementation of new working practices regarded as damaging to health and safety. Here the 'customer' organisation, in this case Nissan, rather than impeding worker resistance, gives these workers an additional bargaining tool: 'Ikeda workers recognised that the JIT relationship with Nissan increased their bargaining position as trade unionists' (Stephenson, 1995: 232). These manufacturing workers were relatively well placed to oppose aspects of managerial innovation, being relatively skilled and adept at organising themselves and bargaining with management as trade unionists. Alternative forms of resistance have to be sought, however, in some of the newer white-collar and service-based organisations.

Call centres are an increasingly common type of work organisation that fit this category. Taylor (1998) shows how, in spite of managerial attempts to monitor work performance and dictate the shape of employee/customer telephone interactions, employees still found ways to resist and create some 'escape' from the worst pressures of intensified work regimes. Employees were able to work out exactly when calls were monitored. Consequently, when they knew they weren't being watched, they were able to interact more 'naturally' with customers, in effect renegotiating the work process on their own terms. But when management was monitoring the interaction, the 'display' of the managerial-sanctioned patterns of interaction with customers was returned to. Employees were able to make distinctions between when it was appropriate to use the 'company personality' and when it was acceptable to use their own. Speaking as 'themselves' became a form of resistance (Taylor, 1998).

New workplace regimes, operating within a framework of contrived consensus, a team-working spirit, internal customer emphasis and quality awareness, can thus be viewed as attempts to obscure and deny access to differing and oppositional interest groups within organisations. We have seen, however, that there is evidence questioning just how effective this is. Nevertheless, questions have to be raised about what sort of pressures for future explosions of conflict on a bigger scale are being built up. Attempts to suppress particularly overt displays of conflict clearly do not negate its presence. Whatever ideological claims made be made for newer employment-management practices, the structured antagonisms of the employment relationship (Edwards, 1986) remain firmly intact. Indeed, to assume that employees are ever going to be fully satisfied with either the terms and conditions under which they 'sell their labour' or the resulting systems of workplace regulation to which they are subjected, and to assume that the interests of employees always coincide with the interests of their employers, is at best naïve and at worst entirely misleading.

Partnership as a way forward?

In this chapter we have sought to emphasise that managing the employment relationship involves both conflict and co-operation. Recently, there has been a resurgence in the use of 'partnership' to characterise the employment relationship. In this section of the chapter we analyse the use of this phrase. Partnership may relate to two sets of relationships within employment – between employer and employee, and between employer and trade union.

A notion of partnership based on the continental European model is put forward by the British Trades Union Congress (TUC). This offers a legitimate role by both governments and employers to trade unions as representatives of employees and their involvement in various institutional fora at the economy and workplace levels. Thus in a document tellingly entitled *Partnership for Progress*, the TUC argued that 'many British companies have recognised the full potential of this EU approach, for example by reaching voluntary agreements on information and consultation bodies in companies operating in this country and other Member States' (TUC, 1997: 21). The TUC's proposed partnership approach has four main prongs:

- employment security and new working practices;
- giving employees a voice in how the company is run;
- fair financial rewards;
- investment in training. (Monks, 1998: 176)

Claydon (1998) has traced the origins of the approach taken by the TUC to the 'new bargaining agenda' of the late 1980s and early 1990s. But he has also demonstrated that by and large this approach was not successful and, rather than entice employers into partnership agreements, the reality of this period was 'an acceleration in the pace of union derecognition since 1988 and its spread across a wider range of employment' (1998:

183). This partnership approach presumes that a bargaining agenda around areas of common concern can be found. The TUC believes that this will be over issues such as training, health and safety and equal opportunities. But Kelly (1996) believes that these three areas are also areas with 'serious conflicts of interest'. This was confirmed by the CBI's insistence that training should not be an automatic subject for collective bargaining following union recognition under the proposed statutory procedures. Moreover, the partnership approach implies that less weight is given to traditional adversarial approaches and issues. Yet significant survey research (Heery, 1996; Kelly and Kelly, 1991) reveals the continued existence of 'us and them' attitudes among employees and their expectations that their trade unions will challenge management on issues that concern them. If instead they move down the path of co-operative issues and agendas, then the membership may react against the incorporation that they fear may take place. Moreover, one of the common areas, health and safety, has been found by Waddington and Whitston (1996) to be the second most common area of grievances that members expected unions to pursue.

The notion of partnership, however, need not necessarily be mediated through trade unions and employers. The concept is also used to characterise the employer–employee relationship whether or not any unions are recognised in the workplace at all. As Beardwell (1998: 202) puts it, this notion of partnership is one 'constructed around the internal relationship within the firm without an external representative agency'. Such an approach has been discussed in Chapter 1 as the high-commitment/indirect-control one; and the ways in which managers have attempted to use forms of employee involvement to enhance employee integration, co-operation and contribution have been explored in Chapter 13. In Kochan's version of this model (Kochan *et al.*, 1986; Kochan, 1995), employees must give commitment, flexibility and loyalty to the organisation in order for it to gain and sustain economic performance. Kochan presents the relationship as one of mutual commitment, but Beardwell (1998) shows that in effect this turns out to be unity on terms defined by the employing firm.

In some presentations of 'partnership', the relationships between employers and employees and unions elide into a single approach. For example, a British government minister justified planned employment legislation as encouraging 'partnership between employer and employees', but at the same time he presented unions as 'partners in the workplace' (Unions 21 newsletter, 1998). But the emphasis in the government's partnership approach is on the relationship between workers and employers, rather than between unions and employers. Indeed, the Unions 21 interpretation of the white paper is that unions are not seen as a collective countervailing force against employers' power, but as the friends for individual workers to help them gain their individual rights (Unions 21, 1998).

Co-operation and partnership mask the tensions and conflict of the employment relationship. The British government's policy prescriptions, based on a mixed and potentially contradictory view of the nature of partnership, also fail to face up to the relationship between co-operation and conflict. By contrast, the approach adopted in this book emphasises the dual nature of the employment relationship, that it involves both co-operation and conflict, not in a polarised, alternative way but intertwined and interrelated. Thus attempts to deny conflict and assert co-operation would appear destined to failure.

Conclusion

Strategic human resourcing is an ongoing process that itself involves co-operative work by managers who may well have different and conflicting priorities and values. This was demonstrated in the O&V Joifel case study back in Chapter 1. But the strategy-making process then has to deal with the challenge of coming to terms with the multiplicity of potentially conflicting groups and individuals that make up the broader organisation. Ways have to found of managing differences and conflicts so that co-operative work can be done to a sufficient level to enable the organisation to continue healthily into the future. In this chapter we have demonstrated the necessity of analysing the events that occur in any specific organisation within a *processual* and *pluralist* framework. This is one that is sensitive both to the depth of the underlying conflicts that exist in workplaces and to the variety of ways in which these conflicts can be expressed or 'brought to the surface'.

We have also identified management–union institutionalised arrangements as one of the strategic options that may be followed to handle conflicts and differences, and this option is set alongside others. However, through reference to a series of research studies and through the use of our own research-based case study in Data-Cables, we have shown that conflicts and their expression in a variety of forms is something that cannot be denied or avoided – in spite of the adoption of newer 'HRM-style' innovations and the development of new workplace regimes.

Summary

In this chapter the following key points have been made:

- People tend to think about employment relations and organisational conflicts in one of two main ways. The first, associated here with Unity Fairweather, sees organisations as big systems that can be managed to achieve consensus and fully shared goals and priorities. This is a systems-based and unitary perspective. The second is a processual and pluralist perspective, argued for here by Polly Politick. This sees managing organisations, and human resourcing issues specifically, as a process of continually adjusting, adapting and changing to cope with the constant interplay of pressures towards co-operation and pressures towards conflict.

- Conflict and co-operation are not opposites. They always exist alongside each other and, indeed, feed off each other.

- Conflicts exist at two levels: at the level of interests and at the level of behaviour and activity.

- At the level of behaviour, underlying conflicts can be expressed in a wide variety of ways – these range from unco-operative behaviour or absenteeism to destructive behaviour or withdrawal of labour.

- Different expressions or manifestations of underlying conflicts are sometimes alternatives to each other (going on strike might replace working to rule, for example) or may reinforce each other (a strike threat might be reinforced by workplace belligerence).

- Trade union membership has declined markedly since 1979, but for an interplay of reasons rather than a single prime cause.

- The proportion of employees whose pay is determined through collective bargaining has also declined and the locus of bargaining has shifted from the industry to the single employer level.

- Various measures of strike activity have also declined, but this is a feature of many western capitalist economies and thus cannot be attributed to a UK-unique feature such as the Conservative government's legislation in the 1980s.

- The decline of strike activity is not to be equated with a decline in conflict in the employment relationship.

- Management–union arrangements represent one human resourcing strategic option relevant to conflict management. An alternative is a substitution approach (where management provides the benefits that union membership can give through other means, typically involving indirect-control/high-commitment practices). Another alternative is to allow a 'black hole' to persist – a relatively 'loose' strategy where there is neither a union–management relationship nor an attempt to build high-commitment relationships directly with employees as individuals.

- 'New workplace regimes' represent a growing development in human resourcing strategies. They combine innovations in work organisation with elements of indirect managerial control. Research demonstrates that these developments in no way lead to the ending of conflicts inherent in employment relations. Investigations also show that attempts to *suppress* conflicts by the adoption of such regimes cannot be wholly successful. In fact, in the long run, they may lead to a dangerous bottling up of dissatisfactions and antagonisms.

- 'Partnership' as a model of the employment relationship is shown to have a variety of meanings and be problematic.

Discussion questions

1 Which perspective is the more 'realistic' about life in work organisations and management – that held by Unity Fairweather or that of Polly Politick? Consider this in the light of what you have personally seen in organisational contexts (including what you might have seen in your school, college or university).

2 How many of the manifestations of conflict in the workplace identified in this chapter have you observed yourself?

3 Think about the typical way in which we tend to hear or read about managerial innovations of the type characterised here as 'new workplace regimes'. How does the type of research-based account we give here compare to the normal stories that we are told?

4 Consider the extent to which 'new workplace regimes' may contain unanticipated costs for employers, particularly when 'voice' mechanisms become closed off to employees (Edwards *et al.*, 1995).

5 To what extent does the fall in strike activity and the adoption of new managerial employment relations strategies mean that there will be a 'build up of steam' in the employment world which, sooner or later, will burst out?

6 What does the notion of 'partnership' mean to you? Is there any evidence of any of the meanings of partnership being practised in a workplace with which you are familiar?

Further reading

For a fuller discussion of conflict, readers are advised to consult Watson (1995b). Edwards (1986) provides both a critique of the Marxist analysis of conflict and an exposition based on a materialist analysis of the employment relationship.

Excellent coverage of issues such as union membership, recognition, collective bargaining and conflict is to be found in Blyton and Turnbull (1998). You could also usefully consult Kessler and Bayliss (1998).

For a consideration of the debate around new workplace regimes, see Thompson and Ackroyd (1995). Many of the issues explored in this chapter are also considered in Ackers *et al.*, (1996).

CONFLICT, CHANGE AND COMPROMISE

Comparative industrial relations and the world automobile industry

Brian Towers

OBJECTIVES

Having completed this chapter and its associated activities, readers should be able to:

- understand the relationship between industrial relations as a practical activity and the assumptions of industrial relations as a field of study;

- have a clear view of the nature of collective bargaining as the central institution in the practice and study of industrial relations, including the explanations and implications of its global decline;

- be able to discuss the purposes, value and limitations of comparative industrial relations;

- see the significance of the automobile industry as an illustrative case study of the value of sectoral, cross-country research in explaining global developments in work, employment and personnel practices.

Introduction

This book is a management text dedicated specifically to that specialism known as human resource management (HRM). The interest in HRM, both as an academic field of study and as a label attached to a practical management activity or set of activities, has grown mightily over the past 20 years. It has not yet eclipsed, but has certainly diminished or partially absorbed, the older academic interest in the practice of industrial relations as well as the study of the long-established management function of personnel management. This is largely explained by the decline of trade unions and contraction of collective bargaining and has meant that industrial relations academics – aside from their somewhat excessive, even dark, preoccupation with measuring and explaining decline – have tended to convert their interests (and job titles!) to HRM. Practitioners have also been busy with conversion, many becoming human resource managers, although interestingly the Institute of Personnel and Development has resisted the revolution in titles – unlike many of its members. Yet despite these changes and transformations, this chapter, apparently perversely, keeps resolutely to the industrial relations road. This course needs some justification.

Although industrial relations, expressed in the data of trade union membership and the coverage of collective bargaining, has undoubtedly been in rapid decline, it is still nowhere near extinction and such a prospect remains wholly unlikely. Even now, some 30 per cent of employees in the UK are trade union members and more than 40 per cent, have their pay and conditions determined by collective bargaining. These figures are indeed much reduced from those of 20 years ago, but in absolute terms they still represent many millions of people. In other countries there has also been decline but not, generally, to the same extent – except in the USA, where decline set in some 40 years ago, marking out that country, as in so many things, as an exceptional case. In a few countries trade union membership is either stable or growing and in many (notably other member states in the European Union) trade unions are a 'social partner', legitimated in both law and practice. Mainland European countries, in their institutions, therefore reflect the continuing importance of industrial relations. However, under management pressures to decentralise, its central locus – in the UK primarily but increasingly elsewhere in Europe – is now the place of work. This is the terrain where the great majority of people still spend a substantial part of their lives as employees and where many still seek, even accounting to a right, to have their interests adequately represented, *vis-à-vis* employers, through either collective bargaining or some alternative or complementary form of representation. It is also a 'contested terrain' (Edwards, 1979; Green and Yanarella, 1996), reflecting the assumption of the industrial relations approach that the interests of employers and employees are, in large measure, in natural 'tension', even though that tension is commonly resolved through collective bargaining and collective agreements. It is also of some note that in those well-managed organisations that do not recognise trade unions, some form of institution to reflect the individual and collective 'voice' of their employees is considered important in achieving enterprise goals and contributing to harmonious relationships between management and employees.

One apparent paradox, though, is that while the study of industrial relations, especially in the UK and USA, is not what it was, its comparative form has been attracting increasing interest as well as growing numbers into its ranks. How is this to be explained? There are perhaps three main reasons.

First, and perhaps the most important, is the increasing internationalisation of national economies, with the associated increase in international competition leading to pressure on organisations to improve their competitiveness. This process has directly influenced the research interests of comparative industrial relations specialists who, over the past few years, have written major global studies of the behaviour of multinational companies in significant industries such as automobiles and telecommunications. One of these global studies, that of automobiles, bringing together a team of academics from 12 countries, is the research case study used in this chapter (Kochan *et al.*, 1997). This industry is also, of course, among the most highly unionised in the world and therefore appropriate for a comparative *industrial relations* study.

Second, and a variation on the competitiveness theme, has been the attention given to the differences between countries' labour-market institutions and behaviour and the role of the state. Thus there has been considerable debate over the alleged tendency of the 'inflexible' German social market 'model', with its institutionalised collective bargaining combined with widely available and generously funded employment protection and social benefits, to generate high and uncompetitive labour costs and impede job creation – in contrast to the supposed virtues of labour-market flexibility, deregulation and limited collective bargaining as the paths to low unemployment and vigorous economic growth. This debate has not only attracted the strong interest of academics – notably, but not surprisingly, from Germany (Buechtemann, 1993), the USA and the UK (Towers, 1997) – but also the close attention of policy makers seeking to achieve politically acceptable levels of unemployment without the use of traditional Keynesian macro-economic instruments that many policy makers now regard (and not necessarily accurately) as inflationary and destabilising.

Third, the liberalisation of world and regional trade, through GATT, NAFTA and the EU's internal market, has generated greater interest in the comparative study of industrial relations employment practices. For example, the ILO's reports have consistently put the case for the wider application and enforcement of internationally acceptable labour standards in trade agreements, and a recent study of The North American Free Trade Agreement (NAFTA) has also considered how far the agreement's rules could be extended to include a social dimension on the EU model (Adams and Turner, 1994).

These, then, are some important reasons for comparative industrial relations being a significant, and growing, area of study and policy interest. The reasons also reveal some of the subject area's current interests. We will touch on a selection of these in this chapter, both in the first part and in the case study.

Comparative industrial relations is, however, a difficult area of study. Comparative methodology, at least in industrial relations, is at an early stage in its development and is only now beginning to move beyond the descriptive, though often rich, collections of country studies or 'models' towards thematic, cross-country projects or multi-country, enterprise research within a single industry or sector. These methodological aspects, important in a text written mainly for postgraduate students, are also discussed in the next section using research themes – such as the employment and industrial relations policies of multinationals and the global future for collective bargaining – as contexts for the discussion.

Finally, in the second half of this chapter the automobile industry is the chosen case study. This is for three reasons. First, though the industry has for long attracted major research interest (including substantial participant observation), recent new approaches to studying it on a global scale (Kochan *et al.*, 1997) illustrate the *general* value of these new methods of comparative analysis. Hence these methods have already been extended to the study of a very different industry, telecommunications (Katz, 1997).

Second, the automobile industry is significant in substantive terms. It has been a frequent pioneer, throughout its history, of new technologies, new working practices and new approaches to the employment relationship. The implementation of these innovations commonly reveals deep-seated tensions between managerial attempts to exert control and the resistance of workers, as well as throwing into focus wider issues of employee rights and social justice. The industry is therefore deserving of study in its own right.

However, and third, the tensions and issues that we observe are not confined to automobiles and are inherent in the capitalist system itself. Printing, newspaper production and, most recently, dock work are industries that have also been subjected to major transformation. Although the form and pace of change in these industries have been unlike that in automobiles, the implementation of change has revealed the same or similar issues, tensions and conflicts. Hence, studying the automobile industry's attempts to reconcile conflicts of interest between capital and labour reflects a wider and continuing phenomenon.

Comparative study: approaches, problems and value

■ Contingencies and multinationals

In Chapter 1, in the discussion of the choices available to managers in their decision making, we are reminded that such choices are influenced or constrained by circumstances or factors that are often largely outside their control. The most obvious – and usually the most powerful and unavoidable – are those political, legal, economic and cultural contexts within which organisations are required to conduct their business. Managers are of course more directly constrained by the nature of the organisation in which they work, i.e. its 'culture' and 'politics'. They also have their own 'human preferences, values, [and] ideologies' (Chapter 1) that can influence commercial considerations in decision making.

The importance of such 'contingencies' is especially evident in the case of organisations that have locations in different countries or in different regions of those countries where regional variations in laws and public policy are significant, as in the USA. The constraints can also change over time, becoming more or less restrictive. For example, although private-sector collective bargaining in the USA is still essentially regulated by the provisions of the 1935 Wagner Act, those provisions were substantially amended by the Taft-Hartley Act in 1947, which shifted the balance of advantage towards employers, an advantage that has since been substantially consolidated by employers themselves, assisted by largely favourable public policy and court decisions (Towers, 1997). In contrast, although the development of the European Union's single market has allowed employers greater freedom to locate or relocate their businesses, the EU's social policies have consistently extended the protections and rights of employees against employers – including informational and consultational rights, though not collective bargaining (Gold, 1993; Rogers and Streeck, 1995). However, although there has been a growth in the EU's regulation of the employment relationship, this remains limited to a 'floor' of employment rights and guarantees of minimum conditions. Beyond the floor, variations remain wide in both the form of regulation and its substance. Germany, for example, provides the highest level of employee protection and non-wage benefits, but the cost of the latter is largely borne by employers themselves. This is in contrast to the UK, where state provision and regulation remain far more important (Freeman, 1994). These contrasts also extend to the institutions of industrial relations (Ferner and Hyman, 1998) so that Germany and the UK can be seen as two 'models' that have different outcomes for the management of enterprises and those employed within them, even though, as we shall discuss later, important global pressures may be beginning to change the distinctiveness and analytical value of such national models (Locke, 1995; Ferner and Hyman, 1998).

Yet despite some evidence of change, variation rather than uniformity remains largely intact, with important implications for employers and employees. For example, in a global context, employers can normally choose to operate in those labour-market conditions, and under those regulations, that allow them to minimise their labour costs and manage with little or no trade union involvement or other form of employee representation. Of course, employers are free to choose otherwise and for a complex of reasons, in addition to the economic and commercial – and may do so. But factors such as profit (or revenue) maximisation, market share and cost minimisation remain important explanations of organisational policy making and behaviour.

Outside the EU, organisations can more easily avoid constraints on their operations. For example, multinationals of EU origin may choose to locate their plants in central and eastern Europe where wages and benefits are lower or the ability to recruit and layoff is subject to fewer controls. This has been especially evident in the case of the German multinational Volkswagen, as well as its American, Japanese, Korean and Italian competitors. In the USA, another prominent German multinational – Mercedes-Benz – has also recently built a new plant in Alabama, a state in which it is relatively easy for Mercedes to establish and maintain a non-union operation and in clear contrast to the company's legally regulated role in collective bargaining and Works Council processes in Germany.

The Mercedes example is one of many instances where the German 'model' is left behind or adapted to local circumstances when German companies locate abroad. The 'culture and politics' of organisations, as well as the 'human preferences, values and ideologies' (Chapter 1) of their managers, do not seem to be good travellers in the German case. Indeed, one German company – the automotive parts company Bosch – adopted a Japanese-style, single-union agreement when establishing its new plant in the UK in South Wales. Nor do Japanese managers always pack their one enterprise union model in their suitcases. In the UK, their approach to trade union representation has pragmatically included multi-union and single-union recognition as well as union avoidance (Oliver and Wilkinson, 1992), the latter most significantly in Honda's new plant in Swindon. In the USA and other countries, Japanese solely owned transplants and joint ventures with US auto companies reveal a wide range of policies and practices towards work organisation, employee relationships and trade union representation (Kenney and Florida, 1993; Elger and Smith, 1994), which suggests a 'horses for courses' approach to the management of labour.

■ Employee interests and collective organisation

National variations in employment law policies and industrial relations institutions and practices are of obvious interest to the managers of multinational companies. These variations (and similarities) are also of interest to those involved in the study of industrial relations, especially where the relationship between management and employees is conducted on a collective basis – although this does not preclude an individual relationship through the contract of employment and those policies that directly impinge on the individual employee. The way in which organisations relate to their employees, both collectively and individually, can also be seen as part of a wider debate on the moral responsibilities (if any) of organisations. An industry that especially attracts this kind of debate is this chapter's case-study industry, as shown in Illustration 15.1.

ILLUSTRATION 15.1

Conflicting interests in the global automobile industry

Is anything more at stake here than another academic debate? Clearly there is . . . the lean production debate is partly about outcomes against which the performance of a strategically important industry should be judged. Is 'leanness' – that is producing high-quality products with minimum labour and capital – the best or only relevant performance measure? Most observers of the auto industry would think not – particularly scholars from the industrial relations field who urge the use of a performance model which recognises the multiplicity of interests or stakeholders with legitimate claims on the industry. These would include not only shareholders but workers, customers, suppliers, and environmentalists, as well as those responsible for macroeconomic policy'.

Source: Kochan *et al.*, 1997: 4–5.

Of this 'multiplicity of interests', this chapter is concerned with the normally conflicting interests of two: managers or employers (representing shareholders) and workers or, more precisely, employees. Although the agenda of employers does not, in practice, exclude wider social, altruistic or humanitarian goals, here it is assumed that their primary purpose in the management of their employees is to maximise efficiency in production (and lately there has also been a strong emphasis on quality) at minimum labour cost. Their employees, in contrast (although the ingredients and their mix are matters of much debate), seek maximum pay and benefits, employment security, good working conditions and job satisfaction. This conflict of interests (as has already been noted earlier) is only rarely conflictual in practice and there can be areas of common interest such as good pay that, together with appropriate levels of productivity, minimise the cost of labour to employers. This explains, for example, why labour costs in the capital-intensive automobile industry are commonly only 10 per cent of total cost. Yet conflicts remain and need to be resolved – if only on a temporary basis – and agreement is normally the outcome. Agreements between the employer and the individual employee (the contract of employment) are protected by the law almost everywhere but, by itself, though it is necessary it is not sufficient. The power imbalance between the individual employee and even a small employer is so great that in many countries agreements (drawing on the collective strength of most or all employees) are also commonly encouraged, or at least protected, by the law. One important exception is the UK, where collective agreements, through still widely accepted custom and practice between employers and trade unions, are not legally enforceable, although an attempt was made to make them so under the 1971 Industrial Relations Act, drawing partly on the experience of the USA. This was an example of institutional borrowing from another country – an occasional outcome of comparative industrial relations – that was a signal failure (Towers, 1997) and, interestingly, the US model is again under scrutiny in the search for a viable British statutory procedure for trade union recognition (Wood, 1997; Institute of Employment Rights, 1998).

Hence the interests of employees can be protected and advanced in two ways, through employees organising themselves or through the law; although these can be complementary as, for example, when the law guarantees individual employment rights at work as well as the right of employees to form and join trade unions or to take industrial action, with the government, and/or its agencies, promoting and encouraging the use and growth of collective bargaining. Employee organisation can of course take different forms, such as independent trade unions, company unions (on the Japanese model), works councils (on the EU member states' model) or some permutation or combination, of which perhaps the best example is still the German system, despite continuing change and development. There trade unions bargain with employers at sectoral level with elected employee works councils working with employers within organisations but not bargaining over pay and conditions – the virtually exclusive preserve of employers and trade unions but outside the plant (Jacobi *et al.*, 1998).

These different forms of employee organisation and the degree to which they are compatible within one system, or transferable to another, are of great interest to students of comparative industrial relations as well as those directly involved in a practical sense, such as trade union and employer organisations and reforming governments and their advisers. However, here we will primarily focus on collective bargaining between trade unions and employers, as the most acceptable and still most effective means of reconciling their conflicting interests (Towers, 1997).

■ The decline of collective bargaining

Despite its acceptability and effectiveness, collective bargaining has been in general (though not universal) decline over the past 20 years and in some countries much longer – notably the USA. This has been directly associated with trade union decline and the corresponding increase in employer power and influence. Analysing and explaining trade union decline (and frequently how to reverse it) has therefore become another important interest of comparative industrial relations scholars, as well as those international agencies with a direct or indirect interest in the health, or otherwise, of trade unions and collective bargaining, such as the OECD and World Bank but, especially, the ILO (*Employment Outlook*, 1994; World Bank, 1995; ILO, 1997).

A recent ILO study of global industrial relations (ILO, 1997) was, not surprisingly, largely concerned with the decline in trade union membership, especially in relation to the worldwide growth in labour forces. The ILO 'density' data (i.e. union membership as a percentage of the non-agricultural labour force) make, for some, gloomy reading:

> Out of a sample of 92 countries for which figures on union membership were available only 14 had a rate of more than 50 per cent in 1995; in 48 countries, in other words in more than half the sample, the rate was less than 20 per cent. (ILO, 1997: 7)

Furthermore, the ILO reports, in most countries the trend is sharply downwards, although it takes some comfort from those countries in which membership and density are relatively stable (such as Belgium, Canada, South Korea and the Nordic group of countries) and in the few where the trend is strongly upwards, notably South Africa, Spain and Finland. It also points out that trade union membership decline is not always associated with a decline in power and influence, citing the continuing central involvement of some trade union movements in political elections and the wider political process as well as the capacity to call for national strike action – as in the French public services in 1995. Trade union candidates are also frequently elected in large numbers to works councils representing employees in European Union countries, notably Germany where they take some 80 per cent of the seats (ILO, 1997; Müller-Jentsch, 1995).

Yet overall the ILO paints a pessimistic picture. It explains such 'adverse developments' in terms of the now familiar collection of factors:

- globalisation of product and labour markets;
- high levels of unemployment;
- decline of manual occupations in favour of white-collar work;
- privatisation and deregulation;
- changes in macro-economic policy away from economic growth and full employment towards balanced budgets and counter-inflation;
- technological transformation of workplaces leading to 'downsizing', 'delayering' and employment insecurity;
- shortcomings of some trade unions' structures and policies.

Such a listing would be widely accepted beyond the ILO, although the extent and significance of 'globalisation' can be challenged, as the ILO cautiously does itself, citing a number of sceptical studies. There are also two important questions to be answered: the *relative* importance of each of the factors (Chaison and Rose 1991; Towers, 1997); and an explanation of how it is that some countries' labour movements continue to prosper without any immunity from adverse global developments. On the second question, the ILO notes that in Belgium, Denmark, Finland, Iceland and Sweden (of the countries with the highest unionisation rates) their unions, in whole or in part, handle the payment of unemployment benefits; while in Taiwan, the payment of medical benefits by the union is the principal reason for taking out membership (ILO, 1997: 24–5).

■ Some problems of comparative analysis

Trying to explain an important phenomenon such as trade union decline reveals certain difficulties inherent to comparative analysis. For example, the rival explanations of decline reflect the different approaches of the academic disciplines. Economists tend to emphasise, usually using quantitative methods, the impact of globalisation and international competition, changing economic structure or – especially in the UK – the effects of macro-economic policy (Disney, 1990; Green, 1992). Industrial relations specialists and labour lawyers, both taking a more qualitative approach, will often differ as to the impact of legislation and public policy (Brown and Ryan, 1997). Political scientists, in contrast, may stress the positive relationship between the tenure of 'leftist' governments and trade union influence (Visser, 1988).

Clearly, there is a good case for avoiding what, to outsiders, seems to be sectarian squabbling and to adopt a cross- or multi-disciplinary approach to comparative analysis and explanation. Trying to understand what is happening outside one's own culture and direct experience may also require an extra quality, i.e. 'the need to adopt an attitude of genuine modesty, humility and respect for the institutions of other peoples' (Schregle, 1981: 29).

A cross- or multi-disciplinary approach, even if combined with caution and modesty, does, however, give rise to other problems. A single discipline may offer limited conclusions, but has the merit of greater precision. Furthermore, *some* outcomes may have monocausal explanations. Multi-disciplinary analysis is also largely associated with the categorisation of countries, or groups of countries, into 'systems' or 'models'. The 1997 ILO study itself adopts this methodology in its search for a viable role for industrial relations and political systems. However, in its identification and use of three major models – the European social model (sometimes referred to as the 'Rhineland model'), the United States and the Japanese – it stresses the importance of placing them in their historical and cultural contexts. This is sensible, but also challenging. Furthermore, even seemingly well-established models change and develop over time arising from internal pressures for change (such as from management) and external changes such as state intervention and pressures from global economic developments. The comprehensive analysis of a model, including a detailed assessment of how far it is changing and adapting to internal and external influences, is especially important when political policy makers and managers are considering adopting some of the institutions and practices of other countries and their enterprises.

Models, whatever the difficulties, clearly have an important place. There is, however, a more fundamental objection to the identification of such models in that they may be such an inaccurate reflection of reality that they are methodologically of limited value. This aspect of the case against national or regional models hinges on the impact of the changes in the world economy discussed earlier undermining the three 'basic assumptions' of traditional (i.e. model-based) research. These basic (macro) assumptions are:

■ national borders and markets coincide;

■ differences *between* national economies are more significant than differences *within* national economies;

- certain national institutions are better than others at adapting to changes in economic and political contexts (Locke *et al.*, 1995).

Richard Locke drawing upon recent research (Locke, 1995) tested his case against the value of models through an 11-country, comparative study focusing on the employment changes at enterprise (micro) level arising from changes in the world economy. The employment changes identified are:

- extensive changes in work organisation such as decentralisation; the introduction of innovations such as team work, job rotation and quality circles; and experiments with new forms of employee participation and involvement;
- downward pressures on pay and labour costs in bargaining and innovations in payment systems for both blue- and white-collar employees;
- an increasing emphasis on training and skill development to meet the changing needs of firms;
- the growth of flexible working arrangements and job insecurity.

The main conclusion of Locke was that in the countries studied (USA, UK, Australia, Spain, Italy, France, Germany, Sweden, Norway, Japan and Canada), there has been 'a significant transformation in industrial relations practices.' He did, however, also report that important variations in the extent of this transformation both within countries and between them. This suggests that although national institutions, practices and laws remain important influences, cross-national pressures leading to changes in employment practices are also significant and worthy of further study.

The research strategy of Locke (and his colleagues) has in fact been applied to two major global industries, i.e. automobiles and telecommunications (Kochan *et al.*, 1997, Katz, 1997) and clearly could be fruitful in research into other global industries such as banking, finance and pharmaceuticals. However, the automobile industry is the case study adopted for this chapter as our example of the use of the comparative approach. The reasons for choosing automobiles were discussed on page 394 and are returned to in the next section.

The world automobile industry: a comparative case study

■ The significance of the automobile industry

The automobile industry has fascinated the popular mind since the inception of mass production at Henry Ford's plants in Michigan at the beginning of the twentieth century. Its products have influenced – and so far (though arguably) mostly for the better – many aspects of economic and social life, although the increasingly negative features of, especially, the private car are now beginning to attract serious public and governmental attention in those countries where rising car ownership is generating unacceptable levels of congestion and pollution, mainly in western, developed economies. In countries relatively new to the lure of mass car ownership, the environmental concerns of the developed west are the subject of much less attention. For the major global producers, establishing production facilities inside countries with lower levels of car ownership but with good growth prospects (such as eastern Europe and China) provides a potentially highly profitable alternative to the sluggish, saturated markets of western Europe, North America and Japan. An illustration of this alternative is shown in Fig. 15.1.

The scale of the investment in eastern Europe by some of the world's leading producers is justified by the market potential of the new plants, especially since the former East Germany is now within EU boundaries and Poland, Hungary and the Czech Republic are being prepared by the EU for membership. Additionally, as the *Financial Times* article (Simonian, 1997) from which Fig. 15.1 is taken points out, the pay and benefits in the new plants are very much lower than in, for example, former West Germany. The article cites the case of a bodyshop worker at the Volkswagen/Skoda plant in the Czech Republic who would earn about one-eighth of that received by her German counterpart. The attraction of low wages is complemented by investment grants and tax incentives in the host countries' regions and, in the case of Volkswagen, political pressure following reunification played a part in its east German investment: 20 per cent of the company is owned by the *Land* of Lower Saxony. The new plants have also provided important opportunities for German companies to test new flexible production methods that would be resisted by their strong, highly unionised workers in the west. The option of shifting production to the east also offers the German management a lever for extracting productivity concessions from their west German plants (Simonian, 1997), a tactic known in the USA as 'whipsawing' and one that is now becoming more common within the EU's internal market.

Innovations in work organisation, employment conditions and payment systems (sought by companies investing in eastern Europe) have been a consistent feature of the automobile industry since its earliest days. Some academics see these innovations as the most important reason for giving the industry such comprehensive and sustained attention with implications much beyond the industry itself: 'as a bellwether of innovation in employment conditions for the industrial relations system and economy as a whole'. (Kochan *et al.*, 1997: 5). They cite, for example, US companies' introduction of long term contracts, cost-of-living clauses and quality-of-working-life programmes; Swedish producers' innovations in alternatives to 'Fordist' mass production; and the introduction in German companies (by negotiation with the powerful IG Metall Union) of new technologies, teamwork and redesigned jobs (Kochan *et al.*, 1997: 6).

This wider, international significance is also evident in the industry's importance to the development plans of emerging industrial economies, as we have seen in the case of eastern Europe. The rapid rise of the Korean economy has also been closely associated with the fast growth, to world status, of its automobile industry, although both its economy and industry are now mutually locked into the serious repercussions of the banking and currency crisis. South American countries and the rapidly developing economy of China also see automobile industry growth as a major stimulus to their economic development. In addition, the industry's large companies have shown a remarkable capacity (as archetypal multinationals) to penetrate foreign economies and establish themselves over long periods – sometimes in joint ventures with other indigenous multinationals. In the USA and UK, for example, the operations of Japanese multinationals, dominated by automobile and electronics corporations, have been important, leading to major studies of their impact on the host economy (Oliver and Wilkinson, 1992; Kenney and Florida, 1993).

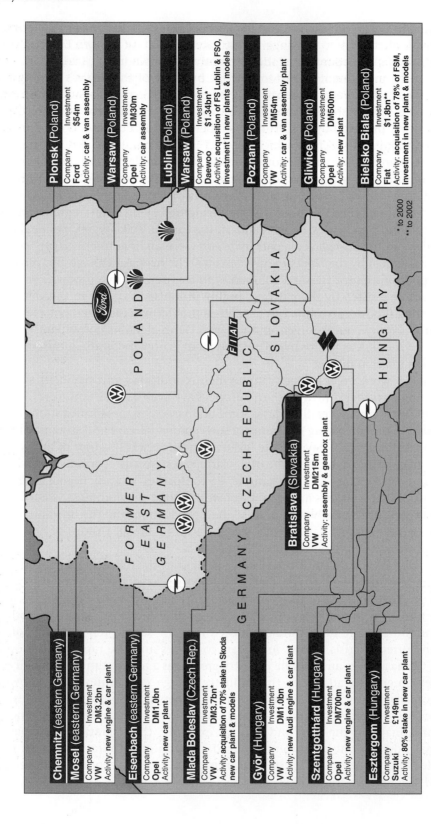

Plonsk (Poland)
Company: Ford
Investment: $54m
Activity: car & van assembly

Warsaw (Poland)
Company: Opel
Investment: DM30m
Activity: car assembly

Lublin (Poland)
Warsaw (Poland)
Company: Daewoo
Investment: $1.34bn*
Activity: acquisition of FS Lublin & FSO, investment in new plants & models

Poznan (Poland)
Company: VW
Investment: DM54m
Activity: car & van assembly plant

Gliwice (Poland)
Company: Opel
Investment: DM500m
Activity: new plant

Bielsko Biala (Poland)
Company: Fiat
Investment: $1.8bn**
Activity: acquisition of 78% of FSM, investment in new plant & models

* to 2000
** to 2002

Bratislava (Slovakia)
Company: VW
Investment: DM215m
Activity: assembly & gearbox plant

Chemnitz (eastern Germany)
Mosel (eastern Germany)
Company: VW
Investment: DM3.2bn
Activity: new engine & car plant

Eisenbach (eastern Germany)
Company: Opel
Investment: DM1.0bn
Activity: new car plant

Mlada Boleslav (Czech Rep.)
Company: VW
Investment: DM3.7bn*
Activity: acquisition of 70% stake in Skoda new car plant & models

Györ (Hungary)
Company: VW
Investment: DM1.0bn
Activity: new Audi engine & car plant

Szentgotthárd (Hungary)
Company: Opel
Investment: DM700m
Activity: new engine & car plant

Esztergom (Hungary)
Company: Suzuki
Investment: £149m
Activity: 80% stake in new car plant

Fig. 15.1 Leading carmakers are investing in eastern Europe

The global significance of the industry is clearly shown in Table 15.1 both in terms of the production and use of the automobile. But perhaps the most studied aspect of the consequences of 'Japanisation' – including a vigorous critique – is the degree to which Japanese working practices, commonly referred to as 'lean production' or 'Toyotism' (reflecting its precise origins), influenced and can further influence traditional mass-production methods developed in the west. This debate also includes discussion of the alternatives to lean production and the possible development of new 'hybrid' production methods (Berggren, 1992; Elger and Smith, 1994; Kochan *et al.*, 1997).

Table 15.1 The world's top 10: production and new registrations of passenger cars, 1995–7 (000s)

	Production		New registrations	
	1995	**1997**	**1995**	**1997**
Japan	7611	8495	4444	4492
USA	6342	6007	8636	8277
Germany	4360	4678	3314	3528
France	3051	3351	1931	1713
South Korea	2003	2308	1074	1159
Spain	1959	2010	834	1016
UK	1532	1693	1945	2171
Italy	1422	1583	1745	2112
Canada	1365	1333	677	740
Brazil	1303	1676	1411	1575
Other	6083	7487	8200	10 117
World	37 031	40 621	34 211	36 900

Source: Extracted from 'World automotive manufacturing' (1998) London: *Financial Times*, 11 May.

■ The evolution of production methods

The earliest production methods in the automobile industry were based on craft principles and early vehicle design and embellishment were strongly influenced by the old crafts involved in the construction of horse-drawn vehicles. Craft principles, even in the USA, did in fact overlap for some years with mass-production techniques, while outside the USA, especially in Europe and Japan, craft traditions continued to survive in the slower development of mass markets and the associated cost benefits of high-volume production. Nor were European, and later Japanese, managers fully committed to Fordist management principles particularly in Europe where unions and their shopfloor members strongly resisted attempts to assert centralised management control. These persistent counter-pressures partly explain the later emergence of alternative 'organising principles' for the industry, i.e. flexible or lean production and the human-centred approach of the Swedish producers; and although the latter seemed to have lost its way by the 1990s it continued to offer a possible legacy for some modification of lean production techniques (MacDuffie, 1997; Berggren, 1992). Hence, while the organising principles of mass production dominated the industry for many years, they co-existed with variations still partly influenced by craft traditions. Additionally, though lean production is now the new, dominant paradigm, mass production – or some variant of the two paradigms – remains important as an organising principle, especially in the 'Big Three' US corporations where resistance to lean production practices remains strong within trade unions and among 'unreconstructed American management' wedded to Fordist labour–management relations (Kenney and Florida, 1993: 287–91). Yet the distinction between the two paradigms has been challenged by those who see lean production as simply a more advanced form of Fordism, maximising work intensity and worker exploitation (Burawoy, 1995; Parker, 1993).

We shall return to this view later. Now we should distinguish more carefully between the organising principles of mass, or Fordist, production and those of lean, or flexible, production.

■ Mass production and lean production

The differences between mass production and lean production are illustrated in Table 15.2. This table inevitably polarises the differences between mass and lean production. As we have already noted, not all producers have shifted to lean production and the way production is currently organised may mix both approaches. For example, joint ventures – such as that of General Motors and Toyota (New United Motor Manufacturing Inc (NUMMI) in Fremont, California) – may be unable to move to full lean production given the constraints of finance, organisational culture and shopfloor resistance. Lean methods may also only be able to be introduced in unionised workplaces able to handle a more innovative form of labour–management relationship, such as the General Motors–United Automobile Workers works partnership agreement at GM's Saturn plant in Tennessee (Towers, 1997). It also follows from the examples of NUMMI and Saturn that, although lean production methods were initially developed by Toyota in Japan in

Table 15.2 Mass production and lean production compared

Mass production	Lean production
■ Standardised products: long production runs	■ Product variety: short, multiple production runs
■ Specialisation of work tasks and functions	■ Team work, multi-skilling, job rotation
■ Assembly line controlled by management	■ Worker ability to stop assembly line
■ Acceptance of minimal level of product quality	■ Intensive quality control: quality circles, total quality management
■ Surplus labour: cover for turnover and absenteeism to avoid line stoppages	■ Minimal labour force: controls on worker selection; absenteeism sanctions
■ Surplus stocks of parts and materials	■ Minimal stock levels: just-in-time systems; close location of suppliers
■ Extensive land area: buffer for large stocks of parts and finished products	■ Minimal land area: limited stocks of parts and finished products
■ Limited, passive, arm's-length relationship with markets and customers	■ Close, active, direct relationship with markets and customers

Sources: MacDuffie, 1997; Kenney and Florida, 1993; Berggren, 1992.

the 1950s and are sometimes therefore referred to as 'Toyotism', they are no longer exclusive to Toyota or even Japanese corporations. Furthermore, lean production methods have perhaps been most influential in countries outside Japan through their 'transplants' and joint ventures. An illustration of the penetration in the 1980s of the US and Canadian markets by Japanese, lean production transplants is shown in Table 15.3.

Table 15.3 Auto transplants in North America, 1990

Company	Location	Year started	Production (000s)	Production planned (000s)	Planned employment level
United States					
Honda	Marysville, Ohio	1982	430	510	8000
Nissan	Smyrna, Tennessee	1983	240	440	5100
NUMMI (Toyota and GM)	Fremont, California	1984	200	300	3400
Mazda	Flat Rock, Michigan	1987	180	240	3400
Diamond Star (Chrysler and Mitsubishi)	Normal, Illinois	1988	150	240	2900
Toyota	Georgetown, Kentucky	1988	220	440	3500
Subaru and Isuzu	Lafayette, Indiana	1989	70	120	1700
Canada					
Honda	Alliston	1988	100	n/a	n/a
Toyota	Cambridge	1988	60	n/a	n/a
CAMI Automotive (Suzuki and GM)	Ingersoll	1990	50	200	2000

Sources: Business Week, 14 August 1989 and *Automotive News,* 7 January 1991, cited in Berggren (1992).

The remarkable reductions in unit and labour costs and gains in productivity, quality and market share achieved by Japanese lean producers and their imitators are essentially explained by the elimination of spare capacity and surpluses of all kinds – including labour – combined with a key emphasis on closely controlled teams responsible for quality as well as the maintenance of production (Womack *et al.,* 1990). As a system, however, its elimination of buffers can render it vulnerable to even minor interruptions of supplies, which explains the need to encourage dependent suppliers to cluster close to assembly plants even though the producer–supplier relationship is more complex than this simplistic model – as we are beginning to understand (Newsome, 1998).

The system is also vulnerable to trade union pressure. The large automobile companies in Japan, as in other industries, took action to break independent, externally located trade unionism in the 1950s (Price, 1997) and, outside Japan, they normally seek the non-union option (as in the USA); or in countries where that option is not so readily available (as in the UK), they will normally want to recognise only one trade union but also heavily circumscribe that union's role (Bassett, 1986; Garrahan and Stewart ,1992).

■ Personnel policies and lean production

The 'high-involvement' work practices of lean producers (team work, multi-skilling or job rotation, the devolving of responsibility for quality to workers in teams) are also normally associated with a special package of personnel policies, i.e. the application of strict criteria in the hiring process; the selection and implementation of incentive wage payment systems and wage structures; the reduction and simplification of job grades; the removal of status differences between manual and white-collar workers (MacDuffie, 1997); and the introduction of involvement and participation programmes. These policies are far from unwelcome to workers in lean production plants, especially when they are combined with reasonable employment security and above-average pay. It is also clear that many employees see the absence of a union presence, or with a strictly curtailed role for the union such as its exclusion from wage determination (as at Nissan, UK), as a price that they are willing to pay for tangible employment benefits. The experience of mass, catastrophic job losses may also be able to transform the 'world view' of highly militant trade union activists, as Turner (1991) commented in his study of the General Motors closure in California followed by its rebirth as NUMMI, noted earlier.

Such evaluative studies of lean production show how research has moved a long way beyond the virtually uncritical acceptance of the inevitability and desirability of lean production by Womack and his colleagues (1990). Recent critical studies of lean production have focused on work intensity, stress and management control (Babson, 1995; Parker, 1993; Parker and Slaughter, 1995). A good example is Parker's description of working with the 'andon' board at NUMMI, as described in Illustration 15.2.

ILLUSTRATION 15.2

Management-by-stress

The 'andon' board illustrates how management-by-stress works. At NUMMI a lighted board above the assembly line – called the andon board – shows the status of each work station. When a worker falls behind or needs help, he or she pulls a cord; bells chime and the board lights up. If the cord is not pulled again within a set period of time (say a minute) the line stops. In one variation of the andon board, the status of each station is indicated with one of three lights: green – production is keeping up and there are no problems; yellow – operator is falling behind or needs help; red – problem requires stopping the line. In the traditional US operation, management would want to see nothing but green lights and would design enough slack into the machinery and procedures so that an operation would almost always run in the green. Individual managers try to protect themselves with excess stock and excess workers to cover glitches or emergencies. CYA (cover your ass) is considered prudent operating procedure.

But in the management-by-stress production system, 'all green' signals inefficiency, workers are not working as hard as they might. If the system is stressed – by speeding up the line for example – the weaker points become evident and the yellow lights go on. A few jobs will go into the red and stop the line. Management can now focus on these few jobs and make necessary adjustments. Once the problems have been corrected, the system can then be further stressed (perhaps by reducing the number of workers) and then rebalanced. The ideal is for the system to run with *all stations* oscillating between green and yellow. Thus the system equilibrates or drives toward being evenly balanced as managers constantly readjust and rebalance to make production ever more efficient. After years of observing waste in traditional plants, some people, including many workers, are attracted to this version of a smoothly functioning, rational management system. In engineering terms, it could be described as a tighter control system with 'fast response inner loops'. The only problem is that it is human beings that are under such rigid control, not machines.

Source: Parker, 1993: 262.

This example of the latent controls available to management under lean production also suggests that the ability of workers to stop the line – i.e. putting the power to control the pace of their work in their own hands and a radical break with the Fordist past – can be more theoretical than real. As Parker argues, once a job has passed through the trial and training period and is working well, as the line speeds up, workers find it more difficult to keep up but management assumes that any problems are the fault of the workers. Then any stopping of the line followed by the chimes and lights *visually* identifies who is responsible. The supervisor goes into action to resolve the problem and restart the line as soon as possible.

The visual identification of who is responsible for stopping the line also invites peer-group pressure, an important aspect of team work, with the members of the team controlling each other to maintain output, quality and earnings. Absenteeism also attracts peer-group pressure, for similar reasons, when replacement workers are not available. From management's perspective, too, attendance is central to the lean production system. In Japanese transplants in the USA, even in unionised plants with formal protection for workers such as NUMMI, dismissal can follow four absences in a year. Yet in Fordist plants, the most strict still allow 15 to 20 unexplained absences in one year without invoking the disciplinary procedure (Kenney and Florida, 1993).

It is therefore at least arguable that lean production, without the buffers and slack of traditional Fordist production methods, is far more stressful to workers. This must be set against the tangible benefits of good pay and employment security, although the latter may lack substance in Japanese companies outside Japan (Kenney and Florida, 1993) and is increasingly under threat within Japan itself, as the economy finds itself in a continuing crisis of recession and financial adjustment (Allinson, 1997).

■ The limits to lean production

As we noted at the beginning of this chapter, the performance of a strategically important global industry such as automobiles should not be judged solely on its 'leanness' or capacity to produce high-quality products with minimum inputs of labour and capital. Hence, this chapter has been mainly concerned with the normally conflicting interests of two of the 'stakeholders' (i.e. employers and employees) involved in any productive enterprise and, specifically, an assessment of the problems as well as the benefits accruing to manual workers under lean production principles and practices.

The benefits contribute to explaining the widespread diffusion of lean production, but the problems have inevitably provoked resistance (and not only from trade unions and workers), which partly explains the absence, so far, of total domination. This resistance is also a factor in the continuing search for possible alternatives to, or the reform of, lean production. This we shall return to at the end of the chapter. What is currently clear, however, is that though lean production is the dominant and still growing influence in the industry, there remains substantial divergence within the wider picture. Kochan *et al.* (1997: 42) have identified four converging and diverging tendencies:

- *stable and lean*, i.e. Japanese-owned plants in Japan and overseas;
- *rapid moves to lean,* i.e. European plants and other 'new-element' countries, such as Korea, that in the past few years have shifted rapidly and comprehensively to lean production practices;
- *sticking with tradition*, i.e. US-owned plants in North America that have maintained or, following experiments, reverted to traditional mass production practices;
- *hybrids*, i.e. assorted plants from various countries that may be moving from mass to lean production or enduring as a 'stable hybrid' or 'as a distinctive model for how to organise work and manage the employment relationship'.

What is also clear is that the competitive advantages of lean production are a powerful force for convergence between *countries*, but between and within *companies*, there remains considerable divergence across a continuum from traditional mass production to lean production. General Motors, for example, within its US operations has enterprises as diverse as the NUMMI joint venture with Toyota – a lean production plant with a union presence – and the innovative Saturn venture combining modified lean working practices but in a context of a fully fledged partnership with the United Automobile Workers (UAW) (Towers, 1997). Saturn, in fact, has attempted to bring together the work organisation innovations of the Swedish model and the lean production system of the Japanese (Kochan *et al.*, 1997). Hence, the experiments of the Swedish automobile companies from the 1970s to the 1990s, though now essentially discontinued, may even yet be influential in the longer-term development of the industry.

Of other influences in explanations of divergence, trade unions are the most significant in an industry that remains highly unionised. According to Kochan *et al.* (1997), they have responded in three ways to management's attempts to introduce lean production work methods and the associated innovations in personnel practices. First, in some cases they have simply accepted the changes because they had little choice, such as at NUMMI where the plant was already closed and would have remained so without acceptance of the management terms, albeit with some negotiation. Similarly, Nissan in the UK was a new plant and the company could dictate the conditions under which it would begin operations. At Rover, again in the UK, the New Deal agreement was seen by the unions as the only means of stopping job losses (Scarbrough and Terry, 1993).

Second, there have been a number a cases of successful resistance where adversarial industrial relations are well entrenched. This is particularly seen in the USA, where the leadership of UAW 'locals' – supported by the membership and sometimes in defiance of national union officials – has been partly responsible for the slow rate of diffusion of lean production principles. Another example is Korea, where management's tactical response to strong labour pressure was the retention of traditional, Fordist, authoritarian management combined with the work-stoppage defences of the buffers of old-fashioned mass production. The outcome was the general strike of 1996.

Third, some unions have conducted partnership agreements with employers, and sometimes have taken the initiative themselves. Saturn remains the best example in the USA – although it has yet to find imitators – and Kochan *et al.* cite similar agreements in Sweden, Germany and South Africa. These innovations undoubtedly reflect local union strength and influence, but they also suggest the inherent problems of lean working practices in motivating employees. Genuine partnerships do, however, remain rare (Verma and Cutcher-Gershenfield, 1993) and their survival and growth are partly conditional on the survival of strong trade unions and co-operative management.

Other influences that may yet play a part in the diffusion or modification of lean production methods and personnel practices include the policies of governments as well as countervailing pressures within automobile companies themselves.

Governments are inevitably attracted to developing those policies that influence the production and labour management policies of automobile companies, especially given the strategic importance of the industry. Some governments (Kochan *et al.* cite Korea, Brazil and South Africa) have restricted foreign competition to facilitate the development of appropriate policies within their own indigenous companies. The development plans of the South African government in particular support lean production practices and human resource development policies in automobile assembly plants. In the European Union, continuing debate over the advantages and problems of flexible labour markets and employment practices has influenced the European Commission to give guarded support to more flexibility in the workplace, although the greater enthusiasm of the British government – as seen in its ambitious learning from Japan programme (Towers, 1997) – has begun to influence other member states, including especially Germany. German automobile companies have for a number of years been introducing lean production practices such as team work and quality circles into the workplace – with the compliance or co-operation of the trade unions and works councils (Turner, 1991; Müller-Jentsch, 1995).

There is, however, some evidence (or belief) that the successful implementation of lean production practices has been handicapped by other policies and practices within organisations. For example, some organisations have experienced early performance gains that they have not been able to maintain (Oliver and Wilkinson, 1992). This may be explained by the absence of organisational flexibility to match the changes in production, or policies that demotivate employees during periods of innovation such as layoffs, 'downsizing' or threats of plant closure used as sanctions (Kochan *et al.*, 1997).

■ The reform of lean production

The diffusion of lean production has clearly been sufficient to accord it 'dominant paradigm' status. This dominance is largely explained by its clear superiority in the workplace in producing vehicles of better quality at lower cost than traditional mass production (Kenney and Florida, 1997). But, as we have noted earlier, the production of good-quality, cheap motor vehicles is not the only way of judging the industry's performance. Furthermore, the continuing survival of mass production is not simply an aberration: it reflects some workers' (and some managers') preferences for a system which, paradoxically given its turbulent industrial relations history, seems to be less stressful than the lean production alternative. Kochan *et al.*, as we have seen, have found that some US plants have even returned to mass production while others by experimenting with 'hybrid' methods and thus combining the two systems may be forming the nucleus of a new way 'to organise work and manage the employment relationship'. The enduring presence of trade unions in the industry also acts as a braking influence on the excesses of lean production and, in some cases, has been the source of new innovations in corporate governance.

The role of trade unions remains important in experiments towards a 'new way' for the automobile industry, possibly bringing together the economic advantages of lean production and a more human-centred approach to the employment relationship. Such discussion and experiment are still influenced by the working practices developed in Swedish automobile companies for over 20 years until the corporate crises that led to the sudden closure of Volvo and Saab's 'alternative production' plants in the early 1990s (Sandberg, 1993; Cressey, 1993; Brulin and Nilsson, 1997).

The contexts of the early Swedish experiments in the 1970s were favourable. Sweden's economy was stable and prosperous and strong, high-membership trade unions were deeply involved. Volvo and Saab were prestigious producers of cars, trucks and buses within the lower-volume, high-quality end of the market and, under full employment conditions, faced acute labour shortages. The case for developing less intensive, more attractive working conditions to overcome labour shortages – while maintaining satisfactory levels of output and productivity – was strong. Given the strength of the trade unions, it was also necessary to integrate trade union representatives in the new approaches to work and its organisation.

The most advanced experimentation took place at Volvo's plants, at Kalmar (opened in 1974) and Uddevalla, which began operations as late as 1989. Uddevalla was the plant that represented the most complete break with the organising principles of Fordist mass production. It has been well described by Sandberg, the research director at the Swedish Centre for Working Life, as shown in Illustration 15.3.

ILLUSTRATION 15.3

Human-centred work organisation at Volvo

Uddevalla represents a fundamental break from the once-dominant Taylorist mode of work-organisation that divides work and controls the workers in detail through machines and supervisors. The assembly-line disappeared and was substituted by a system of well-qualified, autonomous groupwork organisation; advanced automation in the handling of production material; . . . codetermination in . . . planning and a minimum of levels in the organisation. In Uddevalla a small work-group of around 9 built the whole car. There were no supervisors. Instead there was a rotating job – 'group ombudsman' – who related to other groups and to the factory manager. Components were given to the workgroup in kits that make up a complete car. . . . Being engaged in all aspects of work makes the production comprehensible . . . Work-intensity is high as in all group work – making the negotiation of production goals a key union demand.

Source: Sandberg, 1993: 83–4.

Sandberg's claim of a 'fundamental break' is shared by the British academic Peter Cressey (1993), who stresses the participative impact of trade union involvement and the work groups:

> The whole process united indirect participation via trade union representation with direct forms of participation through the creation of autonomous and semi-autonomous work teams. Such a unity offered involvement in both the strategic and the operational aspects of work. (Cressey 1993: 89)

The productivity outcomes were interesting. Volvo's Torslanda plant, using assembly-line work organisation, took 42 man-hours to produce one car. At Uddevalla, one day before its closure, productivity was 36.8 man-hours, although Japanese lean production plants' performance was typically 25 man-hours per car (Sandberg, 1993: 84). Hence, human-centred work organisation could compete with the mass production assembly line, but was significantly below the performance of lean production plants, although the decision to close the Kalmar and Uddevalla operations seemed to be much more closely related to the merger with the lean producer Renault than with Volvo's relative productivity performance (Sandberg, 1993: 86).

In the end, of course, the merger did not last. The closure of Volvo's innovative operations was a considerable setback for the workers and managers who lost their jobs, but also for those who saw 'human-centred' approaches to work organisation as, at least, a moderating influence on lean production, if not a potentially all-conquering new paradigm (Berggren, 1992). Yet, writing after the closures, Berggren (1995) argued that though Volvo had joined the lean producers, it retained some elements of the old system and, not surprisingly in Sweden, the unions remained influential. Even later, at Volvo's Torsland plant, Brulin and Nilsson (1997) still found a strong emphasis on group work co-existing with a lean production system.

Finally, the wheel may now be beginning to turn again, but at Saab. In 1996 General Motors completed its purchase of the Swedish company followed by the appointment, as its head, of an executive from its Saturn Corporation division (Kochan et al., 1997) Saturn is, of course, distinguished for its adoption of some of the more important aspects of the Swedish system, notably autonomous work groups with wide-ranging responsibilities and with the authority, as in Sweden, to elect their own leaders. Saturn is also unionised and the UAW has been a full partner in the partnership innovations extending from shopfloor to boardroom (Towers, 1997). This 'synthesis' of lean and Swedish methods, combined with a major experiment in new forms of corporate governance, remains controversial in both the UAW and GM (Adler et al., 1997) and so far it has not travelled beyond Tennessee – although it may yet find a home in Sweden, justifying Berggren's earlier optimism. However, in the end, much seems to rest on the trade unions retaining enough strength to influence boardroom and workshop outcomes.

CASE STUDY 15.1

Comparative industrial relations policy

You are part of a consultancy team hired by a German multinational manufacturer of luxury cars that has acquired a greenfield site, in rural South Wales, to build a new plant. Your job is to advise on a package of industrial relations and personnel policies that would contribute to commercial success, harmonious industrial relations and company prestige. The company's only stipulation is that it would see advantages in recognising a single trade union for white-collar and manual employees. Additionally, the company will be required, under EU law following the UK's adherence to the Social Chapter, to extend European Works Council representation to its new plant. It may also be required, under an emerging Directive, to set up a Works Council and the company has asked for the consultancy team's recommended strategy on this matter.

Activity 15.1

Prepare a concise, interim, internal report of no more than 1000 words for presentation to your colleagues.

Summary

In this chapter the following key points have been made:

- Industrial relations and comparative industrial relations are principally concerned with studying the processes and consequences of the normally conflicting interests of employers and employees.

- Collective bargaining and its outcomes in collective agreements have been shown to be the most effective and acceptable approaches towards the reconciling of those conflicting interests.

- Comparative industrial relations has revealed that collective bargaining, despite its value, has been in general, though not universal, decline over the past 20 years:
  - this decline has been associated with a parallel, general decline in trade union membership, although analysis has yet to isolate the relative importance of the factors involved or fully explain why some countries' labour movements continue to prosper against the general trend;
  - however, trade union membership decline is not always associated with a decline in national political influence.

- Comparative analysis can involve the specific application of the assumptions and methodologies of single disciplines or a cross- or multi-disciplinary approach:
  - multi-disciplinary research lacks the precision and more sophisticated methodology of the single discipline, but its wider, more inclusive scope offers a better approximation to the realities of complex societies and organisations;

- multi-disciplinary research is closely associated with the identification and use of national 'models';

- a fundamental objection to the use of models in research is that changes in the world economy and markets are blurring the significance of national borders, national economies and national product and labour markets;

- given these changes, studying variations in industrial relations policies and practices *within* countries – such as regional and/or organisational variations – can be at least as revealing as studying variations *between* countries or models;

- this approach can be developed through sectoral, cross-country research in global industries such as automobiles, telecommunications or banking and finance using a common framework such as work, employment and personnel practices.

- The automobile industry is the focus of much academic interest and research because it has been and remains:

- a pioneer in radically new approaches to the organisation of work;

- an important influence on the development of innovations in employment conditions and industrial relations;

- a key sector in many countries' development plans.

- Lean production has replaced 'Fordist' mass production as the leading 'organising principle' in the industry. However:

- while it originated with Japanese companies, it is no longer confined to them;

- its dominance and competitive advantage are largely explained by cost advantages deriving from a package of work practices including team work, job rotation and just-in-time production;

- these radical changes in working practices also seem to require the introduction of a range of personnel practices, including strict hiring criteria, absenteeism control, individual incentive payment systems, limited job grades, single status, employee involvement schemes and an employer preference for non-unionism.

- Critics of lean production maintain that work intensity and stress can be even higher under lean than mass production:

- hence the ability to stop the assembly line is a myth;

- team work, under lean production, increases managerial control of work and workers.

- The diffusion of lean production has not been total and significant pockets of mass production as well as 'hybrid' systems remain, with the potential for retrenchment or growth:

- convergence towards lean production is still taking place between countries but there is also divergence between and within companies;

- some part of this divergence is explained by union resistance and/or co-operation as well as the preferences of some managers – notably in the 'Big Three' in the USA;

- organisational policies and practices have also been important, including attempts to introduce changes in working practices without the associated personnel practices or with demotivating threats of redundancy or plant closure.

■ A potential challenge to the further diffusion of lean production (though as yet limited) lies in the development of 'hybrid' forms combining mass and lean production as responses to the preferences of workers and some managers.

■ In the short and medium term, the 'human-centred' approach to work organisation and the employment relationship has been set back by its collapse in the Swedish automobile industry:

– however, some elements of the system have survived, notably the emphasis on work groups and the close involvement of the trade unions;

– the longer term prospect for a synthesis of lean production and human-centred approaches remains viable, as witness the successful experiments in work reorganisation and corporate governance at GM's Saturn Corporation and the prospects for a similar development at GM's Swedish subsidiary, Saab;

– these prospects seem, however, to depend largely on the trade unions retaining sufficient strength and influence.

Discussion questions

1 To what extent do overseas Japanese companies in the automobile industry export the workplace practices and personnel policies developed in Japan?

2 Discuss the 'stakeholder' view of the enterprise as illustrated in Illustration 15.1.

3 Who should be concerned about the decline of trade union membership? Are trade unions just another 'special interest'?

4 Is 'adversarialism' necessary to the functioning of independent trade unions protecting the interests of their members?

5 How real, in practice, are the distinctions between mass production, lean production and human-centred production? How realistic is a synthesis between the last two?

6 Discuss the nature of team work and its value to organisations. Consider the view that it is an advanced form of managerial control.

7 Discuss the view that even after more than 40 years of European economic and political integration, national industrial relations systems remain intact.

Further reading

For those interested in a global study of the telecommunications industry using the same methodology as that of Kochan *et al.* for the automobile industry, see Katz (1997). This, as does Kochan *et al.*, includes detailed country studies as well as comparative overviews.

There are a number of well-established academic journals (which will be in good university libraries) that publish substantial, up-to-date, authoritative studies of international and comparative industrial relations themes. These include:

- *Industrial Relations Journal (UK)*. The IRJ devotes one-third of its pages to European and international articles as well as publishing a comprehensive annual European review.

- *European Journal of Industrial Relations (UK)*. This new journal specialises in *comparative* European studies.

- *Transfer* (European Trade Union Confederation, Brussels). This is a publication of the ETUC's research institute, the ETUI. It mainly publishes well-researched trade union studies written by academics and researchers in its institute.

- *International Labour Review* (ILO, Geneva). The long-established ILR publishes articles on countries and themes worldwide.

- *Industrial Relations* (USA). One of the two principal US journals that frequently publish international and comparative articles.

- *Industrial and Labour Relations Review* (USA). This journal is the best source of detailed research articles on US themes. It also occasionally publishes articles from non-US sources.

- *International Journal of Human Resource Management* (UK), *Human Resource Management Journal* (UK). These two journals, through carrying HRM titles, regularly publish international and comparative articles that are relevant to this chapter, especially the IJHRM.

For an invaluable, monthly reporting publication, students should consult the *European Industrial Relations Review* (EIRR), published by the London-based Industrial Relations Services. This publication is widely available in university and large public libraries.

AFTERWORD

Successful human resourcing

Ward Griffiths

Assistant Director General, Institute of Personnel and Development
and Visiting Professor of Human Resource Practice,
Nottingham Business School

As the twentieth century draws to a close, we are experiencing the gradual emergence of a new managerial mind-set towards people management and development. The main feature of this is the recognition that optimal organisational performance is increasingly dependent on intellectual capital, innovation and collaborative behaviours. The drive for performance is changing the nature of work, generating demands for increasing and widening knowledge and skills, for the acceptance of increased responsibility by people at work, and for a new focus on work roles and relationships.

As globalisation and continuous changes in markets and technology bring about the erosion of boundaries within and between organisations, 'steady state' hierarchies and fixed roles are no longer viable. Managers are involved with a dynamic set of organisational strategies and underpinning, interrelated, business processes. This book's emphasis on a processual approach to resourcing as the vehicle for relating people management to organisational performance is therefore wholly appropriate. It brings a welcome focus to a way of thinking about human resources strategy-making which is grounded in the realities of organisational life. Strategy can be found in many features of an organisation's planning processes and supporting activities, but is critically about creating and re-creating over time an effective and suitable performance response to the changing performance requirements of the external environment. It is a process of matching organisational capabilities to the forces generated by that environment. And those capabilities, whether they are based on capacity to innovate, or on the maintenance of outstanding quality, or on unique levels of customer trust, are all highly dependent on the effective resourcing and management of the people who work in the business.

Encouragingly, an increasing number of studies show positive associations between human resourcing and performance, suggesting that if an internally integrated set of human resourcing practices is developed continually and aligned with organisation strategies which are likely to be changing and flexible, then higher performance should result.

The Institute of Personnel and Development has recently worked closely with academic researchers to investigate the relationship between people management and performance among UK manufacturing firms varying in size from 60 to 1000 employees. The research concluded that HRM strategies are far more powerful predictors of change in company performance than other factors, including business strategy, quality, the use of advanced manufacturing technology, and research and development (Patterson *et al.*, 1997).

The research nevertheless revealed shortfalls in HRM practices. Half the surveyed organisations had no individual responsible for personnel matters, while more than two-thirds had no written personnel or HRM strategy.

So there remains plenty of room for progress in changing managerial attitudes in such organisations to reflect those of other senior managers in the study who made it clear that human resourcing and employee commitment, satisfaction and participation were the central elements of their business strategy. The evidence is mounting that those who have such positive attitudes to people management and development will benefit. In the USA, research by Mark Huselid, Associate Professor of Human Resource Management at Rutgers University, New Jersey has demonstrated that it is possible to put a price on the benefits of good human resource practice (Huselid, 1995), and Professor Jeffrey Pfeffer of Stanford has also written extensively on organisations whose success can be related to the way they resource their people management and development needs (Pfeffer, 1998).

Of course, the assumptions that have to be built into the 'bundling' of HRM policies, and their link to performance, are complex. Most performance measures are contingent on situational features – and investments in HRM policies and practices may take time to show through. There is little consensus on any 'ideal' design for work practices and – while statistical correlations are impressive – there is little substantive evidence as yet on the underlying causal linkages by which people management practice affects outcomes. So this book's theme of strategies as evolving patterns in a complex, changing picture of organisational activity, rather than as plans which precede activity, will help human resource professionals to effect dynamic, anticipative approaches to their organisations' needs and to provide a flow of value adding contributions.

As economic pressures intensify, the opportunities to make such contributions are increasing. In the summer of l998 IPD interviewed HR Directors in a range of large UK employing organisations. It was striking that all of those interviewed saw themselves as 'business partners', i.e. aiming first and foremost to contribute to the success of their organisations. They described a wide and diverse array of pressures that require a response from them and their function in terms of organisational and people resourcing issues. These included growing the stock of people who can run and manage international businesses, developing a workforce that has good ideas and is innovative, persistent and resourceful, and developing excellence, continuous improvement, integration and business alignment across their people management and development policies and practices. In managing the resourcing process they operate in a variety of roles – as leaders of organisational capability development, as change agents, as internal HR consultants, and as guardians of standards.

The HR directors were agreed that companies are likely to continue to adopt progressive human resource management policies and practices in their search to improve business performance, with a focus on flexibility and continual adjustment to maintain relevance and integration with a wider set of changing strategies. The drivers of the management challenges for their organisations are diverse, as are the management challenges themselves. The pressures are creating multiple questions and issues for HR Directors and those in their function, including envisioning and establishing an infra-structure of systems and processes to resource and enhance 'the people contribution' to organisational goals.

This book helps thinking on human resourcing strategy-making in such circum-stances. It provides valuable insights into how effective, business-focussed employee resourcing can be achieved – what should be done and ideas on how to do it. It illus-trates how to consider the specifics of resourcing strategy in the context of a wider range of strategies and contingencies, and it also offers a guide to ensuring that resourcing processes can produce the workforce behaviours and competences which are needed for particular market circumstances and strategic aims. It should therefore prove to be a useful and reliable source of ideas and interpretation for business-orientated people managers – both specialists and those who have other managerial accountabilities, who recognise that effective human resourcing is a key factor in achieving their own and their organisation's goals.

REFERENCES

A

Ackers, P., Smith, C. and Smith, P. (1996) *The New Workplace and Trade Unionism: Critical Perspectives on Work and Organisation*, London: Routledge.

Adams, J.S. (1965) 'Inequality in social exchange', in L. Berkowitz (ed.) *Advances in Experimental Social Psychology*, Vol. 2, New York: Academic Press, pp. 267–99.

Adams, R.J. and Turner, L. (1994) 'The social dimension of freer trade', in M.L. Cook and H.C. Katz (eds) *Regional Integration and Industrial Relations in North America,* Ithaca, New York: Cornell University Press, pp. 82–104

Adler, N.J. (1997) *International Dimensions of Organisational Behaviour*, 3rd edition, Cincinnati: South-Western College Publishing.

Adler, P.S, Kochan, T.A., MacDuffie, J.P., Frits, K. and Rubinstein, S. (1997) 'United State: variations on a theme', in T.A. Kochan, R.D. Lansbury and J.P. MacDuffie (eds) *After Lean Production: Evolving Employment Practices in the World Auto Industry*, Ithaca, NY: Cornell University Press.

Advisory Conciliation and Arbitration Service Annual Reports 1987–97, ACAS publications, London: ACAS.

Advisory Conciliation and Arbitration Service (1988) *The Development of Payment Systems*, Occasional paper 45, London: ACAS.

Advisory Conciliation and Arbitration Service (1991a) *Consultation and Communication*, Occasional Paper 49, London: ACAS.

Advisory, Conciliation and Arbitration Service (1991b) *Appraisal Related Pay Survey*, London: ACAS.

Allinson, G.D. (1997) *Japan's Postwar History*, Ithaca, New York: Cornell University Press.

Alvesson, M. and Deetz, S. (1996) 'Critical theory and postmodernism approaches to organisation studies', in S.R. Clegg, C. Hardy, and W.R. Nord (eds) *Handbook of Organisation Studies*, London: Sage, pp. 191–217.

Alvesson, M. and Wilmott, H. (1996) *Making Sense of Management: A Critical Introduction,* London: Sage.

Anderson, N. and Herriot, P. (1997) *International Handbook of Selection and Assessment*, Chichester: John Wiley & Sons.

Anderson, N. and Ostroff, C. (1997) 'Selection as socialisation', in N. Anderson and P. Herriot (eds) *International Handbook of Selection and Assessment*, Chichester: John Wiley & Sons, pp. 543–66.

Armstrong, M. (1988) 'Reward management – the changing scene', Institute of Personnel Management, national conference paper, Harrogate, October.

Armstrong, M. (1992) *Human Resource Management: Strategy and Action,* London: Kogan Page.

Armstrong, M. (1994) *Performance Management*, London: Kogan Page.

Armstrong, M. (1995) *Personnel Management Practice*, 5th edition, London: Kogan Page.

Armstrong, M. (1996) *Employee Reward*, London: IPD.

Arnold, J., Cooper, C.L. and Robertson, I.T. (1997) *Work Psychology: Understanding Human Behaviour in the Workplace,* London: Financial Times Pitman Publishing.

Arrowsmith, J. and McGoldrick, A. (1997) 'A flexible future for older workers?', *Personnel Review*, Vol. 26, No. 4, pp. 258–73.

Atkinson, J. (1984) 'Manpower strategies for flexible organisations', *Personnel Management*, August, pp. 28–31.

Atkinson, J. (1987) 'Flexibility or fragmentation? The UK labour market in the eighties', *Labour and Society*, Vol. 12, No. 1, pp. 87–102.

Atkinson, J. (1996) *Temporary Work and the Labour Market*, Report 311, Brighton: Institute of Employment Studies.

Atkinson, J. and Meager, N. (1986) 'Flexibility in firms: a study of changing working patterns and practices', Sussex: Institute of Manpower Studies.

Audit Commission (1993) *Citizen's Charter Indicators: Charting a Course*, London: Audit Commission.

B

Babson, S. (ed.) (1995) *Lean Work: Empowerment and Exploitation in the Global Auto Industry*, Detroit: Wayne State University Press.

Baddon, L., Hunter, L., Hyman, J., Leopold, J. and Ramsay, H. (1989) *People's Capitalism? A Critical Analysis of Profit Sharing and Employee Share Ownership*, London: Routledge.

Bagilhole, B. (1997) *Equal Opportunities and Social Policy*, Essex: Addison Wesley Longman.

Baird, L. and Meshoulam, I. (1988) 'Managing two fits of strategic human resource management', *Academy of Management Review*, Vol. 13, No. 1, pp. 116–28.

Baldry, C., Bain, P. & Taylor, P. (1998) 'Bright satanic offices: intensification, control and team Taylorism', in P. Thompson and C. Warhurst (eds) *Workplaces of the Future*, Basingstoke: Macmillan Business, pp. 163–83.

Ball, R. and Monaghan, C. (1996) 'Performance review: the British experience', *Local Government Studies*, Vol. 22, No. 1, Spring, pp. 40–58.

Bantel, K.A. (1993) 'Strategic clarity in banking: role of top management demography', *Psychological Reports*, No. 73, Vol. 3, Part 2, pp. 1187–201.

Barnett, A. (1996) 'Gas regulator cools cuts', *The Observer*, 11 August, Business Section, p. 3.

Baron, R.A. (1989). 'Impression management by applicants during employment interviews: the "too much of a good thing" effect', in R.W. Eder and G.R. Ferris (eds) *The Employment Interview: Theory, Research and Practice*, Newbury Park, CA: Sage, pp. 204–15.

Bartlett, C.A. and Ghoshal, S. (1989) *Managing across Borders: the Transnational Solution*, Boston: Harvard Business School Press.

Barsoux, J.L. and Lawrence, P. (1990) *Management in France*, London: Cassell.

Bassett, P. (1986) *Strike Free*, London: Macmillan.

Bates, I. (ed.) (1995) 'Special issue on competence and the NVQ framework', *British Journal of Education and Work*, Vol. 8, No. 2.

Baum, T. (1995) *Managing Human Resources in the European Tourism and Hospitality Industry: a Strategic Approach*, London: Chapman & Hall.

Beach, L.R. (1990) *Image Theory: Decision Making in Personal and Organisational Contexts*, Chichester: John Wiley.

Beardwell, I. (1997) 'Into the "black hole"? An examination of the personnel management of non-unionism', *New Zealand Journal of Industrial Relations*, Vol. 22, No. 1, pp. 37–49.

Beardwell, I. (1998) 'Bridging the gap? Employee voice, representation and HRM', in P. Sparrow and M. Marchington (eds) *Human Resource Management: the New Agenda*, London: Financial Times Pitman Publishing, pp. 193–207.

Beatson, M. (1995) *Labour Market Flexibility*, Employment Department Research Series No. 48, London.

Beaumont, J.R., Kinnie, N.J., Arthurs, A.J. and Weatherall, C.B. (1992) *Information Technology and Personnel Management: Issues and Educational Implications*, Bath: School of Management, University of Bath.

Beaumont, P.B. (1987) *The Decline of Trade Union Organisation*, London: Croom Helm.

Beaumont, P.B. (1993) *Human Resource Management*, London: Sage.

Beaver, G. and Harris, L. (1996a) 'Performance management and competitive advantage: issues, contexts and approaches for the smaller organisation', *Business, Growth and Profitability*, Vol. 2, No. 3, pp. 227–38.

Beaver, G. and Harris, L. (1996b) 'The hidden price of the disposable workforce', *Journal of Professional HRM*, Issue 2, pp. 3–8.

Beavis, S. and Barrie, C. (1996) 'Problems lurk in the gas pipeline', *The Guardian*, 2nd August, p. 10.

Beer, M. and Spector, R. (1985) *Human Resource Management: a General Manager's Perspective*, New York: Free Press.

Beer, M., Spector, B., Lawrence, P., Mills, Q. and Walton, R. (1984) *Managing Human Assets*, New York: Free Press.

Beer, M., Eisenstat, R. and Spector, B. (1993) 'Why change programs don't produce change', in C. Mabey and Mayon White (eds) *Managing Change*, 2nd edition, London: Paul Chapman, pp. 91–107.

Bell, W. and Hanson, C. (1984) *Profit Sharing and Employee Shareholding Attitude Survey*, London: Industrial Participation Association.

Bennett, R. and Leduchowicz, T. (1983) 'What makes for an effective trainer?' *Journal of European Industrial Training,* Vol. 7, No. 2, p. 31, Monograph.

Bercusson, B. (1995), 'The conceptualisation of European law', *Industrial Law Journal,* Vol. 24, No. 1, pp. 3–18.

Berggren, C. (1989) 'New production concepts in final assembly in the Swedish experience', in S. Wood (ed.) *The Transformation of Work?*, London: Unwin Hyman.

Berggren, C. (1992) *The Volvo Experience: Alternatives to Lean Production in the Swedish Auto Industry,* Basingstoke: Macmillan.

Berggren, C. (1995) 'A second comeback or a final farewell? The Volvo Trajectory 1974–94', *Paper Presented at the Third GERPISA International Colloquium on the New Industrial Models*, Paris.

Bevan, S. and Thompson, M. (1992) *Pay and Performance – the Employer Experience*, Report 258, Brighton: Institute of Employment Studies.

Billig, M. (1995) *Banal Nationalism,* London: Sage.

Billig, M. (1996) *Arguing and Thinking: a Rhetorical Approach to Social Psychology*, 2nd edition, Cambridge: Cambridge University Press.

Black, J. and Ackers, P. (1988) 'The Japanisation of British industry: a case study of quality circles in the carpet industry', *Employee Relations,* Vol. 10, No. 6, pp. 9–16.

Black, J. and Ackers, P. (1990) 'Voting for employee involvement at General Motors', paper presented to the 8th Labour Process Conference, University of Aston, March.

Blinkhorn, S. and Johnstone, C. (1990) 'The insignificance of personality testing', *Nature,* No. 348, pp. 671–2.

Bluestone, B. (1995) 'Guaranteeing employee rights in the new global marketplace', *Organisation*, Vol. 2, No. 3/4, pp. 396–401, Sage.

Blyton, P. and Morris, J. (1991) *A Flexible Future*, Berlin: Walter De Gruyter.

Blyton, P. and Turnbull, P. (1992) *Reassessing Human Resource Management*, London: Sage.

Blyton, P. and Turnbull, P. (1994) *The Dynamics of Employee Relations*, London: Macmillan.

Blyton, P. and Turnbull, P. (1998) *The Dynamics of Employment Relations* 2nd edition, London: Macmillan.

Bolton, T. (1997) *Human Resource Management: an Introduction*, Oxford: Blackwell.

Bone, A. (1997) 'How studying the law can boost your skills', *People Management*, Vol. 3, No. 14, p. 57.

Booth, A. (1989) 'The bargaining structure of British establishments', *British Journal of Industrial Relations,* Vol. 27, No. 2, pp. 225–34.

Bowen, D.E., Ledford, G.E. and Latham, B.R. (1991) 'Hiring for the organisation, not the job', *Academy of Management Executive*, Vol. 5, No. 4, pp. 35–50.

Bowey, A., Thorpe, R., Mitchell, F., Nicholls, G., Gosnold, D., Savery, L. and Hellier, P. (1982) *Effects of Incentive Payment Systems, United Kingdom 1977–1980,* Department of Employment Research Paper 36, London: DE.

Bowie, N.E. and Duska, R.F. (1990) *Business Ethics*, London: Prentice-Hall International.

Bowles, L.M. and Coates, G. (1993) 'Image and substance: the management of performance as rhetoric or reality', *Personnel Review,* Vol. 22, No. 2, pp. 3–21.

Boxall, P. (1996) 'The strategic HRM debate and the resource-based view of the firm', *Human Resource Management Journal*, Vol. 6, No. 3, pp. 59–75.

Boyatzis, R. (1982) *The Competent Manager,* Chichester: John Wiley.

Boyden, T. and Paddison, L. (1986) 'Banking on equal opportunities', *Personnel Management Journal*, September, pp. 42–6.

Boyer, R. (1987) 'Labour flexibilities: many forms, uncertain effects', *Labour and Society*, Vol. 12, No. 1, pp. 107–29.

Bradley, K. and Hill, S. (1983) 'After Japan: the quality circle transplant and productive efficiency', *British Journal of Industrial Relations,* Vol. 21, No. 5, pp. 291–311.

Bradley, K. and Hill, S. (1987) 'Quality circles and managerial interests', *Industrial Relations*, Vol. 26, No. 1, pp. 68–82.

Bramham, J. (1997) *Human Resource Planning*, London: IPD.

Brannen, P. (1983) *Authority and Participation in Industry*, London: Batsford.

Braverman, H. (1974) *Labour and Monopoly Capital,* New York, Monthly Review Press.

Brewerton, P.A. (1997) '360° feedback: the enthusiasts and the suspicious', unpublished M.Sc. (HRD) dissertation, The Nottingham Trent University.

Brewster, C. (1998) 'Flexible working in Europe: extent, growth and the challenge for HRM', in P. Sparrow and M. Marchington (eds.) *Human Resource Management: the New Agenda,* London: Financial Times Pitman Publishing.

Brewster, C., Hegeswich, A., Lockhart, T. and Mayne, L. (1992) *Issues in People Management No. 6: Flexible Working Patterns in Europe*, London: IPM.

Brewster, C., Hegeswich, A. and Mayne, L. (1994) 'Trends in European HRM', in S. Kirkbride (ed.) *Human Resource Management in Europe*, London: Routledge, pp. 118–32.

Brewster, C., Mayne, L., Tregaskis, O., Parsons, D. and Atterbury, S. (1996) *Working Time and Contract Flexibility in Europe*, Report for the European Commission DGV, Cranfield University School of Management.

Bridges, W. (1995) *JobShift: How to Prosper in a world without Jobs*, London: Nicholas Brearley.

Bristow, E. (1974) 'Profit-sharing, socialism and labour unrest', in K.D. Brown (ed.) *Essays in Anti-Labour History*, London: Macmillan.

Brown, W. (1981) *The Establishment Survey of Warwick 1977/78*, Industrial Relations Research Unit (IRRU).

Brown, W. (1994) 'The consequences of dismantling British Collective Bargaining', *Review of Employment Topics*, Vol. 2, No. 1, pp. 1–11.

Brown, W.D.S. and Ryan, P. (1997) 'The effect of British industrial relations legislation 1979–97', *National Institute Economic Review*, No. 161, July, pp. 69–83.

Brulin, G. and Nilsson, T. (1997) 'Sweden: the Volvo and Saab road beyond lean production', in T.A. Kochan, R.D. Lansbury and J.P. MacDuffie (eds) *After Lean Production: Evolving Employment Practices in the World Auto Industry*, Ithaca, New York: Cornell University Press.

Bryson, C. (1996) 'The use of fixed term contracts in HE: not such a flexible solution for all parties.', paper presented at the International Labour Process Conference, Aston, 27–29 March.

Bryson, C. (1997) 'Do fixed term contracts mean a better or a worse deal for women?', paper presented at the International Labour Process Conference, Edinburgh, 25–27 March.

Bryson, C. and Barnes, N. (1997) 'Professional workers and fixed term contracts: a contradiction in terms', paper presented at the ERU Conference, Cardiff, September.

Bryson, C., Jackson, M. and Leopold, J. (1993) 'Self-determination in the NHS trusts: impact on industrial relations and human resources management', unpublished report, University of Stirling, August.

Buchanan, D. (1994) 'Principles and practice in work design', in K. Sisson (ed.) *Personnel Management*, Oxford: Blackwell.

Buechtemann, C.F. (ed.) (1993) *Employment Security and Labour Market Behaviour: Interdisciplinary Approaches and International Evidence,* Ithaca, New York: ILR Press.

Buglear, J. (1986) 'Appraisal: what it is and why we should fight it', *Evaluation Newsletter*, Society for Research into Higher Education (SRHE), Vol. 10, No. 2, Winter, pp. 20–5.

Bullock Report (1977) *Report of the Committee of Inquiry in Industrial Democracy*, Chairman Lord Bullock, Cmnd 6076, London: HMSO.

Bullock, A. and Stallybrass, O. (1977) *The Fontana Dictionary of Modern Thought,* London: Fontana/Collins.

Burawoy, M. (1985) *The Politics of Production: Factory Regimes under Capitalism and Socialism*, Chicago: University of Chicago Press.

Burchell, B. and Rubery, J. (1990) 'An empirical investigation into the segmentation of the labour supply', *Work, Employment and Society*, Vol. 4, No. 4, pp. 551–75.

Burchill, F. (1997) *Labour Relations*, 2nd edition, Basingstoke: Macmillan.

Burgoyne, J. (1988) 'Management development for the individual and organisation', *Personnel Management*, Vol. 20, No. 6, 40–4.

Burgoyne, J. and Jackson, B. (1997) 'The arena thesis: management development as a pluralistic meeting point', in J. Burgoyne and M. Reynolds (eds) *Management Learning*, London: Sage, pp. 54–70.

Burgoyne, J. and Reynolds, M. (eds) *Management Learning*, London: Sage.

Burns, T. and Stalker, G.S. (1994) *The Management of Innovation* 2nd edition, Oxford: Oxford University Press.

C

CALM (Computer Assisted Learning for Managers) (n.d.) *Setting Objectives*, Brighton: Maxim Training Systems.

Campion, M., Pursell, E. and Brown, B. (1988) 'Structured interviewing: raising the psychometric properties of the employment interview', *Personnel Psychology*, Vol. 41, No. 1, pp. 25–42.

Cannell, M. and Wood, S. (1992) *Incentive Pay*: Impact and Evolution', London: IPM.

Capelli, P. (1995) 'Rethinking employment', *British Journal of Industrial Relations*, Vol. 33, No. 4, pp. 563–602.

Carroll, A.B. (1990) 'Principles of business ethics: their role in decision making and an initial consensus', *Management Decision*, Vol. 28, No. 8, 20–4.

Casey, B. (1988) 'The extent and nature of temporary employment in Britain'. *Cambridge Journal of Economics*, Vol. 12, No. 4, pp. 487–509.

Casey, B. (1995) *Redundancy in Britain*, Research series No. 62, London: Department of Education and Employment.

Casey, B., Metcalf, H. and Millward, N. (1997) *Employers' Use of Flexible Labour*, London: Policy Studies Institute.

Catholic Online (1998) *Out to lunch*, World Wide Web http://www.catholic.org/euthanasia/abort 797.html, visited 27.2.98.

Cattell, R.B. (1965) *The Scientific Analysis of Personality*, Harmondsworth: Penguin.

Cave, K. (1997) 'Zero hours contracts: a report into the incidence and implications of such contracts', University of Huddersfield.

CBI (1989) *Evaluating Your Training*, London: CBI.

Center for the Study of Ethics in the Professions, Illinois Institute of Technology (1998) *Codes of Ethics Online Project*, World Wide Web http://csep.iit.edu./codes/index.html, visited 10.3.98.

Ceriello, V.R. and Freeman, C. (1991) *Human Resource Management Systems: Strategies, Tactics and Techniques*, Lexington, MA: Lexington Books.

Cerveny, R.P., Pegels, C.P. and Sanders, G.L. (1993), 'Strategic information systems for human resource management', in R.P. Cerveny, C.P. Pegels and G.L. Sanders (eds) *Strategic Information Systems for Strategic Manufacturing, Operations, Marketing, Sales,* *Financial and Human Resources Management*, Greenwich, CT: JAI Press, pp. 125–35.

Chacko, T. (1982) 'Women and equal employment: some unintended effects', *Journal of Applied Psychology*, Vol. 67, No. 1, pp. 119–22.

Chaison, G.N. and Rose, J.B. (1991) 'The macrodeterminants of union growth and decline', in G. Strauss, G. Gallagher, G. Daniel and J. Fiorito (eds) *The State of the Unions,* Madison: Industrial Relations Research Association, pp. 3–45.

Challis, D.J. (1981) 'The measurement of outcome in social care of the elderly', *Journal of Social Policy*, Vol. 10, No. 2, pp. 179–208.

Cheung-Judge, L. Mee-Yan (1993) *Equal Opportunities in Management Education and Development,* Oxford: Q&E Consultancy Services.

Chia, R. (1996) *Organisational Analysis as Deconstructive Practice,* Berlin: Walter DeGruyter.

Chia, R. (1997) 'Process philosophy and management learning: cultivating foresight in management', in J. Burgoyne and M. Reynolds (eds) *Management Learning,* London: Sage, pp. 71–88.

Child, J. (1972) 'Organisational structure, environment and performance', *Sociology,* Vol. 6, No. 1, pp. 2–22.

Child, J. (1984) *Organisation*, London: Harper & Row.

Citrine, The Lord (ed.) (1952) *The ABC of Chairmanship*, London: NCLC Publishing.

Clark, H., Chandler, J. and Barry, J (1994) *Organization Identities: Texts and Readings in Organizational Behaviour*, London: Chapman & Hall.

Clark, J. (1993) 'Full flexibility and self-supervision in an automated factory', in J. Clark (ed.) *Human Resource Management and Technical Change*, London: Sage, pp. 116–36.

Claydon, T. (1998) 'Problematising partnership: the prospects for a co-operative bargaining agenda', in P. Sparrow and M. Marchington (eds) *Human Resource Management: the New Agenda*, London: Financial Times Pitman Publishing, pp. 180–92.

Clegg, H. (1985) 'Trade unions as an opposition which can never become a government', in W.E.J. McCarthy (ed.) *Trade Unions*, 2nd edition, Harmondsworth: Pelican, pp. 83–91.

425

Cockburn, C. (1985) *Machinery of Dominance: Men, Women and Technical Know How*, London: Pluto.

Cockburn, C. (1989) 'Equal opportunities: the short and long agenda', *Industrial Relations Journal*, Vol. 20, No. 3, pp. 213–25.

Cockburn, C. (1991) *In the Way of Women: Men's Resistance to Sex Equality in Organisations*, Basingstoke: Macmillan Education.

Collard, R. and Dale, B. (1989) 'Quality circles', in K. Sisson (ed.) *Personnel Management in Britain*, Oxford: Blackwell, pp. 356–77.

Collinson, D. (1987b) 'Who controls selection?', *Personnel Management*, May, pp. 32–6.

Collinson, D. (1991) 'Poachers turned gamekeepers: are personnel managers one of the barriers to equal opportunities?', *Human Resource Management Journal*, Vol. 1, No. 3, Spring, pp. 58–76.

Collinson, D., Knights, D. and Collinson, M. (1990) *Managing to Discriminate*, London: Routledge.

Colwill, N. and Vinnicombe, S. (1991) 'Women's training needs', in J. Firth-Cozens and M. West (eds) *Women at Work,* Milton Keynes: Open University Press, pp. 42–50.

Commission for Racial Equality (1983) *Implementing Equal Employment Opportunity Policies*, London: CRE.

Connock, S. and Johns, T. (1995) *Ethical Leadership*, London: IPD.

Cook, M. (1993) *Personnel Selection and Productivity*, Chichester: John Wiley & Sons.

Cooper, D. and Robertson, I. (1995) *The Psychology of Personality Testing*, London: Routledge.

Coopey, J. (1995) 'The learning organisation, power, politics and ideology' *Management Learning*, Vol. 26, No. 2, pp. 193–213.

Coopey, J. (1996) 'Crucial gaps: power, politics and ideology', in K. Starkey (ed.) *How organizations learn*, London: International Thomson Business Press, pp. 348–67.

Cornford, F.M. (1908) *Microcosmographia Academica: Being a Guide for the Young Academic Politician*, Cambridge: Bowes and Bowes.

Couch, G.M., Hoffman, J.J. and Lamont, B. (1995) 'The effect of firm survival situations on management ethics', *Journal of Employment Counselling,* Vol. 32, June, pp. 79–87.

Cousins, C. (1997) 'Non-standard employment in Europe: a comparison of recent trends in the UK, Sweden, Germany and Spain', paper presented at the International Labour Process Conference, Edinburgh, 25–27 March.

Coussey, M. and Jackson, H. (1991) *Making Equal Opportunities Work*, London: Financial Times Pitman Publishing.

Crainer, S. (1995) *How to Have a Brilliant Career Without Having a Proper Job.* London: Financial Times Pitman Publishing.

Cressey, P. (1993) 'Kalmar and Uddevalla: the demise of Volvo as a European icon', *New Technology, Work and Employment*, Vol. 8, No. 2, pp. 88–90.

Cressey, P. (1998) 'European works councils in practice', *Human Resource Management Journal*, Vol. 8, No. 1, pp. 67–79.

Crompton, R. (1996) 'Gender and class analysis', in D. Lee and B. Turner (eds) *Conflicts about Class: Debating Inequality in Late Industrialism*, Essex: Longman, pp. 115–38.

Crompton, R. and Jones, G. (1984) *White Collar Proletariat: Deskilling and Gender in the Clerical Labour Process*, London: Macmillan.

Cully, M., O'Reilly, A., Millward, N., Forth, J., Woodland, S., Dix, G. and Bryson, A. (1998) *The 1998 Workplace Employee Relations Survey: First Findings*, London: HMSO.

D

Daboub, A.J., Rasheed, A.M.A., Priem, R.L. and Gray, D.A. (1995) 'Top management team characteristics and corporate illegal activity', *Academy of Management Review,* Vol. 20, No. 1, pp. 138–70.

Dachler, M.P. (1994) 'A social-relational perspective of selection', paper presented at the 23rd International Congress of Applied Psychology, Madrid, Spain, July.

Danford, A. (1997) 'The "new industrial relations" and class struggle in the 90s', *Capital and Class*, Issue No. 61, pp. 107–41.

Dastmalchian, A. (1991) 'Workplace flexibility in professional organisations: a study of Canadian hospitals', in P. Blyton and J. Morris (eds) *A Flexible Future*, Berlin: Walter De Gruyter, pp. 329–48.

De Cieri, H. and McGaughey, S. (1998) 'Relocation', in M. Poole and M. Warner (eds) *The IEBM Handbook of Human Resource Management*, London: International Thomson Business Press, pp. 631–42.

De Wit, B. and Meyer, R. (1994) *Strategy: Process, Content, Context*, Minneapolis: West.

Deakin, S. and Wilkinson, F. (1996) *Labour Standards Essential to Economic and Social Progress*, London: Institute of Employment Rights.

Delbridge, R. and Turnbull, P. (1992) 'Human resource maximisation: the management of labour under JIT manufacturing systems', in P. Blyton and P. Turnbull (eds) *Reassessing Human Resource Management*, London: Sage, pp. 56–73.

Department for Education and Employment (1995) *Skills and Enterprise Executive: Issue 5/95*, London: Skills and Enterprise Network Publications.

Department for Education and Employment (1997) *Skill Needs in Britain Survey*, London: IFF Research.

Department of Employment (1971) *Glossary of Training Terms*, London: HMSO.

Department of Employment (1989) *People and Companies: Employee Involvement in Britain*, London: HMSO.

Department of Health (1989) *Working for Patients; Working Paper No. 7: NHS Consultants Appointments, Contracts and Distinction Awards*, London: HMSO.

Devine, M. (ed.) (1990) *The Photofit Manager*, London: Unwin.

Dex, S. and McCulloch, A. (1997) *Flexible Employment: the Future of Britain's Jobs*, Basingstoke: Macmillan.

Dickens, L. (1994) 'Wasted resources? Equal opportunities in employment', in K. Sisson (ed.) *Personnel Management: a Comprehensive Guide to Theory and Practice in Britain*, Oxford: Blackwell, pp. 253–96.

Dickens, L. (1998) 'What HRM means for gender equality', *Human Resource Management Journal*, Vol. 8, No. 1, pp. 23–40.

Dipboye, R.L. (1997) 'Structured selection interviews: why do they work? Why are they underutilized?' in N. Anderson and P. Herriot (eds), *International Handbook of Selection and Assessment*, Chichester: John Wiley & Sons, pp. 543–66.

Disney, R. (1990) 'Explanations of the decline in trade union density in Britain', *British Journal of Industrial Relations*, Vol. 28, No. 2, April, pp. 165–76.

Dobson, J. and Armstrong, M.B. (1995) 'Application of virtue ethics theory: a lesson from architecture', in L.A. Ponemon, M.J.

Epstein and J.C. Gardner, (eds) *Research on Accounting ethics, Vol. 1*, Hampton Hill: JAI Press, pp. 187–202.

Dobson, P. (1989) 'Reference reports', in P. Herriot (ed.) *Assessment and Selection in Organisations*, Chichester: John Wiley & Sons.

Donaldson, J. (1989) *Key Issues in Business Ethics*, London: Academic Press.

Donkin, R. (1997) 'Equity in performance', *Financial Times*, 23 October, p. 13.

Donovan, Lord (1968) *Report of the Royal Commission on Trade Unions and Employers' Associations*, London: HMSO.

Dougherty, R.L., Turban, D.B. and Callender, J.C. (1994) 'Confirming first impressions in the employment interview', *Journal of Applied Psychology*, Vol. 71, No. 1, pp. 9–15.

Dowling, B. and Richardson R. (1997) 'Evaluating performance related pay for managers in the National Health Service', *International Journal of Human Resource Management*, Vol. 8, No. 3, June, pp. 348–67.

Dowling, P.J., Schuler, R.S. and Welch, D.R. (1994) *International Dimensions of Human Resource Management*, 2nd edition, Belmont, CA: Wadsworth.

DTI (1998) Fairness at Work White Paper, http://www.dit.uk.gov/IR/fairness.

Du Gay, P. and Salaman, G. (1992) 'The cult[ure] of the customer', *Journal of Management Studies*, Vol. 29, No. 5, pp. 615–33.

Duncan, C. (1988) 'Why profit-related pay will fail', *Industrial Relations Journal*, Vol. 19, No. 3, pp. 186–200.

Dunivan, L. (1991) 'Implementing a user-driven human resource information system', *Journal of Systems Management*, Vol. 42, No. 10, pp. 13–15.

Dyson, R. (1991) 'Changing labour utilisation in NHS trusts: the reprofiling paper', University of Keele.

E

Eder, R.W. and Ferris, G.R. (1989) *The Employment Interview: Theory, Research and Practice*, Newbury Park, CA: Sage.

Edwards, C.C. (1995) '360 degree feedback', *Management Services*, June, p. 24.

Edwards, P. (1986) *Conflict at Work: a Materialist Analysis of Workplace Relations*, Oxford: Blackwell.

Edwards, P. (1995) 'Strikes and industrial conflict', in P. Edwards (ed.) *Industrial*

Relations: Theory and Practice, Oxford: Blackwell, pp. 434–60.

Edwards, P., Collinson, D. and Della Rocca, G. (1995) 'Workplace resistance in Western Europe' *European Journal of Industrial Relations*, Vol. 1, No. 3, pp. 283–316.

Edwards, P.K. (ed.) (1995) *Industrial Relations: Theory and Practice in Britain*, Oxford: Blackwell.

Edwards, P.K. and Scullion, H. (1982) *The Social Organisation of Industrial Conflict*, Oxford: Blackwell.

Edwards, P.K. and Whitson, C. (1989) 'Industrial discipline, the control of attendance and the subordination of labour', *Work, Employment and Society*, Vol. 3, No. 1, pp. 1–28.

Edwards, R. (1979) *Contested Terrain: the Transformation of the Workplace in the Twentieth Century*, London: Heinemann.

Elger, T. (1991) 'Task flexibility and the intensification of labour in UK manufacturing in the 1980s', in Pollert, A. (ed.) *Farewell to Flexibility*, Oxford: Blackwell, pp. 46–66.

Elger, T. (1996) *Manufacturing Myths and Miracles: Work Re-organisation in British Manufacturing since 79*, University of Warwick, Working Paper, Department of Sociology and Centre for Comparative Labour Studies.

Elger, T. and Smith, C. (1994) *Global Japanization: the Transnational Transformation of the Labour Process,* London and New York: Routledge.

Elliott, L. (1998) 'Globalisation in need of repairs', in *The Guardian Weekly*, 8 February.

Emerson, M. (1988) 'Regulation or deregulation of the labour market', *European Economic Review*, Vol. 32, pp. 775–817.

Employment Europe (1998) European Union Review, 434, pp. 11–18.

Employment Outlook (1994) Paris: Organisation for Economic Cooperation and Development.

Equal Opportunities Commission (1986) *Guidelines for Equal Opportunities Employers,* Manchester: EOC.

Equal Opportunities Review (1998a) No. 78, March/April.

Equal Opportunities Review (1998b) No. 79, May/June.

Equal Opportunities Review (1998c) No. 80, July/August.

Eysenck, H.J. (1953) *The Structure of Human Personality*, London: Methuen.

F

Faichnie, C. (1997) *EOC Research Update*, Issue 6, January.

Farnham D. and Horton. (1996) *Managing the New Public Services,* London: Macmillan.

Ferner, A. (1990) 'The changing influence of the personnel function: privatisation and organisational politics in electricity generation', *Human Resource Management Journal,* Vol. 1, No. 1, pp. 12–29.

Ferner, A. and Hyman, R. (1998) *Changing Industrial Relations in Europe,* 2nd edition, Oxford: Blackwell.

Filipczak, B. (1997) 'Managing a mixed workforce', *Training*, Vol. 34, No. 10, pp. 96–101.

Fischer, F. (1983) 'Ethical discourse in public administration', *Administration and Society*, Vol. 15, No. 1, pp. 5–42.

Fisher, C.M. (1994) 'The differences between appraisal schemes: variation and acceptability', *Personnel Review*, Vol. 23, No. 8, pp. 33–48.

Fisher, C.M. (1995) 'The differences between appraisal schemes: rhetoric and the design of schemes', *Personnel Review*, Vol. 24, No. 1, pp. 51–66.

Fisher, C.M. (1998) *Resource Allocation in the Public Sector: Values, Priorities, and Markets in the Management of Public Services*, London: Routledge.

Fisher, C.M., Rice, C. and Lovell, A.T.A. (1998) 'Downsizing: an Instrument on Perceptions of Ethical Considerations in Human Resource Management and Management Accountancy', unpublished research instrument, Nottingham Business School.

Fisher, D., Merron, K. and Torbert, W.R. (1987) 'Human development and managerial effectiveness', *Group and Organisation Studies*, Vol. 12, No. 3, 257–73.

Fletcher, C. (1989) 'Impression management in the selection interview', in R.A. Giacalone and P. Rosenfeld (eds) *Impression Management in the Organization*, Hillsdale, NJ: Lawrence Erlbaum Associates, pp. 269–81.

Fletcher, C. (1990) 'The relationship between candidate personality, self-presentation strategies, and interviewer assessments in selection interviews: an empirical study', *Human Relations*, Vol. 43, No. 8, pp. 739–49.

Fletcher, C. and Williams, R. (1992) *Performance Management in the UK: an Analysis of the Issues*, London: IPD.

Flood, P., Gannon, M. and Paauwe, J. (1995) *Managing without Traditional Methods: International Innovations in Human Resource Management*, Wokingham: Addison-Wesley.

Floodgate, J.F. and Nixon, A.E. (1994) 'Personal development plans: the challenge of implementation – a case study', *Journal of European Industrial Training*, Vol. 18, No. 11, pp. 43–7.

Fombrun, C.J., Tichy, N. and Devanna, M.A. (1984) *Strategic Human Resource Management*, New York: John Wiley.

Forster, N. (1994) 'The forgotten employees? The experiences of expatriate staff returning to the UK', *The International Journal of Human Resource Management*, Vol. 5, No. 2, pp. 405–25.

Foster, J. (1989) 'Sex discrimination – the enemy of effective resourcing', *Institute of Personnel Management Annual Conference*, Harrogate.

Fowler, A. (1990) 'Performance management: the MBO of the 1990s', *Personnel Management*, July, pp. 47–51.

Fowler, A. (1994) 'Personnel's model army', *Personnel Management*, Vol. 26, No. 9, pp. 34–7.

Fox, A. (1966) *Industrial Sociology and Industrial Relations*, London: HMSO.

Fox, A. (1974) *Beyond Contract: Work, Power and Trust Relations*, London: Faber.

Fox, A. (1979) 'A note on industrial relations pluralism', *Sociology*, Vol. 13, No. 1, pp. 105–9.

Fox, S. (1997) 'From management education and development to the study of management learning', in J. Burgoyne and M. Reynolds (eds) *Management Learning*, London: Sage, pp. 21–37.

Frantzeb, R.B. (1991) 'Human resource managers' IT skills in HR decision making', in Forrer, S.E. and Leibowitz, Z.B. (eds) *Using Computers in Human Resources: How to Select and Make the Best Use of Automated HR Systems*, Oxford: Jossey-Bass, pp. 207–12.

Fredericks, J. and Stewart, J. (1996) 'The strategy–HRD connection', in J. Stewart and J. McGoldrick (eds) *Human Resource Development: Perspectives, Strategies and Practice*, London: Financial Times Pitman Publishing, pp. 101–19.

Fredman, S. (1997) 'Labour law in flux: the changing composition of the workforce', *Industrial Law Journal*, Vol. 26, No. 4, pp. 337–52.

Freeman, R. and Pelletier, J. (1990) 'The impact of industrial relations legislation on British union density', *British Journal of Industrial Relations*, Vol. 28, No. 2, pp. 141–64.

Freeman, R.B. (1994) *Working under Different Rules*, New York: Russell Sage.

French, R. and Bazalgette, J. (1996) 'From learning organization to "teaching-learning organization"', *Management Learning*, Vol. 27, No. 1, pp. 113–28.

Friedman, A.L. (1990) 'Managerial strategies, activities, techniques and technologies: towards a complex theory of the labour process', in D. Knights and H. Willmott (eds) *Labour Process Theory*, London: Macmillan, pp. 177–98.

G

Galagan, P. (1994) 'Reinventing the profession', *Training and Development*, December, pp. 20–7.

Galin, A. (1991) 'Flexible work patterns – why, how, when and where?', *Bulletin of Comparative Labour Relations*, No. 22, pp. 3–18.

Gall, G. (1994) 'The rise of single table bargaining in Britain', *Employee Relations*, Vol. 16, No. 4, pp. 62–71.

Gall, G. and McKay, S. (1994) 'Trade union derecognition in Britain, 1988–1994', *British Journal of Industrial Relations*, Vol. 32, No. 3.

Gall, G. and McKay, S. (1996) *Recognition and Derecognition: the Current Situation*, London: Labour Research Department, pp. 433–48.

Gallie, D. and White, M. (1992) *Employee Commitment and the Skills Revolution*, London: Policy Studies Institute.

Garavan, T. (1991) 'Strategic human resource development', *Journal of European Industrial Training*, Vol. 5, No. 1, pp. 17–31.

Garavan, T. (1995) 'Stakeholders and strategic human resource development' *Journal of European Industrial Training*, Vol. 19, No. 10, pp. 11–16.

Garavan, T. (1997) 'Training, development, education and learning: different or the same?', *Journal of European Industrial Training*, Vol. 21, No. 2, pp. 39–50.

Garavan, T., Costine, P. and Heraty, N. (1995) 'The emergence of strategic HRD', *Journal of*

European Industrial Training, Vol. 19, No. 10, pp. 4–10.

Garrahan, P. and Stewart, P. (1992) *The Nissan Enigma: Flexibility at Work in a Local Economy,* London: Mansell.

Gaugler, B.B., Rosenthal, D.B., Thornton, G.C. and Bentson, C. (1987) 'Meta-analysis of assessment centre validity', *Journal of Applied Psychology*, Vol. 72, No. 3, pp. 493–511.

Geary, J. (1992) 'Employment flexibility and human resource management: the case of three American electronics plants', *Work, Employment and Society,* Vol. 6, No. 2, pp. 251–70.

Geary, J. (1994) 'Task participation: employees' participation enabled or constrained', in K. Sisson (ed.) *Personnel Management*, Oxford: Blackwell, pp. 634–61.

Geary, J. (1995) 'Work practices: the structure of work' in P. Edwards (ed.) *Industrial Relations: Theory and Practice*, Oxford: Blackwell, pp. 368–96.

Gee, J.P., Hull, G. and Lankshear, C. (1996) *The New Work Order: Behind the Language of the New Capitalism,* Colarado: Westview Press.

Gennard, J. and Judge, G. (1997) *Employee Relations*, London: IPD.

Gilbert, N., Burrows, R. and Pollert, A. (1992) *Fordism and Flexibility,* Basingstoke: Macmillan.

Gilmore, D.C. and Ferris, G.R. (1989) 'The effects of applicant impression management tactics on interviewer judgments', *Journal of Management*, No. 15, December, pp. 557–64.

Glaze, T. (1989) 'Cadbury's dictionary of competence', *Personnel Management,* July, pp. 44–8.

Gluck, F.W., Kaufman, S.P. and Walleck, A.S. (1982) 'The four phases of strategic management', *Journal of Business Strategy*, Winter, pp. 9–21.

Gold, M. (ed.) (1993) *The Social Dimension: Employment Policy in the European Community*, Basingstoke: Macmillan.

Goodstein, L.D. and Burke, W.W. (1993) 'Creating successful organization change', in C. Mabey and Mayon White (eds) *Managing Change,* London, Paul Chapman, pp. 164–72.

Goss, D. (1994) *Principles of Human Resource Management,* London: Routledge.

Govindarajan, V. and Gupta, A. (1998a) 'Setting a course for the new global landscape', in *Mastering Global Business*, Financial Times Pitman Publishing, pp. 3–5.

Govindarajan, V. and Gupta A. (1998b) 'Success is all in the mindset', in *Mastering Global Business*, Financial Times Pitman Publishing, pp. 2–3.

Gower (n.d.) *Appraisal Skills*, training video package.

Green, F. (1992) 'Recent trends in British trade union density: how much of a compositional effect?' *British Journal of Industrial Relations*, Vol. 30, No. 3, July, pp. 445–58.

Green, W.C. and Yanarella, E.J. (1996) *North American Auto Unions in Crisis: Lean Production as Contested Terrain,* Albany: State University of New York Press.

Griffin, R. (1988) 'Consequences of quality circles in an industrial setting', *Academy of Management Journal*, Vol. 31, pp. 338–58.

Griffiths, A. and Wall, S. (1996) *Applied Economics*, London: Longman.

Gross, J. (ed.) (1987) *The Oxford Book of Aphorisms*, Oxford: Oxford University Press.

Grubb, D. and Wells, W. (1993) 'Employment regulation and patterns of work in EC countries', *OECD Economic Studies*, Vol. 21, Winter, pp. 7–56.

Gudex, C. (1986) *QALYs and their Use by the Health Service*, Discussion paper No. 20, York: Centre for Health Economics, University of York.

Guest, D. (1982) 'Has the recession really hit personnel management?', *Personnel Management,* Vol. 14, No. 10, pp. 36–9.

Guest, D. (1987) 'Human resource management and industrial relations', *Journal of Management Studies,* Vol. 24, No. 5, pp. 503–21.

Guest, D. (1991) 'Personnel management: the end of orthodoxy?', *British Journal of Industrial Relations*, Vol. 29, No. 2, pp. 149–76.

Guest, D. (1995) 'Human resource management, trade unions and industrial relations', in J. Storey (ed.) *Human Resource Management: a Critical Text,* London: Routledge, pp. 110–41.

Guest, D., Conway, N., Briner, R. and Dickman, M. (1996) 'The state of the psychological contract in employment', *Issues in People Management Report No. 16*, London: IPD.

Guion, R.M. (1997) 'Criterion measures and the criterion dilemma', in N. Anderson and P. Herriot (eds) *International Handbook of*

Selection and Assessment, Chichester: John Wiley & Sons, pp. 543–66.

Gunnigle, P. and Flood, P. (1990) *Personnel Management in Ireland: Practice, Trends and Developments*, Dublin: Gill and Macmillan.

H

Hackman, J.R. and Oldham, G.R. (1976) 'Motivation through the design of work: a test of a theory', *Organisational Behaviour and Human Performance*, Vol. 16, No. 2, pp. 250–79.

Hackman, J.R., Oldham, G.R., Janson, R. and Purdy, K. (1975) 'A new strategy for job enrichment', *California Management Review*, Vol. 17, No. 4, pp. 57–71.

Hakim, C. (1987) 'Trends in the flexible workforce', *Employment Gazette*, No. 95, pp. 549–60.

Hakim, C. (1990) 'Core and periphery in employers' workforce strategies: evidence from the 1987 ELUS survey', *Work, Employment and Society*, Vol. 4, No. 2, pp. 157–88.

Hall, E.J. and Hall, M.R. (1990) *Understanding Cultural Differences*, Yarmouth, ME: Intercultural Press.

Hall, L. (1988) 'Childcare Charter', *Personnel Today*, September.

Hall, L. and Torrington, D. (1989) 'How personnel managers come to terms with the computer', *Personnel Review*, Vol. 18, No. 6, pp. 26–31.

Hall, L. and Torrington, D. (1998) *The Human Resource Function: the Dynamics of Change and Development*, London: Financial Times Management.

Hall, M. (1992) 'Behind the European works councils directives: the European Commission's legislative strategy', *British Journal of Industrial Relations*, Vol. 30, No. 4, pp. 547–61.

Hamblin, A. (1974) *Evaluation and Control of Training*, London: McGraw-Hill.

Hammer, M. and Champy, J. (1994) *Reengineering the Corporation: a Manifesto for Business Revolution*, New York: Hager Business.

Hammermesh, D. (1987) 'The demand for workers and hours and the effects of job security policies: theories and evidence', in R. Hart (ed.) *Employment, Unemployment and Labour Utilisation*, Boston: Unwin, pp. 9–32.

Handy, C. (1994a) *The Empty Raincoat*, London: Hutchinson.

Handy, C. (1994b) *The Future of Work*, London: Hutchinson.

Hannon, J., Jelf, G. and Brandes, D. (1996) 'Human resource information systems: operational issues and strategic considerations in a global environment', *International Journal of Human Resource Management*, Vol. 7, No. 1, pp. 245–69.

Harris, L. (1997) 'New challenges for selection', *Flexible Working Briefing*, Croner Issue No. 20, pp. 5–7.

Harris, L. (1998) 'How performance-related pay can fail to deliver real commitment and adaptability – the view of the middle manager', *Journal of Professional HRM*, No. 10, January.

Harris, L. and Bott, D. (1996) 'Limitation or liberation? The human resource specialist and the law', *Journal of Professional HRM*, No. 4.

Harrison, R. (1993) *Human Resource Management: Issues and Strategies*, Wokingham: Addison-Wesley.

Harrison, R. (1997) *Employee Development*, London: IPD.

Hart, D. and Scott, W. (1973) 'Administrative crisis: the neglect of metaphysical speculation', *Public Administration Review*, Vol. 33, No. 5, September–October, pp. 415–27.

Harzing, A.W. and Ruysseveldt, J.V. (eds) (1995) *International Human Resource Management: an Integrated Approach*, London: Sage.

Heenan, D.A. and Perlmutter, H.V. (1979) *Multinational Organisation Development*, Reading, MA: Addison-Wesley.

Heery, E. (1996) 'The new new unionism', in I. Beardwell (ed.) *Contemporary Industrial Relations: a Critical Analysis*, Oxford: Oxford University Press, pp. 175–202.

Heffcut, A.I. and Arthur, W. (1994) 'Hunter and Hunter (1984) revisited: interview validity for entry-level jobs', *Journal of Applied Psychology*, Vol. 79, No. 2, pp. 184–90

Heider, F. (1958) *The Psychology of Interpersonal Relations*, New York: John Wiley & Sons.

Heinemann, Hope, T. and Hope, J. (1997) 'Chain reaction', *People Management*.

Hendry, C. and Pettigrew A. (1986) 'The practice of human resource management', *Personnel Review*, Vol. 15, No. 5, pp. 3–8.

Hendry, C. and Pettigrew, A. (1992) 'Patterns of strategic change in the development of human resource management', *British Journal of Management*, Vol. 3, No. 3, pp. 137–56.

Hendry, C. (1994a) *Human Resource Management*, Oxford: Butterworth.

Hendry, C. (1994b) *Human Resource Strategies for International Growth*, London: Routledge.

Hendry, C. (1995) *Human Resource Management: a Strategic Approach to Employment,* Oxford: Butterworth-Heinemann.

Hendry, C., Bradley, P. and Perkins, S. (1997) 'Missed a motivator?', *People Management*, Vol. 3, No. 10, May, pp. 21–5.

Heneman, R.L. (1992) *Merit Pay: Linking Pay Increases to Performance Rating*, Reading, MA.: Addison-Wesley.

Henkoff, R. (1992) 'Inside America in biggest private company', *Fortune*, Vol. 126, No. 1, pp. 82–90.

Hepple, B. (1995) 'The future of labour law', *Industrial Law Journal*, Vol. 24, No. 4, pp. 303–22.

Heraty, N. and Morley, M. (1995) 'Line managers and human resource development', *Journal of European Industrial Training,* Vol. 19, No. 10, pp. 31–7.

Herriot, P. (1984) *Down from the Ivory Tower*, Chichester: John Wiley & Sons.

Herriot, P. (1989a) 'Selection as a social process.', in M. Smith and I.T. Robertson (eds) Advances in Selection and Assessment, Chichester: John Wiley & Sons, pp. 171–88.

Herriot, P. (1989b) 'Attribution theory and interview decisions', in R.W. Eder and G.R. Ferris (eds), *The Employment Interview*, London: Sage, pp. 97–109.

Herriot, P. and Anderson, N. (1997) 'Selecting for change: how will personnel and selection psychology survive?', in N. Anderson and P. Herriot (eds), *International Handbook of Selection and Assessment*, Chichester: John Wiley & Sons, pp. 1–38.

Herriot, P. and Pemberton, C. (1995a) 'Psychological contracts – a new deal for middle managers', *People Management,* Vol. 1, No. 12, pp. 32–4.

Herriot, P. and Pemberton, C. (1995b) *New Deals: the Revolution in Managerial Careers*, Chichester: John Wiley & Sons.

Herzberg, F. (1966) *Work and the Nature of Man*, Cleveland, Ohio: World Publishing Company.

Herzberg, F. (1968) 'One more time: how do you motivate employees?', *Harvard Business Review*, Vol. 46, No. 1, pp. 53–62.

Herzberg, F. (1987) 'Workers' needs the same around the world', *Industry Week*, Vol. 21, September, pp. 29–30.

Hesketh, B. and Robertson, I.T. (1993) 'Validating personnel selection: a process model for research and practice', *International Journal of Selection and Assessment*, Vol. 1, No. 1, pp. 3–17.

Hickson, D.J. (1966) 'A convergence in organisation theory', *Administrative Science Quarterly,* Vol. 11, pp. 224–37.

Hickson, D.J., Hinnings, C.R., Lee, C.A., Schneck, R.E. and Pennings, J.M. (1971) 'A strategic contingencies theory of interorganisational power', *Administrative Science Quarterly*, Vol. 11, No. 2, pp. 224–37.

Hill, S. (1991) 'Why quality circles failed but total quality might succeed', *British Journal of Industrial Relations*, Vol. 29, No. 4, pp. 541–69.

Hinrichs, J.R. (1976) 'Personal training', in Dunnette, M.D. (ed.) *Handbook of Organizational and Industrial Psychology*, Chicago: Rand McNally.

Hirsch, W. and Jackson, C. (1995) *Careers in Organisations: Issues for the Future,* Brighton: Institute for Employment Studies.

Hochschild, A.R. (1983) *The Managed Heart: the Commercialisation of Human Feeling*, Berkeley: University of California Press.

Hoecklin, L. (1995) *Managing Cultural Differences: Strategies for Competitive Advantage*, Wokingham: Addison-Wesley.

Hofstede, G. (1980) *Cultures and Consequences*, Beverly Hills, CA: Sage.

Hofstede, G. (1984) *The Game of Budget Control*, London: Tavistock.

Hofstede, G. (1991) *Cultures and Organisations: Software of the Mind*, London: McGraw-Hill.

Hogarth, R. (1980) *Judgement and Choice*, New York: John Wiley & Sons.

Hogg, C. (1998) 'In my opinion . . .', *Croner Reference Book for Employers Magazine,* No. 8, March, p. 5.

Honey, P. (1980) *Solving People-Problems*, London: McGraw-Hill.

Hope, T. and Hope, J. (1997) 'Chain reaction', *People Management*, 25 September, pp. 26–31.

Hope-Hailey, V., Gratton, L., McGovern, P., Stiles, P. and Truss, C, (1997) 'A chameleon function? HRM in the '90s', *Human Resource Management Journal*, Vol. 7, No. 3, pp. 5–18.

Hosking, D.M. and Morley, I.E. (1991) *A Social Psychology of Organising: People, Processes and*

Contexts, Hemel Hempstead: Harvester Wheatsheaf.

Huczynski, A.A. (1983) *Encyclopedia of Management Development Methods*, Aldershot: Gower.

Hughes, E.C. (1937) 'Institutional office and the person', *American Journal of Sociology*, Vol. 4, No. 3, pp. 404–13.

Human Synergistics/Center for Applied Research (n.d.) *Individual Diagnostics*, World Wide Web http://enteract.com/-car/diag2.html, visited 29.1.98.

Hunter, J.E. and Schmidt, F.L. (1990) *Methods of Meta-analysis: Correcting Error and Bias in Research Findings*, Newbury Park, CA: Sage.

Hunter, L. and MacInnes, J. (1991) *Employers' Labour Use Strategies – Case Studies*, Research Paper No. 87, London: Department of Employment.

Hunter, L., McGregor, A., MacInnes, J. and Sproull, A. (1993) 'The "flexible firm": strategy and segmentation', *British Journal of Industrial Relations*, Vol. 31, No. 3, pp. 383–407.

Huselid, M. (1995) 'The impact of human resource management practices on turnover, productivity and corporate financial performance', *Academy of Management Journal*, Vol. 38, No. 3, pp. 635–72.

Hyman, J. and Mason, B. (1995) *Managing Employee Involvement and Participation*, London: Sage.

Hyman, R. (1991) 'Plus ca change? The theory of production and the production of theory', in A. Pollert (ed.) *Farewell to Flexibility*, Oxford: Blackwell, pp. 259–83.

Hyman, R. (1988) 'Flexible specialisation: miracle or myth', in R. Hyman, and W. Streek (eds) *New Technology and Industrial Relations*, Oxford: Blackwell.

Hyman, R. (1989) *Strikes*, 4th edition, London: Macmillan.

I

Ibbetson, A. and Newell, S. (1998) 'Don't blame the provider', *International Journal of Training and Development*, Vol. 1, No. 4, pp. 239–58.

IDS (1997) 'The new agenda, *IDS Focus*, Special Issue, May, Income Data Services.

IDS (1998) 'Pay, conditions and labour market changes', *Report 763*, June, London: IDS.

IDS Study 460 (1990) *Training Strategies*, London: Income Data Services.

IDS Study 626 (1997a) *Performance Management*, London: Income Data Services.

IDS Study 631 (1997b) *Community Personnel Policies*, London: Income Data Services.

IDS Study 634 (1997c) *Recruitment Practices*, London: Income Data Services.

IDS Study 637 (1997d) *European Works Councils*, London: Income Data Services.

IDS Study 638 (1997e) *Suggestion Schemes*, London: Income Data Services.

IDS Study 641 (1998a) *Profit Sharing*, London: Income Data Services.

IDS Study 650 (1998b) *Performance Related Pay*, London: Income Data Services.

IDS Top Pay Unit (1988c) *Paying for Performance*, Income Data Services, Research File No. 9, February.

Illes, P. and Robertson, I. (1997) 'The impact of personnel selection procedures on candidates', in N. Anderson and P. Herriot (eds) *International Handbook of Selection and Assessment*, Chichester: John Wiley & Sons, pp. 543–66.

Industrial Relations Services (IRS) (1994) 'Diversity and change – survey of non-standard working', *IRS Employment Trends*, No. 570, October, pp. 7–18.

Industrial Relations Services (IRS) (1996) 'Holidays and hours: Part I. Entitlements and Changes', *IRS Employment Trends*, 616, September, pp. 5–16.

Inman, K. (1998) 'Fair play', *Employers' Law*, April/May, pp. 11–13.

Institute of Employment Rights (1998) *Need to be Heard at Work: Recognition Laws–Lessons from Abroad*, London: Institute of Employment Rights.

Institute of Management and Manpower plc (1995) *Survey of Long Term Employment Strategies*, London: Institute of Management.

Institute of Personnel and Development (IPD) (1997) *Managing Diversity*, IPD position paper, London: IPD.

Institute of Personnel and Development (IPD) (1998) *Performance Pay Survey Executive Summary*, London: IPD.

Institute of Personnel and Development (IPD) (n.d.) *The IPD Code of Professional Conduct and Disciplinary Procedures*, London: IPD.

Institute of Personnel Management (IPM) (1988) 'Suggestion schemes', *Personnel Management* Factsheet 11, November.

Institute of Personnel Management (IPM) (1992) *Performance Management in the UK: an Analysis of the Issues*, London: IPM.

International Labour Office (ILO) (1997a) *World Labour Report 1997–98: Industrial Relations, Democracy and Social Stability,* Geneva: ILO.

International Labour Office (1997b) *Yearbook of Labour Statistics 1996,* 55th edition, Geneva: ILO.

IRS (1997) 'Culture change', *IRS Management Review,* Issue 1, No. 4.

J

Jackson, M.P., Leopold, J.W. and Tuck, K. (1993) *Decentralisation of Collective Bargaining: an Analysis of Recent Experience in the UK,* Basingstoke: Macmillan.

Jackson, T. (1998) 'The Myth of the global executive', *Financial Times,* 8 October.

Jacobi, O., Keller, B. and Müller-Jentsch, W. (1998) 'Germany: facing new challenges', in A. Ferner, and R. Hyman (eds) *Changing Industrial Relations in Europe,* Oxford: Blackwell, pp. 190–238.

Jacques, E. (1961) *Equitable Payment,* London: Heinemann.

Janz, T., Hellervik, L. and Gilmore, D.C. (1986) *Behaviour Description Interviewing: New, Accurate, Cost-effective,* Boston, MA: Allyn and Bacon.

Jaques, D. (1992) 'Self-appraisal; problems and insights', conference presentation at *Appraisal: Implications for Academic Staff Development in Higher Education,* organised by the Standing Conference on Educational Development (SCED) and Derbyshire College of Higher Education.

Jaques, E. (1956) *Measurement of Responsibility,* London: Tavistock.

Jefferson, M. (1997) *Principles of Employment Law,* 3rd edition, London: Cavendish.

Jenkins, R. (1986) *Racism and Recruitment: Managers, Organisations and Equal Opportunity in the Labour Market,* Cambridge: Cambridge University Press.

Jewson, N. and Mason, D. (1986) 'The theory and practice of equal opportunities policies: liberal and radical approaches', *Sociological Review,* Vol. 34, No. 2, pp. 307–33.

Johnson, G. (1987) *Strategic Change and the Management Process,* Oxford: Basil Blackwell.

Johnson, T. (1977) 'The professions in the class structure', in R. Scase (ed.) *Industrial Society,* London: Allen and Unwin, pp. 93–110.

Jones, A. (1991) 'The role of the management trainer', in Mumford, A. (ed.), *Gower Handbook of Management Development,* Aldershot: Gower, p. 379.

Jones, A.M. and Hendry, C. (1994) 'The learning organisation: adult learning and organisational transformation' *British Journal of Management,* Vol. 5, No. 2, June, pp. 153–62.

Jones, J.E. and Woodcock, M. (1985) *Manual of Management Development,* Aldershot: Gower.

Jones, N. and Fear, N. (1994) 'Continuing professional development: perspectives from human resource professionals', *Personnel Review,* Vol. 23, No. 8, pp. 48–61.

Jones, P. (1988) 'Policy and praxis: local government, a case for treatment', in A. Coyle and J. Skinner (eds) *Women and Work: Positive Action for Change,* Basingstoke: Macmillan Education.

Judge, T.A. and Ferris, G.A. (1992) 'The elusive criterion of fit in human resources staffing decisions', *Human Resource Planning,* Vol. 15, No. 4, pp. 47–67.

K

Kahn-Freund, O. (1972) *Labour and the Law,* London: Stevens and Sons.

Kandola, R. and Fullerton, J. (1994) *Managing the Mosaic: Diversity in action,* London: IPD.

Kanungo, R.N. and Mendonca, M. (1996) *Ethical Dimensions of Leadership,* London: Sage.

Kaplan, R.S. and Norton, D.P. (1992) 'The balanced scorecard – measures that drive performance', *Harvard Business Review,* January/February, pp. 71–9.

Katz, H.C. (ed.) (1997) *Telecommunications: Restructuring Work and Employment Relations Worldwide,* Ithaca, New York: Cornell University Press.

Kauffman, J.R., Jex, S.M., Love, K.G. and Libkuman, T.M. (1993) 'The construct validity of assessment centre performance dimensions', *International Journal of Selection and Assessment,* Vol. 1, No. 4, pp. 213–23.

Kavanagh, M.J., Gueutal, H.G. and Tannenbaum, S.I. (1990) *Human Resource Information Systems: Development and Application,* Boston, MA: PWS-Kent.

Kay, E., Meyer, H.H. and French, J.R.P. (1965) 'Effects of threat in a performance appraisals interview', *Journal of Applied Psychology,* Vol. 49, No. 3, pp. 311–17.

Keenan, T. (1995) 'Graduate recruitment in Britain: a survey of selection methods used by organisations', *Journal of Organisational Behaviour*, Vol. 16, No. 4, pp. 303–17.

Keenan, T. (1997) 'Selection for potential', in N. Anderson and P. Herriot (eds), *International Handbook of Selection and Assessment*, Chichester: John Wiley & Sons, pp. 507–28.

Keeney, M. and Florida, R. (1993) *Beyond Mass Production*, New York: Oxford University Press.

Keenoy, T. (1990) 'HRM, a case of the wolf in sheep's clothing', *Personnel Review*, Vol. 19, No. 2, pp. 3–9.

Keenoy, T. and Anthony, P. (1992) 'HRM: metaphor, meaning and morality', in P. Blyton and P. Turnbull (eds) *Reassessing Human Resource Management*, London: Sage, pp. 233–55.

Keep, E. (1991) 'Corporate training strategies: the vital component?', in J. Storey (ed.) *New Perspectives on Human Resource Management*, London: Routledge, pp. 109–25.

Kelly, A. and Monks, K. (1998) 'View from the bridge and life on deck: contrasts and contradictions in performance-related pay', in C. Mabey, D. Skinner and T. Clark (eds) *Experiencing Human Resource Management*, London: Sage, pp. 113–28.

Kelly, G.A. (1955) *The Psychology of Personal Constructs*, New York: Norton.

Kelly, J. (1982) *Scientific Management, Job Redesign and Work Performance*, London: Academic Press.

Kelly, J. (1988) *Trade Unions and Socialist Politics*, London: Veso.

Kelly, J. (1996) 'Union militancy and social partnership', in P. Ackers, C. Smith and P. Smith (eds) *The New Workplace and Trade Unionism: Critical Perspectives on Work and Organisation*, London: Routledge, pp. 77–109.

Kelly, J. and Kelly, C. (1991) '"Them and us": social psychology and "the new industrial relations"', *British Journal of Industrial Relations*, Vol. 29, No. 1, pp. 25–48.

Kenney, M. and Florida, R. (1993) *Beyond Mass Production: the Japanese System and its Transfer to the US*, New York: Oxford University Press.

Kerr, S. (1991) 'On the folly of rewarding A while hoping for B', in R.M. Steers and L.W. Porter (eds) *Motivation and Work Behaviour*, New York: McGraw-Hill, pp. 485–97

Kessler, I. (1994) 'Performance pay', in K. Sisson (ed.) *Personnel Management: a Comprehensive Guide to Theory and Practice in Britain*, Oxford: Blackwell, pp. 465–93.

Kessler, I. (1995) 'Reward systems' in J. Storey (ed.) *Human Resource Management: a Critical Text*, London: Routledge, pp. 254–79.

Kessler, I. and Bayliss, F. (1995) *Contemporary British Industrial Relations*, 2nd edition, London: Macmillan.

Kessler, I. and Bayliss, F. (1998) *Contemporary British Industrial Relations*, 3rd edition, London: Macmillan.

Kessler, K. and Purcell, J. (1992) 'Performance related pay: objectives and application', *Human Resource Management Journal*, Vol. 2, No. 3, pp. 16–33.

Kingsbury, P. (1997), *IT Answers to HR Questions*, London: IPD.

Kinnie, N. and Arthurs, A. (1993), 'Will personnel people ever learn to love the computer?', *Personnel Management*, June, pp. 46–51.

Kinnie, N. and Lowe D. (1990) 'Performance-related pay on the shop floor', *Personnel Management*, June, pp. 45–9.

Kirk, G. S. (1976) *The Nature of the Greek Myths*, Harmondsworth: Penguin.

Kirkpatrick, D. (1971) *Supervisory Training and Development*, Reading, MA: Addison-Wesley.

Kjonstad, B. and Willmott, H. (1995) 'Business ethics: restrictive or empowering', *Journal of Business Ethics*, Vol. 14, No. 6, pp. 445–64.

Klein, R., Day, P. and Redmayne, S. (1996) *Managing Scarcity: Priority Setting and Rationing in the National Health Service*, Buckingham: Open University Press.

Knights, D. and Raffo, C. (1990) 'Milk round professionalism in personnel recruitment: myth or reality', *Personnel Review*, Vol. 19, No. 1, pp. 28–37.

Kochan, T. (1980) *Collective Bargaining and Industrial Relations*, Homewood, Illinois: Irwin.

Kochan, T. (1995) 'HRM: an American view', in J. Storey (ed.) *Human Resource Management: a Critical Text*, London: Routledge, pp. 332–57.

Kochan, T., Katz, H.C. and McKerzie, R.B. (1986) *The Transformation of American Industrial Relations*, New York: Basic Books.

Kochan, T.A and Barocci, T.A. (1985) *Human Resource Management and Industrial Relations*, Boston: Little Brown.

Kochan, T.A., Lansbury, R.D. and MacDuffie, J.P. (1997) *After Lean Production: Evolving Employment Practices in the World Auto*

Industry, Ithaca, NY: Cornell University Press.

Kohlberg, L. (1969) *Stages in the Development of Moral Thought and Action,* New York: Holt Rinehart and Winston.

Kohlberg, L. (1984) *Essays in Moral Development, Volume 2: the Psychology of Moral Development,* New York: Harper and Row.

Kohn A. (1993) 'Why incentive plans cannot work', *Harvard Business Review,* September/October, pp. 54–63.

Kolb D., Rubin, M.I. and McIntyre, J.M. (1974) *Organizational Psychology: an Experimental Approach*, 2nd edition, Englewood Cliffs, NJ: Prentice-Hall.

Kolb, D.A. (1984) *Experiential Learning,* Englewood Cliffs, NJ: Prentice-Hall.

Kossek, E.E., Young, W., Gash, C. and Nichol, V. (1994) 'Waiting for innovation in the human resource department: Godot implements a human resource information system', *Human Resource Management*, Vol. 33, No. 1, pp. 135–59.

Kotter, J.P. (1982) *The General Manager,* London: Macmillan.

Krafft-Ebbing, R. von (1924) *Psychopathia Sexualis*, 7th edition, Philadelphia: F.A. Davies.

L

Labour Research Department (1993) *Labour Research*, 82/2, February.

Lashley, C. (1997) *Empowering Service Excellence: Beyond the Quick Fix*, London: Cassell.

Latham, G.P., Saari, L.M., Pursell, E.D. and Campion, M. (1980) 'The situational interview', *Journal of Applied Psychology*, Vol. 65, No. 4, pp. 422–7.

Lauermann, E. (1997) 'The NHS and British Airways' in S. Tyson (ed.) *The Practice of Human Resource Strategy*, London: Financial Times Pitman Publishing, pp. 16–26.

Laurent, A. (1983) 'The cultural diversity of western conception of management', *International Studies of Management and Organisation*, Vol. 13, No. 1–2, pp. 75–96.

Lawler, E. and Porter, L. (1968) *Management Attitudes and Behaviour,* Homewood: Irwin-Dorsey.

Lawler, E.E. (1973) *Motivation in Work Organisations,* California: Brook Cole.

Lawler, J.J. (1992) 'Computer-mediated information processing and decision

making in human resource management', *Research in Personnel and Human Resources Management*, Vol. 10, No. 10, pp. 301–44.

Layder, D. (1997) *Modern Social Theory: Key Debates and New Directions*, London: UCL Press.

Lee, M. (1996) 'Action learning as a cross cultural tool', in J. Stewart and J. McGoldrick (eds) *Human Resource Development: Perspectives, Strategies and Practice,* London: Financial Times Pitman Publishing, pp. 240–60.

Lee, M. (1997) 'The developmental approach: a critical reconsideration', in J. Burgoyne and M. Reynolds (eds) *Management Learning,* London: Sage, pp. 199–214.

Lees, S. (1992) 'Ten faces of management development', *Management Education and Development,* Vol. 23, No. 2, pp. 89–105.

Legge, K. (1978) *Power Innovation and Problem-solving in Personnel Management,* Maidenhead: McGraw-Hill.

Legge, K. (1991) 'Human resource management: a critical analysis', in J. Storey (ed.) *New Perspectives on Human Resource Management,* London: Routledge, pp. 19–40.

Legge, K. (1995) *Human Resource Management: Rhetorics and Realities,* London: Macmillan.

Lehrman Brothers (1994) *Jobs Study*, Paris: OECD.

Leighton, P. and Syrett, M. (1989) *New Work Patterns: Putting Policy into Practice,* London: Financial Times Pitman Publishing.

Lengnick-Hall, C. and Lengnick-Hall, M. (1988) 'Strategic human resources management: a review of the literature and a proposed typology', *American Management Review,* Vol. 13, No. 3, pp. 45–70.

Leopold, J. and Beaumont P. (1985) 'Personnel officers in the National Health Service in Scotland: development and change in the 1970s', *Public Administration*, Vol. 63, No. 2, pp. 219–26.

Leopold, J. and Hallier, J. (1997) 'Start-up and ageing in greenfield sites', *Human Resource Management Journal*, Vol. 7, No. 2, pp. 72–88.

Leopold, J. and Hallier, J. (1998) 'Approaches to the employment relationship on greenfield sites: an international comparison', paper presented at the *Sixth Conference on International Human Resource Management*, Paderborn, June.

Lewis, D. (1997) *Essentials of Employment Law,* London: IPD.

Lewis, J. (1995) 'The contractor factor', *Computing Weekly*, 3 January.

Lewis, P. (1991) 'Performance-related pay: pretexts and pitfalls', *Employee Relations*, Vol. 13, No. 1, pp. 12–16.

Lievens, F. (1998) 'Factors which improve the construct validity of assessment centres: a review', *International Journal of Selection and Assessment*, Vol. 6, No. 3, pp. 141–52.

Liff, S. (1989) 'Assessing equal opportunities policies', *Personnel Review*, Vol. 18, No. 1, pp. 27–34.

Liff, S. (1995) 'Equal opportunities', in P. Edwards (ed.) *Industrial Relations: Theory and Practice in Britain*, Oxford: Blackwell, pp. 461–90.

Liff, S. and Wajcman, J. (1996) '"Sameness" and "difference" revisited: which way forward for equal opportunity initiatives?', *Journal of Management Studies,* Vol. 33, No. 1, pp. 79–94.

Limcrick, B. and Heywood, E. (1993) 'Training for women in management', *Women in Management*, Vol. 8, No. 3, pp. 23–30.

Littlefield, D. (1996) 'Councils swop PRP for staff development', *People Management*, 26 September, p. 15.

Local Authority Conditions of Service Advisory Board (1990) *Handbook of Performance Related Pay*, PRP Report, London: LACSAB.

Locke, E. and Latham, G. (1984) *Goal Setting: a Motivational Technique that Works*, Englewood Cliffs, NJ: Prentice-Hall.

Locke, E. and Latham, G. (1990) *A Theory of Goal Setting and Task Performance*, New York: Prentice-Hall.

Locke, E., Shaw, K., Saari, L. and Latham, G. (1981) 'Goal setting and task performance 1969–1980', *Psychological Bulletin*, No. 90, pp. 125–52.

Locke, R. (1995) 'The transformation of industrial relations: a cross-national review', in K.S. Wever and L. Turner (eds) *The Comparative Political Economy of Industrial Relations,* Wisconsin: Industrial Relations Research Association.

Louis, M.R. (1989) 'Systems support for strategic HR: is there a role for OD?', *Human Resource Planning*, Vol. 12, pp. 277–99.

Lovell, A.T.A. (1992) 'Principled dissent and accountancy: ethical dilemmas for individuals, professions and society, unpublished Ph.D. dissertation, The Nottingham Trent University.

Lovell, A.T.A. (1995) 'Moral reasoning and moral atmosphere in the domain of accounting', *Accounting, Auditing & Accountability Journal*, Vol. 8, No. 3, pp. 60–80.

Lovenduski, J. (1985) 'Implementing equal opportunities in the 1980s: an overview', *Public Administration*, Vol. 67, Spring, pp. 7–18.

Loveridge, R. (1983) 'Labour market segmentation and the firm', in J. Edwards *et al.* (ed.) *Manpower Planning: Strategy and Techniques in an Organisational Context*, Chichester: John Wiley & Son, pp. 76–94.

Lowell Bryan, senior partner with McKinsey in New York, quoted by Jackson, T. (1998) 'The myth of the global executive', *Financial Times*, 8 January 1997.

Lowson, C. and Boyce, R. (1990) 'The development of the performance management programme', *Management Services*, September, pp. 6–9.

Lundy, O. and Cowling, A. (1996) *Strategic Human Resource Management*, London: Routledge.

M

Mabbott, J.D. (1967) *The State and the Citizen*, 2nd edition, London: Hutchinson.

Mabey, C. and Mayon White (ed.) (1993) *Managing Change*, 2nd edition, London: The Open University, Paul Chapman.

Mabey, C. and Salaman, G. (1995) *Strategic Human Resource Management*, Oxford: Blackwell.

Macan, T.H., Avedon, M.J., Paese, M. and Smith, D.E. (1994) 'The effects of applicants' reactions to cognitive ability tests and an assessment centre', *Personnel Psychology*, Vol. 47, No. 4, pp. 715–38.

McCabe, D. and Wilkinson, A. (1998) 'The rise and fall of TQM: the vision, meaning and operation of change', *Industrial Relations Journal*, Vol. 29, No. 1, pp. 18–29.

MacDuffie, J.P. and Pil, F.K. (1997) 'Changes in auto industry employment practices: an international overview' in T.A. Kochan, R.D. Lansbury and J.P. MacDuffie (eds) *After Lean Production: Evolving Employment Practices in the World Auto Industry*, Ithaca, New York: Cornell University Press, pp. 9–42.

McEvoy, G.M. (1990) 'Public sector managers' reactions to appraisals by subordinates', *Public Personnel Management*, Vol. 19, No. 2, Summer, pp. 201–12.

McGregor, A. and Sproull, A. (1991) *Employers' Labour Use Strategies: Analysis of an Employer Survey*, Research Paper No. 83, London: Department of Employment.

McGregor, D. (1960) *The Human Side of Enterprise*, New York: McGraw-Hill.

MacInnes, J. (1988) *Thatcherism at Work*, Milton Keynes: Open University Press.

MacInnes, J. (1988) 'The question of flexibility', *Personnel Review*, Vol. 17, No. 3, pp. 12–15.

Mackay, L. and Torrington, D. (1986) *The Changing Nature of Personnel Management*, London: IPM.

McKenna, E. (1994) *Business Psychology and Organisational Behaviour,* Hove: Lawrence Erlbaum Associates.

Mackie, J.L. (1977) *Ethics: Inventing Right and Wrong*, London: Penguin.

McKinlay, A. and Taylor, P. (1996) 'Power, surveillance and resistance: inside the "factory of the future"', in P. Ackers, C. Smith and P. Smith (eds) *The New Workplace and Trade Unionism*, London: Routledge, pp. 279–300.

McLagan, P. and McCullough, R. (1983) *Models for Excellence: the Conclusions and recommendations of the ASTD Training and Development Competency Study,* Washington DC: ASTD.

MacLean Center for Clinical Medical Ethics (1998) *Physician Codes and Oaths,* World Wide Web http://ccme-mac4.bsd.uchicago.edu/CCMEPolicies/Med Codes/Hippo, visited 2/3/1998.

McMahon, F. and Carter, E. (1990) *The Great Training Robbery,* Basingstoke: Falmer Press.

McMullen, J. (1994) 'Contracting out and market testing – the uncertainty ends?', *Industrial Law Journal,* Vol. 23, No. 3, pp. 230–40.

Mahon, T. (1989) 'When line managers welcome equal opportunities', *Personnel Management*, Vol. 21, No. 10, pp 76–9.

March, J.G. and Olsen, J.P. (1976) *Ambiguity and Choice in Organisations,* Oslo: Universitetsforlagtt.

Marchington, M. (1988) 'The four faces of employee consultation', *Personnel Management*, May, pp. 44–7.

Marchington, M. (1992) *Managing the Team*, Oxford: Blackwell.

Marchington, M. (1994) 'The dynamics of joint consultation', in K. Sisson (ed.) *Personnel Management*, Oxford: Blackwell, pp. 662–93.

Marchington, M. (1995) 'Employee relations', in S. Tyson (ed.) *Strategic Prospects for HRM*, London: IPD, pp. 81–111.

Marchington, M. and Parker, P. (1990) *Changing Patterns of Employee Relations*, Hemel Hempstead: Harvester Wheatsheaf.

Marchington, M. and Wilkinson, A. (1996) *Core Personnel and Development,* London: IPD.

Marchington, M., Goodman, J., Wilkinson, A. and Ackers, P. (1992*) New Developments in Employee Involvement*, Research Series No. 2, London: Employment Department.

Marchington, M., Wilkinson, A., Ackers, P. and Goodman, J. (1993) 'The influence of managerial relations on waves of employee involvement', *British Journal of Industrial Relations*, Vol. 31, No. 4, pp. 553–76.

Marginson, P. (1989) 'Employment flexibility in large companies: change and continuity', *Industrial Relations Journal* Vol. 29, No. 2, pp. 101–18.

Marginson, P., Edwards, P.K., Martin, R., Purcell, J. and Sisson, K. (1988) *Beyond the Workplace: Managing Industrial Relations in Multi-Plant Enterprises,* Oxford: Blackwell.

Marinker, M. (ed.) (1990) *Medical Audit and General Practice*, London: British Medical Journal.

Marsden, D. and Richardson, R. (1992) *Motivation and Performance Related Pay in the Public Sector: a Case Study of the Inland Revenue*, Centre for Economic Performance Discussion paper No. 75, London: LSE.

Marsick, V. and Watkins, K. (1997) 'Lessons from informal and incidental learning', in J. Burgoyne and M. Reynolds (eds), *Management Learning: Integrating Perspectives in Theory and Practice,* London: Sage, pp. 295–311.

Martin, P. (1997) 'A future depending on choice', *Financial Times*, November.

Martinez Lucio, M. and Simpson, P. (1992) 'Discontinuity and change in industrial relations: the struggles over its social dimensions and the rise of Human Resource Management', *International Journal of Human Resource Management*, Vol. 3, No. 2, pp. 173–91.

Martinez Lucio, M. and Stewart, P. (1997) 'The paradox of contemporary labour process theory: the rediscovery of labour and the disappearance of collectivism', *Capital and Class*, Vol. 62, June, pp. 49–77.

Mason, E.S. and Mudrack, P.E. (1997) 'Do complex moral reasoners experience greater ethical work conflict?', *Journal of Business Ethics*, Vol. 16 Nos 12–13, pp. 1311–18.

Mason, R. and Bain, P. (1991) 'Trade union recruitment strategies: facing the 1990s', *Industrial Relations Journal*, Vol. 22, No. 1, pp. 36–45.

Mayne, L., Tregaskis, O. and Brewster, C. (1996) 'A comparative analysis of the link between flexibility and HRM strategy', *Employee Relations*, 18(3), pp. 5–24.

Mead, G.H. (1934) *Mind, Self and Society*, Chicago: University of Chicago Press. Reproduced excerpt in H. Clark, J. Chandler and J. Barry (eds) *Organisation and Identities: Text and Readings in Organisational Behaviour*, London: Chapman and Hall, pp. 99–106.

Meager, N. (1985) *Temporary Work in Britain*, Brighton: Institute of Manpower.

Meekings, A. (1995) 'Unlocking the potential of performance measurement: a practical implementation guide', *Public Money and Management*, October/December, pp. 5–12.

Meinhart, D.B. and Davis, D.D. (1993) 'Human resource decision support systems (HRDSS): integrating decision support and human resource information systems', in R.P. Cerveny, C.P. Pegels and G.L. Sanders (eds) *Strategic Information Systems for Strategic Manufacturing, Operations, Marketing, Sales, Financial and Human Resources Management*, Greenwich, CT: JAI Press, pp. 87–103.

Mento, A.J., Steel, R.P. and Karren, R.J. (1987) 'A meta-analytic study of task performance: 1966–1984', *Organisational Behaviour and Human Decision Processes*, Vol. 39, No. 1, pp. 52–83.

Metcalf, D. (1991) 'British unions: dissolution or resurgence?', *Oxford Review of Economic Policy*, Vol. 7, No. 1, pp. 18–32.

Miller, P. (1989) 'Strategic HRM: what it is and what it isn't', *Personnel Management*, February, pp. 36–9.

Miller, P. (1996) 'Strategy and the ethical management of human resources', *Human Resource Management Journal*, Vol. 6, No. 1, pp. 5–18.

Millward, N. and Stevens, M. (1986) *British Workplace Industrial Relations – 1980–1984*, The DE/ESRC/PSI/ACAS Survey, London: Gower.

Millward, N., Stevens, M., Smart, D. and Hawes, W.R. (1992) *Workplace Industrial Relations in Transition*, Aldershot: Dartmouth.

Mintzberg, H. (1973) *The Nature of Managerial Work*, New York: Harper and Row.

Mintzberg, H. (1978) 'Patterns in strategy formation', *Management Science*, Vol. 24, No. 9, pp. 934–48.

Mintzberg, H. (1987) 'Crafting management strategy', *Harvard Business Review*, Vol. 65, No. 4, pp. 66–75.

Mintzberg, H. (1994) *The Rise and Fall of Strategic Planning*, Hemel Hempstead: Prentice-Hall.

Mintzberg, H. and Waters, I.A. (1985) 'Of strategies deliberate and emergent', *Strategic Management Journal*, July/September, Vol. 6, pp. 257–72.

Mohrman Jnr, A., Resnick-West, S.M. and Lawler III, E.E. (1989) *Designing Performance Appraisal Schemes: Aligning Appraisals and Organizational Realities*, San Francisco: Jossey-Bass.

Monks, J. (1998) 'Trade unions, enterprise and the future', in P. Sparrow and M. Marchington (eds) *Human Resource Management: the New Agenda*, London: Financial Times Pitman Publishing, pp. 171–79.

Morgan, G. (1997) *Images of Organisation*, London: Sage.

Morris, J. (1991) 'Action learning: the long haul', in J. Prior (ed.) *Handbook of Training and Development*, Aldershot: Gower.

Morris, M.W. and Peng, K.P. (1994) 'Culture and cause: American and Chinese attributions for social and physical events', *Journal of Personality and Social Psychology*, Vol. 67, No. 6, pp. 949–71.

Motowidlo, S.J. (1986) 'Information processing in personnel decisions', *Research in Personnel and Human Resource Management*, Vol. 4, pp. 41–4.

Müller-Jentsch, W. (1995) 'Germany: from collective voice to co-management', in J. Rogers and W. Streeck (eds) *Works Councils: Consultation, Representation and Cooperation in Industrial Relations*, Chicago and London: University of Chicago Press, pp. 53–78.

Mumford, A. (1993) *Management Development: Strategies for Action*, 2nd edition, London: IPM.

Mumford, A. (1997) *Management Development: Strategies for Action*, 3rd edition, London: IPD.

N

NATFHE (National Association of Teachers in Further and Higher Education) (1991) *Guidelines for Negotiating Appraisal Schemes*, London: NATFHE.

National Economic Development Office (1986) *Changing Work Patterns: How Companies Achieve Flexibility to Meet New Needs*, NEDO: London.

National Health Service Training Authority (1987) *Guide and Model Documentation for Industrial Performance Review* (revised edition) Bristol: NHSTA.

Neathey, F. and Hurstfield, J. (1995) *Flexibility in Practice: Women's Employment and Pay in Retail and Finance*, EOC Research Discussion series, London: IRS.

Neilson, C. (1994) 'New HR software survey shows trends in software useage', *Employment Relations Today*, Vol. 21, No. 3, pp. 277–86.

Newell, S. (1998) 'Editorial: restating and reflecting on the first 5 years of IJSA', *International Journal of Selection and Assessment*, Vol. 6, No. 3, pp. 139–40.

Newsome, K. (1996) 'Beyond the confines: JIT, new buyer–supplier relations and change in the labour process of suppliers', paper delivered to the *14th Annual Labour Process Conference,* University of Aston.

Newsome, K. (1998) *Beyond the Point of Production: JIT, Changing Buyer–Supplier Relations and Change in the Labour Process of Suppliers*. Unpublished PhD thesis: University of Hertfordshire.

Nijhof, W. and de Rijk, R. (1997) 'Roles, competences and outputs of HRD practice: a comparative study in four European countries', *Journal of European Industrial Training*, Vol. 21, No. 6/7, pp. 247–55.

Noon, M. and Blyton, P. (1997) *The Realities of Work*, Basingstoke: Macmillan.

O

O'Doherty, D. (1997) 'Human resource planning: control to seduction?', in I. Beardwell and L. Holden (eds) *Human Resource Management: a Contemporary Perspective*, London: Financial Times Pitman Publishing, pp. 119–63.

O'Reilly, C.A., Chatman, J. and Caldwell, D. (1991) 'People and organisational culture: a profile comparison approach to assessing person–organisation fit', *Academy of Management Journal*, Vol. 3, No. 34, pp. 487–516.

O'Reilly, J. (1992) 'Banking on flexibility: a comparison of the use of flexible employment strategies in the retail banking sector in Britain and France', *International Journal of Human Resource Management*, Vol. 3, No. 1, pp. 35–58.

Oliver, N. and Wilkinson, B. (1992) *The Japanization of British Industry: New Developments in the 1990s,* Oxford: Blackwell.

Olsen, W. (1997) *The Excuse Factory: How Employment Law is Paralysing the American Workplace,* New York: Free Press.

Osterman, P. (1987) 'Choice of employment systems in internal labor markets', *Industrial and Labour Relations Review,* Vol. 47, No. 2, pp. 173–88.

Overell, S. (1997) 'Confusing laws swell discrimination cases', *People Management,* Vol. 3, No. 14, p. 15.

Overell S. (1998) 'Missionary statements' *People Management*, 16 April, pp. 32–7.

Oxford Polytechnic Educational Methods Unit (n.d.) *Academic Staff Development and Appraisal*, Oxford: Oxford Polytechnic.

P

Palmer, G. (1996) 'Reviving resistance: the Japanese factory floor in Britain', *Industrial Relations Journal,* Vol. 27, No. 2, pp. 129–42.

Pandya, N. (1996) 'Afro-Caribbeans hit the cement roof', *The Guardian*, Jobs and Money section, December, p. 20.

Pandya, N. (1997) 'Race to create ethnic balance in the boardroom', *The Guardian*, Jobs and Money section, 1 February, p. 20.

Parker, M. (1993) 'Industrial relations myth and shop-floor reality: the "team concept" in the auto industry', in N. Lichtenstein, and H.J. Harris (eds) *Industrial Democracy in America: the Ambiguous Promise,* Cambridge: Cambridge University Press, pp. 249–74.

Parker, M. and Slaughter, J. (1988) *Choosing Sites: Union and the Team Concept*, Boston, MA: South End Press.

Parker, M. and Slaughter, J. (1995) 'Unions and management by stress', in S. Babson (ed.) *Lean Work: Empowerment and Exploitation in the Global Auto Industry*, Detroit: Wayne State University Press, pp. 41–53.

Patterson, M.G., West, M.A., Lawthorn, R. and Nickell, S. (1997) 'Impact of people management practices on business performance', *Issues in People Management*, No. 22, London: IPD.

Pay and Benefits Bulletin (1997) 'Merit moves on', London: IRS, Jan., pp. 7–11.

Pedler, M. and Boydell, T. (1985) *Managing Yourself,* London: Fontana.

Pedler, M., Burgoyne, J. and Boydell, T. (1991) *The Learning Company,* Maidenhead: McGraw-Hill.

Pedler, M., Burgoyne, J. and Boydell, T. (1994) *A Manager's Guide to Self-Development*, 3rd edition, London: McGraw-Hill.

Pedler, M., Burgoyne, J. and Boydell, T. (1996) *The Learning Company*, 2nd edition, Maidenhead: McGraw-Hill.

Peltu, M. (1996) 'Death to cuts', *Computing*, Vol. 9, May, p. 34.

Pemberton, C. (1995) *Strike a New Career Deal*, London: Financial Times Pitman Publishing.

Pendleton, A. (1997) 'Characteristics of workplaces with financial participation', *Industrial Relations Journal*, Vol. 28, No. 2, pp. 103–19.

Penn, R. (1992) 'Flexibility in Britain during the 1980s: recent empirical evidence', in R. Burrows, N. Gilbert and A. Pollert, *Fordism and Flexibility*, pp. 66-86, Basingstoke: Macmillan.

Perrow, C. (1986) *Complex Organisations: a Critical Study,* London: Tavistock.

Personnel Management Plus (1992) 'Achieving Equality', November, p. 490.

Pettigrew, A. and Whipp, R. (1991) *Managing Change for Competitive Success,* Oxford: Blackwell.

Pettigrew, A., Jones, E. and Reason, P. (1982) *Training and Development Roles in their Organisational Setting*, Sheffield Training Division: MSC.

Pfeffer, J. (1981) *Power in Organisations,* Marshfield, Mass.: Pitman Publishing.

Pfeffer, J. (1994) *Competitive Advantage through People*, Boston, MA: Harvard Business School Press.

Pfeffer, J. (1998a) 'Six dangerous myths about pay', *Harvard Business Review*, May/June, pp. 109–119.

Pfeffer, J. (1998b) *The Human Equation*, Boston: Harvard Business School Press.

Phares, E.J. (1987) *Introduction to Personality*, Columbus, Ohio: Charles E. Merrill.

Pickard, J. (1995) 'Prepare to make a moral judgement', *People Management*, Vol. 1, No. 10, pp. 22–5.

Piore, M. and Sabel, C. (1984) *The Second Industrial Divide,* New York: Basic Books.

Pollert, A. (1988) 'The flexible firm: fiction or fact?' *Work, Employment and Society*, Vol. 2, No. 3, pp. 281–316.

Pollert, A. (1991) *Farewell to Flexibility*, Oxford: Blackwell.

Pollitt, C. (1985) 'Measuring performance: a new system for the NHS', *Policy and Politics*, Vol. 13, No. 1, pp. 1–15.

Poole, M. (1986) *Towards a New Industrial Democracy*, London: Routledge.

Poole, M. and Jenkins, G. (1990) *The Impact of Economic Democracy: Profit Sharing and Employee Shareholding Schemes*, London: Routledge.

Porter, M. (1980) *Competitive Strategies: Technologies for Analyzing Industries and Firms,* New York: Free Press.

Porter, M. (1985) *Competitive Advantage: Creating and Sustaining Superior Performance,* New York: Free Press.

Porter, M.E. (1990) 'The competitive advantage of nations', *Harvard Business Review*, March/April, pp. 73–93.

Powell, P. and Xiao, Z.Z. (1996) 'The extent, mode and quality of IT use in accounting', *Journal of Applied Management Studies*, Vol. 5, No. 2, pp. 143–58.

Premack, S. and Wanous, J.P. (1985) 'A meta-analysis of realistic job preview experiments', *Journal of Applied Psychology*, Vol. 70, No. 4, pp. 706–19.

Price, A.J. (1997) *Human Resource Management in a Business Context,* London: International Thomson Business Press.

Price, C. (1994) 'Gas regulation and competition: substitutes or complements', in J. Bishop, M. Kay and C. Mayer (eds) *Privatisation and Economic Performance*, Oxford: Oxford University Press.

Price, J. (1997) *Japan Works: Power and Paradox in Postwar Industrial Relations,* Ithaca, NY and London: Cornell University Press.

Procter, S., McArdle, L., Rowlinson, M., Forrester, P. and Hassard, J. (1993) 'Performance-related pay in operation: a case study from the electronics industry', *Human Resource Management Journal*, Vol. 3, No. 4, pp. 60–74.

Procter, S.J., Rowlinson, M., McArdle, L., Hassard, J. and Forrester, P. (1994) 'Flexibility, politics and strategy: in defence of the model of the flexible firm', *Work, Employment and Society*, Vol. 8, No. 2, pp. 221–42.

Prowse, K. (1990) 'Assessing the flexible firm', *Personnel Review,* Vol. 19, No. 3, pp. 13–17.

Pucik, V. (1998) 'Creating leaders that are world-class', in *Mastering Global Business*, Financial Times Pitman Publishing, pp. 4–5.

Pugh, D.S. and Hickson, C.D. (1976) *Organisation Structure: Extensions and Replications,* Famborough: Saxon House.

Punnett, B.J. (1998) 'Culture, cross-national', in M. Poole and M. Warner (eds) *The IEBM Handbook of Human Resource Management,* London: International Thompson Business Press, pp. 9–26.

Purcell, J. (1989) 'The impact of corporate strategy on human resource management', in J. Storey (ed.) *New Perspectives on Human Resource Management,* London: Routledge, pp. 67–91.

Purcell, J. (1995) 'Corporate strategy and its link with human resource strategy', in J. Storey (ed.) *Human Resource Management: a Critical Text,* London: Routledge, pp. 63–86.

Purcell, J. and Ahlstrand, B. (1994) *Human Resource Management in the Multidivisional Company,* Oxford: Oxford University Press.

Q

Quinn, J.B. (1980) *Strategies for Change: Logical Incrementalism,* Homewood, IL: Irwin.

Quinn, J.B. (1991) 'Strategies for change', in H. Mintzberg and J.B. Quinn (eds) *The Strategy Process: Concepts, Contexts, Cases,* Englewood Cliffs, NJ: Prentice-Hall International, pp. 2–9.

R

Ramsey, H. (1977) 'Cycles of control: worker participation in sociological and historical perspectives', *Sociology,* Vol. 11, No. 3, September, pp. 481–506.

Ramsey, H. (1983) 'Evolution or cycle? Worker participation in the 1970s and 1980s', in C. Crouch and F. Heller (eds) *Organisational Democracy and Political Processes,* International Yearbook of Industrial Democracy, London: John Wiley & Sons.

Ramsey, H. (1990) *The Joint Consultation Debate: Soft Soap and Hard Cases,* Discussion Paper No. 17, Glasgow: Centre for Research in Industrial Democracy and Participation.

Rawls, J. (1972) *A Theory of Justice,* Oxford: Clarendon Press.

Reber, A.S. (1985) *Dictionary of Psychology,* Harmondsworth: Penguin.

Redman, T. and Snape, E. (1992) 'Upward and onward: can staff appraise their managers?', *Personnel Review,* Vol. 27, No. 7, pp. 32–46.

Reeves, M. (1988) *The Crisis in Higher Education: Competence, Delight and the Common Good,* Milton Keynes: Open University Press and the Society for Research into Higher Education (SRHE).

Reid, M. and Barrington, H. (1994) *Training Interventions,* 4th edition, London: IPD.

Reid, M. and Barrington, H. (1997) *Training Interventions,* 5th edition, London: IPD.

Revans, R.W. (1976) *Action Learning in Hospitals, Diagnosis and Therapy,* Maidenhead: McGraw-Hill.

Revans, R.W. (1980) *Action Learning,* London: Blond and Briggs.

Revans, R.W. (1982) *Origins and Growth of Action Learning,* Bromley: Chartwell and Bratt.

Rice, C. (1993) 'Kolb Revisited', paper presented at *Business Education in Central Europe Conference,* Brno University.

Richards-Carpenter, C. (1991) 'Celebration of an era', *Personnel Management,* February, p. 24.

Richards-Carpenter, C. (1993) 'How a CPIS helps re-engineering', *Personnel Management,* November, p. 23.

Richards-Carpenter, C. (1994) 'Personnel takes pragmatic approach to technology', *Personnel Management,* July, pp. 55.

Robertson, I.T. and Smith, J.M. (1989) 'Personnel selection methods', in J.M. Smith and I.T. Robertson (eds) *Advances in Selection and Assessment,* Chichester: John Wiley & Sons, pp. 89–112.

Robertson, I.T., Illes, P., Gratton, L. and Sharpley, D.S. (1991) 'The impact of personnel selection and assessment methods on candidates', *Human Relations,* No. 44, Vol. 9, pp. 963–82.

Robinson, P. (1997) 'Insecurity and the flexible workforce', paper presented at the ERU conference, Cardiff, September.

Roderick, C. (1993) 'Becoming a learning organisation', *Training & Development,* March, pp. 13–14.

Rodger, A. (1970) *The Seven-point Plan,* London: National Foundation for Educational Research.

Rogers, C.R. (1970) *On Becoming a Person,* Boston, MA: Houghton Mifflin.

Rogers, J. and Streeck, W. (eds) (1995) *Works Councils: Consultation, Representation and Cooperation in Industrial Relations,* Chicago and London: University of Chicago Press.

Rosenfeld, P. (1997) *Impression Management in Organizations,* London: Routledge.

Ross, R. and Schneider, R. (1992) *From Equality to Diversity: a Business Case for Equal*

Opportunities, London: Financial Times Pitman Publishing.

Rothwell, S. (1986) 'Comparative labour costs: getting the right mix', *Manpower Policy and Practice*, Vol. 1, No. 3, pp. 217–35.

Rubery, J. and Wilkinson, F. (1994) *Labour Markets and Flexibility*, Oxford: Oxford University Press.

Rugman, A. (1998) 'Multinationals as regional flagships', in *Mastering Global Business*, Financial Times Pitman Publishing, pp. 6–8.

S

Saggers, R. (1994) 'Training climbs the corporate agenda', *Personnel Management*, Vol. 26, No. 7, pp. 40–5.

Sandberg, Å. (1993) 'Volvo human-centred work organisation – the end of the road?', *New Technology, Work and Employment*, Vol. 8, No. 2, pp. 83–7.

Saville and Holdsworth Ltd (1995) *Work Profiling System* (WPS, updated version), London: Saville and Holdsworth.

Saville and Holdsworth (UK) Ltd (1997) *UK Survey of Views of Performance Appraisal*, Thames Ditton: Saville and Holdsworth.

Scarbrough, H. and Terry, M. (1996) *Industrial Relations and the Reorganisation of Production in the UK Motor Vehicle Industry: a Study of the Rover Group*, Warwick Papers in Industrial Relations No. 58, Warwick University: Industrial Relations Research Unit.

Schneider, B. (1987) 'The people make the place', *Personnel Psychology*, Vol. 3, No. 40, pp. 437–53.

Schneider, B., Goldstein, H. and Smith, D. (1995) 'The ASA framework: an update', *Personnel Psychology*, Vol. 4, No. 48, pp. 747–73.

Schneider, S.C. and Barsoux, J.L. (1997) *Managing Across Cultures*, Hemel Hempstead: Prentice-Hall.

Schon, D.A. (1983) *The Reflective Practitioner: How Professionals Think in Action*, New York: Basic Books.

Schregle, J. (1981) 'Comparative industrial relations: pitfalls and potential', *International Labour Review*, Vol. 120, No. 1, January, pp. 15–30.

Schreier, M. and Groeber, N. (1996) 'Ethical guidelines for the conduct in argumentative discussions: an exploratory study', *Human Relations*, Vol. 49, No. 1, January, pp. 123–32.

Schuler, H. (1993) 'Social validity of selection situations: a concept and some empirical results', in H. Schuler, J.L. Farr, and M. Smith (eds), *Personnel Selection and Assessment: Individual and Organisational Perspectives*, Hillsdale, NJ: Lawrence Erlbaum, pp. 11–26.

Schuler, R. (1998) 'Human resource management', in M. Poole and M. Warner (eds) *The IEBM Handbook of Human Resource Management*, London: International Thomson Business Press, pp. 122–41.

Schuler, R., Dowling, P. and De Cieri, H. (1993) 'An integrative framework of strategic international human resource management', *Journal of Management*, Vol. 19, No. 2, pp. 419–59.

Schuler, R.S. and Jackson, S.E. (1987) 'Linking competitive strategies with human resource management practices', *Academy of Management Executive*, Vol. 1, No. 3, pp. 209–13.

Schuler, R.S. and Jackson, S.E. (1996) *Human Resource Management: Positioning for the 21st Century*, Minneapolis: West.

Scott, R. (1993) 'Getting ready for a move to collective bargaining', *Personnel Management*, September, pp. 38–41.

Seear, N. (1981) 'The management of equal opportunities', in P. Braham, G. Rhodes and M. Pearn, (eds) *Discrimination and Disadvantage in Employment*, London: Harper & Row, p. 295.

Seedhouse, D. (1994) *Fortress NHS: a Philosophical Review of the National Health Service*, Chichester: John Wiley & Sons.

Seligman, D. (1997) 'Talking back to ethicists: what qualifies these professional moralists to tell us how to behave? Not much', *Forbes*, 5 May, Vol. 159, No. 9, p. 192.

Sewell, G. and Wilkinson, B. (1992) 'Empowerment or emasculation? Shopfloor surveillance in a total quality organisation', in P. Blyton and P. Turnbull (eds) *Reassessing Human Resource Management*, London: Sage, pp. 97–115.

Shackleton, V. and Newell, S. (1994) 'European management selection methods: a comparison of 5 countries', *International Journal of Selection and Assessment*, Vol. 2, No. 2, pp. 91–102.

Shackleton, V. and Newell, S. (1997) 'International selection and assessment', in N. Anderson and P. Herriot (eds), *International Handbook of Selection and*

Assessment, Chichester: John Wiley & Sons, pp. 81–96.

Sheppard, B., Lewiicki, R. and Minton, J. (1992) *Organisational Justice*, Lexington: New York.

Shipton, J. and McCauley, J. (1993) 'Issues of power and marginality in personnel', *Human Resource Management Journal*, Vol. 4, No. 1, pp. i–13.

Silverman, D. (1970) *The Theory of Organisations*, London: Heinemann.

Simon, H.A. (1977) *The New Science of Management Decision*, Hemel Hempstead: Prentice-Hall.

Simonian, H. (1997) 'Into the east at full throttle', *Financial Times*, 13 February.

Sisson, K. (1993) 'In search of HRM', *British Journal of Industrial Relations*, Vol. 31, No. 2, pp. 201–10.

Sisson, K. (1994) 'Personnel management paradigms, practice and prospects', in K. Sisson (ed.) *Personnel Management: a Comprehensive Guide to Theory and Practice in Britain*, Oxford: Blackwell, pp. 3–50.

Sisson, K. (1995) 'Human resource management and the personnel function', in J. Storey (ed.), *Human Resource Management: a Critical Text*, London: Routledge, pp. 87–109.

Sloman, M. (1994) 'Coming in from the cold: a new role for trainers', *Personnel Management*, Vol. 26, No. 1, pp. 24–7.

Sly, F. and Stillwell, D. (1997) 'Temporary Workers in Great Britain', *Labour Market Trends*, September, pp. 347–54.

Smith, G. and Cantley, C. (1985) *Evaluating Health Care: a Study in Organisational Evaluation*, Milton Keynes: Open University Press.

Smith, I. (1983) *The Management of Remuneration: Paying for Effectiveness*, London: IPD and Gower.

Smith, M. (1994) 'A theory of the validity of predictors in selection', *Journal of Occupational and Organisational Psychology*, Vol. 2, No. 67, pp. 13–31.

Smith, M., Masi, A., Berg, A. and Smucker, J. (1995) 'External flexibility in Sweden and Canada: a three industry comparison', *Work, Employment and Society*, Vol. 9, No. 4, pp. 689–718.

Smith, P. (1995) 'Performance indicators and outcome in the public sector', *Public Money and Management*, Vol. 15, No. 4, pp. 13–16.

Smith, P. and Morton, G. (1990) 'A change of heart: union exclusion in the provincial newspaper sector', *Work, Employment and Society*, Vol. 4, No. 1, pp. 105–24.

Smith, P. and Morton, G. (1993) 'Union exclusion and the decollectivisation of industrial relations in contemporary Britain', *British Journal of Industrial Relations*, Vol. 31, No. 1, pp. 97–114.

Smith, P. and Morton, G. (1994) 'Union exclusion in Britain: next steps', *Industrial Relations Journal*, Vol. 25, No. 1, pp. 3–14.

Snell, M., Gluklich, P. and Povall, M. (1981) *Equal Pay and Opportunities*, Department of Employment Research Paper 20, London: HMSO.

Snell, R. (1993) *Developing Skills for Ethical Management*, London: Chapman and Hall.

Solomon, R.C. (1993) *Ethics and Excellence: Cooperation and Integrity in Business,* New York: Oxford University Press.

Sparrow, P. (1997) 'Organisational competencies: creating a strategic behavioural framework for selection and assessment', in N. Anderson and P. Herriot (eds) *International Handbook of Selection and Assessment*, Chichester: John Wiley & Sons, pp. 543–66.

Sparrow, P. (1998) 'New organisational forms, processes, jobs and psychological contracts: resolving the HRM issues', in P. Sparrow and M. Marchington (eds) *Human Resource Management: The New Agenda,* London: Financial Times Pitman Publishing, pp. 117–44.

Sparrow, P. and Marchington, M. (1998) *Human Resource Management: The New Agenda*, London: Financial Times Pitman Publishing.

Spinelli, E. (1989) *The Interpreted World*, London: Sage.

Stacey, R. D. (1996) *Strategic Management and Organisational Dynamics,* London: Financial Times Pitman Publishing.

Starkey, K. (ed.) (1996) *How Organizations Learn*, London: International Thomson Business Press.

Stephenson, C. (1996) 'The different experience of trade unionism in two Japanese transplants', in P. Ackers, C. Smith and P. Smith (eds) *The New Workplace and Trade Unionism: Critical Perspectives on Work and Organsiation*, London: Routledge, pp. 210–39.

Stewart, D.W. (1984) 'Managing competing claims: an ethical framework for human resource decision making', *Public*

Administration Review, Vol. 44, No. 1, January/February, pp. 14–22.

Stewart, J. (1996) *Managing Change through Training and Development*, London: Kogan Page, 2nd edition.

Stewart, J. (1991) *Managing Change through Training and Development*, London: Kogan Page.

Stewart, J. (1998) 'Intervention and assessment: the ethics of HRD', *Human Resource Development International,* Vol. 1, No. 1, pp. 9–12.

Stewart, J. (1999) *Employee Development Practice*, London: Financial Times Management.

Stewart, J. and McGoldrick, J. (1996) (eds) *Human Resource Development: Perspectives, Strategies and Practice*, London: Financial Times Pitman Publishing.

Stewart, J. and Sambrook, S. (1995) 'The role of functional analysis in NVQs: a critical appraisal', in I. Bates (ed.) 'Special issue on competence and the NVQ framework', *British Journal of Education and Work*, Vol. 8, No. 2, pp. 93–106.

Stewart, R. (1982) *Choices for the manager,* Maidenhead: McGraw-Hill.

Stiles, P., Gratton, L., Truss, C., Hope-Hailey, V. and McGovern, P. (1997) 'Performance management and the psychological contract', *Human Resource Management Journal*, Vol. 7, No. 1, pp. 57–66.

Stokes, G.S., Hogan, J.B. and Snell, A.F. (1993) 'Comparability of incumbent and applicant samples for the development of biodata keys: the influence of social desirability', *Personnel Psychology*, Vol. 4, No. 46, pp. 739–62.

Stopford, J., Roberts, A., Vagneurk, and Markides, C. (1994) *Building Global Excellence*, London: London Business School.

Storey, J. (1987) *Developments in the Management of Human Resources: an Interim Report*, Warwick Papers in Industrial Relations 17, IRRU, School of Industrial and Business Studies, University of Warwick.

Storey, J. (1989) 'Management development: a literature review', *Personnel Review*, Vol. 18, No. 6, pp. 7–16.

Storey, J. (1991) *New Perspectives on Human Resource Management* (ed.) London: Routledge.

Storey, J. (1992) *Developments in the Management of Human Resources*, Oxford: Blackwell.

Storey, J. (ed.) (1995) *Human Resource Management: a Critical Text,* London: Routledge.

Storey, J. and Sisson, K. (1993) *Managing Human Resources and Industrial Relations*, Buckingham: Open University Press.

Storey, J., Edwards, P.K. and Sisson, K. (1997) *Managers in the Making*, London: Sage.

Straw, J. (1989) *Equal Opportunities: the Way Ahead*, London: IPM.

Stuttaford, T. (1990) 'Privilege to be sniffed at: medical briefing, *The Times*, 1 March.

T

Tailby, S. and Pearson, E. (1998) 'Employee relations in the south west', *Work and Employment*, Issue 6, Spring.

Tate, W. (1995) *Developing Managerial Competence: a Critical Guide to Methods and Materials,* Aldershot: Gower.

Taylor, S. (1998) 'Emotional labour and the new workplace', in P. Thompson and C. Warhurst (eds) *Workplaces of the Future: Critical perspectives on Work and Organisations*, Basingstoke: Macmillan Business, pp. 84–103.

Texas Instruments (1998) *The TI Ethics Quick Test*, World Wide Web http://www.ti.com./corp/docs/ethics/quicktest.htm, visited 10.3.98.

Thomas, K. (1973) *Religion and the Decline of Magic: Studies in Popular Beliefs in the Sixteenth and Seventeenth Centuries*, Harmondsworth: Penguin.

Thompson, P. (1989) *The Nature of Work: An Introduction to Debates on the Labour Process,* London: Macmillan.

Thompson, P. and Ackroyd, S. (1995) 'All quiet on the workplace front: a critique of recent trends in British industrial sociology', *Sociology*, Vol. 29, No. 4, pp. 1–19.

Thompson, P. and Warhurst, C. (eds) (1998) *Workplaces of the Future*, Basingstoke: Macmillan Business.

Thomson, A., Storey, J., Mabey, C., Gray, C., Farmer, E. and Thompson, R. (1997) *A Portrait of Management Development,* London: Institute of Management.

Thouless, R.H. (1953) *Straight and Crooked Thinking,* London: The English Universities' Press.

Thurley, K. (1981) 'Personnel management in the UK – a case for urgent treatment?', *Personnel Management*, August, p. 28.

Torrington, D. (1989) 'Human resource management and the personnel function', in J. Storey (ed.) *New Perspectives on Human Resource Management*, London: Routledge.

Torrington, D. (1994) *International Human Resource Management: Think Globally, Act Locally*, Hemel Hempstead: Prentice-Hall International.

Torrington, D. (1998) 'Crisis and opportunity in HRM: the challenge for the personnel function', in P. Sparrow and M. Marchington (eds) *Human Resource Management: the New Agenda*, London: Financial Times Pitman Publishing, pp. 23–36.

Torrington, D. and Hall, L. (1987) *Personnel Management: a New Approach,* Hemel Hempstead: Prentice-Hall.

Torrington, D. and Hall, L. (1995) *Personnel Management: HRM in Action*, 3rd edition, Hemel Hempstead: Prentice-Hall.

Torrington, D. and Hall, L. (1996) 'Chasing the rainbow. How seeking status through strategy misses the point for the personnel function', *Employee Relations*, Vol. 18, No. 6, pp. 79–97.

Torrington, D. and Hall, L. (1998) *Human Resource Management*, Hemel Hempstead: Prentice-Hall Europe.

Towers, B. (1997) *The Representation Gap: Change and Reform in the British and American Workplace,* Oxford: Oxford University Press.

Townley, B. (1990/1) 'The politics of appraisal: lessons of the introduction of appraisal in UK universities', *Human Resource Management Journal*, Vol. 1, No. 2, pp. 27–42.

Townley, B. (1993) 'Foucault, power/knowledge and its relevance for human resource management', *Academy of Management Review*, Vol. 18, No. 3, pp. 518–45.

Townley, B. (1994) 'Communicating with employees', in K. Sisson (ed.) *Personnel Management*, Oxford: Blackwell.

Trades Union Congress (1994) *Human Resource Management: a Trade Union Response*, London: TUC.

Trades Union Congress (1997) *Partners for Progress: Next Steps for New Unionism*, London: Trades Union Congress.

Trevino, L.K. and Youngblood, S.A. (1990) 'Bad apples in bad barrels: a causal analysis of ethical decision making behaviour', *Journal of Applied Psychology,* Vol. 75, No. 4, pp. 378–85.

Trompenaars, F. (1993) *Riding the Waves of Culture*, London: Nicholas Brealey.

Tuckman, A. (1994) 'The yellow brick road: total quality management and the restructuring of organisational culture', *Organisation Studies*, Vol. 15, No. 5, pp. 727–51.

Tuckman, A. (1995) 'Ideology, quality and TQM', in A. Wilkinson and H. Willmott (eds) *Making Quality Critical: Studies in Organisational Change*, London: Routledge, pp. 54–81.

Tullar, W.L., Mullins, T.W. and Caldwell, S.A. (1979) 'Effects of interview length and applicant quality on interview decision time', *Journal of Applied Psychology*, Vol. 64, No. 6, pp. 669–74.

Tung, R.L. (1998) 'Human resource management, international' in M. Poole and M. Warner (eds) *The IEBM Handbook of Human Resource Management*, London: International Thomson Business Press, pp. 375–90.

Turnbull, P. and Sapsford, D. (1992) 'A sea of discontent: the tides of organised and "unorganised" conflict on the docks', *Sociology*, Vol. 26, No. 2, pp. 291–309.

Turnbull, P. and Wass, V. (1997) 'Job insecurity and labour market lemons: the (mis)management of redundancy in steel-making, coal mining and port transport', *Journal of Management Studies*, Vol. 34, No. 1, pp. 27–52.

Turnbull, P. and Weston, S. (1993) 'Co-operation or control? Capital restructuring and labour relations on the docks', *British Journal of Industrial Relations*, Vol. 31, No. 1, pp. 115–34.

Turner, L. (1991) *Democracy at Work: Changing World Markets and the Future of Labour Unions,* Ithaca, New York and London: Cornell University Press.

Tyson, S. (1995a) *Strategic Prospects for Human Resource Strategy*, London: IPD.

Tyson, S. (1995b) *Human Resource Strategy: Towards a General Theory of Human Resource Management*, London: Financial Times Pitman Publishing.

Tyson, S. (ed.) (1997) *The Practice of Human Resources Strategy*, London: Financial Times Pitman Publishing.

Tyson, S. and Fell, A. (1986) *Evaluating the Personnel Function,* London: Hutchinson.

U

UKCC (United Kingdom Central Council for Nursing, Midwives and Health Visitors) (1996) 'PREP: you and your guide to profiling', *Register*, No. 17, Summer.

Unions 21 (1998) *Fairness at Work White Paper – Preparing a Response*, London: Unions 21.

Ursell, G. (1991) 'Human resource management and labour flexibility', in P. Blyton and J.A. Morris (eds) *A Flexible Future*, Berlin: Walter De Gruyter, pp. 311–28.

V

Valentine, R. and Knights, E. (1998) 'TQM and BPR – can you spot the difference?', *Personnel Review*, Vol. 27, No. 1, pp. 78–85.

Van Vianen, A.E. and Kmieciak, Y.M. (1998) 'The match between recruiters' perceptions of organisational climate and personality of the ideal applicant for a management position', *International Journal of Selection and Assessment*, Vol. 6, No. 3, pp. 153–64.

Vance, C.M., McClaine, S.R., Boje, D.M. and Stage, H.D. (1992) 'An xamination of the transferability of traditional performance appraisal principles across cultural boundaries', *Management International Review*, Vol. 32, No. 4, pp. 313–26.

Vass, P. (1996) 'Regulated industries', in P. Jackson and M. Lavender (eds) *Public Services Yearbook 1996–7*, London: Financial Times Pitman Publishing, pp. 155–68.

Verma, A. and Cutcher-Gershenfeld, N. (1993) 'Joint governance in the workplace: beyond union–management cooperation and worker participation', in B.E. Kaufman, and M.M. Kleiner (eds) *Employee Representation: Alternatives and Future Directions*, Madison: Industrial Relations Research Association, pp. 197–234.

Vinnicombe, S. and Colwill, N. (1995) 'Training, mentoring and networking', in S. Vinnicombe and N. Colwill (eds) *Women in Management*, London: Prentice-Hall, pp. 110–21.

Visser, J. (1988) 'Trade unionism in Europe: present situation and prospects', *Labour and Society*, Vol. 13, No. 1, pp. 125–42.

Vroom, V. (1964) *Work and Motivation*, New York: John Wiley & Sons.

W

Waddington, J. and Whitston, C. (1996) 'Empowerment versus intensification: union perspectives of change in the workplace', in P. Ackers, C. Smith and P. Smith (eds) *The New Workplace and Trade Unionism: Critical Perspectives on Work and Organisation*, London: Routledge, pp. 149–77.

Walby, S. (1989) The Transformation of Work, London: Unwin.

Walsh, D.A. (1992) 'Recruitment for new superstores: A-B-Zee', in D. Winstanley and J. Woodall (eds) *Case Studies in Personnel*, London: IPM, pp. 37–43.

Walsh, T. (1991) 'The reshaping of flexible labour? European policy perspectives', in P. Blyton and J.A. Morris (eds) *Flexible Future*, Berlin: Walter De Gruyter, pp. 349–64.

Walters, M. (1995) *The Performance Management Handbook*, London: IPD.

Walton, R. (1985a) 'Toward a strategy of eliciting employee commitment based on policies of mutuality', in R. Walton and P. Lawrence (eds) *HRM Trends and Challenges*, Boston: Harvard Business School Press.

Walton, R.E. (1985b) 'From control to commitment in the workplace', *Harvard Business Review*, March/April, pp. 77–94.

Wanous, J.P. (1980) *Organisational Entry: Recruitment, Selection and Socialisation of Newcomers*, Reading, MA: Addison-Wesley.

Ward, P. (1995) 'A 360° turn for the better', *People Management*, Vol. 1, No. 3, pp. 20–2.

Watson, G. (1992) 'Hours of work in Great Britain and Europe: evidence from the UK and European Labour Force Surveys', *Employment Gazette*, November, pp. 539–57.

Watson, G. (1994) 'The flexible workforce and patterns of working hours in the UK', *Employment Gazette*, July, pp. 239–47.

Watson, T.J. (1977) *The Personnel Managers*, London: Routledge and Kegan Paul.

Watson, T.J. (1986) *Management, Organisation and Employment Strategy: New Directions in Theory and Practice*, London: Routledge and Kegan Paul.

Watson, T.J. (1994a) *In Search of Management*, London: International Thomson Business Press.

Watson, T.J. (1994b) 'Management "flavours of the month": their role in managers' lives', *International Journal of Human Resource Management*, Vol. 5, No. 4, pp. 889–905.

Watson, T.J. (1995a) 'In search of HRM: beyond the rhetoric and reality distinction or the dog that didn't bark', *Personnel Review*, Vol. 24, No. 4, pp. 6–16.

Watson, T.J. (1995b) *Sociology, Work and Industry*, 3rd edition, London: Routledge.

Watson, T.J. (1997) 'Theorizing managerial work: a pragmatic pluralist approach to interdisciplinary work', *British Journal of Management,* Vol. 8, No. 1, pp. 9–22.

Watson, T.J. and Harris, P. (1996) 'Human resources are strategic too: managerial career strategies, planned or realized', *Strategic Change* Vol. 5, No. 6, pp. 1–12.

Wayne, S.J. and Ferris, G.R. (1990) 'Influence tactics, affect and exchange quality in supervisor-subordinate interactions: a laboratory experiment and field study', *Journal of Applied Psychology*, Vol. 74, No. 3, pp. 487–99.

Webb, J. and Liff, S. (1988) 'Play the white man: the social construction of fairness and competition in equal opportunities policies', *Sociological Review,* Vol. 36, No. 3, pp. 532–51.

Webb, S. (1989) *Blueprint for Success: a Report on Involving Employees in Britain*, London: Industrial Society.

Weber, J. (1996) 'The influence upon managerial moral decision making: nature of the harm and magnitude of consequences', *Human Relations*, Vol. 49, No. 1, January, pp. 1–22.

Webster, B. (1990) 'Beyond the mechanics of HRD', *Personnel Management,* Vol. 22, No. 3, pp. 44–7.

Wedderburn Lord (1986) *The Worker and the Law*, 3rd edition, Harmondsworth: Penguin.

Weick, K.E. (1979) *The Social Psychology of Organising*, Reading, MA: Addison-Wesley.

Weitzman, M. (1984) *The Share Economy*, Cambridge, MA: Harvard University Press.

Weitzner, T.G., Formento, R.J. and Tasso, C.A. (1990) *Human Resource Information Technology: a Current Perspective on Future Directions*, Organization Resources Counselors, Inc, California.

Welch, J. (1997) 'New model army', *People Management*, 4 December, pp. 22–7.

West, M. and Allen, N. (1997) 'Selecting for teamwork', in N. Anderson and P. Herriot (eds) *International Handbook of Selection and Assessment*, Chichester: John Wiley & Sons, pp. 543–66.

Whipp, R. (1992) 'HRM, competition and strategy', in P. Blyton and P. Turnhull (eds) *Reassessing Human Resource Management*, London: Sage, pp. 33–55.

Whitston, C. and Waddington, J. (1994) 'Why join a union?', *New Statesman and Society*, 18 November, pp. 36–8.

Whittington, R. (1993) *What is Strategy and Does it Matter?* London: Routledge.

Wickens, P. (1987) *The Road to Nissan*, London: Macmillan.

Wiersema, M.F. and Bantel, K.A. (1992) 'Top management team demography and corporate strategic change', *Academy of Management Journal*, Vol. 1, No. 35, pp. 91–121.

Wilkinson, A. (1988) 'Empowerment: theory and practice', *Personnel Review*, Vol. 27, No. 1, pp. 40–56.

Wilkinson, A., Marchington, M., Goodman, J. and Ackers, P. (1992) 'Total quality management and employee involvement', *Human Resource Management Journal*, Vol. 2, No. 4, pp. 1–20.

Wilkinson, A., Redman, T., Snape, E. and Marchington, M. (1998) *Managing with Total Quality Management*, London: Macmillan.

Williams, R. (1991) 'Management selection in local government: a survey of practice in England and Wales', *Human Resource Management Journal*, Vol. 3, No. 2, pp. 63–7.

Williamson, O. (1975) *Markets and Hierarchies: Analysis and Anti-Trust Implications*, New York: Free Press.

Willman, P. (1996) 'Merger propensity and merger outcomes among British unions 1986–1995', *Industrial Relations Journal*, Vol. 27, No. 4, pp. 331–8.

Wilson, E. (1996) 'Managing diversity and HRD', in J. Stewart and J. McGoldrick, (eds) *Human Resource Development: Perspectives, Strategies and Practice*, Financial Times Pitman Publishing, pp. 158–79.

Wilson, T. (1991) 'The proletarianisation of academic labour', *Industrial Relations Journal*, Vol. 22. No. 4., pp. 250–62.

Womack, J.P, Jones, D.T. and Roos, D. (1990) *The Machine that Changed the World: the Triumph of Lean Production,* New York: Rawson.

Wood, S. (1995) 'The four pillars of HRM: are they connected?', *Human Resource Management Journal*, Vol. 5, No. 5, pp. 53–8.

Wood, S. (1997) 'Statutory union recognition', *Issues in People Management*, No. 17.

Wood, S. and Albanese, M. (1995) 'Can we speak of high commitment management on the shop floor?', *Journal of Management Studies,* Vol. 32, No. 2, pp. 215–47.

Woodall, J. (1996) 'Human resource management and women: the vision of the gender-blind?', in B. Towers (ed.) *The Handbook of Human Resource Management*, 2nd edition, Oxford: Blackwell, pp. 329–52.

Woodall, J. and Winstanley, D. (1998) *Management Development: Strategy and Practice*, Oxford: Blackwell Business.

Woodward, J. (1994) *Industrial Organisation*, 2nd edition, Oxford: Oxford University Press.

World Bank (1995) *Workers in an Integrating World,* World Development Report, Oxford: Oxford University Press.

World Economic Forum (1998) Geneva, Switzerland.

Wright, G. (1984) *Behavioural Decision Theory: an Introduction*, Harmondsworth: Penguin.

Y

Yeandle, S. (1997) 'Non-standard working: diversity and change in European countries', paper presented at the *International Labour Process Conference*, Edinburgh, 25–27 March.

SUBJECT INDEX

ability tests 156–7
absenteeism 370, 407
ACAS (Advisory, Conciliation and Arbitration Service) 194, 195, 280, 281
surveys 345, 346, 347
acceptability criteria, job 302
accountability 184, 185
Acquired Rights Directive 271, 272, 273
action learning 232, 256
action plans 51–3
ADST (Approved Deferred Share Trust) 352, 353
Advisory, Conciliation and Arbitration Service see ACAS
affirmative action 299
age 78, 79, 83, 297
agendas 206, 240, 241, 256, 300–1
altruism 314, 332
American Society for Training and Development (ASTD) 220, 224
analysis 114, 115, 117, 153, 154
comparative 13, 300, 393, 394–400
'andon' board 406–7
application forms 155–6
appraisal 104, 184–6
360° 169, 180–1, 182, 203
performance 256, 356
see also assessment; evaluation; selection
Approved Deferred Share Trust (ADST) 352, 353
ASA (attraction-selection-attrition) model 149–50
aspirations, employee 70
assessment 7, 130, 154–62, 256, 302
multi-rater assessment 169, 180–1, 182, 203
processual perspective 154, 158, 162
see also appraisal; evaluation; selection
Association of Suggestion Schemes 346
ASTD (American Society for Training and Development) 220, 224
attitude survey 344, 346
attraction-selection-attrition (ASA) model 149–50
attribution theory 138–9
atypical work 70, 294
automobile industry 100, 393, 394, 400–12
Automotive News 405
auxiliary law 269

avoidance 293, 324, 377, 384, 395
penalty 293–4, 295, 296, 300
uncertainty score (Hofstede) 120

balanced scorecard 177, 203
beginners, manager 57, 60
behaviour 160, 184, 205, 229, 245
and conflict 369, 370
Bentham, Jeremy 179
best practice 96, 152
Bett, Sir Michael 304
biodata, selection 155–6
'black hole' strategy 13, 377–8, 380
bonus payments 209
bounded rationality 97
British Gas 197, 198
British Psychological Society (BPS) standards 140
budgets 44, 53–5, 179, 199, 202
Business Week 404
business-related decision making 342, 343

call centres 385
CALM, performance measurement 173
car industry 100, 393, 394, 400–12
careers 27, 222, 224, 257, 258
managed 245
centralisation/decentralisation 69, 93, 194, 205
chance, processual 27, 31, 33
change 13–14, 64, 70, 227, 231
agents 222, 223–4
behavioural 245
cultural see culture change
managing 44, 55, 108, 223
choice 97, 115, 237
constraints 97–8
in international management 94
strategic 28–31, 101, 103, 104, 109
closed shop 271
cloverleaf organisation 69
co-operation and conflict 12–14, 366, 368, 380, 387
defined 365
see also conflict
codes of practice 330–1

collective agreement 274, 396–7
collective bargaining 196, 269, 270, 373, 392
  decline of 397–8
collective learning 244
collective organisation 396–7
Collective Redundancies Directive 273
collective rights 276
collectivism 116, 120, 194, 207
  Hofstede score 119
Commission for Racial Equality (CRE) 293, 299
commitment, employee 195–9
communication 12, 94, 95, 179, 345–6
comparative analysis 13, 300, 393, 394–400
  problems 399–400
compensation agenda 241
competence 185, 209, 256, 260
competition 25, 68, 101, 393, 399
  competitive advantage 45, 49, 96, 177, 408
  league table 101
compliance and penalty avoidance 293–4, 295,
    296, 300
computerisation 55–7, 60, 95, 275
concurrent validity 147, 148
conflict 369–70, 374–5, 379–81, 384–6, 396
  in new work place regime 379–81, 384–6
  see also co-operation and conflict
consequentialism, ethical 319, 320
consultants 223, 286
contingency 96, 97, 207, 260, 394–6
contracts of employment 274, 396, 397
  fixed 75–7, 234
  psychological 83
  subcontracting 66
  temporary 234
  zero hours contract 79–81, 82, 268–9
control 53–5, 93, 380, 407
  direct 42, 43, 256
  indirect 42, 43
core workers 66, 67, 68, 69
core/periphery structure 69, 82
corporate structure 93, 94, 99
  see also organisational structure
counselling 183
covert discrimination 302
CRE (Commission for Racial Equality) 293, 299
criteria-related validity 154, 164
critical management task 26
cross-cultural issues 112, 119–21
cross-validation 155
culture 51, 94, 95, 96, 114
  cultural values 33
  defined 94

employment relationships 115–16
  ethnic 105–6
  and multinationals 104
  national 107
culture change 95, 108, 195, 257, 258
  organisational 196, 231
culture shock 113
cycles, participation 342

Data Protection Act (1984) 275
databases *see* computerisation
decentralisation/centralisation 69, 93, 194, 205
decision making 162–3, 226, 342, 343
  staffing decisions 104, 105
demography 68, 70, 294, 295
demotivation 204
deontology, ethical 320
dependency theory 316–17
derecognition 376, 386
dialectic analysis 318–20, 327
direct control 42, 43, 256
direct involvement 342, 350–1
direct-control/high-commitment 29, 380
direct-control/low-commitment 29, 83, 256, 258,
    260
disabled discrimination 297, 303
disadvantaged groups 297, 299, 300
discrimination 79, 133, 202, 276, 293
  age 83, 297
  covert 302
  disabled 297, 303
  in selection process 162
distancing 66
diversity, managing 258, 296, 304
documentation, appraisal 183
domestic human resourcing 90–8, 106
dominant management 106, 109
downsizing 55, 70, 73, 77, 78
downward communication 345–6
dual resourcing 33, 82, 83, 237, 256
  static dualism 68
duty, ethical 318, 319, 321

early retirement 78, 79
ECJ (European Court of Justice) 206, 266, 271,
    272, 273
ecology heuristic 329, 330
economic factors 30, 115, 399
EITS (Educational and Industrial Test Services)
    157
electronic mail 95
employee involvement 12, 340, 344–54, 387

employee participation 12, 340, 376
  waves or cycles 342–3, 357
employee share ownership plans (ESOPS) 351–2,
    353, 354
employees 77, 82, 109, 110, 114
  age discrimination 79
  age profile 78
  commitment 195–9
  and employer relationships 12–14, 114–15,
    118, 269, 396
  and equal opportunities policies 295
  female 272
  interests 396–7
  manual 194, 209
  pay schemes 209
  personal development 181
  relocation 110
  share-ownership 200, 351–2, 353, 354
  survival anxiety 207
  working hours 79
  see also staff; training and development
employer/employee relationship 12–14, 114–15,
    118, 269, 396
Employers' Labour Use Survey 67
Employment Acts 270, 271, 276–7
employment contracts *see* contracts of
    employment
Employment Europe 82
employment flexibility 68, 70, 71, 83
Employment Gazette 371, 374
employment law 10–11, 268, 269, 396
employment management 19–21, 378
Employment Outlook 397
empowerment 25, 27, 74, 257, 344
environmental analysis 154
epistemology 143
equal opportunities 83, 202, 258, 276, 387
  diversity and 304
  espoused models 292
  legislation on 293
  liberal/radical approaches to 299–300
  managing 10–11, 292, 295, 297
  policies 296–8, 301–3
Equal Pay Act (1970) 270
equity theory 199
ESOPS (employee share-ownership plans) 351–2,
    353, 354
*ESRC Social Change and Economic Life Research
    Initiative* 67
ethics 10–11, 311–14
  codes 330–1
  integrity, dimension of 317–18

moral categories 315–16, 320–3, 325, 327, 330
  moral reasoning 324–8
  purpose 318–20
Ethics Quick Test 330–1
ethnic minorities 83, 105–6, 303
ethnocentric approaches 104–5, 109
EU *see* European Union
European Community *see* European Union
European Court of Justice (ECJ) 206, 266, 271,
    272, 273
European Union 76, 78, 101, 271–5, 280
  and labour market 409
  regulations 70
  and union membership 398
  and worker participation 355
  Works Councils 274, 275, 355, 358
evaluation 7, 149, 228–30
  see also appraisal; assessment; selection
exchange and negotiation selection 133–4
expatriates 110, 113
expectancy theory 169, 196, 198
experiential learning cycle (Kolb) 135–6
experimentation and validity 147–52
external attribution 138
external flexibility 77
externally oriented planning 44

face validity 148, 157, 162
Fair Wages Resolution 269
fairness heuristic 329, 330
feedback 173, 182, 228
felt-fair concept 199–200
female employees 272
femininity score (Hofstede) 120–1
Finance Act (1996) 353
financial flexibility 66, 68
financial involvement 351–4
financial planning, basic 44
Financial Times 100, 101, 203, 277, 401, 403
fit 25–7, 28, 30, 32, 96
  in appraisal schemes 186
  in assessment 161
  processual perspectives 134, 154
  in work setting 149
five-forces framework (Porter) 45
fixed contracts 75–7, 234
flexi-time 79
flexibility 27, 32, 286
  defined 65, 71
  employment 68, 70, 71, 83
  external 77
  financial 66, 68

flexibility (Continued)
  functional 66–7, 68, 69, 71–5
  jobs-based 73
  labour market 82
  locational 71
  numerical 66, 67, 71, 73, 75–9
    redundancy 76, 77–9
  reward 71
  surveys 72
  task 73
  temporal 67, 79–81
flexible firm 5, 27, 66–7, 83
  critiques 67–9
forecasting 44, 180
four-phase management 44
free trade 393
freelance workers 83
full-time workers 66, 82
functional flexibility 66–7, 68, 69, 71–5
functional performance 240–1, 256
fundamental attribution error 139

generic strategy (Porter) 45
geocentric approaches 104, 105, 109
globalisation 6, 92, 99–108, 398, 399
  global mindset 103, 108, 110
  horizontal integration 95
  vertical integration 95
Glossary of Training Terms 218
goal-setting theory 169, 196, 197
golden mean (Aristotle) 311
golden rule 314
government policies 201, 409
graphology 148
Greenbury Committee 353
group-selection 159
Guardian 198

halo and horns effect 139, 183
harassment 274, 297
hard human resource management 41–2, 43, 193
Harvard Business Review 212
Harvard Business School 45
headhunting, reverse 332–4
health and safety 387
hedonism 325
hegemony 302
heuristics 329–30
hidden agendas 206
higher education 76
hire and fire 26, 32, 64, 271
holiday entitlement 274

holistic selection 150, 151
homeworking 71
horizontal integration 28, 32–3, 47, 49–50, 255
  globalised 95, 96
host country employment 109, 114–21
HRIS (human resource information systems)
  55–7, 60
human capital advantage 49
human process advantage 49
human resource information systems (HRIS)
  55–7, 60
human resource management 19–21, 29, 193,
  280–1, 392
human resource maximisation 381
human resource planning 4–5, 39, 40–3, 51–3, 78
  and budgetary control 53–5
  and computerisation 55–7, 60
human resource specialists 208, 258, 282, 285,
  287
  and legislation 277, 278–80
human resources, defined 28, 40
human resourcing
  advantage 49
  analysis *see* analysis
  domestic 90–8, 106
  international 6, 90–108
  national 96–8
  strategies 19–38, 226, 240, 255–8, 356
    concept 20–1
    defined 28
Human Rights Bill (1997) 277
human-centred work organisation 411

idiographic theory, personality 140, 142, 143,
  157
IDS Report 71
IDS Study 71
image, employers 295
impact validity 148
impression management 137–8, 156, 157
in-basket exercise 147
in-tray exercise 158
incrementalisation 24, 28, 45, 68
indirect control 42, 43
indirect representation 342, 343
indirect-control/high-commitment 29, 83, 256,
  257, 380
indirect-control/low-commitment 380
individual need heuristic 329, 330
individual performance-related pay (IPRP) 193,
  196, 200, 203, 209
    measuring and rating 201, 202

public sector 205
individualism 44, 116, 133, 139, 194
  in ethics 325
  Hofstede score 120
  and management development 244, 245
inducement-contribution equilibrium 112
industrial action 281, 373–4
industrial democracy 340
industrial relations 13–14, 392, 393, 396, 399
  surveys 67, 345, 373
Industrial Relations Act (1971) 270, 397
Industrial Training Act (1964) 270
Industrial Tribunals 269, 277, 293
information technology *see* computerisation
inpatriates 110
internal attribution 138
international competition 393, 399
international human resourcing 6, 90–108
  seven Cs (Torrington) 97
international organisation 94–6, 102–3
international relocation 111–14
intervention, minimal 269–71
interviews, job selection 160, 161
IPRP *see* individual performance-related pay
IRS Employment Trends 71

IT (information technology) *see* computerisation
JIT (just-in-time) 73, 380, 381
job analysis 152, 153, 154
job behaviour 229
job description 152, 153, 154
job enrichment 350–1
job performance 149, 153, 256
job redesign 350–1
job specification 134
jobs-based flexibility 73
joint consultation 342, 343
just-in-time (JIT) 73, 380, 381

key decision makers 226
Kohlberg's moral reasoning model 11, 324–8,
  331
  criticisms 327–8

labour costs 81
Labour Force Survey 67, 72, 78, 81
Labour Force Trends 371
labour market 33, 65, 280, 294–5, 393
  deregulation 355
  and European Union 409
  flexible 82
Labour Market Trends 71, 78, 274, 374

labour supply 82
labour utilisation 64, 81
last in, first out (LIFO) 77, 330
law 96, 115, 184, 293, 397
  employment 10–11, 268, 269, 396
lean production 380, 381, 404–11
learning 227, 229, 243, 245
  action 232, 256
  collective 244
  learning cycle 135–6
  management of 232
  natural 226
learning organisations 227, 233
legal process *see* law
liberal/radical approach 299–300
lifelong culture 95
LIFO (last in, first out) 77, 330
line management 205–7, 208, 301
line managers 202, 223, 279, 282–5
  and equal opportunities 301
  and power 301
  and training 224–7
local conditions analysis 115
locational flexibility 71
logical incrementalism 24
London School of Economics 293
long agenda 300–1
long range planning 44
long-term planning 51
Low Pay Commission 275, 276

macro-economic policy 399
mainstream (planned) strategy 23, 25–7
managed careers 245
management 21–2, 44, 104–7, 240, 241, 242
  of change 44, 55, 108, 223
  of conflict 370, 374–5
  of employees 378, 396
  and ethics 311, 317
  of human resources 94, 295
  impression 137–8, 156, 157
  information 55, 57, 60
  latent control 407
  of learning 232
  line 205–7, 208, 301
  performance 7–8, 168–9, 170–1
  personnel management 278, 279, 280, 281,
    286, 301
  problem staff 184
  processual 248, 364, 365, 366, 368
  relocation 111
  self-learning 232

management (Continued)
  self-management 344, 385
  by stress 381
  stretch 349
  style 232
  and trade unions 374–5
  of uncertainty 81–4
  see also total quality management
Management Charter Initiative (MCI) 253
management development 240–4
  approaches 248, 249–52, 256
  defined 9–10, 240, 244–8
  and human resourcing strategy 255–8
  management/manager differences 244
  methods 253–5
  Thomson report 257
  typologies 241, 249–52
Management Today 276
manager/s 57, 97, 223, 301
  pay 201, 203
  training 297
  training manager (role) 222
managerial grid 254–5
managerial ideologies 394, 395
managerial self-development 256
managerial values 394, 395
managerial work 241–2, 244
  see also management development; manager/s
managing 21–2, 241–2, 244, 248
  change 44, 55, 108, 223
  diversity 258, 296, 304
  equal opportunities 10–11, 292, 295, 297
  uncertainty 81–4
manpower planning 40–3, 55
Manpower Services Commission (1978) 223
manual employees 194, 209
marital status discrimination 297
masculinity score (Hofstede) 120
mass production 403, 404–5, 409, 410, 411
MCI (Management Charter Initiative) 253
measurement methods 154–62, 173–8
mechanical metaphors 26
meta-analysis 154
methodology
  management development 253–5
  measurement 154–62, 173–8
  selection 150–1
metrics, monthly 168, 178
mindset 107–8
minimum wage 275, 276
mission statements 52, 53, 94
modification strategy 117

morals *see* ethics
motivation 70, 197, 204
motor industry *see* automobile industry
multi-disciplinary analysis 399
multi-rater assessment 169, 181–2, 183, 203
multi-unit business organisation 92–4
multicultural teams 95
multifunctional workers 66
multinational-polycentric organisation 104
multinationals 99, 101–7, 394–6
multiskilling 71, 72, 73

national culture 95, 107
National Health Service (NHS) 73–4
national human resourcing 96–8
nationalism 95
natural learning 226
network systems 55
new workplace regime 13, 365, 370, 379–81,
    384–6
new-style human resource management 83
newcomer integration 150
NHS (National Health Service) 73–4
nomothetic theory, personality 140, 143, 157
non-disabled male dominance 302, 303
non-management 44
non-standard employment 70, 71
non-standard work 70
non-traditional recruits 294
numerical flexibility 66, 67, 71, 73, 75–9
  redundancy 76, 77–9

objectivity 143
OECD (Organisation for Economic Co-operation
    & Development) 78
older workers 79
on-the-job training 225
ontology 143
operational models, equal opportunity 292, 301–3
Opportunity 2000 297
Oregon experiment 321
Organisation for Economic Co-operation &
    Development (OECD) 78
organisation/employee relationship 396
organisational structures 102, 209, 223, 227, 300
  culture 95, 154, 394, 395
  ethics 311–14, 331
  policy making 395
  politics 394, 395
  see also change; corporate structure; culture
    change
organising 21–2

outsourcing 66, 71
overtime 79–81, 84, 209
ownership 200, 256, 352–3
    employee share 200, 351–2, 353, 354
Oxford Psychologists Press 157

Panoptic gaze (monitoring) 181, 381
PAQ (Position Analysis Questionnaire) 153
parent-country nationals (PCN's) 109
parental leave 274–5, 276
part-time workers 70, 79, 82, 272, 274
particularism 116
partnership 13, 365, 386–7, 409
Partnership for Progress 386
patterned strategy (processual strategy) 23–5,
    27–33
pay
    bonuses 209
    manager/s 201, 203
    matrices 209
    matrix 202
    payment by results 194
    performance pay 8, 186, 193–5, 208–9
    profit-related-pay (PRP) 353, 354
    systems 198, 199, 207, 208–9
    team-based 201
    see also individual performance-related pay
        (IPRP)
payback 233
payroll administration 56
PCN's (parent-country nationals 109
PDP (personal development plan) 182
peer accountability 186
peer assessment 256
peer review 184–5
penalty avoidance and compliance 293–4, 295,
    296, 300
performance appraisal 256, 356
performance management 7–8, 168–9, 170–1
performance measurement 173–8
performance pay 8, 185, 193–5, 208–9
performance tests 158–9
peripheral workers 66, 67, 68–9
person specification 153
personal construct theory 140, 142–7
personal development 169, 183, 231
personal satisfaction and gain heuristic 329,
    330
personality questionnaires 157–8
personality theory
    idiographic 140, 142, 143, 157
    nomothetic 140, 143, 157

questionnaires 157–8
    seven point plan (Rodger) 153
    traits 140–1
personnel management 278, 279, 280, 281, 286,
    301
personnel management/line management tension
    301
personnel managers 282, 301, 302
personnel policies 406–7
picketing 271
piecework 194
planned (mainstream) strategy 23, 25–7
plodders 57
pluralism 364, 366
PM Plus 297
political factors 30, 33, 51, 115, 266
    political correctness 110
political reinforcement agenda 240, 256
polycentric approach 6, 92, 104, 109
polyvalence 71
Position Analysis Questionnaire (PAQ) 153
positive action training 297
positive discrimination 299
Posted Workers Directive (1996) 274
power distance score (Hofstede) 120
power, distribution of 301
pre-departure phase, relocation 112–13
predictive validity 147, 148, 151, 154, 162
    in ability tests 157
private sector 84, 205
processual approach 140
    to selection 133–4, 152, 162
processual management 364, 365, 366, 368
processual perspective
    of assessment 154, 158
    and budgetary control 53, 54
    of human resource planning 52
    and job analysis/description 154
    of managing 248
    of organising 248
    of performance management 171
    of validity 150
processual strategy 4, 23–5, 27–33, 43–7
processual view 82
product innovation strategy 25
product life cycle 26
productive co-operation 207
profit sharing schemes 351
profit-related-pay (PRP) 353, 354
    see also individual performance-related pay
        (IPRP)
programme structures, performance 173

PRP (profit related pay) 353, 354
 see also individual performance-related pay (IPRP)
prudence, ethical 318
psychic defence agenda 240
Psychological Corporation 157
psychology 83, 115, 140, 157
psychometric selection 132–3, 156–8
public sector 69, 78, 79, 84, 197
 and ethics 331–2
 and IPRP 205
 recruitment 283
punishment avoidance 324
puzzles and problems 321–2, 325
 ethical 315, 321, 327, 330

quality circles 346, 347–50
quality of working life 351
questionnaires 153, 157–8, 181–2, 228
quota setting 297, 299

racial discrimination 270, 297, 302
radical managers 57
rating systems, pay 199, 202
rational strategy 45
recognition, union 375–6
recruitment 150, 152, 283, 294, 302–3
 see also selection
redundancy 76, 77–9, 83, 84, 270
 legislation 270, 273
reengineering 56, 349
references, job selection 159–60
regiocentric orientation 6, 104, 105
regulation theory 65
regulative law, employment 269
religious discrimination 297
relocation 110, 111–14, 395
remuneration packages 112
repatriation, relocation 113–14
repertory grid (repgrid) 143, 153
representative participation 343–4
research 83, 148, 399, 400
response presence 45
restrictive law 269
reverse discrimination 299
reward systems 192, 193, 194, 195, 196
 flexibility 71
 in equal opportunities 300
 relocation 112
Rewarding Performance (British Gas) 197, 198
rightsizing 77

Save As You Earn (SAYE) schemes 352, 353

second-generation contractors 272
selection 7, 130
 decisions 162–3
 methods 150–1
 psychometric 132–3, 156–8
 references 159–60
 research on 148
 systemic approach to 131–3, 136, 152, 157, 158
 validity 148, 149
 see also appraisal; assessment; evaluation
self *see* individualism
self-assessment 256
self-awareness 318
self-development 232–3, 234, 256
 see also personal development
self-management 344, 385
self-monitors 137–8
self-report instruments 157
self-serving error 139
self-validating principles 320
semi-structured interviews 161
sex discrimination 270, 274, 297, 302
sexual harassment 274
Seymour Smith and Perez case 272
share ownership 200, 351–2, 353, 354
shift patterns 274
shift premiums 209
short agenda 300–1
single disciplinary research 399
single resourcing 33, 256
single-business organisation 92
single-gender training courses 297–8
situational interview 160
skill-mix 73
SMART targets 197
Social Chapter 271, 274–5, 355
social contract 270, 325
soft human resource planning 41–2, 43, 78
staff appraisal 183–5
staff flows 111
staff, problem 182
staffing decisions 104, 105
staffing policies, transnational 6, 109–14
stakeholders 228, 230, 231, 233, 407
 and performance measurement 177–8
standard employment 69, 84
stars 57, 60
static dualism 68
statistics 178
stereotypes 163, 258
strategic choice, in multinationals 101, 103, 104

strategic facilitators 230
strategic management, history of 44
strategic thrust 25
strategy 21–2
  'black hole' 13, 377–8, 380
  dual resourcing strategy 33, 82, 83, 237, 256
    static dualism 68
  and ethics 311–14
  generic (Porter) 45
  mainstream (planned) 23, 25–7
  modification strategy 117
  patterned (processual strategy) 23–5, 27–33
  product innovation strategy 25
  rational strategy 45
  and unions 377
stress 381, 385, 406, 407
stretch management 349
strikes 281, 373–4
structural form 101, 106
structured antagonism 32, 369
structured interviews 160, 161
subcontracting 66
subculture 95–6
subjectivity 143, 164, 202
substitution strategy, union 377
succession planning 254
suggestion schemes 346–7
suitability criteria, job 302
Sunday Times 201
surveys 67, 72, 78, 81
  ACAS 345, 346, 347
  attitude 344, 346
  flexibility 72
  industrial relations 67, 345, 373
  value model (Hofstede) 119–21
  WERS (workplace employee relations survey)
    73, 297, 352, 356
  WIRS (workplace industrial relations survey)
    67, 345, 346, 373
survival anxiety, employee 207
Süzen v *Zehnacker Gebäudering* (1997) 272
Swedish Centre for Working Life 410
syllogism premise 174–5, 177
systemic approach 140
systemic requirements, assessment centres 162
systemic selection 131–3, 136, 152, 157, 158
systemic validity 154, 164
systems 43–7, 51, 96, 153, 364
  information 55–7, 60
  network 55
  pay 198, 199, 207, 208–9
  perspective 51, 52, 53, 54

reward *see* reward systems
view of planning 51

target appraisal 185
target setting 178–81
task flexibility 73
task participation 342, 345, 350–1
TCN's (third-country nationals) 109
team analysis 154
team briefing 345, 356
team working 73, 207, 351, 407
team-based pay 201
teams, multicultural 95
technology 70, 74, 82, 223
temporal flexibility 67, 79–81
temporary contracts 234
temporary workers 70, 75, 77, 82, 83, 84
third-country nationals (TCN's) 109
Thomson report (management development)
    257
total quality management (TQM) 73, 346,
    347–50, 356–7, 358
  and new workplace 380
TQM *see* total quality management
Trade Union Act (1984) 271
Trade Union and Labour Relations Act (1974)
    270
trade unions 82, 194, 202, 358, 371–9
  avoidance strategy 377, 395
  and discrimination 297
  and European directives 356
  and financial involvement schemes 352, 354
  independent 397
  and lean production 405, 408, 410
  legislation against 270, 271, 280
  membership, decline in 371–3, 392, 398
  recognition of 371–6
  and redundancy 78
  Swedish membership 410
  and total quality management 348, 349
trainers 222, 223–4, 228
training and development 195, 220–1, 231–4,
    237, 297
  courses 225–6, 297
  defined 8–9, 218–20, 242
  ethical 332
  programmes 112, 231
  training manager (role) 222
trait theory 140–1
transnational companies 102, 103, 104, 107
  staffing 6, 109–14
transpatriates 110

Treaty of Rome 270
type theory, personality 140
typologies, management development 241, 249–52
typology, job performance 149

uncertainty 71, 77, 81–4, 120
unemployment 68
unfair dismissal 271, 272, 281
unions *see* trade unions
unitary perspective 364
United States Immigration and Naturalisation
    Service 111
universalism 116
unstructured interviews 160, 161
upskilling 73, 74
upward appraisal 182
upward problem solving 344, 345, 346–50
utility heuristic 320, 329, 330

validity 147–52, 320
    criteria-related 154, 164
    cross-validation 155
    face 148, 157, 162
    predictive 147, 148, 151, 154, 157, 162
value/s
    chain (Porter) 45
    cultural 33
    ethical 320, 329
    managerial 394, 395
    statements 52, 53, 94
    survey model (Hofstede) 119–21

vertical integration 28, 32–3, 47–9, 92, 95
video-conferencing 95
virtual organisation 70
virtue ethics 311
vision statements 52, 53, 94

Wages Councils 269
Warwick Company Level Survey 67
waves, participation 342, 357
WERS (workplace employee relations survey) 73,
    297, 343, 352, 356
whipsawing 401
whistle blowing 325, 332
WIRS (workplace industrial relations survey) 67,
    345, 346, 373
women 68, 70, 75, 83, 303
    training 297–8
Work Profiling System (WPS) 153
work-sampling 158–9
workers *see* employees
working hours 70, 79, 82, 209, 297
Working Time Directive (WTD) 273–4, 276
Workplace Industrial Relations Survey 67, 345, 346,
    373
Works Councils 377, 395, 397
    and European Union 274, 275, 355, 358
world economy 399–400
World Wide Web 55, 100, 106, 330
WPS (Work Profiling System) 153

zero hours contract 79–81, 82, 268–9

NAME INDEX

This index consists of people and organisations.

Ackers, P. 12, 342, 346, 347, 348, 351, 357
Ackroyd, S. 384
Adams, J.S. 112, 199
Adams, R.J. 393
Adler, N.J. 95
Adler, P.S. 411
Advisory Conciliation and Arbitration Service
   (ACAS) 194, 195, 280, 281
Ahlstrand, B. 32
Albanese, M. 29
Algera, J.A. 152
Allen, N. 154
Allinson, G.D. 107
Alvesson, M. 31, 242, 247
Anderson, N. 150, 154, 161
Anthony, P. 31
Armstrong, M. 25, 155, 192, 195, 201, 208, 209
Armstrong, M.B. 311
Arnold, J. 137
Arrowsmith, J. 79
Arthur, W. 161
Arthurs, A. 56
Atkinson, J. 5, 27, 66–7, 68, 69, 76, 77, 133, 266
Audit Commission 177
Avedon, M.J. 161

Babson, S. 381, 406
Baddon, L. 352, 353, 354
Bain, P. 372, 381
Baird, L. 47
Baldry, C. 381
Ball, R. 177
Bantel, K.A. 148, 158
Barnes, N. 75, 77, 83
Barocci, T.A. 26
Baron, R.A. 137
Barrington, H. 253, 254
Barry, J. 142
Barsoux, J.L. 116, 117, 118, 119, 120
Bartlett, C.A. 102, 103
Bassett, P. 372, 405
Bates, I. 253
Baum, T. 219
Bayliss, F. 373, 374

Bazalgette, J. 227
Beach, L.R. 162
Beardwell, I. 378, 387
Beatson, M. 68, 72, 74, 75, 271
Beaumont, J.R. 56
Beaumont, P. 279
Beaumont, P.B. 26, 377
Beaver, G. 206, 208, 267
Beer, M. 25–6, 231, 280
Bell, W. 354
Bennett, R. 8, 220, 221, 237
Bentson, C. 161
Bercusson, B. 271
Berg, A. 82
Berggren, C. 351, 403, 404, 405, 411
Bevan, S. 192, 193
Billig, M. 95, 315
Binet, Alfred 156
Black, J. 348, 351
Blyton, P. 24, 65, 67, 72, 83, 267, 299, 304, 372,
   374, 377
Boje, D.M. 116
Bolton, T. 40
Bond, M. 137
Bone, A. 285
Booth, A. 371
Boring, E.G. 156
Bott, D. 279
Bowen, D.E. 161
Bowey, A. 204
Bowles, L.M. 170, 188
Boxall, P. 20, 207
Boyatzis, R. 253
Boyce, R. 173
Boydell, T. 227, 243, 244, 252, 253, 256
Boyden, T. 294
Boyer, R. 65, 71
Bradley, K. 348
Bradley, P. 192, 205
Bramham, J. 40, 41
Brandes, D. 56
Brannen, P. 342
Braverman, H. 65
Brewerton, P.A. 182

Brewster, C. 68, 70, 82, 266, 286
Bridges, W. 245
Briner, R. 274
Bristow, E. 352
Brown, W. 378
Brown, W.D.S. 399
Brulin, G. 410, 411
Bryson, A. 71, 297, 343, 345, 352, 356, 372, 374
Bryson, C. xi, 69, 74, 75, 76, 77, 83
Buchanan, D. 350, 351
Buechtemann, C.F. 393
Buglear, J. 188
Bullock, A. 325
Bullock Report (1977) 340
Buraway, M. 404
Burchell, B. 82
Burchill, F. 355
Burgoyne, J. 9, 227, 247, 249, 250, 252, 253, 256
Burke, W.W. 231
Burns, T. 30
Burrows, R. 65

Caldwell, D. 149
Caldwell, S.A. 163
Callender, J.C. 139
CALM (Computer Assisted Learning for Managers) 173
Campion, M. 160, 284
Cannell, M. 194
Cannetti, Elias 334
Cantley, C. 177, 178
Capelli, P. 65, 195
Carroll, A.B. 314
Carter, E. 229
Casey, B. 68, 75, 79, 81, 82, 84
Catholic Online 331
Cattell, R.B. 140
Cave, K. 79
CBI (Confederation of British Industry) 229
Center for the Study of Ethics in the Professions 330
Ceriello, V.R. 56
Cerveny, R.P. 56
Chacko, T. 299
Chaison, G.N. 398
Challis, D.J. 175
Champy, J. 349
Chandler, J. 142
Chatman, C.A. 149
Cheung-Judge, L. 258

Chia, R. 242, 243, 244, 248, 251
Child, J. 30
Citrine, The Lord 322
Clark, H. 142
Clark, J. 74
Claydon, T. 386
Clegg, H. 343
Coates, G. 170, 188
Cockburn, C. 11, 300, 301, 308
Collard, R. 347
Collinson, D. 294, 301, 302, 380, 384, 390
Collinson, M. 294, 301, 302
Colwill, N. 298
Commission for Racial Equality 1983 258, 296
Connock, S. 286, 311
Conway, N. 274
Cook, M. 155, 158, 162
Cooper, C.L. 137
Coopey, J. 233, 234
Cornford, F.M. 332
Costine, P. 220, 227
Couch, G.M. 315
Cousins, C. 70
Coussey, M. 305
Crainer, S. 245
Cressey, P. 355, 356, 410, 411
Crompton, R. 11, 302, 303, 305, 308
Crow, Mary xi
Cully, M. 71, 297, 343, 345, 352, 356, 372, 374
Cutcher-Gershenfeld, N. 409

Daboub, A.J. 332
Dachler, M.P. 164
Dale, B. 347
Danford, A. 381
Dastmalchian, A. 69
Davis, D.D. 56
Day, P. 321
De Cieri, H. 102, 103, 111, 112, 113
de Rijk, R. 220, 223, 229
De Wit, B. 45
Deakin, S. 271
Deetz, S. 247
Delbridge, R. 381
Della Rocca, G. 380, 384, 390
Department for Education and Employment (DfEE) 241, 285
Department of Employment 219, 258, 355
Department of Health 186
Department of Trade and Industry (DTI) 82, 371

Devanna, M.A. 26
Devine, M. 253
Dex, S. 84
Dickens, L. 11, 292, 293, 294, 295, 296, 301, 303, 305
Dickman, M. 274
Dipboye, R.L. 139, 161
Disney, R. 371, 399
Dix, G. 71, 297, 343, 345, 352, 356, 372, 374
Dobson, J. 311
Dobson, P. 159
Donaldson, J. 332
Donkin, R. 169, 170, 200
Donovan, Lord 270
Dougherty, R.L. 139
Dowling, B. 203
Dowling, P. 102
Du Gay, P. 381
Dulewicz, V. 162
Duncan, C. 352
Dunivan, L. 56
Dyson, R. 74

Eder, R.W. 160
Edwards, C.C. 181
Edwards, P. 32, 369, 374, 380, 384, 386, 390
Edwards, P.K. 280, 370
Edwards, R. 196, 286, 392
Eisenstat, R. 231
Elger, T. 73, 380, 396, 403
Elliott, L. 99
Emerson, M. 271
Employment Outlook 397
Equal Opportunities Commission (EOC) 293, 295, 296, 299
Equal Opportunities Review 304
European Update 272
Eysenck, H.J. 140

Faichnie, C. 303
Farmer, E. 253, 257, 258
Farnham, D. 69
Fear, N. 182
Fell, A. 280, 281
Ferner, A. 281, 395
Ferris, G.A. 161
Ferris, G.R. 137, 160, 188
Filipczak, B. 83
Fischer, F. 322, 332
Fisher, C.M. xi, 186, 200, 323, 329
Fisher, D. 328
Flanagan, J.A. 153

Fletcher, C. 137, 138, 162, 212
Flood, P. 70, 226
Floodgate, J.F. 183
Florida, R. 380, 396, 401, 404, 407, 409
Fombrun, C.J. 26
Formento, R.J. 56
Forrester, P. 27, 68, 202
Forster, N. 113
Forth, J. 71, 297, 343, 345, 352, 356, 372, 374
Foster, J. 292
Fowler, A. 192, 279, 284–5, 286
Fox, A. 364
Fox, S. 241
Frantzeb, R.B. 56
Fredericks, J. 242
Fredman, S. 271
Freeman, C. 56
Freeman, R. 372
Freeman, R.B. 395
French, J.R.P. 181
French, R. 227
Friedman, A.L. 28
Frits, K. 411
Fullerton, J. 296, 304

Galagan, P. 224–5, 229
Galin, A. 70
Gall, G. 375, 376
Gallie, D. 204
Gannon, M. 70
Garavan, T. 219, 220, 226, 227, 230
Garrahan, P. 75, 405
Gash, C. 56
Gaugler, B.B. 161
Geary, J. 83, 204, 348, 351, 381
Gee, J.P. 380
Gennard, J. 345, 348
Ghoshal, S. 102, 103
Giacalone, R. 137
Gilbert, N. 65
Gilmore, D.C. 137, 160
Glaze, T. 185
Gluck, F.W. 44–5
Gluklich, P. 294
Gold, M. 395
Goldstein, H. 134, 149
Goodman, J. 12, 342, 346, 347, 357
Goodstein, L.D. 231
Gosnold, D. 204
Goss, D. 198, 300, 305, 350
Govindarajan, V. 99, 103, 107, 108
Gower (appraisal skills) 183

Gratton, L. 156, 162, 207, 281, 282
Gray, C. 253, 257, 258
Gray, D.A. 332
Green, F. 399
Green, W.C. 392
Greuter, M.A. 152
Griffin, R. 348
Griffiths, A. 101
Griffiths, Ward 417
Groeber, N. 322
Gross, J. 334
Grubb, D. 271, 274
Guest, D. 195, 274, 279, 280, 282, 378
Gueutal, H.G. 56
Guion, R.M. 148
Gunnigle, P. 226
Gupta, A. 99, 103, 107, 108

Hackman, J.R. 171, 173, 351
Hakim, C. 68, 76, 266
Hall, E.J. 116
Hall, L. 56, 57, 60, 93, 94, 95, 280, 285, 286,
    295
Hall, M. 355
Hall, M.R. 116
Hall, Rachael xi
Hallier, J. 73, 151
Hamblin, A. 228
Hammer, M. 349
Hammermesh, D. 277
Handy, C. 69, 245
Hannon, J. 56
Hanson, C. 354
Harris, L. xi, 196, 198, 204, 206, 208, 267, 279,
    282, 283
Harris, P. 27
Harrison, R. 45, 218, 230, 232, 233, 234, 240,
    241, 242, 244, 246, 247, 253, 254, 255
Hart, D. 320
Hassard, J. 27, 68, 202
Hawes, W.R. 75, 340, 343, 345, 346, 347, 373
Heenan, D.A. 6, 104
Heery, E. 387
Heffcut, A.I. 161
Hegeswich, A. 68, 70
Heider, F. 138
Hellervik, L. 160
Hellier, P. 204
Hendry, C. 24, 27, 40, 102, 103, 104, 105, 109,
    192, 195, 205, 234
Heneman, R.L. 198
Hepple, B. 270, 271

Heraty, N. 220, 226, 227
Herriot, P. 83, 133, 134, 138, 139, 152, 154, 164,
    286
Herzberg, F. 197, 350, 351
Hesketh, B. 164
Heywood, E. 298
Hickson, C.D. 30
Hickson, D.J. 28, 162
Hill, S. 347, 348, 358
Hinnings, C.R. 162
Hinrichs, J.R. 220
Hirsch, W. 245
Hochschild, A.R. 370
Hoecklin, L. 92, 94
Hoffman, J.J. 315
Hofstede, G. 6, 116, 119–21, 178
Hogan, J.B. 156
Hogarth, R. 180
Hogg, C. 197
Honey, P. 183
Hope, J. 53
Hope, T. 53
Hope-Hailey, V. 207, 281, 282
Hosking, D.M. 44
Huczynski, A.A. 253
Hughes, E.C. 45
Hull, G. 380
Human Synergistics/Center for Applied Research
    181
Hunter, J.E. 154
Hunter, L. 68, 82, 352, 353, 354
Huselid, M. 417
Hurstfield, J. 73
Hyman, J. 12, 340, 341, 343, 344, 352, 353, 354,
    355
Hyman, R. 65, 370, 395

Ibbetson, A. 149, 433
IDS *see* Income Data Services
Iles, P. 133, 148, 150, 162, 164
Income Data Services (IDS) 194, 202, 203, 208,
    209, 230, 276, 345, 346, 353, 355, 356
Industrial Relations Services (IRS) 209
Industrial Society 205
Inman, K. 277
Institute of Employment Rights 397
Institute of Management and Manpower plc 78,
    257
Institute of Manpower Studies 56, 66, 193
Institute of Personnel and Development (IPD)
    56, 169, 170, 188, 192, 199, 200, 201, 205,
    208, 272, 285, 299, 304, 392

Institute of Personnel Management (IPM) 188, 193, 194, 279, 346
International Labour Office (ILO) 274, 393, 397, 398
IPD *see* Institute of Personnel and Development
IPM *see* Institute of Personnel Management
IRS 209, 257, 274

Jackson, B. 247, 252
Jackson, C. 245
Jackson, H. 305
Jackson, M. 74
Jackson, M.P. 373
Jackson, S.E. 26, 51
Jackson, T. 101
Jacobi, O. 397
Jacques, E. 199
Janson, R. 351
Janz, T. 160
Jaques, D. 171
Jaques, E. 28
Jeanneret, P.R. 153
Jefferson, M. 266
Jelf, G. 56
Jenkins, G. 354
Jenkins, R. 301, 302
Jewson, N. 299, 300, 303
Jex, S.M. 162
Johns, T. 286, 311
Johnson, G. 24
Johnson, Lyndon 299
Johnson, T. 287
Johnstone, C. 166
Jones, A. 9, 226
Jones, A.M. 234
Jones, D.T. 29, 405
Jones, E. 222, 223
Jones, G. 302, 303
Jones, J.E. 242, 248, 250, 253, 254
Jones, N. 183
Jones, P. 301
Judge, G. 345, 348
Judge, T.A. 161

Kahn-Freund, O. 269
Kandola, R. 296, 304
Kanungo, R.N. 314, 332
Kaplan, R.S. 177, 203
Karren, R.J. 197
Katz, H.C. 387, 394, 400
Kauffman, J.R. 162
Kaufman, S.P 44

Kavanagh, M.J. 56
Kay, E. 182
Keenan, T. 155, 157
Keeney, M. 380
Keenoy, T. 31, 285
Keep, E. 223, 230
Keller, B. 397
Kelly, A. 193
Kelly, C. 387
Kelly, G.A. 142, 143
Kelly, J. 350, 358, 387
Kenney, M. 396, 401, 404, 407, 409
Kerr, S. 198
Kessler, I. 194, 195, 373, 374
Kessler, K. 192, 194, 202
Kingsbury, P. 55
Kinnie, N. 56, 194
Kinnie, N.J. 56
Kirk, G.S. 178
Kirk, Susan xii
Kirkpatrick, D. 228
Kirkpatrick, D.L. 148 9
Kjonstad, B. 326, 331
Klein, R. 321
Kmieciak, Y.M. 150
Knights, D. 155, 294, 301, 302
Knights, E. 350
Kochan, T. 372, 387
Kochan, T.A. 14, 26, 393, 394, 396, 400, 401, 402, 403, 408, 409, 411
Kohlberg, L. 11, 324, 325, 326, 327, 328
Kohn, A. 212
Kolb, D. 7, 135 6
Kossek, E.E. 56
Kotter, J.P. 242
Krafft-Ebbing, R. von 334
Kristof-Brown, A. 134

Labour Research Department 374
Lamont, B. 315
Lankshear, C. 380
Lansbury, R.D. 14, 393, 394, 396, 400, 401, 402, 403, 408, 409, 411
Lashley, C. 351
Latham, B.R. 161
Latham, G. 8, 160, 196
Lauermann, E. 231
Laurent, A. 116
Lawler, E. 197
Lawler, E.E. 192
Lawler III, E.E. 186
Lawler, J.J. 56

Lawrence, P. 119, 280
Layder, D. 45
Ledford, G.E. 161
Leduchowicz, T. 8, 220, 221, 237
Lee, C.A. 162
Lee, M. 9, 243–4, 247, 258
Lees, S. 240
Legge, K. 18, 24, 31, 40, 47, 73, 75, 83, 173, 226, 279, 281, 289, 292, 301, 380
Lehrman Brothers 78
Leighton, P. 76, 77, 83
Lengnick-Hall, C. 26
Lengnick-Hall, M. 26
Leopold, J. xii, 73, 74, 151, 279, 352, 353, 354
Leopold, J.W. 373
Lewiicki, R. 202
Lewis, J. 83
Lewis, P. 199
Libkuman, T.M. 162
Lievens, F. 162
Liff, S. 298, 299, 305
Limerick, B. 298
Littlefield, D. 201
Local Authority Conditions of Service Advisory Board (LACSAB) 194
Locke, E. 8, 196
Locke, R. 395, 400
Louis, M.R. 56
Love, K.G. 162
Lovell, A.T.A. 323, 331
Lovenduski, J. 302
Loveridge, R. 82
Lowe, D. 194
Lowell Bryan 101
Lowson, C. 173

Mabbott, J.D. 319, 320
Mabey, C. 9, 169, 196, 221, 230, 231, 240, 241, 249, 253, 256, 257, 258
Macan, T.H. 161
MacDuffie, J.P. 14, 393, 394, 396, 400, 401, 402, 403, 404, 406, 408, 409, 411
MacInnes, J. 67, 68, 82
Mackay, L. 153
Mackie, J.L. 319
MacLean Center for Clinical Medical Ethics 331
Mahon, T. 301
Manhire, Eileen xii
March, J.G. 31
Marchington, M. 12, 26, 32, 41, 47, 51, 96, 155, 266, 342, 343, 344, 346, 347, 348, 349, 350, 351, 356, 357, 358, 376, 377

Marginson, P. 67, 280
Marinker, M. 185
Marsden, D. 198, 204
Marsick, V. 226
Martin, P. 103
Martin, R. 280
Martinez Lucio, M. 380
Masi, A. 82
Mason, B. 12, 340, 341, 343, 344, 355
Mason, D. 299, 300, 303
Mason, E.S. 324
Mason, R. 372
Mayne, L. 68, 70, 82
McArdle, L. 27, 68, 202
McCabe, D. 356
McClaire, S.R. 116
McCormick, E.J. 153
McCulloch, A. 84
McCullough, R. 224, 225
McEvoy, G.M. 189
McGaughey, S. 111, 112, 113
McGoldrick, A. 79
McGovern, P. 207, 281, 282
McGregor, A. 68, 82
McGregor, D. 316
McIntyre, J.M. 135–6
McKay, S. 376
McKerzie, R.B. 387
McKinlay, A. 385
McLagan, P. 224, 225
McMahon, F. 229
McMullen, J. 271
Mead, G.H. 142
Meager, N. 66, 67, 75
Mecham, R.C. 153
Meehl, P.E. 161
Meekings, A. 178
Meinhart, D.B. 56
Mendonca, M. 314, 332
Mento, A.J. 197
Merron, K. 328
Meshoulam, I. 47
Metcalf, D. 372
Metcalf, H. 79, 81, 82, 84
Meyer, H.H. 182
Meyer, R. 45
Miller, P. 25, 184, 207
Mills, Q. 280
Millward, N. 71, 75, 79, 81, 82, 84, 280, 297, 340, 343, 345, 346, 347, 352, 371, 372, 373, 374
Minton, J. 202
Mintzberg, H. 23, 25, 45, 51, 242, 287

Mitchell, F. 204
Mohrman Jnr., A. 186
Monaghan, C. 177
Monks, J. 358, 386
Monks, K. 193
Morley, I.E. 44
Morley, M. 226
Morris, J. 65, 67, 72
Morris, M.W. 139
Morton, G. 358, 376
Motowidlo, S.J. 56
Mudrack, P.E. 324
Müller-Jentsch, W. 397, 398, 409
Mullins, T.W. 163
Mumford, A. 9, 241, 242, 243, 244, 245, 246,
    247, 249, 250, 251, 252, 253, 254, 255, 256,
    257, 260

National Economic Development Office (NEDO)
    194
Neathey, F. 73
Neilson, C. 56
Newell, S. xii, 148, 149, 155, 157, 159, 160, 165
Newsome, K. xii, 381, 405
Nichol, V. 56
Nicholls, G. 204
Nijhof, W. 220, 223, 229
Nilsson, T. 410, 411
Nixon, 183
Noon, M. 299, 304
Norton, D.P. 177, 203

O'Doherty, D. 41
Oldham, G.R. 171, 173, 351
Oliver, N. 395, 401, 409
Olsen, J.P. 31
Olsen, W. 266
O'Reilly, A. 71, 297, 343, 345, 352, 356, 372, 374
O'Reilly, C.A. 149
O'Reilly, J. 68, 73
Osterman, P. 207
Ostroff, C. 134, 150, 161
Overell, S. 95, 266
Oxford Polytechnic Educational Methods Unit
    185

Paauwe, J. 70
Paddison, L. 294
Paese, M. 161
Palmer, G. 385
Pandya, N. 300
Parker, M. 351, 381, 404, 406, 407

Parker, P. 26, 348
Pearson, E. 346
Pedler, M. 227, 243, 244, 252, 253, 256
Pegels, C.P. 56
Pelletier, J. 372
Peltu, M. 350
Pemberton, C. 83, 245, 286
Pendleton, A. 353
Peng, K.P. 139
Penn, R. 67, 68
Pennings, J.M. 162
Perkins, S. 192, 205
Perlmutter, H.V. 6, 104
Perrow, C. 30
Pettigrew, A. 24, 27, 222, 223
Pfeffer, J. 96, 162, 212, 234, 417
Phares, E.J. 156
Pickard, J. 286
Piore, M. 65
Pollert, A. 65, 68, 69
Pollitt, C. 175
Poole, M. 342, 354
Porter, L. 197
Porter, M.E. 26, 45
Povall, M. 294
Powell, P. 56
Price, A.J. 38
Price, J. 405
Priem, R.L. 332
Proctor, S.J. 27, 68, 202
Prowse, K. 68
Pucik, V. 108, 114
Pugh, D.S. 30
Punnett, B.J. 120, 121
Purcell, J. 26, 32, 192, 194, 202, 280
Purdy, K. 351
Pursell, E. 284

Quinn, J.B. 23, 24, 45

Raffo, C. 155
Ramsey, H. 342, 343, 352, 353, 354
Rasheed, A.M.A. 332
Rawls, J. 320
Reason, P. 222, 223
Reber, A.S. 148, 156
Redman, T. 182, 349, 358
Redmayne, S. 321
Reeves, M. 320
Reid, M. 253, 254
Resnick-West, S.M. 186
Revans, R.W. 232

Rice, C. xii, 136, 323
Richards-Carpenter, C. 55, 56
Richardson, R. 198, 203, 204
Robertson, I. 133, 148
Robertson, I.T. 137, 148, 150, 156, 162, 164
Robinson, P. 70
Roderick, C. 234
Rodger, A. 153
Rogers, C.R. 142
Rogers, J. 395
Roos, D. 29, 405
Rose, J.B. 398
Rosenfeld, P. 137
Rosenthal, D.B. 161
Ross, R. 305
Rothausen, T.J. 134
Rothwell, S. 81
Rowlinson, M. 27, 68, 202
Rubery, J. 65, 82
Rubin, M.I. 135–6
Rubinstein, S. 411
Rugman, A. 101
Ryan, P. 399

Saari, L. 8, 160, 196
Sabel, C. 65
Saggers, R. 223, 225, 226
Salaman, G. 9, 169, 196, 221, 230, 231, 240, 241,
    249, 256, 381
Sambrook, S. 253
Sandberg, A. 410, 411
Sanders, G.L. 56
Sapsford, D. 370
Savery, L. 204
Saville and Holdsworth Ltd 153, 157, 171, 188
Scarbrough, H. 408
Schmidt, F.L. 154
Schneck, R.E. 162
Schneider, B. 134, 149, 154
Schneider, R. 305
Schneider, S.C. 116, 117, 118, 120
Schon, D.A. 363
Schregle, J. 399
Schreier, M. 322
Schuler, H. 161
Schuler, R. 102, 103
Schuler, R.S. 26, 51
Scott, R. 1993 195, 320
Scott, W. 195, 320
Scullion, H. 370
Seear, N. 295
Seedhouse, D. 334

Seligman, D. 334
Sewell, G. 381
Shackleton, V. 148, 155, 157, 159, 160
Sharpley, D.S. 156, 162
Shaw, K. 8, 196
Sheppard, B. 202
Silverman, D. 44
Simon, H.A. 97
Simon, Theodore 156
Simonian, H. 401
Simpson, P. 380
Sisson, K. 29–30, 280, 289, 305, 358
Slaughter, J. 351, 381, 406
Sloman, M. 224, 230
Sly, F. 75
Smart, D. 75, 340, 343, 345, 346, 347, 373
Smith, C. 380, 396, 403
Smith, D. 134, 149
Smith, D.E. 161
Smith, G. 177, 178
Smith, I. 194
Smith, J.M. 148
Smith, M. 82, 149
Smith, P. 175, 358, 376
Smucker, J. 82
Snape, E. 182, 349, 358
Snell, A.F. 156
Snell, M. 294
Snell, R. 320, 324, 328, 331
Snyder, M. 137, 162
Solomon, R.C. 332
Sparrow, P. 73, 153, 266
Spector, B. 231, 280
Spector, R. 25–6
Spinelli, E. 142
Sproull, A. 68, 82
Stacey, R.D. 25
Stage, H.D. 116
Stalker, G.S. 30
Stallybrass, O. 325
Starkey, K. 233
Steel, R.P. 197
Stephenson, C. 385
Stevens, M. 75, 280, 340, 343, 345, 346, 347, 371,
    373
Stewart, D.W. 330
Stewart, J. xii, 182, 223, 227, 231–2, 233, 242,
    243, 248, 253, 254–5, 256
Stewart, P. 75, 405
Stewart, R. 242
Stiles, P. 207, 281, 282
Stillwell, D. 75

Stokes, G.S. 156
Stopford, J. 96
Storey, J. 29–30, 193, 226, 240, 251, 253, 257,
    258, 282, 358
Straw, J. 300
Streeck, W. 395
Stuttaford, T. 319
Syrett, M. 76, 77, 83

Tailby, S. 346
Tannenbaum, S.I. 56
Tansley, Carole xiii, 65
Tasso, C.A. 56
Tate, W. 253
Taylor, P. 381, 385
Taylor, S. 381, 385, 386
Terry, M. 408
Texas Instruments 330
Thomas, K. 168
Thompson, N. 192, 193
Thompson, P. 65, 384
Thompson, R. 253, 257, 258
Thomson, A. 253, 257, 258
Thornton, G.C. 161
Thorpe, R. 204
Thouless, R.H. 322
Tichy, N. 26
Torbert, W.R. 328
Torrington, D. 56, 57, 60, 93, 94, 95, 97, 153,
    199, 279, 280, 285, 286, 287, 290
Towers, B. xiii, 100, 393, 394, 397, 404, 408, 409,
    411
Townley, B. 181, 345, 346
Trades Union Congress (TUC) 345, 386
Tregaskis, O. 82
Trevino, I.K. 324
Trompenaars, F 116
Truss, C. 207, 281, 282
Tuck, K. 373
Tuckman, A. 347, 348
Tullar, W. 163
Tung, R. 104
Turban, D.B. 139
Turnbull, P. 79, 83, 267, 370, 372, 374, 376, 377,
    381
Turner, L. 393, 406, 409
Tyson, S. 24, 45, 47, 280, 281

Unions 21 387
United Kingdom Central Council for Nursing,
    Midwives and Health Visitors (UKCC) 183
Ursell, G. 69

Valentine, R. 350
Van Vianen, A.E. 150
Vance, C.M. 116
Verma, A. 409
Vinnicombe, S. 298
Visser, J. 399
Vroom, V. 8, 196

Waddington, J. 377, 387
Wajcman, J. 305
Walby, S. 83
Wall, S. 101
Walleck, A.S. 44
Walsh, D.A. xiii, 93
Walsh, T. 68
Walters, M. 7, 168, 173
Walton, R. 193, 195, 280
Wanous, J.P. 152, 164
Ward, P. 181
Wass, V. 79
Waters, I.A. 25
Watkins, K. 226
Watson, G. 262
Watson, T.J. xiii, 18, 21, 25, 27, 28, 30, 31, 45,
    65, 73, 83, 90, 91, 92, 134, 173, 195, 206,
    207, 222, 226, 227, 242, 248, 279, 301, 370
Wayne, S.J. 188
Weatherall, C.B. 56
Webb, J. 299
Webb, S. 348
Weber, J. 315
Webster, B. 226
Wedderburn, Lord 269, 270
Weick, K.E. 30
Weitzman, M. 353
Weitzner, T.G. 56
Welch, J. 95
Wells, W. 271, 274
West, M. 154
Weston, S. 376
Whipp, R. 24
White, M. 204
Whitston, C. 370, 377, 387
Whittington, R. 24
Wickens, P. 74
Wiersema, M.F. 148
Wilkinson, A. 12, 32, 41, 47, 51, 96, 155, 342,
    344, 346, 347, 349, 350, 356, 357, 358, 376,
    377
Wilkinson, B. 381, 395, 401, 409
Wilkinson, F. 65, 82, 271
Williams, R. 212, 283

Williamson, O. 65
Willman, P. 372
Willmott, H. 31, 242, 326, 331
Wilson, E. 258
Womack, J.P. 29, 405
Wood, P. 162
Wood, S. 29, 194, 195, 397
Woodall, J. 299, 304
Woodcock, M. 242, 248, 250, 253, 254
Woodland, S. 71, 297, 343, 345, 352, 356, 372, 374

Woodward, J. 30
World Bank 397
World Economic Forum 101
Wright, G. 180, 318

Xiao, Z.Z. 56

Yanarella, E.J. 392
Yeandle, S. 70
Young, W. 56
Youngblood, S.A. 324